T
CRICK
WHO'S WHO
2007

The Future by
JASON RATCLIFFE of the PCA

Foreword by
JUSTIN LANGER

Edited by
CHRIS MARSHALL

Statistics by
RICHARD LOCKWOOD

Photographs by
GETTY IMAGES

This edition first published in the UK in 2007 by Green Umbrella Publishing

© Green Umbrella Publishing 2007
www.greenumbrella.co.uk

Publishers: Jules Gammond and Vanessa Gardner

Editor (for Green Umbrella Publishing): Kirsty Ennever
Picture research: Ellie Charleston
Quiz compiled by Chris Marshall
Cover design by Kevin Gardner
Printed and bound in Italy
By ☙ Grafica Veneta S.p.A.

ACKNOWLEDGEMENTS

Cover photographs by Getty Images, 101 Bayham Street, London, NW1 0AG

The publishers would also like to thank the county clubs, the players
and their families for their assistance in helping to assemble
the information and photographs in this book.

Extra information has also been gathered from the pages of *The Wisden Cricketer*,
The Times, *The Sunday Times*, Cricinfo.com and CricketArchive.com

Thanks also to the following for providing additional photographs:
Andrew Hignell/Glamorgan Cricket Archives, David Griffin, Derby Evening
Telegraph, Empics, Essex CCC, Gerard Farrell, Gloucestershire CCC, ICC, Kent CCC,
Kent Messenger Group, Lancashire CCC, Leicestershire CCC, MCC, Middlesex CCC,
Mike Vimpany, Neville Chadwick Photography, Northamptonshire CCC, Paul Willatts
Photography, Roger Wootton, Sarah Williams, Somerset CCC, Surrey CCC, Sussex
CCC, SWpix, Worcestershire CCC, www.durhamccc.co.uk, Yorkshire CCC

CONTENTS

THE FUTURE
by Jason Ratcliffe
Group Director, PCA

As we enter a new season there is a real sense of *déjà vu* around English cricket in 2007. The Aussies have dominated us to regain the Ashes and many have called for another review of our game. Doom and gloom merchants predict the end is nigh!

Whatever the enquiries and reviews into the defeat, let's not forget that the bulk of the Australian side have dominated worldwide cricket for close on 15 years. Explanations may be required and will no doubt be discussed at length, but some theories are simple: the Aussies were a wounded side after our 2005 win and subsequent celebrations, and we were hit by the loss of several key players from that series. It was never going to be easy on their turf and with some of their ageing players needing to heal their wounds before retirement. Maybe we didn't realise quite how quickly and hard the Australian juggernaut would hit us.

Of course the World Cup will be happening or be over by the time you read this, and if we've done well, will it make any difference to the cricket structure?

The more important review is the structural review that has started in the run-up to the new broadcasting agreement in 2010. We need to take what's good about the last few years and build on that. The positives are strong: central contracts have proved a success; two divisions have improved domestic four-day cricket – and, arguably, we would not have won the Ashes in 2005 but for these developments.

As importantly, the introduction of Twenty20 has injected adrenalin into our domestic and world cricket. It has proved an outstanding success and at a time of disappointment over the recent Ashes, people still generally feel positive about our game. Twenty20 is now seen as a 'jewel in the crown' and must take some credit for the prevalent positive outlook on our game.

But there are also challenges ahead: players have told us for some time that we play too much cricket, but most recent feedback suggests only a small reduction is needed. So changes are needed, but what should they be?

The County Championship, a breeding ground for Test cricketers, should remain in its favoured two-divisional format. However, we need to reduce overs in a day from 104 to 96 to bring the cricket more in line with Test conditions and create more intensity of competition. Whilst key bowlers may dominate more of the cricket, our overuse injury statistics should be reduced.

This season the new ball will be available after 80 overs instead of 90, but this goes only a small way to creating the desired intensity of competition. Many have said that our domestic programme is cluttered with too many competitions and that players – let alone supporters – have a job keeping track of which format they have to play from one day to the next. And commercially does it make sense? Do sponsors really get value for money and differentiation for their naming rights? And are we maximising the potential for this revenue stream? It is, as I and many suggest, cluttered.

The PCA proposals for the structural review involve losing one of the one-day competitions (in all likelihood the Pro40), thus leaving just three competitions overall: a four-day Championship, a 50-over competition and the Twenty20 – all being reflective of international programmes and formats.

Each competition should be tweaked to encourage intensity of competition. The key ingredient is quality of matches and formats. The 50-over tournament could be created from a fresh random draw each year: three pools of six will create 12 zonal games per county, concluding with quarters, semis and a Lord's final. The three-group system has worked well in Twenty20 and, indeed, previous 50-over competitions where a regional basis has been used – for example, the old B&H.

What the structure should provide is encouragement throughout the season that everybody will be in with a good chance of reaching the next stage – thus fewer 'dead games'. Structured correctly, each competition will bubble along to a conclusion in the closing ten weeks of the season, creating longevity, excitement and tough cricket for all.

Will 50 overs be a preferred format at international level in future years? Twenty20 may surpass it since it perhaps reflects our changing society with people having less time to spare in their lives. Whatever the feelings, the game needs to continually be one step ahead of these indicators. Pro40 may not have ignited players and supporters to date, but it may do in time, and, if possible, our domestic structure should follow international cricket trends so that our players are adjusted to the formats they aspire to play.

Sounds simple and all makes sound cricketing sense, but it could never be that simple, could it?

As ever, there are many considerations: stakeholders, supporters, sponsors and broadcasters to take into account and invariably an exhaustive list of different ideas and agendas. Ultimately, the PCA wants to see the best possible cricketing structure, which will be a feeding ground for the next generations of England cricketers. The whole game depends on that, and only a successful England side will enable continued strong broadcasting agreements.

Can we achieve it in time for the next broadcasting negotiations? What this space…!

The PCA continues to be an important stakeholder in the game and we continue to develop and expand. Our support for players past and present grows every year, and 2007 will be no exception with more and more proactivity on and off the pitch (www.thepca.co.uk).

This season sees the launch of the PCA Rankings – an 'MVP' (Most Valuable Player) concept. It's very exciting. Check it out at www.thepca.co.uk/rankings Designed and created by players, it will be the only way to genuinely measure a player's contribution in each domestic competition and overall. Detailed formulae take into account several player performance elements and key performance indicators for each competition. It will be a great talking point daily, weekly and monthly, culminating in an inaugural MVP winner to be honoured at our Annual Awards night at the Royal Albert Hall on 26 September.

Here's to a great summer of rejuvenation, and best wishes to everybody for a successful and enjoyable 2007.

Jason Ratcliffe

Jason Ratcliffe is a director at the PCA and its representative on the ECB Domestic Structure Review Group 2007. He has worked for the PCA for four years after retiring from a cricket career spanning 15 years, with Warwickshire 1988–94 and Surrey 1995–2002. He has achieved winner's medals in every domestic competition.

Professional Cricketers' Association
338 Euston Road
London
NW1 3BT
Direct dial: +44 207 5448668
Fax: +44 207 5448515
Website: www.thepca.co.uk

FOREWORD
by Justin Langer

After Australia lost the Ashes on 12 September 2005, I returned home with my tail between my legs, vowing to make amends next time our two great countries met. Back then, I used an old saying to help keep our last battle in some kind of perspective. Those words of wisdom state, 'the best thing in the world is playing and winning, the second best thing in the world is playing and losing, as long as you are still playing'. In many ways this wisdom summed up how I felt about the last Ashes series in England. Apart from the result, I felt privileged to have been a part of one of the great Test series of modern times and while I was disappointed to have lost to our longest rival, I was thrilled with what had been an inspired contest.

Eighteen months on and having just played in another great Ashes series, I can say for certain that the feeling of winning is so much greater than that of losing – especially when the grand prize is a tiny little urn. What was more satisfying than the result itself was the incredible fulfilment of knowing the hard work, preparation and single-minded commitment and focus to our task had led to such a wonderful reward.

Regardless of what level, or for whom, we play this great game, satisfaction is gained from working and striving towards a goal and seeing positive outcomes both individually and collectively. Heading into 2007, I have no doubt every club in England will be preparing and hoping for their greatest season ever.

Experience has taught me that hard work, vision and commitment are our closest allies if we are to taste that sweet, sweet flavour of success, and in the end it will be the teams who can gain momentum from these invisible friends that will come up triumphant.

Apart from chasing silverware in the first-class and one-day competitions, I am looking forward to another taste of Twenty20 cricket. Coming from an opening batsman in Test cricket, this may surprise many but I was really taken by the game last year at Somerset. I enjoy the entertainment it provides and the intensity of the contest and it is no surprise to me that it has taken many parts of the world by storm.

Although it is obviously a shortened version of the game, I believe Twenty20 provides us as players with a couple of crucial keys to how we should play cricket. We should look to entertain in a selfless fashion, we should look to be athletic and energetic in the field and we should play aggressively and with positive intent in everything we do. By taking this approach to all forms of the game, I am sure we will experience a lot more good days than we have bad ones.

This new season should be one of opportunity in England and all around the globe and I am still so glad to be playing and enjoying the most challenging game in the world.

Justin Langer
February 2007

Editor's Notes

The cricketers listed in this volume include all those who played 1st XI cricket for a first-class county at least once last season, in first-class or one-day (including Twenty20) cricket, and all those registered (at the time of going to press at the beginning of February) to play for the 18 first-class counties in 2007. The umpires' section contains the officials making up the first-class list for 2007. All players' statistics are complete to the end of the last English season (the Stop press section for individual players notes subsequent highlights) and cover first-class, List A and Twenty20 fixtures played that season. Such matches that took place elsewhere in the cricket-playing world during the period, such as the ODI between Ireland and England in Belfast and the European Championship in Scotland, do not feature in the players' season statistics but are recorded in their career tables. Test, ODI and Twenty20 International tallies for umpires are up to and including 9 February 2007.

This year's edition sees the introduction of two new entry headings for the players – ODI debut and, as a reflection of the very short format's arrival at international level, Twenty20 Int debut. It also features a change in the content of the statistics tables. Whereas previously the English domestic one-day competitions were covered individually, figures for these are now conflated in a List A category, which also includes matches such as limited-overs games between the counties and sides touring England. Such matches now qualify as a county debut for the purposes of this book and players' debuts have been adjusted to take account of this change. In addition, just as a player's first-class figures include Test matches, which are also extracted and listed separately, so his List A figures include One-Day Internationals, which are pulled out and appear separately in the same way. Furthermore, in the career tables the List A category contains figures of all the official 'full-length' one-day games in which a player has taken part worldwide, thus giving fuller coverage of his career. The categories 20/20 Int (Twenty20 Internationals) and 20/20 (all Twenty20 matches) have also been introduced and operate in similar fashion to the corresponding first-class and one-day categories.

As in the past, numbers of hundreds given in the statistics tables include all multiples (200s, 300s etc). Tallies of multiple hundreds for players and of one-day hundreds and one-day five-wicket innings for umpires who are former players are shown in the body of the entry, since these cannot be found in the statistics tables. Statistics for 2006 are not given for players whose appearances in first-class cricket or one-day matches that season were only for teams other than a county – e.g. universities (excluding international cricketers on tours to England). These appearances are, however, reflected in their career statistics and reference is made in the Extras section to the team for which they played.

Figures about 1000 runs, 50 wickets and 50 dismissals in a season refer to matches in England only. The figures for batting and bowling averages refer to the full first-class English list for 2006, followed in brackets by the 2005 figures. Inclusion in the batting averages depends on a minimum of six completed innings and an average of at least 10.00; a bowler has to have taken at least ten wickets for inclusion in the bowling averages. Season strike rates for bowlers are allocated according to the same criterion, although any player who has taken a first-class wicket is given a career strike rate. 'Strike rate' refers to a bowler's record of balls bowled per wicket taken.

In the Overseas tours section, the layout 'England to Pakistan 2005-06 (one-day series)', for example, indicates that a player was selected for only the one-day portion of the tour; the layout 'England to Zimbabwe (one-day series) 2004-05', on the other hand, indicates that the tour consisted of a one-day series only.

The following abbreviations apply in the text: ODI means One-Day International; Twenty20 Int means Twenty20 International; * means not out. In statistics tables FC means all first-class matches, including figures for Test matches; List A – 'full-length' one-day matches classified as such by the ICC (e.g. C&G Trophy, NatWest Pro40 and limited-overs matches against touring sides), including figures for One-Day Internationals; 20/20 Int – Twenty20 Internationals; 20/20 – all Twenty20 matches, including figures for Twenty20 Internationals.

Please note that Worcestershire ceased awarding caps in 2001 and now present 'colours' to each player who appears for the county in the Championship; that beginning in 2004 Gloucestershire have awarded caps to players on making their first first-class appearance for the county; that Durham ceased awarding caps after the 2005 season, replacing the cap system with grades of player seniority.

A book of this complexity and detail has to be prepared some months in advance of the new cricket season, and occasionally there are recent changes in a player's circumstances or the structure of the game which cannot be included in time. Many examples of facts, statistics and even opinions which can quickly become outdated in the period between the compilation of the book and its publication, months later, will spring to the reader's mind, and I ask him or her to make the necessary commonsense allowance and adjustments.

Chris Marshall, February 2007

THE PLYAERS

KOLPAK

If a cricketer is a national of a country that has an Association Agreement with the EU (such as South Africa or Zimbabwe) and also has a valid UK work permit, he enjoys the same right to work within the EU as an EU citizen and may be eligible to play county cricket as a domestic (that is, non-overseas) player. Cricketers playing in England under this system are commonly referred to as Kolpak players, after the Kolpak ruling, a judgement in the European Court of Justice that found in favour of Maros Kolpak, a Slovakian handball goalkeeper who challenged his status as a non-EU player in Germany.

MILESTONES AND LANDMARKS

Throughout the book there are 100 quiz questions relating to debuts, firsts, farewells and other milestones and landmarks. Facts and figures are up to 4 February 2007.

ACKERMAN, H. D.   Leicestershire

Name: Hylton Deon (<u>HD</u>) Ackerman
Role: Right-hand bat, right-arm
medium bowler
Born: 14 February 1973, Cape Town,
South Africa
Height: 5ft 11in **Weight:** 13st
County debut: 2005
County cap: 2005
Test debut: 1997-98
1000 runs in a season: 2
1st-Class 200s: 2
1st-Class 300s: 1
Place in batting averages: 5th av. 75.33
(2005 79th av. 38.51)
Parents: Hylton and Dawn
Wife and date of marriage: Katherine,
25 April 2004
Family links with cricket: Father (H. M.
Ackerman) played first-class cricket in South Africa and also for Northamptonshire
Education: Rondebosch Boys' High School, South Africa
Off-season: 'Playing cricket in South Africa'
Overseas tours: South Africa U24 to Sri Lanka 1995; Western Province to Australia
1995-96, to Zimbabwe 1996-97; South Africa A to England 1996, to Sri Lanka 1998,
to Zimbabwe 2004; South Africa to Zimbabwe 2001-02; Leicestershire to Pakistan and
India 2005
Overseas teams played for: Western Province 1993-94 – 2002-03; Gauteng 2003-04;
Lions 2004-05; Cape Cobras 2005-06; Warriors 2006-07
Career highlights to date: 'Being picked for South Africa in 1998'
Cricket moments to forget: 'Being dropped from South African team'
Cricket superstitions: 'None'
Cricketers particularly admired: Steve Waugh
Other sports followed: Football (Manchester United), 'all sport'
Injuries: Out for one and a half weeks with a groin injury
Favourite band: Snow Patrol
Relaxations: 'Golf, movies, reading'
Extras: Scored maiden first-class double century (202*) v Northerns at Centurion in
the SuperSport Series 1997-98, in the process breaking Barry Richards's record for the
most first-class runs by a South African in a domestic season (ended 1997-98 with
1373 at 50.85). Scored century (145) for South Africa A v Sri Lanka A at Matara 1998,
winning Man of the Match award. Man of the SuperSport Series 2000-01. His other
domestic awards include Man of the Match v Griqualand West at Kimberley (81)

and v KwaZulu-Natal at Durban (86*), both in the Standard Bank Cup 2003-04. Captain of Leicestershire 2005. Scored 309* v Glamorgan at Cardiff 2006, setting a new record for the highest individual first-class score by a Leicestershire player; also scored 62 in second innings to set a new record individual match aggregate for the county (371). Leicestershire Cricketer of the Year 2006. Is not considered an overseas player

Opinions on cricket: 'Young players are good for the game, but let's not forget that mature, older players still have a lot to offer. People are too quick to push young players and get rid of experienced ones.'

Best batting: 309* Leicestershire v Glamorgan, Cardiff 2006

2006 Season

	M	Inn	NO	Runs	HS	Avg	100	50	Ct	St	Balls	Runs	Wkts	Avg	BB	5I	10M
Test																	
FC	15	28	4	1808	309 *	75.33	4	14	14	-	0	0	0		-	-	-
ODI																	
List A	13	13	1	321	86	26.75	-	2	4	-	0	0	0		-	-	
20/20 Int																	
20/20	11	11	0	409	87	37.18	-	5	5	-	0	0	0		-	-	

Career Performances

	M	Inn	NO	Runs	HS	Avg	100	50	Ct	St	Balls	Runs	Wkts	Avg	BB	5I	10M
Test	4	8	0	161	57	20.12	-	1	1	-	0	0	0		-	-	-
FC	154	256	26	10408	309 *	45.25	26	62	121	-	102	57	0		-	-	-
ODI																	
List A	160	153	22	4289	114 *	32.74	1	30	57	-	48	52	0		-	-	
20/20 Int																	
20/20	26	26	2	882	87	36.75	-	8	9	-	0	0	0		-	-	

ADAMS, A. R.   Essex

Name: André Ryan Adams
Role: Right-hand bat, right-arm
fast-medium bowler
Born: 17 July 1975, Auckland, New Zealand
Height: 5ft 11in **Weight:** 14st 7lbs
Nickname: Dre, Doctor
County debut: 2004
County cap: 2004
Test debut: 2001-02
ODI debut: 2000-01
Twenty20 Int debut: 2004-05

Place in batting averages: 119th av. 32.85 (2005 115th av. 33.90)
Place in bowling averages: 102nd av. 39.52 (2005 84th av. 33.83)
Strike rate: 79.47 (career 53.05)
Parents: Felise du Chateau and Keith Adams
Wife and date of marriage: Ardene, 5 April 2003
Children: Danté, 24 February 2004
Family links with cricket: 'Parents West Indian!'
Education: West Lake Boys, Auckland
Off-season: Playing for Auckland
Overseas tours: New Zealand to Sharjah (ARY Gold Cup) 2000-01, to Australia 2001-02 (VB Series), to Sharjah (Sharjah Cup) 2001-02, to Pakistan 2002, to Africa (World Cup) 2002-03, to Sri Lanka 2003 (Bank

Alfalah Cup), to England (NatWest Series) 2004, to Bangladesh 2004-05 (one-day series), to Zimbabwe 2005-06 (Videocon Tri-Series), to South Africa (one-day series) 2005-06
Overseas teams played for: Takapuna, Auckland; Auckland 1997-98 –
Career highlights to date: 'Test victory against England in final game (Auckland) in 2002, my Test debut'
Cricket moments to forget: 'Losing to India in 2003 World Cup'
Cricket superstitions: 'None'
Cricketers particularly admired: Viv Richards, Michael Holding
Other sports followed: Rugby (Auckland Blues, All Blacks)
Favourite band: Ryan Edwards
Relaxations: Xbox
Extras: Member of New Zealand team to 1998 Indoor Cricket World Cup. Leading wicket-taker in 1999-2000 Shell Cup one-day competition (28; av. 13.50). His ODI match awards include Man of the Match v India at Queenstown 2002-03 (5-22) and v West Indies at Port Elizabeth in the 2002-03 World Cup (35*/4-44). An overseas player with Essex July to September 2004 (deputising first for Danish Kaneria, then for Scott Brant) and in 2005 and 2006. Scored maiden first-class century (91-ball 124) v Leicestershire at Leicester 2004 in his first Championship innings and batting at No. 9. Took Championship hat-trick (Burns, Jayasuriya, Hildreth) v Somerset at Taunton 2005
Best batting: 124 Essex v Leicestershire, Leicester 2004
Best bowling: 6-25 Auckland v Wellington, Auckland 2004-05

2006 Season

	M	Inn	NO	Runs	HS	Avg	100	50	Ct	St	Balls	Runs	Wkts	Avg	BB	5I	10M
Test																	
FC	8	9	2	230	75	32.85	-	1	4	-	1669	830	21	39.52	4-72	-	-
ODI																	
List A	8	3	1	57	40	28.50	-	-	1	-	341	272	8	34.00	3-59	-	
20/20 Int																	
20/20	3	3	1	49	21	24.50	-	-	1	-	72	95	6	15.83	3-35	-	

Career Performances

	M	Inn	NO	Runs	HS	Avg	100	50	Ct	St	Balls	Runs	Wkts	Avg	BB	5I	10M
Test	1	2	0	18	11	9.00	-	-	1	-	190	105	6	17.50	3-44	-	-
FC	68	88	6	1958	124	23.87	2	9	44	-	13051	6422	246	26.10	6-25	9	1
ODI	39	31	10	409	45	19.47	-	-	7	-	1729	1494	52	28.73	5-22	1	
List A	111	80	21	1127	90 *	19.10	-	1	27	-	5093	4010	144	27.84	5-7	3	
20/20 Int	2	1	0	7	7	7.00	-	-	-	-	48	67	1	67.00	1-27	-	
20/20	13	10	2	110	25	13.75	-	-	2	-	253	337	15	22.46	3-35	-	

ADAMS, C. J. Sussex

Name: Christopher (Chris) John Adams
Role: Right-hand bat, right-arm medium bowler, slip fielder, county captain
Born: 6 May 1970, Whitwell, Derbyshire
Height: 6ft **Weight:** 13st 7lbs
Nickname: Grizzly, Grizwold
County debut: 1988 (Derbyshire), 1998 (Sussex)
County cap: 1992 (Derbyshire), 1998 (Sussex)
Benefit: 2003 (Sussex)
Test debut: 1999-2000
ODI debut: 1998
1000 runs in a season: 8
1st-Class 200s: 4
Place in batting averages: 40th av. 50.75 (2005 64th av. 42.40)
Strike rate: (career 79.31)
Parents: John and Eluned (Lyn)
Wife and date of marriage: Samantha Claire, 26 September 1992
Children: Georgia Louise, 4 October 1993; Sophie Victoria, 13 October 1998
Family links with cricket: Brother David played 2nd XI cricket for Derbyshire and Gloucestershire. Father played for Yorkshire Schools and uncle played for Essex 2nd XI

Education: Chesterfield Boys Grammar School; Repton School
Qualifications: 6 O-levels, NCA coaching awards, Executive Development Certificate in Coaching and Management Skills
Overseas tours: Repton School to Barbados 1987; England NCA North to Northern Ireland 1987; England XI to New Zealand (Cricket Max) 1997; England to South Africa and Zimbabwe 1999-2000; Sussex to Grenada 2001, 2002; Blade to Barbados 2001
Overseas teams played for: Takapuna, New Zealand 1987-88; Te Puke, New Zealand 1989-90; Primrose, Cape Town, South Africa 1991-92; Canberra Comets, Australia 1998-99; University of NSW, Australia 2000-01
Cricket moments to forget: 'The death of Umer Rashid in Grenada [2002]'
Cricketers particularly admired: Ian Botham
Other sports played: Golf, football, 'dabbled a bit with ice hockey'
Other sports followed: Football ('Arsenal!')
Favourite band: Spandau Ballet, Duran Duran
Relaxations: 'Family time'
Extras: Represented English Schools U15 and U19, MCC Schools U19 and, in 1989, England YC. Took two catches as 12th man for England v India at Old Trafford in 1990. Set Derbyshire record for the highest score in the Sunday League (141*) v Kent at Chesterfield 1992. Set record for the highest score by a Derbyshire No. 3, 239 v Hampshire at Southampton 1996. Sussex Player of the Year 1998 and 1999. Set individual one-day record score for Sussex of 163 (off 107 balls) v Middlesex in the National League at Arundel 1999. Sussex 1st XI Fielder of the Season 2000. BBC South Cricketer of the Year 2001. One of *Wisden*'s Five Cricketers of the Year 2004. Scored 200 v Northamptonshire at Hove 2004, in the process becoming the third batsman (after Mark Ramprakash and Carl Hooper) to score a century against all 18 counties. Captain of Sussex since 1998
Best batting: 239 Derbyshire v Hampshire, Southampton 1996
Best bowling: 4-28 Sussex v Durham, Riverside 2001

---

1. Who scored 112 and 83 on Test debut v New Zealand at Lord's 2004?

2006 Season

	M	Inn	NO	Runs	HS	Avg	100	50	Ct	St	Balls	Runs	Wkts	Avg	BB	5I	10M
Test																	
FC	16	25	1	1218	155	50.75	3	7	28	-	6	2	0		-	-	-
ODI																	
List A	15	14	2	342	132 *	28.50	1	1	5	-	0	0	0		-	-	
20/20 Int																	
20/20	8	7	0	169	63	24.14	-	1	2	-	0	0	0		-	-	

Career Performances

	M	Inn	NO	Runs	HS	Avg	100	50	Ct	St	Balls	Runs	Wkts	Avg	BB	5I	10M
Test	5	8	0	104	31	13.00	-	-	6	-	120	59	1	59.00	1-42	-	-
FC	306	499	36	18031	239	38.94	45	88	364	-	3252	1913	41	46.65	4-28	-	-
ODI	5	4	0	71	42	17.75	-	-	3	-	0	0	0		-	-	
List A	346	327	55	10950	163	40.25	20	68	161	-	1391	1217	32	38.03	5-16	1	
20/20 Int																	
20/20	25	21	3	509	63	28.27	-	1	7	-	0	0	0		-	-	

ADAMS, J. H. K.   Hampshire

Name: James (<u>Jimmy</u>) Henry Kenneth Adams
Role: Left-hand bat, left-arm medium bowler
Born: 23 September 1980, Winchester
Height: 6ft 1in **Weight:** 14st 7lbs
Nickname: Bison, Nugget, Hippy, HC
County debut: 2002
County cap: 2006
1000 runs in a season: 1
1st-Class 200s: 1
Place in batting averages: 61st av. 45.11 (2005 190th av. 23.84)
Strike rate: (career 75.57)
Parents: Jenny and Mike
Marital status: Single
Family links with cricket: 'Dad played a bit for Kent Schoolboys. Brothers Ben and Tom, Hampshire age groups'
Education: Sherborne School; Loughborough University
Qualifications: BSc Human Biology, ECB Levels I and II coaching
Career outside cricket: 'Looking into it …'
Off-season: 'Work; Mumbai maybe for a bit'

Overseas tours: England U19 to Sri Lanka (U19 World Cup) 1999-2000; West of England to West Indies 1995; Sherborne School to Pakistan
Overseas teams played for: Woodville, Adelaide 1999-2000; Melville, Perth 2000-01; Bayswater-Morley, Perth 2004-05
Career highlights to date: 'Maiden hundred and county cap'
Cricket moments to forget: 'Kidderminster, June 2000'
Cricket superstitions: 'No superstitions, just habits'
Cricketers particularly admired: 'M. Parker, R. Smith, B. Lara ...'
Young players to look out for: Liam Dawson
Other sports played: 'Little bit of five-a-side football'; hockey (Dorset age group when 14)
Other sports followed: 'Most sports' – football (Aston Villa), NFL
Favourite band: 'Oceansize, Muse, Zeppelin, Blind Melon ...'
Relaxations: 'Reading, eating, music'
Extras: Played in U15 World Cup 1996. Hampshire Young Player of the Year 1998. Represented England U19 2000. Played for Loughborough UCCE 2002-04 (captain 2003), scoring a century in each innings (103/113) v Kent at Canterbury 2002. Represented British Universities 2002-04 (captain 2003). Scored maiden Championship century (168*) as Hampshire scored 404-5 to beat Yorkshire at Headingley 2006. Passed 1000 first-class runs in a season for the first time during his first innings 58 v Warwickshire at The Rose Bowl 2006
Opinions on cricket: 'Fixture list can sometimes seem random, but generally can't complain.'
Best batting: 262* Hampshire v Nottinghamshire, Trent Bridge 2006
Best bowling: 2-16 Hampshire v Durham, Riverside 2004

2006 Season

	M	Inn	NO	Runs	HS	Avg	100	50	Ct	St	Balls	Runs	Wkts	Avg	BB	5I	10M
Test																	
FC	17	31	5	1173	262 *	45.11	2	4	18	-	151	141	1	141.00	1-46	-	-
ODI																	
List A	1	1	0	5	5	5.00	-	-	-	-	0	0	0		-	-	
20/20 Int																	
20/20																	

Career Performances

	M	Inn	NO	Runs	HS	Avg	100	50	Ct	St	Balls	Runs	Wkts	Avg	BB	5I	10M
Test																	
FC	53	95	10	2743	262 *	32.27	3	12	37	-	529	390	7	55.71	2-16	-	-
ODI																	
List A	8	8	0	107	40	13.37	-	-	4	-	1	6	0		-	-	
20/20 Int																	
20/20	7	3	2	33	17 *	33.00	-	-	1	-	6	7	0		-	-	

ADSHEAD, S. J.　　　　　Gloucestershire

Name: <u>Stephen</u> John Adshead
Role: Right-hand bat, wicket-keeper
Born: 29 January 1980, Worcester
Height: 5ft 8in **Weight:** 13st
Nickname: Adders, Top Shelf
County debut: 2000 (Leicestershire), 2003 (Worcestershire), 2004 (Gloucestershire)
County cap: 2003 (Worcestershire colours), 2004 (Gloucestershire)
Place in batting averages: 147th av. 29.86 (2005 140th av. 30.66)
Parents: David and Julie
Wife: Becky
Family links with cricket: Father and brother club cricketers in Worcester; mother keen spectator
Education: Brideley Moor HS, Redditch
Qualifications: 9 GCSEs, 3 A-levels, ECB Level 2 coaching
Career outside cricket: Coaching
Overseas tours: Leicestershire to Potchefstroom, South Africa 2001
Overseas teams played for: Fish Hoek, Cape Town 1998-99; Witwatersrand Technical, Johannesburg 1999-2000; Central Hawke's Bay, New Zealand 2000-01
Career highlights to date: 'Winning C&G final at Lord's 2004'
Cricket moments to forget: 'The whole 2002 season was a fairly miserable one'
Cricket superstitions: 'None'
Cricketers particularly admired: Alec Stewart, Steve Waugh
Young players to look out for: Steve Davies
Favourite band: U2
Relaxations: 'Spending as much time as possible with my wife Becky; gym, eating'
Extras: Scored 187-minute 57* to help save match v Lancashire at Cheltenham 2004
Best batting: 148* Gloucestershire v Surrey, The Oval 2005

2006 Season

	M	Inn	NO	Runs	HS	Avg	100	50	Ct	St	Balls	Runs	Wkts	Avg	BB	5I	10M
Test																	
FC	16	28	5	687	79 *	29.86	-	4	47	2	0	0	0		-	-	-
ODI																	
List A	15	14	5	271	69 *	30.11	-	1	15	9	0	0	0		-	-	
20/20 Int																	
20/20	9	7	4	97	38 *	32.33	-	-	2	4	0	0	0		-	-	

Career Performances

	M	Inn	NO	Runs	HS	Avg	100	50	Ct	St	Balls	Runs	Wkts	Avg	BB	5I	10M
Test																	
FC	52	89	16	2318	148 *	31.75	1	14	133	12	0	0	0		-	-	-
ODI																	
List A	55	49	10	796	77 *	20.41	-	3	65	25	0	0	0		-	-	
20/20 Int																	
20/20	24	17	6	239	81	21.72	-	1	7	11	0	0	0		-	-	

AFZAAL, U.   Northamptonshire

Name: Usman Afzaal
Role: Left-hand bat, slow left-arm bowler
Born: 9 June 1977, Rawalpindi, Pakistan
Height: 6ft **Weight:** 12st 7lbs
Nickname: Saeed, Gulfraz, Usy Bhai, Trevor
County debut: 1995 (Nottinghamshire),
2004 (Northamptonshire)
County cap: 2000 (Nottinghamshire),
2005 (Northamptonshire)
Test debut: 2001
1000 runs in a season: 6
Place in batting averages: 41st av. 50.57
(2005 46th av. 47.48)
Strike rate: (career 95.73)
Parents: Firdous and Shafi Mahmood
Marital status: Single
Family links with cricket: Older brother
Kamran played for NAYC and for
Nottinghamshire U15-U19 ('top player'); younger brother Aqib played for Notts and
England U15; 'Uncle Mac and Uncle Raja great players'
Education: Manvers Pierrepont School; South Notts College
Qualifications: Coaching certificates
Overseas tours: Nottinghamshire to South Africa; England U19 to West Indies 1994-
95, to Zimbabwe 1995-96; 'the great ZRK tour to Lahore, Pakistan' 2000; England A
to West Indies 2000-01; England to India and New Zealand 2001-02
Overseas teams played for: Victoria Park, Perth
Career highlights to date: 'Playing for England in the Ashes [2001]'
Cricket moments to forget: 'Every time I get out'
Cricketers particularly admired: David Gower, Saeed Anwar, Ian Botham,
Clive Rice, Uncle Raja and Uncle Mac
Other sports played: Indoor football

Other sports followed: Football ('a bit of Man U')
Relaxations: 'Praying; spending time with friends and family; listening to Indian music'
Extras: Played for England U15 and U17. Won Denis Compton Award 1996. Took wicket (Adam Gilchrist) with third ball in Test cricket v Australia at The Oval 2001. C&G Man of the Match award for his 3-8 (from four overs) and 64* v Ireland at Clontarf 2002
Best batting: 168* Northamptonshire v Essex, Northampton 2005
Best bowling: 4-101 Nottinghamshire v Gloucestershire, Trent Bridge 1998

2006 Season

	M	Inn	NO	Runs	HS	Avg	100	50	Ct	St	Balls	Runs	Wkts	Avg	BB	5I	10M
Test																	
FC	18	32	6	1315	151	50.57	4	6	6	-	719	471	7	67.28	3-75	-	-
ODI																	
List A	16	16	2	456	108*	32.57	1	1	3	-	20	31	0		-	-	-
20/20 Int																	
20/20	9	8	2	163	64*	27.16	-	1	1	-	24	33	2	16.50	2-15	-	

Career Performances

	M	Inn	NO	Runs	HS	Avg	100	50	Ct	St	Balls	Runs	Wkts	Avg	BB	5I	10M
Test	3	6	1	83	54	16.60	-	1	-	-	54	49	1	49.00	1-49	-	-
FC	182	314	34	10559	168*	37.71	26	51	87	-	7467	4108	78	52.66	4-101	-	-
ODI																	
List A	149	138	21	4232	122*	36.17	4	29	38	-	1041	967	39	24.79	3-4	-	
20/20 Int																	
20/20	25	23	5	382	64*	21.22	-	1	5	-	48	66	2	33.00	2-15	-	

AHMED, J. S.   Essex

Name: Jahid Sheikh Ahmed
Role: Right-hand bat, right-arm medium-fast bowler
Born: 20 February 1986, Chelmsford
Height: 5ft 11in **Weight:** 11st
Nickname: Odd Bod
County debut: 2005
Strike rate: (career 96.00)
Parents: Sheikh Faruque Ahmed
Marital status: Single
Education: St Peters High School; University of East London ('currently studying sports coaching')
Off-season: 'University, training, gym, going away (tour)'
Overseas tours: Essex to South Africa 2006

Career highlights to date: 'Getting 4-32 against Sri Lanka [2006]'
Cricket moments to forget: 'Calling my name "Jihad" on Sky Sports. My name is "JAHID"'
Cricketers particularly admired: Brett Lee, Brian Lara
Young players to look out for: Stuart Broad
Other sports played: Cross country (Essex), badminton
Other sports followed: Football (Arsenal)
Injuries: Out for four weeks with a side injury
Favourite band: Tupac and the Outlawz
Relaxations: Music
Extras: Essex Academy 2004. Community award from Bangladeshi channel, presented by the High Commissioner

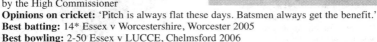

Opinions on cricket: 'Pitch is always flat these days. Batsmen always get the benefit.'
Best batting: 14* Essex v Worcestershire, Worcester 2005
Best bowling: 2-50 Essex v LUCCE, Chelmsford 2006

2006 Season

	M	Inn	NO	Runs	HS	Avg	100	50	Ct	St	Balls	Runs	Wkts	Avg	BB	5I	10M
Test																	
FC	1	0	0	0	0		-	-	1	-	126	76	2	38.00	2-50	-	-
ODI																	
List A	4	0	0	0	0		-	-	-	-	210	170	10	17.00	4-32		
20/20 Int																	
20/20	2	0	0	0	0		-	-	-	-	36	56	2	28.00	1-25	-	

Career Performances

	M	Inn	NO	Runs	HS	Avg	100	50	Ct	St	Balls	Runs	Wkts	Avg	BB	5I	10M
Test																	
FC	2	1	1	14	14 *		-	-	1	-	288	217	3	72.33	2-50	-	-
ODI																	
List A	4	0	0	0	0		-	-	-	-	210	170	10	17.00	4-32	-	
20/20 Int																	
20/20	2	0	0	0	0		-	-	-	-	36	56	2	28.00	1-25	-	

ALI, K.   Worcestershire

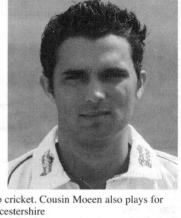

Name: Kabir Ali
Role: Right-hand bat, right-arm
medium-fast bowler
Born: 24 November 1980, Birmingham
Height: 6ft **Weight:** 12st 7lbs
Nickname: Kabby, Taxi
County debut: 1999
County colours: 2002
Test debut: 2003
ODI debut: 2003
50 wickets in a season: 3
Place in batting averages: 261st av. 12.00
(2005 217th av. 20.50)
Place in bowling averages: 36th av. 29.02
(2005 70th av. 30.94)
Strike rate: 50.57 (career 46.65)
Parents: Shabir Ali and M. Begum
Marital status: Single
Family links with cricket: Father played club cricket. Cousin Moeen also plays for
Worcestershire. Cousin Kadeer plays for Gloucestershire
Education: Moseley School; Wolverhampton University
Qualifications: GNVQ Leisure and Tourism, coaching
Overseas tours: Warwickshire U19 to Cape Town 1998; ECB National Academy to
Australia and Sri Lanka 2002-03; England to Australia 2002-03 (VB Series), to South
Africa 2004-05 (one-day series), to Pakistan 2005-06 (one-day series), to India 2005-06
(one-day series); England VI to Hong Kong 2003, 2004, 2005, 2006; England A to
West Indies 2005-06
Overseas teams played for: Midland-Guildford, Perth; Rajasthan, India 2006-07
Career highlights to date: 'Playing for England'
Cricketers particularly admired: Wasim Akram, Glenn McGrath
Young players to look out for: Moeen Ali, Omar Ali, Atif Ali
Other sports played: Football, snooker
Other sports followed: Football, snooker
Relaxations: 'Playing snooker and spending time with family and friends'
Extras: Warwickshire Youth Young Player of the Year award. Represented England
U19. NBC Denis Compton Award for the most promising young Worcestershire player
2000. Junior Royals Player of the Year 2001. Worcestershire Player of the Year 2002.
PCA Young Player of the Year 2002, 2003. Made Test debut in the fourth Test v South
Africa at Headingley 2003, taking a wicket (Neil McKenzie) with his fifth ball.
Worcestershire Young Player of the Year 2003. Don Kenyon Award 2003. Player of the
Final in the Hong Kong Sixes 2004

Best batting: 84* Worcestershire v Durham, Stockton 2003
Best bowling: 8-53 Worcestershire v Yorkshire, Scarborough 2003

2006 Season

	M	Inn	NO	Runs	HS	Avg	100	50	Ct	St	Balls	Runs	Wkts	Avg	BB	5I	10M
Test																	
FC	11	16	2	168	38 *	12.00	-	-	1	-	2023	1161	40	29.02	7-43	3	-
ODI	2	1	0	0	0	0.00	-	-	-	-	96	149	0		-	-	
List A	13	9	2	80	20	11.42	-	-	3	-	558	581	13	44.69	3-8	-	
20/20 Int																	
20/20	2	0	0	0	0		-	-	1	-	46	71	3	23.66	2-43	-	

Career Performances

	M	Inn	NO	Runs	HS	Avg	100	50	Ct	St	Balls	Runs	Wkts	Avg	BB	5I	10M
Test	1	2	0	10	9	5.00	-	-	-	-	216	136	5	27.20	3-80	-	-
FC	81	111	19	1719	84 *	18.68	-	7	22	-	13949	8424	299	28.17	8-53	13	2
ODI	14	9	3	93	39 *	15.50	-	-	1	-	673	682	20	34.10	4-45	-	
List A	130	79	21	911	92	15.70	-	3	23	-	5605	4768	187	25.49	5-36	1	
20/20 Int																	
20/20	9	6	1	85	49	17.00	-	-	5	-	202	268	10	26.80	2-25	-	

ALI, K. Gloucestershire

Name: Kadeer Ali
Role: Right-hand bat, right-arm medium-fast bowler
Born: 7 March 1983, Birmingham
Height: 6ft 2in **Weight:** 13st
Nickname: Kaddy
County debut: 2000 (Worcestershire), 2005 (Gloucestershire)
County cap: 2002 (Worcestershire colours), 2005 (Gloucestershire)
Place in batting averages: 75th av. 39.71 (2005 208th av. 21.47)
Strike rate: (career 152.00)
Parents: Munir Ali and Maqsood Begum
Marital status: Single
Family links with cricket: Brother Moeen and cousin Kabir play for Worcestershire; brother Omar Ali has played county 2nd XI and Minor Counties cricket
Education: Handsworth Grammar; Moseley Sixth Form College

Qualifications: 5 GCSEs, Level 1 coach
Overseas tours: England U19 to India 2000-01, to Australia and (U19 World Cup) New Zealand 2001-02; England A to Malaysia and India 2003-04
Overseas teams played for: WA University, Perth 2002-03
Career highlights to date: 'Being in the national academy. Really enjoyed it'
Cricket moments to forget: 'First-class debut – got a pair against Glamorgan'
Cricket superstitions: 'None'
Cricketers particularly admired: Rahul Dravid, Graeme Hick
Young players to look out for: Moeen Ali ('brother')
Other sports played: Snooker
Other sports followed: Football (Birmingham City FC)
Relaxations: 'Just chilling, spending time with mates, music, movies'
Extras: Young Player awards at Warwickshire CCC. Represented England U19 2000-02. NBC Denis Compton Award for the most promising young Worcestershire player 2001, 2002. Represented ECB National Academy v England XI at Perth 2002-03, scoring a century (100). ECB National Academy 2003-04. Became first player to hit a ball over the Basil D'Oliveira Stand at Worcester, v New Zealanders 2004
Best batting: 145 Gloucestershire v Northamptonshire, Northampton 2006
Best bowling: 1-4 Gloucestershire v Glamorgan, Bristol 2005

2006 Season

	M	Inn	NO	Runs	HS	Avg	100	50	Ct	St	Balls	Runs	Wkts	Avg	BB	5I	10M
Test																	
FC	11	22	1	834	145	39.71	1	5	6	-	84	57	0		-	-	-
ODI																	
List A	2	2	0	41	41	20.50	-	-	1	-	12	14	0		-	-	
20/20 Int																	
20/20	1	1	0	0	0	0.00	-	-	1	-	0	0	0		-	-	

Career Performances

	M	Inn	NO	Runs	HS	Avg	100	50	Ct	St	Balls	Runs	Wkts	Avg	BB	5I	10M
Test																	
FC	49	90	4	2138	145	24.86	1	14	24	-	456	289	3	96.33	1-4	-	-
ODI																	
List A	27	27	1	641	66	24.65	-	5	2	-	63	59	1	59.00	1-4	-	
20/20 Int																	
20/20	6	6	0	122	53	20.33	-	1	3	-	0	0	0		-	-	

ALI, M. M.   Worcestershire

Name: <u>Moeen</u> Munir Ali
Role: Left-hand bat, right-arm
off-spin bowler; 'batter who bowls'
Born: 18 June 1987, Birmingham
Height: 6ft **Weight:** 10st 7lbs
Nickname: Moe, Eddy, Bart, Elvis
County debut: 2005 (Warwickshire)
Place in batting averages: 211th av. 19.66
Strike rate: (career 152.66)
Parents: Munir Ali and Maqsood Begum
Marital status: Single
Family links with cricket: Father is a cricket
coach; cousin Kabir plays for Worcestershire
and England; older brother Kadeer plays for
Gloucestershire; younger brother Omar has
played county 2nd XI and Minor Counties
cricket

Education: Moseley School
Qualifications: GCSEs and Leisure and Tourism
Overseas tours: 'Streets to Arena' to Pakistan 2002; England U19 to India 2004-05,
to Bangladesh 2005-06, to Sri Lanka (U19 World Cup) 2005-06 (c)
Career highlights to date: 'Becoming one of the youngest professional cricketers at
15 years old. Hitting 195* in 20 overs'
Cricket moments to forget: 'None'
Cricket superstitions: 'None'
Cricketers particularly admired: Nick Knight, Sanath Jayasuriya, Saeed Anwar,
Wasim Akram, Kabir Ali, Kadeer Ali, Mohamed Sheikh
Young players to look out for: Omar Munir Ali, Atif Ali, Behram Ali
Other sports played: Football
Other sports followed: Football (Birmingham City)
Favourite band: B21
Extras: Represented England U15 2002. Has won five Warwickshire youth awards
since age of 11. Represented England U19 2004, 2005, 2006. Left Warwickshire at the
end of the 2006 season and has joined Worcestershire for 2007
Best batting: 68 Warwickshire v Nottinghamshire, Trent Bridge 2006
Best bowling: 2-50 Warwickshire v Lancashire, Edgbaston 2006

2006 Season

	M	Inn	NO	Runs	HS	Avg	100	50	Ct	St	Balls	Runs	Wkts	Avg	BB	5I	10M
Test																	
FC	6	9	0	177	68	19.66	-	2	2	-	446	318	3	106.00	2-50	-	-
ODI																	
List A	9	8	1	173	64	24.71	-	2	1	-	124	115	1	115.00	1-9	-	
20/20 Int																	
20/20																	

Career Performances

	M	Inn	NO	Runs	HS	Avg	100	50	Ct	St	Balls	Runs	Wkts	Avg	BB	5I	10M
Test																		
FC	7	10	0	234	68	23.40	-	3	4	-	458	333	3	111.00	2-50	-	-
ODI																	
List A	9	8	1	173	64	24.71	-	2	1	-	124	115	1	115.00	1-9	-	
20/20 Int																	
20/20																	

ALLENBY, J.   Leicestershire

Name: James (<u>Jim</u>) Allenby
Role: Right-hand bat, right-arm medium bowler
Born: 12 September 1982, Perth, Australia
Height: 6ft **Weight:** 13st 8lbs
Nickname: Jimmy, Jay, Jay Bay, Ducktails
County debut: 2005 (one-day), 2006 (first-class)
Parents: Michael and Julie
Marital status: Single
Family links with cricket: 'Great-grandfather played at Yorkshire/Hampshire'
Education: Christ Church Grammar School, Perth
Qualifications: Level 1 coach
Off-season: 'Perth'
Overseas teams played for: Claremont-Nedlands CC, Perth 1993 –
Career highlights to date: 'Playing in and winning Twenty20 [2006]. Hundred (103*) and 68* on Championship debut [v Essex at Leicester 2006]'
Cricket superstitions: 'Put gear on same way each time I bat'
Cricketers particularly admired: Dean Jones

Young players to look out for: David Brown, Stewart Walters
Other sports followed: Football (Leeds United)
Favourite band: Powderfinger
Relaxations: 'Playing golf, swimming/surfing at beach'
Extras: Set record individual score for Western Australia in U19 cricket (180) v Northern Territory 2000-01. Played for Durham Board XI in the 2003 C&G. Set new record for highest individual score in the Durham County League (266*) playing for Brandon 2005. Scored 103* and 68* on Championship debut v Essex at Leicester 2006. Is not considered an overseas player
Opinions on cricket: 'Twenty20 has made the game more watchable for everyone.'
Best batting: 103* Leicestershire v Essex, Leicester 2006

2006 Season

	M	Inn	NO	Runs	HS	Avg	100	50	Ct	St	Balls	Runs	Wkts	Avg	BB	5I	10M
Test																	
FC	2	4	2	239	103*	119.50	1	1	2	-	48	23	0		-	-	-
ODI																	
List A	12	10	3	133	43*	19.00	-	-	6	-	339	243	8	30.37	4-19	-	
20/20 Int																	
20/20	11	8	5	112	64	37.33	-	1	5	-	138	183	8	22.87	2-22	-	

Career Performances

	M	Inn	NO	Runs	HS	Avg	100	50	Ct	St	Balls	Runs	Wkts	Avg	BB	5I	10M
Test																	
FC	2	4	2	239	103*	119.50	1	1	2	-	48	23	0		-	-	-
ODI																	
List A	14	12	4	144	43*	18.00	-	-	6	-	339	243	8	30.37	4-19	-	
20/20 Int																	
20/20	15	11	5	149	64	24.83	-	1	7	-	138	183	8	22.87	2-22	-	

2. Who scored 60 and 104* on Test debut v India at Nagpur 2005-06?

ALLEYNE, D.   Nottinghamshire

Name: David Alleyne
Role: Right-hand bat, wicket-keeper
Born: 17 April 1976, York
Height: 5ft 11in **Weight:** 13st 7lbs
Nickname: Bones, Gears
County debut: 1999 (one-day, Middlesex),
2001 (first-class, Middlesex), 2004
(Nottinghamshire)
Place in batting averages: 155th av. 28.57
Parents: Darcy and Jo
Marital status: Single
Family links with cricket: Father played for
local club Northampton Exiles
Education: Enfield Grammar; Hertford
Regional College, Ware; City and Islington
College
Qualifications: 6 GCSEs, City and Guilds,
BTEC Diploma in Leisure Studies, Level 3
coaching award
Career outside cricket: Coaching; teaching
Overseas tours: Middlesex to Johannesburg 2000-01
Overseas teams played for: Stratford, New Zealand; Inglewood, New Zealand
1997-98; Sturt, Adelaide 1999-2000; Midland-Guildford, Perth 2000-01; Karori CC,
Wellington, New Zealand 2001-02
Cricketers particularly admired: Viv Richards, Desmond Haynes, Carl Hooper,
Jack Russell, Alec Stewart, Keith Piper
Other sports played: Judo, football (Middlesex U15, U16; Enfield Borough U16)
Other sports followed: Football (Liverpool FC)
Extras: Represented Middlesex U11 to U17. London Cricket College (three years).
Middlesex 2nd XI Player of the Year 1999, 2000, 2002. Scored maiden first-class
century (109*) v Warwickshire at Trent Bridge 2006
Best batting: 109* Nottinghamshire v Warwickshire, Trent Bridge 2006

2006 Season

	M	Inn	NO	Runs	HS	Avg	100	50	Ct	St	Balls	Runs	Wkts	Avg	BB	5I	10M
Test																	
FC	12	20	1	543	109 *	28.57	1	4	29	5	0	0	0		-	-	-
ODI																	
List A	6	5	0	62	22	12.40	-	-	7	1	0	0	0		-	-	
20/20 Int																	
20/20	3	1	0	0	0	0.00	-	-	2	-	0	0	0		-	-	

Career Performances

	M	Inn	NO	Runs	HS	Avg	100	50	Ct	St	Balls	Runs	Wkts	Avg	BB	5I	10M
Test																	
FC	22	33	4	849	109 *	29.27	1	4	57	5	0	0	0		-	-	-
ODI																	
List A	38	31	2	321	58	11.06	-	1	29	7	0	0	0		-	-	
20/20 Int																	
20/20	11	5	3	36	24 *	18.00	-	-	6	-	0	0	0		-	-	

AMBROSE, T. R. Warwickshire

Name: Timothy (Tim) Raymond Ambrose
Role: Right-hand bat, wicket-keeper
Born: 1 December 1982, Newcastle,
New South Wales, Australia
Height: 5ft 7in
Nickname: Shambrose, Freak, Mole
County debut: 2001 (Sussex), 2006
(Warwickshire)
County cap: 2003 (Sussex)
Place in batting averages: 111th av. 34.07
(2005 167th av. 27.11)
Parents: Raymond and Sally
Marital status: Single
Family links with cricket: Cousin played
Sydney first grade; father captain of local
grade D4 team
Education: Merewether Selective High,
NSW
Career outside cricket: Greenkeeping
Overseas tours: Sussex to Grenada 2001, 2002
Overseas teams played for: Wallsend, NSW 2000; Nelson Bay, NSW 2001;
Newcastle, NSW 2002
Career highlights to date: 'Winning the Championship 2003. Maiden first-class
century, 149 v Yorkshire'
Cricketers particularly admired: Alec Stewart, Ian Healy, Steve Waugh,
Mushtaq Ahmed
Other sports played: Football, squash, golf, rugby league, rugby union, AFL,
'I'll have a go at anything'
Other sports followed: Rugby league (Newcastle Knights), Australian Rules (Sydney
Swans), football (Tottenham Hotspur)
Favourite band: Jeff Buckley, Ben Harper, Jack Johnson

Relaxations: Guitar, music
Extras: Captained Newcastle (NSW) U16 1999 Bradman Cup winning side. Played for New South Wales U17. Won NSW Junior Cricketer of the Year three years running. C&G Man of the Match award for his 95 v Buckinghamshire at Beaconsfield 2002. Holds a British passport and is not considered an overseas player
Best batting: 149 Sussex v Yorkshire, Headingley 2002

2006 Season

	M	Inn	NO	Runs	HS	Avg	100	50	Ct	St	Balls	Runs	Wkts	Avg	BB	5I	10M
Test																	
FC	9	14	1	443	133	34.07	1	3	30	4	0	0	0		-	-	-
ODI																	
List A	10	8	1	114	31	16.28	-	-	14	3	0	0	0		-	-	
20/20 Int																	
20/20	2	2	1	60	48 *	60.00	-	-	1	1	0	0	0		-	-	

Career Performances

	M	Inn	NO	Runs	HS	Avg	100	50	Ct	St	Balls	Runs	Wkts	Avg	BB	5I	10M
Test																	
FC	56	90	6	2765	149	32.91	3	18	106	14	6	1	0		-	-	-
ODI																	
List A	61	56	5	1220	95	23.92	-	6	68	8	0	0	0		-	-	
20/20 Int																	
20/20	12	9	3	183	54 *	30.50	-	1	9	5	0	0	0		-	-	

ANDERSON, J. M.   Lancashire

Name: <u>James</u> Michael Anderson
Role: Left-hand bat, right-arm fast-medium bowler
Born: 30 July 1982, Burnley
Height: 6ft 2in **Weight:** 13st
Nickname: Jimmy
County debut: 2001 (one-day), 2002 (first-class)
County cap: 2003
Test debut: 2003
ODI debut: 2002-03
50 wickets in a season: 2
Place in batting averages: (2005 278th av. 10.35)
Place in bowling averages: (2005 60th av. 30.21)
Strike rate: (career 46.78)
Parents: Michael and Catherine
Wife and date of marriage: Daniella, February 2006

Family links with cricket: Father and uncle played for Burnley
Education: St Theodore's RC High School; St Theodore's RC Sixth Form Centre – both Burnley
Qualifications: 10 GCSEs, 1 A-level, 1 GNVQ, Level 2 coaching award
Off-season: Touring with England
Overseas tours: Lancashire to Cape Town 2002; ECB National Academy to Australia 2002-03; England to Australia 2002-03 (VB Series), to Africa (World Cup) 2002-03, to Bangladesh and Sri Lanka 2003-04, to West Indies 2003-04, to Zimbabwe (one-day series) 2004-05, to South Africa 2004-05, to Pakistan 2005-06, to India 2005-06, to India (ICC Champions Trophy) 2006-07, to Australia 2006-07; England A to West Indies 2005-06

Career highlights to date: 'Receiving Lancs cap. Playing for England'
Cricket moments to forget: 'England v Australia – 2003 World Cup'
Cricketers particularly admired: Darren Gough, Nasser Hussain, Peter Martin
Other sports played: Golf (12 handicap), football
Other sports followed: Football (Arsenal FC), rugby league, darts
Favourite band: Oasis, U2
Relaxations: 'Watching TV, playing PlayStation, music'
Extras: Represented England U19 2001. Took 50 first-class wickets in his first full season 2002. NBC Denis Compton Award for the most promising young Lancashire player 2002. Won two Man of the Match awards in the 2002-03 World Cup. Took hat-trick (Robinson, Hussain, Jefferson) v Essex at Old Trafford 2003. Recorded a five-wicket innings return (5-73) on Test debut in the first Test v Zimbabwe at Lord's 2003. Became the first England bowler to take an ODI hat-trick (Abdul Razzaq, Shoaib Akhtar, Mohammad Sami) v Pakistan at The Oval in the NatWest Challenge 2003. Cricket Writers' Club Young Player of the Year 2003. Man of the Match in the fifth ODI v Pakistan at Rawalpindi 2005-06 (4-48)
Best batting: 37* Lancashire v Durham, Old Trafford 2005
Best bowling: 6-23 Lancashire v Hampshire, Rose Bowl 2002
Stop press: Made Twenty20 International debut v Australia at Sydney 2006-07. Returned home early from England's tour to Australia 2006-07 with a back complaint

2006 Season

	M	Inn	NO	Runs	HS	Avg	100	50	Ct	St	Balls	Runs	Wkts	Avg	BB	5I	10M
Test																	
FC	1	1	1	7	7*		-	-	1	-	60	38	0		-	-	-
ODI																	
List A	1	0	0	0	0		-	-	-	-	42	31	2	15.50	2-31	-	
20/20 Int																	
20/20																	

Career Performances

	M	Inn	NO	Runs	HS	Avg	100	50	Ct	St	Balls	Runs	Wkts	Avg	BB	5I	10M
Test	13	18	12	89	21*	14.83	-	-	4	-	2221	1353	41	33.00	5-73	2	-
FC	53	62	31	318	37*	10.25	-	-	20	-	8890	5189	190	27.31	6-23	8	1
ODI	50	19	9	69	12*	6.90	-	-	11	-	2452	1972	75	26.29	4-25	-	
List A	88	36	22	149	13*	10.64	-	-	16	-	4220	3293	133	24.75	4-25	-	
20/20 Int																	
20/20	13	3	2	21	16	21.00	-	-	2	-	268	380	12	31.66	2-25	-	

ANDREW, G. M. Somerset

Name: <u>Gareth</u> Mark Andrew
Role: Left-hand bat, right-arm medium-fast bowler
Born: 27 December 1983, Yeovil
Height: 6ft **Weight:** 14st
Nickname: Gaz, Brad, Sobers
County debut: 2003
Place in bowling averages: (2005 127th av. 45.45)
Strike rate: (career 47.75)
Parents: Peter and Susan
Marital status: Single
Family links with cricket: Father and younger brother club cricketers
Education: Ansford Community School; Richard Huish College, Taunton
Qualifications: 10 GCSEs, 3 A-levels, Level 1 coach
Overseas tours: West of England U15 to West Indies 1999; England U17 to Australia 2001; Somerset Academy to Western Australia 2002; Aus Academy to Perth 2003
Overseas teams played for: Swanbourne CC, Perth 2002-03
Career highlights to date: '4-48 against Scotland in totesport League [2004]'

Cricket moments to forget: 'Whenever bowling in the Twenty20'
Cricket superstitions: 'Always put my boots on the right feet'
Cricketers particularly admired: Ian Botham, Andrew Flintoff, Chris Cairns
Young players to look out for: Jack Cooper, Nick Gibbens, Simon Ruddick, Chaz Thomas
Other sports played: Football (Bruton Town FC, Yeovil District U11-U16, Castle Cary AFC)
Other sports followed: Football (Yeovil Town, Man Utd)
Favourite band: 'Too many to mention'
Extras: Represented England U19 v South Africa U19 2003
Best batting: 44 Somerset v Sri Lanka A, Taunton 2004
Best bowling: 4-63 Somerset v Sri Lanka A, Taunton 2004

2006 Season

	M	Inn	NO	Runs	HS	Avg	100	50	Ct	St	Balls	Runs	Wkts	Avg	BB	5I	10M
Test																	
FC																	
ODI																	
List A	11	6	2	59	33	14.75	-	-	2	-	371	345	8	43.12	2-35	-	
20/20 Int																	
20/20	6	2	1	1	1 *	1.00	-	-	3	-	114	195	4	48.75	3-36	-	

Career Performances

	M	Inn	NO	Runs	HS	Avg	100	50	Ct	St	Balls	Runs	Wkts	Avg	BB	5I	10M
Test																	
FC	11	14	1	163	44	12.53	-	-	5	-	1337	989	28	35.32	4-63	-	-
ODI																	
List A	41	23	6	172	33	10.11	-	-	12	-	1321	1360	40	34.00	4-48	-	
20/20 Int																	
20/20	24	11	3	50	12	6.25	-	-	8	-	399	603	23	26.21	4-22	-	

ANYON, J. E. Warwickshire

Name: <u>James</u> Edward Anyon
Role: Left-hand bat, right-arm
fast-medium bowler
Born: 5 May 1983, Lancaster
Height: 6ft 2in **Weight:** 13st 7lbs
Nickname: Jimmy
County debut: 2005
Place in bowling averages: 63rd av. 32.61
(2005 88th av. 35.41)
Strike rate: 66.25 (career 66.28)
Parents: Peter and Christine
Marital status: Single
Family links with cricket: 'Dad used to
play village cricket'
Education: Garstang High School; Preston
College; Loughborough University
Qualifications: GCSEs, 3 A-levels,
BSc Sports Science with Management,
Level 1 coaching
Overseas teams played for: Claremont-Nedlands, Perth 2004-05
Career highlights to date: 'Bowling at Brian Lara'
Cricket moments to forget: 'Losing UCCE final 2004'
Cricketers particularly admired: Glenn McGrath, Michael Atherton
Young players to look out for: Moeen Ali
Other sports played: Football, golf
Other sports followed: Football (Man Utd, Preston North End)
Favourite band: Nuse
Extras: Young Player of the Year awards at Preston CC. Bowler of the Year award at
Farsley CC (Bradford League) 2004. Played for Loughborough UCCE 2003, 2004.
Took Twenty20 hat-trick (Durston, Andrew, Caddick) v Somerset at Edgbaston 2005
Best batting: 21 LUCCE v Leicestershire, Leicester 2003
Best bowling: 5-83 Warwickshire v Nottinghamshire, Edgbaston 2006

2006 Season

	M	Inn	NO	Runs	HS	Avg	100	50	Ct	St	Balls	Runs	Wkts	Avg	BB	5I	10M
Test																	
FC	11	17	6	60	18 *	5.45	-	-	3	-	2054	1011	31	32.61	5-83	1	-
ODI																	
List A	11	5	2	13	12	4.33	-	-	1	-	382	370	13	28.46	3-41	-	
20/20 Int																	
20/20	6	1	1	1	1 *		-	-	1	-	120	198	7	28.28	2-20	-	

Career Performances

	M	Inn	NO	Runs	HS	Avg	100	50	Ct	St	Balls	Runs	Wkts	Avg	BB	5I	10M
Test																	
FC	22	32	14	112	21	6.22	-	-	8	-	3314	1930	50	38.60	5-83	1	-
ODI																	
List A	26	7	2	13	12	2.60	-	-	4	-	964	856	24	35.66	3-41	-	
20/20 Int																	
20/20	13	3	3	16	8 *		-	-	3	-	219	323	16	20.18	3-6	-	

ASTLE, N. J. Lancashire

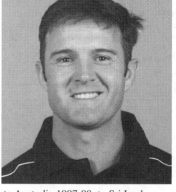

Name: <u>Nathan</u> John Astle
Role: Right-hand bat, right-arm
medium bowler
Born: 15 September 1971, Christchurch,
New Zealand
Height: 5ft 10in
County debut: 1997 (Nottinghamshire),
2005 (Durham), 2006 (Lancashire)
Test debut: 1995-96
ODI debut: 1994-95
Twenty20 Int debut: 2005-06
1st-Class 200s: 2
Place in batting averages: 98th av. 35.75
(2005 112th av. 34.12)
Strike rate: (career 88.56)
Overseas tours: New Zealand to India 1995-
96 (one-day series), to India and Pakistan
(World Cup) 1995-96, to West Indies 1995-
96, to Pakistan 1996-97, to Zimbabwe 1997-98, to Australia 1997-98, to Sri Lanka
1998, to Malaysia (Commonwealth Games) 1998-99, to Bangladesh (Wills
International Cup) 1998-99, to UK, Ireland and Netherlands (World Cup) 1999, to
England 1999, to India 1999-2000, to Zimbabwe 2000-01, to Kenya (ICC Knockout
Trophy) 2000-01, to South Africa 2000-01, to Australia 2001-02, to West Indies 2002,
to Sri Lanka (ICC Champions Trophy) 2002-03, to Africa (World Cup) 2002-03, to
India 2003-04, to England 2004, to England (ICC Champions Trophy) 2004, to
Bangladesh 2004-05, to Australia 2004-05, to Zimbabwe 2005-06, to South Africa
2005-06, to India (ICC Champions Trophy) 2006-07, to Australia (C'wealth Bank
Series) 2006-07, plus other one-day series and tournaments in Sri Lanka, India,
Sharjah, Singapore, Pakistan and South Africa
Overseas teams played for: Canterbury 1991-92 –

Extras: Represented New Zealand U19 1990-91. One of *New Zealand Cricket Almanack*'s two Players of the Year 1995, 1996, 2002. Holds record for the fastest 200 in Tests in terms of balls received (153), scored in the first Test v England at Christchurch 2001-02 (ended up with 222). Has won numerous domestic and international awards, including Man of the [ODI] Series v Zimbabwe 1997-98 and Man of the Match in the final of the Videocon TriSeries 2005-06 v India at Harare (115*). Overseas player with Nottinghamshire 1997; an overseas player with Durham in 2005 as a locum for Mike Hussey; an overseas player with Lancashire during the 2006 season as a locum for Brad Hodge

Best batting: 223 New Zealanders v Queensland, Brisbane 2001-02
Best bowling: 6-22 Canterbury v Otago, Christchurch 1996-97
Stop press: Retired from international cricket in January 2007 during the Commonwealth Bank Series in Australia

2006 Season

	M	Inn	NO	Runs	HS	Avg	100	50	Ct	St	Balls	Runs	Wkts	Avg	BB	5I	10M
Test																	
FC	8	12	0	429	86	35.75	-	3	3	-	351	178	4	44.50	1-9	-	-
ODI																	
List A	8	8	2	231	78	38.50	-	2	2	-	48	51	0		-	-	
20/20 Int																	
20/20	8	8	0	132	40	16.50	-	-	1	-	42	40	1	40.00	1-24	-	

Career Performances

	M	Inn	NO	Runs	HS	Avg	100	50	Ct	St	Balls	Runs	Wkts	Avg	BB	5I	10M
Test	79	133	10	4650	222	37.80	11	24	69	-	5634	2119	51	41.54	3-27	-	-
FC	167	265	23	9165	223	37.87	19	49	128	-	13196	4787	149	32.12	6-22	2	-
ODI	212	207	14	6890	145 *	35.69	16	40	80	-	4768	3741	99	37.78	4-43	-	
List A	366	348	31	11433	145 *	36.06	26	63	143	-	10802	7328	244	30.03	4-14	-	
20/20 Int	2	2	0	15	10	7.50	-	-	3	-	24	20	3	6.66	3-20	-	
20/20	20	20	1	486	75 *	25.57	-	4	7	-	252	278	14	19.85	3-20	-	

AVERIS, J. M. M.   Gloucestershire

Name: <u>James</u> Maxwell Michael Averis
Role: Right-hand bat, right-arm fast-medium bowler
Born: 28 May 1974, Bristol
Height: 5ft 11in **Weight:** 13st 7lbs
Nickname: Avo, Fish, Goat
County debut: 1994 (one-day), 1997 (first-class)
County cap: 2001
Place in batting averages: 217th av. 18.28 (2005 265th av. 12.93)

Place in bowling averages: 135th av. 47.30
(2005 117th av. 43.25)
Strike rate: 64.60 (career 71.25)
Parents: Mike and Carol
Wife and date of marriage: Anna,
26 October 2002
Family links with cricket: Father and
grandfather played
Education: Bristol Cathedral School;
Portsmouth University; St Cross College,
Oxford University
Qualifications: 10 GCSEs, 3 A-levels, BSc
(Hons) Geographical Science, Diploma in
Social Studies (Oxon), FPC I and II
Overseas tours: Bristol Schools to Australia
1990-91; Gloucestershire to Zimbabwe 1997,
to South Africa 1999, to Cape Town 2000, to
Kimberley 2001, to Stellenbosch 2002;

Bristol RFC to South Africa 1996; Oxford University RFC to Japan and Australia 1997
Overseas teams played for: Union CC, Port Elizabeth, South Africa; Kraifontaine,
Boland, South Africa 2001
Career highlights to date: 'Winning treble in 2000'
Cricket moments to forget: 'Dropping the biggest dolly in 2000 NatWest final'
Cricket superstitions: 'Must eat on way to ground. Always use same toilet'
Cricketers particularly admired: Viv Richards, Malcolm Marshall, Ian Botham
Other sports played: Football (Bristol North West), rugby (played for Bristol RFC,
captain of South West U21 1995, Oxford Blue 1996)
Other sports followed: Rugby (Bristol RFC), football (Liverpool FC)
Relaxations: 'Reading, surfing, eating out'
Extras: Oxford Blue 1996, 1997. Played in every one-day game in Gloucestershire's
treble-winning season 2000. Gloucestershire Player of the Year 2001. Had figures of
4-23 in the C&G final v Worcestershire at Lord's 2004, including hat-trick
(Leatherdale, G. Batty, Hall) with the last ball of his ninth over and the first two balls
of his tenth. Released by Gloucestershire at the end of the 2006 season
Best batting: 53 Gloucestershire v Surrey, Bristol 2006
Best bowling: 6-32 Gloucestershire v Northamptonshire, Bristol 2004

2006 Season

	M	Inn	NO	Runs	HS	Avg	100	50	Ct	St	Balls	Runs	Wkts	Avg	BB	5I	10M
Test																	
FC	4	7	0	128	53	18.28	-	1	-	-	646	473	10	47.30	4-75	-	-
ODI																	
List A	14	4	1	15	6 *	5.00	-	-	2	-	654	619	23	26.91	4-17	-	
20/20 Int																	
20/20	1	1	0	10	10	10.00	-	-	-	-	24	36	0		-	-	

Career Performances

	M	Inn	NO	Runs	HS	Avg	100	50	Ct	St	Balls	Runs	Wkts	Avg	BB	5I	10M
Test																	
FC	70	93	17	984	53	12.94	-	1	14	-	11115	6746	156	43.24	6-32	5	-
ODI																	
List A	150	71	34	375	23 *	10.13	-	-	19	-	6806	5534	227	24.37	6-23	4	
20/20 Int																	
20/20	9	3	0	16	10	5.33	-	-	3	-	162	237	12	19.75	3-7	-	

AZHAR MAHMOOD   Surrey

Name: Azhar Mahmood Sagar
Role: Right-hand bat, right-arm
fast-medium bowler; all-rounder
Born: 28 February 1975, Rawalpindi,
Pakistan
Height: 6ft **Weight:** 13st 5lbs
Nickname: Aju
County debut: 2002
County cap: 2004
Test debut: 1997-98
ODI debut: 1996
1st-Class 200s: 1
Place in batting averages: 87th av. 37.50
(2005 25th av. 52.90)
Place in bowling averages: 94th av. 37.45
(2005 85th av. 34.00)
Strike rate: 65.16 (career 49.97)
Parents: Mohammed Aslam Sagar and

Nusrat Perveen
Wife and date of marriage: Ebba Azhar, 13 April 2003
Education: FG No. 1 High School, Islamabad
Qualifications: 'A-level equivalent'
Overseas tours: Pakistan Youth to New Zealand 1994-95; Pakistan A to Bangladesh
1996, to England 1997; Pakistan to India (Pepsi Independence Cup) 1997, to South
Africa and Zimbabwe 1997-98, to Bangladesh (Wills International Cup) 1998-99,
to India 1998-99, to UK, Ireland and Netherlands (World Cup) 1999, to Australia
1999-2000, to Sri Lanka 2000, to Kenya (ICC Knockout Trophy) 2000-01, to New
Zealand 2000-01, to England 2001, to Bangladesh 2001-02, to Australia (Super
Challenge II) 2002, to Morocco (Morocco Cup) 2002, to Zimbabwe 2002-03, to Africa
(World Cup) 2002-03, to England (NatWest Challenge) 2003, to New Zealand 2003-
04, to England (ICC Champions Trophy) 2004, to Australia 2004-05 (VB Series),

to South Africa 2006-07 (one-day series), plus other one-day tournaments in Toronto, Kenya, Sharjah, Bangladesh and Singapore

Overseas teams played for: Islamabad; United Bank; Rawalpindi; Pakistan International Airlines; Habib Bank 2006-07

Career highlights to date: 'First Test match (debut) against South Africa in 1997 in Pakistan (Rawalpindi). I scored 128* in the first innings and 50* in the second, plus two wickets – Man of the Match'

Cricket moments to forget: 'World Cup 1999 – final against Australia (which we lost)'

Cricket superstitions: 'None'

Cricketers particularly admired: Imran Khan, Wasim Akram, Steve Waugh

Other sports played: Snooker, basketball, kite flying

Other sports followed: Football (Man U)

Relaxations: 'Listening to music, training, spending time with my family'

Extras: Scored 128* and 50* on Test debut in the first Test v South Africa at Rawalpindi 1997-98; during first innings shared with Mushtaq Ahmed (59) in a stand of 151, equalling the world tenth-wicket record in Tests. Scored century (136) in the first Test v South Africa at Johannesburg 1997-98, becoming the first Pakistan player to score a Test century in South Africa and achieving feat of scoring a century on Test debuts home and away. Took 6-18 v West Indies in the Coca-Cola Champions Trophy in Sharjah 1999-2000 and 5-28 v Sri Lanka in the final of the same competition, winning the Man of the Match award on both occasions. An overseas player with Surrey at the start of the 2002 season (pending the arrival of Saqlain Mushtaq) and since 2003

Best batting: 204* Surrey v Middlesex, The Oval 2005

Best bowling: 8-61 Surrey v Lancashire, The Oval 2002

Stop press: Called up to the Pakistan squad for the tour to South Africa 2006-07, replacing the injured Shabbir Ahmed

3. Who scored 214 and 100* on Test debut for West Indies 1971-72?

2006 Season

	M	Inn	NO	Runs	HS	Avg	100	50	Ct	St	Balls	Runs	Wkts	Avg	BB	5I	10M
Test																	
FC	13	20	4	600	101	37.50	1	2	18	-	2020	1161	31	37.45	5-69	1	-
ODI																	
List A	10	8	2	227	101 *	37.83	1	-	5	-	383	303	12	25.25	4-17	-	
20/20 Int																	
20/20	10	10	2	217	65 *	27.12	-	1	4	-	187	242	8	30.25	2-6	-	

Career Performances

	M	Inn	NO	Runs	HS	Avg	100	50	Ct	St	Balls	Runs	Wkts	Avg	BB	5I	10M
Test	21	34	4	900	136	30.00	3	1	14	-	3015	1402	39	35.94	4-50	-	-
FC	132	205	26	5566	204 *	31.09	6	29	116	-	22140	11666	443	26.33	8-61	16	3
ODI	139	107	25	1492	67	18.19	-	3	37	-	6148	4741	122	38.86	6-18	3	
List A	244	193	43	3176	101 *	21.17	2	11	73	-	10866	8308	256	32.45	6-18	5	
20/20 Int																	
20/20	26	25	6	555	65 *	29.21	-	2	8	-	499	603	29	20.79	4-20	-	

BALCOMBE, D. J. Hampshire

Name: David John Balcombe
Role: Right-hand bat, right-arm fast-medium bowler
Born: 24 December 1984, City of London
Height: 6ft 4in
Nickname: Balcs, Spalko
County debut: 2006 (one-day)
Strike rate: (career 69.35)
Parents: Peter and Elizabeth
Marital status: Single
Education: St John's School, Leatherhead; Durham University
Qualifications: 9 GCSEs, 3 A-levels, Level 1 coaching award
Career outside cricket: Student and coaching
Off-season: 'Completing final year of degree at Durham University and training'
Overseas tours: Surrey Academy to Perth 2004; MCC A to Canada 2005
Overseas teams played for: Midland-Guildford CC, Western Australia 2003-04
Career highlights to date: 'Taking maiden first-class five-wicket return against Durham, and representing British Universities against Sri Lanka 2006, taking five wickets in the game'

Cricket superstitions: 'Left equipment on first – ie left shoe, left pad'
Cricketers particularly admired: Graeme Fowler, Martin Bicknell
Young players to look out for: Richard Morris, Lee Daggett, Will Smith, Chris Benham
Other sports followed: Rugby (London Wasps), football (Arsenal)
Favourite band: Paolo Nutini, The Kooks
Relaxations: 'Sleeping, socialising'
Extras: Played for Durham UCCE 2005, 2006 (awarded university cap for performances in 2005). Represented British Universities 2006
Opinions on cricket: 'It is continuously moving forward and developing. It is an exciting time to be involved in the game – with new regulations allowing only one overseas player and fewer non-qualified players, younger players will inevitably be given more opportunities.'
Best batting: 73 DUCCE v Leicestershire, Leicester 2005
Best bowling: 5-112 DUCCE v Durham, Durham 2005

2006 Season

	M	Inn	NO	Runs	HS	Avg	100	50	Ct	St	Balls	Runs	Wkts	Avg	BB	5I	10M
Test																	
FC	4	6	1	38	15	7.60	-	-	1	-	626	450	9	50.00	3-67	-	-
ODI																	
List A																	
20/20 Int																	
20/20	1	1	0	3	3	3.00	-	-	-	-	12	15	0		-	-	

Career Performances

	M	Inn	NO	Runs	HS	Avg	100	50	Ct	St	Balls	Runs	Wkts	Avg	BB	5I	10M
Test																	
FC	7	9	1	127	73	15.87	-	1	2	-	1179	841	17	49.47	5-112	1	-
ODI																	
List A																	
20/20 Int																	
20/20	1	1	0	3	3	3.00	-	-	-	-	12	15	0		-	-	

BALL, M. C. J.   Gloucestershire

Name: <u>Martyn</u> Charles John Ball
Role: Right-hand bat, off-spin bowler, slip fielder
Born: 26 April 1970, Bristol
Height: 5ft 9in **Weight:** 12st 10lbs
Nickname: Benny, Barfo
County debut: 1988
County cap: 1996
Benefit: 2002
Place in batting averages: 239th av. 15.35
Place in bowling averages: 76th av. 34.44
Strike rate: 68.40 (career 79.81)
Parents: Kenneth Charles and Pamela Wendy
Wife and date of marriage: Mona, 28 September 1991
Children: Kristina, 9 May 1990; Alexandra, 2 August 1993; Harrison, 5 June 1997
Education: King Edmund Secondary School, Yate; Bath College of Further Education

Qualifications: 6 O-levels, 2 A-levels, advanced cricket coach
Overseas tours: Gloucestershire to Namibia 1991, to Kenya 1992, to Sri Lanka 1993, to Zimbabwe 1996, 1997, to South Africa 1999; MCC to New Zealand 1998-99; England to India 2001-02
Overseas teams played for: North Melbourne, Australia 1988-89; Old Hararians, Zimbabwe 1990-91
Cricketers particularly admired: Ian Botham, Vic Marks, John Emburey, Jack Russell
Other sports played: Rugby, football (both to county schoolboys level); 'enjoy golf and skiing'
Other sports followed: 'All sport – massive Man City fan'
Relaxations: 'Spending some quality time at home with family'
Extras: Represented county schools. Played for Young England 1989. Produced best match bowling figures for the Britannic County Championship 1993 season – 14-169 against Somerset at Taunton. Called up for England Test tour of India 2001-02 after withdrawal of Robert Croft. Retired from county cricket during the 2006-07 off-season
Best batting: 75 Gloucestershire v Somerset, Taunton 2003
Best bowling: 8-46 Gloucestershire v Somerset, Taunton 1993

	M	Inn	NO	Runs	HS	Avg	100	50	Ct	St		Balls	Runs	Wkts	Avg	BB	5I	10M
Test																		
FC	10	15	1	215	58	15.35	-	1	16	-		1847	930	27	34.44	6-134	1	-
ODI																		
List A	13	8	4	31	9	7.75	-	-	10	-		576	426	23	18.52	5-48	1	
20/20 Int																		
20/20	9	4	2	47	27 *	23.50	-	-	3	-		158	210	9	23.33	3-23		

Career Performances

	M	Inn	NO	Runs	HS	Avg	100	50	Ct	St		Balls	Runs	Wkts	Avg	BB	5I	10M
Test																		
FC	193	295	54	4633	75	19.22	-	16	233	-		31048	14682	389	37.74	8-46	13	1
ODI																		
List A	282	196	69	1776	51	13.98	-	1	137	-		11602	8777	288	30.47	5-33	3	
20/20 Int																		
20/20	29	12	5	113	27 *	16.14	-	-	13	-		530	661	27	24.48	3-23	-	

BALLANCE, G. S.   Derbyshire

Name: <u>Gary</u> Simon Ballance
Role: Left-hand top-order bat, occasional right-arm leg-spin bowler
Born: 22 November 1989, Harare, Zimbabwe
Nickname: Gazza
County debut: 2006 (one-day)
Parents: Simon and Gail
Marital status: Single
Family links with cricket: 'Father – Zimbabwe Country Districts.' Uncle David Houghton is Derbyshire director of cricket and former captain of Zimbabwe
Education: Peterhouse, Zimbabwe; Harrow School
Overseas tours: Zimbabwe U19 to Sri Lanka (U19 World Cup) 2005-06
Career highlights to date: 'Making 73 for Derbyshire first team against Hampshire last season'
Cricket superstitions: 'None'
Cricketers particularly admired: Andy Flower, Shane Warne
Other sports played: Golf, tennis, rugby

Other sports followed: Football (Liverpool)
Favourite band: Blink-182, The Killers
Relaxations: 'Watching TV'
Extras: Man of the Match v England U19 at Colombo in the U19 World Cup 2005-06 (3-21/47). Made county one-day debut aged 16 v West Indies A in a 50-over match at Derby 2006, scoring 48; made Pro40 debut v Hampshire at The Rose Bowl 2006, scoring 73

2006 Season

	M	Inn	NO	Runs	HS	Avg	100	50	Ct	St	Balls	Runs	Wkts	Avg	BB	5I	10M
Test																	
FC																	
ODI																	
List A	3	3	0	127	73	42.33	-	1	1	-	0	0	0		-	-	
20/20 Int																	
20/20																	

Career Performances

	M	Inn	NO	Runs	HS	Avg	100	50	Ct	St	Balls	Runs	Wkts	Avg	BB	5I	10M
Test																	
FC																	
ODI																	
List A	3	3	0	127	73	42.33	-	1	1	-	0	0	0		-	-	
20/20 Int																	
20/20																	

BANERJEE, V. Gloucestershire

Name: Vikram Banerjee
Role: Left-hand bat, left-arm orthodox spin bowler
Born: 20 March 1984, Bradford
Height: 6ft **Weight:** 11st
Nickname: Banners
County debut: 2006
County cap: 2006
Place in bowling averages: 145th av. 57.21
Strike rate: 98.35 (career 116.81)
Parents: Biren and Shyamli
Marital status: Single
Education: King Edward's School, Birmingham; Cambridge University
Qualifications: 12 GCSEs, 4 A-levels, BA (Econ), coaching Level 2
Overseas tours: ECB Emerging Players to Mumbai (World Cricket Academy) 2006-07

Overseas teams played for: Shivaji Park Gymkhana, Mumbai 2003
Career highlights to date: 'Winning at Lord's in 2005 Varsity Match. First wicket for Gloucestershire (Mark Butcher)'
Cricket moments to forget: 'Innings defeat to Somerset on debut'
Cricket superstitions: 'Right pad on first'
Cricketers particularly admired: Viv Richards, Sachin Tendulkar, Bishan Bedi
Other sports followed: Football (Aston Villa)
Favourite band: U2, Status Quo, Sting, Jack Johnson, Coldplay
Relaxations: 'Movies, reading, spending time with mates'
Extras: Cambridge Blue 2004-06. Played for Cambridge UCCE 2006. ECB National Skills Set. NBC Denis Compton Award for the most promising young Gloucestershire player 2006
Best batting: 29 Cambridge University v Oxford University, Fenner's 2005
Best bowling: 4-150 Gloucestershire v Glamorgan, Cardiff 2006

2006 Season

	M	Inn	NO	Runs	HS	Avg	100	50	Ct	St	Balls	Runs	Wkts	Avg	BB	5I	10M
Test																	
FC	7	11	3	72	28	9.00	-	-	2	-	1377	801	14	57.21	4-150	-	-
ODI																	
List A																		
20/20 Int																		
20/20																		

Career Performances

	M	Inn	NO	Runs	HS	Avg	100	50	Ct	St	Balls	Runs	Wkts	Avg	BB	5I	10M
Test																		
FC	9	15	3	139	29	11.58	-	-	2	-	1869	1089	16	68.06	4-150	-	-
ODI																		
List A																		
20/20 Int																		
20/20																		

BARNES, M. W. Warwickshire

Name: <u>Michael</u> William Barnes
Role: Right-hand bat, wicket-keeper
Born: 3 April 1985, Frimley, Surrey
Height: 5ft 11in **Weight:** 11st
Nickname: Barnesy, Barndog, Barno,
'anything with a Barn!'
County debut: No first-team appearance
Parents: Sharon and Doug
Marital status: Single
Family links with cricket: 'Dad used
to play'
Education: Bohunt School, Liphook;
South Downs College
Qualifications: 11 GCSEs
Off-season: 'Winter training at Edgbaston
and a couple of months abroad playing'
Overseas tours: West of England U15 to
West Indies 2000

Overseas teams played for: Westville CC, South Africa 2006
Career highlights to date: 'First hundred against Middlesex. Winning 2nd XI Trophy
with Warwickshire and joining the Bears'
Cricket moments to forget: 'Any dropped catches'
Cricket superstitions: 'Must wink at the number 14 after I've seen the number 13 –
very strange but I can't help it'
Cricketers particularly admired: Alec Stewart, Ricky Ponting, Matthew Scott
Young players to look out for: Mitchell Stokes, James Manning
Other sports played: Football (Chelsea and West Ham Youth teams)
Other sports followed: Football (Chelsea), Australian Rules football (Essendon
Bombers), 'England in anything'
Favourite band: Aerosmith, Jimmy Barnes
Relaxations: 'Watching TV (*Family Guy*), golf; spending time with the Mannings and
enjoying Shazza's cooking'
Extras: Took hat-trick of stumpings at the age of 12
Opinions on cricket: 'Needs to be taken into the present time and not be dragged
down by old-fashioned opinions.'

BARRICK, D. J.　　　　　Durham

Name: <u>David</u> James Barrick
Role: Right-hand bat, leg-spin bowler; all-rounder
Born: 4 January 1984, Pontefract, Yorkshire
Height: 5ft 8in **Weight:** 11st 7lbs
Nickname: Baz
County debut: 2005 (one-day)
Parents: Janet and Dave
Marital status: Single
Education: Malet Lambert School; Wilberforce College
Qualifications: 10 GCSEs, 3 A-levels, Levels 1 and 2 cricket coaching
Overseas tours: England U17 to Australia 2001; Durham to Dubai 2005
Overseas teams played for: Adelaide Buffalos CC 2002; Bulleen Bulls CC, Melbourne 2003-04

Career highlights to date: 'Playing for England U17'
Cricket moments to forget: 'Involved in run-out, missed ball, broke finger, whilst doing 12th man – right laugh!'
Cricket superstitions: 'None'
Cricketers particularly admired: Ricky Ponting, Shane Warne, Herschelle Gibbs
Other sports played: Golf, football
Other sports followed: Football (Sheffield Wednesday)
Favourite band: Linkin Park
Relaxations: 'Music, watching sport and films, eating out, and the gym?!'
Extras: Released by Durham at the end of the 2006 season

4. Who scored 222* on Test debut for South Africa 2003?

2006 Season

	M	Inn	NO	Runs	HS	Avg	100	50	Ct	St	Balls	Runs	Wkts	Avg	BB	5I	10M
Test																	
FC																	
ODI																	
List A																	
20/20 Int																	
20/20	2	2	0	9	7	4.50	-	-	-	-	42	65	2	32.50	2-34	-	

Career Performances

	M	Inn	NO	Runs	HS	Avg	100	50	Ct	St	Balls	Runs	Wkts	Avg	BB	5I	10M
Test																	
FC																	
ODI																	
List A	1	1	1	24	24 *		-	-	1	-	30	41	0		-	-	
20/20 Int																	
20/20	2	2	0	9	7	4.50	-	-	-	-	42	65	2	32.50	2-34	-	

BATTY, G. J. Worcestershire

Name: <u>Gareth</u> Jon Batty
Role: Right-hand bat, off-spin bowler, county vice-captain; all-rounder
Born: 13 October 1977, Bradford, Yorkshire
Height: 5ft 11in **Weight:** 12st 7lbs
Nickname: Batts, Boris, Stuta
County debut: 1997 (Yorkshire), 1998 (one-day, Surrey), 1999 (first-class, Surrey), 2002 (Worcestershire)
County colours: 2002 (Worcestershire)
Test debut: 2003-04
ODI debut: 2002-03
50 wickets in a season: 2
Place in batting averages: 58th av. 46.50 (2005 162nd av. 28.50)
Place in bowling averages: 69th av. 33.46 (2005 96th av. 37.57)
Strike rate: 69.23 (career 66.02)
Parents: David and Rosemary
Marital status: Single
Family links with cricket: Father was Yorkshire Academy coach; brother played for Yorkshire and Somerset

Education: Bingley Grammar
Qualifications: 9 GCSEs, BTEC Art and Design, coaching certificate
Career outside cricket: 'Property development'
Overseas tours: England U15 to South Africa 1993; England U19 to Zimbabwe 1995-96, to Pakistan 1996-97; ECB National Academy to Australia and Sri Lanka 2002-03; England to Bangladesh and Sri Lanka 2003-04, to West Indies 2003-04, to Zimbabwe (one-day series) 2004-05, to South Africa 2004-05, to India 2005-06 (one-day series); England A to West Indies 2005-06
Overseas teams played for: Marist Newman, Australia 1999
Career highlights to date: 'Playing for England'
Cricket moments to forget: 'Every time we lose'
Cricket superstitions: 'None'
Cricketers particularly admired: Adam Hollioake 'to name but one'
Young players to look out for: Ravi Bopara, Steve Davies, Daryl Mitchell
Other sports played: Golf, rugby
Other sports followed: Rugby union (Bradford & Bingley), rugby league (Leeds Rhinos)
Favourite band: Frank Sinatra
Relaxations: 'Property and spending time with family and friends'
Extras: *Daily Telegraph* Young Player of the Year 1993. Surrey Supporters' Club Most Improved Player Award and Young Player of the Year Award 2001. Surrey CCC Young Player of the Year Award 2001. ECB 2nd XI Player of the Year 2001. Leading all-rounder in the inaugural Twenty20 Cup 2003. Made Test debut in the first Test v Bangladesh at Dhaka 2003-04, taking a wicket (Alok Kapali) with his third ball. Vice-captain of Worcestershire since 2005. ECB National Academy 2005-06
Opinions on cricket: 'I think Twenty20 is great and keeps kids interested.'
Best batting: 133 Worcestershire v Surrey, The Oval 2004
Best bowling: 7-52 Worcestershire v Northamptonshire, Northampton 2004

5. Which England great made a pair on Test debut
v Australia at Edgbaston 1975?

2006 Season

	M	Inn	NO	Runs	HS	Avg	100	50	Ct	St	Balls	Runs	Wkts	Avg	BB	5I	10M
Test																	
FC	15	24	8	744	112 *	46.50	1	3	14	-	2977	1439	43	33.46	6-119	1	-
ODI																	
List A	17	14	2	116	22	9.66	-	-	7	-	753	478	25	19.12	4-27	-	
20/20 Int																	
20/20	8	8	3	67	35	13.40	-	-	3	-	162	259	6	43.16	3-38	-	

Career Performances

	M	Inn	NO	Runs	HS	Avg	100	50	Ct	St	Balls	Runs	Wkts	Avg	BB	5I	10M
Test	7	8	1	144	38	20.57	-	-	3	-	1394	733	11	66.63	3-55	-	-
FC	93	144	27	3152	133	26.94	2	15	68	-	18488	8887	280	31.73	7-52	10	1
ODI	7	5	1	6	3	1.50	-	-	4	-	362	294	4	73.50	2-40	-	
List A	133	110	23	1452	83 *	16.68	-	4	51	-	5280	3922	121	32.41	4-27	-	
20/20 Int																	
20/20	26	25	5	323	87	16.15	-	1	8	-	474	684	21	32.57	3-38	-	

BATTY, J. N. Surrey

Name: Jonathan (<u>Jon</u>) Neil Batty
Role: Right-hand bat, wicket-keeper
Born: 18 April 1974, Chesterfield
Height: 5ft 10in **Weight:** 11st 6lbs
Nickname: JB
County debut: 1997
County cap: 2001
1000 runs in a season: 1
50 dismissals in a season: 4
Place in batting averages: 99th av. 35.34
(2005 59th av. 43.68)
Strike rate: (career 58.00)
Parents: Roger and Jill
Marital status: Single
Family links with cricket: Father played to a
high standard of club cricket
Education: Wheatley Park; Repton; Durham
University (St Chad's); Keble College,
Oxford
Qualifications: 10 GCSEs, 4 A-levels, BSc (Hons) in Natural Sciences, Diploma in
Social Studies (Oxon)
Overseas tours: Repton School to Netherlands 1991; MCC to Bangladesh 1996;
Surrey to South Africa 1997, 2001

Overseas teams played for: Mount Lawley CC, Perth 1997-2002
Career highlights to date: 'Winning three County Championships'
Cricket moments to forget: 'None!'
Cricketers particularly admired: David Gower, Alec Stewart, Jack Russell
Other sports played: Golf, squash
Other sports followed: Football (Nottingham Forest)
Relaxations: Reading, listening to music, movies
Extras: Represented Combined Universities 1994, 1995. Oxford Blue 1996. Surrey Supporters' Club Most Improved Player 2002, 2003. BBC Radio London Listeners' Cricketer of the Year 2003. Became second wicket-keeper (after Kent's Steve Marsh in 1991) to take eight catches in an innings (a new Surrey record) and score a century (129) in the same match, v Kent at The Oval 2004. Achieved double of 1000 (1025) runs and 50 (53) dismissals in first-class cricket 2006. Captain of Surrey 2004
Best batting: 168* Surrey v Essex, Chelmsford 2003
Best bowling: 1-21 Surrey v Lancashire, Old Trafford 2000

2006 Season

	M	Inn	NO	Runs	HS	Avg	100	50	Ct	St	Balls	Runs	Wkts	Avg	BB	5I	10M
Test																	
FC	17	29	0	1025	133	35.34	2	7	44	9	0	0	0		-	-	-
ODI																	
List A	15	13	1	325	53	27.08	-	3	8	5	0	0	0		-	-	
20/20 Int																	
20/20	10	8	2	166	59	27.66	-	2	8	9	0	0	0		-	-	

Career Performances

	M	Inn	NO	Runs	HS	Avg	100	50	Ct	St	Balls	Runs	Wkts	Avg	BB	5I	10M
Test																	
FC	144	218	27	6270	168 *	32.82	12	31	378	51	78	61	1	61.00	1-21	-	-
ODI																	
List A	148	117	22	2054	158 *	21.62	1	10	138	25	0	0	0		-	-	
20/20 Int																	
20/20	34	28	10	383	59	21.27	-	2	23	12	0	0	0		-	-	

BELL, I. R.   Warwickshire

Name: <u>Ian</u> Ronald Bell
Role: Right-hand bat, right-arm
medium bowler
Born: 11 April 1982, Coventry
Height: 5ft 10in **Weight:** 11st
Nickname: Belly
County debut: 1999
County cap: 2001
Test debut: 2004
ODI debut: 2004-05
Twenty20 Int debut: 2006
1000 runs in a season: 2
1st-Class 200s: 2
Place in batting averages: 22nd av. 59.41
(2005 52nd av. 44.91)
Strike rate: (career 57.72)
Parents: Terry and Barbara
Marital status: Single
Family links with cricket: Brother Keith played for England U18
Education: Princethorpe College, Rugby
Overseas tours: Warwickshire U19 to Cape Town 1998-99; England U19 to New
Zealand 1998-99, to Malaysia and (U19 World Cup) Sri Lanka 1999-2000, to India
2000-01 (c); England A to West Indies 2000-01, to Sri Lanka 2004-05 (c); ECB
National Academy to Australia 2001-02, to Sri Lanka 2002-03; England to
Zimbabwe (one-day series) 2004-05, to South Africa 2004-05, to Pakistan 2005-06,
to India 2005-06, to India (ICC Champions Trophy) 2006-07, to Australia 2006-07
Overseas teams played for: University of Western Australia, Perth 2003-04
Cricket moments to forget: 'Being bowled for a duck when making county debut'
Cricketers particularly admired: Michael Atherton, Steve Waugh, Alec Stewart,
Nick Knight
Other sports played: Football (was at Coventry City School of Excellence),
rugby, golf
Other sports followed: Football (Aston Villa), rugby union (Northampton Saints)
Relaxations: Golf, listening to music
Extras: Played for England U14, U15, U16, U17; captained England U19. NBC Denis
Compton Award for the most promising young Warwickshire player 1999, 2000, 2001.
Gray-Nicolls Trophy for Best Young Schools Cricketer 2000. Cricket Society's Most
Promising Young Cricketer of the Year Award 2001. Recorded maiden one-day century
(125) and maiden one-day five-wicket return (5-41) v Essex at Chelmsford in the NCL
2003. Scored maiden first-class double century (262*) v Sussex at Horsham 2004, in
the process setting with Tony Frost (135*) a new Warwickshire record partnership for

the seventh wicket (289*). Cricket Writers' Club Young Cricketer of the Year 2004. PCA Young Player of the Year award 2004. ECB National Academy 2004-05. Made ODI debut in the first ODI v Zimbabwe at Harare 2004-05, scoring 75 and winning Man of the Match award. Appointed MBE in 2006 New Year Honours as part of 2005 Ashes-winning England team. Recalled to the Test side for series v Pakistan 2006, scoring three hundreds (100*, 106*, 119) in successive Tests. Man of the Match in the fourth ODI v Pakistan at Trent Bridge 2006 (86*). England 12-month central contract 2006-07

Best batting: 262* Warwickshire v Sussex, Horsham 2004
Best bowling: 4-4 Warwickshire v Middlesex, Lord's 2004
Stop press: ICC Emerging Player of the Year award 2006

2006 Season

	M	Inn	NO	Runs	HS	Avg	100	50	Ct	St	Balls	Runs	Wkts	Avg	BB	5I	10M
Test	4	7	3	375	119	93.75	3	-	2	-	0	0	0		-	-	-
FC	9	16	4	713	119	59.41	3	4	4	-	210	111	5	22.20	2-59	-	-
ODI	10	10	1	399	88	44.33	-	3	-	-	36	40	1	40.00	1-13		
List A	14	12	1	477	88	43.36	-	4	2	-	48	59	1	59.00	1-13	-	
20/20 Int	1	1	0	14	14	14.00	-	-	1	-	0	0	0		-	-	
20/20	1	1	0	14	14	14.00	-	-	1	-	0	0	0		-	-	

Career Performances

	M	Inn	NO	Runs	HS	Avg	100	50	Ct	St	Balls	Runs	Wkts	Avg	BB	5I	10M
Test	18	32	5	1287	162 *	47.66	5	7	18	-	102	64	1	64.00	1-33	-	-
FC	100	172	17	6756	262 *	43.58	17	35	61	-	2713	1478	47	31.44	4-4	-	-
ODI	23	21	3	783	88	43.50	-	6	2	-	88	88	6	14.66	3-9	-	
List A	112	105	11	3490	137	37.12	2	29	35	-	1290	1138	33	34.48	5-41	1	
20/20 Int	1	1	0	14	14	14.00	-	-	1	-	0	0	0		-	-	
20/20	19	18	4	260	66 *	18.57	-	1	8	-	132	186	3	62.00	1-12	-	

6. Who scored 114 on Test debut for Bangladesh 2001-02?

BENHAM, C. C.   Hampshire

Name: Christopher (<u>Chris</u>) Charles Benham
Role: Right-hand bat, right-arm
off-spin bowler
Born: 24 March 1983, Frimley, Surrey
Height: 6ft 2in **Weight:** 13st
Nickname: Cut-snake, Togo, Benoit, Benny
County debut: 2004
Place in batting averages: 113th av. 33.60
(2005 272nd av. 11.70)
Parents: Frank and Sandie
Marital status: Single
Family links with cricket: 'Both older
brothers, Nick and Andy, played local
club cricket'
Education: Yateley Comprehensive School;
Yateley Sixth Form College; Loughborough
University
Qualifications: 10 GCSEs, 3 A-levels
Off-season: 'Spending time in Sydney and Melbourne, relaxing, training and watching
the Ashes'
Overseas tours: West of England U15 to West Indies 1998
Overseas teams played for: Perth CC 2004-05
Career highlights to date: '158 (off 130 balls) in Pro40 play-off match v Glamorgan
at The Rose Bowl, September 2006, which we won to gain promotion to first division'
Cricket moments to forget: 'Getting a king pair in a pre-season friendly match
against Essex in 2005'
Cricket superstitions: 'There's a few!'
Cricketers particularly admired: Steve Waugh, Graham Thorpe, Shane Warne,
John Crawley, Darren Lehmann
Young players to look out for: Liam Dawson, Richard Morris
Other sports played: Football (school, district and county sides; trials with Swindon
and Crystal Palace), tennis, golf
Other sports followed: Football (Reading FC), 'follow all sports'
Favourite band: The Fratellis, Razorlight, Jack Johnson
Relaxations: 'Reading, music, PlayStation, "Champ Man"'
Extras: Played for ESCA U15 and England U16. Played for Loughborough UCCE
2002, 2004. Represented British Universities 2004. Scored 74 on Championship debut
v Derbyshire at Derby 2004. NBC Denis Compton Award for the most promising
young Hampshire player 2006. Scored 130-ball 158 v Glamorgan at The Rose Bowl in
Pro40 play-off 2006, winning Man of the Match award
Best batting: 95 Hampshire v Warwickshire, Rose Bowl 2006

2006 Season

	M	Inn	NO	Runs	HS	Avg	100	50	Ct	St	Balls	Runs	Wkts	Avg	BB	5I	10M
Test																	
FC	9	15	0	504	95	33.60	-	4	9	-	30	37	0		-	-	-
ODI																	
List A	11	10	1	487	158	54.11	2	3	4	-	0	0	0		-	-	
20/20 Int																	
20/20	8	6	0	120	59	20.00	-	1	4	-	0	0	0		-	-	

Career Performances

	M	Inn	NO	Runs	HS	Avg	100	50	Ct	St	Balls	Runs	Wkts	Avg	BB	5I	10M
Test																	
FC	18	31	1	823	95	27.43	-	5	14	-	30	37	0		-	-	-
ODI																	
List A	12	11	1	487	158	48.70	2	3	4	-	0	0	0		-	-	
20/20 Int																	
20/20	8	6	0	120	59	20.00	-	1	4	-	0	0	0		-	-	

BENKENSTEIN, D. M. Durham

Name: Dale Martin Benkenstein
Role: Right-hand bat, right-arm off-break
or medium bowler, county captain
Born: 9 June 1974, Harare, Zimbabwe
County debut: 2005
ODI debut: 1998-99
1000 runs in a season: 2
1st-Class 200s: 2
Place in batting averages: 36th av. 51.72
(2005 16th av. 58.85)
Place in bowling averages: 101st av. 39.42
(2005 45th av. 27.75)
Strike rate: 62.64 (career 68.98)
Family links with cricket: Father, Martin,
and two brothers, Brett and Boyd, played
first-class cricket
Education: Michaelhouse, KwaZulu-Natal
Overseas tours: KwaZulu-Natal to Australia
(Champions Cup) 2000-01; South Africa U24 to Sri Lanka 1995; South Africa A to Sri
Lanka 1998, to West Indies 2000; South Africa to Malaysia (Commonwealth Games)
1998-99, to Bangladesh (Wills International Cup) 1998-99, to New Zealand 1998-99,
to Sri Lanka (ICC Champions Trophy) 2002-03, plus one-day series and tournaments
in Kenya, India and Sharjah

Overseas teams played for: Natal/KwaZulu-Natal 1992-93 – 2003-04; Dolphins 2004-05 –

Extras: Captained Natal Schools and South Africa Schools. One of *South African Cricket Annual*'s five Cricketers of the Year 1997. Was captain of KwaZulu-Natal, leading the side to the double (SuperSport Series and Standard Bank Cup) in 1996-97 and 2001-02. Has won numerous domestic awards, including Man of the Match in the final of the Standard Bank Cup 2001-02 at Durban (77*) and in the final of the SuperSport Series 2005-06 at Durban (151). Scored century (125) v Middlesex at Lord's 2006, in the process sharing with Gareth Breese (110) in a new record fifth-wicket partnership for Durham (222). Scored century (151) v Yorkshire at Headingley 2006, in the process sharing with Ottis Gibson (155) in a new record seventh-wicket partnership for Durham (315). Captain of Durham since 2006. Is not considered an overseas player

Best batting: 259 KwaZulu-Natal v Northerns, Durban 2001-02

Best bowling: 4-16 Dolphins v Warriors, Durban 2005-06

2006 Season

	M	Inn	NO	Runs	HS	Avg	100	50	Ct	St	Balls	Runs	Wkts	Avg	BB	5I	10M
Test																	
FC	17	31	2	1500	151	51.72	3	7	8	-	877	552	14	39.42	3-16	-	-
ODI																	
List A	15	15	4	484	84	44.00	-	4	5	-	336	300	7	42.85	3-42		
20/20 Int																	
20/20	6	6	1	89	56 *	17.80	-	1	5	-	102	119	3	39.66	2-23		

Career Performances

	M	Inn	NO	Runs	HS	Avg	100	50	Ct	St	Balls	Runs	Wkts	Avg	BB	5I	10M
Test																	
FC	157	234	28	9575	259	46.48	24	48	113	-	5657	2771	82	33.79	4-16	-	-
ODI	23	20	3	305	69	17.94	-	1	3	-	65	44	4	11.00	3-5	-	
List A	212	189	47	4872	107 *	34.30	1	27	75	-	2240	1814	68	26.67	4-16	-	
20/20 Int																	
20/20	23	23	5	489	56 *	27.16	-	2	9	-	234	294	14	21.00	3-10	-	

BENNING, J. G. E.   Surrey

Name: <u>James</u> Graham Edward Benning
Role: Right-hand bat, right-arm medium bowler; batting all-rounder
Born: 4 May 1983, Mill Hill, London
Height: 5ft 11in **Weight:** 13st
Nickname: Benno
County debut: 2002 (one-day), 2003 (first-class)
Place in batting averages: 63rd av. 44.36 (2005 48th av. 46.42)
Strike rate: (career 75.54)
Parents: Sandy and David
Marital status: Single
Family links with cricket: 'Dad played for Middlesex'
Education: Caterham School
Qualifications: 12 GCSEs, 3 AS-levels
Overseas tours: Surrey YC to Barbados 1999-2000, to Sri Lanka 2002

Overseas teams played for: North Dandenong, Australia 2001-02
Career highlights to date: 'Making County Championship debut'
Cricket moments to forget: 'Dropping two catches in front of a lively crowd at Canterbury, live on Sky'
Cricket superstitions: 'Order in which I put my kit on'
Cricketers particularly admired: Alec Stewart, Adam Hollioake
Other sports played: Rugby, football
Other sports followed: Football (Watford)
Favourite band: 'Listen to almost all music apart from thrash metal'
Relaxations: 'Going to the gym, music, spending time around friends'
Extras: Played for England U15-U19. First recipient of Ben Hollioake Scholarship. NBC Denis Compton Award for the most promising young Surrey player 2003. Scored maiden Championship century from 100 balls (finishing with 112) v Gloucestershire at The Oval 2006 on his 23rd birthday. Carried bat for 146-ball 189* as Surrey fell two short of Gloucestershire's 339-8 at Bristol in the C&G 2006
Best batting: 128 Surrey v OUCCE, The Parks 2004
Best bowling: 3-57 Surrey v Kent, Tunbridge Wells 2005

2006 Season

	M	Inn	NO	Runs	HS	Avg	100	50	Ct	St	Balls	Runs	Wkts	Avg	BB	5I	10M
Test																	
FC	8	13	2	488	122 *	44.36	2	2	4	-	252	237	3	79.00	2-58	-	-
ODI																	
List A	12	12	2	612	189 *	61.20	1	5	3	-	78	104	1	104.00	1-27	-	
20/20 Int																	
20/20	10	10	1	326	88	36.22	-	4	3	-	0	0	0			-	-

Career Performances

	M	Inn	NO	Runs	HS	Avg	100	50	Ct	St	Balls	Runs	Wkts	Avg	BB	5I	10M
Test																	
FC	20	34	3	1165	128	37.58	4	5	8	-	831	703	11	63.90	3-57	-	-
ODI																	
List A	47	46	2	1546	189 *	35.13	1	12	11	-	800	867	26	33.34	4-43	-	
20/20 Int																	
20/20	30	30	1	683	88	23.55	-	5	7	-	30	43	2	21.50	1-7	-	

BETTS, M. M.   Middlesex

Name: <u>Melvyn</u> Morris Betts
Role: Right-hand bat, right-arm
fast-medium bowler
Born: 26 March 1975, County Durham
Height: 5ft 11in   **Weight:** 12st 4lbs
Nickname: Mel B, Betsy
County debut: 1993 (Durham),
2001 (Warwickshire), 2004 (Middlesex)
County cap: 1998 (Durham),
2001 (Warwickshire)
Place in batting averages: (2005 244th
av. 17.00)
Place in bowling averages: (2005 98th
av. 38.09)
Strike rate: (career 52.40)
Parents: Melvyn and Shirley
Wife and date of marriage: Angela,
3 October 1998
Children: Chloe, 16 July 1999; Megan, 14 May 2002
Family links with cricket: 'Dad played for local team Sacriston'
Education: Fyndoune Community College
Qualifications: 9 GCSEs, plus qualifications in engineering and sports and
recreational studies

Overseas tours: England U19 to Sri Lanka 1993-94; England A to Zimbabwe and South Africa 1998-99; Durham CCC to South Africa 1996; MCC to Namibia and Uganda 2004-05

Career highlights to date: 'Taking 9-64 v Northamptonshire'

Cricket superstitions: 'None'

Cricketers particularly admired: David Boon

Young players to look out for: Chris Whelan

Other sports followed: Football (Newcastle United FC)

Favourite band: U2

Relaxations: 'Golf and catching up with friends'

Extras: Represented England U19 1994. Took 5-22 on Championship debut for Warwickshire against his old county, Durham, at Edgbaston 2001. Released by Middlesex at the end of the 2006 season

Opinions on cricket: 'There should be 96 overs in a day's play to make lunch and tea longer.'

Best batting: 73 Warwickshire v Lancashire, Edgbaston 2003

Best bowling: 9-64 Durham v Northamptonshire, Northampton 1997

2006 Season

	M	Inn	NO	Runs	HS	Avg	100	50	Ct	St	Balls	Runs	Wkts	Avg	BB	5I	10M
Test																	
FC	2	4	0	18	7	4.50	-	-	1	-	156	88	4	22.00	2-29	-	-
ODI																	
List A	2	2	0	10	8	5.00	-	-	-	-	72	74	2	37.00	2-57	-	
20/20 Int																	
20/20																	

Career Performances

	M	Inn	NO	Runs	HS	Avg	100	50	Ct	St	Balls	Runs	Wkts	Avg	BB	5I	10M
Test																	
FC	117	168	37	1897	73	14.48	-	5	38	-	18184	10723	347	30.90	9-64	14	2
ODI																	
List A	97	63	25	368	21	9.68	-	-	16	-	4290	3526	118	29.88	4-15	-	
20/20 Int																	
20/20	11	3	1	17	13 *	8.50	-	-	2	-	222	347	6	57.83	2-51	-	

BICHEL, A. J. Essex

Name: Andrew (<u>Andy</u>) John Bichel
Role: Right-hand bat, right-arm
fast-medium bowler
Born: 27 August 1970, Laidley,
Queensland, Australia
Height: 5ft 11in **Weight:** 13st 13lbs
Nickname: Bic, Andre
County debut: 2001 (Worcestershire),
2005 (Hampshire), 2006 (Essex)
County cap: 2001; colours 2002 (both
Worcestershire)
Test debut: 1996-97
ODI debut: 1996-97
50 wickets in a season: 1
Place in batting averages: 83rd av. 37.85
Place in bowling averages: 52nd av. 30.96
(2005 72nd av. 31.50)
Strike rate: 52.65 (career 49.47)
Parents: Trevor and Shirley

Wife and date of marriage: Dionn, 18 April 1997
Children: Keegan, 26 October 1999; Darcy, 24 October 2002
Family links with cricket: 'Dad played local Queensland country cricket. Uncle Don played for Queensland. Best game was against England'
Education: Laidley High; Ipswich TAFE
Qualifications: Carpentry; cricket coaching
Overseas tours: Queensland Academy to South Africa 1994; Australian Academy to South Africa 1996; Australia A to Scotland and Ireland 1998; Australia to South Africa 1996-97, to England 1997, to New Zealand (one-day series) 1997-98, to Malaysia (Commonwealth Games) 1998-99, to West Indies 1998-99, to South Africa 2001-02, to Kenya (PSO Tri-Nation Tournament) 2002, to Sri Lanka (ICC Champions Trophy) 2002-03, to Sri Lanka and Sharjah (v Pakistan) 2002-03, to Africa (World Cup) 2002-03, to West Indies 2002-03, to India (TVS Cup) 2003-04; FICA World XI to New Zealand 2004-05
Overseas teams played for: Queensland 1992-93 –
Career highlights to date: 'World Cup 2003'
Cricket moments to forget: 'Being sick on the field against India in India'
Cricket superstitions: 'Like my gear in its place before the game'
Cricketers particularly admired: Allan Border, Sachin Tendulkar, Glenn McGrath, Dennis Lillee
Other sports played: Rugby league (first grade TRL); tennis (first grade LTA)
Other sports followed: Rugby league (Brisbane Broncos), AFL (Brisbane Lions)

Favourite band: U2, Cold Chisel
Relaxations: 'Beach, fishing, golf, hanging out on the islands just off Queensland coast'
Extras: Sheffield Shield Player of the Year 1996-97. Queensland Player of the Year 1998-99. An overseas player with Worcestershire 2001-02, 2004. Won the Dick Lygon Award 2001 as Worcestershire's Player of the Year; was also the Worcestershire Supporters' Association Player of the Year 2001 and the winner of the inaugural Don Kenyon Award. Man of the Match v South Africa at Sydney in the VB Series 2001-02 (5-19) and v England at Port Elizabeth in the World Cup 2002-03 (34* following 7-20, the third best bowling return in ODI history). Named Australia's State Player of the Year at the 2005 Allan Border Medal awards. Named Man of the Series in the Pura Cup 2005-06. Has same birthday as the late Sir Donald Bradman. Was a temporary overseas player with Hampshire during the 2005 season, scoring 138 on debut v Gloucestershire at Cheltenham and in the process sharing with Nic Pothas (139) in a new Hampshire record partnership for the eighth wicket (257). An overseas player with Essex 2006; has returned for the second part of the 2007 season
Best batting: 142 Worcestershire v Northamptonshire, Worcester 2004
Best bowling: 9-93 Worcestershire v Gloucestershire, Worcester 2002

2006 Season

	M	Inn	NO	Runs	HS	Avg	100	50	Ct	St	Balls	Runs	Wkts	Avg	BB	5I	10M
Test																	
FC	8	8	1	265	75 *	37.85	-	2	-	-	1685	991	32	30.96	6-38	1	-
ODI																	
List A	9	4	0	100	41	25.00	-	-	3	-	363	272	21	12.95	5-44	1	
20/20 Int																	
20/20	10	5	2	28	12 *	9.33	-	-	4	-	240	324	14	23.14	4-23	-	

Career Performances

	M	Inn	NO	Runs	HS	Avg	100	50	Ct	St	Balls	Runs	Wkts	Avg	BB	5I	10M
Test	19	22	1	355	71	16.90	-	1	16	-	3336	1870	58	32.24	5-60	1	-
FC	166	214	21	4954	142	25.66	6	21	79	-	33644	17839	680	26.23	9-93	32	6
ODI	67	36	13	471	64	20.47	-	1	19	-	3257	2463	78	31.57	7-20	2	
List A	217	149	35	2280	100	20.00	1	5	69	-	10514	7634	293	26.05	7-20	4	
20/20 Int																	
20/20	17	12	5	215	58 *	30.71	-	1	9	-	373	488	22	22.18	4-23	-	

BICKNELL, D. J.　　　Nottinghamshire

Name: <u>Darren</u> John Bicknell
Role: Left-hand opening bat, occasional slow left-arm bowler
Born: 24 June 1967, Guildford
Height: 6ft 4½in　**Weight:** 14st 9lbs
Nickname: Denz, Bickers
County debut: 1987 (Surrey), 2000 (Notts)
County cap: 1990 (Surrey), 2000 (Notts)
Benefit: 1999 (Surrey)
1000 runs in a season: 9
1st-Class 200s: 2
Place in batting averages: 152nd av. 29.34 (2005 32nd av. 50.91)
Strike rate: (career 54.10)
Parents: Vic and Valerie
Wife and date of marriage: Rebecca, 21 September 1992
Children: Lauren Elizabeth, 21 September 1993; Sam, 9 November 1995; Emily, 16 December 1997
Family links with cricket: Brother Martin played for Surrey
Education: Robert Haining County Secondary; Guildford County College of Technology
Qualifications: 8 O-levels, 2 A-levels, senior coaching award, Diploma in Golf Club Management, 'Sage Accountancy 10-day passport to competency'
Overseas tours: Surrey to Sharjah 1988, 1989, to Dubai 1990, to Perth 1995; Nottinghamshire to Johannesburg 2000, 2001, 2002; England A to Zimbabwe and Kenya 1989-90, to Pakistan 1990-91, to Bermuda and West Indies 1991-92
Overseas teams played for: Coburg, Melbourne 1986-87
Career highlights: 'England A call-up. Debut for Surrey. Being capped by Notts and Surrey. Every time I reach a hundred'
Cricket moments to forget: 'My first-ball dismissal in my debut A "Test" match v Zimbabwe, and brother Martin getting me out twice'
Cricket superstitions: 'Try and wear same clothes if successful previously'
Cricketers particularly admired: Mark Taylor, David Gower, Angus Fraser, Martin Bicknell
Young players to look out for: Samit Patel, Josh Mierkalns
Other sports played: Golf (11 handicap), five-a-side football
Other sports followed: Football (West Ham United, Nottingham Forest)
Favourite band: Anastacia
Relaxations: Family, golf and TV
Extras: Won the Walter Lawrence Trophy 1989 (fastest first-class century of the

season) for his 69-ball hundred v Essex at The Oval. Shared Surrey record third-wicket stand of 413 with David Ward v Kent at Canterbury in 1990. Surrey Batsman of the Year four times. Became first English cricketer to take part in more than one Championship partnership of 400-plus when he scored 180* in a first-wicket stand of 406* with Guy Welton (200*) v Warwickshire at Edgbaston 2000; the stand broke several records, including that for the highest Nottinghamshire partnership for any wicket. Was acting captain of Nottinghamshire in 2001 during the absence through injury of Jason Gallian. Retired at the end of the 2006 season

Best batting: 235* Surrey v Nottinghamshire, Trent Bridge 1994
Best bowling: 3-7 Surrey v Sussex, Guildford 1996

2006 Season

	M	Inn	NO	Runs	HS	Avg	100	50	Ct	St	Balls	Runs	Wkts	Avg	BB	5I	10M
Test																	
FC	18	29	0	851	95	29.34	-	4	3	-	0	0	0		-	-	-
ODI																	
List A	1	1	1	53	53 *		-	1	-	-	0	0	0		-	-	
20/20 Int																	
20/20																	

Career Performances

	M	Inn	NO	Runs	HS	Avg	100	50	Ct	St	Balls	Runs	Wkts	Avg	BB	5I	10M
Test																	
FC	324	560	43	19931	235 *	38.55	46	91	107	-	1569	1015	29	35.00	3-7	-	-
ODI																	
List A	236	229	28	7522	135 *	37.42	10	52	55	-	84	82	3	27.33	1-11	-	
20/20 Int																	
20/20	1	1	0	10	10	10.00	-	-	-	-	0	0	0		-	-	

7. Which current first-class umpire took a wicket with his
first ball in Test cricket, v West Indies at Trent Bridge 1991?

BICKNELL, M. P.   Surrey

Name: <u>Martin</u> Paul Bicknell
Role: Right-hand bat, right-arm
fast-medium bowler
Born: 14 January 1969, Guildford
Height: 6ft 4in   **Weight:** 15st
Nickname: Bickers
County debut: 1986
County cap: 1989
Benefit: 1997; testimonial 2006
Test debut: 1993
ODI debut: 1990-91
50 wickets in a season: 11
Place in batting averages: (2005 78th
av. 38.55)
Place in bowling averages: (2005 62nd
av. 30.37)
Strike rate: (career 52.23)
Parents: Vic and Val

Wife and date of marriage: Loraine, 29 September 1995
Children: Eleanor, 31 March 1995; Charlotte, 22 July 1996
Family links with cricket: Brother played for Surrey and Nottinghamshire
Education: Robert Haining County Secondary
Qualifications: 2 O-levels, NCA coach
Overseas tours: England YC to Sri Lanka 1986-87, to Australia 1987-88; England A
to Zimbabwe and Kenya 1989-90, to Bermuda and West Indies 1991-92, to South
Africa 1993-94; England to Australia 1990-91
Career highlights: 'A *Wisden* Cricketer of the Year 2001'
Cricket moments to forget: 'It's all been an experience!!'
Cricketers particularly admired: 'All honest county trundlers'
Other sports played: Golf
Other sports followed: Football (Leeds United), golf
Relaxations: 'Playing golf, reading; spending time with my children'
Extras: Took 7-30 in National League v Glamorgan at The Oval 1999, the best one-
day return by a Surrey bowler. Had match figures of 16-119 (9-47 in the second
innings) v Leicestershire at Guildford in 2000. One of *Wisden*'s Five Cricketers of the
Year 2001. Wetherell Award for the Cricket Society's leading all-rounder in English
first-class cricket 2000 and 2001. Surrey Supporters' Player of the Year 1993, 1997,
1999, 2000, 2001. Surrey Players' Player of the Year 1997, 1998, 1999, 2000, 2001.
Surrey CCC Bowler of the Season Award 2001. Took 6-42 v Kent at The Oval 2002,
in the process achieving the feat of having recorded a five-wicket innings return
against all 17 counties besides his own. His 5-128 v Kent at The Oval 2004 included

his 1000th first-class wicket (Matthew Dennington). His 5-93 v Somerset at Bath 2006 included his 1000th Championship wicket (Andrew Caddick). Retired at the end of the 2006 season, becoming Master in Charge of Cricket at Charterhouse School

Best batting: 141 Surrey v Essex, Chelmsford 2003
Best bowling: 9-45 Surrey v Cambridge University, The Oval 1988

2006 Season

	M	Inn	NO	Runs	HS	Avg	100	50	Ct	St	Balls	Runs	Wkts	Avg	BB	5I	10M
Test																	
FC	4	6	2	156	59	39.00	-	1	2	-	606	303	7	43.28	5-93	1	-
ODI																	
List A																	
20/20 Int																	
20/20																	

Career Performances

	M	Inn	NO	Runs	HS	Avg	100	50	Ct	St	Balls	Runs	Wkts	Avg	BB	5I	10M
Test	4	7	0	45	15	6.42	-	-	2	-	1080	543	14	38.78	4-84	-	-
FC	292	358	87	6740	141	24.87	3	26	103	-	55420	26589	1061	25.06	9-45	44	4
ODI	7	6	2	96	31 *	24.00	-	-	2	-	413	347	13	26.69	3-55	-	
List A	334	174	72	1589	66 *	15.57	-	2	78	-	16191	10790	429	25.15	7-30	3	
20/20 Int																	
20/20	3	2	2	11	10 *		-	-	1	-	66	61	4	15.25	2-11	-	

8. Who had match figures of 16-137 on Test debut at Lord's 1972?

BIRCH. D. J.   Derbyshire

Name: Daniel (<u>Dan</u>) John Birch
Role: Left-hand bat, right-arm
medium bowler
Born: 21 January 1981, Nottingham
Height: 6ft 3in **Weight:** 16st
Nickname: Birchy
County debut: No first-team appearance
Marital status: Single
Family links with cricket: 'Dad John Birch
played for Notts CCC in 1970s and 1980s
and was [Notts] manager'
Education: Kimberley Comprehensive
Career outside cricket: 'Manager and coach
at John Birch Sports Centre Ltd'
Off-season: 'Working!'
Overseas teams played for: Frankston
Peninsula CC, Melbourne 2002-03
Career highlights to date: 'Top score
of 181*'

Cricketers particularly admired: Shane Warne, Brian Lara
Young players to look out for: 'Daniel Birch'
Other sports followed: Football (Nottingham Forest)
Relaxations: 'Weight training, fishing, pub'
Extras: Played for both Kent and Derbyshire 2nd XIs 2006

BIRT, T. R.   Derbyshire

Name: <u>Travis</u> Rodney Birt
Role: Left-hand bat, 'right-arm fast bowler', wicket-keeper 'sometimes'
Born: 9 December 1981, Sale, Victoria, Australia
Height: 5ft 11in **Weight:** 14st
Nickname: Trevor
County debut: 2006
1000 runs in a season: 1
Place in batting averages: 50th av. 48.13
Strike rate: (career 75.50)
Parents: Rod and Wendy
Marital status: Single
Family links with cricket: 'Uncle still dominates local cricket in Melbourne'

Education: Catholic College, Sale, Victoria
Career outside cricket: 'Helicopter pilot'
Off-season: 'Playing golf'
Overseas tours: Commonwealth Bank Centre of Excellence to India 2004
Overseas teams played for: Tasmania 2003-04 –
Career highlights to date: 'Deceiving HD Ackerman with my lack of pace and removing his middle stump with my first ball in one-day cricket'
Cricket moments to forget: 'In Under 12s I dropped the same batsman three times in four balls'
Cricket superstitions: 'Left pad first; bottom strap followed by the top strap'
Young players to look out for: Tim Paine
Other sports followed: Football (Man United)
Favourite band: Linkin Park
Relaxations: 'PlayStation, shopping'
Extras: Represented Australia U19 2000-01. Set record for the highest individual score for Tasmania in a List A match with his 145 v South Australia at Hobart in the ING Cup 2004-05, also winning Man of the Match award. Represented Australia A in the Top End Series 2006, scoring century (130) v India A at Cairns. An overseas player with Derbyshire since 2006
Opinions on cricket: 'Five-over games are four times as good as Twenty20.'
Best batting: 181 Derbyshire v Gloucestershire, Bristol 2006
Best bowling: 1-24 Derbyshire v Surrey, The Oval 2006

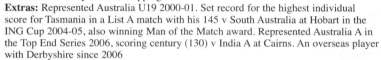

9. Who achieved a hat-trick on Test debut for Australia
v Pakistan at Rawalpindi 1994-95?

2006 Season

	M	Inn	NO	Runs	HS	Avg	100	50	Ct	St	Balls	Runs	Wkts	Avg	BB	5I	10M
Test																	
FC	14	24	2	1059	181	48.13	3	6	7	-	151	119	2	59.50	1-24	-	-
ODI																	
List A	15	15	0	564	108	37.60	1	5	3	-	90	85	5	17.00	2-15	-	
20/20 Int																	
20/20																	

Career Performances

	M	Inn	NO	Runs	HS	Avg	100	50	Ct	St	Balls	Runs	Wkts	Avg	BB	5I	10M
Test																	
FC	34	62	3	2382	181	40.37	6	13	15	-	151	119	2	59.50	1-24	-	-
ODI																	
List A	38	38	0	1141	145	30.02	2	6	14	-	90	85	5	17.00	2-15	-	
20/20 Int																	
20/20	3	3	1	8	4 *	4.00	-	-	2	-	0	0	0		-	-	

BLACKWELL, I. D.   Somerset

Name: Ian David Blackwell
Role: Left-hand bat, slow left-arm bowler;
all-rounder
Born: 10 June 1978, Chesterfield
Height: 6ft 2in
Nickname: Donkey, Le Donk, Blackdog,
Donk
County debut: 1997 (Derbyshire),
2000 (Somerset)
County cap: 2001 (Somerset)
Test debut: 2005-06
ODI debut: 2002-03
1000 runs in a season: 2
1st-Class 200s: 1
Place in batting averages: (2005 28th
av. 52.33)
Place in bowling averages: (2005 143rd
av. 56.03)
Strike rate: (career 92.15)
Parents: John and Marilyn
Wife and date of marriage: Elizabeth (Beth), 30 September 2006
Family links with cricket: 'Father played for Derbyshire Over 50s and also league
cricket'

Education: Manor School (GCSEs); Brookfield Community School (A-levels)
Qualifications: 9 GCSEs, 1 A-level, Level 2 coaching award
Career outside cricket: 'Property tycoon!'
Off-season: 'Doing Level 3 coaching course; reducing my golf handicap; and spending numerous hours at Esporta gym!'
Overseas tours: Somerset to Cape Town 2000, 2001; England VI to Hong Kong 2001; England to Sri Lanka (ICC Champions Trophy) 2002-03, to Australia 2002-03 (VB Series), to Africa (World Cup) 2002-03, to Bangladesh and Sri Lanka 2003-04 (one-day series), to West Indies 2003-04 (one-day series), to Pakistan 2005-06 (one-day series), to India 2005-06; ECB National Academy to Australia 2002-03
Overseas teams played for: Delacombe Park CC, Melbourne 1997, 1999; Spotswood CC, Melbourne
Career highlights to date: 'Playing one Test match and 34 One-Day Internationals. 247* v Derbyshire [2003]'
Cricket moments to forget: 'Any of my numerous noughts for England'
Cricket superstitions: 'Always chew gum. Box first, inner thigh pad, thigh pad, right pad, left pad – routine not superstition'
Cricketers particularly admired: Ricky Ponting, Graeme Smith, Andrew Caddick, Mark Ramprakash, James Hildreth
Young players to look out for: 'Schnitzleburger, Kratz Jnr and Oli Jnr'
Other sports played: Football (Sheffield Wednesday Young Owls), golf (6 handicap)
Other sports followed: Football (Chesterfield FC), 'any golf tournaments'
Injuries: Out for two weeks with disc problems in the lower back; for three months with a SLAP lesion of the left shoulder
Favourite band: Eminem, Oasis, Arctic Monkeys
Relaxations: 'PS2, going to the races'
Extras: Became first batsman in Championship history to score two centuries (103/122) in a match batting at No. 7, v Northants at Northampton 2001. Scored 134-ball double century (finishing with 247*) v Derbyshire at Taunton 2003, the fastest double century on record by an Englishman in terms of balls received. Won the Walter Lawrence Trophy 2005 (fastest first-class century of the season) for his 67-ball hundred (finishing with 107) v Derbyshire at Taunton. Captain of Somerset July 2005-2006, although absent injured for most of the 2006 season
Opinions on cricket: 'Twenty20 game flying – more games are needed. Maybe drop Pro40 and play teams home and away. Return C&G to knockout trophy – FA Cup of cricket.'
Best batting: 247* Somerset v Derbyshire, Taunton 2003
Best bowling: 7-90 Somerset v Glamorgan, Taunton 2004
  7-90 Somerset v Nottinghamshire, Trent Bridge 2004

2006 Season

	M	Inn	NO	Runs	HS	Avg	100	50	Ct	St	Balls	Runs	Wkts	Avg	BB	5I	10M
Test																	
FC	2	2	0	92	49	46.00	-	-	-	-	276	139	3	46.33	2-63	-	-
ODI																	
List A	3	2	1	42	27 *	42.00	-	-	1	-	48	23	0			-	-
20/20 Int																	
20/20																	

Career Performances

	M	Inn	NO	Runs	HS	Avg	100	50	Ct	St	Balls	Runs	Wkts	Avg	BB	5I	10M
Test	1	1	0	4	4	4.00	-	-	-	-	114	71	0		-	-	-
FC	115	177	13	6372	247 *	38.85	16	29	45	-	17329	8238	188	43.81	7-90	7	-
ODI	34	29	2	403	82	14.92	-	1	8	-	1230	877	24	36.54	3-26	-	
List A	194	176	16	4294	134 *	26.83	3	25	48	-	6386	5117	141	36.29	5-26	1	
20/20 Int																	
20/20	21	21	4	354	82	20.82	-	1	8	-	398	474	18	26.33	4-26	-	

BLAIN, J. A. R.   Yorkshire

Name: <u>John</u> Angus Rae Blain
Role: Right-hand bat, right-arm
fast-medium bowler
Born: 4 January 1979, Edinburgh
Height: 6ft 2in **Weight:** 13st 7lbs
Nickname: Blainy, Haggis, William, JB
County debut: 1997 (Northamptonshire),
2004 (Yorkshire)
ODI debut: 1999
Strike rate: (career 51.96)
Parents: John and Elma
Marital status: Single
Education: Penicuik HS; Jewel and Esk
Valley College
Qualifications: 8 GCSEs, 1 A-level, HNC
Leisure and Recreation, Level 1 coaching
award
Off-season: October to mid-November – ICC
High Performance Camp, Pretoria, South Africa; mid-December to end December –
ODIs v Bangladesh; January to February – Kenya and Sharjah; March – World Cup,
West Indies
Overseas tours: Northants CCC to Zimbabwe 1997, to Grenada 2001, 2002; Scotland

U19 to Netherlands (International Youth Tournament) 1994-95, to Bermuda (International Youth Tournament) 1997, to South Africa (U19 World Cup) 1997-98 (c); Scotland to Denmark (European Championships) 1996, to Malaysia (ICC Trophy) 1996-97, to Malaysia (Commonwealth Games) 1998-99, to Sharjah ('World Cup warm-up') 1999, to Canada (ICC Trophy) 2001, to UAE (ICC Six Nations Challenge) 2003-04, to UAE (ICC Inter-Continental Cup) 2004, to Bangladesh (one-day series) 2006-07, to Kenya (including ICC World Cricket League) 2006-07, to Sharjah 2006-07, to West Indies (World Cup) 2006-07

Overseas teams played for: New Plymouth Old Boys, New Zealand 1998-99; Taranaki Cricket Association, New Zealand 1998-99

Career highlights to date: 'World Cup 1999, England. Signing for Yorkshire CCC'

Cricket moments to forget: 'Not qualifying for the 2003 World Cup, failing to qualify by losing the last match by six runs in Canada 2001; not qualifying for the Champions Trophy in England 2004, losing last game to the USA in Dubai 2004' (*USA qualified for the Champions Trophy ahead of Scotland by virtue of a net run rate that was superior by just 0.028 runs*)

Cricket superstitions: 'Keeping a tidy kitbag'

Cricketers particularly admired: Devon Malcolm, Darren Lehmann

Young players to look out for: David Wainwright

Other sports played: Football (schoolboy forms with Hibernian FC and Falkirk FC, making youth and reserve team appearances)

Other sports followed: Rugby

Relaxations: 'Listening to music, going out for a beer; spending time with my girlfriend and going home to Scotland to see family; watching football, going to the gym, and sleeping!'

Extras: Has played for Scotland in first-class cricket and in the B&H and NatWest competitions; also played for Scottish Saltires in NCL. Took 5-24 on Sunday League debut for Northamptonshire v Derbyshire at Derby 1997. Represented Scotland in the 1999 World Cup, taking 10 wickets and finishing top of the strike rate chart for the tournament. Man of the Match in the final of the ICC Inter-Continental Cup v Canada in the UAE 2004, returning match figures of 7-55 (3-27/4-28). Released by Yorkshire at the end of the 2006 season

Opinions on cricket: 'Too many so-called British- or English-qualified imports coming into the game. County players are underestimated in world cricket. The instant success of "newcomers" to the England team shows just that.'

Best batting: 53 Scotland v Ireland, Aberdeen 2006

Best bowling: 6-42 Northamptonshire v Kent, Canterbury 2001

2006 Season

	M	Inn	NO	Runs	HS	Avg	100	50	Ct	St	Balls	Runs	Wkts	Avg	BB	5I	10M
Test																	
FC	3	3	0	24	12	8.00	-	-	2	-	354	287	5	57.40	2-72	-	-
ODI																	
List A	1	1	0	7	7	7.00	-	-	-	-	18	21	1	21.00	1-21		
20/20 Int																	
20/20																	

Career Performances

	M	Inn	NO	Runs	HS	Avg	100	50	Ct	St	Balls	Runs	Wkts	Avg	BB	5I	10M
Test																	
FC	37	42	16	349	53	13.42	-	1	9	-	5093	3748	98	38.24	6-42	2	-
ODI	8	7	1	31	16	5.16	-	-	2	-	337	316	13	24.30	4-37	-	
List A	56	29	13	158	29	9.87	-	-	14	-	2342	2006	78	25.71	5-24	2	
20/20 Int																	
20/20																	

BOPARA, R. S. Essex

Name: Ravinder (<u>Ravi</u>) Singh Bopara
Role: Right-hand top-order bat, right-arm medium bowler
Born: 4 May 1985, Newham, London
Height: 5ft 10in **Weight:** 12st
Nickname: Puppy
County debut: 2002
County cap: 2005
Place in batting averages: 100th av. 35.28 (2005 95th av. 36.66)
Place in bowling averages: 129th av. 45.00 (2005 135th av. 47.95)
Strike rate: 67.47 (career 70.80)
Parents: Baldish and Charanjit
Marital status: Single
Education: Brampton Manor School; Barking Abbey Sports College
Qualifications: 7 GCSEs, ECB Level 1 coaching
Overseas tours: England U19 to Australia 2002-03, to Bangladesh (U19 World Cup) 2003-04; England A to West Indies 2005-06, to Bangladesh 2006-07; England to Australia 2006-07 (C'wealth Bank Series)

Career highlights to date: 'Playing against India and Pakistan overseas teams. Meeting Sachin Tendulkar; facing Shoaib Akhtar and Mohammad Sami'
Cricket moments to forget: 'I went out to bat once and didn't realise I didn't have a box on until I got hit there'
Cricketers particularly admired: Sachin Tendulkar, Viv Richards, Carl Hooper
Young players to look out for: Bilal Shafayat, 'and any players who are hungry for success'
Other sports followed: Football (Arsenal)
Favourite band: Tupac and the Outlawz
Extras: Played for Development of Excellence XI (South) v West Indies U19 2001. Represented England U19 2003 and 2004. C&G Man of the Match award v Devon at Exmouth 2005 (65*). Scored 135 v Australians in a two-day game at Chelmsford 2005. Represented England A v Sri Lankans and v Pakistanis 2006. ECB National Academy 2005-06, 2006-07
Best batting: 159 Essex v Glamorgan, Cardiff 2006
Best bowling: 5-75 Essex v Surrey, Colchester 2006
Stop press: Called up to the England squad for the Commonwealth Bank Series in Australia 2006-07, replacing the injured Kevin Pietersen; made ODI debut v Australia at Sydney

2006 Season

	M	Inn	NO	Runs	HS	Avg	100	50	Ct	St	Balls	Runs	Wkts	Avg	BB	5I	10M
Test																	
FC	18	28	3	882	159	35.28	2	3	14	-	1551	1035	23	45.00	5-75	1	-
ODI																	
List A	17	14	3	424	101*	38.54	1	4	6	-	524	481	18	26.72	3-23	-	
20/20 Int																	
20/20	8	8	1	133	83	19.00	-	1	2	-	132	179	7	25.57	2-2	-	

Career Performances

	M	Inn	NO	Runs	HS	Avg	100	50	Ct	St	Balls	Runs	Wkts	Avg	BB	5I	10M
Test																	
FC	48	79	13	2246	159	34.03	3	8	35	-	3257	2298	46	49.95	5-75	1	-
ODI																	
List A	60	55	14	1202	101*	29.31	1	7	18	-	1264	1111	38	29.23	3-23	-	
20/20 Int																	
20/20	25	19	2	279	83	16.41	-	1	6	-	276	383	14	27.35	3-18	-	

BORRINGTON, P. M.   Derbyshire

Name: <u>Paul</u> Michael Borrington
Role: Right-hand opening bat, right-arm off-spin bowler, occasional wicket-keeper
Born: 24 May 1988, Nottingham
Height: 5ft 10in   **Weight:** 10st 3lbs
Nickname: Borrers, Boz, Bozza
County debut: 2005
Parents: Tony and Sheila
Marital status: Single
Family links with cricket: Father played for Derbyshire 1970-82
Education: Chellaston School; Repton School (sixth form); Loughborough University
Qualifications: 10 GCSEs, 3 A-levels
Career outside cricket: Student
Off-season: 'Studying at Loughborough University'

Overseas tours: Derbyshire U15 to South Africa 2003; England U16 to South Africa 2004; Repton School to Sri Lanka 2005; Derbyshire Academy to South Africa 2006
Career highlights to date: 'Captaining the Midlands to victory in the 2003 Bunbury Festival. First-class debut v Leicestershire at the age of 17'
Cricket moments to forget: 'Leaving a straight ball on my first-class debut'
Cricket superstitions: 'None'
Cricketers particularly admired: Michael Vaughan
Young players to look out for: 'The current Derbyshire Academy'
Other sports played: Football, occasional golf
Other sports followed: Football (Crewe Alexandra)
Favourite band: Razorlight
Relaxations: 'Spending time with my friends'
Extras: NBC Denis Compton Award 2005. Derbyshire Academy Player of the Year 2006
Opinions on cricket: 'Very impressed with the structure, organisation and coaching at the England age-group levels. Introduction and development of county academies has been a huge success – English cricket will reap the benefits in the next few years.'
Best batting: 38 Derbyshire v Surrey, Derby 2006

2006 Season

	M	Inn	NO	Runs	HS	Avg	100	50	Ct	St	Balls	Runs	Wkts	Avg	BB	5I	10M
Test																	
FC	1	2	0	56	38	28.00	-	-	-	-	0	0	0		-	-	-
ODI																	
List A																		
20/20 Int																		
20/20																		

Career Performances

	M	Inn	NO	Runs	HS	Avg	100	50	Ct	St	Balls	Runs	Wkts	Avg	BB	5I	10M
Test																		
FC	3	4	0	88	38	22.00	-	-	-	-	0	0	0		-	-	-
ODI																		
List A																		
20/20 Int																		
20/20																		

BOTHA, A. G.   Derbyshire

Name: Anthony (<u>Ant</u>) Greyvensteyn Botha
Role: Left-hand bat, slow left-arm bowler
Born: 17 November 1976, Pretoria,
South Africa
Height: 6ft **Weight:** 12st 7lbs
Nickname: Boats
County debut: 2004
County cap: 2004
Place in batting averages: 177th av. 24.73
(2005 80th av. 38.47)
Place in bowling averages: 98th av. 38.75
(2005 128th av. 45.63)
Strike rate: 68.79 (career 71.21)
Parents: Elise and Ian
Marital status: Single
Education: Maritzburg College;
Natal Tech
Qualifications: Marketing Manager Diploma
Off-season: 'Will be in South Africa – Durban for six weeks'
Overseas tours: South Africa U19 to India 1995-96
Overseas teams played for: Natal/KwaZulu-Natal 1995-96 – 1998-99; Easterns
1999-2000 – 2002-03; Joondalup CC, Perth 2005-06

Career highlights to date: 'Winning the four-day championship with Easterns 2002'
Cricket moments to forget: 'Getting badly injured in 2004 against Yorkshire'
Cricket superstitions: 'None'
Cricketers particularly admired: Steve Waugh, Jonty Rhodes
Young players to look out for: Greg Smith (Derbyshire)
Other sports played: Hockey, tennis
Other sports followed: Football (Liverpool), rugby (Sharks)
Favourite band: Live
Relaxations: 'Watersports, beach'
Extras: Represented South African Schools 1995. Played for South African Academy 1997. Scored maiden first-class century (103) v Durham UCCE at Derby 2004, then took 5-55 in the DUCCE second innings to become the first Derbyshire player since 1937 to score a century and record a five-wicket innings return in the same first-class match. C&G Man of the Match award v Durham at Riverside 2005 (4-44/34*). Is England-qualified
Best batting: 156* Derbyshire v Yorkshire, Derby 2005
Best bowling: 8-53 Natal B v Northerns B, Centurion 1997-98

2006 Season

	M	Inn	NO	Runs	HS	Avg	100	50	Ct	St	Balls	Runs	Wkts	Avg	BB	5I	10M
Test																	
FC	12	21	2	470	100	24.73	1	4	14	-	1995	1124	29	38.75	6-117	1	-
ODI																	
List A	17	16	5	338	46 *	30.72	-	-	8	-	777	656	17	38.58	5-60	1	
20/20 Int																	
20/20	7	4	1	41	16	13.66	-	-	3	-	114	151	6	25.16	2-46	-	

Career Performances

	M	Inn	NO	Runs	HS	Avg	100	50	Ct	St	Balls	Runs	Wkts	Avg	BB	5I	10M
Test																	
FC	84	137	21	2889	156 *	24.90	3	12	62	-	14599	7084	205	34.55	8-53	5	1
ODI																	
List A	94	72	21	1061	60 *	20.80	-	2	41	-	3467	2752	94	29.27	5-60	1	
20/20 Int																	
20/20	19	14	5	142	25 *	15.77	-	-	6	-	366	439	18	24.38	2-16	-	

BOYCE, M. A. G.   Leicestershire

Name: Matthew (<u>Matt</u>) Andrew Golding Boyce
Role: Left-hand opening bat, 'very occasional' right-arm off-spin bowler
Born: 13 August 1985, Cheltenham
Height: 5ft 10in **Weight:** 10st 12lbs
Nickname: Boycey
County debut: 2006
Parents: Anne and Andrew
Marital status: Single
Family links with cricket: 'Father played recreational cricket for over 20 years and coached youth cricket for ten years. Aunt played for Cambridge University. Brother played for Oakham School for three years in 1st XI'
Education: Oakham School; Nottingham University
Qualifications: 9 GCSEs, 3 A-levels
Overseas tours: Leicestershire U13 to South Africa 1998; Oakham School to South Africa 2000
Overseas teams played for: Hoppers Crossing, Melbourne 2003-04
Career highlights to date: 'Scoring first century (105) v Northants for Leics 2nd XI. Scoring 2570 runs in 2004 season for Egerton Park and Market Overton and Leics, including record score of 225 (150 balls; 30 x 4, 5 x 6) in the Rutland Championship side v Peterborough. Playing for England Development Squad v Bangladesh 2004'
Cricket moments to forget: 'Walking out to bat against Northamptonshire without a box on and facing the first over before admitting to that fact!'
Cricket superstitions: 'None'
Cricketers particularly admired: David Gower, Andrew Strauss, Brian Lara
Other sports played: Hockey (Leicestershire and Midlands Schoolboys, England trialist), rugby (Oakham School; played scrum half in two *Daily Mail* Cup final winning sides at Twickenham), football (for university), squash (for hall at university)
Other sports followed: Football (Manchester United), rugby (Leicester Tigers)
Favourite band: Midtown, Queen
Relaxations: Sport – squash, gym, swimming, football, rugby; socialising, PlayStation, music
Extras: County Council Special Award for Youth Cricket. *Rutland Times* Young Cricketer of the Year. Sporting Moment of the Year 2004 (225; *see above*). Rutland League Teenage Cricketer of the Year. Leading batsman in Leicestershire League
Best batting: 6 Leicestershire v Pakistanis, Leicester 2006

2006 Season

	M	Inn	NO	Runs	HS	Avg	100	50	Ct	St	Balls	Runs	Wkts	Avg	BB	5I	10M
Test																	
FC	1	2	0	10	6	5.00	-	-	-	-	0	0	0		-	-	-
ODI																	
List A																	
20/20 Int																	
20/20																	

Career Performances

	M	Inn	NO	Runs	HS	Avg	100	50	Ct	St	Balls	Runs	Wkts	Avg	BB	5I	10M
Test																	
FC	1	2	0	10	6	5.00	-	-	-	-	0	0	0		-	-	-
ODI																	
List A																	
20/20 Int																	
20/20																	

10. Who took 7-43 on Test debut v West Indies at Lord's 1995?

BRAGG, W. D.   Glamorgan

Name: William (<u>Will</u>) David Bragg
Role: Left-hand bat, wicket-keeper
Born: 24 October 1986, Gwent, South Wales
Height: 5ft 10in **Weight:** 12st 6lbs
Nickname: Braggy, Milf, Braggpot, Pottsy
County debut: No first-team appearance
(*see Extras*)
Parents: Susan and Steven
Marital status: Single
Family links with cricket: 'Father and
brother have both played for local sides
(Malpas CC)'
Education: Rougemont Independent School;
Cardiff University

Qualifications: 11 GCSEs, 4 A-levels,
'studying for degree'
Career outside cricket: 'Civil engineering'
Off-season: 'Studying; pots; girlfriend
(Jodie)'
Career highlights to date: 'Playing for Glamorgan'
Cricket moments to forget: 'Dropping easy catches'
Cricket superstitions: 'Put box on last'
Cricketers particularly admired: Matthew Maynard, Alan Jones, Brian Lara
Young players to look out for: Tom Maynard, Ben Wright, Mike O'Shea,
James Harris
Other sports played: Rugby (for school), football (Gwent County)
Other sports followed: Football (Tottenham)
Favourite band: Razorlight
Relaxations: 'Pots with mates; girlfriend'
Extras: Scored most runs by any batsman for Wales U15. Played for Wales Minor
Counties in the C&G 2005 and in Minor Counties competitions 2004-06. Played for
Glamorgan in the Twenty20 Floodlit Cup 2006 but has yet to appear for the county in
first-class cricket or major domestic competition
Opinions on cricket: 'One-day cricket seems to pull in the crowds, exciting. Four-day
cricket seems far slower and more boring.'

2006 Season (did not make any first-class or one-day appearances)

Career Performances

	M	Inn	NO	Runs	HS	Avg	100	50	Ct	St	Balls	Runs	Wkts	Avg	BB	5I	10M
Test																	
FC																	
ODI																	
List A	1	1	1	41	41 *		-	-	1	-	0	0	0		-	-	
20/20 Int																	
20/20																	

BRAVO, D. J. Kent

Name: <u>Dwayne</u> John Bravo
Role: Right-hand bat, right-arm medium-fast bowler; all-rounder
Born: 7 October 1983, Santa Cruz, Trinidad
Nickname: Johnny
County debut: 2006
Test debut: 2004
ODI debut: 2003-04
Twenty20 Int debut: 2005-06
Place in batting averages: 172nd av. 26.00
Strike rate: (career 54.94)
Overseas tours: West Indies U19 to New Zealand (U19 World Cup) 2001-02; West Indies A to England 2002; West Indies to England (ICC Champions Trophy) 2004, to Australia (VB Series) 2004-05, to Australia 2005-06, to New Zealand 2005-06, to Malaysia (DLF Cup) 2006-07, to India (ICC Champions Trophy) 2006-07, to Pakistan 2006-07
Overseas teams played for: Trinidad and Tobago 2001-02 –
Extras: Took 6-55 following a first innings 77 in his third Test match, v England at Old Trafford 2004. His awards include Man of the Match v India in the fourth ODI (3-32/61*) and the fifth ODI (44-ball 62*), both at Port of Spain 2006. An overseas player with Kent during the 2006 season as a locum for Andrew Hall
Best batting: 197 Trinidad and Tobago v West Indies B, Couva 2003-04
Best bowling: 6-11 Trinidad and Tobago v Windward Islands, St George's 2002-03

2006 Season

	M	Inn	NO	Runs	HS	Avg	100	50	Ct	St	Balls	Runs	Wkts	Avg	BB	5I	10M
Test																	
FC	5	8	0	208	76	26.00	-	1	-	-	529	435	8	54.37	6-112	1	-
ODI																	
List A	7	6	1	129	50	25.80	-	1	1	-	227	183	8	22.87	2-33	-	-
20/20 Int																	
20/20	1	1	1	0	0 *		-	-	-	-	18	17	0			-	-

Career Performances

	M	Inn	NO	Runs	HS	Avg	100	50	Ct	St	Balls	Runs	Wkts	Avg	BB	5I	10M
Test	16	30	1	956	113	32.96	2	5	13	-	2403	1295	36	35.97	6-55	2	-
FC	66	122	6	3490	197	30.08	7	17	47	-	6044	3319	110	30.17	6-11	6	-
ODI	48	37	11	576	62 *	22.15	-	2	16	-	1862	1661	49	33.89	3-24	-	
List A	77	63	14	1006	62 *	20.53	-	3	28	-	2654	2297	78	29.44	4-34	-	
20/20 Int	1	1	1	19	19 *		-	-	-	-	16	16	2	8.00	2-16	-	
20/20	2	2	2	19	19 *		-	-	-	-	34	33	2	16.50	2-16	-	

BREESE, G. R.   Durham

Name: <u>Gareth</u> Rohan Breese
Role: Right-hand bat, right-arm off-spin bowler; all-rounder
Born: 9 January 1976, Montego Bay, Jamaica
Height: 5ft 8in **Weight:** 13st
Nickname: Briggy
County debut: 2004
Test debut: 2002-03
Place in batting averages: 203rd av. 21.48 (2005 121st av. 32.50)
Place in bowling averages: 136th av. 48.03 (2005 87th av. 34.83)
Strike rate: 82.55 (career 64.57)
Parents: Brian and Jean
Marital status: Single
Family links with cricket: Father played league cricket in Somerset and Wales; also played representative cricket for two parishes in Jamaica as wicket-keeper/batsman. He is currently the cricket operations officer of the Jamaica Board
Education: Wolmer's Boys School, Kingston; University of Technology, Kingston
Qualifications: Level 2 coach, Diploma in Hotel and Resort Management

Off-season: Playing as overseas player for Jamaica
Overseas tours: West Indies U19 to Pakistan and Bangladesh 1995-96; Jamaica to Malaysia (Commonwealth Games) 1998-99; West Indies A to England 2002; West Indies to India 2002-03
Overseas teams played for: Jamaica 1995-96 –
Career highlights to date: 'Playing at the highest level and representing Durham over the last three seasons'
Cricket moments to forget: 'My two Test innings'
Cricket superstitions: 'None'
Cricketers particularly admired: Jimmy Adams, Courtney Walsh, Delroy Morgan (Jamaica), Dale Benkenstein, Gordon Muchall
Young players to look out for: Gordon Muchall, Nick Cook, Ben Harmison
Other sports played: Pool
Relaxations: 'My computer; music, shopping; hanging out with team-mates/friends'
Extras: Represented West Indies U19 1994-95. Second-highest wicket-taker in the Busta Cup 2000-01 with 36 (av. 15.11) and in 2001-02 with 44 (av. 20.18). Captain of Jamaica in first-class cricket 2003-04 and in one-day cricket 2004-05. Scored 165* as Durham made 453-9 to beat Somerset at Taunton 2004. Scored century (110) v Middlesex at Lord's 2006, in the process sharing with Dale Benkenstein (125) in a new record fifth-wicket partnership for Durham (222). Is a British passport-holder and is not considered an overseas player
Opinions on cricket: 'The longer format of the game, mainly at first-class level, has lost a lot of its support through possible lack of interest, so we see smaller crowds. I think we as players should do our best to play hard, exciting cricket at all times to try and force results and attract the spectator support which the game previously enjoyed.'
Best batting: 165* Durham v Somerset, Taunton 2004
Best bowling: 7-60 Jamaica v Barbados, Bridgetown 2000-01

2006 Season

	M	Inn	NO	Runs	HS	Avg	100	50	Ct	St	Balls	Runs	Wkts	Avg	BB	5I	10M
Test																	
FC	17	29	0	623	110	21.48	1	1	14	-	2229	1297	27	48.03	4-75	-	-
ODI																	
List A	15	13	3	229	50	22.90	-	1	10	-	612	507	19	26.68	4-36	-	
20/20 Int																	
20/20	7	6	1	46	15	9.20	-	-	4	-	114	128	7	18.28	3-35	-	

Career Performances

	M	Inn	NO	Runs	HS	Avg	100	50	Ct	St	Balls	Runs	Wkts	Avg	BB	5I	10M
Test	1	2	0	5	5	2.50	-	-	1	-	188	135	2	67.50	2-108	-	-
FC	105	168	18	3941	165*	26.27	3	25	85	-	17306	7898	268	29.47	7-60	12	3
ODI																	
List A	86	64	14	929	52*	18.58	-	2	42	-	3379	2465	87	28.33	4-24	-	
20/20 Int																	
20/20	19	17	3	121	24*	8.64	-	-	8	-	366	426	21	20.28	4-14	-	

BRESNAN, T. T. Yorkshire

Name: Timothy (<u>Tim</u>) Thomas Bresnan
Role: Right-hand bat, right-arm fast bowler; all-rounder
Born: 28 February 1985, Pontefract
Height: 6ft 1in **Weight:** 14st 7lbs
Nickname: Brez, Brezzie, Tikka
County debut: 2001 (one-day), 2003 (first-class)
County cap: 2006
ODI debut: 2006
Twenty20 Int debut: 2006
Place in batting averages: 184th av. 24.18 (2005 220th av. 19.94)
Place in bowling averages: 61st av. 32.06 (2005 80th av. 33.42)
Strike rate: 57.72 (career 58.62)
Parents: Julie and Ray
Marital status: Single
Family links with cricket: 'Dad played local league cricket'
Education: Castleford High School; Pontefract New College
Qualifications: 11 GCSEs, UKCC 2 cricket coaching, Advanced Scuba Diver Level II
Overseas tours: Yorkshire U16 to Cape Town 2001; England U17 to Australia 2000-01; England U19 to Australia and (U19 World Cup) New Zealand 2001-02, to Australia 2002-03, to Bangladesh (U19 World Cup) 2003-04; England VI to Hong Kong 2006; England A to Bangladesh 2006-07
Overseas teams played for: Sutherland CC, Sydney 2005-06
Career highlights to date: 'Making England debut, Lord's 2006'
Cricket moments to forget: 'First big injury, June 2006'
Cricket superstitions: 'None'
Cricketers particularly admired: Ian Botham
Young players to look out for: Jack Hughes
Other sports played: Golf
Other sports followed: Football (Sheffield United)
Injuries: Out for two months with a stress reaction in the back
Favourite band: Razorlight, Snow Patrol
Relaxations: 'PlayStation, cinema'
Extras: Bunbury Festival Best All-rounder and Most Outstanding Player. Made one-day debut v Kent at Headingley 2001 aged 16 years 102 days, making him the youngest player to represent Yorkshire since Paul Jarvis in 1981. NBC Denis Compton Award for the most promising young Yorkshire player 2002, 2003. Represented England U19 2002 and 2003

Opinions on cricket: 'Should be three two-hour sessions, 96 overs in a day (every day).'
Best batting: 94 MCC v Nottinghamshire, Lord's 2006
Best bowling: 5-42 Yorkshire v Worcestershire, Worcester 2005

2006 Season

	M	Inn	NO	Runs	HS	Avg	100	50	Ct	St	Balls	Runs	Wkts	Avg	BB	5I	10M
Test																	
FC	12	17	1	387	94	24.18	-	2	4	-	1905	1058	33	32.06	5-58	1	-
ODI	4	4	1	51	20	17.00	-	-	1	-	150	169	2	84.50	1-38	-	
List A	11	7	2	148	47 *	29.60	-	-	3	-	468	466	11	42.36	3-46	-	
20/20 Int	1	1	1	6	6 *		-	-	-	-	12	20	0		-	-	
20/20	4	2	1	14	8	14.00	-	-	-	-	54	65	6	10.83	3-21	-	

Career Performances

	M	Inn	NO	Runs	HS	Avg	100	50	Ct	St	Balls	Runs	Wkts	Avg	BB	5I	10M
Test																	
FC	41	56	7	950	94	19.38	-	6	12	-	6097	3445	104	33.12	5-42	2	-
ODI	4	4	1	51	20	17.00	-	-	1	-	150	169	2	84.50	1-38	-	
List A	90	62	17	769	61	17.08	-	1	28	-	3669	3058	78	39.20	4-25	-	
20/20 Int	1	1	1	6	6 *		-	-	-	-	12	20	0		-	-	
20/20	22	16	7	223	42	24.77	-	-	7	-	428	534	26	20.53	3-21	-	

BRIDGE, G. D. Durham

Name: <u>Graeme</u> David Bridge
Role: Right-hand bat, slow left-arm bowler
Born: 4 September 1980, Sunderland
Height: 5ft 8in **Weight:** 12st 12lbs
Nickname: Bridgey, Teet
County debut: 1999
Strike rate: (career 70.23)
Parents: Anne and John
Wife and date of marriage: Leanne,
2 October 2004
Children: Olivia Molly, 13 September 2003
Family links with cricket: 'Dad and brother played club cricket'
Education: Southmoor School, Sunderland
Qualifications: 5 GCSEs, Level 1 coaching
Overseas tours: England U19 to New Zealand 1998-99, to Malaysia and (U19 World Cup) Sri Lanka 1999-2000;

Durham to South Africa 2002; Durham Academy to India

Career highlights to date: 'Making first-team debut'

Cricket moments to forget: 'Pulling up with twisted ankle on TV'

Cricket superstitions: 'Don't be late'

Cricketers particularly admired: Martin Love, David Boon

Other sports played: Football

Other sports followed: Football (Sunderland AFC 'home or away')

Favourite band: 'Anything'; Stone Roses

Relaxations: 'Horse racing (jumps)'

Extras: Played in U15 World Cup 1996. Represented England U19 1999. C&G Man of the Match award on county one-day debut for his 3-44 v Gloucestershire at Bristol 2001. Released by Durham at the end of the 2006 season

Best batting: 52 Durham v Leicestershire, Riverside 2004

Best bowling: 6-84 Durham v Hampshire, Riverside 2001

2006 Season

	M	Inn	NO	Runs	HS	Avg	100	50	Ct	St	Balls	Runs	Wkts	Avg	BB	5I	10M
Test																	
FC	1	2	0	48	43	24.00	-	-	-	-	96	73	1	73.00	1-73	-	-
ODI																	
List A	1	0	0	0	0		-	-	-	-	42	41	1	41.00	1-41		
20/20 Int																	
20/20	6	4	1	22	11 *	7.33	-	-	1	-	92	113	3	37.66	2-16	-	

Career Performances

	M	Inn	NO	Runs	HS	Avg	100	50	Ct	St	Balls	Runs	Wkts	Avg	BB	5I	10M
Test																	
FC	40	66	12	966	52	17.88	-	3	20	-	6251	3141	89	35.29	6-84	1	-
ODI																	
List A	49	35	13	332	50 *	15.09	-	1	8	-	2096	1538	55	27.96	4-20	-	
20/20 Int																	
20/20	11	7	1	41	11 *	6.83	-	-	2	-	205	214	10	21.40	2-16	-	

BROAD, S. C. J.　　Leicestershire

Name: <u>Stuart</u> Christopher John Broad
Role: Left-hand bat, right-arm
fast-medium bowler
Born: 24 June 1986, Nottingham
Height: 6ft 6in **Weight:** 13st
Nickname: Broady
County debut: 2005
ODI debut: 2006
Twenty20 Int debut: 2006
Place in batting averages: 204th av. 21.46
(2005 274th av. 10.70)
Place in bowling averages: 53rd av. 31.06
(2005 43rd av. 27.70)
Strike rate: 50.35 (career 48.00)
Parents: Carole and Chris
Marital status: Single
Family links with cricket: 'Dad played for
Glos, Notts and England'
Education: Oakham School
Qualifications: 10 GCSEs, 3 A-levels
Off-season: 'ECB National Academy in Perth'
Overseas tours: Oakham School to South Africa 2000-01; England A to West Indies
2005-06, to Bangladesh 2006-07
Overseas teams played for: Hoppers Crossing CC, Melbourne 2004-05
Career highlights to date: 'England ODI debut v Pakistan 2006. Winning Twenty20
Cup 2006 with Leicestershire'
Cricket superstitions: 'Three warm-up balls before I bowl a new spell'
Cricketers particularly admired: Glenn McGrath, Shaun Pollock
Young players to look out for: Mark Collier
Other sports played: Hockey (Midlands age-groups), golf
Other sports followed: Football (Nottingham Forest), rugby (Leicester Tigers)
Favourite band: Snow Patrol
Relaxations: 'PSP, playing golf, films'
Extras: Leicestershire Young Cricketers' Batsman of the Year 2003. Represented
England U19 2005. Cricket Writers' Club Young Cricketer of the Year 2006. Cricket
Society Most Promising Young Cricketer of the Year 2006. ECB National Academy
2005-06, 2006-07
Opinions on cricket: 'From what I've seen, Kolpak cricketers [*see page 13*] improve
the standard of cricket in England, but it is good to see the ECB controlling the
number of players that come over. The best youngsters still break through. Playing
against better players can only make England stronger in the future because youngsters
have to improve their game to compete.'

Best batting: 65* Leicestershire v Derbyshire, Leicester 2006
Best bowling: 5-83 Leicestershire v Gloucestershire, Leicester 2006
Stop press: Called up to England squad for the Commonwealth Bank Series in Australia 2006-07 as cover in the pace-bowling department

2006 Season

	M	Inn	NO	Runs	HS	Avg	100	50	Ct	St	Balls	Runs	Wkts	Avg	BB	5I	10M
Test																	
FC	14	17	4	279	65 *	21.46	-	2	6	-	2417	1491	48	31.06	5-83	4	-
ODI	5	3	3	9	8 *		-	-	1	-	214	185	5	37.00	3-57	-	
List A	11	5	4	31	11 *	31.00	-	-	2	-	486	457	10	45.70	3-57	-	
20/20 Int	1	0	0	0	0		-	-	-	-	24	35	2	17.50	2-35	-	
20/20	9	0	0	0	0		-	-	1	-	216	179	14	12.78	3-13	-	

Career Performances

	M	Inn	NO	Runs	HS	Avg	100	50	Ct	St	Balls	Runs	Wkts	Avg	BB	5I	10M
Test																	
FC	25	31	8	387	65 *	16.82	-	2	8	-	3840	2402	80	30.02	5-83	4	-
ODI	5	3	3	9	8 *		-	-	1	-	214	185	5	37.00	3-57	-	
List A	12	5	4	31	11 *	31.00	-	-	2	-	528	492	12	41.00	3-57	-	
20/20 Int	1	0	0	0	0		-	-	-	-	24	35	2	17.50	2-35	-	
20/20	9	0	0	0	0		-	-	1	-	216	179	14	12.78	3-13	-	

BROPHY, G. L. Yorkshire

Name: <u>Gerard</u> Louis Brophy
Role: Right-hand bat, wicket-keeper
Born: 26 November 1975, Welkom, South Africa
Height: 5ft 11in **Weight:** 12st
Nickname: Scuba, Broph
County debut: 2002 (Northamptonshire), 2006 (Yorkshire)
Place in batting averages: 236th av. 15.68
Parents: Gerard and Trish
Wife and date of marriage: Alison, 3 January 2004
Education: Christian Brothers College, Boksburg; Wits Technikon (both South Africa)
Qualifications: Marketing Diploma, Level 2 coach

Overseas tours: South Africa U17 to England 1993; South African Academy to Zimbabwe 1998-99
Overseas teams played for: Gauteng 1996-97 – 1998-99; Free State 1999-2000 – 2000-01
Career highlights to date: 'Captaincy of Free State 2000-01. First dismissal [in collaboration] with Allan Donald'
Cricket moments to forget: 'Messing up a live TV interview'
Cricket superstitions: 'Right pad on first and right glove on first'
Cricketers particularly admired: Ray Jennings, Ian Healy, Allan Donald, Hansie Cronje
Other sports played: Golf, rugby
Other sports followed: Golf, rugby
Favourite band: Coldplay
Relaxations: 'Fishing, travelling, braais, scuba diving'
Extras: Captained South Africa U17. Played for Ireland in the NatWest 2000. Holds a British passport and is not considered an overseas player
Best batting: 185 South African Academy v ZCU President's XI, Harare 1998-99

2006 Season

	M	Inn	NO	Runs	HS	Avg	100	50	Ct	St	Balls	Runs	Wkts	Avg	BB	5I	10M
Test																	
FC	10	16	0	251	97	15.68	-	1	26	3	0	0	0		-	-	-
ODI																	
List A	12	8	1	112	32	16.00	-	-	7	2	0	0	0		-	-	
20/20 Int																	
20/20	9	7	2	152	57	30.40	-	1	2	-	0	0	0		-	-	

Career Performances

	M	Inn	NO	Runs	HS	Avg	100	50	Ct	St	Balls	Runs	Wkts	Avg	BB	5I	10M
Test																	
FC	63	102	14	2759	185	31.35	5	13	151	10	6	1	0		-	-	-
ODI																	
List A	67	52	9	941	57 *	21.88	-	4	58	13	0	0	0		-	-	
20/20 Int																	
20/20	15	12	4	211	57	26.37	-	1	5	1	0	0	0		-	-	

BROWN, A. D.   Surrey

Name: <u>Alistair</u> Duncan Brown
Role: Right-hand bat, right-arm off-spin
bowler, occasional wicket-keeper
Born: 11 February 1970, Beckenham
Height: 5ft 10in **Weight:** 12st 7lbs
Nickname: The Lord
County debut: 1990 (one-day),
1992 (first-class)
County cap: 1994
Benefit: 2002
ODI debut: 1996
1000 runs in a season: 8
1st-Class 200s: 3
List A 200s: 2
Place in batting averages: 30th av. 54.95
(2005 50th av. 45.61)
Strike rate: (career 228.00)
Parents: Robert and Ann
Wife and date of marriage: Sarah, 10 October 1998
Children: Max Charles, 9 March 2001; Joe Robert, 11 March 2003
Family links with cricket: Father played for Surrey Young Amateurs in the 1950s
Education: Caterham School
Qualifications: 5 O-levels, Level II coach
Overseas tours: England VI to Singapore 1993, 1994, 1995, to Hong Kong 1997;
England to Sharjah (Champions Trophy) 1997-98, to Bangladesh (Wills International
Cup) 1998-99
Overseas teams played for: North Perth, Western Australia 1989-90
Career highlights to date: '118 v India at Old Trafford 1996; 203 v Hampshire at
Guildford 1997; 268 v Glamorgan at The Oval 2002'
Cricket moments to forget: 'A great couple of days in Ireland!'
Cricket superstitions: 'Always get to the ground before 11 a.m.'
Cricketers particularly admired: Ian Botham, Viv Richards
Other sports played: Football, golf
Other sports followed: Football (West Ham United), rugby union (London Wasps)
Favourite band: Roachford, Snow Patrol
Relaxations: 'Golf and sleep (when the children allow)'
Extras: Man of the Match for his 118 against India in the third ODI at Old Trafford
1996. Recorded the highest-ever score in the Sunday League with 203 off 119 balls
against Hampshire at Guildford in 1997 and received an individual award at the PCA
dinner for that achievement. Joint winner (with Carl Hooper) of the EDS Walter
Lawrence Trophy for the fastest first-class 100 of the 1998 season (72 balls v

Northants at The Oval). Surrey CCC Batsman of the Season 2001. Scored 160-ball 268 out of 438-5 v Glamorgan at The Oval in the C&G 2002; it set a new record for the highest individual score in professional one-day cricket worldwide and Brown also became the first batsman to have scored two double centuries in one-day cricket. Scored 154 v Lancashire at Old Trafford 2004 to complete full set of first-class hundreds against all 17 other counties

Best batting: 295* Surrey v Leicestershire, Oakham School 2000
Best bowling: 3-25 Surrey v Somerset, Guildford 2006

2006 Season

	M	Inn	NO	Runs	HS	Avg	100	50	Ct	St	Balls	Runs	Wkts	Avg	BB	5I	10M
Test																	
FC	16	27	4	1264	215	54.95	5	4	9	-	143	74	3	24.66	3-25	-	-
ODI																	
List A	15	14	1	456	106	35.07	1	2	4	-	54	47	1	47.00	1-23	-	
20/20 Int																	
20/20	10	10	0	247	83	24.70	-	1	5	-	0	0	0		-	-	

Career Performances

	M	Inn	NO	Runs	HS	Avg	100	50	Ct	St	Balls	Runs	Wkts	Avg	BB	5I	10M
Test																	
FC	231	365	39	14428	295 *	44.25	44	57	235	1	1140	592	5	118.40	3-25	-	-
ODI	16	16	0	354	118	22.12	1	1	6	-	6	5	0		-	-	
List A	354	340	17	10287	268	31.84	18	47	122	-	423	438	12	36.50	3-39	-	
20/20 Int																	
20/20	34	34	1	854	83	25.87	-	6	26	-	2	2	0		-	-	

11. Who holds the record for being the oldest
player to appear in a Test, having played in his final Test
in 1929-30 at more than 52 years of age?

BROWN, D. O.   Gloucestershire

Name: <u>David</u> Owen Brown
Role: Right-hand bat, right-arm medium bowler
Born: 8 December 1982, Burnley
Height: 6ft **Weight:** 13st 7lbs
Nickname: Wally, Browny
County debut: 2006
County cap: 2006
Strike rate: (career 83.40)
Parents: Peter and Valerie
Marital status: Single
Family links with cricket: 'Father played for 30 years with Burnley and Southgate. Brother Michael opens the batting for Hampshire CCC'
Education: Queen Elizabeth's Grammar School, Blackburn; Collingwood College, Durham University
Qualifications: 10 GCSEs, 4 A-levels, BA (Hons) Sport in the Community
Overseas tours: MCC B to Nepal 2003; MCC A to Canada 2005
Overseas teams played for: Claremont-Nedlands, Perth 2001-02; Perth CC 2005-06
Career highlights to date: 'Signing for Gloucestershire CCC. Playing for Durham University'
Cricket moments to forget: 'First-class debut v Notts for Durham University 2003 – got golden duck and went the distance. Any time I self-destruct'
Cricket superstitions: 'None'
Cricketers particularly admired: Dale Benkenstein, Andrew Flintoff, Ricky Ponting, James Anderson
Young players to look out for: Will Smith, Ali Maiden, David Balcombe, Jonathan Clare, James Allenby, Luke Ronchi, Lee Daggett
Other sports played: Golf, football
Other sports followed: Football (Burnley FC)
Favourite band: Dire Straits, Fleetwood Mac, Eagles, 'any "cheese"'
Relaxations: 'Championship Manager; watching *The Office*, *Alan Partridge*; golf, DVDs, cinema, socialising, sleeping'
Extras: Played for Durham UCCE 2003-05. Represented British Universities 2005. Struck 26-ball 63* on one-day debut v Surrey at Bristol in the C&G 2006
Opinions on cricket: 'Too many games; not enough time for quality practice. MCC Universities a good method of providing counties with young talented cricketers. Twenty20 looks like a great format as long as authorities don't "overkill" it through too much expansion.'

Best batting: 77 DUCCE v Leicestershire, Leicester 2005
Best bowling: 2-48 DUCCE v Northamptonshire, Northampton 2004

2006 Season

	M	Inn	NO	Runs	HS	Avg	100	50	Ct	St	Balls	Runs	Wkts	Avg	BB	5I	10M
Test																	
FC	1	2	0	56	34	28.00	-	-	-	-	54	30	0		-	-	-
ODI																	
List A	2	2	1	77	63 *	77.00	-	1	-	-	30	47	0		-	-	
20/20 Int																	
20/20	9	8	1	138	36	19.71	-	-	2	-	0	0	0		-	-	

Career Performances

	M	Inn	NO	Runs	HS	Avg	100	50	Ct	St	Balls	Runs	Wkts	Avg	BB	5I	10M
Test																	
FC	11	18	0	498	77	27.66	-	4	7	-	834	679	10	67.90	2-48	-	-
ODI																	
List A	2	2	1	77	63 *	77.00	-	1	-	-	30	47	0		-	-	
20/20 Int																	
20/20	9	8	1	138	36	19.71	-	-	2	-	0	0	0		-	-	

BROWN, D. R.   Warwickshire

Name: Douglas (<u>Dougie</u>) Robert Brown
Role: Right-hand bat, right-arm fast-medium bowler; all-rounder
Born: 29 October 1969, Stirling, Scotland
Height: 6ft 2in **Weight:** 14st 7lbs
Nickname: Hoots
County debut: 1991 (one-day), 1991-92 (first-class)
County cap: 1995
Benefit: 2005
ODI debut: 1997-98
1000 runs in a season: 1
50 wickets in a season: 4
1st-Class 200s: 1
Place in batting averages: 208th av. 20.44 (2005 178th av. 25.66)
Place in bowling averages: 32nd av. 28.48 (2005 67th av. 30.80)
Strike rate: 59.00 (career 54.42)
Parents: Alastair and Janette

Children: Lauren, 14 September 1998
Family links with cricket: 'Both grandads played a bit'
Education: Alloa Academy; West London Institute of Higher Education (Borough Road College)
Qualifications: 9 O-Grades, 5 Higher Grades, BEd (Hons) Physical Education, ECB Level III coach
Career outside cricket: PE teacher
Overseas tours: Scotland XI to Pakistan 1988-89; England VI to Hong Kong 1997, 2001, 2003; England A to Kenya and Sri Lanka 1997-98; England to Sharjah (Champions Trophy) 1997-98, to West Indies 1997-98 (one-day series), to Bangladesh (Wills International Cup) 1998-99; Scotland to UAE (ICC Six Nations Challenge) 2003-04, to Ireland (ICC Trophy) 2005, to Bangladesh (one-day series) 2006-07
Overseas teams played for: Primrose, Cape Town 1992-93; Vredenburg Saldhana, Cape Town 1993-94; Eastern Suburbs, Wellington 1995-96; Wellington, New Zealand 1995-96; Namibia 2002-03
Career highlights to date: 'Playing first Lord's final v Northants 1995. England debut in Sharjah'
Cricket moments to forget: 'Phone call from David Graveney (chairman of selectors) saying you are dropped!'
Cricket superstitions: 'None'
Cricketers particularly admired: Ian Botham, Wasim Akram, Dermot Reeve 'and everyone who gives 100 per cent'
Other sports played: Golf
Other sports followed: Football (Alloa Athletic, 'and all the Midlands football teams')
Favourite band: Oasis, U2
Relaxations: 'Music, time with Lauren'
Extras: Played football at Hampden Park for Scotland U18. Has played first-class and one-day cricket for Scotland; has played ODI cricket for England and Scotland. Scored 1118 runs and took 109 wickets in all first-team county cricket 1997. Vice-captain of Warwickshire 2002-03. Warwickshire All-rounder of the Year 2002. Scored 108 v Essex at Edgbaston in the C&G 2003, winning Man of the Match award and sharing with Ashley Giles (71*) in a competition record seventh-wicket partnership (170). Scored century (108*) then returned first innings figures of 5-53 v Northamptonshire at Northampton 2004. Took 500th first-class wicket for Warwickshire (Ed Smith), v Middlesex at Lord's 2006
Opinions on cricket: 'Still a great game!'
Best batting: 203 Warwickshire v Sussex, Hove 2000
Best bowling: 8-89 First-Class Counties XI v Pakistan A, Chelmsford 1997

2006 Season

	M	Inn	NO	Runs	HS	Avg	100	50	Ct	St	Balls	Runs	Wkts	Avg	BB	5I	10M
Test																	
FC	11	19	1	368	69	20.44	-	2	4	-	1947	940	33	28.48	4-45	-	-
ODI																	
List A	8	5	0	95	27	19.00	-	-	-	-	276	230	9	25.55	3-37	-	
20/20 Int																	
20/20	8	5	1	50	22	12.50	-	-	4	-	168	239	7	34.14	2-16	-	

Career Performances

	M	Inn	NO	Runs	HS	Avg	100	50	Ct	St	Balls	Runs	Wkts	Avg	BB	5I	10M
Test																	
FC	208	317	40	8455	203	30.52	10	44	129	-	30750	16136	565	28.55	8-89	21	4
ODI	11	10	4	114	21	19.00	-	-	1	-	390	344	9	38.22	2-28	-	
List A	300	242	40	4678	108	23.15	1	22	73	-	12379	9404	357	26.34	5-31	2	
20/20 Int																	
20/20	27	20	1	223	37	11.73	-	-	9	-	480	611	23	26.56	3-21	-	

BROWN, J. F.   Northamptonshire

Name: <u>Jason</u> Fred Brown
Role: Right-hand bat, off-spin bowler
Born: 10 October 1974,
Newcastle-under-Lyme
Height: 6ft **Weight:** 13st
Nickname: Cheese, Fish, Brownie
County debut: 1996
County cap: 2000
50 wickets in a season: 3
Place in bowling averages: 139th av. 50.42
(2005 51st av. 28.20)
Strike rate: 101.82 (career 71.46)
Parents: Peter and Cynthia
Wife and date of marriage: Sam,
26 September 1998
Children: Millie
Education: St Margaret Ward RC School,
Stoke-on-Trent
Qualifications: 9 GCSEs, Level 1 coaching qualification
Overseas tours: Kidsgrove League U18 to Australia 1990; Northants CCC to
Zimbabwe 1998, to Grenada 2000; England A to West Indies 2000-01; England
to Sri Lanka 2000-01

Overseas teams played for: North East Valley, Dunedin, New Zealand 1996-97
Cricketers particularly admired: John Emburey, Carl Hooper
Other sports played: Golf
Other sports followed: Football (Port Vale)
Relaxations: 'Reading, listening to music'
Extras: Represented Staffordshire at all junior levels, in Minor Counties, and in the NatWest 1995. Once took 10-16 in a Kidsgrove League game against Haslington U18 playing for Sandyford U18. Took 100th first-class wicket in 23rd match, v Sussex at Northampton 2000, going on to take his 50th wicket of the season in the same game, only his seventh of the summer. Took 5-27 v Somerset at Northampton 2003, the best return by a Northants bowler in the Twenty20 Cup. C&G Man of the Match award for his 5-19 v Cambridgeshire at Northampton 2004
Best batting: 38 Northamptonshire v Hampshire, Northampton 2003
Best bowling: 7-69 Northamptonshire v Durham, Riverside 2003

2006 Season

	M	Inn	NO	Runs	HS	Avg	100	50	Ct	St	Balls	Runs	Wkts	Avg	BB	5I	10M
Test																	
FC	15	19	5	85	20 *	6.07	-	-	3	-	3564	1765	35	50.42	5-82	1	-
ODI																	
List A	15	5	4	9	7 *	9.00	-	-	1	-	678	528	14	37.71	2-32	-	
20/20 Int																	
20/20	9	2	1	9	6 *	9.00	-	-	3	-	210	257	10	25.70	2-17	-	

Career Performances

	M	Inn	NO	Runs	HS	Avg	100	50	Ct	St	Balls	Runs	Wkts	Avg	BB	5I	10M
Test																	
FC	105	123	51	508	38	7.05	-	-	21	-	26727	11975	374	32.01	7-69	21	5
ODI																	
List A	129	48	29	107	16	5.63	-	-	26	-	6160	4426	119	37.19	5-19	1	
20/20 Int																	
20/20	26	2	1	9	6 *	9.00	-	-	6	-	545	689	28	24.60	5-27	1	

BROWN, K. R. Lancashire

Name: <u>Karl</u> Robert Brown
Role: Right-hand bat, right-arm
medium bowler
Born: 17 May 1988, Bolton
Height: 5ft 10in **Weight:** 10st 11lbs
Nickname: Brownie, Charlie
County debut: 2006
Parents: Paul and Lorraine
Marital status: Single
Family links with cricket: Father has played
club cricket for over 30 years and had two
seasons as club professional at Clifton CC in
the Bolton Association
Education: Hesketh Fletcher CE, Atherton,
Lancashire
Qualifications: 8 GCSEs
Off-season: 'England U19 tour to Malaysia,
23 January to 24 February 2007'
Overseas tours: England U16 to South Africa 2003-04; England U19 to Bangladesh
2005-06, to Malaysia 2006-07
Cricket superstitions: 'None'
Cricketers particularly admired: Andrew Flintoff
Young players to look out for: Tom Smith
Other sports played: 'Used to play football'; golf
Other sports followed: Football (Bolton Wanderers), golf
Favourite band/music: Floorfillers 4
Relaxations: 'Watching Bolton Wanderers FC'
Extras: Lancashire Junior Player of the Year 2004
Best batting: 32 Lancashire v DUCCE, Durham 2006

2006 Season

	M	Inn	NO	Runs	HS	Avg	100	50	Ct	St	Balls	Runs	Wkts	Avg	BB	5I	10M
Test																	
FC	1	2	0	34	32	17.00	-	-	-	-	0	0	0		-	-	-
ODI																	
List A																	
20/20 Int																	
20/20																	

	M	Inn	NO	Runs	HS	Avg	100	50	Ct	St	Balls	Runs	Wkts	Avg	BB	5I	10M
Test																	
FC	1	2	0	34	32	17.00	-	-	-	-	0	0	0		-	-	-
ODI																	
List A																	
20/20 Int																	
20/20																	

BROWN, M. J. Hampshire

Name: <u>Michael</u> James Brown
Role: Right-hand bat, wicket-keeper
Born: 9 February 1980, Burnley
Height: 6ft **Weight:** 12st
Nickname: Weasel, Dawson
County debut: 1999 (Middlesex),
2004 (Hampshire)
Place in batting averages: 122nd av. 32.71
(2005 195th av. 23.33)
Parents: Peter and Valerie
Marital status: Single
Family links with cricket: 'Father played
league cricket for 30 years. Mum makes great
tuna sandwiches.' Brother David played for
DUCCE and is now with Gloucestershire
Education: Queen Elizabeth's Grammar
School, Blackburn; Durham University
Qualifications: 10 GCSEs, 4 A-levels, 2.1
Economics/Politics

Career outside cricket: 'Stockbroker?'
Off-season: 'Working for Teather and Greenwood in the City, then off to Perth after
Christmas'
Overseas teams played for: Western Province CC, Cape Town 1998-99; Fremantle
CC 2002-05; South Perth CC 2005-06
Career highlights to date: 'First first-class hundred v Leicestershire; C&G win;
all wins'
Cricket moments to forget: 'Leaving straight balls'
Cricket superstitions: 'Always tap non-striker's end four times at end of over when
at that end'
Cricketers particularly admired: Dale Benkenstein, Nic Pothas, Michael Yardy
Young players to look out for: David Brown, Liam Dawson

Other sports played: Football ('badly'), golf ('occasional bandit')
Other sports followed: Football (Burnley FC)
Favourite band: REM
Relaxations: 'Examining tough ethical questions with Chris Tremlett; learning about dinosaurs; helping Chris Tremlett with his modelling career'
Extras: Represented ECB U19 A v Pakistan U19 1998. Played for Durham UCCE and represented British Universities 2001, 2002. 'Was at non-striker's end as five wickets fell in one over, Middlesex 2nd XI v Glamorgan 2nd XI, July 2001'
Opinions on cricket: 'Twenty20 cricket [should be] played at end of season. Second XI cricket should mirror first-class cricket. Wickets and practice facilities in 2nd XI still disgraceful.'
Best batting: 133 Hampshire v LUCCE, Rose Bowl 2006

2006 Season

	M	Inn	NO	Runs	HS	Avg	100	50	Ct	St	Balls	Runs	Wkts	Avg	BB	5I	10M
Test																	
FC	5	8	1	229	133	32.71	1	-	3	-	0	0	0		-	-	-
ODI																	
List A	3	3	0	149	76	49.66	-	1	1	-	0	0	0		-	-	
20/20 Int																	
20/20																	

Career Performances

	M	Inn	NO	Runs	HS	Avg	100	50	Ct	St	Balls	Runs	Wkts	Avg	BB	5I	10M
Test																	
FC	46	81	8	2121	133	29.05	3	13	40	-	0	0	0		-	-	-
ODI																	
List A	8	8	0	227	76	28.37	-	1	3	-	0	0	0		-	-	
20/20 Int																	
20/20	3	3	0	19	14	6.33	-	-	-	-	0	0	0		-	-	

12. Who made his final Test appearance for England in
1976 at the age of 45?

BROWNING, R. J.   Northamptonshire

Name: Richard (<u>Rich</u>) James Browning
Role: Right-hand bat, right-arm
medium-fast bowler
Born: 9 October 1987, Wolverhampton
Height: 6ft 3in **Weight:** 14st 11lbs
Nickname: Browndog
County debut: 2006 (one-day, Derbyshire)
Parents: Tim and Carolyn
Marital status: Single
Family links with cricket: 'Father once
fielded for England in the 1980 Test match at
Headingley against West Indies as Botham
was injured. He and my grandfather also
played decent standard club cricket'
Education: Wolverhampton Grammar School

Qualifications: 10 GCSEs, 3 A-levels, Level
2 cricket coaching
Career outside cricket: Student
Off-season: 'In South Africa with Derbyshire Academy, tour to Port Elizabeth'
Overseas tours: Derbyshire Academy to Port Elizabeth 2006
Career highlights to date: 'Making my first-team debut away to Worcestershire in a
Pro40 game on Sky Sports'
Cricket moments to forget: 'Giving Hassan Adnan and Graeme Welch throw-downs
before the Pro40 game at Grace Road and physically not being able to let go of the
ball'
Cricketers particularly admired: Andrew Flintoff, Glenn McGrath, Brett Lee
Young players to look out for: Moeen Ali, Chris Paget, Paul Borrington, Dan
Redfern, Jake Needham
Other sports played: Football ('used to play Wolverhampton Schools')
Other sports followed: Football (Leeds United – 'grandfather used to play for them
and Sheffield United in the 1960s')
Injuries: Out for three to four weeks on and off with compartment syndrome
Relaxations: 'Driving, listening to music and socialising with mates'
Extras: Represented England Schools v India U19 2006. Played for North Regional
U19 in regional tournament at Loughborough 2006. Left Derbyshire at the end of the
2006 season and has joined Northamptonshire for 2007
Opinions on cricket: 'Game is becoming increasingly more well known and followed
and I believe this is thanks to the excitement of the Twenty20 and Pro40 introductions.
Keep it coming!'

2006 Season

	M	Inn	NO	Runs	HS	Avg	100	50	Ct	St	Balls	Runs	Wkts	Avg	BB	5I	10M
Test																	
FC																	
ODI																	
List A	1	1	0	2	2	2.00	-	-	-	-	18	26	0			-	-
20/20 Int																	
20/20																	

Career Performances

	M	Inn	NO	Runs	HS	Avg	100	50	Ct	St	Balls	Runs	Wkts	Avg	BB	5I	10M
Test																	
FC																	
ODI																	
List A	1	1	0	2	2	2.00	-	-	-	-	18	26	0			-	-
20/20 Int																	
20/20																	

BRUCE, J. T. A.   Hampshire

Name: <u>James</u> Thomas Anthony Bruce
Role: Right-hand bat, right-arm
fast-medium bowler
Born: 17 December 1979, Hammersmith,
London
Height: 6ft 1in **Weight:** 13st 10lbs
Nickname: Brucey, Bula, Bear, Eugene
County debut: 2003
County cap: 2006
Place in bowling averages: 39th av. 29.18
(2005 14th av. 23.14)
Strike rate: 51.63 (career 56.32)
Parents: Andrew and Claire
Marital status: Single
Family links with cricket: 'All three of my
brothers have played youth cricket for
Hampshire'
Education: Eton College; Durham University
Qualifications: BA (Hons) Geography, Level 1 coaching
Off-season: 'Work experience in London. Stock Exchange cricket tour to South
Africa'
Overseas tours: West of England U15 to West Indies 1995; Eton College to South

Africa 1998-99; Durham University to South Africa 2001; Yellowhammers to South Africa 2001-02

Overseas teams played for: Balmain Tigers, Sydney 2002-03; South Perth CC, Perth 2003-05

Career highlights to date: 'Making my Championship debut against Somerset. Making my NCL debut in a day/night game on Sky v Notts at Trent Bridge [2003]. Playing in Twenty20 competition'

Cricket moments to forget: 'Having my box split in two by Mike Kasprowicz'

Cricket superstitions: 'Too many to mention'

Cricketers particularly admired: Robin Smith, Shane Warne, John Crawley, Bruce Reid

Young players to look out for: Kevin Latouf, Mitchell Stokes, Edward Bruce

Other sports played: Rugby, golf

Injuries: Out for seven weeks with a right pectoral tendon tear

Favourite band: Powderfinger

Relaxations: 'I like spending time on the beach, watching TV and sleeping'

Extras: Played for DUCCE in 2001 and 2002. Played for Cumberland in the C&G 2002

Best batting: 21* Hampshire v Glamorgan, Rose Bowl 2003

Best bowling: 5-43 Hampshire v Nottinghamshire, Rose Bowl 2006

2006 Season

	M	Inn	NO	Runs	HS	Avg	100	50	Ct	St	Balls	Runs	Wkts	Avg	BB	5I	10M
Test																	
FC	13	14	8	52	17	8.66	-	-	2	-	1962	1109	38	29.18	5-43	1	-
ODI																	
List A	12	8	4	37	19 *	9.25	-	-	6	-	472	345	25	13.80	4-18	-	
20/20 Int																	
20/20																	

Career Performances

	M	Inn	NO	Runs	HS	Avg	100	50	Ct	St	Balls	Runs	Wkts	Avg	BB	5I	10M
Test																	
FC	35	39	16	159	21 *	6.91	-	-	10	-	4788	3026	85	35.60	5-43	1	-
ODI																	
List A	21	12	7	59	19 *	11.80	-	-	7	-	806	619	33	18.75	4-18	-	
20/20 Int																	
20/20	13	4	1	18	12	6.00	-	-	6	-	180	235	11	21.36	3-20	-	

BURROWS, T. G.   Hampshire

Name: Thomas (<u>Tom</u>) George Burrows
Role: Right-hand bat, wicket-keeper
Born: 5 May 1985, Reading
Height: 5ft 8in **Weight:** 10st 10lbs
Nickname: TB
County debut: 2005 (*see Extras*)
Parents: Tony and Victoria
Marital status: Single
Family links with cricket: 'My father was
briefly on Gloucestershire groundstaff and
played club cricket'
Education: Reading School; Solent
University
Qualifications: 12 GCSEs, 4 AS-levels,
3 A-levels, Level 1 cricket coach
Career outside cricket: 'Studying for law
degree'
Off-season: 'Studying'
Overseas tours: MCC to Namibia and Uganda 2004-05
Overseas teams played for: Melville CC, Perth 2003-04
Career highlights to date: 'First-class debut v Kent, scoring 42 and putting on 131
with Shane Warne when we were 130-7'
Cricket moments to forget: 'Any dropped catch'
Cricket superstitions: 'Left pad on first'
Cricketers particularly admired: Adi Aymes, Jack Russell, Steve Waugh,
John Crawley
Young players to look out for: David Balcombe, Mitchell Stokes, Richard Morris
Other sports played: Rugby, football
Other sports followed: Football (Chelsea), rugby (London Irish)
Favourite band: Gavin DeGraw
Relaxations: 'Watching films'
Extras: Appeared as substitute wicket-keeper for Hampshire v Yorkshire at The Rose
Bowl 2002 but did not make full debut until 2005. Played for Berkshire in the C&G
2003
Best batting: 42 Hampshire v Kent, Canterbury 2005

2006 Season

	M	Inn	NO	Runs	HS	Avg	100	50	Ct	St	Balls	Runs	Wkts	Avg	BB	5I	10M
Test																	
FC	2	3	0	49	20	16.33	-	-	5	-	0	0	0		-	-	-
ODI																	
List A	2	2	1	17	16	17.00	-	-	2	2	0	0	0		-	-	
20/20 Int																	
20/20																	

Career Performances

	M	Inn	NO	Runs	HS	Avg	100	50	Ct	St	Balls	Runs	Wkts	Avg	BB	5I	10M
Test																	
FC	3	5	0	104	42	20.80	-	-	10	-	0	0	0		-	-	-
ODI																	
List A	3	3	1	18	16	9.00	-	-	3	2	0	0	0		-	-	
20/20 Int																	
20/20	1	0	0	0	0		-	-	-	-	0	0	0		-	-	

BURTON, D. A. Gloucestershire

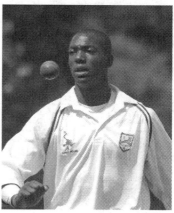

Name: <u>David</u> Alexander Burton
Role: Right-hand bat, right-arm fast bowler
Born: 23 August 1985, London
Height: 5ft 11in **Weight:** 11st 11lbs
Nickname: Burts, Burtna, DB
County debut: 2006
County cap: 2006
Parents: Denise Careless and
Cuthbert Burton
Marital status: Single
Education: Sacred Heart RC Secondary
School, Camberwell; Lambeth College,
Vauxhall, both London
Qualifications: 2 GCSEs, First Diploma in
Electronic Engineering, Diploma in
Electronics and PC Systems, ECB Levels 1
and 2 coaching
Off-season: 'Cricket coaching and training'
Career highlights to date: '52* v Glamorgan [2006]'
Cricketers particularly admired: Darren Gough, Curtly Ambrose, Mark Butcher,
Allan Donald
Young players to look out for: Chris Thompson

Other sports played: Mountain biking, basketball
Other sports followed: Basketball (Houston Rockets)
Favourite band: Jagged Edge, Lil Jon, David Banner, Monica
Relaxations: 'Reading, chilling with my girlfriend, cycling, running'
Extras: Played for South London Schools Hobbs Trophy runners-up side 2000.
Dulwich CC Player of the Year 2006. Scored 52* on first-class debut at Cardiff 2006,
in the process sharing with Mark Hardinges (101) in a record ninth-wicket partnership
for Gloucestershire in matches v Glamorgan (128)
Opinions on cricket: 'Keep it simple and clear at all times, with the highest intensity
of consistency.'
Best batting: 52* Gloucestershire v Glamorgan, Cardiff 2006

2006 Season

	M	Inn	NO	Runs	HS	Avg	100	50	Ct	St	Balls	Runs	Wkts	Avg	BB	5I	10M
Test																	
FC	1	2	1	53	52 *	53.00	-	1	-	-	120	129	0		-	-	-
ODI																	
List A																	
20/20 Int																	
20/20																	

Career Performances

	M	Inn	NO	Runs	HS	Avg	100	50	Ct	St	Balls	Runs	Wkts	Avg	BB	5I	10M
Test																	
FC	1	2	1	53	52 *	53.00	-	1	-	-	120	129	0		-	-	-
ODI																	
List A																	
20/20 Int																	
20/20																	

BUTCHER, M. A.   Surrey

Name: <u>Mark</u> Alan Butcher
Role: Left-hand bat, right-arm medium bowler, county captain
Born: 23 August 1972, Croydon
Height: 5ft 11in   **Weight:** 13st
Nickname: Butch, Baz
County debut: 1991 (one-day), 1992 (first-class)
County cap: 1996
Benefit: 2005
Test debut: 1997
1000 runs in a season: 8
1st-Class 200s: 2

Place in batting averages: 25th av. 58.60 (2005 101st av. 35.37)
Strike rate: (career 61.31)
Parents: Alan and Elaine
Children: Alita, 1999
Family links with cricket: Father Alan played for Glamorgan, Surrey and England and is now coach with Surrey; brother Gary played for Glamorgan and Surrey; uncle Ian played for Gloucestershire and Leicestershire; uncle Martin played for Surrey
Education: Trinity School; Archbishop Tenison's, Croydon
Qualifications: 5 O-levels, senior coaching award
Career outside cricket: Singer, guitar player
Overseas tours: England YC to New Zealand 1990-91; Surrey to Dubai 1990, 1993, to Perth 1995; England A to Australia 1996-97; England to West Indies 1997-98, to Australia 1998-99, to South Africa 1999-2000, to India and New Zealand 2001-02, to Australia 2002-03, to Bangladesh and Sri Lanka 2003-04, to West Indies 2003-04, to South Africa 2004-05
Overseas teams played for: South Melbourne, Australia 1993-94; North Perth 1994-95
Cricketers particularly admired: Ian Botham, David Gower, Viv Richards, Larry Gomes, Graham Thorpe, Alec Stewart, Michael Holding
Other sports followed: Football (Crystal Palace)
Relaxations: Music, playing the guitar, novels, wine
Extras: Played his first game for Surrey in 1991 against his father's Glamorgan in the Refuge Assurance League at The Oval, the first-ever match of any sort between first-class counties in which a father and son have been in opposition. Captained England in the third Test v New Zealand at Old Trafford 1999, deputising for the injured Nasser Hussain. Scored match-winning 173* in the fourth Test v Australia at Headingley 2001, winning Man of the Match award, and was England's Man of the Series with 456 runs (more than any other batsman on either side) at an average of 50.66. His other Test awards include England's Man of the Series v Sri Lanka 2002 and v Zimbabwe 2003. Slazenger Sheer Instinct Award 2001 for the cricketer who has impressed the most in the recent season. Scored century in each innings (151/108) v Glamorgan at The Oval 2006, emulating achievement of his father, Alan (117*/114), in the corresponding fixture in 1984. Captain of Surrey since 2005
Best batting: 259 Surrey v Leicestershire, Leicester 1999
Best bowling: 5-86 Surrey v Lancashire, Old Trafford 2000
Stop press: Reached the final of BBC celebrity singing show *Just the Two of Us* in January 2007 with Sarah Brightman

2006 Season

	M	Inn	NO	Runs	HS	Avg	100	50	Ct	St	Balls	Runs	Wkts	Avg	BB	5I	10M
Test																	
FC	17	29	4	1465	151	58.60	5	8	17	-	30	8	1	8.00	1-8	-	-
ODI																	
List A	14	14	3	540	88 *	49.09	-	5	1	-	0	0	0			-	-
20/20 Int																	
20/20	2	2	0	6	5	3.00	-	-	1	-	0	0	0			-	-

Career Performances

	M	Inn	NO	Runs	HS	Avg	100	50	Ct	St	Balls	Runs	Wkts	Avg	BB	5I	10M
Test	71	131	7	4288	173 *	34.58	8	23	61	-	901	541	15	36.06	4-42	-	-
FC	255	439	34	16346	259	40.36	34	90	235	-	7664	4209	125	33.67	5-86	1	-
ODI																	
List A	174	156	29	3732	104	29.38	1	22	55	-	2527	2210	49	45.10	3-23	-	
20/20 Int																	
20/20	5	5	0	154	60	30.80	-	2	1	-	0	0	0			-	-

CADDICK, A. R.   Somerset

Name: <u>Andrew</u> Richard Caddick
Role: Right-hand bat, right-arm
fast-medium bowler
Born: 21 November 1968, Christchurch,
New Zealand
Height: 6ft 5in **Weight:** 14st 13lbs
Nickname: Des, Shack
County debut: 1990 (one-day),
1991 (first-class)
County cap: 1992
Benefit: 1999
Test debut: 1993
ODI debut: 1993
50 wickets in a season: 10
100 wickets in a season: 1
Place in batting averages: 230th av. 17.05
(2005 221st av. 19.69)
Place in bowling averages: 86th av. 35.85
(2005 46th av. 27.79)
Strike rate: 58.07 (career 50.40)
Parents: Christopher and Audrey
Wife and date of marriage: Sarah, 27 January 1995

Children: Ashton Faye, 24 August 1998; Fraser Michael, 12 October 2001
Education: Papanui High School, Christchurch, New Zealand
Qualifications: Qualified plasterer and tiler. Qualified helicopter pilot
Overseas tours: New Zealand YC to Australia (U19 World Cup) 1987-88, to England 1988; England A to Australia 1992-93; England to West Indies 1993-94, to Zimbabwe and New Zealand 1996-97, to West Indies 1997-98, to South Africa and Zimbabwe 1999-2000, to Kenya (ICC Knockout Trophy) 2000-01, to Pakistan and Sri Lanka 2000-01, to India (one-day series) and New Zealand 2001-02, to Sri Lanka (ICC Champions Trophy) 2002-03, to Australia 2002-03, to Africa (World Cup) 2002-03
Career highlights to date: 'Bowling West Indies out at Lord's [2000] and thus getting my name up on the board'
Cricketers particularly admired: Dennis Lillee, Richard Hadlee, Robin Smith, Jimmy Cook
Other sports followed: 'Mostly all'
Relaxations: Golf
Extras: Whyte and Mackay Bowler of the Year 1997. Took 105 first-class wickets in 1998 season. Leading wicket-taker in the single-division four-day era of the County Championship with 422 wickets (av. 22.48) 1993-99. Cornhill England Player of the Year 1999-2000. Took 5-16 from 13 overs as West Indies were bowled out for 54 in their second innings in the second Test at Lord's 2000. Took 5-14 in fourth Test v West Indies at Headingley 2000, including four wickets (Jacobs, McLean, Ambrose, King) in an over. One of *Wisden*'s Five Cricketers of the Year 2001. Took 200th Test wicket (Craig McMillan) in the third Test v New Zealand at Auckland 2001-02. His international awards include England's Man of the Series v New Zealand 1999 and joint Man of the Match (with Gary Kirsten) in the third Test v South Africa at Durban 1999-2000. Retired from ODI cricket in March 2003. Took 1000th first-class wicket (Joe Sayers) v Yorkshire at Taunton 2005
Best batting: 92 Somerset v Worcestershire, Worcester 1995
Best bowling: 9-32 Somerset v Lancashire, Taunton 1993

13. Who was the first player to make 100 ODI appearances?

2006 Season

	M	Inn	NO	Runs	HS	Avg	100	50	Ct	St	Balls	Runs	Wkts	Avg	BB	5I	10M
Test																	
FC	16	25	5	341	68	17.05	-	1	5	-	3659	2259	63	35.85	5-40	4	-
ODI																	
List A	12	6	3	43	11	14.33	-	-	5	-	480	448	18	24.88	3-36	-	
20/20 Int																	
20/20	2	0	0	0	0		-	-	-	-	42	88	3	29.33	2-37	-	

Career Performances

	M	Inn	NO	Runs	HS	Avg	100	50	Ct	St	Balls	Runs	Wkts	Avg	BB	5I	10M
Test	62	95	12	861	49 *	10.37	-	-	21	-	13558	6999	234	29.91	7-46	13	1
FC	244	328	63	3957	92	14.93	-	8	83	-	53931	28082	1070	26.24	9-32	73	16
ODI	54	38	18	249	36	12.45	-	-	9	-	2937	1965	69	28.47	4-19	-	
List A	252	130	55	801	39	10.68	-	-	41	-	12394	8674	329	26.36	6-30	4	
20/20 Int																	
20/20	12	1	0	0	0	0.00	-	-	1	-	216	349	10	34.90	2-12	-	

CAIRNS, C. L. Nottinghamshire

Name: Christopher (<u>Chris</u>) Lance Cairns
Role: Right-hand bat, right-arm
fast-medium bowler
Born: 13 June 1970, Picton, New Zealand
Height: 6ft 2in **Weight:** 14st
County debut: 1988
County cap: 1993
Test debut: 1989-90
ODI debut: 1990-91
Twenty20 Int debut: 2004-05
1000 runs in a season: 1
50 wickets in a season: 3
Strike rate: (career 52.93)
Parents: Lance and Sue
Family links with cricket: Father played for
New Zealand; uncle played first-class cricket
in New Zealand
Education: Christchurch Boys' High School,
New Zealand
Qualifications: Fifth and Sixth form certificates
Overseas tours: New Zealand YC to Australia (U19 World Cup) 1987-88; New
Zealand Young Internationals to Zimbabwe 1988-89; New Zealand to Australia

1989-90, 1993-94, to India 1995-96, to India and Pakistan (World Cup) 1995-96, to West Indies 1995-96, to Pakistan 1996-97, to Zimbabwe 1997-98, to Australia 1997-98, to Sri Lanka 1998, to UK, Ireland and Netherlands (World Cup) 1999, to England 1999, to India 1999-2000, to Zimbabwe and South Africa 2000-01, to Kenya (ICC Knockout Trophy) 2000-01, to Australia 2001-02, to Africa (World Cup) 2002-03, to Pakistan (one-day series) 2003-04, to England 2004, to England (ICC Champions Trophy) 2004, to Bangladesh 2004-05 (one-day series), to Australia 2004-05 (one-day series), plus other one-day tournaments in Sharjah, India, Singapore, Sri Lanka and Zimbabwe; ICC World XI to Australia (Tsunami Relief) 2004-05

Overseas teams played for: Northern Districts 1988-89; Canterbury 1990-91 – 2005-06

Cricketers particularly admired: Mick Newell, Richard Hadlee, Dennis Lillee

Extras: Won the Walter Lawrence Trophy for the fastest first-class hundred of the season 1995 (65 balls for Notts v Cambridge University at Fenner's). Cricket Society's Wetherell Award for leading all-rounder in English first-class cricket 1995. One of *New Zealand Cricket Almanack*'s two Players of the Year 1998, 1999, 2000. One of *Indian Cricket*'s five Cricketers of the Year 2000. One of *Wisden*'s Five Cricketers of the Year 2000. Had match figures of 10-100 v West Indies at Hamilton 1999-2000 to make himself and his father Lance the first father and son to have taken ten wickets in a Test match; also won Man of the Match award. His other Test and ODI awards include New Zealand's Man of the Series v England 1999 and Man of the Match for his 102* in the ICC Knockout Trophy final v India in Kenya 2000-01. Took 200th ODI wicket (Tillakaratne Dilshan) v Sri Lanka at Christchurch 2005-06. An overseas player with Notts 1988-89, 1992-93, 1995-96, 2003 (one-day captain 2003) and as a locum for Stephen Fleming for the early part of 2006. Retired from Test cricket in 2004 after the third Test v England at Trent Bridge; announced his retirement from all international cricket in early 2006

Best batting: 158 New Zealand v South Africa, Auckland 2003-04
Best bowling: 8-47 Nottinghamshire v Sussex, Arundel 1995

2006 Season

	M	Inn	NO	Runs	HS	Avg	100	50	Ct	St	Balls	Runs	Wkts	Avg	BB	5I	10M
Test																	
FC																	
ODI																	
List A	2	1	0	27	27	27.00	-	-	-	-	102	70	6	11.66	4-30	-	
20/20 Int																	
20/20																	

Career Performances

	M	Inn	NO	Runs	HS	Avg	100	50	Ct	St	Balls	Runs	Wkts	Avg	BB	5I	10M
Test	62	104	5	3320	158	33.53	5	22	14	-	11698	6410	218	29.40	7-27	13	1
FC	217	341	38	10702	158	35.32	13	71	78	-	34252	18322	647	28.31	8-47	30	6
ODI	215	193	25	4950	115	29.46	4	26	66	-	8168	6594	201	32.80	5-42	1	
List A	425	377	59	10364	143	32.59	9	55	118	-	16578	12711	455	27.93	6-12	6	
20/20 Int	2	2	0	3	2	1.50	-	-	1	-	48	52	1	52.00	1-28	-	
20/20	5	5	1	23	15	5.75	-	-	4	-	108	126	5	25.20	2-24	-	

CARBERRY, M. A.   Hampshire

Name: <u>Michael</u> Alexander Carberry
Role: Left-hand bat, right-arm medium bowler
Born: 29 September 1980, Croydon
Height: 5ft 11in   **Weight:** 14st 7lbs
Nickname: Carbs
County debut: 2001 (Surrey), 2003 (Kent), 2006 (Hampshire)
County cap: 2006 (Hampshire)
Place in batting averages: 93rd av. 36.07
Strike rate: (career 86.40)
Parents: Maria and Neville
Marital status: Single
Family links with cricket: 'My dad played club cricket'
Education: St John Rigby College
Qualifications: 10 GCSEs
Overseas tours: Surrey U17 to South Africa 1997; England U19 to New Zealand 1998-99, to Malaysia and (U19 World Cup) Sri Lanka 1999-2000; England A to Bangladesh 2006-07
Overseas teams played for: Portland CC, Melbourne; University CC, Perth 2005
Career highlights to date: 'Every day is a highlight'

Cricket moments to forget: 'None'
Cricketers particularly admired: Ricky Ponting, Brian Lara
Relaxations: 'Sleeping'
Extras: Scored century (126*) for ECB U18 v Pakistan U19 at Abergavenny 1998. Represented England U19 1999, 2000. NBC Denis Compton Award for the most promising young Surrey player 1999, 2000. Scored century (137) on Kent debut v Cambridge UCCE at Fenner's 2003. Scored 112 as Kent scored a then county record fourth-innings 429-5 to beat Worcestershire at Canterbury 2004
Best batting: 153* Surrey v CUCCE, Fenner's 2002
Best bowling: 2-85 Hampshire v Durham, Riverside 2006

2006 Season

	M	Inn	NO	Runs	HS	Avg	100	50	Ct	St	Balls	Runs	Wkts	Avg	BB	5I	10M
Test																	
FC	15	28	2	938	104	36.07	2	5	8	-	132	114	2	57.00	2-85	-	-
ODI																	
List A	16	15	0	541	88	36.06	-	6	4	-	0	0	0			-	-
20/20 Int																	
20/20	8	8	0	222	90	27.75	-	2	4	-	0	0	0			-	-

Career Performances

	M	Inn	NO	Runs	HS	Avg	100	50	Ct	St	Balls	Runs	Wkts	Avg	BB	5I	10M
Test																	
FC	50	87	8	2982	153 *	37.74	6	16	24	-	432	365	5	73.00	2-85	-	-
ODI																	
List A	64	59	3	1368	88	24.42	-	12	22	-	42	41	1	41.00	1-21	-	
20/20 Int																	
20/20	25	23	5	508	90	28.22	-	4	10	-	0	0	0			-	-

---

14. Who scored 115* on ODI debut for Zimbabwe v Sri Lanka
at New Plymouth 1991-92?

CARTER, N. M.   Warwickshire

Name: <u>Neil</u> Miller Carter
Role: Left-hand bat, left-arm medium-fast bowler
Born: 29 January 1975, Cape Town, South Africa
Height: 6ft 2in **Weight:** 15st
Nickname: Carts
County debut: 2001
County cap: 2005
Place in batting averages: 237th av. 15.62 (2005 226th av. 19.45)
Place in bowling averages: 109th av. 40.94 (2005 82nd av. 33.60)
Strike rate: 69.23 (career 65.31)
Parents: John and Heather
Marital status: Single
Education: Hottentots Holland High School; Cape Technikon; ITI
Qualifications: Diploma in Financial Information Systems, Certified Novell Engineer, Level 2 coaching
Career outside cricket: Computer engineering/networking; stocks and shares
Off-season: 'Buying and selling shares'
Overseas tours: SA Country Schools U15 to England 1992; Warwickshire to Cape Town 2001, 2002
Overseas teams played for: Boland 1998-99 – 2003-04
Career highlights to date: 'My first-class hundred and one-day hundred. Last B&H winners 2002. County Championship 2004'
Cricket moments to forget: 'Losing C&G final 2005'
Cricketers particularly admired: Allan Donald, Shaun Pollock, Jacques Kallis
Young players to look out for: Moeen Ali
Other sports played: Hockey (Pinelands Indoor 1st team), golf, squash
Other sports followed: Rugby union (Stormers in Super 14; Springboks), golf (USPGA tour), baseball (LA Angels)
Favourite band: Madison Avenue
Relaxations: Gricing (steam train photography)
Extras: Won Man of the Match award in first one-day match for Warwickshire (4-21 and a 43-ball 40), in C&G v Essex at Edgbaston 2001. Warwickshire Player of the Year 2005 (1088 runs and 94 wickets in all cricket and, including Twenty20, equalled Allan Donald's club season record of 53 one-day wickets). Is England-qualified
Opinions on cricket: 'Two up/two down is better. Play-off [in Pro40] is not needed,

seeing that you only play eight games. Still a lot of cricket played. Wickets need to be relaid to get the bounce/pace back in the game.'

Best batting: 103 Warwickshire v Sussex, Hove 2002
Best bowling: 6-63 Boland v Griqualand West, Kimberley 2000-01

2006 Season

	M	Inn	NO	Runs	HS	Avg	100	50	Ct	St	Balls	Runs	Wkts	Avg	BB	5I	10M
Test																	
FC	13	20	4	250	36	15.62	-	-	1	-	2354	1392	34	40.94	6-63	1	-
ODI																	
List A	17	13	2	247	135	22.45	1	-	-	-	636	563	22	25.59	4-37	-	
20/20 Int																	
20/20	8	7	1	84	29	14.00	-	-	1	-	171	204	6	34.00	3-28	-	

Career Performances

	M	Inn	NO	Runs	HS	Avg	100	50	Ct	St	Balls	Runs	Wkts	Avg	BB	5I	10M
Test																	
FC	71	96	19	1451	103	18.84	1	3	20	-	11691	6864	179	38.34	6-63	5	-
ODI																	
List A	120	99	12	1633	135	18.77	1	4	12	-	5324	4228	166	25.46	5-31	2	
20/20 Int																	
20/20	30	29	1	475	47	16.96	-	-	6	-	608	714	32	22.31	5-19	1	

CHAMBERS, D. J. Kent

Name: <u>Dominic</u> James Chambers
Role: Right-hand opening bat, right-arm medium-fast bowler
Born: 6 January 1984, Canterbury
Height: 6ft **Weight:** 13st 5lbs
Nickname: Poppa, Chambo, Dwaine
County debut: 2006
Parents: David and Jane
Marital status: Single
Family links with cricket: 'Uncle (Arthur Underwood) used to play for Notts. Grandfather a life member at Kent'
Education: St Edmund's, Canterbury; Canterbury College; 'going to Christ Church, Canterbury'
Qualifications: 9 GCSEs, 2 A-levels, ECB Level 2 coach
Career outside cricket: 'Coach, student'

Off-season: 'Coaching for Sporting Image and Cowdrey class coaching'
Overseas tours: South of England to West Indies 1998
Overseas teams played for: Claremont-Nedlands, Perth 2005-06
Career highlights to date: 'Making first-class debut against Cambridge UCCE, May 2006'
Cricket moments to forget: 'Being dropped after carrying my bat scoring 92* for Kent 2nd XI. Not being selected for Public Schools XI at Bunbury Festival'
Cricket superstitions: 'Left pad on first'
Cricketers particularly admired: Shane Warne, Sachin Tendulkar, Kevin Pietersen
Young players to look out for: Neil Dexter, Joe Denly, Sam Northeast
Other sports played: Football, hockey, badminton
Other sports followed: Football (Arsenal)
Favourite band: Coldplay
Relaxations: 'Reading, socialising, cinema, dancing'
Extras: Plays for St Lawrence and Highland Court CC. Scored record 2701 runs (av. 67.00) for St Edmund's School 1st XI 1999-2002. Robin Jackman Trophy. East Kent League Player of the Year 2006. Kent Academy scholar
Opinions on cricket: 'More chances should be given to home-grown players.'
Best batting: 12 Kent v CUCCE, Fenner's 2006

2006 Season

	M	Inn	NO	Runs	HS	Avg	100	50	Ct	St	Balls	Runs	Wkts	Avg	BB	5I	10M
Test																	
FC	1	1	0	12	12	12.00	-	-	1	-	0	0	0		-	-	-
ODI																	
List A																	
20/20 Int																	
20/20																	

Career Performances

	M	Inn	NO	Runs	HS	Avg	100	50	Ct	St	Balls	Runs	Wkts	Avg	BB	5I	10M
Test																	
FC	1	1	0	12	12	12.00	-	-	1	-	0	0	0		-	-	-
ODI																	
List A																	
20/20 Int																	
20/20																	

CHAMBERS, M. A.   Essex

Name: Maurice Anthony Chambers
Role: Right-hand bat, right-arm fast bowler
Born: 14 September 1987, Port Antonio, Portland, Jamaica
Height: 6ft 3in   **Weight:** 13st
Nickname: Moza
County debut: 2005
Strike rate: (career 96.00)
Parents: Melinda Fenton
Marital status: Single
Education: Homerton College of Technology; Sir George Monoux College
Career outside cricket: 'Playing basketball and studying'
Off-season: 'Going to the gym and also going to India with Essex Academy'
Overseas tours: Essex Academy to India 2006-07; England U19 to Malaysia 2006-07
Career highlights to date: 'Playing for Essex 2nd XI v Middlesex [2006] and bowling 16 overs, 7 maidens, and taking 3 wickets for 25 runs'
Cricket moments to forget: 'Playing for England U19 v India, we were eight wickets down with two balls to go and I was the last batsman. I told myself I was not going to pad up, and then my mate was out and I went in to bat with no Abdo Guard or gloves'
Cricketers particularly admired: Curtly Ambrose, Courtney Walsh, Stephen Harmison, Brian Lara, Andrew Strauss, Andrew Flintoff
Young players to look out for: Ben Wright, Moeen Ali, Mervyn Westfield, Varun Chopra, Jahid Ahmed, Andy Miller
Other sports played: Basketball
Other sports followed: Football (Manchester United)
Injuries: A spur in the back of the ankle pre-season 2006
Favourite band: G-Unit
Relaxations: 'Listening to music; playing PS2'
Extras: London Schools Cricket Association Best Bowling Award 2003. Played for MCC Young Cricketers 2004. Wanstead CC Bowler of the Year
Best batting: 2* Essex v Derbyshire, Chelmsford 2005
Best bowling: 1-73 Essex v Derbyshire, Chelmsford 2005

2006 Season (did not make any first-class or one-day appearances)

Career Performances

	M	Inn	NO	Runs	HS	Avg	100	50	Ct	St	Balls	Runs	Wkts	Avg	BB	5I	10M
Test																	
FC	1	1	1	2	2*	-	-	-	-	-	96	84	1	84.00	1-73	-	-
ODI																	
List A																	
20/20 Int																	
20/20																	

CHAPPLE, G.   Lancashire

Name: Glen Chapple
Role: Right-hand bat, right-arm
medium-fast bowler; all-rounder
Born: 23 January 1974, Skipton, Yorkshire
Height: 6ft 1in **Weight:** 13st
Nickname: Chappy
County debut: 1992
County cap: 1994
Benefit: 2004
ODI debut: 2006
50 wickets in a season: 4
Place in batting averages: 126th av. 32.22
(2005 202nd av. 22.21)
Place in bowling averages: 28th av. 27.41
(2005 7th av. 21.48)
Strike rate: 62.24 (career 56.83)
Parents: Mike and Eileen
Wife and date of marriage: Kerry,
31 January 2004
Children: Annie, 6 August 2003; Joe, 16 January 2006
Family links with cricket: Father played in Lancashire League for Nelson and was a
professional for Darwen and Earby
Education: West Craven High School; Nelson and Colne College
Qualifications: 8 GCSEs, 2 A-levels
Off-season: 'Grafting'
Overseas tours: England U18 to Canada (International Youth Tournament) 1991;
England YC to New Zealand 1990-91; England U19 to Pakistan 1991-92, to India
1992-93; England A to India 1994-95, to Australia 1996-97; England VI to Hong Kong
2002, 2003, 2004, 2006

Cricket superstitions: 'None'
Cricketers particularly admired: Dennis Lillee, Robin Smith
Other sports followed: Football (Liverpool), golf
Favourite band: U2, Oasis, Stone Roses
Relaxations: 'Golf'
Extras: Set record for fastest century in first-class cricket (21 minutes; against declaration bowling) v Glamorgan at Old Trafford 1993. Man of the Match in the 1996 NatWest final against Essex at Lord's for his 6-18. Lancashire Player of the Year 2002
Opinions on cricket: 'How long do people have to keep banging on about playing too much cricket? It's not difficult to see and it's annoying that nothing will change until my boots are in the bin! Cheers!'
Best batting: 155 Lancashire v Somerset, Old Trafford 2001
Best bowling: 6-30 Lancashire v Somerset, Blackpool 2002

2006 Season

	M	Inn	NO	Runs	HS	Avg	100	50	Ct	St	Balls	Runs	Wkts	Avg	BB	5I	10M
Test																	
FC	14	19	1	580	82	32.22	-	3	6	-	2552	1124	41	27.41	6-35	1	-
ODI																	
List A	13	8	1	89	28 *	12.71	-	-	-	-	546	377	17	22.17	4-23	-	
20/20 Int																	
20/20																	

Career Performances

	M	Inn	NO	Runs	HS	Avg	100	50	Ct	St	Balls	Runs	Wkts	Avg	BB	5I	10M
Test																	
FC	204	281	54	5685	155	25.04	6	25	68	-	34330	17325	604	28.68	6-30	24	1
ODI	1	1	0	14	14	14.00	-	-	-	-	24	14	0		-	-	
List A	244	138	35	1736	81 *	16.85	-	8	54	-	10509	7902	273	28.94	6-18	4	
20/20 Int																	
20/20	21	14	3	135	55 *	12.27	-	1	8	-	354	475	21	22.61	2-13	-	

15. Don Bradman famously recorded a duck in his final Test innings. Who dismissed him?

CHERRY, D. D.   Glamorgan

Name: <u>Daniel</u> David Cherry
Role: Left-hand bat, right-arm
spin bowler
Born: 7 February 1980, Newport, Gwent
Height: 5ft 9in **Weight:** 12st 6lbs
Nickname: Spikes, McNab, Kiwi,
Banners, Rhino
County debut: 1998
1st-Class 200s: 1
Place in batting averages: 134th av. 31.29
(2005 135th av. 31.03)
Parents: David and Elizabeth
Marital status: Single
Family links with cricket: Father played
club cricket for Cresselly CC and now
coaches
Education: Tonbridge School, Kent;
University of Wales, Swansea

Qualifications: 10 GCSEs, 3 A-levels, BA History, Level 2 coach
Career outside cricket: 'Criminal analysis or criminology'
Off-season: 'Going back to university to do master's in criminology'
Overseas tours: Tonbridge School to Australia 1996-97; Glamorgan to Cape
Town 2002
Overseas teams played for: Doutta Stars, Melbourne 2002-03
Career highlights to date: 'Maiden first-class hundred (226 v Middlesex 2005)'
Cricket moments to forget: 'Getting hit on the hand by a Shoaib Akhtar beamer!'
Cricket superstitions: 'None'
Cricketers particularly admired: Michael Atherton, Graham Thorpe,
Steve James
Young players to look out for: James Harris, Gareth Rees, Willy Bragg
Other sports played: Rugby, rackets (Public Schools doubles champion)
Other sports followed: Rugby (Neath-Swansea Ospreys), football (Everton)
Favourite band: Super Furry Animals
Relaxations: Reading true crime books, listening to music; 'socialising with the
high-quality clientele that frequents Pembrokeshire's premier nightspot – "The Sands
Discotheque Deluxe"'
Extras: Played for ECB U19 XI v Pakistan U19 1998. Awarded Glamorgan 2nd XI
cap 2002. Glamorgan Young Player of the Year 2005. First Glamorgan player to score
a double hundred as maiden first-class century (226 v Middlesex at Southgate 2005)
Opinions on cricket: 'Work hard, back your ability and most importantly – enjoy it!'
Best batting: 226 Glamorgan v Middlesex, Southgate 2005

2006 Season

	M	Inn	NO	Runs	HS	Avg	100	50	Ct	St	Balls	Runs	Wkts	Avg	BB	5I	10M
Test																	
FC	9	17	0	532	121	31.29	1	3	4	-	4	4	0		-	-	-
ODI																	
List A	10	9	0	80	21	8.88	-	-	2	-	60	82	1	82.00	1-26	-	
20/20 Int																	
20/20																	

Career Performances

	M	Inn	NO	Runs	HS	Avg	100	50	Ct	St	Balls	Runs	Wkts	Avg	BB	5I	10M
Test																	
FC	33	59	1	1626	226	28.03	3	4	9	-	40	13	0		-	-	-
ODI																	
List A	22	20	0	312	42	15.60	-	-	5	-	66	91	1	91.00	1-26	-	
20/20 Int																	
20/20	3	3	1	55	43 *	27.50	-	-	1	-	6	6	2	3.00	2-6	-	

CHILTON, M. J.   Lancashire

Name: <u>Mark</u> James Chilton
Role: Right-hand bat, right-arm medium bowler, county captain
Born: 2 October 1976, Sheffield
Height: 6ft 2in   **Weight:** 12st 10lbs
Nickname: Dip, Chill
County debut: 1997
County cap: 2002
1000 runs in a season: 1
Place in batting averages: 128th av. 31.91 (2005 99th av. 35.80)
Strike rate: (career 127.50)
Parents: Jim and Sue
Marital status: Single
Family links with cricket: Father played local cricket
Education: Manchester Grammar School; Durham University
Qualifications: 10 GCSEs, 3 A-levels, BA (Hons) Business Economics, senior coaching award
Overseas tours: Manchester Grammar School to Barbados 1993-94, to South Africa 1995-96; Durham University to Zimbabwe 1997-98

Overseas teams played for: East Torrens, Adelaide 2000-01; North Sydney CC, Sydney 2002-03

Career highlights to date: 'Lord's final 2006'

Cricket moments to forget: 'Lord's final 2006!'

Cricket superstitions: 'None'

Cricketers particularly admired: Michael Atherton, David Gower

Young players to look out for: Karl Brown, Steven Croft

Other sports played: Football, golf

Other sports followed: 'Interest in most sports', football (Manchester United)

Favourite band: Coldplay, Embrace

Relaxations: 'Guitar and music'

Extras: Represented England U14, U15, U17. England U15 Batsman of the Year award 1992. Played for North of England v New Zealand U19 in 1996. Played for British Universities in 1997 Benson and Hedges Cup, winning the Gold Award against Sussex at Fenner's (34/5-26). Captain of Lancashire since 2005

Opinions on cricket: 'Things have moved in the right direction, but I still feel improvements could be made. We should look to mirror international cricket as closely as we can (e.g. 40-over cricket? Reduce overs to 90/96 in four-day).'

Best batting: 131 Lancashire v Kent, Old Trafford 2006

Best bowling: 1-1 Lancashire v Sri Lanka A, Old Trafford 1999

2006 Season

	M	Inn	NO	Runs	HS	Avg	100	50	Ct	St	Balls	Runs	Wkts	Avg	BB	5I	10M
Test																	
FC	16	25	1	766	131	31.91	1	4	13	-	111	52	2	26.00	1-1	-	-
ODI																	
List A	16	16	3	446	76 *	34.30	-	2	3	-	0	0	0			-	-
20/20 Int																	
20/20	8	7	2	93	38	18.60	-	-	4	-	0	0	0			-	-

Career Performances

	M	Inn	NO	Runs	HS	Avg	100	50	Ct	St	Balls	Runs	Wkts	Avg	BB	5I	10M
Test																	
FC	129	209	14	6349	131	32.55	16	23	103	-	1275	636	10	63.60	1-1	-	-
ODI																	
List A	147	140	19	3679	115	30.40	4	18	46	-	1082	992	41	24.19	5-26	1	
20/20 Int																	
20/20	26	19	7	206	38	17.16	-	-	11	-	0	0	0			-	-

CHOPRA, V.   Essex

Name: Varun Chopra
Role: Right-hand bat, right-arm
off-spin bowler
Born: 21 June 1987, Ilford, Essex
Height: 6ft 1in **Weight:** 12st 2lbs
Nickname: Tidz
County debut: 2006
Place in batting averages: 82nd av. 37.93
Parents: Chander and Surinder
Marital status: Single
Education: Ilford County HS
Qualifications: 11 GCSEs, 3 A-levels
Off-season: 'Paul Terry Academy, Perth;
World Cricket Academy, Mumbai'
Overseas tours: England U19 to Bangladesh
2005-06 (c), to Sri Lanka (U19 World Cup)
2005-06; Essex to South Africa 2006
Career highlights to date: 'Century [106

plus 50* in second innings] on Championship debut v Gloucestershire [at Chelmsford
2006]. Captaining England U19. Man of Series v India U19'
Cricket moments to forget: 'U19 World Cup semi-final [2005-06]' (*England lost to
India by 234 runs, having been bowled out for 58*)
Cricket superstitions: 'Left pad on first'
Cricketers particularly admired: Sachin Tendulkar, Rahul Dravid, Andy Flower
Young players to look out for: Mervyn Westfield
Other sports played: Football
Favourite band: T.I.
Relaxations: 'All sports, poker; Pro Evo, 24'
Extras: Lord's Taverners Player of the Year U13, U15, U19. Sony Sports Personality
of the Year runner-up. Essex Academy. Captained England U19 2005 and 2006; Man
of the Match v Bangladesh U19 at Colombo in the quarter-finals of the U19 World
Cup 2005-06 and Man of the Series v India U19 2006, scoring a century in each
innings (123/164) in the second 'Test' at Taunton. Scored century (106) on
Championship debut v Gloucestershire at Chelmsford 2006, in the process becoming
the youngest player to score a Championship hundred for Essex
Opinions on cricket: 'Two overseas players are good for the standard of county
cricket.'
Best batting: 106 Essex v Gloucestershire, Chelmsford 2006

2006 Season

	M	Inn	NO	Runs	HS	Avg	100	50	Ct	St	Balls	Runs	Wkts	Avg	BB	5I	10M
Test																	
FC	9	16	1	569	106	37.93	1	4	7	-	0	0	0		-	-	-
ODI																	
List A	2	2	0	7	6	3.50	-	-	-	-	0	0	0		-	-	
20/20 Int																	
20/20	1	1	1	1	1 *		-	-	-	-	0	0	0		-	-	

Career Performances

	M	Inn	NO	Runs	HS	Avg	100	50	Ct	St	Balls	Runs	Wkts	Avg	BB	5I	10M
Test																	
FC	9	16	1	569	106	37.93	1	4	7	-	0	0	0		-	-	-
ODI																	
List A	2	2	0	7	6	3.50	-	-	-	-	0	0	0		-	-	
20/20 Int																	
20/20	1	1	1	1	1 *		-	-	-	-	0	0	0		-	-	

CLARK, S. G.   Leicestershire

Name: Steven (Steve) George Clark
Role: Right-hand bat, right-arm medium-fast bowler; all-rounder
Born: 17 November 1982, Doncaster
Height: 6ft 1in **Weight:** 13st 1lb
Nickname: Clarky, Mushroom, Fish Head
County debut: 2006
Strike rate: (career 44.46)
Parents: Tom and Mo
Marital status: Single
Education: Worksop College; Loughborough University
Qualifications: 3 A-levels, 2:1 degree, Level 1 coaching
Off-season: 'Overseas playing in Perth'
Overseas teams played for: Bendigo United CC, Victoria 2000-01; Rygersdal CC, Cape Town 2005-06
Career highlights to date: 'Making first-class debut [for Leicestershire] v Somerset [2006]'
Cricket moments to forget: 'Averaging six with the bat in first half of season in Cape Town!'

Cricket superstitions: 'None'
Cricketers particularly admired: Kevin Pietersen, Michael Clarke
Young players to look out for: Jo Root
Other sports played: Football (Sheffield United Juniors), golf
Other sports followed: Football (Sheffield United)
Injuries: Out for two weeks with a sore lower back
Favourite band: Zero 7
Relaxations: 'Playing golf and being with friends'
Extras: Played for Yorkshire Board XI in the 2003 C&G. Played for Loughborough UCCE 2005. Played three first-class matches for Leicestershire 2006
Opinions on cricket: 'The Twenty20 format has moved the game forward in all areas, and I'm looking forward to seeing where it goes next.'
Best batting: 47* LUCCE v Nottinghamshire, Trent Bridge 2005
Best bowling: 5-29 LUCCE v Worcestershire, Kidderminster 2005

2006 Season

	M	Inn	NO	Runs	HS	Avg	100	50	Ct	St	Balls	Runs	Wkts	Avg	BB	5I	10M
Test																	
FC	3	5	1	45	23*	11.25	-	-	1	-	72	69	2	34.50	1-29	-	-
ODI																	
List A																	
20/20 Int																	
20/20																	

Career Performances

	M	Inn	NO	Runs	HS	Avg	100	50	Ct	St	Balls	Runs	Wkts	Avg	BB	5I	10M
Test																	
FC	6	8	2	102	47*	17.00	-	-	2	-	578	323	13	24.84	5-29	1	-
ODI																	
List A	2	2	0	53	52	26.50	-	1	-	-	18	31	1	31.00	1-31	-	
20/20 Int																	
20/20																	

CLARKE, R.   Surrey

Name: Rikki Clarke
Role: Right-hand bat, right-arm fast-medium
bowler, county vice-captain; all-rounder
Born: 29 September 1981, Orsett, Essex
Height: 6ft 4½in   **Weight:** 14st
Nickname: Clarkey, Crouchy
County debut: 2001 (one-day),
2002 (first-class)
County cap: 2005
Test debut: 2003-04
ODI debut: 2003
1000 runs in a season: 1
1st-Class 200s: 1
Place in batting averages: 27th av. 57.05
(2005 60th av. 43.11)
Place in bowling averages: 110th av. 41.40
(2005 104th av. 39.33)
Strike rate: 64.00 (career 59.86)
Parents: Bob and Janet
Marital status: Single
Family links with cricket: 'Dad played a bit but not any more'
Education: Broadwater; Godalming College
Qualifications: 5 GCSEs, GNVQ Leisure and Tourism
Career outside cricket: 'Poker player'
Off-season: 'England tour and Academy tour'
Overseas tours: Surrey U19 to Barbados; MCC Young Cricketers to Cape Town;
England to Sri Lanka (ICC Champions Trophy) 2002-03, to Bangladesh and Sri Lanka
2003-04, to West Indies 2003-04, to India (ICC Champions Trophy) 2006-07; ECB
National Academy to Australia and Sri Lanka 2002-03; England A to Sri Lanka 2004-
05, to West Indies 2005-06
Career highlights to date: 'Playing for England and being made vice-captain of
Surrey'
Cricket moments to forget: 'None'
Cricket superstitions: 'Left pad first'
Cricketers particularly admired: Andrew Flintoff, Darren Gough
Young players to look out for: Jade Dernbach, Stuart Broad, James Benning
Other sports played: Snooker, poker
Other sports followed: Football (Tottenham)
Injuries: Out for two weeks with a thumb injury
Favourite band: Ne-Yo
Relaxations: 'Watching films and playing poker'

Extras: Named after former Tottenham Hotspur and Argentina footballer Ricky Villa. Represented England U17. Scored maiden first-class century (107*) on first-class debut v Cambridge UCCE at Fenner's 2002. NBC Denis Compton Award for the most promising young Surrey player 2002. Cricket Writers' Club Young Player of the Year 2002. Surrey Supporters' Young Player of the Year 2002. Surrey Sponsors' Young Player of the Year 2002. Made ODI debut v Pakistan at Old Trafford in the NatWest Challenge 2003, taking the wicket of Imran Nazir with his first ball in international cricket. ECB National Academy 2004-05, 2005-06, 2006-07. Vice-captain of Surrey since 2006

Best batting: 214 Surrey v Somerset, Guildford 2006
Best bowling: 4-21 Surrey v Leicestershire, Leicester 2003

2006 Season

	M	Inn	NO	Runs	HS	Avg	100	50	Ct	St	Balls	Runs	Wkts	Avg	BB	5I	10M
Test																	
FC	13	21	3	1027	214	57.05	3	3	14	-	1408	911	22	41.40	4-45	-	-
ODI	3	3	0	45	39	15.00	-	-	-	-	65	64	1	64.00	1-37	-	
List A	14	13	1	260	40	21.66	-	-	3	-	281	314	4	78.50	1-26	-	
20/20 Int																	
20/20	10	10	2	196	79 *	24.50	-	1	3		132	143	10	14.30	3-18	-	

Career Performances

	M	Inn	NO	Runs	HS	Avg	100	50	Ct	St	Balls	Runs	Wkts	Avg	BB	5I	10M
Test	2	3	0	96	55	32.00	-	1	1	-	174	60	4	15.00	2-7	-	-
FC	66	108	12	3900	214	40.62	10	15	77	-	5687	3952	95	41.60	4-21	-	-
ODI	20	13	0	144	39	11.07	-	-	11	-	469	415	11	37.72	2-28	-	
List A	104	91	12	1944	98 *	24.60	-	9	40	-	2629	2499	65	38.44	4-49	-	
20/20 Int																	
20/20	27	26	6	461	79 *	23.05	-	2	14	-	359	435	23	18.91	3-11	-	

CLAYDON, M. E.   Durham

Name: <u>Mitchell</u> Eric Claydon
Role: Left-hand bat, right-arm fast bowler
Born: 25 November 1982, Fairfield, Australia
Height: 6ft 4in   **Weight:** 15st 9lbs
Nickname: Lips
County debut: 2005 (Yorkshire)
Strike rate: (career 134.00)
Parents: Robert (Tosh) and Sue
Marital status: Single
Children: Lachlan Robert Bickhoff-Claydon, 25 February 2004
Family links with cricket: Father played for Markington CC in the Nidderdale League
Education: Westfields Sports High School, Sydney
Qualifications: Level 1 coaching
Career outside cricket: 'Real estate agent'
Overseas teams played for: Campbelltown-Camden Ghosts 1999 –
Career highlights to date: 'First-class debut against Bangladesh at Headingley. Taking first first-class wicket'
Cricket moments to forget: 'While participating in a fielding drill consisting of high catches, I misjudged the height of the ball; the next thing I knew I was lying on the physio table with an ice pack on my forehead'
Cricket superstitions: 'Must wear my gold chain that has a photo of my sister who died in 2003'
Cricketers particularly admired: Steve Waugh
Young players to look out for: Richard Pyrah, Mark Lawson
Other sports played: Rugby league, rugby union
Other sports followed: Rugby league (West Tigers), football (Leeds United)
Favourite band: Powderfinger
Relaxations: 'Surfing whilst home in Australia; golf'
Extras: Only player in history of Campbelltown-Camden Ghosts to have taken two first grade hat-tricks. Holds a British passport and is not considered an overseas player. Released by Yorkshire at the end of the 2006 season and has joined Durham for 2007
Opinions on cricket: 'My opinion is all cricket should play two-hour sessions, 90 overs in a day as they do in Test cricket. Second XI cricket should play four days instead of three, and I believe Twenty20 cricket will take over.'
Best batting: 38 Yorkshire v Durham, Riverside 2006
Best bowling: 1-27 Yorkshire v Bangladesh A, Headingley 2005

2006 Season

	M	Inn	NO	Runs	HS	Avg	100	50	Ct	St	Balls	Runs	Wkts	Avg	BB	5I	10M
Test																	
FC	2	2	0	38	38	19.00	-	-	-	-	258	171	2	85.50	1-42	-	-
ODI																	
List A	7	2	0	15	9	7.50	-	-	-	-	342	293	8	36.62	2-41	-	
20/20 Int																	
20/20	7	2	2	14	12 *			-	-	2	-	139	188	5	37.60	2-6	-

Career Performances

	M	Inn	NO	Runs	HS	Avg	100	50	Ct	St	Balls	Runs	Wkts	Avg	BB	5I	10M
Test																	
FC	3	2	0	38	38	19.00	-	-	-	-	402	263	3	87.66	1-27	-	-
ODI																	
List A	7	2	0	15	9	7.50	-	-	-	-	342	293	8	36.62	2-41	-	
20/20 Int																	
20/20	7	2	2	14	12 *			-	-	2	-	139	188	5	37.60	2-6	-

CLINTON, R. S. Surrey

Name: <u>Richard</u> Selvey Clinton
Role: Left-hand opening bat, right-arm medium bowler
Born: 1 September 1981, Sidcup, Kent
Height: 6ft 3in **Weight:** 15st 9lbs
Nickname: Clint
County debut: 2001 (Essex), 2004 (Surrey)
Place in batting averages: (2005 133rd av. 31.19)
Strike rate: (career 96.50)
Parents: Cathy and Grahame
Marital status: Single
Family links with cricket: 'Father played for Surrey. Uncles, cousin and brother play high standard of club cricket in Kent Premier League'
Education: Colfes School, London; Loughborough University
Qualifications: 9 GCSEs, 3 A-levels
Overseas teams played for: Kensington CC, Adelaide; Valleys CC, Brisbane 2000-02
Cricket superstitions: 'Just a tried and tested routine'
Cricketers particularly admired: Graham Thorpe, Mark Butcher

Other sports played: Football, squash
Other sports followed: Motor racing (Formula One)
Favourite band: Aqua, The Sometime Maybes
Extras: Scored 36 and 58* on first-class debut v Surrey at Ilford 2001; scored 56 the following day on Norwich Union League debut v Durham at the same ground. Played for Loughborough UCCE 2004-06. Represented British Universities 2004, 2005, 2006. Joined Surrey during the 2004 season, scoring 73 on Championship debut v Worcestershire at The Oval
Best batting: 108* LUCCE v Essex, Chelmsford 2006
Best bowling: 2-30 Essex v Australians, Chelmsford 2001

2006 Season

	M	Inn	NO	Runs	HS		Avg	100	50	Ct	St	Balls	Runs	Wkts	Avg	BB	5I	10M
Test																		
FC	4	7	2	236	108	*	47.20	1	-	1	-	0	0	0		-	-	-
ODI																		
List A	2	2	0	15	10		7.50	-	-	-	-	0	0	0		-	-	
20/20 Int																		
20/20																		

Career Performances

	M	Inn	NO	Runs	HS		Avg	100	50	Ct	St	Balls	Runs	Wkts	Avg	BB	5I	10M
Test																		
FC	39	68	5	1837	108	*	29.15	4	9	23	-	193	152	2	76.00	2-30	-	-
ODI																		
List A	18	15	3	189	56		15.75	-	1	3	-	48	58	2	29.00	2-16	-	
20/20 Int																		
20/20																		

CLOUGH, G. D.   Nottinghamshire

Name: Gareth David Clough
Role: Right-hand bat, right-arm medium bowler; all-rounder
Born: 23 May 1978, Leeds
Height: 6ft **Weight:** 12st
Nickname: Garth, Banga
County debut: 1998 (Yorkshire), 2001 (Nottinghamshire)
Strike rate: (career 88.50)
Parents: David and Gillian
Marital status: Single
Education: Pudsey Grangefield
Qualifications: 9 GCSEs, 3 A-levels, Level 1 cricket coach

Career outside cricket: 'Still working on one'

Off-season: 'Gaining qualifications for future career'

Overseas tours: Yorkshire to Durban and Cape Town 1999; Nottinghamshire to Johannesburg 2001-03

Overseas teams played for: Somerset West, Cape Town 1996-97; Deepdene Bears, Melbourne 1999-2000, 2001-02

Career highlights to date: '2006 Twenty20 finals day'

Cricket moments to forget: 'Result at end of Twenty20 final'

Cricketers particularly admired: Ian Botham, Steve Waugh

Young players to look out for: Samit Patel

Other sports played: Golf, football, poker, darts

Other sports followed: 'All sports'; football (Everton), rugby league (Leeds Rhinos)

Injuries: Out for four weeks with a torn oblique muscle

Favourite band: Razorlight

Relaxations: 'Dining out, socialising with friends, golf'

Extras: Topped Nottinghamshire 2nd XI bowling averages 2000 with 37 wickets at 19.05 and also scored 400 runs. Took 6-25 v Sussex at Trent Bridge in the Pro40 2006, the best one-day return by a Notts bowler since 1994

Opinions on cricket: 'Just keeps on getting better and better.'

Best batting: 55 Nottinghamshire v India A, Trent Bridge 2003

Best bowling: 3-69 Nottinghamshire v Gloucestershire, Trent Bridge 2001

16. Who scored a century (105) on the Queen Mother's 100th birthday in his 100th Test match?

2006 Season

	M	Inn	NO	Runs	HS	Avg	100	50	Ct	St	Balls	Runs	Wkts	Avg	BB	5I	10M
Test																	
FC	1	0	0	0	0		-	-	1	-	78	56	2	28.00	2-56	-	-
ODI																	
List A	13	8	1	86	26	12.28	-	-	3	-	318	274	13	21.07	6-25	1	
20/20 Int																	
20/20	10	4	2	79	40 *	39.50	-	-	-	-	132	158	8	19.75	2-17	-	

Career Performances

	M	Inn	NO	Runs	HS	Avg	100	50	Ct	St	Balls	Runs	Wkts	Avg	BB	5I	10M
Test																	
FC	11	15	2	147	55	11.30	-	1	4	-	1062	684	12	57.00	3-69	-	-
ODI																	
List A	86	50	16	585	42 *	17.20	-	-	27	-	2900	2485	79	31.45	6-25	1	
20/20 Int																	
20/20	28	18	4	269	40 *	19.21	-	-	4	-	444	570	24	23.75	2-17	-	

COETZER, K. J.   Durham

Name: <u>Kyle</u> James Coetzer
Role: Right-hand bat, right-arm medium bowler
Born: 14 April 1984, Aberdeen
Height: 5ft 11in
Nickname: Costa
County debut: 2004
Parents: Peter and Megan
Marital status: Single
Family links with cricket: 'All of my family plays, including two older brothers'
Education: Aberdeen Grammar School
Qualifications: Standard grades, 4 Intermediate 2s
Off-season: 'Studying a few courses and hopefully a few weeks playing in Cape Town'
Overseas tours: Scotland U19 to New Zealand (U19 World Cup) 2001-02, to Netherlands (ECC U19 Championships) 2003 (c), to Bangladesh (U19 World Cup) 2003-04 (c), to Ireland, to Denmark; Scotland to UAE (ICC Inter-Continental Cup) 2004, to Ireland (ICC Trophy) 2005, to Barbados 2006; Durham to Dubai 2005, 2006, to Mumbai 2006

Overseas teams played for: Cape Town CC 2002-03, 2003-04, 2004, 2005-06; Gosnells CC 2005
Cricket moments to forget: 'Most of 2006 season'
Cricket superstitions: 'Touch bat in crease after "over" is called'
Cricketers particularly admired: Jacques Kallis, Michael Hussey
Young players to look out for: Andrew Smith, Moneeb Iqbal
Other sports played: Golf, basketball, football
Other sports followed: Football (Aberdeen, Arsenal)
Injuries: Broken finger; bad back
Favourite band: Jack Johnson 'and a good mix of music'
Relaxations: 'Listening to music'
Extras: Man of the Match (146*) v Italy in the ECC U19 Championships at Deventer 2003. Has played for Scotland in first-class and one-day cricket, including NCL 2003 and C&G 2003, 2004 and 2006. Scored 67 on first-class debut, for Durham v Glamorgan at Cardiff 2004
Best batting: 133* Scotland v Kenya, Abu Dhabi 2004

2006 Season

	M	Inn	NO	Runs	HS	Avg	100	50	Ct	St	Balls	Runs	Wkts	Avg	BB	5I	10M
Test																	
FC	1	2	0	98	63	49.00	-	1	-	-	18	19	0		-	-	-
ODI																	
List A	1	1	0	0	0	0.00	-	-	-	-	0	0	0		-	-	
20/20 Int																	
20/20																	

Career Performances

	M	Inn	NO	Runs	HS	Avg	100	50	Ct	St	Balls	Runs	Wkts	Avg	BB	5I	10M
Test																	
FC	9	15	3	456	133 *	38.00	1	2	-	-	54	22	0		-	-	-
ODI																	
List A	10	9	1	86	30	10.75	-	-	3	-	60	47	0		-	-	
20/20 Int																	
20/20																	

COLLINGWOOD, P. D. Durham

Name: <u>Paul</u> David Collingwood
Role: Right-hand bat, right-arm
medium bowler
Born: 26 May 1976, Shotley Bridge,
Tyneside
Height: 5ft 11in **Weight:** 12st
Nickname: Colly
County debut: 1995 (one-day),
1996 (first-class)
County cap: 1998
Benefit: 2007
Test debut: 2003-04
ODI debut: 2001
Twenty20 Int debut: 2005
1000 runs in a season: 2
Place in batting averages: 70th av. 41.81
(2005 33rd av. 50.90)
Place in bowling averages: (2005 77th
av. 32.71)
Strike rate: (career 79.76)
Parents: David and Janet
Wife: Vicki
Children: Shannon, 2006
Family links with cricket: Father and brother play in the Tyneside Senior League for
Shotley Bridge CC
Education: Blackfyne Comprehensive School; Derwentside College
Qualifications: 9 GCSEs, 2 A-levels
Overseas tours: Durham Cricket Academy to Sri Lanka 1996 (c); England VI
to Hong Kong 2001, 2002; England to Zimbabwe (one-day series) 2001-02, to India
and New Zealand 2001-02 (one-day series), to Australia 2002-03, to Africa (World
Cup) 2002-03, to Bangladesh and Sri Lanka 2003-04, to West Indies 2003-04, to
Zimbabwe (one-day series) 2004-05, to South Africa 2004-05, to Pakistan 2005-06, to
India 2005-06, to India (ICC Champions Trophy) 2006-07, to Australia 2006-07
Overseas teams played for: Bulleen CC, Melbourne 1995-96, 1996-97 ('won flag on
both occasions'); Cornwall CC, Auckland 1997-98; Alberton CC, Johannesburg 1998-
99; Richmond CC, Melbourne 2000-01
Cricket moments to forget: 'Being Matthew Walker's (Kent) first first-class wicket'
Cricket superstitions: 'Left pad on first, and wearing them on the wrong legs'
Cricketers particularly admired: Steve Waugh, Jacques Kallis, Glenn McGrath,
Shane Warne
Other sports played: Golf (9 handicap)
Other sports followed: Football ('The Red and Whites' – Sunderland)

Extras: Took wicket (David Capel) with first ball on first-class debut against Northants, then scored 91 in Durham's first innings. Durham Player of the Year 2000. Awarded the Ron Brierley Scholarship 2000 through the ECB in conjunction with the Victorian Cricket Association, Australia; joint (and first English) winner of the Jack Ryder Medal, awarded by the umpires, for his performances in Victorian Premier Cricket 2000-01. Scored 112* and took England ODI best 6-31 v Bangladesh at Trent Bridge in the NatWest Series 2005, winning Man of the Match award. His other ODI awards include Man of the Match v Sri Lanka in the VB Series at Perth 2002-03 (100) and v Zimbabwe at Edgbaston in the ICC Champions Trophy 2004 (80*). Slazenger Sheer Instinct Award 2005. Appointed MBE in 2006 New Year Honours as part of 2005 Ashes-winning England team. England 12-month central contract 2006-07. Vice-captain of Durham 2005-06

Best batting: 190 Durham v Sri Lankans, Riverside 2002
190 Durham v Derbyshire, Derby 2005
Best bowling: 5-52 Durham v Somerset, Stockton 2005
Stop press: Scored 206 in the second Test at Adelaide 2006-07, becoming the first England batsman to score a Test double century in Australia since Wally Hammond in 1936-37 and sharing with Kevin Pietersen (158) in a record fourth-wicket stand for England v Australia (310). Man of the Match v New Zealand at Brisbane in the Commonwealth Bank Series 2006-07 (106/2-46), in the following game (first final) v Australia at Melbourne (120* plus a catch and two run-outs) and in the following game (second final) v Australia at Sydney (70/2-26)

2006 Season

	M	Inn	NO	Runs	HS	Avg	100	50	Ct	St	Balls	Runs	Wkts	Avg	BB	5I	10M
Test	7	12	1	460	186	41.81	1	1	10	-	234	134	1	134.00	1-33	-	-
FC	7	12	1	460	186	41.81	1	1	10	-	234	134	1	134.00	1-33	-	-
ODI	8	7	0	221	61	31.57	-	2	4	-	234	162	4	40.50	2-23	-	
List A	10	9	0	307	61	34.11	-	3	5	-	294	221	5	44.20	2-23	-	
20/20 Int	2	2	0	7	5	3.50	-	-	-	-	36	41	4	10.25	4-22	-	
20/20	2	2	0	7	5	3.50	-	-	-	-	36	41	4	10.25	4-22	-	

Career Performances

	M	Inn	NO	Runs	HS	Avg	100	50	Ct	St	Balls	Runs	Wkts	Avg	BB	5I	10M
Test	15	28	3	1027	186	41.08	2	3	20	-	432	245	1	245.00	1-33	-	-
FC	132	231	17	7446	190	34.79	16	35	138	-	7976	4021	100	40.21	5-52	1	-
ODI	100	89	20	2251	112 *	32.62	2	12	54	-	2271	1900	50	38.00	6-31	1	
List A	257	240	42	6300	118 *	31.81	4	37	125	-	6491	5166	150	34.44	6-31	1	
20/20 Int	3	3	0	53	46	17.66	-	-	-	-	48	49	6	8.16	4-22	-	
20/20	3	3	0	53	46	17.66	-	-	-	-	48	49	6	8.16	4-22	-	

Name: Nicholas (Nick) Richard Denis Compton
Role: Right-hand bat, right-arm off-spin bowler
Born: 26 June 1983, Durban, South Africa
Height: 6ft 1in **Weight:** 13st 1lb
Nickname: Compo, Lord
County debut: 2001 (one-day), 2004 (first-class)
County cap: 2006
1000 runs in a season: 1
Place in batting averages: 53rd av. 46.96
Strike rate: (career 42.00)
Parents: Richard and Glynis
Marital status: 'Available'
Family links with cricket: Grandfather Denis Compton played football and cricket for England
Education: Harrow School; Durham University
Qualifications: 3 A-levels, ECB coach Level 1
Career outside cricket: 'Media'
Off-season: 'Build on experiences this season; time away from cricket – travelling and a few beach weights! Return a better player next year'
Overseas tours: England U19 to Australia and (U19 World Cup) New Zealand 2001-02; MCC to Canada 2005-06; England A to Bangladesh 2006-07
Overseas teams played for: University of Western Australia, Perth 2001; Berea Rovers, Durban; University of Cape Town
Career highlights to date: 'Reaching 100 at Lord's with a six v Kent to score my first Championship century [2006] – champagne moment!'
Cricket moments to forget: 'Relegation to second division'
Cricketers particularly admired: Rahul Dravid, Jacques Kallis, Steve Waugh, Ed Joyce
Young players to look out for: Billy Godleman, Steve Finn
Other sports played: Golf (6 handicap), waterskiing, represented Natal at junior level at tennis
Other sports followed: Football (Arsenal), rugby union (Natal Sharks)
Favourite band: Killers
Relaxations: 'Diving; hair gel'
Extras: Played for Natal U13 and U15. Natal Academy award 1997. Middlesex U17 Batsman of the Season 1999. Middlesex U19 Player of the Season 2000. NBC Denis Compton Award for the most promising young Middlesex player 2001, 2002, 2006.

Represented England U19 2002. Scored maiden first-class century (101) v OUCCE at The Parks 2006 and maiden Championship century (124) in the following match v Kent at Lord's 2006. Carried bat for 105* v Nottinghamshire at Lord's 2006, in the process passing 1000 first-class runs for the season in his first full season of county cricket. Is England-qualified

Opinions on cricket: 'A great time to be involved in English cricket.'
Best batting: 190 Middlesex v Durham, Lord's 2006
Best bowling: 1-94 Middlesex v Sussex, Southgate 2006

2006 Season

	M	Inn	NO	Runs	HS	Avg	100	50	Ct	St	Balls	Runs	Wkts	Avg	BB	5I	10M
Test																	
FC	17	31	3	1315	190	46.96	6	4	7	-	42	103	1	103.00	1-94	-	-
ODI																	
List A	13	10	0	235	60	23.50	-	2	7	-	0	0	0			-	-
20/20 Int																	
20/20	8	8	1	117	50 *	16.71	-	1	4	-	0	0	0			-	-

Career Performances

	M	Inn	NO	Runs	HS	Avg	100	50	Ct	St	Balls	Runs	Wkts	Avg	BB	5I	10M
Test																	
FC	22	40	7	1521	190	46.09	6	5	10	-	42	103	1	103.00	1-94	-	-
ODI																	
List A	28	23	4	449	86 *	23.63	-	3	9	-	30	20	0			-	-
20/20 Int																	
20/20	17	13	1	144	50 *	12.00	-	1	10	-	0	0	0			-	-

17. Which player appeared for Sri Lanka in their
inaugural Test, v England in 1981-82, and in their 100th,
v Pakistan in 2000-01?

COOK, A. N.   Essex

Name: <u>Alastair</u> Nathan Cook
Role: Left-hand opening bat, right-arm
off-spin bowler
Born: 25 December 1984, Gloucester
Height: 6ft 2in **Weight:** 12st 10lbs
Nickname: Ali, Cooky, Chef
County debut: 2003
County cap: 2005
Test debut: 2005-06
ODI debut: 2006
1000 runs in a season: 2
Place in batting averages: 11th av. 64.38
(2005 27th av. 52.35)
Strike rate: (career 50.00)
Parents: Graham and Elizabeth
Marital status: Single
Family links with cricket: 'Dad played for
village side; brothers play for Maldon CC'
Education: Bedford School
Qualifications: 9 GCSEs, 3 A-levels

Overseas tours: Bedford School to Barbados 2001; England U19 to Bangladesh (U19 World Cup) 2003-04 (c); England A to Sri Lanka 2004-05, to West Indies 2005-06; England to Pakistan 2005-06, to India 2005-06, to Australia 2006-07
Cricket moments to forget: 'Running myself out first ball in U15 World Cup game against India'
Cricket superstitions: 'A few!'
Cricketers particularly admired: Graham Thorpe, Andy Flower, Graham Gooch
Young players to look out for: Ravi Bopara, James Hildreth, Mark Pettini
Other sports played: Squash, golf
Other sports followed: 'All sports'
Relaxations: 'Spending time with friends'
Extras: Played for England U15 in U15 World Cup 2000. Represented England U19 2003 and (as captain) 2004. Scored 69* on first-class debut v Nottinghamshire at Chelmsford 2003 and a further two half-centuries in his next two Championship matches. Had consecutive scores of 108*, 108* and 87 in the U19 World Cup 2003-04 in Bangladesh. NBC Denis Compton Award for the most promising young Essex player 2003. Scored 214 v Australians at Chelmsford in a two-day game 2005. Cricket Writers' Club Young Player of the Year 2005. PCA Young Player of the Year 2005, 2006. Called up as a replacement to the England tour of India 2005-06, scoring century (104*) on Test debut in the first Test at Nagpur (following 60 in first innings). ECB National Academy 2004-05 (part-time), 2005-06. England 12-month central contract 2006-07

Best batting: 195 Essex v Northamptonshire, Northampton 2005
Best bowling: 3-13 Essex v Northamptonshire, Chelmsford 2005
Stop press: Scored maiden Ashes century (116) in the third Test at Perth 2006-07, becoming the first England player to score four Test hundreds before his 22nd birthday

2006 Season

	M	Inn	NO	Runs	HS	Avg	100	50	Ct	St	Balls	Runs	Wkts	Avg	BB	5I	10M
Test	7	12	1	578	127	52.54	2	2	6	-	0	0	0		-	-	-
FC	13	23	5	1159	132	64.38	4	6	15	-	24	8	0		-	-	-
ODI	2	2	0	80	41	40.00	-	-	-	-	0	0	0		-	-	
List A	5	5	2	228	91 *	76.00	-	1	4	-	0	0	0		-	-	
20/20 Int																	
20/20	1	1	0	9	9	9.00	-	-	-	-	0	0	0		-	-	

Career Performances

	M	Inn	NO	Runs	HS	Avg	100	50	Ct	St	Balls	Runs	Wkts	Avg	BB	5I	10M
Test	9	16	2	761	127	54.35	3	3	7	-	0	0	0		-	-	-
FC	52	92	11	3915	195	48.33	11	22	56	-	150	111	3	37.00	3-13	-	-
ODI	2	2	0	80	41	40.00	-	-	-	-	0	0	0		-	-	
List A	25	24	3	626	94	29.80	-	3	11	-	18	10	0		-	-	
20/20 Int																	
20/20	2	2	0	11	9	5.50	-	-	-	-	0	0	0		-	-	

COOK, S. J.   Kent

Name: Simon James Cook
Role: Right-hand bat, right-arm fast-medium bowler
Born: 15 January 1977, Oxford
Height: 6ft 4in **Weight:** 13st
Nickname: Cookie, Donk, Chef
County debut: 1997 (one-day, Middlesex), 1999 (first-class, Middlesex), 2005 (Kent)
County cap: 2003 (Middlesex)
Place in batting averages: 253rd av. 14.00 (2005 268th av. 12.06)
Place in bowling averages: 66th av. 33.03 (2005 63rd av. 30.41)
Strike rate: 63.00 (career 60.59)
Parents: Phil and Sue
Marital status: Single
Family links with cricket: Brothers play for Oxfordshire

Education: Matthew Arnold School
Qualifications: GCSEs, NVQ Business Administration II, Level 3 ECB coach
Career outside cricket: Coaching and property development
Overseas tours: Middlesex to South Africa 2000
Overseas teams played for: Rockingham, Perth 2001, 2002
Career highlights to date: 'Beating Australia in one-day game at Lord's; winning division two of NCL and equalling league record for wickets in a season (39)'
Cricket moments to forget: 'Being outside the circle in a one-day game when I was supposed to be in it. Danny Law was bowled, the ball went for four [off the stumps, making six no-balls in total] and he went on to win the game for Durham'
Cricket superstitions: 'None'
Cricketers particularly admired: Angus Fraser, Glenn McGrath
Young players to look out for: Billy Godleman, Eoin Morgan, Joe Denly
Other sports followed: Football (Liverpool), 'any other ball sport'
Player website: www.vcamcricket.co.uk
Extras: Scored career best 93* v Nottinghamshire at Lord's 2001, helping Middlesex to avoid the follow-on, then took a wicket with the first ball of his opening spell. Equalled Adam Hollioake's record for the most wickets in a one-day league season (39) 2004
Opinions on cricket: 'I would like to see all our domestic competitions run in line with international regulations. Also lunch and tea breaks extended!'
Best batting: 93* Middlesex v Nottinghamshire, Lord's 2001
Best bowling: 8-63 Middlesex v Northamptonshire, Northampton 2002

2006 Season

	M	Inn	NO	Runs	HS	Avg	100	50	Ct	St	Balls	Runs	Wkts	Avg	BB	5I	10M
Test																	
FC	11	14	0	196	71	14.00	-	1	1	-	1763	925	28	33.03	6-74	2	-
ODI																	
List A	10	3	2	27	22	27.00	-	-	2	-	474	427	12	35.58	3-54	-	
20/20 Int																	
20/20	1	1	0	1	1	1.00	-	-	-	-	6	16	0		-	-	

Career Performances

	M	Inn	NO	Runs	HS	Avg	100	50	Ct	St	Balls	Runs	Wkts	Avg	BB	5I	10M
Test																	
FC	91	119	13	1736	93 *	16.37	-	4	27	-	14361	7582	237	31.99	8-63	8	-
ODI																	
List A	135	88	28	1028	67 *	17.13	-	2	18	-	5971	4710	166	28.37	6-37	2	
20/20 Int																	
20/20	16	11	4	81	20	11.57	-	-	3	-	320	415	22	18.86	3-14	-	

CORK, D. G. Lancashire

Name: Dominic Gerald Cork
Role: Right-hand bat, right-arm
fast-medium bowler
Born: 7 August 1971, Newcastle-under-
Lyme, Staffordshire
Height: 6ft 2½in **Weight:** 14st
Nickname: Corky
County debut: 1990 (Derbyshire),
2004 (Lancashire)
County cap: 1993 (Derbyshire),
2004 (Lancashire)
Benefit: 2001 (Derbyshire)
Test debut: 1995
ODI debut: 1992
50 wickets in a season: 7
1st-Class 200s: 1
Place in batting averages: 188th av. 23.60
(2005 129th av. 31.76)
Place in bowling averages: 19th av. 25.50 (2005 29th av. 26.00)
Strike rate: 55.59 (career 53.37)
Parents: Gerald and Mary
Wife and date of marriage: Donna, 28 August 2000
Children: Ashleigh, 28 April 1990; Gregory, 29 September 1994
Family links with cricket: 'Father and two brothers played in the same side at Betley
CC in Staffordshire'
Education: St Joseph's College, Trent Vale, Stoke-on-Trent; Newcastle College
Qualifications: 2 O-levels, Level 2 coach
Career outside cricket: 'None at the moment, but once I retire I would like to go into
the media side'
Overseas tours: England YC to Australia 1989-90; England A to Bermuda and West
Indies 1991-92, to Australia 1992-93, to South Africa 1993-94, to India 1994-95;
England to South Africa 1995-96, to India and Pakistan (World Cup) 1995-96,
to New Zealand 1996-97, to Australia 1998-99, to Pakistan and Sri Lanka 2000-01,
to Sri Lanka (ICC Champions Trophy) 2002-03; England VI to Hong Kong 2005,
2006 (c)
Overseas teams played for: East Shirley, Christchurch, New Zealand 1990-91
Career highlights to date: 'Making my debut for England'
Cricket moments to forget: 'Every time the team loses'
Cricket superstitions: 'None'
Cricketers particularly admired: Kim Barnett, Mike Atherton, Ian Botham,
Malcolm Marshall

Other sports played: Golf, football
Other sports followed: Football (Stoke City)
Favourite band: 'Anything R&B'
Relaxations: 'Listening to music'
Extras: Scored century as nightwatchman for England Young Cricketers v Pakistan Young Cricketers at Taunton 1990. Took 8-53 before lunch on his 20th birthday, v Essex at Derby 1991. Selected for England A in 1991 – his first full season of first-class cricket. PCA Young Player of the Year 1991. Took 7-43 on Test debut against West Indies at Lord's 1995, the best innings figures by an England debutant. Took hat-trick (Richardson, Murray, Hooper) against the West Indies at Old Trafford in the fourth Test 1995. PCA Player of the Year 1995. Finished top of the Whyte and Mackay bowling ratings 1995. Cornhill England Player of the Year 1995-96. One of *Wisden*'s Five Cricketers of the Year 1996. Man of the Match in the second Test v West Indies at Lord's 2000; on his recall to the Test side he had match figures of 7-52 followed by a match-winning 33* in England's second innings. Derbyshire captain 1998-2003. Took Twenty20 hat-trick (Pietersen, Ealham, Patel) v Nottinghamshire at Old Trafford 2004
Best batting: 200* Derbyshire v Durham, Derby 2000
Best bowling: 9-43 Derbyshire v Northamptonshire, Derby 1995

2006 Season

	M	Inn	NO	Runs	HS	Avg	100	50	Ct	St	Balls	Runs	Wkts	Avg	BB	5I	10M
Test																	
FC	14	17	2	354	154	23.60	1	1	11	-	2335	1071	42	25.50	6-53	1	-
ODI																	
List A	14	8	3	168	46	33.60	-	-	2	-	570	389	19	20.47	4-35	-	
20/20 Int																	
20/20	5	4	0	37	22	9.25	-	-	1	-	102	101	8	12.62	4-16	-	

Career Performances

	M	Inn	NO	Runs	HS	Avg	100	50	Ct	St	Balls	Runs	Wkts	Avg	BB	5I	10M
Test	37	56	8	864	59	18.00	-	3	18	-	7678	3906	131	29.81	7-43	5	-
FC	265	390	50	8636	200 *	25.40	8	50	196	-	45106	22266	845	26.35	9-43	32	5
ODI	32	21	3	180	31 *	10.00	-	-	6	-	1772	1368	41	33.36	3-27	-	
List A	273	212	30	3872	93	21.27	-	19	103	-	13034	9196	338	27.20	6-21	4	
20/20 Int																	
20/20	27	23	2	241	28	11.47	-	-	5	-	390	439	21	20.90	4-16	-	

COSGROVE, M. J.   Glamorgan

Name: <u>Mark</u> James Cosgrove
Role: Left-hand bat, right-arm
medium bowler
Born: 14 June 1984, Adelaide,
South Australia
Height: 5ft 9in
Nickname: Cozzie, Baby Boof
County debut: 2006
County cap: 2006
ODI debut: 2005-06
1st-Class 200s: 1
Place in batting averages: 42nd av. 50.35
Strike rate: (career 74.76)
Overseas tours: Australia U19 to New
Zealand (U19 World Cup) 2001-02; Australia
to Malaysia (DLF Cup) 2006-07
Overseas teams played for: Northern
Districts, Adelaide; South Australia
2002-03 –
Extras: Made A Grade debut for Northern Districts aged 14. Represented Australia
U19. Attended Commonwealth Bank [Australian] Cricket Academy 2002. Played for
Swalwell in the Northumberland and Tyneside Senior League 2005. Won Man of the
Match award for his 69-ball 74 on ODI debut v Bangladesh at Fatullah 2005-06.
Named Bradman Young Cricketer of the Year at the 2005 Allan Border Medal awards.
ING Cup Player of the Year 2005-06. An overseas player with Glamorgan 2006
Best batting: 233 Glamorgan v Derbyshire, Derby 2006
Best bowling: 1-0 South Australia v New South Wales, Adelaide 2003-04

18. Whose 8-64 in the second Test v India
at Kolkata 1996-97 remains the best innings return
by a South African on debut?

2006 Season

	M	Inn	NO	Runs	HS	Avg	100	50	Ct	St	Balls	Runs	Wkts	Avg	BB	5I	10M
Test																	
FC	10	19	2	856	233	50.35	2	6	5	-	420	234	5	46.80	1-8	-	-
ODI																	
List A	11	10	0	345	75	34.50	-	3	8	-	155	179	1	179.00	1-33	-	
20/20 Int																	
20/20																	

Career Performances

	M	Inn	NO	Runs	HS	Avg	100	50	Ct	St	Balls	Runs	Wkts	Avg	BB	5I	10M
Test																	
FC	36	66	4	2624	233	42.32	6	17	28	-	972	579	13	44.53	1-0	-	-
ODI	3	3	0	112	74	37.33	-	1	-	-	30	13	1	13.00	1-1	-	
List A	50	49	3	1625	121	35.32	2	12	17	-	354	375	5	75.00	2-21	-	
20/20 Int																	
20/20	4	4	0	80	44	20.00	-	-	1	-	6	14	0			-	-

COSKER, D. A.   Glamorgan

Name: <u>Dean</u> Andrew Cosker
Role: Right-hand bat, left-arm spin bowler
Born: 7 January 1978, Weymouth, Dorset
Height: 5ft 11in **Weight:** 12st 7lbs
Nickname: Lurks, The Lurker
County debut: 1996
County cap: 2000
Place in batting averages: 231st av. 16.80 (2005 194th av. 23.38)
Place in bowling averages: 130th av. 45.03 (2005 137th av. 50.17)
Strike rate: 91.42 (career 80.11)
Parents: Des and Carol
Wife and date of marriage: Katie, 24 November 2006
Family links with cricket: 'Brother dabbled in Welsh League. Father still plays village cricket but refuses to give up the ghost'
Education: Millfield School
Qualifications: 10 GCSEs, 4 A-levels, 'degree in construction'
Career outside cricket: 'Land "guru" and crane driving'

Off-season: 'Generally relaxing, preferably on the golf course'

Overseas tours: West of England U15 to West Indies 1993-94; Millfield School to Sri Lanka 1994-95; England U17 to Netherlands 1995; England U19 to Pakistan 1996-97; England A to Kenya and Sri Lanka 1997-98, to Zimbabwe and South Africa 1998-99; Glamorgan CCC to Cape Town and Jersey

Overseas teams played for: Gordon CC, Sydney 1996-97; Crusaders, Durban 2001-02

Career highlights to date: 'Every time we win the toss and field'

Cricket moments to forget: 'Every time we field for more than 150 overs'

Cricket superstitions: 'Get out of bed on the left when we field; get out of bed on the right when we bat'

Cricketers particularly admired: Graham Gooch, Graham Thorpe

Young players to look out for: Gareth Rees, Richard Grant

Other sports played: Golf

Other sports followed: Football ('Spurs and the Swans')

Injuries: Out for one week with 'poppadom knee'; 'my right jelly knee has caused particular nuisance all year'

Favourite band: 'Starship'

Relaxations: 'Trying to dig up Cardiff "indoor school of death" during the winter as it's a graveyard for all bowlers'

Extras: England U15, U17 and U19. Played for U19 TCCB Development of Excellence XI v South Africa U19 1995. Leading wicket-taker on England A tour of Zimbabwe and South Africa 1998-99 (22; av. 22.90). Third youngest Glamorgan player to receive county cap

Opinions on cricket: 'Players play with too many egos. We tend to forget that we are only cricketers and not superhuman. There is the real world we all have to go into after the cricket "goldfish bowl". [Let's] just enjoy playing professional sport while we can.'

Best batting: 52 Glamorgan v Gloucestershire, Bristol 2005

Best bowling: 6-140 Glamorgan v Lancashire, Colwyn Bay 1998

19. Who captained England on his Test debut in the first Test v India at Delhi 1972-73?

2006 Season

	M	Inn	NO	Runs	HS	Avg	100	50	Ct	St	Balls	Runs	Wkts	Avg	BB	5I	10M
Test																	
FC	13	16	6	168	39	16.80	-	-	9	-	3017	1486	33	45.03	4-78	-	-
ODI																	
List A	16	9	6	60	14 *	20.00	-	-	10	-	727	582	15	38.80	3-37	-	
20/20 Int																	
20/20	8	1	1	3	3 *		-	-	-	-	138	190	5	38.00	2-20	-	

Career Performances

	M	Inn	NO	Runs	HS	Avg	100	50	Ct	St	Balls	Runs	Wkts	Avg	BB	5I	10M
Test																	
FC	134	166	54	1487	52	13.27	-	1	92	-	25476	12302	318	38.68	6-140	2	-
ODI																	
List A	151	75	32	.357	27 *	8.30	-	-	59	-	6552	5209	156	33.39	5-54	1	
20/20 Int																	
20/20	26	8	7	30	10 *	30.00	-	-	10	-	420	606	19	31.89	2-20	-	

COVERDALE, P. S.　　　Northamptonshire

Name: <u>Paul</u> Stephen Coverdale
Role: Right-hand bat, right-arm medium-fast bowler
Born: 24 July 1983, Harrogate
Height: 5ft 10in **Weight:** 12st 6lbs
Nickname: Covers, Flaps, Drill Sergeant, Machine
County debut: No first-team appearance
Parents: Stephen and Jane
Marital status: Single
Family links with cricket: 'Father played for Yorkshire CCC and Cambridge University and is the former Chief Executive of Northamptonshire'
Education: Wellingborough School; Loughborough University
Qualifications: 9 GCSEs, 3 A-levels, BSc (Hons) Information Management and Business Studies, Level 1 coach
Career outside cricket: 'Since completing university have set up a sporting memorabilia and exhibitions company (CaptureSport), specialising in creating memorabilia products for sports personalities' testimonials and benefits and for clubs'

Overseas tours: Northamptonshire U19 to South Africa 2000

Overseas teams played for: Swanbourne, Perth 2002

Cricket moments to forget: 'Leaving a straight one first ball on a pair in a 2nd XI match a few years ago and then breaking my hand punching the dressing-room wall!'

Cricketers particularly admired: Allan Lamb, Steve Waugh, Matthew Hayden, Mike Hussey, Jacques Kallis

Other sports played: 'Pub golf'

Other sports followed: Rugby union (Northampton Saints), football (Aston Villa)

Favourite band: Bon Jovi, Dire Straits, Whitesnake ('think the lead singer is a distant relative!')

Player website: www.capturesport.com

Extras: Played county age groups, captaining at U14, U15, U17 and U19. Represented East England Schools U18. Played for Northamptonshire Board XI in the C&G 2001, 2002 and 2003. Represented English Universities in the Home Nations Tournament 2003. Captained English Universities 2004

Opinions on cricket: 'The format of the county competitions and the pressures put on counties to hold their own as financially viable businesses force "short-termism" to occur. Counties have to be successful in the immediate and short term in order to survive. This is why staff turnover has increased rapidly and we're seeing an influx of players on short contracts from overseas, often at the expense of counties' youth systems. The counties cannot be blamed for this but it does not bode well for their future progression and long-term improvement.'

2006 Season (did not make any first-class or one-day appearances)

Career Performances

	M	Inn	NO	Runs	HS	Avg	100	50	Ct	St	Balls	Runs	Wkts	Avg	BB	5I	10M
Test																	
FC																	
ODI																	
List A	3	3	0	33	19	11.00	-	-	3	-	96	48	1	48.00	1-21	-	
20/20 Int																	
20/20																	

CRAWLEY, J. P. Hampshire

Name: <u>John</u> Paul Crawley
Role: Right-hand bat, occasional
wicket-keeper
Born: 21 September 1971, Maldon, Essex
Height: 6ft 2in **Weight:** 13st 7lbs
Nickname: Creepy, Jonty, JC
County debut: 1990 (Lancashire),
2002 (Hampshire)
County cap: 1994 (Lancashire),
2002 (Hampshire)
Test debut: 1994
ODI debut: 1994-95
1000 runs in a season: 10
1st-Class 200s: 6
1st-Class 300s: 2
Place in batting averages: 7th av. 66.80
(2005 49th av. 46.14)
Strike rate: (career 101.50)
Parents: Frank and Jean (deceased)
Marital status: Married

Family links with cricket: Father played in Manchester Association; brother Mark
played for Lancashire and Nottinghamshire; brother Peter plays for Warrington CC
and has played for Scottish Universities and Cambridge University; uncle was
excellent fast bowler; godfather umpires in Manchester Association
Education: Manchester Grammar School; Trinity College, Cambridge;
Open University Business School
Qualifications: 10 O-levels, 2 AO-Levels, 3 A-levels, 2 S-levels, BA in History,
MA (Cantab), Professional Certificate in Management
Overseas tours: England YC to Australia 1989-90, to New Zealand 1990-91 (c);
England A to South Africa 1993-94, to West Indies 2000-01; England to Australia
1994-95, to South Africa 1995-96, to Zimbabwe and New Zealand 1996-97, to West
Indies 1997-98, to Australia 1998-99, 2002-03
Overseas teams played for: Midland-Guildford, Perth 1990
Cricketers particularly admired: Michael Atherton, Neil Fairbrother,
Graham Gooch, Alec Stewart, David Gower, Allan Donald, Ian Salisbury
Other sports followed: Football (Manchester United), golf
Relaxations: 'Playing or trying to play the guitar'
Extras: Sir John Hobbs Silver Jubilee Memorial Prize 1987. Played for England YC
1989, 1990 and (as captain) 1991; first to score 1000 runs in U19 'Tests'. Lancashire
vice-captain 1998. Topped English first-class batting averages for 1998 season (1851
runs; av. 74.04). Lancashire Player of the Year 1998. Lancashire captain 1999-2001.

Scored 272 on debut for Hampshire v Kent at Canterbury 2002, a Hampshire debut record. Captain of Hampshire 2003. Hampshire Player of the Year 2006
Best batting: 311* Hampshire v Nottinghamshire, Rose Bowl 2005
Best bowling: 1-7 Hampshire v Surrey, The Oval 2005

2006 Season

	M	Inn	NO	Runs	HS	Avg	100	50	Ct	St	Balls	Runs	Wkts	Avg	BB	5I	10M
Test																	
FC	16	27	1	1737	189	66.80	6	7	8	-	30	29	0		-	-	-
ODI																	
List A	15	14	1	421	100	32.38	1	1	4	-	0	0	0		-	-	
20/20 Int																	
20/20																	

Career Performances

	M	Inn	NO	Runs	HS	Avg	100	50	Ct	St	Balls	Runs	Wkts	Avg	BB	5I	10M
Test	37	61	9	1800	156 *	34.61	4	9	29	-	0	0	0		-	-	-
FC	319	527	51	22771	311 *	47.83	52	123	207	1	203	261	2	130.50	1-7	-	-
ODI	13	12	1	235	73	21.36	-	2	1	1	0	0	0		-	-	
List A	286	273	22	7945	114	31.65	7	49	85	4	6	4	0		-	-	
20/20 Int																	
20/20	10	10	1	107	23	11.88	-	-	3	-	0	0	0		-	-	

CROFT, R. D. B.   Glamorgan

Name: <u>Robert</u> Damien Bale Croft
Role: Right-hand bat, off-spin bowler
Born: 25 May 1970, Morriston, Swansea
Height: 5ft 11in **Weight:** 13st 7lbs
Nickname: Crofty
County debut: 1989
County cap: 1992
Benefit: 2000
Test debut: 1996
ODI debut: 1996
50 wickets in a season: 8
Place in batting averages: 131st av. 31.63 (2005 172nd av. 26.53)
Place in bowling averages: 60th av. 32.00 (2005 136th av. 49.62)
Strike rate: 63.86 (career 77.54)
Parents: Malcolm and Susan
Wife: Marie

Children: Callum James Bale Croft
Family links with cricket: Father and grandfather played league cricket
Education: St John Lloyd Catholic School, Llanelli; Neath Tertiary College;
West Glamorgan Institute of Higher Education
Qualifications: 6 O-levels, OND Business Studies, HND Business Studies,
NCA senior coaching certificate
Overseas tours: England A to Bermuda and West Indies 1991-92, to South Africa
1993-94; England to Zimbabwe and New Zealand 1996-97, to West Indies 1997-98,
to Australia 1998-99, to Sharjah (Coca-Cola Cup) 1998-99, to Sri Lanka 2000-01,
2003-04; England VI to Hong Kong 2003, 2005 (c)
Career highlights to date: 'Playing for England and winning the Championship with
Glamorgan in 1997'
Cricket moments to forget: 'None. This career is too short to forget any of it'
Cricketers particularly admired: Ian Botham, Viv Richards, Shane Warne
Other sports played: 'Give anything a go'
Other sports followed: Football (Liverpool FC), rugby (Llanelli and Wales)
Interests/relaxations: 'Everything'
Extras: Captained England South to victory in International Youth Tournament 1989
and was voted Player of the Tournament. Glamorgan Young Player of the Year 1992.
Scored Test best 37* in the third Test at Old Trafford 1998, resisting for 190 minutes
to deny South Africa victory. Represented England in the 1999 World Cup. Honorary
fellow of West Glamorgan Institute of Higher Education. Scored 69-ball 119 v Surrey
at The Oval in the C&G 2002 as Glamorgan made 429 in reply to Surrey's 438-5.
Glamorgan Player of the Year 2003 (jointly with Michael Kasprowicz) and 2004.
Glamorgan vice-captain 2002-03; appointed captain during 2003, taking over from the
injured Steve James; stood down as captain in mid-September 2006. Man of the Match
in England's victory v Pakistan in the final of the Hong Kong Sixes 2003. Retired
from international cricket in January 2004. Cricket Society's Wetherell Award 2004 for
the leading all-rounder in English first-class cricket. His 5-56 v Derbyshire at Derby
2006 included his 900th first-class wicket (Ian Hunter)
Best batting: 143 Glamorgan v Somerset, Taunton 1995
Best bowling: 8-66 Glamorgan v Warwickshire, Swansea 1992

2006 Season

	M	Inn	NO	Runs	HS	Avg	100	50	Ct	St	Balls	Runs	Wkts	Avg	BB	5I	10M
Test																	
FC	16	24	5	601	72	31.63	-	3	9	-	4215	2112	66	32.00	7-67	3	1
ODI																	
List A	15	12	0	200	54	16.66	-	1	4	-	578	495	12	41.25	2-19	-	
20/20 Int																	
20/20	8	2	1	22	21	22.00	-	-	4	-	150	183	6	30.50	2-35	-	

Career Performances

	M	Inn	NO	Runs	HS	Avg	100	50	Ct	St	Balls	Runs	Wkts	Avg	BB	5I	10M
Test	21	34	8	421	37 *	16.19	-	-	10	-	4619	1825	49	37.24	5-95	1	-
FC	334	495	90	10722	143	26.47	6	48	159	-	73511	34324	948	36.20	8-66	41	8
ODI	50	36	12	345	32	14.37	-	-	11	-	2466	1743	45	38.73	3-51	-	
List A	374	312	57	6127	143	24.02	4	31	89	-	17323	12468	384	32.46	6-20	1	
20/20 Int																	
20/20	27	18	4	325	62 *	23.21	-	2	14	-	564	756	31	24.38	3-32	-	

CROFT, S. J. Lancashire

Name: <u>Steven</u> John Croft
Role: Right-hand bat, right-arm medium-fast bowler; all-rounder
Born: 11 October 1984, Blackpool
Height: 5ft 11in **Weight:** 14st
Nickname: Crofty
County debut: 2005
Parents: Elizabeth and Lawrence
Marital status: Single
Family links with cricket: Father played for local team
Education: Highfield High, Blackpool; Myerscough College
Qualifications: 10 GCSEs, First Diploma in Sports Studies, Level 2 cricket coach
Career outside cricket: Coaching
Overseas teams played for: St Kilda, Melbourne 2005-06
Career highlights to date: 'Signing for Lancashire CCC'
Cricket moments to forget: 'Duck on 2nd XI debut'
Cricket superstitions: 'Left pad on first'
Cricketers particularly admired: Andrew Flintoff, Stuart Law, Jacques Kallis
Young players to look out for: Karl Brown, Tom Smith, Gareth Cross
Other sports played: Football ('played for Blackpool town team and trialled at Oldham FC and Wimbledon FC')
Other sports followed: Football (Newcastle)
Favourite band: Oasis, The Killers, Blink-182
Relaxations: 'Socialising with friends; music, movies, sport'
Extras: Played for Lancashire Board XI in the C&G 2003. Only third amateur to score over 1000 runs in a season in the Northern Premier League

Opinions on cricket: 'Too many Kolpak [*see page 13*] players in the game, leading to English talent not coming through. Twenty20 has been good for the game.'
Best batting: 17 Lancashire v DUCCE, Durham 2006

2006 Season

	M	Inn	NO	Runs	HS	Avg	100	50	Ct	St	Balls	Runs	Wkts	Avg	BB	5I	10M
Test																	
FC	1	1	0	17	17	17.00	-	-	1	-	0	0	0		-	-	-
ODI																	
List A	7	5	0	140	56	28.00	-	1	6	-	127	165	7	23.57	4-59	-	
20/20 Int																	
20/20	8	8	1	102	31	14.57	-	-	5	-	86	121	4	30.25	2-10	-	

Career Performances

	M	Inn	NO	Runs	HS	Avg	100	50	Ct	St	Balls	Runs	Wkts	Avg	BB	5I	10M
Test																	
FC	2	2	0	23	17	11.50	-	-	1	-	66	49	0		-	-	-
ODI																	
List A	10	8	1	151	56	21.57	-	1	7	-	175	199	8	24.87	4-59	-	
20/20 Int																	
20/20	8	8	1	102	31	14.57	-	-	5	-	86	121	4	30.25	2-10	-	

CROOK, A. R.   Northamptonshire

Name: Andrew (<u>Andy</u>) Richard Crook
Role: Right-hand bat, right-arm
off-spin bowler
Born: 14 October 1980, Adelaide, South
Australia
Height: 6ft 4in **Weight:** 14st 5lbs
Nickname: Crooky, Gonk
County debut: 2004 (Lancashire)
Strike rate: (career 111.42)
Parents: Sue (mother) and Doug (stepfather);
Martyn (father)
Marital status: Engaged to Louise
Children: 'Expecting our first baby in
June 2007'
Family links with cricket: 'Brother, Steve,
also at Northants'
Education: Rostrevor College
Career outside cricket: 'Have been working

in the Lancashire indoor centre, coaching a variety of players and tutoring college cricketers'

Off-season: 'Two months in Australia for Christmas'

Overseas teams played for: South Australia 1998-99; Northern Districts, South Australia; East Torrens CC, Adelaide

Career highlights to date: '2005 Twenty20 finals day'

Cricket moments to forget: 'Being the last man out on my Old Trafford debut, and my wicket meant Lancashire were relegated to Division Two of the County Championship'

Cricketers particularly admired: Gary Kirsten

Young players to look out for: Karl Brown

Other sports followed: Football (Blackburn Rovers), AFL (Essendon Bombers)

Favourite band: Snow Patrol, U2, Counting Crows

Extras: Made first-class debut for South Australia v England XI at Adelaide 1998-99. Made new Lancashire record individual one-day score (162*), v Buckinghamshire at Wormsley in the C&G 2005, winning Man of the Match award. Released by Lancashire at the end of the 2006 season and has joined Northamptonshire for 2007. Is not considered an overseas player

Best batting: 88 Lancashire v OUCCE, The Parks 2005

Best bowling: 3-71 Lancashire v Essex, Old Trafford 2005

2006 Season

	M	Inn	NO	Runs	HS	Avg	100	50	Ct	St	Balls	Runs	Wkts	Avg	BB	5I	10M
Test																	
FC																	
ODI																	
List A	2	2	0	73	42	36.50	-	-	-	-	0	0	0		-	-	
20/20 Int																	
20/20																	

Career Performances

	M	Inn	NO	Runs	HS	Avg	100	50	Ct	St	Balls	Runs	Wkts	Avg	BB	5I	10M
Test																	
FC	5	7	0	200	88	28.57	-	1	4	-	780	509	7	72.71	3-71	-	-
ODI																	
List A	16	14	2	361	162*	30.08	1	-	4	-	353	319	10	31.90	3-32	-	
20/20 Int																	
20/20	10	7	3	51	15	12.75	-	-	3	-	126	201	7	28.71	2-25	-	

CROOK, S. P.   Northamptonshire

Name: <u>Steven</u> Paul Crook
Role: Right-hand bat, right-arm medium-fast bowler; all-rounder
Born: 28 May 1983, Adelaide, South Australia
Height: 5ft 11in **Weight:** 13st 3lbs
Nickname: Crooky, Crookster
County debut: 2003 (Lancashire), 2005 (Northamptonshire)
Place in batting averages: 227th av. 17.25
Place in bowling averages: 133rd av. 46.00
Strike rate: 61.82 (career 75.31)
Parents: 'Dad – Martyn, mum – Sue and stepfather – Doug'
Marital status: Single
Family links with sport: Brother Andrew also at Northamptonshire. Father, Martyn, played professional football

Education: Rostrevor College
Qualifications: Matriculation
Overseas tours: Lancashire to Cape Town 2003, 2004
Overseas teams played for: Northern Districts, South Australia
Career highlights to date: 'Playing semi-final of Twenty20 2004'
Cricket moments to forget: 'Getting beaten in semi of Twenty20 2004'
Cricketers particularly admired: Andrew Flintoff, Stuart Law
Young players to look out for: Tom Smith, Steve Croft, Andy Crook
Other sports followed: Football (Tottenham Hotspur FC)
Favourite band: The Doors, The Strokes
Relaxations: 'Hanging out with mates'
Extras: Attended South Australia Cricket Academy. Represented South Australia U13-U19. Selected for Australia U19 preliminary World Cup squad 2001-02. Is not considered an overseas player
Opinions on cricket: 'More Twenty20!!'
Best batting: 97 Northamptonshire v Yorkshire, Northampton 2005
Best bowling: 3-46 Northamptonshire v Leicestershire, Northampton 2006

2006 Season

	M	Inn	NO	Runs	HS	Avg	100	50	Ct	St	Balls	Runs	Wkts	Avg	BB	5I	10M
Test																	
FC	8	10	2	138	44	17.25	-	-	5	-	1051	782	17	46.00	3-46	-	-
ODI																	
List A	6	4	0	49	23	12.25	-	-	1	-	198	144	5	28.80	4-20	-	
20/20 Int																	
20/20																	

Career Performances

	M	Inn	NO	Runs	HS	Avg	100	50	Ct	St	Balls	Runs	Wkts	Avg	BB	5I	10M
Test																	
FC	19	22	4	610	97	33.88	-	4	7	-	2184	1532	29	52.82	3-46	-	-
ODI																	
List A	19	14	1	146	23	11.23	-	-	4	-	576	574	13	44.15	4-20	-	
20/20 Int																	
20/20	11	8	1	124	27	17.71	-	-	1	-	12	22	0		-	-	

CROSS, G. D. Lancashire

Name: <u>Gareth</u> David Cross
Role: Right-hand bat, wicket-keeper
Born: 20 June 1984, Bury
Height: 5ft 9in **Weight:** 11st 9lbs
Nickname: Crossy
County debut: 2005
Place in batting averages: 169th av. 27.00
Parents: Duncan and Margaret
Marital status: Single
Family links with cricket: 'Dad played for
Prestwich. Brother Matthew plays for
Monton and Weaste'
Education: Moorside High School; Eccles
College
Qualifications: 9 GCSEs, GNVQ Science
Overseas teams played for: St Kilda,
Melbourne 2002-04
Cricket moments to forget: 'Tim Rees top-
edging the ball into my head whilst I was keeping for Salford against Bolton'
Cricket superstitions: 'Just putting batting gear on in the same order'
Cricketers particularly admired: Ian Healy, Adam Gilchrist, Graeme Rummans
Young players to look out for: Steven Croft, Steven Crook

Other sports played: Football ('had a trial for Man United when I was 13')
Other sports followed: Football (Man United)
Favourite band: Eminem, Oasis
Relaxations: 'Watching football; five-a-side football'
Extras: Manchester Association Young Player of the Year. Bolton Association Young Player of the Year 2000. ECB Premier League Young Player of the Year. Liverpool Competition Player of the Year 2004. Played for Lancashire Board XI in the C&G 2003. Made five dismissals in first innings of Championship debut v Leicestershire at Old Trafford 2005
Opinions on cricket: 'Bigger crowds because of Twenty20. More cricket in schools.'
Best batting: 72 Lancashire v Kent, Canterbury 2006

2006 Season

	M	Inn	NO	Runs	HS	Avg	100	50	Ct	St	Balls	Runs	Wkts	Avg	BB	5I	10M
Test																	
FC	4	6	0	162	72	27.00	-	2	13	4	0	0	0		-	-	-
ODI																	
List A	4	2	0	34	20	17.00	-	-	-	1	0	0	0		-	-	
20/20 Int																	
20/20	8	7	0	61	36	8.71	-	-	7	3	0	0	0		-	-	

Career Performances

	M	Inn	NO	Runs	HS	Avg	100	50	Ct	St	Balls	Runs	Wkts	Avg	BB	5I	10M
Test																	
FC	6	9	0	200	72	22.22	-	2	22	6	0	0	0		-	-	-
ODI																	
List A	9	7	1	87	21	14.50	-	-	6	5	0	0	0		-	-	
20/20 Int																	
20/20	8	7	0	61	36	8.71	-	-	7	3	0	0	0		-	-	

20. Against which country playing its inaugural Test
did Maurice Allom take four wickets in five balls, including a
hat-trick, on his Test debut in 1929-30?

CULLEN, D. J. Somerset

Name: Daniel (<u>Dan</u>) James Cullen
Role: Right-hand bat, right-arm
off-spin bowler
Born: 10 April 1984, Adelaide, South
Australia
County debut: 2006
Test debut: 2005-06
ODI debut: 2005-06
Strike rate: (career 75.71)
Overseas tours: Australia A to Pakistan
2005-06; Australia to Bangladesh 2005-06,
to Malaysia (DLF Cup) 2006-07
Overseas teams played for: South Australia
2004-05 –
Extras: Represented Australia U19. Man of
the Match v Western Australia at Perth in the
Pura Cup 2004-05. Named Bradman Young
Cricketer of the Year at the 2006 Allan

Border Medal awards. Australia contract 2006-07. An overseas player with
Somerset 2006
Best batting: 42 South Australia v Tasmania, Hobart 2004-05
Best bowling: 5-38 South Australia v Western Australia, Perth 2004-05

2006 Season

	M	Inn	NO	Runs	HS	Avg	100	50	Ct	St	Balls	Runs	Wkts	Avg	BB	5I	10M
Test																	
FC	4	6	4	81	24 *	40.50	-	-	1	-	714	381	7	54.42	5-137	1	-
ODI																	
List A	3	0	0	0	0		-	-	-	-	78	53	2	26.50	2-32	-	
20/20 Int																	
20/20																	

Career Performances

	M	Inn	NO	Runs	HS	Avg	100	50	Ct	St	Balls	Runs	Wkts	Avg	BB	5I	10M
Test	1	0	0	0	0		-	-	-	-	84	54	1	54.00	1-25	-	-
FC	26	34	14	334	42	16.70	-	-	7	-	6284	3347	83	40.32	5-38	4	-
ODI	5	1	1	2	2 *		-	-	2	-	213	147	2	73.50	2-25	-	
List A	27	10	4	59	13 *	9.83	-	-	7	-	1148	901	28	32.17	3-28	-	
20/20 Int																	
20/20	4	3	0	18	10	6.00	-	-	1	-	84	90	6	15.00	3-23	-	

CUMMINS, R. A. G.   Leicestershire

Name: <u>Ryan</u> Anthony Gilbert Cummins
Role: Right-hand lower-order bat, right-arm medium-fast bowler
Born: 14 April 1984, Sutton, Surrey
Height: 6ft 4in **Weight:** 13st 4lbs
Nickname: Rhino, Yummins
County debut: 2005
Place in bowling averages: 126th av. 44.53 (2005 81st av. 33.42)
Strike rate: 66.00 (career 73.44)
Parents: Tony and Sheila
Marital status: Single
Family links with cricket: 'Great-grandfather, Gilly Reay, played for Surrey. Father played county 2nd XI and sister plays county cricket for Northants'
Education: Wallington County Grammar School for Boys; Loughborough University
Qualifications: 11 GCSEs, 4 A-levels, BSc (Hons) Geography (2.2), Level 2 cricket coach, Level 1 hockey coach
Off-season: 'Spending time at home in London with my family and friends. Also interspersed with visits to Loughborough University and Leicestershire'
Career highlights to date: 'Playing in the winning Twenty20 side of 2006'
Cricket moments to forget: 'Bowling the way I did in the Twenty20 final! Nerves got the better of me!'
Cricketers particularly admired: Phil DeFreitas, Brian Lara, Adam Hollioake
Other sports played: 'County swimming, hockey, squash, golf, tennis'
Other sports followed: Rugby (Leicester Tigers), golf
Favourite band: Counting Crows, Jack Johnson
Relaxations: 'Golf, spending time with my girlfriend and seeing mates'
Extras: Played for Loughborough UCCE 2003-05. Represented British Universities 2005
Opinions on cricket: 'Level of professionalism in the game must continue to improve, so as to improve both individuals and the standard of English cricket.'
Best batting: 26 LUCCE v Sussex, Hove 2005
Best bowling: 4-46 Leicestershire v West Indies A, Leicester 2006

2006 Season

	M	Inn	NO	Runs	HS	Avg	100	50	Ct	St	Balls	Runs	Wkts	Avg	BB	5I	10M
Test																	
FC	7	8	4	38	13	9.50	-	-	2	-	858	579	13	44.53	4-46	-	-
ODI																	
List A	11	3	1	3	2	1.50	-	-	3	-	396	292	15	19.46	2-14	-	
20/20 Int																	
20/20	1	0	0	0	0		-	-	1	-	18	40	0		-	-	

Career Performances

	M	Inn	NO	Runs	HS	Avg	100	50	Ct	St	Balls	Runs	Wkts	Avg	BB	5I	10M
Test																	
FC	15	16	8	73	26	9.12	-	-	3	-	2130	1404	29	48.41	4-46	-	-
ODI																	
List A	11	3	1	3	2	1.50	-	-	3	-	396	292	15	19.46	2-14	-	
20/20 Int																	
20/20	1	0	0	0	0		-	-	1	-	18	40	0		-	-	

CUSDEN, S. M. J.   Derbyshire

Name: <u>Simon</u> Mark James Cusden
Role: Right-hand bat, right-arm fast-medium bowler
Born: 21 February 1985, Margate, Kent
Height: 6ft 6in **Weight:** 16st
Nickname: Big Ron, Village, Ronnie Villarge, Cuzzy, Cuzbee, Cuzman, Freak, Boris
County debut: 2004 (Kent)
Strike rate: (career 48.83)
Parents: Mark and Karen
Marital status: Engaged
Family links with cricket: 'Dad Beltinge legend'
Education: Simon Langton GS for Boys
Qualifications: 3 A-levels
Off-season: 'Working at Simon Langton GS'
Overseas tours: England U19 to Australia 2002-03
Career highlights to date: 'St Lawrence six-a-side trophy winners'
Cricket moments to forget: 'Losing my off pole to Lewis Jenkins'
Cricketers particularly admired: Matthew Walker

Players to look out for: Jimmy Lincoln, Rob Clift, Theron Tickridge, Clive Medhurst
Other sports played: Snooker, squash, rugby
Favourite band: The Fray
Relaxations: 'Playing guitar; spending time with fiancée and mates'
Extras: Represented England U19 2004. Took wicket (Mal Loye) with his first ball for Kent, v Lancashire at Tunbridge Wells in the totesport League 2004. Kent Academy Scholar of the Year 2004. Released by Kent at the end of the 2006 season and has joined Derbyshire for 2007
Best batting: 12* Kent v Sussex, Canterbury 2004
Best bowling: 4-68 Kent v Northamptonshire, Canterbury 2004

2006 Season

	M	Inn	NO	Runs	HS	Avg	100	50	Ct	St	Balls	Runs	Wkts	Avg	BB	5I	10M
Test																	
FC	1	0	0	0	0		-	-	-	-	108	83	2	41.50	2-62	-	-
ODI																	
List A	1	0	0	0	0		-	-	-	-	24	32	1	32.00	1-32	-	
20/20 Int																	
20/20																	

Career Performances

	M	Inn	NO	Runs	HS	Avg	100	50	Ct	St	Balls	Runs	Wkts	Avg	BB	5I	10M
Test																	
FC	6	7	5	28	12 *	14.00	-	-	2	-	879	594	18	33.00	4-68	-	-
ODI																	
List A	6	3	1	5	3	2.50	-	-	-	-	192	193	4	48.25	1-29	-	
20/20 Int																	
20/20																	

DAGGETT, L. M.   Warwickshire

Name: Lee Martin Daggett
Role: Right-hand bat, right-arm fast-medium bowler
Born: 1 October 1982, Bury, Lancashire
Height: 6ft **Weight:** 13st 7lbs
Nickname: Dags, Len, Lenny
County debut: 2006
Place in bowling averages: 18th av. 25.31
Strike rate: 43.37 (career 58.51)
Parents: Peter and Kathleen
Marital status: Single

Family links with cricket: 'Dad captained Ramsbottom CC in the Lancashire League and now coaches Ramsbottom CC 1st XI'

Education: Woodhey High School, Bury; Holy Cross College, Bury; Durham University

Qualifications: BA (Hons) Sport, Health and Exercise (dissertation on sportsmanship, ethics and morals in cricket)

Overseas tours: British Universities to South Africa 2004

Overseas teams played for: Joondalup CC, Perth 2001-02, 2006

Career highlights to date: '8-94 v Durham CCC in 2004 for DUCCE'

Cricket moments to forget: 'The whole feeling and uncertainty of being a trialist'

Cricket superstitions: 'Not really'

Cricketers particularly admired: 'My father', Brett Lee, Allan Donald, Graeme Fowler

Young players to look out for: William Rew Smith

Other sports played: Football ('used to play for Bury School of Excellence; played at the old Wembley')

Other sports followed: Football (Manchester United), rugby (Western Force)

Favourite band: Ocean Colour Scene, Oasis

Relaxations: 'Cinema, running, darts, gym'

Extras: Played for Durham UCCE 2003-05. Durham University Sportsman of the Year 2004. Represented British Universities 2004-05

Opinions on cricket: 'Twenty20 is the way forward. Need better structure in league cricket in England. We could learn a lot from the structure used in Australia.'

Best batting: 12* Warwickshire v Lancashire, Blackpool 2006

Best bowling: 8-94 DUCCE v Durham, Riverside 2004

2006 Season

	M	Inn	NO	Runs	HS	Avg	100	50	Ct	St	Balls	Runs	Wkts	Avg	BB	5I	10M
Test																	
FC	5	9	4	37	12 *	7.40	-	-	1	-	694	405	16	25.31	6-30	1	-
ODI																	
List A	7	3	3	14	5 *		-	-	-	-	296	251	7	35.85	2-33	-	
20/20 Int																	
20/20																	

Career Performances

	M	Inn	NO	Runs	HS	Avg	100	50	Ct	St	Balls	Runs	Wkts	Avg	BB	5I	10M
Test																	
FC	14	20	10	58	12 *	5.80	-	-	1	-	1931	1212	33	36.72	8-94	2	-
ODI																	
List A	7	3	3	14	5 *		-	-	-	-	296	251	7	35.85	2-33	-	
20/20 Int																	
20/20																	

DALRYMPLE, J. W. M.   Middlesex

Name: James (Jamie) William Murray Dalrymple
Role: Right-hand bat, off-spin bowler
Born: 21 January 1981, Nairobi, Kenya
Height: 6ft **Weight:** 13st 7lbs
Nickname: JD, Pest
County debut: 2000 (one-day), 2001 (first-class)
County cap: 2004
ODI debut: 2006
Twenty20 Int debut: 2006
1st-Class 200s: 2
Place in batting averages: 107th av. 34.42 (2005 110th av. 34.33)
Place in bowling averages: 93rd av. 37.37 (2005 108th av. 40.86)
Strike rate: 73.58 (career 78.30)
Parents: Douglas and Patricia
Marital status: Single
Family links with cricket: 'Dad played lots of club cricket.' Brother Simon played for Oxford University in 2002 and 2004
Education: Radley College, Abingdon; St Peter's College, Oxford University

Qualifications: 10 GCSEs, 5 A-levels, degree in History
Overseas tours: Middlesex to South Africa 2000; England A to West Indies 2005-06; England to India (ICC Champions Trophy) 2006-07, to Australia 2006-07
Cricket moments to forget: 'Middlesex v Warwickshire at Edgbaston 2003 – being part of the loss of eight wickets in a session, and the match'
Cricketers particularly admired: David Gower, Carl Hooper, Ian Botham, Mark Waugh
Other sports played: Rugby (college), hockey (university)
Other sports followed: Rugby (Northampton RUFC)
Favourite band: 'Don't have a favourite'
Relaxations: Reading, golf
Extras: Represented England U19 2000. Played for Oxford UCCE 2001 and (as captain) 2002. Represented British Universities 2001 and (as captain) 2002. Oxford Blue 2001, 2002 (captain) and 2003 (captain). Scored double century (236*) in the Varsity Match at Fenner's 2003 and took 5-49 in the Cambridge first innings. C&G Man of the Match awards v Wales Minor Counties at Lamphey (104*; second fifty in 14 balls) and v Glamorgan at Lord's (107) 2004. ECB National Academy 2005-06, 2006-07
Best batting: 244 Middlesex v Surrey, The Oval 2004
Best bowling: 5-49 Oxford University v Cambridge University, Fenner's 2003
Stop press: Called up to England Test squad for tour of Australia 2006-07 as replacement for Ashley Giles

2006 Season

	M	Inn	NO	Runs	HS	Avg	100	50	Ct	St	Balls	Runs	Wkts	Avg	BB	5I	10M
Test																	
FC	12	19	0	654	96	34.42	-	5	6	-	2134	1084	29	37.37	4-61	-	-
ODI	10	9	0	304	67	33.77	-	2	5	-	420	300	8	37.50	2-13	-	
List A	20	18	2	544	82	34.00	-	4	8	-	873	660	22	30.00	3-61	-	
20/20 Int	2	2	0	28	27	14.00	-	-	-	-	24	27	2	13.50	1-10	-	
20/20	5	4	0	48	27	12.00	-	-	1	-	78	94	4	23.50	2-22	-	

Career Performances

	M	Inn	NO	Runs	HS	Avg	100	50	Ct	St	Balls	Runs	Wkts	Avg	BB	5I	10M
Test																	
FC	63	105	10	3422	244	36.02	5	18	35	-	8457	4681	108	43.34	5-49	1	-
ODI	11	10	0	321	67	32.10	-	2	5	-	474	351	9	39.00	2-13	-	
List A	95	84	18	2012	107	30.48	2	12	40	-	3006	2441	74	32.98	4-14	-	
20/20 Int	2	2	0	28	27	14.00	-	-	-	-	24	27	2	13.50	1-10	-	
20/20	18	16	3	275	39	21.15	-	-	4	-	198	284	10	28.40	2-22	-	

DANISH KANERIA Essex

Name: Danish Prabha Shanker Kaneria
Role: Right-hand bat, right-arm
leg-spin and googly bowler
Born: 16 December 1980, Karachi, Pakistan
Height: 6ft 1in
Nickname: Danny Boy, Dani
County debut: 2004
County cap: 2004
Test debut: 2000-01
ODI debut: 2001-02
50 wickets in a season: 1
Place in bowling averages: 106th av. 40.17
(2005 79th av. 33.40)
Strike rate: 80.08 (career 56.48)
Parents: Prabha Shanker Kaneria and Babita
P. Kaneria
Wife and date of marriage: Dharmeta
Danish Kaneria, 15 February 2004
Family links with cricket: Cousin, wicket-keeper Anil Dalpat, played nine Tests for
Pakistan 1983-84
Education: St Patrick's High School, Karachi
Overseas tours: Pakistan U19 to Sri Lanka (U19 World Cup) 1999-2000; Pakistan A
to Kenya 2000, to Sri Lanka 2001; Pakistan to Bangladesh 2001-02, to Sharjah (v
West Indies) 2001-02, to Sharjah (v Australia) 2002-03, to England (NatWest
Challenge) 2003, to New Zealand 2003-04, to Australia 2004-05, to India 2004-05, to
West Indies 2004-05, to Sri Lanka 2005-06, to England 2006, plus other one-day
tournaments in Sharjah and Sri Lanka
Overseas teams played for: Pakistan National Shipping Corporation 1998-99;
Karachi Whites 1998-99, 2000-02; Pakistan Reserves 1999-2000; Habib Bank 1999 –
2006-07; Karachi 2003-04; Karachi Blues 2004-05
Career highlights to date: 'Playing for Pakistan. English county cricket'
Cricket moments to forget: 'The first Test match played for Pakistan' (*2-89/0-30 in
the drawn second Test at Faisalabad 2000-01*)
Cricket superstitions: 'I kiss the ground when taking the field'
Cricketers particularly admired: Abdul Qadir, Viv Richards, Joel Garner
Other sports played: Football, table tennis
Other sports followed: Football (Brazil)
Favourite band: 'I like Indian music'
Relaxations: 'Listening to music and being with family'
Extras: Represented Pakistan U19 1998-99. The second Hindu to play in Tests for
Pakistan, after his cousin Anil Dalpat. Had match figures of 12-94 (6-42/6-52) v

Bangladesh at Multan in the first match of the Asian Test Championship 2001-02, winning Man of the Match award. His other international awards include Man of the [Test] Series v Bangladesh 2001-02 and Man of the Match in the second Test v Sri Lanka at Karachi 2004-05 (3-72/7-118). Returned first innings figures of 7-188 (from 49.3 overs) in the third Test v Australia at Sydney 2004-05, in the process taking his 100th Test wicket (Shane Warne). An overseas player with Essex 2004-05; has returned for 2007

Best batting: 47 Karachi Blues v Karachi Whites, Karachi 2004-05
Best bowling: 7-39 Karachi Whites v Gujranwala, Karachi 2000-01

2006 Season

	M	Inn	NO	Runs	HS	Avg	100	50	Ct	St	Balls	Runs	Wkts	Avg	BB	5I	10M
Test	4	6	3	49	29	16.33	-	-	-	-	1338	651	13	50.07	3-77	-	-
FC	6	7	3	49	29	12.25	-	-	-	-	1842	924	23	40.17	4-32	-	-
ODI																	
List A																	
20/20 Int																	
20/20																	

Career Performances

	M	Inn	NO	Runs	HS	Avg	100	50	Ct	St	Balls	Runs	Wkts	Avg	BB	5I	10M
Test	40	54	27	175	29	6.48	-	-	11	-	11035	5565	169	32.92	7-77	11	2
FC	99	120	61	511	47	8.66	-	-	32	-	26377	12586	467	26.95	7-39	33	5
ODI	16	8	6	6	3 *	3.00	-	-	2	-	776	589	12	49.08	3-31	-	
List A	92	44	22	130	16	5.90	-	-	18	-	4731	3214	138	23.28	5-21	3	
20/20 Int																	
20/20	12	3	0	7	5	2.33	-	-	2	-	215	305	11	27.72	4-31	-	

21. Who had to postpone his wedding when called up for an unexpected Test debut v New Zealand at Christchurch in 1983-84?

DAVIES, A. P.   Glamorgan

Name: <u>Andrew</u> Philip Davies
Role: Left-hand bat, right-arm
medium-fast bowler
Born: 7 November 1976, Neath
Height: 6ft **Weight:** 12st 3lbs
Nickname: Diver
County debut: 1995
Place in batting averages: (2005 207th
av. 21.50)
Place in bowling averages: (2005 138th
av. 51.07)
Strike rate: (career 71.09)
Parents: Anne and Phil
Wife and date of marriage: Nerys,
1 February 2003
Children: Aaron and Joseph, 1 July 2005
Family links with cricket: 'Father and
brother play local league cricket'
Education: Dwr-y-Felin, Neath; Christ College, Brecon
Qualifications: GCSEs, A-levels, Level 2 coach
Off-season: 'Looking after my twin boys and computer course'
Overseas tours: Wales MC to Barbados; Glamorgan to Pretoria, to Cape Town
Overseas teams played for: Marist CC, Whangarei, New Zealand 1995-96; Marist
Old Boys, Napier, New Zealand
Career highlights to date: 'Winning two one-day championships'
Cricket moments to forget: 'Any hammering'
Cricket superstitions: 'None'
Cricketers particularly admired: Matthew Maynard, Steve Watkin
Young players to look out for: Ben Wright, Tom Maynard
Other sports followed: Football (Tottenham Hotspur)
Injuries: Out for a 'few weeks' with a slight side strain and an ankle injury
Favourite band: Oasis
Relaxations: 'Music'
Extras: Wales U19 Player of the Year 1995. Wales Player of the Year 1996. 2nd XI
cap 1998. 2nd XI Player of the Year 1998, 1999. 1st XI Player of the Month August-
September 1998. Glamorgan's leading wicket-taker (21) in the NUL 2001. Fastest
Glamorgan player to 100 one-day wickets
Best batting: 41* Glamorgan v Nottinghamshire, Trent Bridge 2005
Best bowling: 5-79 Glamorgan v Worcestershire, Cardiff 2002

2006 Season

	M	Inn	NO	Runs	HS	Avg	100	50	Ct	St	Balls	Runs	Wkts	Avg	BB	5I	10M
Test																	
FC	4	6	3	51	16	17.00	-	-	1	-	744	402	8	50.25	2-28	-	-
ODI																	
List A	14	8	4	107	24	26.75	-	-	3	-	621	594	20	29.70	3-27	-	
20/20 Int																	
20/20	5	1	1	3	3 *		-	-	1	-	114	190	4	47.50	3-34	-	

Career Performances

	M	Inn	NO	Runs	HS	Avg	100	50	Ct	St	Balls	Runs	Wkts	Avg	BB	5I	10M
Test																	
FC	34	46	11	487	41 *	13.91	-	-	8	-	4692	2858	66	43.30	5-79	1	-
ODI																	
List A	98	45	26	265	24	13.94	-	-	13	-	4277	3703	141	26.26	5-19	2	
20/20 Int																	
20/20	18	7	2	23	11	4.60	-	-	5	-	408	579	22	26.31	3-17	-	

DAVIES, M. A.   Durham

Name: <u>Mark</u> Anthony Davies
Role: Right-hand bat, right-arm fast-medium bowler
Born: 4 October 1980, Stockton-on-Tees
Height: 6ft 3in **Weight:** 13st
Nickname: Davo
County debut: 1998 (one-day), 2002 (first-class)
County cap: 2005
50 wickets in a season: 1
Place in batting averages: (2005 262nd av. 13.33)
Place in bowling averages: (2005 2nd av. 16.53)
Strike rate: (career 46.20)
Parents: Howard and Mandy
Marital status: Single
Education: Northfield School, Billingham; Stockton Sixth Form College
Qualifications: 5 GCSEs, NVQ Level 3 Sport and Recreation
Overseas tours: Durham to South Africa 2002
Overseas teams played for: North Kalgoorlie CC, Western Australia

Cricketers particularly admired: Glenn McGrath
Other sports played: Football, golf, boxing
Other sports followed: Football (Middlesbrough)
Relaxations: Socialising, golf
Extras: Represented England U19 2000. Attended Durham Academy. Was the first bowler to reach 50 first-class wickets in 2004
Best batting: 62 Durham v Somerset, Stockton 2005
Best bowling: 6-32 Durham v Worcestershire, Riverside 2005

2006 Season

	M	Inn	NO	Runs	HS	Avg	100	50	Ct	St	Balls	Runs	Wkts	Avg	BB	5I	10M
Test																	
FC	2	2	0	10	10	5.00	-	-	2	-	192	99	2	49.50	1-9	-	-
ODI																	
List A																	
20/20 Int																	
20/20																	

Career Performances

	M	Inn	NO	Runs	HS	Avg	100	50	Ct	St	Balls	Runs	Wkts	Avg	BB	5I	10M
Test																	
FC	43	65	23	488	62	11.61	-	1	9	-	6839	3298	148	22.28	6-32	7	-
ODI																	
List A	63	34	12	164	31 *	7.45	-	-	9	-	2562	1772	60	29.53	4-13	-	
20/20 Int																	
20/20	9	4	3	11	6	11.00	-	-	2	-	204	241	8	30.12	2-14	-	

DAVIES, S. M.   Worcestershire

Name: Steven (<u>Steve</u>) Michael Davies
Role: Left-hand bat, wicket-keeper
Born: 17 June 1986, Bromsgrove
Height: 5ft 11in **Weight:** 11st 7lbs
Nickname: Davo
County debut: 2004 (one-day), 2005 (first-class)
County colours: 2005
1000 runs in a season: 1
50 dismissals in a season: 1
Place in batting averages: 85th av. 37.57 (2005 103rd av. 34.83)
Parents: Lin and Michael
Marital status: Single
Education: King Charles I School
Qualifications: 9 GCSEs, 1 A-level, 2 AS-levels

Off-season: ECB National Academy
Overseas tours: England U17 to Netherlands 2003; England U19 to Bangladesh (U19 World Cup) 2003-04, to India 2004-05 (c); England A to West Indies 2005-06, to Bangladesh 2006-07
Career highlights to date: 'Maiden first-class century against Somerset'
Cricket superstitions: 'None'
Cricketers particularly admired: Adam Gilchrist, Chris Read
Young players to look out for: Adam Harrison, Will Gifford
Other sports played: Basketball (trials for England), golf
Other sports followed: Football (Arsenal)
Favourite band: Usher
Relaxations: 'Playing golf and basketball; socialising with friends; listening to music'

Extras: Represented England U19 2004, 2005. Took six catches in Leicestershire's first innings at Worcester 2006, equalling Worcestershire record for wicket-keeping catches in a first-class innings. Achieved double of 1000 (1052) runs and 50 (68) dismissals in first-class cricket 2006. ECB National Academy 2004-05 (part-time), 2005-06 (including visit to World Academy, India), 2006-07
Opinions on cricket: 'More Twenty20 cricket.'
Best batting: 192 Worcestershire v Gloucestershire, Bristol 2006

2006 Season

	M	Inn	NO	Runs	HS	Avg	100	50	Ct	St	Balls	Runs	Wkts	Avg	BB	5I	10M
Test																	
FC	17	29	1	1052	192	37.57	3	3	63	5	0	0	0		-	-	-
ODI																	
List A	17	14	2	177	52	14.75	-	1	19	7	0	0	0		-	-	
20/20 Int																	
20/20	8	6	1	97	27	19.40	-	-	2	-	0	0	0		-	-	

Career Performances

	M	Inn	NO	Runs	HS	Avg	100	50	Ct	St	Balls	Runs	Wkts	Avg	BB	5I	10M
Test																	
FC	28	48	2	1679	192	36.50	4	5	74	8	0	0	0		-	-	-
ODI																	
List A	32	27	5	374	52	17.00	-	1	31	10	0	0	0		-	-	
20/20 Int																	
20/20	8	6	1	97	27	19.40	-	-	2	-	0	0	0		-	-	

DAVIS, M. J. G. Sussex

Name: <u>Mark</u> Jeffrey Gronow Davis
Role: Right-hand bat, right-arm
off-spin bowler
Born: 10 October 1971, Port Elizabeth,
South Africa
Height: 6ft 2in **Weight:** 12st 8lbs
Nickname: Davo, Doxy, Sparky
County debut: 2001
County cap: 2002
Place in batting averages: (2005 260th
av. 14.00)
Strike rate: (career 79.63)
Parents: Jeremy and Marilyn
Wife and date of marriage: Candice,
8 April 2000
Family links with cricket: 'Father supports
Sussex. My brothers, William and Patrick,
play league cricket in Sussex'

Education: Grey High School; University of Pretoria
Qualifications: BA Psychology and English
Career outside cricket: Coach of UPE International Cricket Academy in Port
Elizabeth
Overseas tours: South Africa U24 to Sri Lanka 1995; Northern Transvaal to
Zimbabwe 1992-93, to Kenya 1994-95, 1995-96
Overseas teams played for: Northern Transvaal/Northerns 1990-91 – 1999-2000
Career highlights: 'Winning the County Championship [2003]. It was second to none,
unbelievable! That and my 168 v Middlesex the same season'
Cricket superstitions: 'None'
Cricketers particularly admired: 'All my team-mates', Tim May, Shane Warne
Other sports played: Golf, tennis
Other sports followed: Rugby ('support the Springboks'), football (Middlesbrough)
Favourite band: 'Very eclectic tastes – no real favourite'
Relaxations: 'Golf, music, going out with friends, watching good movies'
Extras: Represented South Africa A 1995. Captain of Northern Transvaal/Northerns
1997-2000, during which time the province won the first two trophies in its history.
Member of MCC. Scored maiden first-class century (111) v Somerset at Taunton 2002,
in the process sharing with Robin Martin-Jenkins (205*) in a record eighth-wicket
partnership for Sussex (291); the stand fell one run short of the record eighth-wicket
partnership in English first-class cricket, set in 1896. Retired at the end of the 2005
season to become club coach but registration retained. Is not considered an overseas
player

Best batting: 168 Sussex v Middlesex, Hove 2003
Best bowling: 8-37 Northerns B v North West, Potchefstroom 1994-95

2006 Season (did not make any first-class or one-day appearances)

Career Performances

	M	Inn	NO	Runs	HS	Avg	100	50	Ct	St	Balls	Runs	Wkts	Avg	BB	5I	10M
Test																	
FC	127	187	30	2941	168	18.73	2	8	69	-	18475	8368	232	36.06	8-37	5	1
ODI																	
List A	160	90	35	946	37	17.20	-	-	34	-	7306	5316	142	37.43	4-14	-	
20/20 Int																	
20/20	17	9	5	78	20 *	19.50	-	-	5	-	276	343	13	26.38	3-13	-	

DAWSON, L. A. Hampshire

Name: Liam Andrew Dawson
Role: Right-hand bat, slow left-arm bowler; all-rounder
Born: 1 March 1990, Swindon
Height: 5ft 8in **Weight:** 10st 7lbs
Nickname: Daws, Lemmy
County debut: No first-team appearance
Parents: Andy and Bev
Marital status: Single
Family links with cricket: 'Dad played for Goatacre and Chippenham and played representative games for Wiltshire CCC. Brother plays for Goatacre'
Education: John Bentley School
Qualifications: GCSEs
Off-season: 'Playing in Australia and training.' England U19 tour
Overseas tours: West of England U15 to

West Indies 2005; England U16 to South Africa 2006; England U19 to Malaysia 2006-07
Overseas teams played for: Melville, Perth 2006-07
Career highlights to date: 'Being given a county contract and representing England age-groups'
Cricket moments to forget: 'Being hit for 27 in a three-day game in one over!'
Cricket superstitions: 'Not really'
Cricketers particularly admired: Shane Warne, Dan Vettori

Young players to look out for: Sam Northeast, Benny Howell, Mitchell Stokes
Other sports played: Football (Calne Town)
Other sports followed: Football (Bury)
Favourite band: Coldplay
Relaxations: 'Football, going out with mates, golf'
Extras: Hampshire Academy Player of the Year 2005. Bunbury Festival All-rounder of the Tournament 2005. Played for Wiltshire in Minor Counties competitions 2006
Opinions on cricket: 'Twenty20 has brought cricket up a level with bigger crowds, which is good for the game. C&G should be a straight knockout competition, which makes it more entertaining and better games to play and watch.'

DAWSON, R. K. J.   Northamptonshire

Name: <u>Richard</u> Kevin James Dawson
Role: Right-hand bat, right-arm off-spin bowler
Born: 4 August 1980, Doncaster
Height: 6ft 4in **Weight:** 11st 4lbs
Nickname: Billy Dog
County debut: 2001 (Yorkshire)
County cap: 2004 (Yorkshire)
Test debut: 2001-02
Place in batting averages: 269th av. 10.58 (2005 139th av. 30.71)
Place in bowling averages: (2005 107th av. 40.66)
Strike rate: (career 75.75)
Parents: Kevin and Pat
Marital status: Single
Family links with cricket: Brother Gareth plays for Doncaster Town CC
Education: Batley GS; Exeter University
Qualifications: 10 GCSEs, 4 A-levels, degree in Exercise and Sports Science
Overseas tours: England U18 to Bermuda 1997; England U19 to New Zealand 1998-99; England to India and New Zealand 2001-02, to Australia 2002-03; ECB National Academy to Sri Lanka 2002-03; England A to Sri Lanka 2004-05
Cricketers particularly admired: Steve Waugh, Graeme Swann
Other sports played: Football
Other sports followed: Football (Doncaster Rovers FC)
Relaxations: Sleeping, listening to music
Extras: Captained England U15. Sir John Hobbs Silver Jubilee Memorial Prize 1995. Represented England U19 1999. Captained British Universities 2000. NBC Denis

Compton Award for the most promising young Yorkshire player 2001. Made Test debut in the first Test v India at Mohali 2001-02, taking 4-134 in India's first innings. Released by Yorkshire at the end of the 2006 season and has joined Northamptonshire for 2007

Best batting: 87 Yorkshire v Kent, Canterbury 2002
Best bowling: 6-82 Yorkshire v Glamorgan, Scarborough 2001

2006 Season

	M	Inn	NO	Runs	HS	Avg	100	50	Ct	St	Balls	Runs	Wkts	Avg	BB	5I	10M
Test																	
FC	8	13	1	127	56	10.58	-	1	2	-	1176	701	8	87.62	4-151	-	-
ODI																	
List A	13	7	0	50	24	7.14	-	-	7	-	533	435	8	54.37	3-56	-	
20/20 Int																	
20/20	9	5	2	58	22	19.33	-	-	6	-	158	203	10	20.30	3-24	-	

Career Performances

	M	Inn	NO	Runs	HS	Avg	100	50	Ct	St	Balls	Runs	Wkts	Avg	BB	5I	10M
Test	7	13	3	114	19 *	11.40	-	-	3	-	1116	677	11	61.54	4-134	-	-
FC	88	132	15	2496	87	21.33	-	11	46	-	13711	7646	181	42.24	6-82	5	-
ODI																	
List A	100	63	14	478	41	9.75	-	-	35	-	3881	3038	105	28.93	4-13	-	
20/20 Int																	
20/20	22	8	3	71	22	14.20	-	-	7	-	449	558	24	23.25	3-24	-	

22. Who was the first player to make 300 ODI appearances?

DEAN, K. J.   Derbyshire

Name: <u>Kevin</u> James Dean
Role: Left-hand bat, left-arm medium bowler
Born: 16 October 1975, Derby
Height: 6ft 5in **Weight:** 14st
Nickname: Deany, Red Face, The Wall,
George
County debut: 1996
County cap: 1998
Benefit: 2006
50 wickets in a season: 2
Strike rate: (career 45.87)
Parents: Ken and Dorothy
Marital status: Engaged to Sharon
Education: Leek High School; Leek College
of Further Education
Qualifications: 8 GCSEs, 1 AS-level,
3 A-levels, ECB Level 2 coaching
Career outside cricket: 'Professional
gambler/tipster'

Off-season: 'Continued work on becoming a professional punter and tipster [with]
sessions at Uttoxeter Racecourse'
Overseas tours: MCC to Australia 2002-03
Overseas teams played for: Sturt CC, Adelaide 1996-97
Career highlights to date: 'Can't split – 1) Hitting the winning runs against Australia
for Derbyshire in 1997; 2) Getting either hat-trick'
Cricket moments to forget: 'Spending time out injured'
Cricket superstitions: 'Last person out of changing room for first session of fielding'
Cricketers particularly admired: Dominic Cork, Wasim Akram, Michael Holding
Young players to look out for: Dan Redfern
Other sports played: Football, golf, tennis, snooker
Other sports followed: Football (Derby County), horse racing
Favourite band: Stereophonics
Extras: Achieved first-class hat-trick (E. Smith, Hooper, Llong) against Kent at Derby
1998. Took second first-class hat-trick (Habib, Kumble, Ormond) v Leicestershire at
Leicester 2000. Joint leading wicket-taker in English first-class cricket 2002 (with
Martin Saggers) with 83 wickets (av. 23.50). Derbyshire Player of the Year 2002
(jointly with Michael DiVenuto)
Best batting: 54* Derbyshire v Worcestershire, Derby 2002
Best bowling: 8-52 Derbyshire v Kent, Canterbury 2000

2006 Season

	M	Inn	NO	Runs	HS	Avg	100	50	Ct	St	Balls	Runs	Wkts	Avg	BB	5I	10M
Test																	
FC	5	5	2	19	18	6.33	-	-	-	-	539	364	6	60.66	2-32	-	-
ODI																	
List A	13	6	2	4	3	1.00	-	-	-	-	612	500	18	27.77	3-39	-	
20/20 Int																	
20/20	8	3	3	8	8 *		-	-	2	-	164	217	8	27.12	2-14	-	

Career Performances

	M	Inn	NO	Runs	HS	Avg	100	50	Ct	St	Balls	Runs	Wkts	Avg	BB	5I	10M
Test																	
FC	105	141	44	1130	54 *	11.64	-	2	20	-	16698	9549	364	26.23	8-52	15	4
ODI																	
List A	137	62	32	239	16 *	7.96	-	-	24	-	6047	4612	156	29.56	5-32	2	
20/20 Int																	
20/20	15	4	4	11	8 *		-	-	4	-	278	363	11	33.00	2-14	-	

DENLY, J. L.   Kent

Name: Joseph (<u>Joe</u>) Liam Denly
Role: Right-hand bat,
leg-spin bowler
Born: 16 March 1986, Canterbury
Height: 6ft **Weight:** 11st 9lbs
Nickname: No Pants
County debut: 2004
Strike rate: (career 54.00)
Parents: Jayne and Nick
Marital status: Single
Family links with cricket: 'Dad and brother
play local cricket'
Education: Chaucer Technology School
Qualifications: 10 GCSEs, Level 1 coach
Off-season: 'Sydney, Australia'
Overseas tours: England U18 to Netherlands
2003; England U19 to India 2004-05
Overseas teams played for: Hamersley
Carine, Perth 2003; UTS Balmain Tigers, Sydney 2005-07
Career highlights to date: 'First first-class hundred'
Cricket moments to forget: 'Golden duck on first-class debut'
Cricket superstitions: 'Left pad on first'

Cricketers particularly admired: Steve Waugh
Young players to look out for: Sam Denly
Other sports played: Football (Charlton Athletic U14, U15)
Other sports followed: Football (Arsenal)
Favourite band: Westlife
Extras: Has represented England U17, U18 and U19
Opinions on cricket: 'It's great.'
Best batting: 115 Kent v CUCCE, Fenner's 2006
Best bowling: 2-40 Kent v CUCCE, Fenner's 2006

2006 Season

	M	Inn	NO	Runs	HS	Avg	100	50	Ct	St	Balls	Runs	Wkts	Avg	BB	5I	10M
Test																	
FC	3	5	1	387	115	96.75	2	2	1	-	216	104	4	26.00	2-40	-	-
ODI																	
List A	4	4	1	115	70	38.33	-	1	2	-	0	0	0			-	-
20/20 Int																	
20/20	1	1	0	2	2	2.00	-	-	-	-	0	0	0			-	-

Career Performances

	M	Inn	NO	Runs	HS	Avg	100	50	Ct	St	Balls	Runs	Wkts	Avg	BB	5I	10M
Test																	
FC	5	8	1	401	115	57.28	2	2	1	-	216	104	4	26.00	2-40	-	-
ODI																	
List A	11	11	2	193	70	21.44	-	1	2	-	0	0	0			-	-
20/20 Int																	
20/20	4	2	0	6	4	3.00	-	-	2	-	0	0	0			-	-

DENNINGTON, M. J.   Kent

Name: Matthew (<u>Matt</u>) John Dennington
Role: Right-hand bat, right-arm medium-fast bowler
Born: 16 October 1982, Durban, South Africa
Height: 6ft 1in **Weight:** 12st 10lbs
Nickname: Denners, Denzel
County debut: 2003 (one-day), 2004 (first-class)
Place in batting averages: (2005 198th av. 23.00)
Strike rate: (career 57.21)
Parents: John and Yvonne
Marital status: Single
Education: Northwood Boys, Durban; Varsity College and University of South Africa (UNISA)
Qualifications: Matriculation

Overseas teams played for: Crusaders CC, Durban 1998-2002; KwaZulu-Natal B 2002-03

Career highlights to date: 'Taking three wickets in a Championship game against Surrey and getting 50* to save the game'

Cricket moments to forget: 'Colliding with team-mate going for a catch on the boundary and breaking my kneecap'

Cricket superstitions: 'Not a superstitious cricketer'

Cricketers particularly admired: Paddy Clift, Allan Donald

Other sports played: Golf

Other sports followed: Rugby (Natal Sharks)

Favourite band: Red Hot Chili Peppers

Relaxations: 'Going to gym; surfing and other watersports; playing golf'

Extras: Natal Schools 1999-2000. Natal Academy 2001-02. Natal B 2002. Released by Kent at the end of the 2006 season

Best batting: 55 Kent v Hampshire, Canterbury 2005

Best bowling: 3-23 Kent v Bangladesh A, Canterbury 2005

2006 Season

	M	Inn	NO	Runs	HS	Avg	100	50	Ct	St	Balls	Runs	Wkts	Avg	BB	5I	10M
Test																	
FC	1	1	1	2	2*		-	-	-	-	156	50	3	16.66	2-21	-	-
ODI																	
List A	1	0	0	0	0		-	-	-	-	60	63	0			-	-
20/20 Int																	
20/20																	

Career Performances

	M	Inn	NO	Runs	HS	Avg	100	50	Ct	St	Balls	Runs	Wkts	Avg	BB	5I	10M
Test																	
FC	12	18	4	271	55	19.35	-	3	5	-	1087	624	19	32.84	3-23	-	-
ODI																	
List A	17	12	4	99	26*	12.37	-	-	3	-	600	634	7	90.57	3-53	-	
20/20 Int																	
20/20	8	3	0	22	12	7.33	-	-	2	-	144	222	9	24.66	4-28	-	

DERNBACH, J. W. — Surrey

Name: <u>Jade</u> Winston Dernbach
Role: Right-hand bat, right-arm fast bowler
Born: 3 March 1986, Johannesburg,
South Africa
Height: 6ft 2in **Weight:** 13st
County debut: 2003
Strike rate: (career 70.44)
Parents: Carmen and Graeme
Marital status: Single
Education: St John the Baptist
Overseas tours: La Manga tournament,
Spain 2003
Career highlights to date: 'Making my first-
team debut for Surrey against India A'
Cricket moments to forget: 'Going out first
ball in the ECB U17 final in 2003'
Cricketers particularly admired: Jacques
Kallis, Jonty Rhodes, James Anderson,
Rikki Clarke

Other sports played: Rugby (Surrey U16)
Other sports followed: Football (Arsenal)
Favourite band: Usher
Relaxations: 'Going out with friends; swimming, playing football and rugby; listening
to music'
Extras: Sir Jack Hobbs Fair Play Award. Surrey U19 Player of the Year. Made first-
class debut v India A at The Oval 2003 aged 17, becoming the youngest player for 30
years to play first-class cricket for Surrey. Surrey Academy 2003, 2004
Best batting: 9 Surrey v Gloucestershire, Bristol 2006
Best bowling: 3-67 Surrey v Gloucestershire, Bristol 2006

2006 Season

	M	Inn	NO	Runs	HS	Avg	100	50	Ct	St	Balls	Runs	Wkts	Avg	BB	5I	10M
Test																	
FC	2	3	2	13	9	13.00	-	-	-	-	266	165	4	41.25	3-67	-	-
ODI																	
List A	12	5	1	7	4	1.75	-	-	4	-	402	453	16	28.31	3-36	-	
20/20 Int																	
20/20	8	2	0	1	1	.50	-	-	2	-	131	215	5	43.00	1-19	-	

Career Performances

	M	Inn	NO	Runs	HS	Avg	100	50	Ct	St	Balls	Runs	Wkts	Avg	BB	5I	10M
Test																	
FC	6	7	4	18	9	6.00	-	-	1	-	634	500	9	55.55	3-67	-	-
ODI																	
List A	19	7	1	29	21	4.83	-	-	6	-	666	703	26	27.03	4-36	-	
20/20 Int																	
20/20	9	2	0	1	1	.50	-	-	3	-	155	267	5	53.40	1-19	-	

DEXTER, N. J.   Kent

Name: <u>Neil</u> John Dexter
Role: Right-hand bat, right-arm medium bowler; all-rounder
Born: 21 August 1984, Johannesburg, South Africa
Height: 6ft **Weight:** 11st 4lbs
Nickname: Ted, Dex, Sexy Dexy
County debut: 2005
Place in batting averages: 26th av. 57.87
Strike rate: (career 90.75)
Parents: John and Susan
Marital status: Single
Education: Northwood School, Durban; UNISA (University of South Africa)
Qualifications: Matriculation
Off-season: 'Going back to Durban; working on all-round fitness'
Overseas teams played for: Crusaders CC 2000-06
Career highlights to date: 'Scoring first ton against Glamorgan 2006'
Cricket moments to forget: 'Being hit for 25 in one over against Worcester'
Cricketers particularly admired: Steve Waugh, Brett Lee
Young players to look out for: Alex Blake, Sam Northeast, Joe Denly
Other sports played: Golf, tennis, 'most sports'
Other sports followed: Football (Man Utd)
Favourite band: Simple Plan, Goo Goo Dolls
Relaxations: 'Lying around doing nothing'
Extras: Played for Natal U13-19, Natal Academy and Natal A. Is not considered an overseas player
Opinions on cricket: 'Very professional with lots of opportunities.'
Best batting : 131* Kent v Nottinghamshire, Canterbury 2006
Best bowling : 2-40 Kent v Lancashire, Old Trafford 2006

2006 Season

	M	Inn	NO	Runs	HS	Avg	100	50	Ct	St	Balls	Runs	Wkts	Avg	BB	5I	10M
Test																	
FC	8	12	4	463	131 *	57.87	2	1	3	-	534	281	6	46.83	2-40	-	-
ODI																	
List A	15	13	1	437	135 *	36.41	1	1	3	-	186	158	7	22.57	3-17	-	
20/20 Int																	
20/20	9	9	0	167	36	18.55	-	-	7	-	90	155	4	38.75	3-27	-	

Career Performances

	M	Inn	NO	Runs	HS	Avg	100	50	Ct	St	Balls	Runs	Wkts	Avg	BB	5I	10M
Test																	
FC	11	18	5	639	131 *	49.15	2	3	7	-	726	442	8	55.25	2-40	-	-
ODI																	
List A	17	15	1	442	135 *	31.57	1	1	3	-	246	226	10	22.60	3-17	-	
20/20 Int																	
20/20	9	9	0	167	36	18.55	-	-	7	-	90	155	4	38.75	3-27	-	

DIVENUTO, M. J.   Durham

Name: <u>Michael</u> James DiVenuto
Role: Left-hand bat, right-arm medium/
leg-break bowler
Born: 12 December 1973, Hobart, Tasmania
Height: 5ft 11in **Weight:** 12st 12lbs
Nickname: Diva
County debut: 1999 (Sussex),
2000 (Derbyshire)
County cap: 1999 (Sussex),
2000 (Derbyshire)
ODI debut: 1996-97
1000 runs in a season: 6
1st-Class 200s: 2
Place in batting averages: 31st av. 54.45
(2005 37th av. 49.70)
Strike rate: (career 160.20)
Parents: Enrico and Elizabeth
Wife and date of marriage: Renae,
31 December 2003
Children: Sophia Lily, 21 March 2005
Family links with cricket: 'Dad and older brother Peter both played grade cricket in
Tasmania.' Brother Peter also played for Italy

Education: St Virgil's College, Hobart

Qualifications: HSC (5 x Level III subjects), Level 3 cricket coach

Off-season: 'Playing for Tasmania'

Overseas tours: Australian Cricket Academy to India and Sri Lanka 1993, to South Africa 1996; Australia A to Malaysia (Super 8s) 1997 (c), to Scotland and Ireland 1998 (c), to Los Angeles 1999; Australia to South Africa 1996-97 (one-day series), to Hong Kong (Super 6s) 1997, to Malaysia (Super 8s) 1998; Tasmania to Zimbabwe 1995-96

Overseas teams played for: North Hobart CC, Tasmania; Kingborough, Tasmania; Tasmania 1991-92 –

Career highlights to date: 'Playing for Australia. Man of the Match award v South Africa at Johannesburg 1997. Dismissing Jamie Cox at Taunton in 1999, my first wicket in first-class cricket'

Cricket moments to forget: 'Being dismissed by Jamie Cox at Taunton in 1999, *his* first wicket in first-class cricket'

Cricketers particularly admired: David Boon, Dean Jones, Kepler Wessels, Mark and Steve Waugh

Other sports played: Australian Rules (Tasmanian U15, U16 and Sandy Bay FC)

Other sports followed: Australian Rules football (Geelong Cats)

Injuries: Out for the last few weeks of the 2006 season with a groin injury

Favourite band: U2

Relaxations: Golf, sleeping and eating

Extras: Man of the Match for his 89 in fifth ODI v South Africa at Johannesburg 1997. Was Sussex overseas player 1999; an overseas player with Derbyshire 2000-06. Scored 173* v Derbyshire Board XI at Derby in NatWest 2000, a record for Derbyshire in one-day cricket. Carried his bat for 192* v Middlesex at Lord's 2002; also scored 113 in the second innings. Derbyshire Player of the Year 2002 (jointly with Kevin Dean). First batsman to 1000 Championship runs 2003. Vice-captain of Derbyshire 2002-06 (was appointed captain for 2004 but was unable to take up post due to back surgery). Has joined Durham as an overseas player for 2007

Opinions on cricket: 'I think the game is in great shape at the moment. Plenty of interest in cricket thanks to the Ashes [2005]. In domestic cricket players need more time between games for recovery and preparation.'

Best batting: 230 Derbyshire v Northamptonshire, Derby 2002

Best bowling: 1-0 Tasmania v Queensland, Brisbane 1999-2000

2006 Season

	M	Inn	NO	Runs	HS	Avg	100	50	Ct	St	Balls	Runs	Wkts	Avg	BB	5I	10M
Test																	
FC	14	23	1	1198	161 *	54.45	3	7	19	-	0	0	0		-	-	-
ODI																	
List A	11	11	1	294	93 *	29.40	-	2	4	-	0	0	0		-	-	
20/20 Int																	
20/20	8	7	0	146	53	20.85	-	1	1	-	0	0	0		-	-	

Career Performances

	M	Inn	NO	Runs	HS	Avg	100	50	Ct	St	Balls	Runs	Wkts	Avg	BB	5I	10M
Test																	
FC	231	409	20	16745	230	43.04	36	101	261	-	801	480	5	96.00	1-0	-	-
ODI	9	9	0	241	89	26.77	-	2	1	-	0	0	0		-	-	
List A	244	239	16	7617	173 *	34.15	13	38	92	-	200	181	5	36.20	1-10	-	
20/20 Int																	
20/20	23	22	3	553	77 *	29.10	-	5	3	-	78	88	5	17.60	3-19	-	

DIXEY, P. G.   Kent

Name: <u>Paul</u> Garrod Dixey
Role: Right-hand bat, wicket-keeper
Born: 2 November 1987, Canterbury
Height: 5ft 8in **Weight:** 10st 7lbs
Nickname: Dix
County debut: 2005
Parents: James and Lindsay
Marital status: Single
Family links with cricket: 'Dad used to play club cricket for St Lawrence and Highland Court'
Education: King's School, Canterbury; Durham University (Hatfield College)
Qualifications: 8 GCSEs, 4 AS-levels, 3 A-levels
Off-season: 'Studying Geology at Durham University; training with Durham UCCE'
Overseas tours: England U16 to South Africa
Career highlights to date: 'First-class debut against Bangladesh A at Canterbury'
Cricket moments to forget: 'Losing to Western Province U17 at Fairbairn College off the last ball of a closely fought two-day game'

Cricket superstitions: 'None'
Cricketers particularly admired: Adam Gilchrist, Ian Healy, Alan Knott
Young players to look out for: Alex Blake, Sam Northeast, James Iles
Other sports played: Hockey, rugby
Other sports followed: Rugby ('follow the Premiership')
Favourite band: Ne-Yo
Relaxations: 'Skiing, fly fishing, listening to music'
Extras: *Daily Telegraph* Bunbury ESCA Wicket-keeping Scholarship Award 2003; Magic Moment Award (Bunbury 2003). Represented England U19 2006
Opinions on cricket: 'As a young player hoping to make my way in the game, I am pleased to see the new ruling of limiting overseas players to one per county.'
Best batting: 24 Kent v Bangladesh A, Canterbury 2005

2006 Season

	M	Inn	NO	Runs	HS	Avg	100	50	Ct	St	Balls	Runs	Wkts	Avg	BB	5I	10M
Test																	
FC	1	1	0	0	0	0.00	-	-	3	-	0	0	0		-	-	-
ODI																	
List A																	
20/20 Int																	
20/20																	

Career Performances

	M	Inn	NO	Runs	HS	Avg	100	50	Ct	St	Balls	Runs	Wkts	Avg	BB	5I	10M
Test																	
FC	2	3	1	40	24	20.00	-	-	6	-	0	0	0		-	-	-
ODI																	
List A																	
20/20 Int																	
20/20																	

23. Which current batsman won a
NatWest Man of the Match award on his competition
debut in the final at Lord's 1988?

DOSHI, N. D.　　　　　　　　　　　　　Surrey

Name: <u>Nayan</u> Dilip Doshi
Role: Right-hand bat, left-arm spin bowler
Born: 6 October 1978, Nottingham
Height: 6ft 4in
Nickname: Dosh, Troll, Turtlehead
County debut: 2004
County cap: 2006
50 wickets in a season: 1
Place in bowling averages: 31st av. 28.11
(2005 134th av. 47.26)
Strike rate: 55.15 (career 66.42)
Parents: Dilip and Kalindi
Marital status: Married
Family links with cricket: Father is former
India Test and ODI spin bowler Dilip Doshi,
who also played for Nottinghamshire and
Warwickshire
Education: King Alfred School, London
Career outside cricket: Family business
Overseas teams played for: Saurashtra, India 2001-02 –
Career highlights to date: 'Twenty20 semi-final 2004'
Cricket moments to forget: 'Too many'
Cricketers particularly admired: Viv Richards, Sachin Tendulkar, Garfield Sobers
Favourite band: 'Like lots of them'
Relaxations: Wildlife photography
Extras: Made first-class debut for Saurashtra v Baroda at Rajkot 2001-02. Recorded
maiden first-class ten-wicket match return (5-125/6-57) v Lancashire at Old Trafford
2004 and another (3-73/7-110) v Sussex at Hove in the following Championship
match. Took 21 wickets in the Twenty20 Cup 2006, breaking the competition season
record of 20 held by Adam Hollioake. Is England-qualified
Best batting: 37 Saurashtra v Vidarbha, Rajkot 2005-06
Best bowling: 7-110 Surrey v Sussex, Hove 2004

2006 Season

	M	Inn	NO	Runs	HS	Avg	100	50	Ct	St	Balls	Runs	Wkts	Avg	BB	5I	10M
Test																	
FC	14	13	8	106	32	21.20	-	-	3	-	2813	1434	51	28.11	6-91	1	1
ODI																	
List A	14	7	0	37	24	5.28	-	-	6	-	634	677	25	27.08	5-30	1	
20/20 Int																	
20/20	10	3	2	2	1 *	2.00	-	-	3	-	210	243	21	11.57	4-22	-	

Career Performances

	M	Inn	NO	Runs	HS	Avg	100	50	Ct	St	Balls	Runs	Wkts	Avg	BB	5I	10M
Test																	
FC	47	61	15	451	37	9.80	-	-	7	-	8170	4261	123	34.64	7-110	5	3
ODI																	
List A	55	25	6	190	38 *	10.00	-	-	13	-	2287	2136	52	41.07	5-30	1	
20/20 Int																	
20/20	27	6	4	4	1 *	2.00	-	-	9	-	540	634	46	13.78	4-22	-	

DURSTON, W. J. Somerset

Name: Wesley (<u>Wes</u>) John Durston
Role: Right-hand bat, right-arm off-spin bowler, 'very occasional' wicket-keeper
Born: 6 October 1980, Taunton
Height: 5ft 10in **Weight:** 12st 7lbs
Nickname: Bestie
County debut: 2002
Place in batting averages: 81st av. 38.25 (2005 98th av. 35.88)
Place in bowling averages: 112th av. 41.60
Strike rate: 67.50 (career 73.37)
Parents: Gill and Steve
Wife and date of marriage: Christina, 4 October 2003
Children: Daisy, 4 July 2004; Joseph, 29 September 2006
Family links with cricket: 'Dad and my two brothers, Dan and Greg, all play. On occasions all four played in same local team (Compton Dundon)'
Education: Millfield School; University College Worcester
Qualifications: 3 A-levels, BSc Sport & Exercise Science, ECB Level II cricket coaching, Level 1 hockey coaching, Level 1 football coaching
Career outside cricket: 'Coaching at Millfield School'
Off-season: 'Working at my game and fitness in Taunton, whilst coaching hockey and cricket at Millfield School'
Overseas tours: West of England to West Indies 1996; Somerset to Cape Town 2006
Career highlights to date: 'Winning the Twenty20 trophy with Somerset CCC in 2005. Maiden first-class century v Derbyshire (August 2005)'
Cricket moments to forget: 'Being out lbw for first-ball duck on Sky Sports (v Kent 2006)'
Cricket superstitions: 'Right foot on to and off field first. Saluting magpies'

Cricketers particularly admired: Ian Botham
Young players to look out for: Rory Hamilton-Brown, Craig Kieswetter, Joseph Durston
Other sports played: Hockey (Taunton Vale), golf, 'any pub sport'
Other sports followed: Football (Man Utd)
Injuries: Out for three weeks with a fractured finger
Favourite band: Barenaked Ladies
Relaxations: 'Time at home with family; playing cards'
Extras: Captained winning Lord's Taverners team v Shrewsbury School at Trent Bridge 1996. Wetherell Schools All-rounder Award 1999; scored 956 runs and took 35 wickets. Has captained Somerset 2nd XI on occasion. Scored 44-ball 55 on first-class debut at Taunton 2002 as Somerset, chasing 454 to win, tied with West Indies A. Attended World Cricket Academy, Mumbai, 2005
Opinions on cricket: 'With the success of Twenty20 it may be very easy to lose sight of the importance of Championship cricket, which would be very detrimental to the game, as it provides English cricket with the only specific grooming for the Test arena.'
Best batting: 146* Somerset v Derbyshire, Derby 2005
Best bowling: 3-23 Somerset v Sri Lanka A, Taunton 2004

2006 Season

	M	Inn	NO	Runs	HS	Avg	100	50	Ct	St	Balls	Runs	Wkts	Avg	BB	5I	10M
Test																	
FC	13	23	3	765	89	38.25	-	7	15	-	675	416	10	41.60	2-31	-	-
ODI																	
List A	17	14	4	248	62 *	24.80	-	2	5	-	228	234	8	29.25	3-44	-	
20/20 Int																	
20/20	6	4	1	17	7	5.66	-	-	1	-	58	80	2	40.00	2-25	-	

Career Performances

	M	Inn	NO	Runs	HS	Avg	100	50	Ct	St	Balls	Runs	Wkts	Avg	BB	5I	10M
Test																	
FC	25	43	6	1303	146 *	35.21	1	8	33	-	1761	1170	24	48.75	3-23	-	-
ODI																	
List A	38	33	12	677	62 *	32.23	-	5	9	-	648	652	18	36.22	3-44	-	
20/20 Int																	
20/20	24	19	5	218	34	15.57	-	-	7	-	136	211	10	21.10	3-25	-	

EALHAM, M. A.   Nottinghamshire

Name: <u>Mark</u> Alan Ealham
Role: Right-hand bat, right-arm
medium bowler; all-rounder
Born: 27 August 1969, Ashford, Kent
Height: 5ft 10in **Weight:** 14st
Nickname: Ealy, Border, Skater
County debut: 1989 (Kent),
2004 (Nottinghamshire)
County cap: 1992 (Kent),
2004 (Nottinghamshire)
Benefit: 2003 (Kent)
Test debut: 1996
ODI debut: 1996
1000 runs in a season: 1
50 wickets in a season: 1
Place in batting averages: 129th av. 31.82
(2005 147th av. 30.25)
Place in bowling averages: 5th av. 20.78
(2005 5th av. 20.80)
Strike rate: 46.91 (career 57.83)
Parents: Alan and Sue
Wife and date of marriage: Kirsty, 24 February 1996
Children: George, 8 March 2002
Family links with cricket: Father played for Kent
Education: Stour Valley Secondary School
Qualifications: 9 CSEs
Career outside cricket: Plumber

Overseas tours: England A to Australia 1996-97, to Kenya and Sri Lanka 1997-98;
England VI to Hong Kong 1997, 2001; England to Sharjah (Champions Trophy) 1997-
98, to Bangladesh (Wills International Cup) 1998-99, to Australia 1998-99 (CUB
Series), to Sharjah (Coca-Cola Cup) 1998-99, to South Africa and Zimbabwe 1999-
2000 (one-day series), to Kenya (ICC Knockout Trophy) 2000-01, to Pakistan and Sri
Lanka 2000-01 (one-day series)
Overseas teams played for: South Perth, Australia 1992-93; University, Perth
1993-94
Cricketers particularly admired: Ian Botham, Viv Richards, Robin Smith,
Steve Waugh, Paul Blackmore and Albert 'for his F and G'
Other sports followed: Football (Manchester United), 'and most other sports'
Relaxations: Playing golf and snooker, watching films
Extras: Set then record for fastest Sunday League century (44 balls), v Derbyshire at
Maidstone 1995. Represented England in the 1999 World Cup. Returned a then

England best ODI bowling analysis with his 5-15 v Zimbabwe at Kimberley in January 2000; all five were lbw. Vice-captain of Kent 2001. Won the Walter Lawrence Trophy 2006 (fastest first-class century of the season) for his 45-ball hundred (finishing with 112*) v MCC at Lord's

Best batting: 153* Kent v Northamptonshire, Canterbury 2001
Best bowling: 8-36 Kent v Warwickshire, Edgbaston 1996

2006 Season

	M	Inn	NO	Runs	HS	Avg	100	50	Ct	St	Balls	Runs	Wkts	Avg	BB	5I	10M
Test																	
FC	17	26	3	732	112 *	31.82	2	4	13	-	2158	956	46	20.78	5-59	2	-
ODI																	
List A	11	9	0	107	51	11.88	-	1	5	-	396	265	14	18.92	4-53	-	
20/20 Int																	
20/20	11	9	4	129	39 *	25.80	-	-	1	-	250	289	9	32.11	2-27	-	

Career Performances

	M	Inn	NO	Runs	HS	Avg	100	50	Ct	St	Balls	Runs	Wkts	Avg	BB	5I	10M
Test	8	13	3	210	53 *	21.00	-	2	4	-	1060	488	17	28.70	4-21	-	-
FC	240	369	55	10227	153 *	32.57	12	63	127	-	31982	15206	553	27.49	8-36	22	1
ODI	64	45	4	716	45	17.46	-	-	9	-	3227	2197	67	32.79	5-15	2	
List A	385	317	69	6061	112	24.43	1	26	104	-	17141	11699	432	27.08	6-53	4	
20/20 Int																	
20/20	27	25	5	416	91	20.80	-	1	2	-	608	692	23	30.08	2-22	-	

24. Which landmark match took place at Oxford
from 14 to 16 April 1992?

EDWARDS, N. J. Somerset

Name: <u>Neil</u> James Edwards
Role: Left-hand bat, occasional
right-arm medium bowler
Born: 14 October 1983, Truro, Cornwall
Height: 6ft 3in **Weight:** 14st
Nickname: Toastie, Shanksy
County debut: 2002
Place in batting averages: 136th av. 30.90
Strike rate: (career 140.50)
Parents: Lynn and John
Marital status: Single
Family links with cricket: 'Cousin played
first-class cricket for Worcestershire'
Education: Cape Cornwall School; Richard
Huish College
Qualifications: 11 GCSEs, 3 A-levels,
Level 1 coach
Overseas tours: Cornwall U13 to South

Africa 1997; West of England to West Indies 1999; Somerset Academy to Australia
2002; England U19 to Australia 2002-03
Career highlights to date: '160 for Somerset v Hampshire in County Championship
2003'
Cricket moments to forget: 'Duck on debut for Cornwall'
Cricket superstitions: 'Never change batting gloves when batting'
Cricketers particularly admired: Marcus Trescothick, Matthew Hayden
Other sports played: Football
Other sports followed: Football (Stoke City FC)
Favourite band: 'I listen to any music'
Extras: Scored 213 for Cornwall U19 v Dorset U19 at 16 years old. Scored a second
innings 97 in England U19's victory over Australia U19 in the first 'Test' at Adelaide
2002-03. Represented England U19 2003. Somerset Wyverns Award for Best
Performance by an Uncapped Player 2003 (160 v Hampshire)
Best batting: 160 Somerset v Hampshire, Taunton 2003
Best bowling: 1-16 Somerset v Derbyshire, Taunton 2004

2006 Season

	M	Inn	NO	Runs	HS	Avg	100	50	Ct	St	Balls	Runs	Wkts	Avg	BB	5I	10M
Test																	
FC	7	10	0	309	77	30.90	-	2	4	-	18	12	0		-	-	-
ODI																	
List A	5	5	0	113	65	22.60	-	1	1	-	0	0	0		-	-	
20/20 Int																	
20/20																	

Career Performances

	M	Inn	NO	Runs	HS	Avg	100	50	Ct	St	Balls	Runs	Wkts	Avg	BB	5I	10M
Test																	
FC	24	41	0	1306	160	31.85	1	5	17	-	281	193	2	96.50	1-16	-	-
ODI																	
List A	5	5	0	113	65	22.60	-	1	1	-	0	0	0		-	-	
20/20 Int																	
20/20	1	1	0	1	1	1.00	-	-	-	-	0	0	0		-	-	

ELLIOTT, M. T. G.   Yorkshire

Name: <u>Matthew</u> Thomas Gray Elliott
Role: Left-hand bat, left-arm
orthodox bowler
Born: 28 September 1971, Chelsea,
Victoria, Australia
Height: 6ft 3in **Weight:** 13st 8lbs
Nickname: Hoarse, Herb
County debut: 2000 (Glamorgan),
2002 (Yorkshire)
County cap: 2000 (Glamorgan)
Test debut: 1996-97
ODI debut: 1997
1000 runs in a season: 2
1st-Class 200s: 2
Place in batting averages: (2005 23rd
av. 53.28)
Strike rate: (career 95.53)
Parents: John and Glenda
Wife and date of marriage: Megan, 11 December 1994
Children: Zachary, 22 November 1997; Samuel, 18 February 2000;
William, June 2004
Education: Kyabram Secondary College

Qualifications: VCE
Overseas tours: Young Australia (Australia A) to England and Netherlands 1995; Australia to South Africa 1996-97, to England 1997, to West Indies 1998-99; FICA World XI to New Zealand 2004-05
Overseas teams played for: Victoria 1992-93 – 2004-05; South Australia 2005-06 –
Career highlights to date: 'Taking the 2002 C&G Trophy through Scarborough on an open-top bus with a police escort!'
Cricket moments to forget: 'Being dismissed by Dean Cosker at Sophia Gardens in '97!'
Cricket superstitions: 'Always put left shoe on first'
Cricketers particularly admired: Shane Warne, Allan Border, Steve Waugh
Other sports played: Australian Rules football
Other sports followed: Australian Rules football (Collingwood FC)
Relaxations: 'Fishing; reading biographies; drinking Corona'
Extras: Scored 556 runs (av. 55.60) in the 1997 Ashes series. One of *Wisden*'s Five Cricketers of the Year 1998. Sheffield Shield Player of the Year 1995-96 and 1998-99. An overseas player with Glamorgan 2000, 2004 and 2005. Scored 177 and shared in a Glamorgan record first-wicket partnership of 374 with Stephen James v Sussex at Colwyn Bay 2000. Was Yorkshire's overseas player for the latter part of 2002 and has returned for the first part of 2007 as a locum for Younus Khan. C&G Man of the Match award for his 128* in the final v Somerset at Lord's 2002. Pura Cup Player of the Year 2003-04 and Man of the Match in the final v Queensland at Melbourne (155/55*). *Wisden Australia*'s Pura Cup Cricketer of the Year 2004-05
Best batting: 203 Victoria v Tasmania, Melbourne 1995-96
Best bowling: 3-68 Victoria v Queensland, Melbourne 2004-05

2006 Season (did not make any first-class or one-day appearances)

Career Performances

	M	Inn	NO	Runs	HS	Avg	100	50	Ct	St	Balls	Runs	Wkts	Avg	BB	5I	10M
Test	21	36	1	1172	199	33.48	3	4	14	-	12	4	0		-	-	
FC	194	357	27	16312	203	49.43	50	77	213	-	1242	754	13	58.00	3-68	-	-
ODI	1	1	0	1	1	1.00	-	-	-	-	0	0	0		-	-	
List A	140	136	19	5125	156	43.80	13	30	55	-	92	92	0		-	-	
20/20 Int																	
20/20	9	9	1	276	52 *	34.50	-	2	3	-	0	0	0		-	-	

ERVINE, S. M.   Hampshire

Name: <u>Sean</u> Michael Ervine
Role: Left-hand bat, right-arm
medium-fast bowler; all-rounder
Born: 6 December 1982, Harare, Zimbabwe
Height: 6ft 2in **Weight:** 14st
Nickname: Slug
County debut: 2005
County cap: 2005
Test debut: 2003
ODI debut: 2001-02
Place in batting averages: 180th av. 24.42
(2005 144th av. 30.40)
Place in bowling averages: 107th av. 40.76
(2005 75th av. 32.38)
Strike rate: 68.34 (career 60.62)
Parents: Rory and Judy
Marital status: Single
Family links with cricket: 'Grandfather
played cricket for Rhodesia and father and uncle both played for Rhodesia'
Education: Lomagundi College, Zimbabwe
Qualifications: 5 O-levels, Levels 1 and 2 coaching
Off-season: 'Playing for Western Australia'
Overseas tours: Zimbabwe U19 to Sri Lanka (U19 World Cup) 1999-2000, to New
Zealand (U19 World Cup) 2001-02; Zimbabwe to Bangladesh 2001-02, to Sri Lanka
2001-02 (one-day series), to Sri Lanka (ICC Champions Trophy) 2002-03, to England
2003, to Australia 2003-04, plus one-day tournaments in Sharjah
Overseas teams played for: Midlands, Zimbabwe 2001-02 – 2003-04; Western
Australia 2006-07
Cricket moments to forget: 'Fielding the ball off my own bowling and rupturing my
knee, needing a total knee reconstruction'
Cricket superstitions: 'None'
Cricketers particularly admired: Andy Flower, Shane Warne
Young players to look out for: Shaun Marsh (Western Australia)
Other sports played: Golf, tennis, squash, fishing
Other sports followed: AFL (Kangaroos)
Injuries: Out for the Twenty20 Cup with a knee injury; for the last two weeks of the
season with an ankle injury
Favourite band: Snow Patrol
Relaxations: 'Music, art'
Extras: CFX [Zimbabwean] Academy 2000-01. Represented Zimbabwe in the World
Cup 2002-03. Struck 99-ball century (100) at Adelaide in the VB Series 2003-04 as
Zimbabwe fell just three runs short of India's 280-7. Man of the Match in the first Test

v Bangladesh at Harare 2003-04 (86/74). C&G Man of the Match awards in the semi-final v Yorkshire at The Rose Bowl (100) and in the final v Warwickshire at Lord's (104) 2005. Holds an Irish passport and is not considered an overseas player
Opinions on cricket: 'Too many overs in a day in four-day cricket. No rest time for players in between games.'
Best batting: 126 Midlands v Manicaland, Mutare 2002-03
Best bowling: 6-82 Midlands v Mashonaland, Kwekwe 2002-03

2006 Season

	M	Inn	NO	Runs	HS	Avg	100	50	Ct	St	Balls	Runs	Wkts	Avg	BB	5I	10M
Test																	
FC	15	22	3	464	50 *	24.42	-	1	14	-	1777	1060	26	40.76	3-57	-	-
ODI																	
List A	14	14	3	269	45	24.45	-	-	6	-	419	334	13	25.69	4-24	-	
20/20 Int																	
20/20																	

Career Performances

	M	Inn	NO	Runs	HS	Avg	100	50	Ct	St	Balls	Runs	Wkts	Avg	BB	5I	10M
Test	5	8	0	261	86	32.62	-	3	7	-	570	388	9	43.11	4-146	-	-
FC	61	98	10	2795	126	31.76	4	16	58	-	7457	4611	123	37.48	6-82	5	-
ODI	42	34	7	698	100	25.85	1	2	5	-	1649	1561	41	38.07	3-29	-	
List A	102	89	15	2113	104	28.55	3	7	22	-	3894	3404	108	31.51	5-50	2	
20/20 Int																	
20/20	7	6	0	116	46	19.33	-	-	1	-	90	117	8	14.62	2-13	-	

25. What 50-year-old tradition was broken with for the second Test v Bangladesh at Riverside 2005?

EVANS, L.   Surrey

Name: Laurie Evans
Role: Right-hand bat, right-arm fast-medium bowler; all-rounder
Born: 12 October 1987, Lambeth, London
Height: 6ft **Weight:** 13st 3lbs
Nickname: Lau, Evs, Augustus ('because I eat a lot')
County debut: No first-team appearance
Parents: Sue and Marcus
Marital status: Single
Education: John Fisher, Purley; Whitgift School, South Croydon; Durham University
Qualifications: BTEC Sport, 3 A-levels, 'taking cricket coaching level 2'
Career outside cricket: 'None – want to be a chef'
Off-season: 'In the Durham UCCE Academy and going away to India'
Overseas tours: Surrey Academy to South Africa 2006
Career highlights to date: 1) 135* (75 balls, 10 x 4, 10 x 6) for John Fisher 1st XI v Millfield 1st XI in schools national Twenty20 final at Edgbaston 2006. It was the occasion that made it special. 2) 139 Surrey 2nd XI v Essex 2nd XI at The Oval 2006
Cricket moments to forget: 'I only dropped three catches all season in 2005 and they were all in the U17 national final v Yorkshire'
Cricket superstitions: 'None'
Cricketers particularly admired: Mark Ramprakash
Young players to look out for: Simon King (Surrey), Zafar Ansari (Surrey Academy – 'he's 14 and he's just unreal')
Other sports played: Rugby (Harlequins Academy; won U15 *Daily Mail* National Schools Cup with Whitgift v Millfield at Twickenham 2003)
Other sports followed: Football (Arsenal)
Injuries: Undersurface tear of labrum in the right shoulder
Favourite band: James Brown, 112, Usher, Arctic Monkeys
Relaxations: 'Love cooking, clothes'
Extras: Represented ECB Development of Excellence XI v India U19 2006
Opinions on cricket: 'The game today is more exciting than ever. It's got quicker and more interesting to spectators. However, I think that it shouldn't be changed too much, otherwise it will lose its history and essence.'

EVANS, L.   Durham

Name: Luke Evans
Role: Right-hand bat, right-arm fast bowler
Born: 26 April 1987, Sunderland
Height: 6ft 7in **Weight:** 13st
Nickname: Longshanks, Scarecrow,
Pencil, Tripod
County debut: No first-team appearance
Parents: Gayle and Stephen
Marital status: Single
Family links with cricket: 'I feel obliged to
mention my dad's role as an anchor batsman
for Farringdon School in the 1970s...so he
says'
Education: St Aidan's Comprehensive
RC School
Qualifications: 10 GCSEs, 2 A-levels
Career outside cricket: 'I am now
independently studying music and would like
to start tutoring guitar and bass'
Off-season: 'Training and conditioning, then hopefully doing some bowling in India'
Overseas tours: Durham CCC to Dubai 2006
Career highlights to date: 'Although it was a cup tie for the Academy, recording
figures of 6-18 off nine overs is still a proud moment for me'
Cricket superstitions: 'None'
Cricketers particularly admired: Curtly Ambrose, Jason Gillespie,
Stephen Harmison
Young players to look out for: Andrew Smith
Other sports played: 'I play darts casually from time to time'
Other sports followed: 'I couldn't be called a diehard Sunderland fan, but I'd like to
see them do well'
Injuries: Out for two weeks with an impingement of the rib
Favourite band: Audioslave, Black Label Society, Pantera, Soundgarden 'and more'
Relaxations: 'Playing guitar and drawing'
Extras: Represented ECB Development of Excellence XI v Bangladesh U19 2004.
Represented England U17 v MCC YC. City of Sunderland Young Achievers Award for
Sport 2004. Sue Wright Sporting Achievement Award (from school)
Opinions on cricket: 'I think that the Dukes ball should be used worldwide in Test
matches. I also think more pitches should be friendly to both batsman and bowler –
true bounce but good value if you hit the deck and hit the seam. It's also great to see
more public interest in cricket.'

FERLEY, R. S.   Nottinghamshire

Name: <u>Robert</u> Steven Ferley
Role: Right-hand bat, left-arm spin bowler
Born: 4 February 1982, Norwich
Height: 5ft 8in **Weight:** 12st 4lbs
Nickname: Mr Shaky Shake, Billy Bob,
Bob Turkey
County debut: 2003 (Kent)
Strike rate: (career 69.77)
Parents: Pam and Tim (divorced)
Marital status: Single
Education: King Edward VII High School;
Sutton Valence School (A-levels); Grey
College, Durham University
Qualifications: 10 GCSEs, 3 A-levels
Overseas tours: England U19 to India 2000-
01; British Universities to South Africa 2002
Cricketers particularly admired: Steve
Waugh, Steve Marsh, Min Patel,
Charles Clarke
Other sports played: Rugby, hockey, tennis, football
Other sports followed: Football (Liverpool)
Relaxations: 'Films, interior design, keeping fit'
Extras: Represented England U17 1999. Played for Durham UCCE 2001, 2002 and
2003. Represented British Universities 2001, 2002 and 2003. Represented England
U19 2001. Took 4-76 on Championship debut v Surrey at The Oval 2003. Left Kent at
the end of the 2006 season and has joined Nottinghamshire for 2007
Best batting: 78* DUCCE v Durham, Durham 2003
Best bowling: 6-136 Kent v Middlesex, Canterbury 2006

2006 Season

	M	Inn	NO	Runs	HS	Avg	100	50	Ct	St	Balls	Runs	Wkts	Avg	BB	5I	10M
Test																	
FC	3	3	0	36	22	12.00	-	-	-	-	734	378	9	42.00	6-136	1	-
ODI																	
List A	4	1	0	26	26	26.00	-	-	2	-	167	141	9	15.66	4-33	-	
20/20 Int																	
20/20																	

Career Performances

	M	Inn	NO	Runs	HS	Avg	100	50	Ct	St	Balls	Runs	Wkts	Avg	BB	5I	10M
Test																	
FC	26	34	7	502	78 *	18.59	-	2	8	-	3768	2268	54	42.00	6-136	1	-
ODI																	
List A	32	18	5	226	42	17.38	-	-	12	-	1426	1114	41	27.17	4-33	-	
20/20 Int																	
20/20	6	2	2	17	16 *		-	-	2	-	90	140	2	70.00	1-9	-	

FINN, S. T.   Middlesex

Name: <u>Steven</u> Thomas Finn
Role: Right-hand bat, right-arm medium-fast bowler
Born: 4 April 1989, Watford
Height: 6ft 8in **Weight:** 13st 12lbs
Nickname: Finny
County debut: 2005
Strike rate: (career 60.00)
Parents: Diana and Terry
Marital status: Single
Family links with cricket: 'Dad and Grandad played club cricket'
Education: Parmiter's School, Watford, Herts
Qualifications: 10 GCSEs, 4 AS-levels
Career outside cricket: 'Student'
Off-season: 'Working for A-levels and training for 2007'
Overseas tours: England U16 to South Africa 2004-05; England U19 to Malaysia 2006-07
Career highlights to date: 'Playing against India U19 as a 17-year-old in 2006'
Cricket moments to forget: 'Third man out in a hat-trick v India U19 during second "One-Day International" 2006'
Cricketers particularly admired: Glenn McGrath
Young players to look out for: Billy Godleman, Dan Housego, Rhys Williams, Shaun Levy
Other sports played: Basketball (county), football (district)
Other sports followed: Football (Watford)
Favourite band: Coldplay
Relaxations: 'Music, PlayStation, films'
Extras: Has represented England U15, U16, U17 and U19

Opinions on cricket: 'Happy with the numerous opportunities that are given to young players like myself.'
Best bowling: 1-16 Middlesex v CUCCE, Fenner's 2005

2006 Season (did not make any first-class or one-day appearances)

Career Performances

	M	Inn	NO	Runs	HS	Avg	100	50	Ct	St	Balls	Runs	Wkts	Avg	BB	5I	10M
Test																	
FC	1	0	0	0	0		-	-	-	-	120	53	2	26.50	1-16	-	-
ODI																	
List A																	
20/20 Int																	
20/20																	

FISHER, I. D. Gloucestershire

Name: Ian Douglas Fisher
Role: Left-hand bat, left-arm spin bowler
Born: 31 March 1976, Bradford
Height: 5ft 11in **Weight:** 13st 6lbs
Nickname: Fish, Flash, Fishy
County debut: 1995-96 (Yorkshire),
2002 (Gloucestershire)
County cap: 2004 (Gloucestershire)
Place in batting averages: 161st av. 28.00
(2005 216th av. 20.66)
Place in bowling averages: 147th av. 75.50
(2005 123rd av. 44.68)
Strike rate: 120.80 (career 77.80)
Parents: Geoff and Linda
Marital status: Single
Family links with cricket: Father played
club cricket
Education: Beckfoot Grammar School

Qualifications: 9 GCSEs, NCA coaching award, sports leader's award, lifesaver
(bronze), YMCA gym instructor
Overseas tours: Yorkshire to Zimbabwe 1996, to South Africa 1998, 1999, 2001,
to Perth 2000; MCC to Sri Lanka 2001
Overseas teams played for: Somerset West, Cape Town 1994-95; Petone Riverside,
Wellington, New Zealand 1997-98
Career highlights to date: 'Winning the Championship with Yorkshire [2001]'
Cricket moments to forget: 'My pair'

Cricketers particularly admired: Darren Lehmann, Shane Warne
Other sports played: Football (Westbrook)
Other sports followed: Football (Leeds United)
Relaxations: Music, movies, catching up with friends, shopping, eating out
Extras: Played England U17 and Yorkshire Schools U15, U16 and Yorkshire U19.
Bowled the last first-class ball delivered at Northlands Road, Southampton, September 2000. Recorded three Championship five-wicket returns in successive innings 2003, including maiden ten-wicket match (5-30/5-93) v Durham at Bristol
Best batting: 103* Gloucestershire v Essex, Gloucester 2002
Best bowling: 5-30 Gloucestershire v Durham, Bristol 2003

2006 Season

	M	Inn	NO	Runs	HS	Avg	100	50	Ct	St	Balls	Runs	Wkts	Avg	BB	5I	10M
Test																	
FC	5	8	2	168	45	28.00	-	-	1	-	1208	755	10	75.50	3-110	-	-
ODI																	
List A	11	7	2	77	25 *	15.40	-	-	4	-	426	319	9	35.44	3-41	-	
20/20 Int																	
20/20	8	3	2	21	9 *	21.00	-	-	3	-	120	185	7	26.42	2-4	-	

Career Performances

	M	Inn	NO	Runs	HS	Avg	100	50	Ct	St	Balls	Runs	Wkts	Avg	BB	5I	10M
Test																	
FC	75	112	19	2130	103 *	22.90	1	7	26	-	12060	6553	155	42.27	5-30	7	1
ODI																	
List A	54	32	11	194	25 *	9.23	-	-	17	-	2098	1523	58	26.25	3-18	-	
20/20 Int																	
20/20	16	5	3	30	9 *	15.00	-	-	7	-	204	305	14	21.78	4-22	-	

26. Who bowed out of county cricket in 2006 with 339
in his final Championship innings?

FLEMING, S. P.   Nottinghamshire

Name: Stephen Paul Fleming
Role: Left-hand bat, occasional right-arm
slow-medium bowler, county captain
Born: 1 April 1973, Christchurch,
New Zealand
Height: 6ft 3in
County debut: 2001 (Middlesex),
2003 (Yorkshire), 2005 (Nottinghamshire)
County cap: 2001 (Middlesex), 2005 (Notts)
Test debut: 1993-94
ODI debut: 1993-94
Twenty20 Int debut: 2004-05
1000 runs in a season: 1
1st-Class 200s: 4
Place in batting averages: 45th av. 49.60
(2005 13th av. 60.53)
Education: Cashmere High School;
Christchurch College of Education

Overseas tours: New Zealand U19 to India 1991-92; New Zealand to England 1994, to South Africa 1994-95, to India 1995-96, to India and Pakistan (World Cup) 1995-96, to West Indies 1995-96, to Pakistan 1996-97, to Zimbabwe 1997-98 (c), to Australia 1997-98 (c), to Sri Lanka 1997-98 (c), to Bangladesh (Wills International Cup) 1998-99 (c), to UK, Ireland and Netherlands (World Cup) 1999 (c), to England 1999 (c), to India 1999-2000 (c), to Zimbabwe 2000-01 (c), to Kenya (ICC Knockout Trophy) 2000-01 (c), to South Africa 2000-01 (c), to Australia 2001-02 (c), to Pakistan 2002 (c), to West Indies 2002 (c), to Sri Lanka (ICC Champions Trophy) 2002-03 (c), to Africa (World Cup) 2002-03 (c), to Sri Lanka 2003 (c), to India 2003-04 (c), to England 2004 (c), to England (ICC Champions Trophy) 2004 (c), to Bangladesh 2004-05 (c), to Australia 2004-05 (c), to Zimbabwe 2005-06 (c), to South Africa 2005-06 (c), to India (ICC Champions Trophy) 2006-07 (c), to Australia (C'wealth Bank Series) 2006-07 (c), plus other one-day tournaments in Sharjah, India, Singapore and Sri Lanka; ICC World XI to Australia (Tsunami Relief) 2004-05

Overseas teams played for: Canterbury 1991-92 – 1999-2000; Wellington 2000-01 –
Extras: Captain of New Zealand since 1996-97. Led his country to series victory in England in 1999, which included New Zealand's first wins at Lord's and The Oval. His Test awards include Man of the Match in the first Test v Pakistan at Hamilton 2003-04 (192) and in the second Test v South Africa at Cape Town 2005-06 (262). Has won numerous ODI awards, including Man of the Match for his 134* v South Africa at Johannesburg in the 2002-03 World Cup and Man of the NatWest Series in England 2004. One of *New Zealand Cricket Almanack*'s two Players of the Year 1998, 2003, 2004. Is New Zealand's most-capped Test player and highest Test run-scorer. Was

Middlesex overseas player in 2001; was a Yorkshire overseas player in 2003; an overseas player with Nottinghamshire and captain since 2005
Best batting: 274* New Zealand v Sri Lanka, Colombo 2002-03
Stop press: Man of the Match v South Africa at Mumbai (89) and v Pakistan at Mohali (80), both in the ICC Champions Trophy 2006-07

2006 Season

	M	Inn	NO	Runs	HS	Avg	100	50	Ct	St	Balls	Runs	Wkts	Avg	BB	5I	10M
Test																	
FC	13	22	2	992	192	49.60	2	8	17	-	0	0	0		-	-	-
ODI																	
List A	13	12	1	310	121 *	28.18	1	-	10	-	0	0	0		-	-	
20/20 Int																	
20/20	10	10	1	336	64 *	37.33	-	3	2	-	0	0	0		-	-	

Career Performances

	M	Inn	NO	Runs	HS	Avg	100	50	Ct	St	Balls	Runs	Wkts	Avg	BB	5I	10M
Test	102	173	10	6545	274 *	40.15	9	41	152	-	0	0	0		-	-	-
FC	224	368	31	14759	274 *	43.79	31	86	299	-	102	129	0		-	-	-
ODI	253	243	19	7184	134 *	32.07	6	43	116	-	29	28	1	28.00	1-8	-	
List A	418	397	36	12430	139 *	34.43	19	73	199	-	35	31	2	15.50	1-3	-	
20/20 Int	3	3	0	55	31	18.33	-	-	1	-	0	0	0		-	-	
20/20	25	25	1	583	64 *	24.29	-	5	6	-	0	0	0		-	-	

27. Who made his county debut in 1991 only to find his father playing for the opposition?

FLINTOFF, A. Lancashire

Name: Andrew Flintoff
Role: Right-hand bat, right-arm
fast-medium bowler
Born: 6 December 1977, Preston
Height: 6ft 4in
Nickname: Freddie
County debut: 1995
County cap: 1998
Benefit: 2006
Test debut: 1998
ODI debut: 1998-99
Twenty20 Int debut: 2005
Place in batting averages: (2005 74th
av. 39.06)
Place in bowling averages: 41st av. 29.28
(2005 22nd av. 25.05)
Strike rate: 65.07 (career 64.24)
Parents: Colin and Susan
Wife and date of marriage: Rachael, 5 March 2005
Children: Holly, 6 September 2004; Corey, 8 March 2006
Family links with cricket: Brother Chris and father both local league cricketers
Education: Ribbleton Hall High School
Qualifications: 9 GCSEs
Off-season: Touring with England
Overseas tours: England Schools U15 to South Africa 1993; England U19 to West
Indies 1994-95, to Zimbabwe 1995-96, to Pakistan 1996-97 (c); England A to Kenya
and Sri Lanka 1997-98, to Zimbabwe and South Africa 1998-99; England to Sharjah
(Coca-Cola Cup) 1998-99, to South Africa and Zimbabwe 1999-2000, to Kenya (ICC
Knockout Trophy) 2000-01, to Pakistan and (one-day series) Sri Lanka 2000-01, to
Zimbabwe (one-day series) 2001-02, to India and New Zealand 2001-02, to Australia
2002-03, to Africa (World Cup) 2002-03, to Bangladesh and Sri Lanka 2003-04, to
West Indies 2003-04, to South Africa 2004-05, to Pakistan 2005-06, to India 2005-06, to
India (ICC Champions Trophy) 2006-07 (c), to Australia 2006-07 (Test c); ECB
National Academy to Australia 2001-02; England VI to Hong Kong 2001; ICC World
XI to Australia (Super Series) 2005-06
Other sports/games played: Represented Lancashire Schools at chess
Extras: Represented England U14 to U19. Cricket Writers' Club Young Player of the
Year and PCA Young Player of the Year 1998. Scored first century before lunch by a
Lancashire batsman in a Roses match, v Yorkshire at Old Trafford 1999. Won the EDS
Walter Lawrence Trophy 1999 (for the fastest first-class century of the season).
Lancashire Player of the Year 2000. Vice-captain of Lancashire 2002. BBC North West

Sports Personality of the Year 2003. One of *Wisden*'s Five Cricketers of the Year 2004. Vodafone England Cricketer of the Year 2003-04 and 2005-06. Shared with Andrew Strauss in a record stand for any wicket for England in ODIs (226) v West Indies at Lord's in the NatWest Series 2004. His Test awards include England's Man of the Series v West Indies 2004 and v Australia 2005 (plus the inaugural Compton-Miller Medal 2005 for Ashes Player of the Series), and Man of the Series v India 2005-06. His ODI awards include Man of the NatWest Series 2003 and Man of the Series v Bangladesh 2003-04. Winner of inaugural ICC One-Day Player of the Year award 2003-04. PCA Player of the Year award 2004, 2005. ICC Player of the Year award (jointly with Jacques Kallis) 2005. BBC Sports Personality of the Year 2005. Appointed MBE in 2006 New Year Honours as part of 2005 Ashes-winning England team. Captained England (when fit) in the absence of Michael Vaughan. England 12-month central contract 2006-07

Best batting: 167 England v West Indies, Edgbaston 2004

Best bowling: 5-24 Lancashire v Hampshire, Southampton 1999

Stop press: Captained England for much of the Commonwealth Bank Series 2006-07 in Australia after injury to Michael Vaughan. Man of the Match v New Zealand at Hobart in the Commonwealth Bank Series 2006-07 (2-37/72*)

2006 Season

	M	Inn	NO	Runs	HS	Avg	100	50	Ct	St	Balls	Runs	Wkts	Avg	BB	5I	10M
Test	3	5	2	47	33*	15.66	-	-	4	-	773	354	12	29.50	3-52	-	-
FC	4	7	2	88	37	17.60	-	-	6	-	911	410	14	29.28	3-52	-	-
ODI																	
List A	1	0	0	0	0		-	-	1	-	54	30	3	10.00	3-30	-	
20/20 Int																	
20/20	2	2	0	57	47	28.50	-	-	1	-	30	22	3	7.33	3-4	-	

Career Performances

	M	Inn	NO	Runs	HS	Avg	100	50	Ct	St	Balls	Runs	Wkts	Avg	BB	5I	10M
Test	62	100	5	3127	167	32.91	5	22	44	-	11685	5827	186	31.32	5-58	2	-
FC	154	242	17	7914	167	35.17	15	46	164	-	17989	8798	280	31.42	5-24	3	-
ODI	102	90	12	2674	123	34.28	3	15	33	-	3882	2840	110	25.81	4-14	-	
List A	236	212	23	5748	143	30.41	6	30	90	-	7464	5153	224	23.00	4-11	-	
20/20 Int	1	1	0	6	6	6.00	-	-	1	-	18	15	0		-	-	
20/20	8	8	0	245	85	30.62	-	1	3	-	131	139	8	17.37	3-4	-	

FLOWER, A. Essex

Name: Andrew (<u>Andy</u>) Flower
Role: Left-hand bat, wicket-keeper,
occasional right-arm medium/off-spin bowler
Born: 28 April 1968, Cape Town,
South Africa
Height: 5ft 10in
Nickname: Petals
County debut: 2002
County cap: 2002
Test debut: 1992-93
ODI debut: 1991-92
1000 runs in a season: 5
1st-Class 200s: 4
Place in batting averages: 6th av. 73.14
(2005 5th av. 71.00)
Strike rate: (career 89.85)
Parents: Bill and Jean
Family links with cricket: Younger brother
Grant played for Zimbabwe and also plays for Essex
Education: Vainona High School
Overseas tours: Zimbabwe to Australia and New Zealand (World Cup) 1991-92,
to India 1992-93, to Pakistan 1993-94 (c), to Australia 1994-95 (c), to New Zealand
1995-96 (c), to India and Pakistan (World Cup) 1995-96 (c), to Sri Lanka and Pakistan
1996-97, to Sri Lanka and New Zealand 1997-98, to Bangladesh (Wills International
Cup) 1998-99, to Pakistan 1998-99, to UK, Ireland and Netherlands (World Cup)
1999, to South Africa 1999-2000, to West Indies 1999-2000 (c), to England 2000 (c),
to Kenya (ICC Knockout Trophy) 2000-01, to India 2000-01, to New Zealand and
Australia 2000-01, to Bangladesh, Sri Lanka and India 2001-02, to Sri Lanka (ICC
Champions Trophy) 2002-03, plus other one-day tournaments in Sharjah, South Africa,
Kenya, India, Bangladesh and Singapore
Overseas teams played for: Mashonaland 1993-94 – 2002-03; South Australia
2003-04
Other sports played: Tennis, squash; rugby, hockey (at school)
Extras: Scored century (115*) on ODI debut v Sri Lanka at New Plymouth in the
1992 World Cup. Appeared in Zimbabwe's inaugural Test, v India at Harare 1992-93.
Scored 156 v Pakistan at Harare 1994-95 in Zimbabwe's first Test win, in the process
sharing with Grant Flower (201*) in a record fourth-wicket stand for Zimbabwe in
Tests (269). Man of the Series v India 2000-01 (232*, 183*, 70 and 55; av. 270.00).
FICA International Player of the Year 2001. Scored 142 and 199* v South Africa in the
first Test at Harare 2001, becoming the first wicket-keeper to score a century in each
innings of a Test match and the first to go to the top of the PricewaterhouseCoopers

ratings for Test batsmen. Scored 142* v England at Harare 2001-02, in the process sharing with Heath Streak in a new world record seventh-wicket partnership for ODIs (130). One of *Wisden*'s Five Cricketers of the Year 2002. Overseas player with Essex since 2002. A former captain of Zimbabwe. Retired from international cricket after the 2002-03 World Cup. Is England-qualified

Best batting: 271* Essex v Northamptonshire, Northampton 2006
Best bowling: 1-1 Mashonaland v Mashonaland CD, Harare South 1993-94

2006 Season

	M	Inn	NO	Runs	HS	Avg	100	50	Ct	St	Balls	Runs	Wkts	Avg	BB	5I	10M
Test																	
FC	17	27	6	1536	271 *	73.14	7	3	18	-	48	20	1	20.00	1-20	-	-
ODI																	
List A	14	12	3	541	81	60.11	-	5	4	-	0	0	0		-	-	
20/20 Int																	
20/20	4	4	0	50	22	12.50	-	-	1	-	0	0	0		-	-	

Career Performances

	M	Inn	NO	Runs	HS	Avg	100	50	Ct	St	Balls	Runs	Wkts	Avg	BB	5I	10M
Test	63	112	19	4794	232 *	51.54	12	27	151	9	3	4	0		-	-	-
FC	223	372	69	16379	271 *	54.05	49	75	361	21	629	270	7	38.57	1-1	-	-
ODI	213	208	16	6786	145	35.34	4	55	141	32	30	23	0		-	-	
List A	380	366	45	12511	145	38.97	12	97	254	48	132	103	1	103.00	1-21	-	
20/20 Int																	
20/20	21	20	2	595	83	33.05	-	4	6	-	0	0	0		-	-	

28. Who scored 203* in his first Test match as
West Indies captain 2004-05?

FLOWER, G. W.   Essex

Name: <u>Grant</u> William Flower
Role: Right-hand bat, left-arm spin bowler; all-rounder
Born: 20 December 1970, Harare, Zimbabwe
Height: 5ft 10in
Nickname: Gobby
County debut: 2002 (Leicestershire), 2005 (Essex)
County cap: 2005 (Essex)
Test debut: 1992-93
ODI debut: 1992-93
1st-Class 200s: 3
Place in batting averages: 116th av. 33.09 (2005 215th av. 20.89)
Strike rate: (career 75.52)
Parents: Bill and Jean
Marital status: Single
Family links with cricket: Younger brother of Andy Flower (also plays for Essex)
Education: St George's College, Harare
Career outside cricket: Coaching
Off-season: 'Coaching Essex Academy; doing Level 3 coaching course; personal training course'
Overseas tours: Zimbabwe to India 1992-93, to Pakistan 1993-94, to Australia (one-day series) 1994-95, to New Zealand 1995-96, to India and Pakistan (World Cup) 1995-96, to Sri Lanka and Pakistan 1996-97, to Sri Lanka and New Zealand 1997-98, to Bangladesh (Wills International Cup) 1998-99, to Pakistan 1998-99, to UK, Ireland and Netherlands (World Cup) 1999, to South Africa 1999-2000, to West Indies 1999-2000, to England 2000, to Kenya (ICC Knockout Trophy) 2000-01, to India 2000-01, to New Zealand and Australia 2000-01, to Bangladesh, Sri Lanka and India 2001-02, to Sri Lanka (ICC Champions Trophy) 2002-03, to England 2003, to Australia 2003-04 (VB Series), plus other one-day tournaments in Sharjah, South Africa, Kenya, India, Bangladesh and Singapore
Overseas teams played for: Mashonaland 1994-95 – 2003-04
Career highlights to date: 'Scoring 201* v Pakistan in 1994-95 in our first Test match victory in Harare'
Cricket moments to forget: 'Losing to Kenya in the last World Cup for Zimbabwe'
Cricket superstitions: 'None'
Cricketers particularly admired: Sachin Tendulkar, Graeme Hick, Andrew Flower
Young players to look out for: Mark Pettini, Ravi Bopara
Other sports played: Tennis, squash, hockey

Other sports followed: Rugby, golf

Relaxations: 'Gym, beer and fishing …'

Extras: Appeared in Zimbabwe's inaugural Test, v India at Harare 1992-93. Scored 201* v Pakistan at Harare 1994-95 in Zimbabwe's first Test win, in the process sharing with Andy Flower (156) in a record fourth-wicket stand for Zimbabwe in Tests (269). Became the first player to score a hundred in each innings of a Test for Zimbabwe (104/151) in the first Test v New Zealand at Harare 1997-98. His Test awards include Man of the Series v New Zealand 1997-98. His ODI awards include Zimbabwe's Man of the Series v Pakistan 1996-97, as well as Man of the Match v England at Trent Bridge in the NatWest Series 2003 (96*) and v Australia at Adelaide in the VB Series 2003-04 (94). Was Leicestershire's overseas player during June 2002. Announced his retirement from international cricket in 2004. Is no longer considered an overseas player

Opinions on cricket: 'Too much international cricket leading to burn-out, injuries etc. Championship cricket should be reduced, giving more time to recover and prepare for next game?'

Best batting: 243* Mashonaland v Matabeleland, Harare 1996-97

Best bowling: 7-31 Zimbabweans v Lahore Division, Lahore 1998-99

2006 Season

	M	Inn	NO	Runs	HS	Avg	100	50	Ct	St	Balls	Runs	Wkts	Avg	BB	5I	10M
Test																	
FC	7	11	0	364	101	33.09	1	3	7	-	349	190	8	23.75	3-28	-	-
ODI																	
List A	9	5	0	118	61	23.60	-	1	4	-	306	235	6	39.16	2-32	-	
20/20 Int																	
20/20	2	0	0	0	0		-	-	-	-	42	69	2	34.50	2-40	-	

Career Performances

	M	Inn	NO	Runs	HS	Avg	100	50	Ct	St	Balls	Runs	Wkts	Avg	BB	5I	10M
Test	67	123	6	3457	201*	29.54	6	15	43	-	3378	1537	25	61.48	4-41	-	-
FC	168	289	22	10068	243*	37.70	21	57	151	-	12235	5450	162	33.64	7-31	3	-
ODI	219	212	18	6536	142*	33.69	6	40	86	-	5420	4187	104	40.25	4-32	-	
List A	314	300	26	9313	148*	33.98	11	59	125	-	8242	6082	176	34.55	4-32	-	
20/20 Int																	
20/20	9	3	2	7	4	7.00	-	-	3	-	142	194	10	19.40	3-20	-	

FOOTITT, M. H. A.   Nottinghamshire

Name: <u>Mark</u> Harold Alan Footitt
Role: Right-hand bat, left-arm fast bowler
Born: 25 November 1985, Nottingham
Height: 6ft 2in **Weight:** 12st 7lbs
Nickname: Footy
County debut: 2005
Strike rate: (career 43.15)
Parents: Graham and Julie
Marital status: Engaged to Kerry Ann
Pashley
Family links with cricket: 'Dad and grandad
played local cricket'
Education: Carlton le Willows School
Qualifications: 3 GCSEs, Level 1 coaching
Overseas tours: Nottinghamshire to South
Africa 2006
Career highlights to date: 'Playing my first
game for Notts. Being picked for the National
Academy 2006'
Cricket moments to forget: 'My first Twenty20 game'
Cricket superstitions: 'None'
Cricketers particularly admired: Brett Lee
Other sports played: Football
Other sports followed: Football (Man Utd)
Favourite band: The Killers
Relaxations: 'Playing on PS2 and PC; watching TV/DVDs'
Extras: Attended MRF Pace Foundation, India 2000, 2001, 2006. Played for Notts
Board XI in the 2002 C&G. Represented England U19 2005. ECB National Academy
2005-06
Best batting: 19* Nottinghamshire v Hampshire, Rose Bowl 2005
Best bowling: 5-45 Nottinghamshire v West Indies A, Trent Bridge 2006

2006 Season

	M	Inn	NO	Runs	HS	Avg	100	50	Ct	St	Balls	Runs	Wkts	Avg	BB	5I	10M
Test																	
FC	3	3	3	5	5 *		-	-	-	-	300	220	7	31.42	5-45	1	-
ODI																	
List A																	
20/20 Int																	
20/20																	

Career Performances

	M	Inn	NO	Runs	HS	Avg	100	50	Ct	St	Balls	Runs	Wkts	Avg	BB	5I	10M
Test																	
FC	5	6	4	40	19 *	20.00	-	-	1	-	561	480	13	36.92	5-45	1	-
ODI																	
List A	1	0	0	0	0		-	-	-	-	18	18	0			-	-
20/20 Int																	
20/20	1	0	0	0	0		-	-	-	-	12	34	0			-	-

FOSTER, E. J. Worcestershire

Name: Edward (Ed) John Foster
Role: Left-hand bat, wicket-keeper
Born: 21 January 1985, Shrewsbury
Height: 6ft 1in **Weight:** 11st 8lbs
Nickname: Fos, Fossie
County debut: No first-team appearance
Parents: John and Jean
Marital status: Single
Family links with cricket: Father captained
Shropshire CCC; brother Robert plays for
Shropshire CCC
Education: Meole Brace Secondary;
Loughborough University
Qualifications: '10½ GCSEs', 3 A-levels,
1 AS-level, ECB Level 2 coaching
Career outside cricket: Student
Off-season: 'Perth, WA – training with
batting coach Noddy Holder, playing grade
cricket'
Overseas teams played for: Claremont-Nedlands CC, Perth
Career highlights to date: '105 v Essex for Loughborough UCCE [2006]'
Cricket superstitions: 'Left pad on first'
Cricketers particularly admired: Alec Stewart, Graham Thorpe
Young players to look out for: James Taylor
Other sports played: Football (recreational)
Other sports followed: Football (Arsenal, Shrewsbury Town)
Relaxations: TV, computer games
Extras: Worcestershire Academy 2002-03. Played for Loughborough UCCE 2005,
2006. Midland Club Cricket Conference Player of the Year 2005
Opinions on cricket: 'All one-day domestic cricket should be 50 overs.'
Best batting: 105 LUCCE v Essex, Chelmsford 2006

2006 Season (did not make any first-class or one-day appearances for his county)

Career Performances

	M	Inn	NO	Runs	HS	Avg	100	50	Ct	St	Balls	Runs	Wkts	Avg	BB	5I	10M
Test																	
FC	3	4	1	210	105	70.00	1	1	1	-		0	0	0		-	-	-
ODI																	
List A																		
20/20 Int																		
20/20																		

FOSTER, J. S. Essex

Name: James Savin Foster
Role: Right-hand bat, wicket-keeper
Born: 15 April 1980, Whipps Cross, London
Height: 6ft **Weight:** 12st
Nickname: Fozzy, Chief
County debut: 2000
County cap: 2001
Test debut: 2001-02
ODI debut: 2001-02
1000 runs in a season: 1
50 dismissals in a season: 3
1st-Class 200s: 1
Place in batting averages: 49th av. 48.35
(2005 93rd av. 36.71)
Parents: Martin and Diana
Marital status: Single
Family links with cricket: 'Dad played for
Essex Amateurs'
Education: Forest School; Durham University
Qualifications: 10 GCSEs, 3 A-levels, hockey and cricket Level 1 coaching awards
Overseas tours: BUSA to South Africa 1999; Durham University to South Africa
1999, to Vienna (European Indoor Championships) 1999; England A to West Indies
2000-01; England to Zimbabwe (one-day series) 2001-02, to India and New Zealand
2001-02, to Australia 2002-03
Overseas teams played for: Claremont-Nedlands, Perth 2006-07
Career highlights to date: 'Playing for my country'
Cricketers particularly admired: Nasser Hussain, Stuart Law, Robert Rollins,
Ian Healy, Jack Russell, Alec Stewart, Adam Gilchrist
Other sports played: Hockey (Essex U21), tennis (played for GB U14 v Sweden
U14; national training squad)

Other sports followed: Football
Relaxations: Socialising
Extras: Essex U17 Player of the Year 1997. Represented ECB U19 1998 and England U19 1999. Represented BUSA 1999, 2000 and 2001. Voted Essex Cricket Society 2nd XI Player of the Year 2000. Played for Durham UCCE 2001. NBC Denis Compton Award for the most promising young Essex player 2001. Achieved double (1037 runs plus 51 dismissals) 2004
Best batting: 212 Essex v Leicestershire, Chelmsford 2004

2006 Season

	M	Inn	NO	Runs	HS	Avg	100	50	Ct	St	Balls	Runs	Wkts	Avg	BB	5I	10M
Test																	
FC	17	21	4	822	103	48.35	2	6	65	3	0	0	0		-	-	-
ODI																	
List A	17	12	4	301	67	37.62	-	1	19	5	0	0	0		-	-	
20/20 Int																	
20/20	10	9	1	122	47 *	15.25	-	-	3	4	0	0	0		-	-	

Career Performances

	M	Inn	NO	Runs	HS	Avg	100	50	Ct	St	Balls	Runs	Wkts	Avg	BB	5I	10M
Test	7	12	3	226	48	25.11	-	-	17	1	0	0	0		-	-	-
FC	106	154	21	4588	212	34.49	8	22	276	28	12	6	0		-	-	-
ODI	11	6	3	41	13	13.66	-	-	13	7	0	0	0		-	-	
List A	102	76	21	1241	67	22.56	-	3	127	27	0	0	0		-	-	
20/20 Int																	
20/20	26	20	4	239	62 *	14.93	-	1	10	10	0	0	0		-	-	

29. Who, in 1975-76, became the only player yet to have scored a century in each innings in his first Test as captain?

FOSTER, P. J.   Northamptonshire

Name: Patrick John Foster
Role: Right-hand bat, right-arm
medium-fast bowler
Born: 20 March 1987, Nairobi, Kenya
Height: 6ft 2in   **Weight:** 13st 8lbs
Nickname: Fozzie
County debut: No first-team appearance
Parents: Richard and Rachel
Marital status: Single
Family links with cricket: 'Father plays club
cricket. Brother plays junior county cricket'
Education: Oundle School; Durham
University
Qualifications: 10 GCSEs, 3 A-levels,
Levels 1 and 2 cricket coaching, emergency
aid
Career outside cricket: 'Want to go into
sports management or agency'
Off-season: 'First year of university at Durham, reading Combined Social Sciences
and training in the Centre of Excellence. Going to India with Durham UCCE in
March'
Overseas tours: Oundle School to Sri Lanka 2003, to South Africa 2005
Career highlights to date: 'Representing ECB Development of Excellence XI v India
U19, July 2006'
Cricket moments to forget: 'Getting a golden duck in my first second-team game'
Cricket superstitions: 'As I walk on to the pitch, just over the rope I pick up a bit of
grass and throw it over my shoulder'
Cricketers particularly admired: Glenn McGrath, Shaun Pollock, Matthew Hoggard
Young players to look out for: Alex Wakely, Ben Howgego, Joe Buttleman, Paul
Dixey, Greg Smith
Other sports played: Hockey (England Schools), rugby, squash, golf, tennis
Other sports followed: Rugby (Leicester Tigers), football (Liverpool)
Favourite band: Counting Crows
Relaxations: 'Music, TV, films, other sports'
Extras: Represented ECB Development of Excellence XI v India U19 2006
Opinions on cricket: 'Believe that the newer formats of the game have improved
county cricket massively. Think that Twenty20 is great for the counties and the game,
and think there should be a second-team Twenty20 competition. Like the way more
and more youngsters are being given opportunities in the first team earlier. Think that
this will only become more evident when the limit of overseas players is just one.
Having said that, I believe it's superb the way the best cricketers in the world come
over and play county cricket and improve the quality so much.'

FRANCIS, J. D.   Somerset

Name: <u>John</u> Daniel Francis
Role: Left-hand bat, slow left-arm bowler
Born: 13 November 1980, Bromley, Kent
Height: 5ft 11in **Weight:** 13st
Nickname: Long John, Franky, Junior
County debut: 2001 (Hampshire),
2004 (Somerset)
1000 runs in a season: 1
Place in batting averages: 248th av. 14.55
(2005 68th av. 40.84)
Strike rate: (career 68.25)
Parents: Linda and Daniel
Marital status: Single
Family links with cricket: Brother Simon
played for Hampshire and Somerset. Father
played club cricket. Grandfather played in the
services

Education: King Edward VI, Southampton;
Durham and Loughborough Universities
Qualifications: 10 GCSEs, 3 A-levels, BSc Sports Science, ECB Level 1
coaching award
Overseas tours: Twyford School to Barbados 1993; West of England U15 to West
Indies 1995; King Edward VI, Southampton to South Africa 1998; Durham University
to South Africa 2000; British Universities to South Africa 2002
Career highlights to date: 'Scoring maiden first-class century for Somerset v
Yorkshire at Scarborough 2004, sharing in a partnership of 197 runs with Ricky
Ponting'
Cricket moments to forget: 'Getting first ever pair, in a match v Yorkshire'
Cricket superstitions: 'Too many to say'
Cricketers particularly admired: Graham Thorpe, Adam Hollioake, Mike Hussey,
Simon Francis
Young players to look out for: James Hildreth, Matt Wood, Ben Riches,
Andrew Dunn
Other sports played: Hockey (England U18), golf, squash
Favourite band: David Gray
Relaxations: Drawing and painting, socialising
Extras: Hampshire Young Sportsman of the Year 1995. Sir John Hobbs Silver Jubilee
Memorial Prize for outstanding U16 player of the year 1996. Leading run-scorer in
U15 World Cup 1996. Played for Loughborough UCCE 2001, 2002 and 2003. NBC
Denis Compton Award for the most promising young Hampshire player 2002.
Represented British Universities 2002 and 2003

Best batting: 125* Somerset v Yorkshire, Headingley 2005
Best bowling: 1-1 Hampshire v Leicestershire, Leicester 2002

2006 Season

	M	Inn	NO	Runs	HS	Avg	100	50	Ct	St	Balls	Runs	Wkts	Avg	BB	5I	10M
Test																	
FC	5	9	0	131	41	14.55	-	-	5	-	6	9	0		-	-	-
ODI																	
List A	4	3	1	89	51	44.50	-	1	2	-	0	0	0		-	-	
20/20 Int																	
20/20	1	1	0	9	9	9.00	-	-	-	-	0	0	0		-	-	

Career Performances

	M	Inn	NO	Runs	HS	Avg	100	50	Ct	St	Balls	Runs	Wkts	Avg	BB	5I	10M
Test																	
FC	54	96	8	2638	125 *	29.97	6	14	32	-	273	164	4	41.00	1-1	-	-
ODI																	
List A	65	61	10	1745	103 *	34.21	1	12	15	-	0	0	0		-	-	
20/20 Int																	
20/20	10	10	3	221	49	31.57	-	-	-	-	0	0	0		-	-	

FRANCIS, S. R. G. Somerset

Name: <u>Simon</u> Richard George Francis
Role: Right-hand bat, right-arm
medium-fast bowler
Born: 15 August 1978, Bromley, Kent
Height: 6ft 1in **Weight:** 14st
Nickname: Franco, Guru
County debut: 1997 (Hampshire),
2002 (Somerset)
Strike rate: (career 63.04)
Parents: Daniel and Linda
Marital status: Single
Family links with cricket: Brother John
plays at Somerset. Father played club cricket.
Grandfather played for the Navy
Education: King Edward VI, Southampton;
Durham University
Qualifications: 9 GCSEs, 1 AS-Level,
3 A-levels, BA (Hons) Sport in the
Community, Level 1 coaching in hockey, Level III coaching in cricket
Career outside cricket: Cricket and hockey coaching

Overseas tours: England U17 to Netherlands (International Youth Tournament) 1995; England U19 to Pakistan 1996-97; Durham University to Zimbabwe 1997-98; Hampshire to Boland 2001; England A to Malaysia and India 2003-04
Overseas teams played for: Maties (Stellenbosch University), South Africa 2000; Melville CC, Perth 2001
Cricket moments to forget: 'Whole of the B&H competition 2002'
Cricketers particularly admired: Malcolm Marshall, Richard Hadlee, Allan Donald, Graham Dilley
Other sports played: Golf, hockey (England U18 1995)
Relaxations: 'Films, sleeping, reading, listening to music'
Extras: Played in Durham University's BUSA Championship-winning side 1999. Took hat-trick v Loughborough UCCE at Taunton 2003. ECB National Academy 2003-04. His 8-66 v Derbyshire at Derby in the C&G 2004 is the best return by a Somerset bowler in one-day cricket. Released by Somerset at the end of the 2006 season
Best batting: 44 Somerset v Yorkshire, Taunton 2003
Best bowling: 5-42 Somerset v Glamorgan, Taunton 2004

2006 Season

	M	Inn	NO	Runs	HS	Avg	100	50	Ct	St	Balls	Runs	Wkts	Avg	BB	5I	10M
Test																	
FC	3	5	1	85	38	21.25	-	-	1	-	330	237	4	59.25	3-61	-	-
ODI																	
List A	1	0	0	0	0		-	-	1	-	48	41	0		-	-	
20/20 Int																	
20/20	1	0	0	0	0		-	-	-	-	18	47	0		-	-	

Career Performances

	M	Inn	NO	Runs	HS	Avg	100	50	Ct	St	Balls	Runs	Wkts	Avg	BB	5I	10M
Test																	
FC	58	77	33	509	44	11.56	-	-	18	-	8511	5521	135	40.89	5-42	3	-
ODI																	
List A	70	36	17	240	33 *	12.63	-	-	16	-	2929	2644	77	34.33	8-66	1	
20/20 Int																	
20/20	20	9	4	31	9 *	6.20	-	-	4	-	360	598	10	59.80	2-22	-	

FRANKLIN, J. E. C. — Glamorgan

Name: James Edward Charles Franklin
Role: Left-hand bat, left-arm
fast-medium bowler; all-rounder
Born: 7 November 1980, Wellington,
New Zealand
Height: 6ft 4in **Weight:** 15st
Nickname: Tank
County debut: 2004 (Gloucestershire),
2006 (Glamorgan)
County cap: 2004 (Gloucestershire),
2006 (Glamorgan)
Test debut: 2000-01
ODI debut: 2000-01
Twenty20 Int debut: 2005-06
1st-Class 200s: 1
Place in batting averages: 178th av. 24.71
Place in bowling averages: 49th av. 30.64
Strike rate: 48.70 (career 46.76)
Parents: Monica and Russell
Marital status: Engaged
Family links with cricket: 'No family links, which means I am not related to Trevor Franklin and Clive Franklin!'
Education: Wellington College, New Zealand
Off-season: 'Playing more cricket back home'
Overseas tours: New Zealand U19 to South Africa (U19 World Cup) 1997-98, to Sri Lanka (U19 World Cup) 1999-2000; New Zealand A to South Africa 2004-05, to Sri Lanka 2005-06; New Zealand to Australia 2001-02 (VB Series), to England 2004, to Bangladesh 2004-05, to Australia 2004-05, to Zimbabwe 2005-06, to South Africa 2005-06, to India (ICC Champions Trophy) 2006-07, to Australia (C'wealth Bank Series) 2006-07, plus one-day tournaments in Sharjah
Overseas teams played for: Wellington 1998-99 –
Career highlights to date: 'Winning Test matches'
Cricket moments to forget: 'Being hit for four consecutive sixes by Shaun Pollock!'
Cricket superstitions: 'None. Plenty of routines, though'
Cricketers particularly admired: Wasim Akram, Mark Waugh
Young players to look out for: Ross Taylor, Jesse Ryder, Richard Sherlock
Other sports played: Football ('college 1st XI; could have gone on, chose cricket!')
Other sports followed: Rugby (Hurricanes, All Blacks), football (Liverpool FC), baseball (NY Yankees)
Injuries: Knee and back injuries
Favourite band: Fat Freddys Drop

Relaxations: 'Watching TV; taking the p--- out of Gareth Rees and Robert Croft'
Extras: Represented New Zealand U19. New Zealand Academy 1999-2000. Man of the Match v England at Riverside in the NatWest Series 2004 (5-42). Was an overseas player with Gloucestershire for part of the 2004 season. Took 7-60 v Lancashire at Cheltenham 2004, the best figures by a bowler on Championship debut for Gloucestershire since 1900. Became the second New Zealand cricketer to take a Test hat-trick (Manjural Islam Rana, Mohammad Rafique, Tapash Baisya), in the first Test v Bangladesh at Dhaka 2004-05. Scored maiden Test century (122*) in the second Test v South Africa at Cape Town 2005-06, batting at No. 9. An overseas player with Glamorgan 2006
Opinions on cricket: 'We need longer lunch and tea breaks. Let's get crowds back to four- and five-day cricket. More cricket games should be played at Colwyn Bay CC.'
Best batting: 208 Wellington v Auckland, Wellington 2005-06
Best bowling: 7-30 Wellington v Central Districts, Wellington 2005-06

2006 Season

	M	Inn	NO	Runs	HS	Avg	100	50	Ct	St	Balls	Runs	Wkts	Avg	BB	5I	10M
Test																	
FC	9	15	1	346	94	24.71	-	2	4	-	1510	950	31	30.64	5-68	1	-
ODI																	
List A	10	9	4	209	68 *	41.80	-	1	1	-	372	367	9	40.77	2-26	-	
20/20 Int																	
20/20	8	6	2	127	69 *	31.75	-	1	-	-	155	229	5	45.80	1-23	-	

Career Performances

	M	Inn	NO	Runs	HS	Avg	100	50	Ct	St	Balls	Runs	Wkts	Avg	BB	5I	10M
Test	19	25	5	460	122 *	23.00	1	1	7	-	3205	1970	70	28.14	6-119	3	-
FC	85	125	19	2921	208	27.55	3	12	27	-	13983	7334	299	24.52	7-30	11	1
ODI	41	25	6	221	29 *	11.63	-	-	13	-	1692	1468	37	39.67	5-42	1	
List A	110	84	27	1243	76	21.80	-	5	36	-	4874	3824	118	32.40	5-42	1	
20/20 Int	1	1	1	13	13 *		-	-	1	-	24	21	0		-	-	
20/20	12	10	3	233	69 *	33.28	-	1	3	-	245	337	5	67.40	1-23	-	

FRANKS, P. J.   Nottinghamshire

Name: <u>Paul</u> John Franks
Role: Left-hand bat, right-arm
fast-medium bowler; all-rounder
Born: 3 February 1979, Sutton-in-Ashfield
Height: 6ft 2in **Weight:** 14st
Nickname: Franksie, Pike
County debut: 1996
County cap: 1999
Benefit: 2007
ODI debut: 2000
50 wickets in a season: 2
Place in batting averages: 199th av. 22.11
Place in bowling averages: 146th av. 59.50
Strike rate: 93.05 (career 56.95)
Parents: Patricia and John
Wife and date of marriage: Helen,
1 October 2005
Family links with cricket: 'Dad was league
legend for 25 years'
Education: Minster School, Southwell; West Notts College
Qualifications: 7 GCSEs, GNVQ (Advanced) Leisure Management, coaching Level 1
Overseas tours: England U19 to Pakistan 1996-97, to South Africa (including U19
World Cup) 1997-98; England A to Zimbabwe and South Africa 1998-99, to
Bangladesh and New Zealand 1999-2000, to West Indies 2000-01, to Sri Lanka 2004-
05; Notts CCC to South Africa 1998, 1999
Overseas teams played for: Bellville CC, Cape Town 2006
Career highlights to date: 'England debut. Notts Championship win 2005. Twenty20
finals day 2006'
Cricket moments to forget: 'Being injured'
Cricketers particularly admired: Ian Botham, Andrew Flintoff, Chris Cairns,
Mark Ealham
Young players to look out for: Lewis Bramley, Andy Bell, Michael Bell, Sam Wood
Other sports played: Golf
Other sports followed: Football (Mansfield Town)
Injuries: Broken toe – no time out ('big heart')
Favourite band: The Killers, Red Hot Chili Peppers
Relaxations: 'TV; temperature control of Guinness!'
Extras: Took Championship hat-trick (Penney, Brown, Welch) v Warwickshire at
Trent Bridge 1997 (aged 18 years 163 days). Won U19 World Cup winner's medal in
Johannesburg 1998. NBC Denis Compton Award 1999. Cricket Writers' Young Player
of the Year 2000. Vice-captain of Nottinghamshire 2003-04. ECB National Academy
2004-05. 'Youngest Notts player to be awarded a benefit year, aged 28'

Opinions on cricket: 'Pitches better; balls crap; game great!'
Best batting: 123* Nottinghamshire v Leicestershire, Leicester 2003
Best bowling: 7-56 Nottinghamshire v Middlesex, Lord's 2000

2006 Season

	M	Inn	NO	Runs	HS	Avg	100	50	Ct	St	Balls	Runs	Wkts	Avg	BB	5I	10M
Test																	
FC	14	20	3	376	64	22.11	-	3	1	-	1675	1071	18	59.50	2-24	-	-
ODI																	
List A	10	8	1	107	40	15.28	-	-	-	-	159	154	4	38.50	2-5	-	
20/20 Int																	
20/20	10	3	1	11	11	5.50	-	-	1	-	90	143	6	23.83	2-19	-	

Career Performances

	M	Inn	NO	Runs	HS	Avg	100	50	Ct	St	Balls	Runs	Wkts	Avg	BB	5I	10M
Test																	
FC	135	197	40	4157	123 *	26.47	3	20	44	-	20675	11406	363	31.42	7-56	11	-
ODI	1	1	0	4	4	4.00	-	-	1	-	54	48	0		-	-	
List A	135	101	29	1527	84 *	21.20	-	4	20	-	5339	4273	159	26.87	6-27	2	
20/20 Int																	
20/20	26	17	7	196	29 *	19.60	-	-	4	-	129	194	9	21.55	2-19	-	

FROST, T.   Warwickshire

Name: Tony Frost
Role: Right-hand bat, wicket-keeper
Born: 17 November 1975, Stoke-on-Trent
Height: 5ft 10in **Weight:** 10st 6lbs
County debut: 1997
County cap: 1999
50 dismissals in a season: 1
Place in batting averages: 32nd av. 53.87
(2005 214th av. 20.95)
Parents: Ivan and Christine
Marital status: Single
Family links with cricket: Father played for
Staffordshire
Education: James Brinkley High School;
Stoke-on-Trent College
Qualifications: 5 GCSEs
Overseas tours: Kidsgrove U18 to Australia
1990-91
Other sports followed: Football, golf

Extras: Represented Staffordshire at all levels from U11 to U19. Won Texaco U16 competition with Staffordshire in 1992. Played for Development of Excellence XI U17, U18, and U19. Scored century (135*) v Sussex at Horsham 2004, in the process setting with Ian Bell (262*) a new Warwickshire record partnership for the seventh wicket (289*). C&G Man of the Match award in the semi-final v Lancashire at Edgbaston 2005. Retired at the end of the 2006 season

Best batting: 135* Warwickshire v Sussex, Horsham 2004

2006 Season

	M	Inn	NO	Runs	HS	Avg	100	50	Ct	St	Balls	Runs	Wkts	Avg	BB	5I	10M
Test																	
FC	8	13	5	431	96	53.87	-	4	20	-	0	0	0		-	-	-
ODI																	
List A	6	4	1	71	30	23.66	-	-	6	1	0	0	0		-	-	
20/20 Int																	
20/20	6	3	1	42	33 *	21.00	-	-	4	1	0	0	0		-	-	

Career Performances

	M	Inn	NO	Runs	HS	Avg	100	50	Ct	St	Balls	Runs	Wkts	Avg	BB	5I	10M
Test																	
FC	92	134	21	3178	135 *	28.12	3	16	225	16	12	15	0		-	-	-
ODI																	
List A	79	43	16	485	47	17.96	-	-	76	19	0	0	0		-	-	
20/20 Int																	
20/20	13	7	2	92	33 *	18.40	-	-	10	8	0	0	0		-	-	

FULTON, D. P.   Kent

Name: David (Dave) Paul Fulton
Role: Right-hand top-order bat, left-arm spin bowler, occasional wicket-keeper
Born: 15 November 1971, Lewisham
Height: 6ft 2in **Weight:** 12st 7lbs
Nickname: Tav, Rave
County debut: 1992
County cap: 1998
Benefit: 2006
1000 runs in a season: 3
1st-Class 200s: 2
Place in batting averages: 80th av. 38.76 (2005 153rd av. 29.75)
Strike rate: (career 193.00)
Parents: John and Ann
Wife and date of marriage: Claudine Kay Tomlin, 19 December 2003
Children: Freddie Tom, 30 September 2004

Family links with cricket: Father played for village

Education: The Judd School, Tonbridge; University of Kent at Canterbury

Qualifications: 10 GCSEs, 3 A-levels, BA (Hons) Politics and International Relations, advanced cricket coach, rugby coach, gym instructor qualification

Career outside cricket: Journalist

Overseas tours: Kent SCA U17 to Singapore and New Zealand 1987-88; Kent to France 1998, to Port Elizabeth 2001

Overseas teams played for: Avendale CC, Cape Town 1993-94; Victoria CC, Cape Town 1994-95; University of WA, Perth 1995-96; Petersham-Marrickville CC, Sydney 1998-99, 1999-2000

Career highlights: 'Will Kendall caught and bowled Fulton (first and only first-class victim). PCA Player of the Year 2001'

Cricket moments to forget: 'Already forgotten'

Cricketers particularly admired: Gordon Greenidge, Graham Gooch, Courtney Walsh, Steve Waugh

Other sports played: Chess (England junior), table tennis ('top 10 in UK as a junior'; played for South England juniors); rugby, football, tennis, golf, squash

Other sports followed: Football (Nottingham Forest), rugby (Harlequins)

Relaxations: 'Reading, music, fitness; walking Poppy, our dog'

Player website: www.davidfulton2006.com

Extras: Was the last person to catch Viv Richards in a first-class match, in 1993. Scored double century (208*) and century (104*) v Somerset at Canterbury 2001, also taking seven catches in the match. First batsman to 1000 first-class runs in 2001 and the season's leading English batsman in terms of runs scored and average with 1892 runs (av. 75.68). Kent Batsman of the Year (Denness Award) 2001. PCA Player of the Year 2001. Captain of Kent in County Championship 2002; overall captain of Kent 2003-05. Retired at the end of the 2006 season

Best batting: 208* Kent v Somerset, Canterbury 2001

Best bowling: 1-37 Kent v Oxford University, Canterbury 1996

2006 Season

	M	Inn	NO	Runs	HS	Avg	100	50	Ct	St	Balls	Runs	Wkts	Avg	BB	5I	10M
Test																	
FC	15	26	1	969	155	38.76	2	6	7	-		6	3	0		-	-
ODI																	
List A																	
20/20 Int																	
20/20																	

	M	Inn	NO	Runs	HS	Avg	100	50	Ct	St	Balls	Runs	Wkts	Avg	BB	5I	10M
Test																	
FC	200	352	20	12125	208 *	36.52	28	53	266	-	193	120	1	120.00	1-37	-	-
ODI																	
List A	108	99	5	1962	82	20.87	-	7	46	-	6	9	0		-	-	
20/20 Int																	
20/20	5	4	2	40	15	20.00	-	-	1	-	0	0	0		-	-	

GALE, A. W. Yorkshire

Name: <u>Andrew</u> William Gale
Role: Left-hand bat, right-arm off-spin bowler, part-time wicket-keeper
Born: 28 November 1983, Dewsbury
Height: 6ft 2in **Weight:** 13st 7lbs
Nickname: Galey, G-Unit, G-Banger
County debut: 2004
Place in batting averages: 182nd av. 24.33
Parents: Denise and Alan
Marital status: 'Attached'
Family links with cricket: 'Grandad'
Education: Whitcliffe Mount; Heckmondwike Grammar
Qualifications: 10 GCSEs, 3 A-levels, Level 3 cricket coaching
Career outside cricket: 'Cricket coaching company'
Off-season: 'Improving business'

Overseas tours: England U17 to Australia 2001; England U19 to Australia 2002-03; Yorkshire to Grenada 2001, to India 2005
Overseas teams played for: Blacktown, Sydney 2004-05
Career highlights to date: 'Scoring maiden first-class hundred'
Cricket moments to forget: 'Dropping catch at Old Trafford'
Cricket superstitions: 'No odd numbers'
Cricketers particularly admired: Marcus Trescothick, Darren Lehmann
Young players to look out for: Mark Lawson, Adil Rashid, Joe Sayers
Other sports played: Football (Batley Old Boys)
Other sports followed: Football (Huddersfield Town), rugby league (Bradford Bulls)
Favourite band: Simply Red
Relaxations: 'PlayStation'
Extras: Played for England age-groups from U15. Yorkshire League Young Batsman of the Year 2002

Opinions on cricket: 'No Kolpaks [*see page 13*], one overseas – will allow more English talent to come through and express themselves. Can only be better for England team.'

Best batting: 149 Yorkshire v Warwickshire, Scarborough 2006

2006 Season

	M	Inn	NO	Runs	HS	Avg	100	50	Ct	St	Balls	Runs	Wkts	Avg	BB	5I	10M
Test																	
FC	5	9	0	219	149	24.33	1	-	2	-	0	0	0		-	-	-
ODI																	
List A	9	7	1	211	63 *	35.16	-	1	1	-	0	0	0		-	-	
20/20 Int																	
20/20	9	7	1	109	50	18.16	-	1	5	-	0	0	0		-	-	

Career Performances

	M	Inn	NO	Runs	HS	Avg	100	50	Ct	St	Balls	Runs	Wkts	Avg	BB	5I	10M
Test																	
FC	9	16	0	297	149	18.56	1	-	4	-	0	0	0		-	-	-
ODI																	
List A	26	24	2	515	70 *	23.40	-	2	7	-	0	0	0		-	-	
20/20 Int																	
20/20	12	10	1	165	50	18.33	-	1	7	-	0	0	0		-	-	

GALLIAN, J. E. R.   Nottinghamshire

Name: <u>Jason</u> Edward Riche Gallian
Role: Right-hand bat, right-arm
medium bowler
Born: 25 June 1971, Manly, NSW, Australia
Height: 6ft **Weight:** 14st 7lbs
Nickname: Gal
County debut: 1990 (Lancashire),
1998 (Nottinghamshire)
County cap: 1994 (Lancashire),
1998 (Nottinghamshire)
Benefit: 2005 (Nottinghamshire)
Test debut: 1995
1000 runs in a season: 6
1st-Class 300s: 1
Place in batting averages: 160th av. 28.29
(2005 24th av. 53.04)
Strike rate: (career 74.50)
Parents: Ray and Marilyn

Wife and date of marriage: Charlotte, 2 October 1999
Children: Tom, 11 May 2001; Harry, 8 September 2003; Emily, 6 October 2006
Family links with cricket: Father played for Stockport
Education: The Pittwater House Schools, Australia; Oxford University
Qualifications: Higher School Certificate, Diploma in Social Studies (Keble College, Oxford)
Career outside cricket: 'Involved in a media training company'
Overseas tours: Australia U20 to West Indies 1989-90; England A to India 1994-95, to Pakistan 1995-96, to Australia 1996-97; England to South Africa 1995-96; Nottinghamshire to Johannesburg 2000, to South Africa 2001; MCC to UAE and Oman 2004
Overseas teams played for: NSW U19 1988-89; NSW Colts and NSW 2nd XI 1990-91; Manly 1993-94
Career highlights to date: 'First Test match'
Cricket moments to forget: 'Breaking a finger in my first Test match'
Cricket superstitions: 'None'
Cricketers particularly admired: Desmond Haynes, Mike Gatting
Young players to look out for: Charlie Shreck, Samit Patel
Other sports followed: Rugby league and union, football
Injuries: Out for six weeks with a stress fracture of the foot
Favourite band: Midnight Oil
Relaxations: 'Looking after the kids'
Extras: Represented Australia YC 1988-90 (captain v England YC 1989-90); also represented Australia U20 and U21 1991-92. Took wicket of D. A. Hagan of Oxford University with his first ball in first-class cricket 1990. Played for Oxford University and Combined Universities 1992; captained Oxford University 1993. Qualified to play for England 1994. Recorded highest individual score in history of Old Trafford with his 312 v Derbyshire in 1996. Captain of Nottinghamshire from part-way through the 1998 season to 2002 and in 2004; Nottinghamshire club captain and captain in first-class cricket 2003
Opinions on cricket: 'Four-day cricket should be more in line with Test matches – two-hour sessions, time made up if lost during game. More 50-over cricket to develop World Cup cricketers.'
Best batting: 312 Lancashire v Derbyshire, Old Trafford 1996
Best bowling: 6-115 Lancashire v Surrey, Southport 1996

2006 Season

	M	Inn	NO	Runs	HS	Avg	100	50	Ct	St	Balls	Runs	Wkts	Avg	BB	5I	10M
Test																	
FC	14	24	0	679	171	28.29	2	3	17	-	0	0	0		-	-	-
ODI																	
List A	3	3	0	100	91	33.33	-	1	3	-	0	0	0		-	-	
20/20 Int																	
20/20																	

Career Performances

	M	Inn	NO	Runs	HS	Avg	100	50	Ct	St	Balls	Runs	Wkts	Avg	BB	5I	10M
Test	3	6	0	74	28	12.33	-	-	1	-	84	62	0		-	-	
FC	218	374	35	13233	312	39.03	34	63	191	-	7078	4099	95	43.14	6-115	1	-
ODI																	
List A	209	205	15	5855	134	30.81	8	36	71	-	2049	1808	55	32.87	5-15	1	
20/20 Int																	
20/20	8	8	0	152	62	19.00	-	1	1	-	0	0	0		-	-	

GANGULY, S. C. Northamptonshire

Name: <u>Sourav</u> Chandidas Ganguly
Role: Left-hand bat, right-arm medium bowler
Born: 8 July 1972, Kolkata (Calcutta), India
Height: 5ft 11in
County debut: 2000 (Lancashire), 2005 (Glamorgan), 2006 (Northamptonshire)
Test debut: 1996
ODI debut: 1991-92
1st-Class 200s: 2
Place in batting averages: (2005 10th av. 62.57)
Strike rate: (career 65.50)
Family links with cricket: Brother Snehasish played for Bengal 1986-87 – 1996-97
Education: St Xavier's College
Overseas tours: India U19 to Bangladesh (Beximco Asia Youth Cup) 1989-90; India to Australia 1991-92, to England 1996, to South Africa 1996-97, to West Indies 1996-97, to Sri Lanka 1997, to Zimbabwe 1998-99, to Bangladesh (Wills International Cup) 1998-99, to New Zealand 1998-99, to UK, Ireland and Netherlands (World Cup) 1999, to Australia 1999-2000, to Kenya (ICC Knockout Trophy) 2000-01 (c), to Bangladesh 2000-01 (c), to Zimbabwe 2001 (c), to Sri Lanka 2001 (c), to South Africa 2001-02 (c), to West Indies 2001-02 (c), to England 2002 (c), to Sri Lanka (ICC Champions Trophy) 2002-03 (c), to New Zealand 2002-03 (c), to Africa (World Cup) 2002-03 (c), to Australia 2003-04 (c), to Pakistan 2003-04 (c), to England (ICC Champions Trophy) 2004 (c), to Bangladesh 2004-05 (c), to Zimbabwe 2005-06 (c), to Pakistan 2005-06, to South Africa 2006-07, plus other one-day tournaments in Sri Lanka, Toronto, Pakistan, Sharjah, Bangladesh, Singapore, Kenya, Netherlands, England; Asian Cricket Council XI to Australia (Tsunami Relief) 2004-05 (c)
Overseas teams played for: Bengal 1989-90 –

Extras: Scored century (131) on Test debut, v England at Lord's 1996, and another (136) in the following Test at Trent Bridge to become the third player, after Lawrence Rowe and Alvin Kallicharran, to score a century in his first two Test innings. Was one of *Indian Cricket*'s five Cricketers of the Year 1996. Scored 183 v Sri Lanka at Taunton in the 1999 World Cup, sharing with Rahul Dravid in a second-wicket stand of 318, a then ODI (and still a World Cup) record for any wicket. CEAT International Player of the Year 2000. His many, many awards include Man of the [ODI] Series v West Indies 2001-02 and Man of the Match in the first Test v Australia at Brisbane 2003-04 (144). Captain of India from February 2000 to October 2005. Was Lancashire's overseas player in 2000; an overseas player with Glamorgan in 2005; and an overseas player with Northamptonshire during the 2006 season as a locum for Chris Rogers

Best batting: 200* Bengal v Tripura, Kolkata 1993-94
200* Bengal v Bihar, Kolkata 1994-95
Best bowling: 6-46 Bengal v Orissa, Kolkata 2000-01

2006 Season

	M	Inn	NO	Runs	HS	Avg	100	50	Ct	St	Balls	Runs	Wkts	Avg	BB	5I	10M
Test																	
FC	4	6	1	24	9	4.80	-	-	-	-	252	131	3	43.66	1-19	-	-
ODI																	
List A	2	2	0	80	71	40.00	-	1	-	-	78	65	0			-	-
20/20 Int																	
20/20	9	9	1	220	73	27.50	-	1	5	-	186	249	11	22.63	2-17	-	

Career Performances

	M	Inn	NO	Runs	HS	Avg	100	50	Ct	St	Balls	Runs	Wkts	Avg	BB	5I	10M
Test	88	140	12	5221	173	40.78	12	25	59	-	2516	1419	26	54.57	3-28	-	-
FC	207	320	38	12277	200 *	43.53	25	71	149	-	9695	5505	148	37.19	6-46	4	-
ODI	279	270	21	10123	183	40.65	22	60	96	-	4123	3470	93	37.31	5-16	2	
List A	385	371	39	13840	183	41.68	31	81	124	-	7319	5928	161	36.81	5-16	2	
20/20 Int																	
20/20	15	14	1	334	73	25.69	-	1	6	-	264	353	16	22.06	3-27	-	

GAZZARD, C. M. Somerset

Name: <u>Carl</u> Matthew Gazzard
Role: Right-hand bat, wicket-keeper
Born: 15 April 1982, Penzance
Height: 6ft **Weight:** 13st
Nickname: Gazza, Sling Boy, Coral
County debut: 2002
Place in batting averages: 241st av. 15.25
(2005 191st av. 23.75)
Parents: Paul and Alison
Marital status: Single
Family links with cricket: Father and
brother both played for Cornwall Schools;
mother's a keen follower
Education: Mounts Bay Comprehensive;
Richard Huish College, Taunton
Qualifications: 10 GCSEs, 2 A-levels,
Levels 1 and 2 coaching
Overseas tours: Cornwall Schools U13 to

Johannesburg; West of England U15 to West Indies; Somerset Academy to
Durban 1999
Overseas teams played for: Subiaco-Floreat, Perth 2000-01; Scarborough, Perth
2002-03
Career highlights to date: '157 v Derby in totesport game [2004]'
Cricket moments to forget: 'Dislocating my shoulder in Perth – kept me out for
2001 season'
Cricket superstitions: 'None'
Cricketers particularly admired: Marcus Trescothick, Graham Rose
Young players to look out for: James Hildreth
Other sports played: Football (played through the age groups for Cornwall)
Other sports followed: Football (West Ham United)
Favourite band: Red Hot Chili Peppers
Relaxations: 'Walking Stella and Elle. Following the Pilgrims with JP'
Extras: Played for England U13, U14, U15, U19. Won the Graham Kersey Award for
Best Wicket-keeper at Bunbury Festival. Played for Cornwall in Minor Counties aged
16. Scored 136-ball 157 (his maiden one-day century) v Derbyshire at Derby in the
totesport League 2004. Man of the Match in Twenty20 Cup semi-final v Leicestershire
at The Oval 2005
Best batting: 74 Somerset v Worcestershire, Worcester 2005

2006 Season

	M	Inn	NO	Runs	HS	Avg	100	50	Ct	St	Balls	Runs	Wkts	Avg	BB	5I	10M
Test																	
FC	13	22	2	305	35	15.25	-	-	32	-	0	0	0		-	-	-
ODI																	
List A	14	11	2	91	16	10.11	-	-	15	1	0	0	0		-	-	
20/20 Int																	
20/20	8	3	1	19	10 *	9.50	-	-	6	1	0	0	0		-	-	

Career Performances

	M	Inn	NO	Runs	HS	Avg	100	50	Ct	St	Balls	Runs	Wkts	Avg	BB	5I	10M
Test																	
FC	27	42	6	732	74	20.33	-	1	58	1	0	0	0		-	-	
ODI																	
List A	52	44	4	924	157	23.10	1	4	48	6	0	0	0		-	-	
20/20 Int																	
20/20	25	17	4	221	39	17.00	-	-	13	5	0	0	0		-	-	

GIBSON, O. D.   Durham

Name: <u>Ottis</u> Delroy Gibson
Role: Right-hand bat, 'right-arm gas' bowler; bowling all-rounder
Born: 16 March 1969, Barbados
Height: 6ft 2in **Weight:** 13st 7lbs
Nickname: Gibbo
County debut: 1994 (Glamorgan), 2004 (Leicestershire), 2006 (Durham)
County cap: 2004 (Leicestershire)
Test debut: 1995
ODI debut: 1995-96
50 wickets in a season: 2
Place in batting averages: 115th av. 33.11 (2005 230th av. 18.95)
Place in bowling averages: 44th av. 29.75 (2005 95th av. 37.37)
Strike rate: 48.32 (career 51.05)
Parents: Barry
Marital status: 'Girlfriend'
Children: Michael James
Education: Ellerslie Secondary School, Barbados
Qualifications: Level 4 coaching certificate

Career outside cricket: Coaching
Off-season: Coaching
Overseas tours: West Indies A to Sri Lanka 1996-97, to South Africa 1997-98; West Indies to England 1995, to Australia 1995-96, to India and Pakistan (World Cup) 1995-96, to Malaysia (Commonwealth Games) 1998-99, to South Africa 1998-99, plus one-day tournament in Sharjah
Overseas teams played for: Barbados 1990-91 – 1997-98; Border 1992-93 – 1994-95; Griqualand West 1998-99 – 1999-2000; Gauteng 2000-01
Career highlights to date: 'Making debut for West Indies'
Cricket moments to forget: 'My 14 overs for 101 v Hampshire this season [2006]'
Cricket superstitions: 'None'
Cricketers particularly admired: Malcolm Marshall, Courtney Walsh, Allan Donald
Young players to look out for: Ben Harmison, Stuart Broad
Other sports played: Basketball (district), football, golf
Other sports followed: 'All sports', football (Man United), basketball (Lakers)
Injuries: Out for four weeks for a groin operation; also suffered broken wrist
Favourite band: Oasis, 'any reggae band'
Relaxations: 'Watching TV'
Extras: One of *South African Cricket Annual*'s five Cricketers of the Year 1993. Was Glamorgan overseas player 1994-96. Scored maiden first-class century (101*) from 69 balls for West Indians v Somerset at Taunton 1995, batting at No. 9. Has won numerous domestic match awards and was also Man of the Match v Australia at Brisbane in B&H World Series Cup 1995-96 (40-ball 52/2-38). Leicestershire Player of the Year 2004. Scored century (155) v Yorkshire at Headingley 2006, in the process sharing with Dale Benkenstein (151) in a new record seventh-wicket partnership for Durham (315). Is UK resident and no longer considered an overseas player
Opinions on cricket: 'Championship should be maximum 96 overs in a day; early start to make up lost time.'
Best batting: 155 Durham v Yorkshire, Headingley 2006
Best bowling: 7-55 Border v Natal, Durban 1994-95

2006 Season

	M	Inn	NO	Runs	HS	Avg	100	50	Ct	St	Balls	Runs	Wkts	Avg	BB	5I	10M
Test																	
FC	13	22	4	596	155	33.11	1	2	5	-	2368	1458	49	29.75	6-110	1	-
ODI																	
List A	10	5	1	32	13	8.00	-	-	3	-	476	403	13	31.00	4-63	-	
20/20 Int																	
20/20	1	1	0	2	2	2.00	-	-	1	-	18	32	0		-	-	

Career Performances

	M	Inn	NO	Runs	HS	Avg	100	50	Ct	St	Balls	Runs	Wkts	Avg	BB	5I	10M
Test	2	4	0	93	37	23.25	-	-	-	-	472	275	3	91.66	2-81	-	-
FC	162	244	34	5026	155	23.93	2	25	62	-	29562	16659	579	28.77	7-55	24	5
ODI	15	11	1	141	52	14.10	-	1	3	-	739	621	34	18.26	5-40	2	
List A	194	148	32	2428	102 *	20.93	1	5	55	-	9042	6852	276	24.82	5-19	5	
20/20 Int																	
20/20	19	14	2	141	18	11.75	-	-	6	-	385	480	16	30.00	2-20	-	

GIDMAN, A. P. R.   Gloucestershire

Name: Alexander (<u>Alex</u>) Peter Richard Gidman
Role: Right-hand bat, right-arm medium bowler, county vice-captain
Born: 22 June 1981, High Wycombe
Height: 6ft 2in **Weight:** 14st
Nickname: G, Giddo
County debut: 2001 (one-day), 2002 (first-class)
County cap: 2004
1000 runs in a season: 2
Place in batting averages: 44th av. 49.76 (2005 85th av. 37.48)
Place in bowling averages: 127th av. 44.82 (2005 103rd av. 39.07)
Strike rate: 81.88 (career 72.23)
Parents: Alistair and Jane
Marital status: Single
Family links with cricket: Brother is at Durham CCC
Education: Wycliffe College, Stonehouse, Gloucestershire
Qualifications: 6 GCSEs, 1 A-level, GNVQ Level 2 in Leisure and Tourism
Overseas tours: MCC Young Cricketers to Cape Town 1999; Gloucestershire to South Africa; England A to Malaysia and India 2003-04 (c), to Sri Lanka 2004-05

Overseas teams played for: Albion CC, New Zealand 2001
Career highlights to date: 'Two C&G Trophy final victories. Academy captain'
Cricket moments to forget: 'C&G quarter-final loss to Kent 2002'
Cricket superstitions: 'None'
Cricketers particularly admired: Steve Waugh
Young players to look out for: Steve Snell
Other sports played: Golf
Other sports followed: Football (Wolves), rugby (Gloucester)
Favourite band: Matchbox Twenty, Train
Relaxations: 'Just chilling out; movies, golf'
Extras: Gloucestershire Young Player of the Year 2002, 2003. NBC Denis Compton Award for the most promising young Gloucestershire player 2002, 2003. ECB National Academy 2003-04, 2004-05. Gloucestershire Players' Player of the Year 2006. Vice-captain of Gloucestershire since 2006
Best batting: 142 Gloucestershire v Surrey, Bristol 2005
Best bowling: 4-47 Gloucestershire v Glamorgan, Cardiff 2005

2006 Season

	M	Inn	NO	Runs	HS	Avg	100	50	Ct	St	Balls	Runs	Wkts	Avg	BB	5I	10M
Test																	
FC	16	31	6	1244	120	49.76	4	7	2	-	1392	762	17	44.82	3-38	-	-
ODI																	
List A	15	14	1	336	84	25.84	-	2	4	-	330	295	11	26.81	3-21	-	
20/20 Int																	
20/20	8	8	3	175	52 *	35.00	-	1	2	-	36	59	2	29.50	1-2	-	

Career Performances

	M	Inn	NO	Runs	HS	Avg	100	50	Ct	St	Balls	Runs	Wkts	Avg	BB	5I	10M
Test																	
FC	68	121	13	4111	142	38.06	8	26	42	-	4695	3025	65	46.53	4-47	-	-
ODI																	
List A	86	78	10	1656	84	24.35	-	8	31	-	1360	1188	28	42.42	3-21	-	
20/20 Int																	
20/20	22	17	4	345	61	26.53	-	2	7	-	48	84	3	28.00	1-2	-	

GIDMAN, W. R. S.   Durham

Name: William (<u>Will</u>) Robert Simon Gidman
Role: Left-hand bat, right-arm medium bowler; all-rounder
Born: 14 February 1985, High Wycombe
Height: 6ft 2in   **Weight:** 12st 7lbs
Nickname: Gidders, Giddo
County debut: No first-team appearance
Parents: Alistair and Jane
Marital status: Single
Family links with cricket: Brother of Alex Gidman, vice-captain of Gloucestershire
Education: Wycliffe College, Stonehouse, Gloucestershire; Berkshire College of Agriculture
Qualifications: 7 GCSEs, Level 2 cricket coaching, Level 1 rugby and football coaching
Career outside cricket: 'Part-time teacher'
Off-season: 'I have spent a couple of winters working as a part-time teacher at Wycliffe College'
Overseas tours: Wycliffe College to South Africa 2000; MCC YC to Sri Lanka 2004, to India 2005, to Lanzarote 2006
Overseas teams played for: Gold Coast Dolphins, Australia 2004-05
Career highlights to date: 'Signing for Durham CCC'
Cricket moments to forget: 'Giving away four overthrows off Freddie Flintoff's bowling whilst doing 12th man duties for England against Bangladesh'
Cricket superstitions: 'None'
Cricketers particularly admired: Gary Sobers, Graham Thorpe, Mike Hussey, Alex Gidman
Young players to look out for: Kevin Jones
Other sports played: Football (Stroud and District), rugby, golf, table tennis
Other sports followed: Football (Wolves), rugby (Gloucester)
Favourite band: Embrace
Relaxations: 'Music, TV, walking the dog, Sudoku'
Extras: Was first Gloucestershire U10 to score a hundred. Played for Gloucestershire Board XI in the 2003 C&G. MCC YC cap
Opinions on cricket: 'I love the traditions of our game and the thought of things like drop-in pitches and taking too many decisions away from the umpires in the middle, I am not sure about.'

Career Performances

	M	Inn	NO	Runs	HS	Avg	100	50	Ct	St	Balls	Runs	Wkts	Avg	BB	5I	10M
Test																	
FC																	
ODI																	
List A	1	1	0	12	12	12.00	-	-	-	-	0	0	0		-	-	
20/20 Int																	
20/20																	

GIFFORD, W. M. Worcestershire

Name: William (<u>Will</u>) McLean Gifford
Role: Right-hand bat, right-arm fast-medium bowler
Born: 10 October 1985, Sutton Coldfield
Height: 5ft 11in **Weight:** 13st
Nickname: Giff
County debut: 2006 (one-day)
Parents: Andy and Kim
Marital status: Single
Family links with cricket: 'Dad played local cricket. Brother plays'
Education: Malvern College; Loughborough University
Qualifications: 10 GCSEs, 3 A-levels
Off-season: 'Last year at university'
Overseas tours: Staffordshire U16 to Barbados; Malvern College to South Africa; England U19 to India 2004-05
Career highlights to date: 'England U19 tour and getting contract at Worcestershire'
Cricket superstitions: 'Left pad on first'
Cricketers particularly admired: Graeme Hick, Ricky Ponting
Young players to look out for: Steve Davies, Will Gallimore, Keith Bradley
Other sports played: Hockey (Midlands age-groups), football (England Independent Schools)
Other sports followed: Football (West Brom), rugby (Worcester)
Favourite band: Jimmy Eat World, All-American Rejects
Relaxations: 'A drink with friends, listening to music'
Extras: Captained Loughborough UCCE 2005, 2006. Represented British Universities 2005. Is not related to Norman Gifford

Opinions on cricket: 'Top drawer.'
Best batting: 33 LUCCE v Nottinghamshire, Trent Bridge 2005

2006 Season

	M	Inn	NO	Runs	HS	Avg	100	50	Ct	St	Balls	Runs	Wkts	Avg	BB	5I	10M
Test																	
FC	2	2	0	0	0	0.00	-	-	-	-	0	0	0		-	-	-
ODI																	
List A	1	1	0	1	1	1.00	-	-	-	-	0	0	0		-	-	
20/20 Int																	
20/20																	

Career Performances

	M	Inn	NO	Runs	HS	Avg	100	50	Ct	St	Balls	Runs	Wkts	Avg	BB	5I	10M
Test																	
FC	5	7	1	78	33	13.00	-	-	3	-	0	0	0		-	-	-
ODI																	
List A	1	1	0	1	1	1.00	-	-	-	-	0	0	0		-	-	
20/20 Int																	
20/20																	

GILBERT, C. R.   Yorkshire

Name: Christopher (<u>Chris</u>) Robert Gilbert
Role: Right-hand bat, right-arm medium bowler; all-rounder
Born: 16 April 1984, Scarborough
Height: 5ft 10in **Weight:** 12st 11lbs
Nickname: Gilly
County debut: 2006 (one-day)
Parents: Roger and Vicky
Marital status: Single
Family links with cricket: 'Dad sports teacher and played some representative. Brother plays for Scarborough and played Yorkshire senior schools'
Education: Scarborough College
Qualifications: Level 2 coaching
Career outside cricket: Coaching
Overseas tours: England U17 to Australia 2001; England U19 to Australia and (U19 World Cup) New Zealand 2001-02

Overseas teams played for: Scarborough, Perth; Upper Valley, New Zealand

Career highlights to date: 'Gaining a contract with Yorkshire'
Cricket moments to forget: 'Getting out to my brother in the league!'
Cricket superstitions: 'None'
Cricketers particularly admired: Craig White, Darren Gough
Young players to look out for: Greg Wood, Mark Lawson
Other sports played: Hockey (England U16, U18)
Other sports followed: Premiership football and rugby
Favourite band: Green Day, Arctic Monkeys, Kaiser Chiefs
Relaxations: 'Travelling'
Extras: Played for Yorkshire Board XI in the 2003 C&G
Opinions on cricket: 'Quick and energetic – good to play and watch.'

2006 Season

	M	Inn	NO	Runs	HS	Avg	100	50	Ct	St	Balls	Runs	Wkts	Avg	BB	5I	10M
Test																	
FC																	
ODI																	
List A	3	3	0	18	9	6.00	-	-	-	-	112	130	6	21.66	3-33	-	
20/20 Int																	
20/20	6	4	1	64	36 *	21.33	-	-	3	-	0	0	0		-	-	

Career Performances

	M	Inn	NO	Runs	HS	Avg	100	50	Ct	St	Balls	Runs	Wkts	Avg	BB	5I	10M
Test																	
FC																	
ODI																	
List A	4	4	0	31	13	7.75	-	-	1	-	154	163	6	27.16	3-33	-	
20/20 Int																	
20/20	6	4	1	64	36 *	21.33	-	-	3	-	0	0	0		-	-	

30. Who played a record 591 matches before he scored
his maiden first-class century?

GILES, A. F. Warwickshire

Name: <u>Ashley</u> Fraser Giles
Role: Right-hand bat, slow left-arm bowler
Born: 19 March 1973, Chertsey, Surrey
Height: 6ft 4in **Weight:** 15st 7lbs
Nickname: Splash, Skinny, Gilo
County debut: 1993
County cap: 1996
Benefit: 2006
Test debut: 1998
ODI debut: 1997
50 wickets in a season: 2
Place in batting averages: (2005 212th av. 21.07)
Place in bowling averages: (2005 58th av. 30.08)
Strike rate: (career 68.67)
Parents: Michael and Paula
Wife and date of marriage: Stine, 9 October 1999
Children: Anders Fraser, 29 May 2000; Matilde, February 2002
Family links with cricket: Father played and brother Andrew a club cricketer at Ripley, Surrey
Education: George Abbott County Secondary, Burpham, Guildford
Qualifications: 9 GCSEs, 2 A-levels, coaching certificate
Overseas tours: Surrey U19 to Barbados 1990-91; Warwickshire to Cape Town 1996, 1997, to Bloemfontein 1998; England A to Australia 1996-97, to Kenya and Sri Lanka 1997-98; England to Sharjah (Champions Trophy) 1997-98, to Bangladesh (Wills International Cup) 1998-99, to Australia 1998-99 (CUB Series), to South Africa and Zimbabwe 1999-2000 (one-day series), to Kenya (ICC Knockout Trophy) 2000-01, to Pakistan and Sri Lanka 2000-01, to India and New Zealand 2001-02, to Sri Lanka (ICC Champions Trophy) 2002-03, to Australia 2002-03, to Africa (World Cup) 2002-03, to Bangladesh and Sri Lanka 2003-04, to West Indies 2003-04, to Zimbabwe (one-day series) 2004-05, to South Africa 2004-05, to Pakistan 2005-06, to Australia 2006-07
Overseas teams played for: Vredenburg/Saldanha, Cape Town 1992-95; Avendale CC, Cape Town 1995-96
Cricketers particularly admired: Dermot Reeve, Tim Munton, Dougie Brown, Ian Botham
Other sports played: Golf (14 handicap), football
Other sports followed: Football (QPR)
Relaxations: 'Cinema, music, spending lots of time with my family'
Extras: Surrey Young Cricketer of the Year 1991. NBC Denis Compton Award for

Warwickshire 1996. Warwickshire Player of the Year 1996 and 2000. Warwickshire Most Improved Player 1996. Cricket Society's Leading Young All-rounder 1996. Scored hundred (123*) and had five-wicket innings return (5-28) v Oxford University at The Parks 1999. Took 17 Test wickets v Pakistan 2000-01, the highest total by an England bowler in a series in Pakistan. Man of the Match in ODI v India at Delhi 2001-02 (5-57). Scored 71* v Essex at Edgbaston in the C&G 2003, sharing with Dougie Brown (108) in a competition record seventh-wicket partnership (170). Man of the Match in the first Test v West Indies at Lord's 2004 (4-129/5-81). One of *Wisden*'s Five Cricketers of the Year 2005. Appointed MBE in 2006 New Year Honours as part of 2005 Ashes-winning England team. England 12-month central contract 2006-07
Best batting: 128* Warwickshire v Sussex, Hove 2000
Best bowling: 8-90 Warwickshire v Northamptonshire, Northampton 2000
Stop press: Returned home early from England tour of Australia 2006-07 to be with his wife, who had been taken ill

---

2006 Season (did not make any first-class or one-day appearances)

Career Performances

	M	Inn	NO	Runs	HS	Avg	100	50	Ct	St	Balls	Runs	Wkts	Avg	BB	5I	10M
Test	52	77	12	1347	59	20.72	-	4	32	-	11688	5544	140	39.60	5-57	5	-
FC	176	245	45	5272	128 *	26.36	3	22	79	-	36812	15696	536	29.28	8-90	26	3
ODI	62	35	13	385	41	17.50	-	-	22	-	2856	2069	55	37.61	5-57	1	
List A	224	141	41	2089	107	20.89	1	5	73	-	9729	6961	272	25.59	5-21	3	
20/20 Int																	
20/20	2	1	1	0	0 *	-	-	-	-	-	42	34	2	17.00	2-21	-	

31. Whose 311, scored at Old Trafford in 1964,
was his maiden Test century?

GILLESPIE, J. N. Yorkshire

Name: <u>Jason</u> Neil Gillespie
Role: Right-hand bat, right-arm fast bowler
Born: 19 April 1975, Darlinghurst,
Australia
Height: 6ft 5in **Weight:** 14st 9lbs
Nickname: Dizzy
County debut: 2006
Test debut: 1996-97
ODI debut: 1996
Twenty20 Int debut: 2005
1st-Class 200s: 1
Place in batting averages: 179th av. 24.66
(2005 182nd av. 24.83)
Place in bowling averages: 72nd av. 33.61
Strike rate: 72.41 (career 54.43)
Parents: Neil and Vicki
Wife and date of marriage: Anna,
20 September 2003
Children: Sapphire, 2 March 1995; Jackson Anderson, 1 February 2006
Education: Cabra College, Adelaide
Career outside cricket: 'Many and varied!'
Off-season: 'Playing for the Southern Redbacks in Australia'
Overseas tours: Australia U19 to India 1993-94; Australia A to Scotland and Ireland 1998; Australia to Sri Lanka (Singer World Series) 1996, to South Africa 1996-97, to England 1997, to West Indies 1998-99, to Sri Lanka 1999, to Kenya (ICC Knockout Trophy) 2000-01, to India 2000-01, to England 2001, to South Africa 2001-02, to Sri Lanka (ICC Champions Trophy) 2002-03, to Sri Lanka and Sharjah (v Pakistan) 2002-03, to Africa (World Cup) 2002-03, to West Indies 2002-03, to Sri Lanka 2003-04, to England (ICC Champions Trophy) 2004, to India 2004-05, to New Zealand 2004-05, to England 2005, to Bangladesh 2005-06, plus other one-day series and tournaments in India, Kenya, Zimbabwe, Netherlands and England
Overseas teams played for: Adelaide CC 1986 – ; South Australia 1994-95 –
Career highlights to date: 'Playing for Australia'
Cricket moments to forget: 'Colliding with Steve Waugh in a Test match' (*During the first Test v Sri Lanka in Kandy 1999, Waugh and Gillespie collided while attempting to catch Mahela Jayawardene. Waugh's nose was broken; Gillespie suffered a broken leg*)
Cricket superstitions: 'Too many to mention!'
Cricketers particularly admired: Malcolm Marshall, Merv Hughes, Adam Gilchrist, Darren Lehmann, Glenn McGrath, Jamie Siddons
Young players to look out for: Shaun Tait, Adil Rashid

Other sports played: Basketball ('badly')
Other sports followed: AFL (Western Bulldogs), rugby league (South Sydney, Leeds Rhinos), football (Portsmouth, Altrincham), basketball (Adelaide 36ers)
Favourite band: Metallica, Van Halen, Led Zeppelin
Relaxations: 'Long lunches, BBQs, family time'
Extras: Is the first known male cricketer of indigenous descent (great-grandson of a Kamilaroi warrior) to have played Test cricket for Australia. One of *Wisden*'s Five Cricketers of the Year 2002. Is fifth in the all-time list of Australia's Test wicket-takers. Scored 201* batting as nightwatchman in the second Test v Bangladesh at Chittagong 2005-06, reaching his double century on his 31st birthday. His match awards include Man of the Match v England in the fourth Test at Headingley 1997 (7-37/2-65) and v India at Centurion in the 2002-03 World Cup (3-13 from 10 overs). An overseas player with Yorkshire since 2006. Australia contract 2006-07
Opinions on cricket: 'Batsmen should not be allowed a runner. Abolish leg byes. No raising of bats upon reaching fifty. If the ball stays in field of play, it is not four, regardless of whether fielder is touching rope.'
Best batting: 201* Australia v Bangladesh, Chittagong 2005-06
Best bowling: 8-50 South Australia v New South Wales, Sydney 2001-02

2006 Season

	M	Inn	NO	Runs	HS	Avg	100	50	Ct	St	Balls	Runs	Wkts	Avg	BB	5I	10M
Test																	
FC	14	21	6	370	45	24.66	-	-	1	-	2607	1210	36	33.61	6-37	1	-
ODI																	
List A	8	2	0	14	11	7.00	-	-	3	-	366	300	7	42.85	3-41	-	
20/20 Int																	
20/20	9	1	0	3	3	3.00	-	-	1	-	187	228	9	25.33	2-29	-	

Career Performances

	M	Inn	NO	Runs	HS	Avg	100	50	Ct	St	Balls	Runs	Wkts	Avg	BB	5I	10M
Test	71	93	28	1218	201 *	18.73	1	2	27	-	14234	6770	259	26.13	7-37	8	-
FC	143	189	48	2552	201 *	18.09	1	6	56	-	27654	12936	508	25.46	8-50	19	1
ODI	97	39	16	289	44 *	12.56	-	-	10	-	5144	3611	142	25.42	5-22	3	
List A	149	66	27	490	44 *	12.56	-	-	20	-	7998	5612	210	26.72	5-22	3	
20/20 Int	1	1	0	24	24	24.00	-	-	-	-	24	49	1	49.00	1-49	-	
20/20	10	2	0	27	24	13.50	-	-	1	-	211	277	10	27.70	2-29	-	

GODDARD, L. J.   Derbyshire

Name: <u>Lee</u> James Goddard
Role: Right-hand bat, wicket-keeper
Born: 22 October 1982, Dewsbury
Height: 5ft 10in   **Weight:** 11st 4lbs
Nickname: Godders, Goddy
County debut: 2004
Parents: Steven and Lynda
Marital status: Single ('long-term girlfriend')
Family links with cricket: 'Dad likes to think he was good at cricket'
Education: Batley Grammar School; Huddersfield Technical College; Loughborough University
Qualifications: 9 GCSEs, Foundation degree in Sports Science, ECB Level 1 coaching
Career outside cricket: 'Estate agents'
Off-season: 'Hopefully pre-season tour somewhere'

Overseas teams played for: Parramatta, Sydney 2001-02
Career highlights to date: 'First team debut v Hampshire 2004 (five catches). Maiden fifty v Surrey 2006'
Cricket moments to forget: 'None to date'
Cricket superstitions: 'Left pad on first'
Cricketers particularly admired: Ian Healy, Adam Gilchrist, Alec Stewart
Young players to look out for: Jake Needham, Wayne White, Paul Borrington
Other sports played: Football (Huddersfield Town 9-15 years), golf (12 handicap), snooker
Other sports followed: Football (Leeds United), rugby league (Leeds Rhinos)
Favourite band: Maroon 5, Jack Johnson
Relaxations: 'Listening to music, shopping, spending time with girlfriend (Kelly)'
Extras: Played in Yorkshire's U17 County Championship winning side. Played for Yorkshire Board XI in the 2003 C&G. Played for Loughborough UCCE in 2003. Was in British Universities squad for match v Zimbabweans 2003. Derbyshire CCC 2nd XI Player of the Year 2004. Released by Derbyshire at the end of the 2006 season
Opinions on cricket: 'Less Kolpaks [*see page 13*]. Give youth the chance instead.'
Best batting: 91 Derbyshire v Surrey, Derby 2006

	M	Inn	NO	Runs	HS	Avg	100	50	Ct	St	Balls	Runs	Wkts	Avg	BB	5I	10M
Test																	
FC	4	6	2	209	91	52.25	-	1	8	-	0	0	0		-	-	-
ODI																	
List A	4	3	1	50	36	25.00	-	-	3	-	0	0	0		-	-	
20/20 Int																	
20/20																	

Career Performances

	M	Inn	NO	Runs	HS	Avg	100	50	Ct	St	Balls	Runs	Wkts	Avg	BB	5I	10M
Test																	
FC	9	12	4	265	91	33.12	-	1	17	-	0	0	0		-	-	-
ODI																	
List A	6	5	2	69	36	23.00	-	-	8	-	0	0	0		-	-	
20/20 Int																	
20/20																	

GODLEMAN, B-A.   Middlesex

Name: Billy-Ashley (<u>Billy</u>) Godleman
Role: Left-hand bat
Born: 11 February 1989, Islington, London
Height: 6ft 3in **Weight:** 13st 7lbs
County debut: 2005
Parents: Ashley Fitzgerald and Johnny Godleman
Marital status: Single
Family links with cricket: 'Dad played and coached'
Education: Islington Green School
Qualifications: 8 GCSEs
Overseas tours: England U16 to South Africa 2004-05; England U19 to Malaysia 2006-07
Career highlights to date: 'Scoring 69* on my first-class debut v Cambridge UCCE. Three second-team 100s (v Sussex, Essex and Surrey); 820 runs, av. 64'
Cricket moments to forget: 'Drawing final league game of season against Hampstead for my club Brondesbury – had them nine down but couldn't bowl them out to win league'

Cricket superstitions: 'Check bat alignment every ball'
Cricketers particularly admired: Andy Flower, Graeme Smith
Young players to look out for: Johnny Godleman Jnr, Steven Finn, Eoin Morgan
Other sports played: Football
Other sports followed: Football (Liverpool FC), rugby union, cricket (Brondesbury)
Favourite band: Nas, Tupac, Pink Floyd, Steely Dan, Van Morrison
Relaxations: 'Music, watching football (specifically Liverpool), watching cricket'
Extras: Named best player in country U13, U14 and U15 at regional tournaments;
scored 168-ball 143 for South v West at Bunbury U15 Festival at Nottingham 2004.
Made 2nd XI Trophy debut for Middlesex 2003. Represented England U19 2006
Opinions on cricket: 'You get out what you put in.'
Best batting: 69* Middlesex v CUCCE, Fenner's 2005

2006 Season

	M	Inn	NO	Runs	HS	Avg	100	50	Ct	St	Balls	Runs	Wkts	Avg	BB	5I	10M
Test																	
FC																	
ODI																	
List A																	
20/20 Int																	
20/20	4	3	0	71	41	23.66	-	-	-	-	0	0	0		-	-	

Career Performances

	M	Inn	NO	Runs	HS	Avg	100	50	Ct	St	Balls	Runs	Wkts	Avg	BB	5I	10M
Test																	
FC	1	1	1	69	69 *		-	1	-	-	0	0	0		-	-	-
ODI																	
List A																	
20/20 Int																	
20/20	4	3	0	71	41	23.66	-	-	-	-	0	0	0		-	-	

32. Which future Surrey leg-spinner took a wicket
with his first ball in Test cricket, v Australia 1959-60?

GOODWIN, M. W. Sussex

Name: <u>Murray</u> William Goodwin
Role: Right-hand bat, right-arm medium/
leg-spin bowler
Born: 11 December 1972, Harare, Zimbabwe
Height: 5ft 9in **Weight:** 11st 2lbs
Nickname: Muzza, Fuzz, Goodie
County debut: 2001
County cap: 2001
Test debut: 1997-98
ODI debut: 1997-98
1000 runs in a season: 5
1st-Class 200s: 5
1st-Class 300s: 1
Place in batting averages: 12th av. 63.42
(2005 18th av. 57.50)
Strike rate: (career 99.28)
Parents: Penny and George
Wife and date of marriage: Tarsha,
13 December 1997
Children: Jayden William; Ashton George, 19 November 2006
Family links with cricket: 'Dad is a coach. Eldest brother played for Zimbabwe'
Education: St John's, Harare, Zimbabwe; Newtonmoore Senior High, Bunbury,
Western Australia
Qualifications: Level II coach
Off-season: Playing for Warriors, South Africa
Overseas tours: Australian Cricket Academy to South Africa 1992, to Sri Lanka and
India 1993; Zimbabwe to Sri Lanka and New Zealand 1997-98, to Bangladesh (Wills
International Cup) 1998-99, to Pakistan 1998-99, to UK, Ireland and Netherlands
(World Cup) 1999, to South Africa 1999-2000, to West Indies 1999-2000, to England
2000
Overseas teams played for: Excelsior, Netherlands 1997; Mashonaland 1997-98 –
1998-99; Western Australia 1994-95 – 1996-97, 2000-01 – 2005-06; Warriors
2006-07 –
Career highlights to date: 'Becoming the highest individual scorer in Sussex's
history – 335* v Leicestershire, September 2003 at Hove. Broke Duleepsinhji's record
of 333 in 1930'
Cricketers particularly admired: Allan Border, Steve Waugh, Curtly Ambrose,
Sachin Tendulkar
Other sports played: Hockey (WA Country), golf, tennis
Other sports followed: 'All'
Favourite band: 'No real favourites; I have a very eclectic collection'

Relaxations: 'Socialising with friends'

Extras: Attended Australian Cricket Academy. Scored 166* v Pakistan at Bulawayo 1997-98, in the process sharing with Andy Flower (100*) in the highest partnership for Zimbabwe for any wicket in Tests (277*). His international awards include Man of the Match in ODI v Sri Lanka at Colombo 1997-98 (111) and in the second Test v England at Trent Bridge 2000 (148*). Retired from international cricket in 2000. Scored double century (203*) and century (115) v Nottinghamshire at Trent Bridge 2001. Joint Sussex Player of the Year (with Richard Montgomerie) 2001. Scored 335* v Leicestershire at Hove 2003, surpassing K. S. Duleepsinhji's 333 in 1930 to set a new record for the highest individual score for Sussex (and winning the Sussex Outstanding Performance of the Year Award 2003). Scored 214* v Warwickshire at Hove 2006, in the process sharing with Michael Yardy (159*) in a new Sussex record partnership for the third wicket (385*). Overseas player with Sussex 2001-04. Is no longer considered an overseas player

Best batting: 335* Sussex v Leicestershire, Hove 2003
Best bowling: 2-23 Zimbabweans v Lahore Division, Lahore 1998-99

2006 Season

	M	Inn	NO	Runs	HS	Avg	100	50	Ct	St	Balls	Runs	Wkts	Avg	BB	5I	10M
Test																	
FC	16	27	1	1649	235	63.42	6	7	4	-	0	0	0		-	-	-
ODI																	
List A	17	17	4	603	158 *	46.38	1	3	8	-	0	0	0		-	-	
20/20 Int																	
20/20	5	5	1	133	67 *	33.25	-	1	1	-	0	0	0		-	-	

Career Performances

	M	Inn	NO	Runs	HS	Avg	100	50	Ct	St	Balls	Runs	Wkts	Avg	BB	5I	10M
Test	19	37	4	1414	166 *	42.84	3	8	10	-	119	69	0		-	-	-
FC	194	339	24	15148	335 *	48.08	46	65	116	-	695	357	7	51.00	2-23	-	-
ODI	71	70	3	1818	112 *	27.13	2	8	20	-	248	210	4	52.50	1-12	-	
List A	275	267	29	8333	167	35.01	11	52	91	-	351	306	7	43.71	1-9	-	
20/20 Int																	
20/20	22	17	1	281	67 *	17.56	-	1	4	-	0	0	0		-	-	

GOUGH, D. Essex

Name: Darren Gough
Role: Right-hand bat, right-arm fast bowler, county vice-captain
Born: 18 September 1970, Barnsley
Height: 5ft 11in **Weight:** 13st 9lbs
Nickname: Rhino, Dazzler
County debut: 1989 (Yorkshire), 2004 (Essex)
County cap: 1993 (Yorkshire), 2004 (Essex)
Benefit: 2001 (Yorkshire)
Test debut: 1994
ODI debut: 1994
Twenty20 Int debut: 2005
50 wickets in a season: 4
Place in batting averages: (2005 88th av. 37.00)
Place in bowling averages: 35th av. 28.96 (2005 71st av. 31.07)
Strike rate: 55.72 (career 51.17)
Parents: Trevor and Christine
Children: Liam James, 24 November 1994; Brennan Kyle, 9 December 1997
Education: Priory Comprehensive; Airedale and Wharfedale College (part-time)
Qualifications: 2 O-levels, 5 CSEs, BTEC Leisure, NCA coaching award
Overseas tours: England YC to Australia 1989-90; Yorkshire to Barbados 1989-90, to South Africa 1991-92, 1992-93; England A to South Africa 1993-94; England to Australia 1994-95, to South Africa 1995-96, to India and Pakistan (World Cup) 1995-96, to Zimbabwe and New Zealand 1996-97, to Australia 1998-99, to Sharjah (Coca-Cola Cup) 1998-99, to South Africa and Zimbabwe 1999-2000, to Kenya (ICC Knockout Trophy) 2000-01, to Pakistan and Sri Lanka 2000-01, to India and New Zealand 2001-02 (one-day series), to Australia 2002-03, to West Indies 2003-04 (one-day series), to Zimbabwe (one-day series) 2004-05, to South Africa 2004-05 (one-day series); ICC World XI to Australia (Tsunami Relief) 2004-05; England VI to Hong Kong 2006
Overseas teams played for: East Shirley, Christchurch, New Zealand 1991-92
Cricketers particularly admired: Shane Warne, Steve Waugh, Ian Botham, Michael Atherton, Malcolm Marshall
Other sports played: Golf, football
Other sports followed: Football (Barnsley and Tottenham Hotspur)
Relaxations: Golf, cinema
Extras: Yorkshire Sports Personality of the Year 1994. Cornhill England Player of the Year 1994-95, 1998-99. Whyte and Mackay Bowler of the Year 1996. Took Test hat-trick (Healy, MacGill, Miller) v Australia at Sydney 1998-99. *Sheffield Star* Sports

Personality of the Year. One of *Wisden*'s Five Cricketers of the Year 1999. Won Freeserve Fast Ball award 2000 for a delivery timed at 93.1 mph during the first Test v Zimbabwe at Lord's. Vodafone England Cricketer of the Year 2000-01. *GQ* Sportsman of the Year 2001. Took 200th Test wicket (Rashid Latif) v Pakistan at Lord's 2001 in his 50th Test. His international awards include Man of the [Test] Series v Sri Lanka 2000-01 and England's Man of the [Test] Series v West Indies 2000. Retired from Test cricket during the 2003 season. Granted Freedom of the City of London in March 2004. Took 200th ODI wicket (Harbhajan Singh) v India at Lord's in the NatWest Challenge 2004, becoming the first England bowler to reach the milestone. Winner, with Lilia Kopylova, of *Strictly Come Dancing*, December 2005. Vice-captain of Essex since 2005
Best batting: 121 Yorkshire v Warwickshire, Headingley 1996
Best bowling: 7-28 Yorkshire v Lancashire, Headingley 1995

2006 Season

	M	Inn	NO	Runs	HS		Avg	100	50	Ct	St	Balls	Runs	Wkts	Avg	BB	5I	10M
Test																		
FC	7	7	4	173	52	*	57.66	-	2	1	-	1393	724	25	28.96	5-82	1	-
ODI	2	2	0	19	18		9.50	-	-	-	-	72	72	0		-	-	
List A	13	8	2	149	53	*	24.83	-	1	3	-	479	365	14	26.07	4-39	-	
20/20 Int	1	0	0	0	0			-	-	-	-	23	33	0		-	-	
20/20	11	8	0	128	37		16.00	-	-	-	-	251	331	11	30.09	2-8	-	

Career Performances

	M	Inn	NO	Runs	HS		Avg	100	50	Ct	St	Balls	Runs	Wkts	Avg	BB	5I	10M
Test	58	86	18	855	65		12.57	-	2	13	-	11821	6503	229	28.39	6-42	9	-
FC	226	300	58	4240	121		17.52	1	19	45	-	41403	21813	809	26.96	7-28	30	3
ODI	159	87	38	609	46	*	12.42	-	-	25	-	8470	6209	235	26.42	5-44	2	
List A	390	215	70	1979	72	*	13.64	-	2	64	-	19422	13492	554	24.35	7-27	7	
20/20 Int	2	0	0	0	0			-	-	-	-	41	49	3	16.33	3-16	-	
20/20	15	11	2	163	37		18.11	-	-	-	-	335	414	17	24.35	3-16	-	

GRANT, R. N. Glamorgan

Name: <u>Richard</u> Neil Grant
Role: Right-hand bat, right-arm medium bowler; 'batter who bowls a little'
Born: 5 June 1984, Neath
Height: 5ft 10in **Weight:** 13st 8lbs
Nickname: Pingu, Wig
County debut: 2004 (one-day), 2005 (first-class)
Place in batting averages: 222nd av. 17.81 (2005 241st av. 17.16)
Strike rate: (career 57.66)
Parents: Kevin ('Sven-Göran Eriksson') and Moira

Marital status: Single ('long-term girlfriend Samantha')
Family links with cricket: 'Brother Glamorgan 2nd XI, MCC YC (groundstaff); Dad local cricket (not very good, though)'
Education: Cefn Saeson Comprehensive, Neath; Neath Port Talbot College
Qualifications: 6 GCSEs, NVQ Level II Carpentry, Level II coaching award
Career outside cricket: '12-month contract'
Off-season: 'Fitness training, golf (playing) and working as a carpenter'
Overseas tours: South Wales Junior League to Australia 1998; Wales U16 to Jersey 2000; Neath Port Talbot College to Goa 2001, to Malta 2002, to South Africa 2003
Overseas teams played for: Havelock North, Napier, New Zealand 2003-04

Career highlights to date: 'totesport League debut'
Cricket moments to forget: 'None, they have all been great'
Cricket superstitions: 'Left pad on first'
Cricketers particularly admired: Simon Jones ('coming back from serious injury')
Young players to look out for: Gareth Rees, James Harris
Other sports played: Golf
Other sports followed: Football (Swansea City, Blackburn), rugby (Ospreys)
Favourite band: Coldplay
Relaxations: 'Spending time with girlfriend Samantha'
Extras: Neath Port Talbot College Sportsman of the Year 2002; Neath Port Talbot County Borough Council Sportsman of the Year 2002. Glamorgan 2nd XI Player of the Year 2005
Opinions on cricket: 'Ninety overs in the day plus longer tea break.'
Best batting: 44 Glamorgan v Essex, Chelmsford 2006
Best bowling: 1-9 Glamorgan v Essex, Chelmsford 2006

2006 Season

	M	Inn	NO	Runs	HS	Avg	100	50	Ct	St	Balls	Runs	Wkts	Avg	BB	5I	10M
Test																	
FC	7	11	0	196	44	17.81	-	-	3	-	155	128	3	42.66	1-9	-	-
ODI																	
List A	16	15	0	333	45	22.20	-	-	3	-	85	114	4	28.50	2-21	-	
20/20 Int																	
20/20	8	8	1	206	77	29.42	-	2	2	-	33	80	3	26.66	2-18	-	

Career Performances

	M	Inn	NO	Runs	HS	Avg	100	50	Ct	St	Balls	Runs	Wkts	Avg	BB	5I	10M
Test																	
FC	11	18	1	299	44	17.58	-	-	4	-	173	146	3	48.66	1-9	-	-
ODI																	
List A	30	27	2	516	45	20.64	-	-	6	-	223	273	6	45.50	2-21	-	
20/20 Int																	
20/20	10	9	1	242	77	30.25	-	2	3	-	63	130	7	18.57	4-38	-	

GRAY, A. K. D.   Derbyshire

Name: Andrew (<u>Andy</u>) Kenneth Donovan Gray
Role: Right-hand bat, right-arm off-spin bowler
Born: 19 May 1974, Armadale, Western Australia
Nickname: Graysie
County debut: 2001 (Yorkshire), 2005 (Derbyshire)
Place in batting averages: 220th av. 18.00 (2005 154th av. 29.62)
Place in bowling averages: 132nd av. 45.35 (2005 133rd av. 47.08)
Strike rate: 82.14 (career 87.82)
Overseas teams played for: Willetton, Western Australia
Extras: Scored maiden first-class century (104) v Somerset at Taunton 2003. Is not considered an overseas player. Released by Derbyshire at the end of the 2006 season
Best batting: 104 Yorkshire v Somerset, Taunton 2003
Best bowling: 4-128 Yorkshire v Surrey, The Oval 2001

2006 Season

	M	Inn	NO	Runs	HS	Avg	100	50	Ct	St	Balls	Runs	Wkts	Avg	BB	5I	10M
Test																	
FC	8	11	2	162	29	18.00	-	-	-	-	1150	635	14	45.35	3-106	-	-
ODI																	
List A	5	4	2	41	15	20.50	-	-	1	-	282	206	7	29.42	3-44	-	
20/20 Int																	
20/20	1	0	0	0	0		-	-	-	-	24	23	0			-	-

Career Performances

	M	Inn	NO	Runs	HS	Avg	100	50	Ct	St	Balls	Runs	Wkts	Avg	BB	5I	10M
Test																	
FC	34	50	10	1048	104	26.20	1	3	25	-	4918	2559	56	45.69	4-128	-	-
ODI																	
List A	49	27	10	189	30 *	11.11	-	-	13	-	1736	1384	47	29.44	4-34	-	
20/20 Int																	
20/20	16	5	0	19	13	3.80	-	-	5	-	321	410	16	25.62	3-18	-	

GREENIDGE, C. G. — Gloucestershire

Name: <u>Carl</u> Gary Greenidge
Role: Right-hand bat, right-arm fast-medium bowler
Born: 20 April 1978, Basingstoke
Height: 5ft 10in **Weight:** 12st 8lbs
Nickname: Carlos, Gs, Jackal
County debut: 1998 (one-day, Surrey), 1999 (first-class, Surrey), 2002 (Northamptonshire), 2005 (Gloucestershire)
County cap: 2005 (Gloucestershire)
50 wickets in a season: 1
Strike rate: (career 56.03)
Parents: Gordon and Anita
Marital status: Single
Family links with cricket: Father Gordon played for Hampshire and West Indies, as did cousin (on mother's side) Andy Roberts
Education: St Michael's, Barbados; Heathcote School, Chingford; City of Westminster College
Qualifications: GNVQ Leisure and Tourism, NCA senior coaching award
Cricket moments to forget: 'Yorkshire v Northants, April 2003, first game of the season – easily my worst ever game' (*Northants conceded 673 runs and lost by an innings*)

Cricket superstitions: 'None'
Cricketers particularly admired: Malcolm Marshall, Michael Holding, Viv Richards
Other sports played: Football ('PlayStation!')
Other sports followed: Football (Arsenal), basketball (LA Lakers)
Favourite band: Bob Marley and the Wailers
Relaxations: 'PlayStation, movies, reading, music'
Extras: Spent a year on Lord's groundstaff. Took 5-60 (8-124 the match) on
Championship debut for Surrey, v Yorkshire at The Oval 1999
Best batting: 46 Northamptonshire v Derbyshire, Derby 2002
Best bowling: 6-40 Northamptonshire v Durham, Riverside 2002

2006 Season

	M	Inn	NO	Runs	HS	Avg	100	50	Ct	St	Balls	Runs	Wkts	Avg	BB	5I	10M
Test																	
FC	5	8	0	42	20	5.25	-	-	3	-	657	533	9	59.22	3-50	-	-
ODI																	
List A	3	2	2	13	13 *		-	-	-	-	143	164	7	23.42	4-40	-	
20/20 Int																	
20/20	8	1	0	1	1	1.00	-	-	5	-	186	281	9	31.22	3-37	-	

Career Performances

	M	Inn	NO	Runs	HS	Avg	100	50	Ct	St	Balls	Runs	Wkts	Avg	BB	5I	10M
Test																	
FC	41	49	7	348	46	8.28	-	-	15	-	6276	4220	112	37.67	6-40	4	-
ODI																	
List A	54	23	9	101	20	7.21	-	-	15	-	2347	2168	63	34.41	4-40	-	
20/20 Int																	
20/20	20	5	3	9	5 *	4.50	-	-	8	-	420	608	25	24.32	3-15	-	

33. Which England seamer had match figures of 10-70
on Test debut v India at Delhi 1976-77?

GRIFFITH, A. R.   Leicestershire

Name: <u>Adam</u> Richard Griffith
Role: Right-hand bat, right-arm fast-medium
bowler
Born: 11 February 1978, Launceston,
Tasmania
Height: 6ft 6in
Nickname: Big
County debut: 2006
Place in bowling averages: 144th av. 56.45
Strike rate: 99.63 (career 58.26)
Overseas teams played for: Tasmania
2002-03 –

Extras: Represented Australia A 2003-04.
Top wicket-taker for Tasmania in the Pura
Cup 2004-05 (45; av. 28.78) and 2005-06
(48; 25.85). Played for Bacup in the
Lancashire League 2005. Tasmania's Pura
Cup Player of the Year and Player of the Year
2005-06. His awards include Man of the Match v New South Wales at Newcastle in
the ING Cup 2004-05 (3-43) and v Victoria at Melbourne in the ING Cup 2005-06
(4-36). An overseas player with Leicestershire during the 2006 season as a locum for
Mohammad Asif
Best batting: 41* Leicestershire v Gloucestershire, Leicester 2006
Best bowling: 7-54 Tasmania v Victoria, Hobart 2004-05

2006 Season

	M	Inn	NO	Runs	HS		Avg	100	50	Ct	St	Balls	Runs	Wkts	Avg	BB	5I	10M
Test																		
FC	5	6	2	84	41	*	21.00	-	-	-	-	1096	621	11	56.45	3-34	-	-
ODI																		
List A	5	2	1	19	19		19.00	-	-	2	-	174	214	5	42.80	3-61	-	
20/20 Int																		
20/20	10	2	1	1	1	*	1.00	-	-	-	-	213	228	18	12.66	3-14	-	

Career Performances

	M	Inn	NO	Runs	HS		Avg	100	50	Ct	St	Balls	Runs	Wkts	Avg	BB	5I	10M
Test																		
FC	35	55	14	441	41	*	10.75	-	-	5	-	7749	4323	133	32.50	7-54	7	1
ODI																		
List A	45	19	8	83	33		7.54	-	-	8	-	2315	1863	55	33.87	4-36	-	
20/20 Int																		
20/20	12	3	1	7	6		3.50	-	-	-	-	261	289	19	15.21	3-14	-	

GRIFFITHS, D. A. Hampshire

Name: <u>David</u> Andrew Griffiths
Role: Left-hand bat, right-arm
fast bowler
Born: 10 September 1985, Newport,
Isle of Wight
Height: 6ft 1in **Weight:** 12st 7lbs
Nickname: Griff
County debut: 2006
Parents: Adrian Griffiths and Lizbeth Porter;
Dave Porter (stepfather); Sharon Griffiths
(stepmother)
Marital status: Single
Family links with cricket: 'Father captained
Wales. Stepfather captained Isle of Wight.
Uncles play league cricket'
Education: Sandown High School, Isle of
Wight

Qualifications: Level 1 cricket coaching
Career outside cricket: Handyman
Overseas tours: West of England U15 to West Indies 2001; England U19 to India
2004-05
Career highlights to date: 'England U19 v Essex 2nd XI – 5-9 in seven overs,
including a hat-trick'
Cricket moments to forget: 'Not being able to play in 2005 [due to stress fracture]'
Cricket superstitions: 'At end of run-up always turn left to run in to bowl'
Cricketers particularly admired: Brian Lara, Darren Gough
Young players to look out for: Kevin Latouf, Joe Denly, Ben Harmison, Moeen Ali
Other sports played: Football (Isle of Wight U11-U18), rugby (IOW)
Other sports followed: Football (Man Utd), rugby league (St Helens)
Favourite band: Jack Johnson
Relaxations: Golf, skiing
Extras: Represented England U19 2004. Southern League Young Player of the Year
2004
Opinions on cricket: 'Twenty20 is awesome, bringing in younger crowds and
families who have a great enthusiasm for the game.'
Best batting: 16* Hampshire v LUCCE, Rose Bowl 2006

2006 Season

	M	Inn	NO	Runs	HS	Avg	100	50	Ct	St	Balls	Runs	Wkts	Avg	BB	5I	10M
Test																	
FC	1	1	1	16	16 *		-	-	-	-	36	29	0		-	-	-
ODI																	
List A																	
20/20 Int																	
20/20																	

Career Performances

	M	Inn	NO	Runs	HS	Avg	100	50	Ct	St	Balls	Runs	Wkts	Avg	BB	5I	10M
Test																		
FC	1	1	1	16	16 *		-	-	-	-	36	29	0		-	-	-
ODI																	
List A																	
20/20 Int																	
20/20																	

GROENEWALD, T. D.   Warwickshire

Name: Timothy (Tim) Duncan Groenewald
Role: Right-hand bat, right-arm fast-medium bowler; all-rounder
Born: 10 January 1984, Pietermaritzburg, South Africa
Height: 6ft 2in **Weight:** 14st
Nickname: TG, Groenie
County debut: 2006
Place in batting averages: 192nd av. 22.42
Strike rate: (career 117.00)
Parents: Neil and Tessa
Marital status: Single
Education: Maritzburg College, Natal; University of South Africa
Qualifications: Marketing degree
Overseas teams played for: Zingari CC, Natal 1998-2006; Natal Inland 2002-05
Career highlights to date: 'Opening the bowling for Natal Dolphins with Lance Klusener. Getting contracted to Warwickshire'
Cricket moments to forget: 'Getting out for 99 (aged 10)'
Cricket superstitions: 'None. Not superstitious'
Cricketers particularly admired: Allan Donald, Steve Waugh, Hansie Cronje

Young players to look out for: Chris Woakes
Other sports played: Hockey (Midlands U21 A 2003), tennis and golf ('socially')
Other sports followed: Rugby (Natal Sharks)
Favourite band: Green Day, Coldplay
Relaxations: 'Listening to music, watching sport, sleeping, spending time with friends'
Extras: Leading wicket-taker at National U19 Week and represented South African Schools Colts U19
Opinions on cricket: 'Really enjoy the shorter games such as Twenty20 – think it does a lot for the game and brings more people to cricket. I think that there should be more positive results in four-day cricket.'
Best batting: 76 Warwickshire v Durham, Riverside 2006
Best bowling: 2-36 Warwickshire v Yorkshire, Edgbaston 2006

2006 Season

	M	Inn	NO	Runs	HS	Avg	100	50	Ct	St	Balls	Runs	Wkts	Avg	BB	5I	10M
Test																	
FC	6	9	2	157	76	22.42	-	1	1	-	702	396	6	66.00	2-36	-	-
ODI																	
List A	5	3	1	9	9 *	4.50	-	-	1	-	120	138	2	69.00	2-42	-	
20/20 Int																	
20/20	2	0	0	0	0		-	-	1	-	24	43	0		-	-	

Career Performances

	M	Inn	NO	Runs	HS	Avg	100	50	Ct	St	Balls	Runs	Wkts	Avg	BB	5I	10M
Test																	
FC	6	9	2	157	76	22.42	-	1	1	-	702	396	6	66.00	2-36	-	-
ODI																	
List A	5	3	1	9	9 *	4.50	-	-	1	-	120	138	2	69.00	2-42	-	
20/20 Int																	
20/20	2	0	0	0	0		-	-	1	-	24	43	0		-	-	

34. In which year did Durham's Riverside Ground host its first Test match and who were England's opponents?

GURNEY, H. F.   Leicestershire

Name: <u>Harry</u> Frederick Gurney
Role: Right-hand bat, left-arm seam bowler
Born: 25 October 1986, Nottingham
Height: 6ft 2in   **Weight:** 12st
Nickname: Gurns
County debut: No first-team appearance
Parents: Jane and John
Marital status: Single
Education: Garendon High School;
Loughborough Grammar School; University
of Leeds
Qualifications: 9 GCSEs, 4 A-levels
Career outside cricket: 'Student'
Off-season: 'University'
Overseas tours: Loughborough GS to Cape
Town 2004; Leicestershire Academy/U19 to
India 2005-06
Career highlights to date: 'Gaining my
contract'
Cricket moments to forget: 'My performance in first game against first-class
opposition – Yorkshire at Headingley'
Cricket superstitions: 'None'
Cricketers particularly admired: Glenn McGrath, Courtney Walsh
Young players to look out for: Sam Reddish, Johnny and Alfie Gurney
Other sports played: 'Recreational football'
Other sports followed: Football (West Ham United)
Injuries: Out for two weeks with a strained hamstring
Favourite band: ELO, Queen
Relaxations: 'Poker'
Extras: Played for Bradford/Leeds UCCE 2006
Opinions on cricket: 'Glad the [2005] Ashes win and Twenty20 success is creating a
resurgence in cricket's popularity.'

GUY, S. M.   Yorkshire

Name: <u>Simon</u> Mark Guy
Role: Right-hand bat, wicket-keeper
Born: 17 November 1978, Rotherham
Height: 5ft 7in **Weight:** 10st 7lbs
Nickname: Rat
County debut: 2000
Place in batting averages: 176th av. 25.00
Parents: Darrell and Denise
Wife and date of marriage: Suzanne,
13 October 2001
Children: Isaac Simon, 15 January 2004
Family links with cricket: 'Father played for
Nottinghamshire and Worcestershire 2nd XI
and for Rotherham Town CC. Brothers play
local cricket for Treeton CC'
Education: Wickersley Comprehensive
School

Qualifications: GNVQ in Leisure and
Recreation, Level 3 coaching award
Overseas tours: Yorkshire to South Africa 1999, 2001, to Grenada 2002
Overseas teams played for: Orange CYMS, NSW 1999-2000
Career highlights to date: 'Playing the last ever County Championship game at
Southampton [Northlands Road in 2000] and winning off the last ball with 13
Yorkshire and past Yorkshire men on the pitch at the same time'
Cricket moments to forget: 'On my debut against the Zimbabweans, smashing a door
after getting out – but I still say it was an accident'
Cricket superstitions: 'Just a lot of routines'
Cricketers particularly admired: Jack Russell, Darren Lehmann
Young players to look out for: Joe Sayers
Other sports played: 'I like to play all sports', rugby (played for South Yorkshire
and Yorkshire)
Other sports followed: Rugby (Rotherham RUFC), 'Treeton Welfare CC, where all
my family play'
Favourite band: Pink
Relaxations: 'Playing all sports, socialising with friends, watching cartoons, and
eating a lot'
Extras: Topped Yorkshire 2nd XI batting averages 1998 (106.00). Awarded 2nd XI
cap 2000. Took five catches in an innings for first time for Yorkshire 1st XI v Surrey
at Scarborough 2000
Best batting: 52* Yorkshire v Durham, Headingley 2006

2006 Season

	M	Inn	NO	Runs	HS	Avg	100	50	Ct	St	Balls	Runs	Wkts	Avg	BB	5I	10M
Test																	
FC	6	8	2	150	52 *	25.00	-	1	15	5	0	0	0		-	-	-
ODI																	
List A	3	2	0	11	8	5.50	-	-	3	2	0	0	0		-	-	
20/20 Int																	
20/20																	

Career Performances

	M	Inn	NO	Runs	HS	Avg	100	50	Ct	St	Balls	Runs	Wkts	Avg	BB	5I	10M
Test																	
FC	32	45	6	612	52 *	15.69	-	1	86	12	24	8	0		-	-	-
ODI																	
List A	19	14	3	195	40	17.72	-	-	18	7	0	0	0		-	-	
20/20 Int																	
20/20																	

HABIB, A.   Leicestershire

Name: Aftab Habib
Role: Right-hand bat, 'very, very slow bowler'
Born: 7 February 1972, Reading
Height: 5ft 9in **Weight:** 13st
Nickname: Afie, Tabby, Inzy, Habiby
County debut: 1992 (Middlesex), 1995 (Leicestershire), 2002 (Essex)
County cap: 1998 (Leicestershire), 2002 (Essex)
Test debut: 1999
1000 runs in a season: 2
1st-Class 200s: 1
Place in batting averages: (2005 87th av. 37.10)
Strike rate: (career 106.00)
Parents: Tahira (deceased) and Hussain
Marital status: Single
Family links with cricket: Cousin of Zahid Sadiq (ex-Surrey and Derbyshire)
Education: Taunton School
Qualifications: 7 GCSEs, Level 2 coaching
Career outside cricket: Property management

Overseas tours: Berkshire CCC to South Africa 1996; England YC to Australia 1989-90, to New Zealand 1990-91; England A to Bangladesh and New Zealand 1999-2000, to West Indies 2000-01

Overseas teams played for: Globe Wakatu, Nelson, New Zealand 1992-93, 1996-97; Riccarton CC, Christchurch, New Zealand 1997-98; Kingborough CC, Hobart

Career highlights to date: 'Playing for England in 1999'

Cricket moments to forget: 'Losing three one-day finals and a Test match at Lord's'

Cricketers particularly admired: Sachin Tendulkar, Mark Waugh, Ricky Ponting

Young players to look out for: Ravi Bopara

Other sports played: 'Enjoy most sports', football (Reading Schools)

Other sports followed: Football (Reading FC, Liverpool), rugby (Leicester Tigers, New Zealand All Blacks)

Favourite band: Adnan Sami

Relaxations: 'Music, reading, golf, cinema'

Extras: Played for England U15-U19. Middlesex 2nd XI Seaxe Player of the Year 1992. Leicestershire 2nd XI Player of the Year 1995. Championship medals with Leicestershire in 1996 and 1998. Scored 101* for England A v New Zealand A to help save the first 'Test' at Lincoln 1999-2000. Left Essex at the end of the 2004 season and rejoined Leicestershire for 2005; released by Leicestershire at the end of the 2006 season

Best batting: 215 Leicestershire v Worcestershire, Leicester 1996

Best bowling: 1-10 Essex v Kent, Chelmsford 2003

2006 Season

	M	Inn	NO	Runs	HS	Avg	100	50	Ct	St	Balls	Runs	Wkts	Avg	BB	5I	10M
Test																	
FC	1	1	0	4	4	4.00	-	-	1	-	0	0	0		-	-	-
ODI																	
List A																	
20/20 Int																	
20/20																	

Career Performances

	M	Inn	NO	Runs	HS	Avg	100	50	Ct	St	Balls	Runs	Wkts	Avg	BB	5I	10M
Test	2	3	0	26	19	8.66	-	-	-	-	0	0	0		-	-	-
FC	159	241	29	8873	215	41.85	21	46	80	-	106	80	1	80.00	1-10	-	-
ODI																	
List A	168	148	26	3212	111	26.32	1	14	59	-	59	58	2	29.00	2-5	-	
20/20 Int																	
20/20	2	2	1	26	16 *	26.00	-	-	1	-	0	0	0		-	-	

HALL, A. J.   Kent

Name: <u>Andrew</u> James Hall
Role: Right-hand bat, right-arm
fast-medium bowler; all-rounder
Born: 31 July 1975, Johannesburg,
South Africa
County debut: 2003 (Worcestershire),
2005 (Kent)
County cap: 2003 (Worcestershire colours),
2005 (Kent)
Test debut: 2001-02
ODI debut: 1998-99
Twenty20 Int debut: 2005-06
Place in batting averages: (2005 81st
av. 38.42)
Place in bowling averages: 10th av. 23.85
(2005 25th av. 25.70)
Strike rate: 55.07 (career 56.25)
Wife: Leanie
Education: Hoërskool Alberton

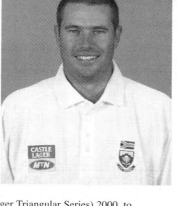

Overseas tours: South Africa to Sri Lanka (Singer Triangular Series) 2000, to
Australia (Super Challenge) 2000, to Singapore (Godrej Singapore Challenge) 2000-
01, to Kenya (ICC Knockout Trophy) 2000-01, to Bangladesh (TVS Cup) 2003, to
England 2003, to Pakistan 2003-04, to India 2004-05, to West Indies 2004-05, to India
(one-day series) 2005-06, to Australia 2005-06 (VB Series), to Sri Lanka 2006, to
India (ICC Champions Trophy) 2006-07
Overseas teams played for: Transvaal/Gauteng 1994-95 – 2000-01;
Easterns 2001-02 – 2003-04; Lions 2004-05 – 2005-06; Dolphins 2006-07 –
Extras: Played for South Africa Academy 1997. Was shot in the hand and face by a
mugger in Johannesburg in 1999 and was car-jacked in 2002. Man of the Match in tied
indoor ODI v Australia at Melbourne 2000. His other international awards include
Man of the Match in the first Test v India at Kanpur 2004-05 (163) and in the fifth
ODI v New Zealand at Centurion 2005-06 (4-23). One of *South African Cricket
Annual*'s five Cricketers of the Year 2002. His South African domestic awards include
Man of the SuperSport Series 2002-03 and Man of the Match in the final (6-77/5-22).
An overseas player with Worcestershire 2003-04. Man of the Match v Lancashire in
the C&G semi-final at Worcester 2003. An overseas player with Kent since 2005
Best batting: 163 South Africa v India, Kanpur 2004-05
Best bowling: 6-77 Easterns v Western Province, Benoni 2002-03

2006 Season

	M	Inn	NO	Runs	HS	Avg	100	50	Ct	St	Balls	Runs	Wkts	Avg	BB	5I	10M
Test																	
FC	4	5	2	237	68 *	79.00	-	2	3	-	771	334	14	23.85	3-27	-	-
ODI																	
List A	5	4	0	164	100	41.00	1	-	2	-	253	247	9	27.44	3-15	-	
20/20 Int																	
20/20	8	8	0	174	36	21.75	-	-	7	-	161	186	13	14.30	3-15	-	

Career Performances

	M	Inn	NO	Runs	HS	Avg	100	50	Ct	St	Balls	Runs	Wkts	Avg	BB	5I	10M
Test	19	30	4	735	163	28.26	1	3	15	-	2838	1511	39	38.74	3-1	-	-
FC	115	169	23	4999	163	34.23	5	34	83	-	19802	9186	352	26.09	6-77	12	1
ODI	70	46	11	761	81	21.74	-	2	24	-	2512	1900	68	27.94	4-23	-	
List A	216	171	31	4268	129 *	30.48	4	23	61	-	8730	6530	240	27.20	4-23	-	
20/20 Int	2	1	0	11	11	11.00	-	-	-	-	48	60	3	20.00	3-22	-	
20/20	30	29	2	596	59	22.07	-	1	10	-	606	790	35	22.57	3-15	-	

HAMILTON-BROWN, R. J.   Surrey

Name: <u>Rory</u> James Hamilton-Brown
Role: Right-hand bat, right-arm
off-spin bowler
Born: 3 September 1987, London
Height: 6ft **Weight:** 13st 7lbs
Nickname: Bear, Stewi, RHB
County debut: 2005
Parents: Roger and Holly
Marital status: Single
Family links with cricket: 'Dad played for
Warwickshire'
Education: Millfield School
Qualifications: 9 GCSEs, 3 A-levels
Overseas tours: England U16 to South
Africa; England U19 to Bangladesh 2005-06,
to Sri Lanka (U19 World Cup) 2005-06
Career highlights to date: 'Facing Mushtaq
Ahmed on debut against Sussex in the
totesport League

Cricket moments to forget: 'Dropping a very simple catch which single-handedly
meant Surrey U19 were knocked out of national competition'
Cricket superstitions: 'None'

Cricketers particularly admired: Damien Martyn, Mark Ramprakash, Alec Stewart
Young players to look out for: Billy Godleman, Ben Wright
Other sports played: Rugby (England U16, England Junior National Academy)
Other sports followed: Football (Birmingham City)
Favourite band: Donnel Jones, Trey Songz
Relaxations: 'Relaxing with friends'
Extras: Captained England U15. *Daily Telegraph* Bunbury Scholar (Batsman) 2003. Broke Millfield batting record 2004 at 16. Made 2nd XI Championship debut 2004, scoring 43 and 84 v Sussex 2nd XI at Hove. Represented England U19 2006
Best batting: 9 Surrey v Bangladesh A, The Oval 2005
Stop press: Forced to withdraw from England U19 tour to Malaysia 2006-07, which he was due to captain, after failing to recover sufficiently from shoulder surgery

2006 Season

	M	Inn	NO	Runs	HS	Avg	100	50	Ct	St	Balls	Runs	Wkts	Avg	BB	5I	10M
Test																	
FC																	
ODI																	
List A	2	2	0	23	17	11.50	-	-	-	-	0	0	0		-	-	
20/20 Int																	
20/20																	

Career Performances

	M	Inn	NO	Runs	HS	Avg	100	50	Ct	St	Balls	Runs	Wkts	Avg	BB	5I	10M
Test																	
FC	1	2	0	14	9	7.00	-	-	1	-	0	0	0		-	-	-
ODI																	
List A	4	3	0	43	20	14.33	-	-	-	-	0	0	0		-	-	
20/20 Int																	
20/20																	

35. Which ground hosted the first Twenty20 International
to be played in England?

HARDINGES, M. A.　　　Gloucestershire

Name: <u>Mark</u> Andrew Hardinges
Role: Right-hand bat, right-arm
medium-fast bowler
Born: 5 February 1978, Gloucester
Height: 6ft 1in **Weight:** 13st 7lbs
Nickname: Dinges
County debut: 1999
County cap: 2004
Place in batting averages: 110th av. 34.15
(2005 239th av. 17.56)
Place in bowling averages: 123rd av. 43.95
(2005 54th av. 28.59)
Strike rate: 70.60 (career 65.34)
Parents: David and Jean
Marital status: Single
Family links with cricket: Brother and
father played club cricket
Education: Malvern College; Bath
University

Qualifications: 10 GCSEs, 3 A-levels, BSc (Hons) Economics and Politics
Overseas tours: Malvern College to South Africa 1996; Gloucestershire to South
Africa 1999, 2000
Overseas teams played for: Newtown and Chilwell, Geelong, Australia 1997
Career highlights to date: 'Norwich Union debut v Notts 2001 – scored 65 and set
[then] domestic one-day seventh-wicket partnership record (164) with J. Snape. Also
Lord's final v Surrey'
Cricket moments to forget: 'Glos v Somerset [Norwich Union 2001] – bowled three
overs for 30 and was run out for 0 on Sky TV'
Cricketers particularly admired: Kim Barnett, Steve Waugh, Mark Alleyne
Other sports played: Golf, tennis (Gloucester U14), football (university first team)
Other sports followed: Football (Tottenham)
Relaxations: Golf
Extras: Represented British Universities 2000. C&G Man of the Match award for his
4-19 v Shropshire at Shrewsbury School 2002. Scored maiden one-day century (111*)
v Lancashire at Old Trafford in the totesport League 2005, in the process sharing with
Ramnaresh Sarwan (118*) in a new competition record fifth-wicket partnership (221*)
Best batting: 172 Gloucestershire v OUCCE, The Parks 2002
Best bowling: 5-51 Gloucestershire v Kent, Maidstone 2005

2006 Season

	M	Inn	NO	Runs	HS	Avg	100	50	Ct	St	Balls	Runs	Wkts	Avg	BB	5I	10M
Test																	
FC	11	15	2	444	107 *	34.15	2	1	-	-	1624	1011	23	43.95	4-127	-	-
ODI																	
List A	10	8	1	161	60	23.00	-	1	4	-	382	370	15	24.66	3-22	-	
20/20 Int																	
20/20	9	9	1	195	94 *	24.37	-	2	3	-	150	282	2	141.00	1-27	-	

Career Performances

	M	Inn	NO	Runs	HS	Avg	100	50	Ct	St	Balls	Runs	Wkts	Avg	BB	5I	10M
Test																	
FC	35	52	6	1175	172	25.54	3	3	16	-	4509	2663	69	38.59	5-51	1	-
ODI																	
List A	59	52	7	772	111 *	17.15	1	3	23	-	2047	1784	50	35.68	4-19	-	
20/20 Int																	
20/20	27	20	3	354	94 *	20.82	-	2	7	-	323	551	15	36.73	3-18	-	

HARINATH, A. Surrey

Name: Arun Harinath
Role: Left-hand bat, off-spin bowler
Born: 26 March 1987, Carshalton, Surrey
Height: 5ft 11in **Weight:** 11st 10lbs
Nickname: The Baron
County debut: No first-team appearance
Parents: Mala and Suppiah
Marital status: Single
Family links with cricket: Brother
Muhunthan played for Surrey 2nd XI 2006
Education: Tiffin Boys Grammar School;
Loughborough University
Career outside cricket: 'Student'
Off-season: 'Studying and being a member
of the UCCE at Loughborough University'
Overseas tours: Surrey U19 to Sri Lanka
2002, to Cape Town 2005; Surrey Academy
to Perth 2004; England U17 to Netherlands
2004
Overseas teams played for: Randwick Petersham, Sydney 2005-06
Career highlights to date: 'Maiden 2nd XI hundred'
Cricket moments to forget: 'Dropping Samit Patel against Nottinghamshire 2nds
at Sutton'

Cricketers particularly admired: Steve Waugh, Michael Hussey, Justin Langer, Brian Lara, Rahul Dravid, Mohammad Yousuf
Young players to look out for: Muhunthan Harinath
Other sports played: Rugby, badminton
Other sports followed: Rugby (Bath), NFL (Atlanta Falcons)
Injuries: Out for the last week of the season with split webbing on the right hand
Favourite band: The Strokes, Inspector Gajan
Relaxations: 'Films and music mainly'
Extras: Made 2nd XI Championship debut 2003
Opinions on cricket: 'The harder you work, the more you will get out of the game.'

HARMISON, B. W.   Durham

Name: <u>Ben</u> William Harmison
Role: Left-hand bat, right-arm fast-medium bowler; all-rounder
Born: 9 January 1986, Ashington, Northumberland
Height: 6ft 5in **Weight:** 14st
Nickname: Harmy
County debut: 2005 (one-day), 2006 (first-class)
Place in batting averages: 86th av. 37.53
Parents: Margaret and Jim
Marital status: Single
Family links with cricket: Brother Stephen plays for Durham and England. Father Jim and brother James play league cricket for Ashington CC
Education: Ashington High School
Career outside cricket: 'Bit of this, bit of that'
Off-season: 'Relaxing; working on my game'
Overseas tours: England U19 to Bangladesh (U19 World Cup) 2003-04, to India 2004-05; Durham to India 2005
Career highlights to date: 'Two hundreds in my first two [first-class] games for Durham'
Cricket moments to forget: 'Getting a first-baller v Bangladesh A in a one-dayer'
Cricket superstitions: 'Left pad first'
Cricketers particularly admired: Andrew Flintoff
Young players to look out for: Moeen Ali 'and Durham Academy lads'
Other sports played: Golf, fishing, football
Other sports followed: Football (Newcastle United)

Injuries: Unable to bowl for months because of a stress fracture of the back; 'heavily scabbed kneecap'
Favourite band: 'Enjoy watching Girls Aloud videos'
Relaxations: 'Fishing, listening to music'
Extras: Represented England U19 2005. Scored century (110) on first-class debut v Oxford UCCE at The Parks 2006 and another (105) in his next first-class match v West Indies A at Riverside 2006
Opinions on cricket: 'More time for rest and preparation for the next game!'
Best batting: 110 Durham v OUCCE, The Parks 2006

2006 Season

	M	Inn	NO	Runs	HS	Avg	100	50	Ct	St	Balls	Runs	Wkts	Avg	BB	5I	10M
Test																	
FC	9	17	2	563	110	37.53	2	3	5	-	0	0	0		-	-	-
ODI																	
List A	7	7	0	142	57	20.28	-	1	4	-	0	0	0		-	-	
20/20 Int																	
20/20	2	2	0	8	5	4.00	-	-	1	-	0	0	0		-	-	

Career Performances

	M	Inn	NO	Runs	HS	Avg	100	50	Ct	St	Balls	Runs	Wkts	Avg	BB	5I	10M
Test																	
FC	9	17	2	563	110	37.53	2	3	5	-	0	0	0		-	-	-
ODI																	
List A	8	8	0	142	57	17.75	-	1	5	-	30	51	1	51.00	1-51	-	
20/20 Int																	
20/20	2	2	0	8	5	4.00	-	-	1	-	0	0	0		-	-	

36. In 2001 who became the first player to score a century in each innings of his Championship debut?

HARMISON, S. J.   Durham

Name: <u>Stephen</u> James Harmison
Role: Right-hand bat, right-arm
fast bowler
Born: 23 October 1978, Ashington,
Northumberland
Height: 6ft 4in **Weight:** 14st
Nickname: Harmy
County debut: 1996
County cap: 1999
Test debut: 2002
ODI debut: 2002-03
Twenty20 Int debut: 2005
50 wickets in a season: 3
Place in batting averages: 224th av. 17.50
Place in bowling averages: 24th av. 26.54
(2005 6th av. 21.14)
Strike rate: 45.87 (career 56.17)
Parents: Jimmy and Margaret
Wife and date of marriage: Hayley, 8 October 1999
Children: Emily Alice, 1 June 1999; Abbie Meg; Isabel Grace, May 2006
Family links with cricket: Brother James has played for Northumberland; brother
Ben played for England U19 and is now at Durham
Education: Ashington High School
Overseas tours: England U19 to Pakistan 1996-97; England A to Zimbabwe and
South Africa 1998-99; ECB National Academy to Australia 2001-02; England to
Australia 2002-03, to Africa (World Cup) 2002-03, to Bangladesh 2003-04, to West
Indies 2003-04, to South Africa 2004-05, to Pakistan 2005-06, to India 2005-06, to India
(ICC Champions Trophy) 2006-07, to Australia 2006-07; ICC World XI to Australia
(Super Series) 2005-06
Cricketers particularly admired: David Boon, Courtney Walsh
Other sports played: Football (played for Ashington in Northern League), golf,
snooker
Other sports followed: Football (Newcastle United)
Relaxations: Spending time with family
Extras: Man of the [Test] Series v West Indies 2003-04 (23 wickets at 14.86,
including 7-12 at Kingston) and England's Man of the [Test] Series v New Zealand
2004 (21 wickets at 22.09). Had match figures of 9-121 (6-46/3-75) in the fourth Test
v West Indies at The Oval 2004 to go to the top of the PricewaterhouseCoopers ratings
for Test bowlers. His other international awards include Man of the Match in the
second Test v Pakistan at Old Trafford 2006 (6-19/5-57). Became second England
bowler (after James Anderson) to take an ODI hat-trick (Kaif, Balaji, Nehra), v India

at Trent Bridge in the NatWest Challenge 2004. One of *Wisden*'s Five Cricketers of the Year 2005. Became first bowler to take a first-class hat-trick for Durham (Pipe, Mason, Wigley) v Worcestershire at Riverside 2005. Appointed MBE in 2006 New Year Honours as part of 2005 Ashes-winning England team. England 12-month central contract 2006-07

Best batting: 42 England v South Africa, Cape Town 2004-05
Best bowling: 7-12 England v West Indies, Kingston 2003-04
Stop press: Retired from ODI cricket in December 2006

2006 Season

	M	Inn	NO	Runs	HS	Avg	100	50	Ct	St	Balls	Runs	Wkts	Avg	BB	5I	10M
Test	4	5	1	76	36	19.00	-	-	1	-	909	542	20	27.10	6-19	2	1
FC	6	8	2	105	36	17.50	-	-	1	-	1101	637	24	26.54	6-19	2	1
ODI	5	3	2	9	5 *	9.00	-	-	-	-	300	286	8	35.75	3-31	-	
List A	8	5	3	33	17	16.50	-	-	-	-	468	412	13	31.69	3-31	-	
20/20 Int	1	0	0	0	0		-	-	-	-	24	29	0		-	-	
20/20	1	0	0	0	0		-	-	-	-	24	29	0		-	-	

Career Performances

	M	Inn	NO	Runs	HS	Avg	100	50	Ct	St	Balls	Runs	Wkts	Avg	BB	5I	10M
Test	45	60	16	505	42	11.47	-	-	6	-	9866	5157	179	28.81	7-12	8	1
FC	130	179	49	1258	42	9.67	-	-	22	-	25449	13167	453	29.06	7-12	15	1
ODI	44	20	12	64	13 *	8.00	-	-	8	-	2378	1978	64	30.90	5-33	1	
List A	101	46	23	139	17	6.04	-	-	15	-	5052	4111	131	31.38	5-33	1	
20/20 Int	2	0	0	0	0		-	-	1	-	39	42	1	42.00	1-13	-	
20/20	3	0	0	0	0		-	-	1	-	63	61	2	30.50	1-13	-	

37. Which current first-class umpire took
5-50 in Pakistan's second innings on his Test
debut at Headingley in 1992?

HARRIS, A. J. Nottinghamshire

Name: <u>Andrew</u> James Harris
Role: Right-hand bat, right-arm
fast-medium bowler
Born: 26 June 1973, Ashton-under-Lyne,
Lancashire
Height: 6ft **Weight:** 11st 9lbs
Nickname: AJ, Honest
County debut: 1994 (Derbyshire),
2000 (Nottinghamshire)
County cap: 1996 (Derbyshire),
2000 (Nottinghamshire)
50 wickets in a season: 1
Place in bowling averages: 46th av. 30.28
(2005 34th av. 26.38)
Strike rate: 54.60 (career 51.64)
Parents: Norman (deceased) and Joyce
Wife and date of marriage: Kate,
7 October 2000
Children: Jacob Alexander, 28 August 2002
Education: Hadfield Comprehensive School; Glossopdale Community College
Qualifications: 6 GCSEs, 1 A-level
Overseas tours: England A to Australia 1996-97
Overseas teams played for: Ginninderra West Belconnen, Australian Capital Territory
1992-93; Victoria University of Wellington CC, New Zealand 1997-98
Cricket superstitions: 'None'
Cricketers particularly admired: Merv Hughes, Allan Donald
Other sports played: Golf, snooker, football
Other sports followed: Football (Man City)
Relaxations: 'Good food, good wine and the odd game of golf'
Extras: Nottinghamshire Player of the Year 2002. Had the misfortune to be 'timed
out' v Durham UCCE at Trent Bridge 2003 (was suffering from groin injury)
Best batting: 41* Nottinghamshire v Northamptonshire, Northampton 2002
Best bowling: 7-54 Nottinghamshire v Northamptonshire, Trent Bridge 2002

2006 Season

	M	Inn	NO	Runs	HS	Avg	100	50	Ct	St	Balls	Runs	Wkts	Avg	BB	5I	10M
Test																	
FC	13	17	2	119	28*	7.93	-	-	2	-	2075	1151	38	30.28	5-53	1	-
ODI																	
List A	11	5	0	51	34	10.20	-	-	1	-	457	343	16	21.43	4-30	-	
20/20 Int																	
20/20	5	1	0	6	6	6.00	-	-	-	-	96	116	5	23.20	2-13	-	

Career Performances

	M	Inn	NO	Runs	HS	Avg	100	50	Ct	St	Balls	Runs	Wkts	Avg	BB	5I	10M
Test																	
FC	117	158	39	1030	41 *	8.65	-	-	34	-	19985	11955	387	30.89	7-54	16	3
ODI																	
List A	133	50	19	211	34	6.80	-	-	27	-	5902	4940	175	28.22	5-35	1	
20/20 Int																	
20/20	18	4	2	6	6	3.00	-	-	4	-	298	455	14	32.50	2-13	-	

HARRIS, J. A. R.   Glamorgan

Name: <u>James</u> Alexander Russell Harris
Role: Right-hand bat, right-arm fast-medium bowler; all-rounder
Born: 16 May 1990, Morriston, Swansea
Height: 6ft **Weight:** 10st 7lbs
Nickname: Rolf, Bones
County debut: No first-team appearance (*see **Extras***)
Parents: Helen and Russ
Marital status: Single
Family links with cricket: 'Father played for British Colleges'
Education: Pontarddulais Comprehensive; Gorseinon College
Qualifications: 9 GCSEs
Off-season: 'No tours planned as yet. Hard work'
Overseas tours: West of England U15 to West Indies 2004-05 (c); England U16 to South Africa 2005-06 (c)
Career highlights to date: 'Taking 3-44 on my second-team debut as a 14-year-old. Second youngest player to represent Glamorgan in a one-day game [*see **Extras***] at 16 years 120 days'
Cricketers particularly admired: Steve Waugh, Sachin Tendulkar, Shane Warne, Glenn McGrath
Young players to look out for: Sam Northeast, Mike O'Shea, Ben Wright, Will Bragg
Other sports followed: Football (Newcastle)
Injuries: Out for two weeks with a finger injury
Favourite band: Lighthouse Family, John Legend
Relaxations: 'Shopping for clothes; music'
Extras: 2005 Bunbury Scholarship to National Academy. Signed professional contract aged 16 years 9 days. Played for Glamorgan in the Twenty20 Floodlit Cup 2006 but has yet to appear for the county in first-class cricket or a major domestic competition

HARRIS, P. L. Warwickshire

Name: Paul Lee Harris
Role: Right-hand bat, slow left-arm bowler
Born: 2 November 1978, Harare, Zimbabwe
County debut: 2006
Place in batting averages: 254th av. 14.00
Place in bowling averages: 40th av. 29.19
Strike rate: 67.22 (career 62.52)
Overseas teams played for: Western
Province 1998-99 – 2001-02; Northerns
2002-03 – 2005-06; Titans 2004-05 –
Extras: Man of the Match v Dolphins at
Durban in the SuperSport Series 2005-06
(5-32/3-58). Joint leading wicket-taker (with
Dale Steyn) in the SuperSport Series 2005-06
with 49 at 21.48
Best batting: 47 Northerns v North West,
Potchefstroom 2005-06
Best bowling: 6-54 Titans v Cape Cobras,
Benoni 2005-06

Stop press: Made Test debut for South Africa in the third Test v India at Cape Town
2006-07, taking 4-129 in India's first innings (but losing his Kolpak status – *see page
13* – and has returned to Warwickshire as an overseas player for the second part of the
2007 season)

2006 Season

	M	Inn	NO	Runs	HS	Avg	100	50	Ct	St	Balls	Runs	Wkts	Avg	BB	5I	10M
Test																	
FC	8	11	1	140	32	14.00	-	-	3	-	2084	905	31	29.19	6-80	4	-
ODI																	
List A	8	3	1	2	1	1.00	-	-	1	-	324	232	12	19.33	3-33	-	
20/20 Int																	
20/20	3	1	1	1	1 *		-	-	-	-	54	97	2	48.50	2-45	-	

Career Performances

	M	Inn	NO	Runs	HS	Avg	100	50	Ct	St	Balls	Runs	Wkts	Avg	BB	5I	10M
Test																	
FC	40	49	9	625	47	15.62	-	-	17	-	8754	4039	140	28.85	6-54	9	-
ODI																	
List A	28	7	2	25	10	5.00	-	-	12	-	1188	893	29	30.79	3-33	-	
20/20 Int																	
20/20	4	2	1	4	3	4.00	-	-	1	-	72	120	4	30.00	2-23	-	

Name: <u>Adam</u> James Harrison
Role: Right-hand bat, right-arm medium-fast bowler
Born: 30 October 1985, Newport, Gwent
Height: 6ft **Weight:** 13st
Nickname: Worm, Ceedo
County debut: 2005
Strike rate: (career 74.00)
Parents: Stuart and Susan
Marital status: Single
Family links with cricket: 'Father played in 1970s for Glamorgan. Brother [David] currently on staff'
Education: West Monmouth Comprehensive School; St Albans High School
Qualifications: 10 GCSEs, 2 A-levels, Level 1 coaching award
Career outside cricket: 'Training to be bricklayer'
Off-season: 'Rehabilitation from second ankle operation; trip to Perth'
Overseas tours: West of England U15 to West Indies 2001; England U18 to Netherlands 2003; England U19 to Qatar 2003, to Bangladesh (U19 World Cup) 2003-04, to India 2004-05
Career highlights to date: 'Glamorgan debut 2005. First-class debut 2004 (MCC). U19 World Cup 2004'
Cricket moments to forget: 'Losing semi-final of U19 World Cup 2004 against West Indies'
Cricket superstitions: 'Left boot first'
Cricketers particularly admired: Steve Watkin, Alex Wharf, Andrew Flintoff
Young players to look out for: Steve Davies, Will Bragg
Other sports played: Golf, squash (Wales U11-U13), football ('keeper for Football Association of Wales 2002-03')
Other sports followed: Football (Manchester United)
Injuries: Out for six weeks after a second operation for a posterior impingement (ankle spur)
Relaxations: 'Socialising with friends; Sky Plus, FIFA 07'
Extras: BBC *Test Match Special* U15 Cricketer of the Year 2001. Sir John Hobbs Memorial Award 2001. Royal Variety Club Outstanding Newcomer Award 2002. NBC Denis Compton Award for the most promising young Glamorgan player 2003. Represented England U19 2003, 2004, 2005. Made first-class debut for MCC v Sussex at Lord's 2004. ECB National Academy 2004-05 (part-time)

Opinions on cricket: 'Lunch and tea 30 minutes each. Should be able to shake hands on dead game earlier.'
Best batting: 34* MCC v Sussex, Lord's 2004
Best bowling: 2-65 MCC v Sussex, Lord's 2004

2006 Season

	M	Inn	NO	Runs	HS	Avg	100	50	Ct	St	Balls	Runs	Wkts	Avg	BB	5I	10M
Test																	
FC	1	1	0	3	3	3.00	-	-	-	-	126	81	1	81.00	1-81	-	-
ODI																	
List A	1	1	0	6	6	6.00	-	-	1	-	54	59	1	59.00	1-59	-	
20/20 Int																	
20/20																	

Career Performances

	M	Inn	NO	Runs	HS	Avg	100	50	Ct	St	Balls	Runs	Wkts	Avg	BB	5I	10M
Test																	
FC	3	3	1	37	34 *	18.50	-	-	-	-	370	243	5	48.60	2-65	-	-
ODI																	
List A	1	1	0	6	6	6.00	-	-	1	-	54	59	1	59.00	1-59	-	
20/20 Int																	
20/20	3	1	1	1	1 *		-	-	2	-	67	92	5	18.40	2-12	-	

HARRISON, D. S. — Glamorgan

Name: David Stuart Harrison
Role: Right-hand bat, right-arm
fast-medium bowler
Born: 31 July 1981, Newport, Gwent
Height: 6ft 5in **Weight:** 16st
Nickname: Harry, Hazza, Des, Desmond,
Roof, Morehead, Pass Me, Cus, Dogs, Ceedo,
Your Eyes, Get Off My Train, Dai, Sammy
County debut: 1999
County cap: 2006
50 wickets in a season: 1
Place in batting averages: 201st av. 21.61
(2005 270th av. 11.77)
Place in bowling averages: 103rd av. 39.62
(2005 141st av. 53.19)
Strike rate: 72.02 (career 62.54)
Parents: Stuart and Susan
Marital status: Single

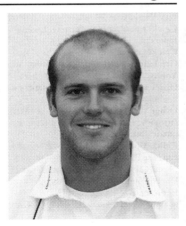

Family links with cricket: 'Brother ("The Worm") also plays for Glamorgan. Father played for Glamorgan'

Education: West Monmouth Comprehensive; Usk/Pontypool College; UWIC

Qualifications: 5 GCSEs, BTEC Diploma Sports Studies/Science (distinction), City & Guilds Level 2 IT, qualified high school caretaker

Off-season: 'Studying master's degree at UWIC. Touring with MCC. Bowling for three hours at a time indoors then batting for two minutes against Wally at the EWO'

Overseas tours: Wales U15 to Ireland; Gwent YC to South Africa 1996; Wales U16 to Jersey 1997, 1998; England U19 to Malaysia and (U19 World Cup) Sri Lanka 1999-2000; Glamorgan to Cape Town 2002; England A to Sri Lanka 2004-05; MCC to Bahrain 2005-06; 'Dean Cosker Invitational to Guernsey and Berlin 2006'

Overseas teams played for: Claremont, Cape Town 2002 (one game during Glamorgan tour)

Career highlights to date: 'Winning National League 2002. Glamorgan debut 1999. England A tour 2005'

Cricket superstitions: 'Always brush my hair before bowling'

Cricketers particularly admired: Jon Lewis, Paul Franks, Nasser Hussain

Young players to look out for: Adam Harrison

Other sports played: Squash (Wales junior squad), rugby (East Wales U11 caps), football, volleyball, tennis, badminton

Other sports followed: Rugby (Newport Gwent Dragons), football (Man Utd)

Injuries: Out for six weeks with a bruised toe

Favourite band: 'All the live bands down my local, "The Lower"'

Relaxations: 'Socialising, golf'

Extras: Has played for Glamorgan from U12, becoming seventh youngest to play for 1st XI, aged 17. Represented England at U17, U18 and U19. Glamorgan Young Player of the Year 2003, 2004. ECB National Academy 2004-05

Best batting: 88 Glamorgan v Essex, Chelmsford 2004

Best bowling: 5-48 Glamorgan v Somerset, Swansea 2004

2006 Season

	M	Inn	NO	Runs	HS	Avg	100	50	Ct	St	Balls	Runs	Wkts	Avg	BB	5I	10M
Test																	
FC	13	16	3	281	64	21.61	-	1	4	-	2521	1387	35	39.62	5-76	1	-
ODI																	
List A	11	8	3	115	30	23.00	-	-	1	-	510	357	15	23.80	4-31	-	
20/20 Int																	
20/20	4	0	0	0	0		-	-	1	-	51	87	1	87.00	1-30	-	

Career Performances

	M	Inn	NO	Runs	HS	Avg	100	50	Ct	St	Balls	Runs	Wkts	Avg	BB	5I	10M
Test																	
FC	68	98	14	1341	88	15.96	-	4	24	-	10633	6200	170	36.47	5-48	6	-
ODI																	
List A	58	37	12	357	37 *	14.28	-	-	6	-	2446	1850	68	27.20	5-26	2	
20/20 Int																	
20/20	10	3	0	5	4	1.66	-	-	3	-	177	252	9	28.00	2-17	-	

HARRISON, P. W. Leicestershire

Name: Paul William Harrison
Role: Right-hand bat, wicket-keeper
Born: 22 May 1984, Cuckfield, West Sussex
Height: 6ft 2in **Weight:** 12st 12lbs
Nickname: Harry, Potter
County debut: 2005 (Warwickshire), 2005 (one-day, Leicestershire), 2006 (first-class, Leicestershire)
Parents: Angela and Brian
Marital status: Single
Family links with cricket: 'Dad and uncle played league cricket in Sussex. Brother Leigh played YCs and 2nd XI at Sussex'
Education: The Forest School; College of Richard Collyer, Horsham; Loughborough University
Qualifications: 3 A-levels, Level 1 coaching
Overseas tours: Sussex Young Cricketers to Sri Lanka 2001, to South Africa 2003
Overseas teams played for: Tuart Hill, Perth 2002
Career highlights to date: 'Beating Worcestershire first team with Loughborough UCCE 2005'

Cricket moments to forget: 'Dropping a catch on the boundary for my club that would have got us promoted to the premier division'
Cricketers particularly admired: Mark Waugh, Alec Stewart, Adam Gilchrist
Young players to look out for: David Wainwright, Ryan Cummins
Other sports played: Football (county U18), golf (Mannings Heath; 7 handicap)
Other sports followed: Football (Arsenal, Brighton & Hove Albion)
Favourite band: Red Hot Chili Peppers
Extras: Sussex U19 Player of the Year. Played for Loughborough UCCE 2004-06. Played one first-class game for Warwickshire 2005 and played for Leicestershire in the International Twenty20 Club Championship 2005. Represented British Universities 2006
Best batting: 54 LUCCE v Nottinghamshire, Trent Bridge 2005

2006 Season

	M	Inn	NO	Runs	HS	Avg	100	50	Ct	St	Balls	Runs	Wkts	Avg	BB	5I	10M
Test																	
FC	3	6	1	77	28 *	15.40	-	-	6	-	0	0	0		-	-	-
ODI																	
List A	3	3	0	98	61	32.66	-	1	3	-	0	0	0		-	-	
20/20 Int																	
20/20	6	5	1	46	18	11.50	-	-	1	-	0	0	0		-	-	

Career Performances

	M	Inn	NO	Runs	HS	Avg	100	50	Ct	St	Balls	Runs	Wkts	Avg	BB	5I	10M
Test																	
FC	10	16	4	297	54	24.75	-	1	15	-	0	0	0		-	-	-
ODI																	
List A	3	3	0	98	61	32.66	-	1	3	-	0	0	0		-	-	
20/20 Int																	
20/20	7	6	1	49	18	9.80	-	-	1	-	0	0	0		-	-	

HARVEY, I. J.   Derbyshire

Name: <u>Ian</u> Joseph Harvey
Role: Right-hand bat, right-arm
fast-medium bowler
Born: 10 April 1972, Wonthaggi,
Victoria, Australia
Height: 5ft 9in **Weight:** 12st 8lbs
Nickname: Freak
County debut: 1999 (Gloucestershire),
2004 (Yorkshire)
County cap: 1999 (Gloucestershire),
2005 (Yorkshire)
ODI debut: 1997-98
1st-Class 200s: 1
Place in batting averages: 28th av. 56.10
(2005 62nd av. 42.88)
Place in bowling averages: 37th av. 29.07
(2005 32nd av. 26.26)
Strike rate: 65.69 (career 56.95)
Family links with cricket: Brothers club
cricketers in Australia
Education: Wonthaggi Technical College

Overseas tours: Australian Academy to New Zealand 1994-95; Australia to Sharjah
(Coca-Cola Cup) 1997-98, to New Zealand 1999-2000 (one-day series), to Kenya
(ICC Knockout Trophy) 2000-01, to India 2000-01 (one-day series), to England 2001
(one-day series), to South Africa 2001-02 (one-day series), to Africa (World Cup)
2002-03, to West Indies 2002-03 (one-day series), to India (TVS Cup) 2003-04, to Sri
Lanka 2003-04 (one-day series), to Zimbabwe (one-day series) 2004, to Netherlands
(Videocon Cup) 2004, to England (ICC Champions Trophy) 2004; Australia A to
South Africa 2002-03; FICA World XI to New Zealand 2004-05
Overseas teams played for: Victoria 1993-94 – 2004-05; Cape Cobras 2005-06 –
Extras: The nickname 'Freak' is a reference to his brilliant fielding and was
reportedly coined by Shane Warne. Attended Commonwealth Bank [Australian]
Cricket Academy 1994. An overseas player with Gloucestershire 1999-2003 and in
2006; an overseas player with Yorkshire 2004-05. Man of the Match in the Carlton
Series first final v West Indies at Sydney 2000-01 (47*/2-5). Won the Walter Lawrence
Trophy 2001 for the season's fastest first-class hundred with his 61-ball century v
Derbyshire at Bristol; also took 5-89 in Derbyshire's second innings. Has won
numerous Australian and English domestic awards, including C&G Man of the Match
in the final v Worcestershire at Lord's 2003 (2-37 and a 36-ball 61). Scored the first
ever century in the Twenty20 Cup (100* from 50 balls), v Warwickshire at Edgbaston
2003. One of *Wisden*'s Five Cricketers of the Year 2004. Has joined Derbyshire for
2007; is no longer considered an overseas player

Best batting: 209* Yorkshire v Somerset, Headingley 2005
Best bowling: 8-101 Australia A v South Africa A, Adelaide 2002-03

2006 Season

	M	Inn	NO	Runs	HS	Avg	100	50	Ct	St	Balls	Runs	Wkts	Avg	BB	5I	10M
Test																	
FC	9	15	5	561	114	56.10	2	2	4	-	854	378	13	29.07	3-25	-	-
ODI																	
List A	11	11	1	537	112	53.70	2	2	2	-	458	343	11	31.18	2-22	-	
20/20 Int																	
20/20	8	8	0	206	56	25.75	-	1	3	-	174	286	7	40.85	3-42	-	

Career Performances

	M	Inn	NO	Runs	HS	Avg	100	50	Ct	St	Balls	Runs	Wkts	Avg	BB	5I	10M
Test																	
FC	163	269	28	8120	209 *	33.69	13	46	110	-	24094	11577	423	27.36	8-101	15	2
ODI	73	51	11	715	48 *	17.87	-	-	17	-	3279	2577	85	30.31	4-16	-	
List A	302	265	26	5906	112	24.71	2	27	81	-	13493	9872	445	22.18	5-19	9	
20/20 Int																	
20/20	32	31	3	993	109	35.46	3	4	8	-	629	844	33	25.57	3-28	-	

38. Which former England captain went to a
century as he struck the winning runs in his final Test,
v New Zealand at Lord's 2004?

HASSAN ADNAN   Derbyshire

Name: Mohammad Hassan Adnan Syed
Role: Right-hand bat, right-arm
off-spin bowler
Born: 15 May 1975, Lahore, Punjab
Height: 5ft 8½in **Weight:** 11st 8lbs
Nickname: Hassy
County debut: 2003
County cap: 2004
1000 runs in a season: 1
Place in batting averages: 117th av. 33.07
(2005 159th av. 29.17)
Strike rate: (career 110.25)
Parents: Syed Inam Ali and Methab Bano
Wife and date of marriage: Naila, 18
January 2006
Education: MAO College, Lahore
Off-season: 'Coaching and training'
Overseas teams played for: Islamabad
1994-95, 2000-01; Gujranwala 1997-98 – 1998-99; Water and Power Development
Authority (WAPDA) 1997-98 – 2004-05
Career highlights to date: 'Being a capped player'
Cricket superstitions: 'None'
Cricketers particularly admired: Steve Waugh
Young players to look out for: Gary Ballance, Jake Needham
Other sports played: Badminton
Other sports followed: Football
Relaxations: 'Playing computer games; listening to music'
Extras: Won two Man of the Match awards in the Tissot Cup domestic competition in
Pakistan. Scored century (113*) as Derbyshire beat New Zealanders in 50-over match
at Derby 2004. Scored 1247 County Championship runs in his first full season 2004.
Derbyshire Supporters' Club Player of the Year 2004. Is England-qualified
Opinions on cricket: 'Twenty20 cricket has brought a lot of excitement to the game.
It has attracted a lot of new fans.'
Best batting: 191 Derbyshire v Somerset, Taunton 2005
Best bowling: 1-4 Derbyshire v Yorkshire, Derby 2004
              1-4 WAPDA v Allied Bank, Karachi 2004-05
              1-4 Derbyshire v Gloucestershire, Derby 2006

2006 Season

	M	Inn	NO	Runs	HS	Avg	100	50	Ct	St	Balls	Runs	Wkts	Avg	BB	5I	10M
Test																	
FC	18	29	2	893	117	33.07	1	5	4	-	54	37	1	37.00	1-4	-	-
ODI																	
List A	12	11	0	247	45	22.45	-	-	8	-	36	33	1	33.00	1-20	-	
20/20 Int																	
20/20	5	4	2	80	54 *	40.00	-	1	2	-	18	19	1	19.00	1-19	-	

Career Performances

	M	Inn	NO	Runs	HS	Avg	100	50	Ct	St	Balls	Runs	Wkts	Avg	BB	5I	10M
Test																	
FC	116	192	22	6812	191	40.07	10	46	62	-	453	318	4	79.50	1-4	-	-
ODI																	
List A	69	66	9	1789	113 *	31.38	2	13	26	-	187	162	6	27.00	2-13	-	
20/20 Int																	
20/20	11	9	2	167	54 *	23.85	-	1	4	-	54	68	2	34.00	1-18	-	

HEATHER, S. A. Sussex

Name: <u>Sean</u> Andrew Heather
Role: Right-hand bat, right-arm medium bowler
Born: 5 February 1982, Chichester
Height: 6ft **Weight:** 12st
Nickname: Seany, Badger, Road Kill, Lucky
County debut: 2005
Parents: Andrew and Carole
Marital status: Engaged to Bridget
Education: Chichester High School for Boys; Chichester High School Sixth Form College
Qualifications: 4 GCSEs, Advanced GNVQ Leisure and Tourism
Career outside cricket: Computer analyst for West Sussex County Council
Overseas teams played for: Swanbourne, Perth 2000-01; Sydenham, Christchurch 2005
Career highlights to date: 'Breaking the Sussex Premier League's run-scoring record in 2004, scoring 1086 runs in the season'
Cricketers particularly admired: Darren Gough, James Kirtley
Young players to look out for: Luke Wright

Other sports played: Golf, football
Other sports followed: Football (Liverpool FC)
Favourite band: Queen
Relaxations: Playing snooker
Extras: *Wisden* Cockspur Club Cricketer of the Year 2004. Released by Sussex at the end of the 2006 season
Best batting: 7 Sussex v Bangladeshis, Hove 2005

2006 Season

	M	Inn	NO	Runs	HS	Avg	100	50	Ct	St	Balls	Runs	Wkts	Avg	BB	5I	10M
Test																	
FC	1	1	0	0	0	0.00	-	-	1	-	0	0	0		-	-	-
ODI																	
List A	2	2	0	15	11	7.50	-	-	2	-	0	0	0		-	-	
20/20 Int																	
20/20	7	4	2	20	8	10.00	-	-	1	-	42	53	4	13.25	3-16	-	

Career Performances

	M	Inn	NO	Runs	HS	Avg	100	50	Ct	St	Balls	Runs	Wkts	Avg	BB	5I	10M
Test																	
FC	2	2	0	7	7	3.50	-	-	1	-	0	0	0		-	-	-
ODI																	
List A	2	2	0	15	11	7.50	-	-	2	-	0	0	0		-	-	
20/20 Int																	
20/20	7	4	2	20	8	10.00	-	-	1	-	42	53	4	13.25	3-16	-	

HEMP, D. L.   Glamorgan

Name: <u>David</u> Lloyd Hemp
Role: Left-hand bat, county captain
Born: 15 November 1970, Hamilton, Bermuda
Height: 6ft 1in **Weight:** 12st 7lbs
Nickname: Hempy, Gramps, Mad Dog
County debut: 1991 (Glamorgan), 1997 (Warwickshire)
County cap: 1994 (Glamorgan), 1997 (Warwickshire)
1000 runs in a season: 6
Place in batting averages: 97th av. 35.82 (2005 58th av. 44.16)
Strike rate: (career 60.70)
Parents: Clive and Elisabeth
Wife and date of marriage: Angela, 16 March 1996
Children: Cameron, January 2002
Family links with cricket: Father and brother both played for Swansea CC
Education: Olchfa Comprehensive School; Millfield School; Birmingham University

Qualifications: 5 O-levels, 2 A-levels, MBA, Level III coaching award

Career outside cricket: PR/marketing; coaching

Off-season: 'Working for Nyans Communications (marketing and PR company); playing for Bermuda'

Overseas tours: Welsh Cricket Association U18 to Barbados 1986; Welsh Schools U19 to Australia 1987-88; Glamorgan to Trinidad 1990; South Wales Cricket Association to New Zealand and Australia 1991-92; England A to India 1994-95; Bermuda to Kenya 2006-07, to South Africa (ICC Associates Tri-Series) 2006-07

Overseas teams played for: Crusaders, Durban 1992-98

Career highlights to date: '99* England A v India A, Calcutta "Test" match 1994-95'

Cricket moments to forget: 'None'

Cricket superstitions: 'None'

Cricketers particularly admired: Brian Lara, Graeme Hick, Mark Ramprakash

Young players to look out for: Ben Wright, James Harris, Neil Saker

Other sports played: Football, golf

Other sports followed: Football (Swansea City, West Ham United)

Favourite band: Manic Street Preachers, Stereophonics

Relaxations: Golf, reading

Extras: In 1989 scored 104* and 101* for Welsh Schools U19 v Scottish Schools U19 and 120 and 102* v Irish Schools U19. Scored 258* for Wales v MCC 1991. Scored two 100s (138/114*) v Hampshire at Southampton 1997. Vice-captain of Warwickshire 2001. Left Warwickshire in the 2001-02 off-season and rejoined Glamorgan for 2002. Scored 88-ball 102 v Surrey at The Oval in the C&G 2002 as Glamorgan made 429 in reply to Surrey's 438-5. Won Glamorgan's Byron Denning Award 2004. Glamorgan Player of the Year 2005. Glamorgan captain since Robert Croft stood down in mid-September 2006

Opinions on cricket: 'Slightly reduce amount of cricket played, which would allow for more quality practices. Practice facilities, although improving, still need to get better. No overseas players as the best are not available, which would therefore hopefully give more opportunities to home-grown players.'

Best batting: 186* Warwickshire v Worcestershire, Edgbaston 2001

Best bowling: 3-23 Glamorgan v South Africa A, Cardiff 1996

Stop press: Represented Bermuda in the ICC Inter-Continental Cup 2006, scoring 247* v Netherlands at Pretoria, and made ODI debut for Bermuda in series v Kenya in Mombasa 2006-07

2006 Season

	M	Inn	NO	Runs	HS	Avg	100	50	Ct	St	Balls	Runs	Wkts	Avg	BB	5I	10M
Test																	
FC	16	29	1	1003	155	35.82	3	2	18	-	0	0	0		-	-	-
ODI																	
List A	16	15	2	333	79 *	25.61	-	2	5	-	0	0	0		-	-	
20/20 Int																	
20/20	8	7	3	234	74	58.50	-	2	6	-	0	0	0		-	-	

Career Performances

	M	Inn	NO	Runs	HS	Avg	100	50	Ct	St	Balls	Runs	Wkts	Avg	BB	5I	10M
Test																	
FC	234	399	35	13069	186 *	35.90	25	71	160	-	1032	778	17	45.76	3-23	-	-
ODI																	
List A	243	213	27	4997	121	26.86	5	25	88	-	189	178	11	16.18	4-32	-	
20/20 Int																	
20/20	27	25	5	611	74	30.55	-	3	16	-	0	0	0		-	-	

HENDERSON, C. W.   Leicestershire

Name: <u>Claude</u> William Henderson
Role: Right-hand bat, left-arm spin bowler
Born: 14 June 1972, Worcester, South Africa
Height: 6ft 2in **Weight:** 14st 2lbs
Nickname: Hendy, Hendo
County debut: 2004
County cap: 2004
Test debut: 2001-02
ODI debut: 2001-02
Place in batting averages: 144th av. 30.27
(2005 188th av. 24.29)
Place in bowling averages: 114th av. 41.91
(2005 116th av. 42.90)
Strike rate: 76.00 (career 73.53)
Parents: Henry and Susan
Wife and date of marriage: Nicci,
29 March 2003
Family links with cricket: Brother James
played first-class cricket
Education: Worcester High School
Qualifications: Level 2 coaching, basic computer skills, basic bookkeeping skills
Career outside cricket: 'Family business'

Off-season: 'Playing for Highveld Lions, Johannesburg'
Overseas tours: South Africa A to Sri Lanka 1998; South Africa to Zimbabwe 2001-02, to Australia 2001-02
Overseas teams played for: Boland 1990-91 – 1997-98; Western Province 1998-99-2003-04; Highveld Lions 2006-07
Career highlights to date: 'Playing for South Africa'
Cricket moments to forget: 'Losing to Devon in C&G 2004'
Cricket superstitions: 'None'
Cricketers particularly admired: Shane Warne, Jacques Kallis
Young players to look out for: Stuart Broad
Other sports played: Golf, tennis, fishing
Other sports followed: Rugby (Leicester Tigers)
Favourite band: U2
Relaxations: 'Cinema, travelling, spending time with family'
Extras: Has won several match awards in South African domestic cricket. Scored fifty (63) and recorded five-wicket innings return (5-28) on Championship debut for Leicestershire v Glamorgan at Leicester 2004; recorded a further five-wicket return (5-24) on one-day debut v Yorkshire at Headingley in the totesport League 2004. Is not considered an overseas player
Best batting: 71 Western Province v KwaZulu-Natal, Cape Town 2003-04
Best bowling: 7-57 Boland v Eastern Province, Paarl 1994-95

2006 Season

	M	Inn	NO	Runs	HS	Avg	100	50	Ct	St	Balls	Runs	Wkts	Avg	BB	5I	10M
Test																	
FC	17	24	6	545	62 *	30.27	-	1	7	-	3724	2054	49	41.91	5-69	2	-
ODI																	
List A	12	11	5	134	29 *	22.33	-	-	2	-	516	351	13	27.00	3-36	-	
20/20 Int																	
20/20	4	1	0	1	1	1.00	-	-	3	-	72	89	2	44.50	1-25	-	

Career Performances

	M	Inn	NO	Runs	HS	Avg	100	50	Ct	St	Balls	Runs	Wkts	Avg	BB	5I	10M
Test	7	7	0	65	30	9.28	-	-	2	-	1962	928	22	42.18	4-116	-	-
FC	163	220	54	3031	71	18.25	-	8	63	-	40885	17501	556	31.47	7-57	18	-
ODI	4	0	0	0	0		-	-	-	-	217	132	7	18.85	4-17	-	
List A	176	97	52	775	32	17.22	-	-	44	-	8018	5479	220	24.90	6-29	2	
20/20 Int																	
20/20	20	8	2	20	9 *	3.33	-	-	7	-	289	350	15	23.33	3-26	-	

HENDERSON, T.　　　　　　　　　　　　　　　Kent

Name: Tyron Henderson
Role: Right-hand bat, right-arm fast-medium
bowler; all-rounder
Born: 1 August 1974, Durban, South Africa
Nickname: The Blacksmith
County debut: 2006
Place in batting averages: 218th av. 18.25
Strike rate: (career 62.36)
Family links with cricket: Grandfather
(J. K. Henderson) and great-uncle (W. A.
Henderson) played first-class cricket for
North Eastern Transvaal
Overseas tours: South African Academy to
Ireland and Scotland 1999; South Africa A to
Sri Lanka 2005-06
Overseas teams played for: Border 1998-99
– 2003-04; Eastern Cape 2003-04; Warriors
2004-05 – 2005-06; Lions 2006-07 –

Extras: Played for Berkshire in the 2003 C&G. Has represented South Africa A. His
awards include Man of the Match v Griqualand West at Kimberley in the Standard
Bank Cup 2003-04 (3-45/126*) and v Dolphins at Port Elizabeth in the Standard Bank
Pro20 Series 2004-05 (3-24/44). An overseas player with Kent during the 2006 season
as a locum for Justin Kemp
Best batting: 81 Border v Gauteng, Johannesburg 1999-2000
Best bowling: 6-56 Border v Free State, Bloemfontein 2000-01
Stop press: Made Twenty20 International debut v India at Johannesburg 2006-07

2006 Season	M	Inn	NO	Runs	HS	Avg	100	50	Ct	St	Balls	Runs	Wkts	Avg	BB	5I	10M
Test																	
FC	6	9	1	146	59	18.25	-	1	2	-	864	505	9	56.11	4-29	-	-
ODI																	
List A	7	6	0	82	20	13.66	-	-	4	-	318	231	10	23.10	5-28	1	
20/20 Int																	
20/20	9	8	2	148	63	24.66	-	1	1	-	210	259	7	37.00	3-17	-	

Career Performances

	M	Inn	NO	Runs	HS	Avg	100	50	Ct	St	Balls	Runs	Wkts	Avg	BB	5I	10M
Test																	
FC	73	117	16	1749	81	17.31	-	6	23	-	13222	5922	212	27.93	6-56	6	-
ODI																	
List A	81	63	16	1123	126 *	23.89	1	6	18	-	3639	2522	101	24.97	5-5	3	
20/20 Int																	
20/20	28	25	2	559	85	24.30	-	5	2	-	596	697	29	24.03	3-11	-	

HICK, G. A.   Worcestershire

Name: <u>Graeme</u> Ashley Hick
Role: Right-hand bat, off-spin bowler
Born: 23 May 1966, Harare, Zimbabwe
Height: 6ft 3in   **Weight:** 14st 4lbs
Nickname: Hicky, Ash
County debut: 1984
County cap: 1986; colours 2002
Benefit: 1999; testimonial 2006
Test debut: 1991
ODI debut: 1991
1000 runs in a season: 19
1st-Class 200s: 13
1st-Class 300s: 2
1st-Class 400s: 1
Place in batting averages: 47th av. 48.71 (2005 107th av. 34.51)
Strike rate: (career 90.03)
Parents: John and Eve
Wife and date of marriage: Jackie, 5 October 1991
Children: Lauren Amy, 12 September 1992; Jordan Ashley, 5 September 1995
Family links with cricket: Father has served on Zimbabwe Cricket Union Board of Control and played representative cricket in Zimbabwe
Education: Prince Edward Boys' High School, Zimbabwe
Qualifications: 4 O-levels, NCA coaching award
Overseas tours: Zimbabwe to England (World Cup) 1983, to Sri Lanka 1983-84, to England 1985; England to Australia and New Zealand (World Cup) 1991-92, to India and Sri Lanka 1992-93, to West Indies 1993-94, to Australia 1994-95, to South Africa 1995-96, to India and Pakistan (World Cup) 1995-96, to Sharjah (Akai Singer Champions Trophy) 1997-98, to West Indies 1997-98 (one-day series), to Bangladesh (Wills International Cup) 1998-99, to Australia 1998-99, to Sharjah (Coca-Cola Cup) 1998-99, to South Africa and Zimbabwe 1999-2000 (one-day series), to Kenya (ICC

Knockout Trophy) 2000-01, to Pakistan and Sri Lanka 2000-01; FICA World XI to New Zealand 2004-05

Overseas teams played for: Old Hararians, Zimbabwe 1982-90; Northern Districts, New Zealand 1987-89; Queensland 1990-91; Auckland 1997-98

Cricketers particularly admired: Steve Waugh, Glenn McGrath

Other sports played: Golf ('relaxation'), hockey (played for Zimbabwe)

Other sports followed: Football (Liverpool FC), golf, tennis, squash, hockey

Extras: One of *Wisden*'s Five Cricketers of the Year 1987. In 1988 he made 405* v Somerset at Taunton and scored 1000 first-class runs by the end of May. Qualified to play for England 1991. Scored 100th first-class century (132) v Sussex at Worcester 1998; at the age of 32, he became the second youngest player after Wally Hammond to score 100 centuries. Won ODI Man of the Match awards v Zimbabwe, the country of his birth, for his match-winning 87* at Bulawayo and his 80 and 5-33 at Harare, February 2000. Scored 200* v Durham at Riverside 2001, in the process achieving the feat of having recorded centuries against each of the other 17 counties, both home and away. Captain of Worcestershire 2000-02. Became leading run-scorer in the history of the one-day league, v Middlesex at Lord's 2005. Took eight catches in match v Essex at Chelmsford 2005, equalling the Worcestershire record. Scored 130th career first-class century (139) v Northamptonshire at Worcester 2006 to move into eighth spot on the all-time first-class century-makers' list and become the eighth batsman (the first for Worcestershire) to register 100 first-class centuries for a single county

Best batting: 405* Worcestershire v Somerset, Taunton 1988

Best bowling: 5-18 Worcestershire v Leicestershire, Worcester 1995

2006 Season

	M	Inn	NO	Runs	HS	Avg	100	50	Ct	St	Balls	Runs	Wkts	Avg	BB	5I	10M
Test																	
FC	14	23	2	1023	182	48.71	4	3	36	-	0	0	0		-	-	-
ODI																	
List A	15	15	6	374	50 *	41.55	-	1	8	-	0	0	0		-	-	
20/20 Int																	
20/20	8	8	1	298	97 *	42.57	-	3	1	-	0	0	0		-	-	

Career Performances

	M	Inn	NO	Runs	HS	Avg	100	50	Ct	St	Balls	Runs	Wkts	Avg	BB	5I	10M
Test	65	114	6	3383	178	31.32	6	18	90	-	3057	1306	23	56.78	4-126	-	-
FC	500	829	80	39460	405 *	52.68	132	150	668	-	20889	10308	232	44.43	5-18	5	1
ODI	120	118	15	3846	126 *	37.33	5	27	64	-	1236	1026	30	34.20	5-33	1	
List A	625	605	90	21180	172 *	41.12	39	134	277	-	8603	6649	225	29.55	5-19	4	
20/20 Int																	
20/20	21	21	2	736	116 *	38.73	1	7	7	-	0	0	0		-	-	

HILDRETH, J. C. Somerset

Name: <u>James</u> Charles Hildreth
Role: Right-hand bat, right-arm medium
bowler; all-rounder
Born: 9 September 1984, Milton Keynes
Height: 5ft 10in **Weight:** 12st
Nickname: Hildy, Hildz
County debut: 2003
1st-Class 200s: 1
Place in batting averages: 103rd av. 34.69
(2005 86th av. 37.48)
Strike rate: (career 111.00)
Parents: David and Judy
Marital status: Single
Family links with cricket: 'Dad played
county league cricket in Kent and Northants'
Education: Millfield School
Qualifications: 10 GCSEs, 3 A-levels, ECB
Level 1 coaching

Overseas tours: 'West' to West Indies 1999, 2000; Millfield to Sri Lanka 2001;
England U19 to Bangladesh (U19 World Cup) 2003-04
Cricket moments to forget: 'Being bowled first ball by Shoaib Akhtar'
Cricket superstitions: 'Left pad before right when getting padded up'
Other sports played: Hockey (West of England), squash (South of England), tennis
(South of England), football (England Independent Schools, Luton Town), rugby
(Millfield)
Other sports followed: Football (Charlton Athletic)
Favourite band: Jack Johnson
Relaxations: Travelling, snowboarding, music
Extras: NBC Denis Compton Award for the most promising young Somerset player
2003. Scored maiden first-class century (101) plus 72 in the second innings v Durham
at Taunton 2004 in his second Championship match. Represented England U19 v
Bangladesh U19 2004, scoring 210 in second 'Test' at Taunton. Cricket Society's Most
Promising Young Cricketer of the Year 2004. Scored maiden first-class double century
(227*) at Taunton 2006, setting a new record for the highest score by a Somerset
batsman v Northamptonshire. ECB National Academy 2004-05 (part-time)
Best batting: 227* Somerset v Northamptonshire, Taunton 2006
Best bowling: 2-39 Somerset v Hampshire, Taunton 2004

2006 Season

	M	Inn	NO	Runs	HS	Avg	100	50	Ct	St	Balls	Runs	Wkts	Avg	BB	5I	10M
Test																	
FC	14	24	1	798	227 *	34.69	1	3	11	-	30	27	0		-	-	-
ODI																	
List A	18	17	2	495	122	33.00	1	2	2	-	36	56	1	56.00	1-20	-	
20/20 Int																	
20/20	8	8	2	78	27 *	13.00	-	-	4	-	0	0	0		-	-	

Career Performances

	M	Inn	NO	Runs	HS	Avg	100	50	Ct	St	Balls	Runs	Wkts	Avg	BB	5I	10M
Test																	
FC	44	75	7	2504	227 *	36.82	5	14	38	-	222	176	2	88.00	2-39	-	-
ODI																	
List A	62	59	10	1469	122	29.97	1	6	18	-	90	117	2	58.50	1-20	-	
20/20 Int																	
20/20	26	26	3	437	71	19.00	-	3	9	-	136	190	10	19.00	3-24	-	

HODD, A. J. Sussex

Name: <u>Andrew</u> John Hodd
Role: Right-hand bat, wicket-keeper
Born: 12 January 1984, Chichester
Height: 5ft 9½in **Weight:** 11st 8lbs
Nickname: Hoddy
County debut: 2002 (one-day, Sussex),
2003 (first-class, Sussex), 2005 (Surrey)
Parents: Karen and Adrian
Marital status: Single
Family links with cricket: 'Long line of
enthusiastic club cricketers'
Education: Bexhill High School; Bexhill
College; 'short stint at Loughborough Uni'
Qualifications: 9 GCSEs, 4 A-levels,
Level 1 coach
Career outside cricket: Coaching
Overseas tours: South of England U14 to
West Indies 1998; Sussex Academy to Cape
Town 1999, to Sri Lanka 2001; England U17 to Australia 2000-01; England U19 to
Australia 2002-03
Career highlights to date: 'Achieving a contract with Sussex'
Cricket superstitions: 'Too many! Must drink coffee the morning of a game'

Cricketers particularly admired: David Hussey, Matt Prior
Young players to look out for: Luke Wright, Ollie Rayner, Ben Brown
Other sports played: Golf, football, boxing
Other sports followed: Football (Brighton & Hove Albion)
Favourite band: Hard-Fi
Relaxations: 'Cinema, DVDs, gym, going out'
Extras: Played for England U14, U15, U17 and U19. Graham Kersey Trophy, Bunbury 1999. Several junior Player of the Year awards at Sussex. Sussex County League Young Player of the Year 2002. Sussex 2nd XI Player of the Year 2003. Joined Surrey for 2004, leaving at the end of the 2005 season to rejoin Sussex for 2006
Best batting: 57* Surrey v Bangladesh A, The Oval 2005

2006 Season

	M	Inn	NO	Runs	HS	Avg	100	50	Ct	St	Balls	Runs	Wkts	Avg	BB	5I	10M
Test																	
FC	3	4	0	29	18	7.25	-	-	8	-	0	0	0		-	-	-
ODI																	
List A																	
20/20 Int																	
20/20																	

Career Performances

	M	Inn	NO	Runs	HS	Avg	100	50	Ct	St	Balls	Runs	Wkts	Avg	BB	5I	10M
Test																	
FC	5	6	2	141	57 *	35.25	-	2	11	-	0	0	0		-	-	-
ODI																	
List A	3	3	0	13	9	4.33	-	-	3	-	0	0	0		-	-	
20/20 Int																	
20/20	1	0	0	0	0		-	-	-	-	0	0	0		-	-	

---

39. Which member of a famous cricketing family
had match figures of 9-99 on his Test debut when South Africa
met New Zealand at Durban in 1961-62?

HODGE, B. J. Lancashire

Name: Bradley (<u>Brad</u>) John Hodge
Role: Right-hand bat, right-arm
off-spin bowler
Born: 29 December 1974, Sandringham,
Melbourne, Australia
Height: 5ft 7½in **Weight:** 12st 8lbs
Nickname: Bunk
County debut: 2002 (Durham), 2003
(Leicestershire), 2005 (Lancashire)
County cap: 2003 (Leicestershire),
2006 (Lancashire)
Test debut: 2005-06
ODI debut: 2005-06
1000 runs in a season: 2
1st-Class 200s: 7
1st-Class 300s: 1
Place in batting averages: (2005 122nd
av. 32.50)

Strike rate: (career 71.42)
Parents: John and Val
Wife: Megan
Children: Jesse
Education: St Bede's College, Mentone; Deakin University
Overseas tours: Australia U19 to New Zealand 1992-93; Commonwealth Bank
[Australian] Cricket Academy to Zimbabwe 1998-99; Australia A to Los Angeles
(Moov America Challenge) 1999, to Pakistan 2005-06; Australia to India 2004-05, to
New Zealand 2004-05, to England 2005, to New Zealand (one-day series) 2005-06
Overseas teams played for: Victoria 1993-94 –
Cricketers particularly admired: Allan Border, Dennis Lillee, Dean Jones,
Sachin Tendulkar
Other sports played/followed: Australian Rules football (Melbourne), golf, tennis,
soccer, skiing
Extras: Attended Commonwealth Bank [Australian] Cricket Academy 1993. Leading
run-scorer for Victoria in the Sheffield Shield in his first season (1993-94) with 903
runs (av. 50.16). Victoria's Pura Cup Player of the Year 2000-01 and 2001-02; winner
of the national Pura Cup Player of the Season Award 2001-02 (jointly with Jimmy
Maher of Queensland). Was Durham's overseas player 2002 from late July; an
overseas player with Leicestershire 2003-04 (appointed vice-captain for 2004; assumed
the captaincy in July on the resignation of Phillip DeFreitas). Scored 202* v
Loughborough UCCE at Leicester 2003, in the process sharing with Darren Maddy
(229*) in a record partnership for any wicket for Leicestershire (436*). His 302* v

Nottinghamshire at Trent Bridge 2003 was the then highest individual first-class score by a Leicestershire player. ING Cup Player of the Year 2003-04. Has won numerous Australian and English domestic awards, including Man of the Match in the Twenty20 Cup final at Edgbaston 2004 for his 53-ball 77*. Man of the Match in the first Test v South Africa at Perth 2005-06 (41/203*). Australia contract 2006-07. An overseas player with Lancashire since 2005

Best batting: 302* Leicestershire v Nottinghamshire, Trent Bridge 2003
Best bowling: 4-17 Australia A v West Indians, Hobart 2000-01

2006 Season

	M	Inn	NO	Runs	HS	Avg	100	50	Ct	St	Balls	Runs	Wkts	Avg	BB	5I	10M
Test																	
FC	6	7	2	505	161	101.00	3	-	4	-	210	97	5	19.40	3-21	-	-
ODI																	
List A	6	5	2	268	118	89.33	1	1	1	-	24	28	0			-	-
20/20 Int																	
20/20																	

Career Performances

	M	Inn	NO	Runs	HS	Avg	100	50	Ct	St	Balls	Runs	Wkts	Avg	BB	5I	10M
Test	5	9	2	409	203 *	58.42	1	1	9	-	12	8	0			-	-
FC	184	324	31	13970	302 *	47.67	43	50	108	-	4857	2737	68	40.25	4-17	-	-
ODI	5	5	0	79	59	15.80	-	1	1	-	18	16	0			-	-
List A	171	165	17	5674	164	38.33	12	30	65	-	1260	1124	30	37.46	5-28	1	
20/20 Int																	
20/20	23	23	3	1039	106	51.95	1	8	13	-	222	265	19	13.94	4-17	-	

40. Who celebrated becoming the first player to appear in 100 Tests by scoring 104 v Australia in 1968?

HODNETT, G. P. Gloucestershire

Name: <u>Grant</u> Phillip Hodnett
Role: Right-hand top-order bat, right-arm
leg-spin bowler, occasional wicket-keeper
Born: 17 August 1982, Johannesburg,
South Africa
Height: 6ft 4in **Weight:** 14st
Nickname: Hodders, Hoddy
County debut: 2005
County cap: 2005
Parents: Phillip and Julia
Marital status: Single
Family links with cricket: Brother Kyle an
MCC Young Cricketer
Education: Northwood High School, Durban
Qualifications: Matriculation, ECB Level 1
coach, GFA Fitness Instructor
Career outside cricket: 'Personal trainer;
cricket coach; sports nutrition sales'

Overseas tours: Gloucestershire to South Africa 2006
Overseas teams played for: Durban Collegians 2005-06
Career highlights to date: 'First-class and Championship debut against Warwickshire
at Edgbaston 2005'
Cricket moments to forget: 'I've forgotten it already'
Cricket superstitions: 'None'
Cricketers particularly admired: Hansie Cronje, Jonty Rhodes, Steve Waugh,
Andrew Flintoff, Michael Atherton
Young players to look out for: Kyle Hodnett, Neil Dexter, Steve Snell
Other sports played: Golf, squash, bodyboarding, football, rugby
Other sports followed: Rugby union (England), football (Newcastle United)
Favourite band: Blink-182
Relaxations: 'Going to gym; swimming; reading sports magazines'
Extras: Represented KwaZulu-Natal Schools. West of England Premier League
Batsman of the Year 2004. Is not considered an overseas player
Opinions on cricket: 'I am in favour of the more traditional game of cricket, although
I can understand the need to bring the game to the people – i.e. Twenty20 – from an
entertainment and financial point of view.'
Best batting: 49 Gloucestershire v Warwickshire, Edgbaston 2005

2006 Season

	M	Inn	NO	Runs	HS	Avg	100	50	Ct	St	Balls	Runs	Wkts	Avg	BB	5I	10M
Test																	
FC																	
ODI																	
List A	1	1	0	7	7	7.00	-	-	-	-	0	0	0		-	-	
20/20 Int																	
20/20																	

Career Performances

	M	Inn	NO	Runs	HS	Avg	100	50	Ct	St	Balls	Runs	Wkts	Avg	BB	5I	10M
Test																	
FC	1	2	0	59	49	29.50	-	-	1	-	0	0	0		-	-	-
ODI																	
List A	1	1	0	7	7	7.00	-	-	-	-	0	0	0		-	-	
20/20 Int																	
20/20																	

HOGG, K. W. Lancashire

Name: <u>Kyle</u> William Hogg
Role: Left-hand bat, right-arm
fast-medium bowler; all-rounder
Born: 2 July 1983, Birmingham
Height: 6ft 4in **Weight:** 13st
Nickname: Boss, Hoggy
County debut: 2001
Place in batting averages: 92nd av. 36.28
Place in bowling averages: 81st av. 35.20
Strike rate: 77.60 (career 69.14)
Parents: Sharon and William
Marital status: Single
Family links with cricket: Father played for
Lancashire and Warwickshire; grandfather
Sonny Ramadhin played for Lancashire and
West Indies
Education: Saddleworth High School
Qualifications: GCSEs
Overseas tours: England U19 to India 2000-01, to Australia and (U19 World Cup)
New Zealand 2001-02; Lancashire to South Africa, to Grenada; ECB National
Academy to Australia and Sri Lanka 2002-03
Overseas teams played for: Otago 2006-07

Cricket moments to forget: '[B&H 2002] semi-final v Warwickshire'
Cricket superstitions: 'None'
Cricketers particularly admired: Andrew Flintoff, David Byas, Stuart Law, Carl Hooper
Other sports played: Football
Other sports followed: Football (Man Utd)
Favourite band: Stone Roses, Red Hot Chili Peppers, Bob Marley
Relaxations: 'Relaxing with friends'
Extras: Represented England U19 2001, 2002. NBC Denis Compton Award for the most promising young Lancashire player 2001. Recorded maiden first-class five-wicket return (5-48) on Championship debut v Leicestershire at Old Trafford 2002. Included in provisional England squad of 30 for the 2002-03 World Cup
Best batting: 70 Lancashire v Middlesex, Lord's 2006
Best bowling: 5-48 Lancashire v Leicestershire, Old Trafford 2002

2006 Season

	M	Inn	NO	Runs	HS	Avg	100	50	Ct	St	Balls	Runs	Wkts	Avg	BB	5I	10M
Test																	
FC	8	8	1	254	70	36.28	-	2	1	-	1164	528	15	35.20	2-33	-	-
ODI																	
List A	15	10	3	101	28	14.42	-	-	1	-	562	356	16	22.25	2-16	-	
20/20 Int																	
20/20	3	2	0	44	25	22.00	-	-	-	-	12	22	2	11.00	2-10	-	

Career Performances

	M	Inn	NO	Runs	HS	Avg	100	50	Ct	St	Balls	Runs	Wkts	Avg	BB	5I	10M
Test																	
FC	29	37	2	702	70	20.05	-	5	10	-	3734	2037	54	37.72	5-48	1	-
ODI																	
List A	78	47	15	544	41 *	17.00	-	-	14	-	2783	2169	78	27.80	4-20	-	
20/20 Int																	
20/20	5	4	0	53	25	13.25	-	-	-	-	37	69	3	23.00	2-10	-	

HOGGARD, M. J.   Yorkshire

Name: <u>Matthew</u> James Hoggard
Role: Right-hand bat, right-arm
fast-medium bowler
Born: 31 December 1976, Leeds
Height: 6ft 2in **Weight:** 14st
Nickname: Oggie
County debut: 1996
County cap: 2000
Test debut: 2000
ODI debut: 2001-02
50 wickets in a season: 2
Place in batting averages: (2005 267th
av. 12.38)
Place in bowling averages: 79th av. 34.72
(2005 44th av. 27.72)
Strike rate: 67.45 (career 53.39)
Parents: Margaret and John
Wife and date of marriage: Sarah,
2 October 2004

Family links with cricket: 'Dad is a cricket badger'
Education: Pudsey Grangefield
Qualifications: GCSEs and A-levels
Off-season: Touring with England
Overseas tours: Yorkshire CCC to South Africa; England U19 to Zimbabwe 1995-96;
England to Kenya (ICC Knockout Trophy) 2000-01, to Pakistan and Sri Lanka
2000-01, to Zimbabwe (one-day series) 2001-02, to India and New Zealand 2001-02,
to Sri Lanka (ICC Champions Trophy) 2002-03, to Australia 2002-03, to Africa (World
Cup) 2002-03, to Bangladesh and Sri Lanka 2003-04, to West Indies 2003-04, to South
Africa 2004-05, to Pakistan 2005-06, to India 2005-06, to Australia 2006-07
Overseas teams played for: Pirates, Johannesburg 1995-97; Free State 1998-2000
Cricketers particularly admired: Allan Donald, Courtney Walsh
Other sports played: Rugby
Other sports followed: Rugby league (Leeds Rhinos)
Relaxations: Dog walking
Extras: Was top wicket-taker in the 2000 National League competition with 37
wickets at 12.37. PCA Young Player of the Year 2000. Took 7-63 v New Zealand in the
first Test at Christchurch 2001-02, the best innings return by an England pace bowler
in Tests v New Zealand. Took Test hat-trick (Sarwan, Chanderpaul, Ryan Hinds) in the
third Test v West Indies at Bridgetown 2003-04. His international awards include Man
of the [Test] Series v Bangladesh 2003-04 as well as Man of the Match in the fourth
Test v South Africa at Johannesburg 2004-05 (5-144/7-61) and in the first Test v India

at Nagpur 2005-06 (6-57). Appointed MBE in 2006 New Year Honours as part of 2005 Ashes-winning England team. One of *Wisden*'s Five Cricketers of the Year 2006. Took 200th Test wicket (Farveez Maharoof) in the first Test v Sri Lanka at Lord's 2006. England 12-month central contract 2006-07

Best batting: 89* Yorkshire v Glamorgan, Headingley 2004
Best bowling: 7-49 Yorkshire v Somerset, Headingley 2003
Stop press: Had first innings figures of 7-109 in the second Test v Australia at Adelaide 2006-07; took 235th Test wicket (Michael Hussey) in the fourth Test v Australia at Melbourne 2006-07 to move into seventh place in the England list of Test wicket-takers

2006 Season

	M	Inn	NO	Runs	HS	Avg	100	50	Ct	St	Balls	Runs	Wkts	Avg	BB	5I	10M
Test	7	10	1	66	13	7.33	-	-	2	-	1638	842	25	33.68	4-27	-	-
FC	11	16	2	81	13	5.78	-	-	3	-	2220	1146	33	34.72	4-27	-	-
ODI																	
List A																		
20/20 Int																		
20/20																		

Career Performances

	M	Inn	NO	Runs	HS	Avg	100	50	Ct	St	Balls	Runs	Wkts	Avg	BB	5I	10M
Test	58	79	26	414	38	7.81	-	-	23	-	12162	6607	222	29.76	7-61	6	1
FC	142	184	58	1112	89 *	8.82	-	2	43	-	26909	13803	504	27.38	7-49	15	1
ODI	26	6	2	17	7	4.25	-	-	5	-	1306	1152	32	36.00	5-49	1	
List A	120	36	19	61	7 *	3.58	-	-	15	-	5677	4168	172	24.23	5-28	4	
20/20 Int																	
20/20	6	2	1	19	18	19.00	-	-	1	-	132	221	7	31.57	3-23	-	

41. Which batsman, who eventually appeared in 79 Tests, captained England only once, v Australia at Headingley 1968?

HOLE, S. M.   Warwickshire

Name: <u>Stuart</u> Mark Hole
Role: Right-hand bat, right-arm seam bowler
Born: 17 July 1985, Oxford
Height: 6ft 1in   **Weight:** 12st 7lbs
Nickname: Holey
County debut: No first-team appearance
Parents: Les and Sally
Marital status: Single
Education: Bartholomew School; Premier
Training fitness course
Qualifications: Qualified personal trainer
and sports masseur
Career outside cricket: Personal trainer
Off-season: 'In Australia'
Career highlights to date: 'Winning the 2nd
XI Trophy with Warwickshire. And signing
my first pro contract'
Cricket moments to forget: 'Haven't had
any as yet…'
Cricketers particularly admired: Michael Powell
Young players to look out for: Moeen Ali
Other sports played: Football ('played at Wycombe Wanderers FC for four years')
Other sports followed: Football (Liverpool, Wycombe Wanderers)
Injuries: Out for one month with lower back problems
Relaxations: 'Listening to music – R&B and dancehall'
Extras: Played for Oxfordshire in Minor Counties competitions 2005-06

42. Which ground hosted the first ODI played in England, in 1972?

HOPKINSON, C. D. Sussex

Name: <u>Carl</u> Daniel Hopkinson
Role: Right-hand bat, right-arm medium-fast bowler; 'batter that bowls'
Born: 14 September 1981, Brighton
Height: 5ft 11in
Nickname: Hoppo
County debut: 2001 (one-day), 2002 (first-class)
Place in batting averages: 173rd av. 25.82 (2005 176th av. 26.23)
Strike rate: (career 122.00)
Parents: Jane and Jerry
Marital status: Single
Family links with cricket: 'Dad played in the local team, which got me interested, and coached me from a young age'
Education: Chailey; Brighton College
Qualifications: 7 GCSEs, 3 A-levels, Level 1 coaching

Overseas tours: Tours to India 1997-98, to South Africa 1999
Overseas teams played for: Rockingham-Mandurah, Western Australia 2000-01
Cricket moments to forget: 'Playing on my debut and taking guard before the incoming batsman was announced; in other words, they didn't know who I was!'
Cricketers particularly admired: Dennis Lillee, Ian Botham, Viv Richards, Graham Thorpe
Other sports played: Rugby ('won Rosslyn Park National Sevens'), squash, football
Other sports followed: Football (West Ham)
Favourite band: 50 Cent
Relaxations: 'Going out in Brighton with my mates, cinema etc.'
Extras: South of England and England squads until U17. Sussex Young Player of the Year 2000. Sussex 2nd XI Fielder of the Year 2001, 2003. Took wicket (John Wood) with his third ball on county debut, in the Norwich Union League v Lancashire at Hove 2001. C&G Man of the Match award v Nottinghamshire at Hove 2005 (51 plus run-out of Stephen Fleming)
Best batting: 74 Sussex v Nottinghamshire, Hove 2006
Best bowling: 1-20 Sussex v LUCCE, Hove 2004

2006 Season

	M	Inn	NO	Runs	HS	Avg	100	50	Ct	St	Balls	Runs	Wkts	Avg	BB	5I	10M
Test																	
FC	17	28	0	723	74	25.82	-	6	10	-	58	48	0		-	-	-
ODI																	
List A	18	15	2	391	69 *	30.07	-	4	7	-	0	0	0		-	-	
20/20 Int																	
20/20	8	6	2	54	22 *	13.50	-	-	3	-	0	0	0		-	-	

Career Performances

	M	Inn	NO	Runs	HS	Avg	100	50	Ct	St	Balls	Runs	Wkts	Avg	BB	5I	10M
Test																	
FC	28	46	1	1126	74	25.02	-	9	15	-	244	167	2	83.50	1-20	-	-
ODI																	
List A	65	51	6	987	69 *	21.93	-	6	32	-	512	506	14	36.14	3-19	-	
20/20 Int																	
20/20	15	10	3	74	22 *	10.57	-	-	3	-	0	0	0		-	-	

HORTON, P. J.   Lancashire

Name: <u>Paul</u> James Horton
Role: Right-hand bat, right-arm medium/off-spin bowler
Born: 20 September 1982, Sydney, Australia
Height: 5ft 10in **Weight:** 11st 3lbs
Nickname: Horts, Ozzy
County debut: 2003
Place in batting averages: (2005 76th av. 38.88)
Parents: Donald William and Norma
Marital status: Single
Education: Colo High School, Sydney/Broadgreen Comprehensive, Liverpool; St Margaret's High School
Qualifications: 11 GCSEs, 3 A-levels, Level 2 ECB coach
Overseas tours: Hawkesbury U15 to New Zealand 1997; Lancashire to Cape Town 2002-03, to Grenada 2003
Overseas teams played for: Hawkesbury, Sydney 1992-93 – 1997-98; Penrith, NSW 2002-03
Career highlights to date: 'First-class debut v Durham UCCE 2003'

Cricket moments to forget: 'First 2nd XI game for Lancashire at Old Trafford – out for 0'
Cricket superstitions: 'None'
Cricketers particularly admired: Dean Jones, Sachin Tendulkar, Mark Waugh
Other sports played: Football, golf, squash, tennis, badminton
Other sports followed: Football (Liverpool)
Favourite band: Red Hot Chili Peppers
Relaxations: 'Golf, socialising with friends, watching sport'
Extras: Captained Lancashire U17 and U19. Captained Lancashire Board XI in the C&G 2003. Lancashire Young Player of the Year Award 2001, 2002. Leading run-scorer for Lancashire 2nd XI in the 2nd XI Championship 2003 (861 runs; av. 50.65)
Best batting: 99 Lancashire v Essex, Old Trafford 2005

2006 Season

	M	Inn	NO	Runs	HS	Avg	100	50	Ct	St	Balls	Runs	Wkts	Avg	BB	5I	10M
Test																	
FC	4	7	2	227	79	45.40	-	2	3	-	0	0	0		-	-	-
ODI																	
List A	3	2	0	2	2	1.00	-	-	-	-	0	0	0		-	-	
20/20 Int																	
20/20	4	3	1	17	10 *	8.50	-	-	2	-	0	0	0		-	-	

Career Performances

	M	Inn	NO	Runs	HS	Avg	100	50	Ct	St	Balls	Runs	Wkts	Avg	BB	5I	10M
Test																	
FC	12	18	3	601	99	40.06	-	4	6	1	0	0	0		-	-	-
ODI																	
List A	10	7	0	143	46	20.42	-	-	-	-	0	0	0		-	-	
20/20 Int																	
20/20	5	4	1	28	11	9.33	-	-	2	-	0	0	0		-	-	

HOUSEGO, D. M.   Middlesex

Name: Daniel (Dan) Mark Housego
Role: Right-hand bat, off-spin bowler
Born: 12 October 1988, Windsor
Height: 5ft 8in **Weight:** 11st 3lbs
County debut: No first-team appearance
Parents: Beryl and Jim
Marital status: Single
Education: The Oratory School, Woodcote, Reading
Qualifications: 8 GCSEs, Level 1 coaching
Career outside cricket: 'Training to be a gym assistant'

Off-season: 'A-levels/gym'
Overseas tours: England U16 to South Africa 2002, 2004
Career highlights to date: '138* v Somerset 2nd XI; 161 v Derbyshire 2nd XI; 170* Berkshire v Shropshire'
Cricket moments to forget: 'I wouldn't forget any'
Cricket superstitions: 'None'
Cricketers particularly admired: Ian Bell
Young players to look out for: Billy Godleman, Steve Finn
Other sports played: Football (Oxford United FC), athletics (U12 200m national champion)
Other sports followed: Golf, football (Oxford United)
Favourite band: Chris Brown
Relaxations: 'Fishing, golf'

Extras: Represented England U15, U16, U17. Played for Berkshire in the Minor Counties Championship 2006
Opinions on cricket: 'Love every minute of it! Enjoy improving.'

HUGHES, L. D.   Derbyshire

Name: <u>Liam</u> Daniel Hughes
Role: Right-hand bat, right-arm medium-fast bowler
Born: 21 March 1988, Wordsley, West Midlands
Height: 6ft 1in
Nickname: Yozza
County debut: No first-team appearance
Parents: Angela and Malcolm
Marital status: Single
Education: Ounsdale High School; Wolverhampton University
Qualifications: 2 A-levels
Career highlights to date: 'Taking a wicket with my first ball in second-team cricket for Derbyshire v Lancashire'
Cricket moments to forget: 'A pair v Yorkshire'

Cricketers particularly admired: Glenn McGrath
Other sports followed: Football (Wolves), American football (St Louis Rams)
Injuries: Out for the second half of the season with a stress fracture
Favourite band: Pussycat Dolls
Extras: Played for Staffordshire U15. Selected for ECB Midlands Regional Academy Squad 2005. Made 2nd XI Championship debut 2005

HUNTER, I. D. Derbyshire

Name: Ian David Hunter
Role: Right-hand bat, right-arm fast-medium bowler
Born: 11 September 1979, Durham City
Height: 6ft 2in **Weight:** 12st 7lbs
Nickname: Sticks, Hunts
County debut: 1999 (one-day, Durham), 2000 (first-class, Durham), 2004 (Derbyshire)
Place in batting averages: 247th av. 14.57 (2005 251st av. 15.14)
Place in bowling averages: 90th av. 36.88 (2005 120th av. 44.29)
Strike rate: 61.50 (career 64.77)
Parents: Ken and Linda
Marital status: Single
Family links with cricket: Brother local village cricketer
Education: Fyndoune Community College, Sacriston; New College, Durham
Qualifications: 9 GCSEs, 1 A-level (PE), BTEC National Diploma in Sports Science, Level I and II cricket coaching awards
Overseas tours: Durham U21 to Sri Lanka 1996; Durham to Cape Town 2002
Career highlights to date: 'Scoring 63 on first-class debut' (*v Leicestershire at Riverside 2000 as nightwatchman*)
Cricket superstitions: 'Always put my left pad on first'
Cricketers particularly admired: Allan Donald, Steve Waugh
Other sports played: Football, golf
Other sports followed: Football (Durham City AFC)
Relaxations: Socialising with friends; keeping fit, golf, football
Extras: Set a new Durham best analysis for the 2nd XI Championship with his 11-155 v Lancashire 2nd XI 1999. Represented England U19 1999
Best batting: 65 Durham v Northamptonshire, Northampton 2002
Best bowling: 5-63 Derbyshire v Durham, Riverside 2005

2006 Season

	M	Inn	NO	Runs	HS	Avg	100	50	Ct	St	Balls	Runs	Wkts	Avg	BB	5I	10M
Test																	
FC	14	13	6	102	48	14.57	-	-	6	-	2214	1328	36	36.88	4-22	-	-
ODI																	
List A	4	3	1	6	5 *	3.00	-	-	-	-	179	150	2	75.00	2-53	-	
20/20 Int																	
20/20	1	0	0	0	0		-	-	-	-	18	33	0		-	-	

Career Performances

	M	Inn	NO	Runs	HS	Avg	100	50	Ct	St	Balls	Runs	Wkts	Avg	BB	5I	10M
Test																	
FC	49	67	16	897	65	17.58	-	2	15	-	7644	4780	118	40.50	5-63	1	-
ODI																	
List A	72	45	10	274	39	7.82	-	-	14	-	3137	2558	76	33.65	4-29	-	
20/20 Int																	
20/20	12	4	2	39	25 *	19.50	-	-	3	-	252	363	14	25.92	3-26	-	

HUSSEY, D. J.   Nottinghamshire

Name: David (<u>Dave</u>) John Hussey
Role: Right-hand bat, right-arm
off-spin bowler, occasional wicket-keeper
Born: 15 July 1977, Perth, Western Australia
Height: 5ft 11in **Weight:** 13st 3lbs
Nickname: Huss, Hussa, Husscat
County debut: 2004
County cap: 2004
1000 runs in a season: 3
1st-Class 200s: 2
Place in batting averages: 51st av. 47.62
(2005 6th av. 68.05)
Strike rate: (career 76.63)
Parents: Helen and Ted
Marital status: Single
Family links with cricket: Brother Mike
plays for Australia and Western Australia and
has played for Northamptonshire,
Gloucestershire and Durham
Education: Prendiville Catholic College; Edith Cowan University
Qualifications: Bachelor of Business (Sports Management and Sports Science)
Career outside cricket: 'Marine biology'

Off-season: 'In Victoria, Australia, playing'
Overseas tours: Commonwealth Bank [Australian] Cricket Academy to Sri Lanka 1997-98
Overseas teams played for: Wanneroo DCC, Perth 1992-2001; Prahran CC, Victoria 2001 – ; Victoria 2002-03 –
Career highlights to date: 'Winning Pura Cup with Victoria 2004. Winning Championship with Notts 2005'
Cricket moments to forget: 'Debut for Victoria – dropped S. Waugh on 4; he went on to make 211'
Cricket superstitions: 'Left shoe on first'
Cricketers particularly admired: Brendon Julian, Mark Waugh, Damien Martyn
Young players to look out for: Andrew Hodd
Other sports played: Australian Rules football, squash, tennis, football
Other sports followed: AFL (St Kilda FC), football (Brighton & Hove Albion)
Favourite band: Keane, Foo Fighters
Relaxations: 'Reading'
Extras: Played for Western Australia U19 and 2nd XI. Represented Australia U19 1995-96. Has represented Australia A. Scored 212* and won Man of the Match award as Victoria scored 455-7 to beat New South Wales at Newcastle in the Pura Cup 2003-04. His other awards include Man of the Match v New South Wales at Melbourne in the Pura Cup 2003-04 (120/50) and v South Australia at Adelaide in the ING Cup 2003-04 (113). An overseas player with Nottinghamshire since 2004
Opinions on cricket: 'Too many administrators in the game who have too many poor opinions.'
Best batting: 232* Nottinghamshire v Warwickshire, Trent Bridge 2005
Best bowling: 4-105 Nottinghamshire v Hampshire, Trent Bridge 2005

2006 Season

	M	Inn	NO	Runs	HS	Avg	100	50	Ct	St	Balls	Runs	Wkts	Avg	BB	5I	10M
Test																	
FC	17	28	4	1143	164	47.62	5	1	14	-	270	236	6	39.33	2-66	-	-
ODI																	
List A	14	11	2	273	81	30.33	-	2	9	-	32	25	0			-	-
20/20 Int																	
20/20	11	10	3	394	71	56.28	-	2	6	-	0	0	0			-	-

Career Performances

	M	Inn	NO	Runs	HS	Avg	100	50	Ct	St	Balls	Runs	Wkts	Avg	BB	5I	10M
Test																	
FC	83	126	15	5641	232 *	50.81	21	21	91	-	1456	1010	19	53.15	4-105	-	-
ODI																	
List A	89	82	15	2643	130	39.44	4	13	44	-	421	431	9	47.88	3-48	-	
20/20 Int																	
20/20	28	26	3	658	71	28.60	-	3	16	-	22	22	0			-	-

HUTTON, B. L.   Middlesex

Name: Benjamin (<u>Ben</u>) Leonard Hutton
Role: Left-hand bat, right-arm
medium bowler
Born: 29 January 1977, Johannesburg,
South Africa
Height: 6ft 1½in   **Weight:** 12st
Nickname: Gibbo
County debut: 1999
County cap: 2003
1000 runs in a season: 2
Place in batting averages: 139th av. 30.68
(2005 104th av. 34.82)
Strike rate: (career 100.28)
Parents: Charmaine and Richard
Marital status: Single
Family links with cricket: Sir Leonard
Hutton (grandfather) Yorkshire and England;
Richard Hutton (father) Yorkshire and

England; Ben Brocklehurst (grandfather) Somerset; Oliver Hutton (brother)
Oxford University
Education: Radley College; Durham University
Qualifications: 10 GCSEs, 3 A-levels, BA (Hons) Social Sciences, NCA
coaching award
Overseas tours: Durham University to Zimbabwe 1997-98; Middlesex to Portugal
1996, 1997, 1998, to South Africa 1999, to Malta 2001, to Mumbai 2003;
MCC to Italy
Overseas teams played for: Pirates CC, Johannesburg 1996; Wanderers CC,
Johannesburg 1997; Gosnells, Perth 2001-02
Cricket moments to forget: 'Breaking my hand v Gloucestershire 2001. Two
Championship pairs'
Cricket superstitions: 'None'
Cricketers particularly admired: Sir Leonard Hutton, Justin Langer, Mark
Ramprakash, Andy Flower
Young players to look out for: Nick Compton, Eoin Morgan
Other sports played: Golf (12 handicap)
Other sports followed: 'All sport, except motor racing'
Favourite band: 'Too many to mention'
Relaxations: 'Reading and listening to music'
Extras: Played in Durham University's BUSA Championship winning side 1997, 1998
(shared) and 1999. Opened for Middlesex v Essex at Southend 1999 with Andrew
Strauss, his former opening partner at Radley. Scored century in each innings
(100/107) v Kent at Southgate 2004. Captain of Middlesex 2005-06

Best batting: 152 Middlesex v Kent, Lord's 2005
Best bowling: 4-37 Middlesex v Sri Lankans, Shenley 2002

2006 Season

	M	Inn	NO	Runs	HS	Avg	100	50	Ct	St	Balls	Runs	Wkts	Avg	BB	5I	10M
Test																	
FC	11	20	1	583	105	30.68	2	1	16	-	352	263	3	87.66	2-20	-	-
ODI																	
List A	9	8	1	145	40	20.71	-	-	6	-	84	73	3	24.33	2-24	-	
20/20 Int																	
20/20																	

Career Performances

	M	Inn	NO	Runs	HS	Avg	100	50	Ct	St	Balls	Runs	Wkts	Avg	BB	5I	10M
Test																	
FC	106	182	15	5516	152	33.02	17	18	132	-	3510	2211	35	63.17	4-37	-	-
ODI																	
List A	118	96	17	1577	77	19.96	-	7	59	-	1727	1591	51	31.19	5-45	1	
20/20 Int																	
20/20	18	14	3	114	27 *	10.36	-	-	8	-	84	129	4	32.25	2-21	-	

ILES, J. A.   Kent

Name: <u>James</u> Alexander Iles
Role: Right-hand bat, right-arm
fast-medium bowler
Born: 11 February 1990, Chatham, Kent
Height: 6ft 4in **Weight:** 14st 7lbs
Nickname: Ilo
County debut: 2006
Strike rate: (career 78.00)
Parents: Diane and Peter
Marital status: Single
Education: Maidstone Grammar School
for Boys
Qualifications: 10 GCSEs
Career outside cricket: 'Student'
Off-season: 'Staying at home, training in
Canterbury'
Overseas tours: England U16 to South
Africa 2005-06
Career highlights to date: 'First-class debut, 17 May 2006 v Cambridge UCCE'
Cricket moments to forget: 'Whilst playing for my club as a colt, I chased a ball to

the boundary with no bearing where the sightscreen was – I slid straight into it, cutting my shin open'

Cricket superstitions: 'I have to put my left pad on before my right'

Cricketers particularly admired: Andrew Flintoff

Other sports played: Rugby ('Kent, three years')

Other sports followed: Football (Arsenal), rugby (Wasps)

Injuries: Out for two weeks in August with shin splints; 'lower back stress fracture September-December this winter [2006]'

Favourite band: Brian McKnight

Relaxations: 'Watching my local rugby team; listening to music'

Extras: Kent Academy scholar. Youngest player to make first-class debut for Kent, aged 16 years 92 days

Opinions on cricket: 'I believe that teams should only be allowed one overseas or Kolpak player [*see page 13*] per season. This will allow younger, home-grown players to be given the opportunity to play first-class cricket.'

Best bowling: 1-27 Kent v CUCCE, Fenner's 2006

2006 Season

	M	Inn	NO	Runs	HS	Avg	100	50	Ct	St	Balls	Runs	Wkts	Avg	BB	5I	10M
Test																	
FC	1	0	0	0	0		-	-	-	-	78	37	1	37.00	1-27	-	-
ODI																	
List A																	
20/20 Int																	
20/20																	

Career Performances

	M	Inn	NO	Runs	HS	Avg	100	50	Ct	St	Balls	Runs	Wkts	Avg	BB	5I	10M
Test																	
FC	1	0	0	0	0		-	-	-	-	78	37	1	37.00	1-27	-	-
ODI																	
List A																	
20/20 Int																	
20/20																	

IQBAL, M. M.   Durham

Name: <u>Moneeb</u> Mohammed Iqbal
Role: Right-hand bat, leg-break bowler
Born: 28 February 1986, Glasgow, Scotland
County debut: 2006
Strike rate: (career 54.11)
Family links with cricket: Brother-in-law
Mohammad Ramzan played Test cricket for
Pakistan
Overseas tours: Scotland U19 to New
Zealand (U19 World Cup) 2001-02, to
Bangladesh (U19 World Cup) 2003-04, to Sri
Lanka (U19 World Cup) 2005-06, plus
various Scotland age-group tours to Europe
Extras: Man of the Match v Kenya U19 at
Carisbrook in the U19 World Cup 2001-02
(2-16/40) and v Nepal U19 at Chittagong in
the U19 World Cup 2003-04 (2-34/67).
Played for Scotland in the C&G 2002, aged
16. Durham Academy
Best batting: 20 Durham v Kent, Stockton 2006
Best bowling: 4-36 Durham v OUCCE, The Parks 2006

2006 Season

	M	Inn	NO	Runs	HS	Avg	100	50	Ct	St	Balls	Runs	Wkts	Avg	BB	5I	10M
Test																	
FC	4	8	3	53	20	10.60	-	-	2	-	487	417	9	46.33	4-36	-	-
ODI																	
List A																	
20/20 Int																	
20/20																	

Career Performances

	M	Inn	NO	Runs	HS	Avg	100	50	Ct	St	Balls	Runs	Wkts	Avg	BB	5I	10M
Test																		
FC	4	8	3	53	20	10.60	-	-	2	-	487	417	9	46.33	4-36	-	-
ODI																	
List A	1	0	0	0	0		-	-	-	-	18	24	0		-	-
20/20 Int																	
20/20																	

IRANI, R. C.   Essex

Name: Ronald (<u>Ronnie</u>) Charles Irani
Role: Right-hand bat, county captain
Born: 26 October 1971, Leigh, Lancashire
Height: 6ft 4in **Weight:** 14st 8lbs
Nickname: Reggie
County debut: 1990 (Lancashire),
1994 (Essex)
County cap: 1994 (Essex)
Benefit: 2003 (Essex)
Test debut: 1996
ODI debut: 1996
1000 runs in a season: 7
50 wickets in a season: 1
1st-Class 200s: 1
Place in batting averages: 19th av. 59.72
(2005 20th av. 57.23)
Strike rate: (career 60.13)
Parents: Jimmy and Anne
Wife: Lorraine
Children: Simone, 25 September 2000; Maria, 6 January 2002
Family links with cricket: 'Father played league cricket for over 30 years. Mum did
teas for years as well'
Education: Smithills Comprehensive School
Qualifications: 9 GCSEs
Overseas tours: England YC to Australia 1989-90; England A to Pakistan 1995-96,
to Bangladesh and New Zealand 1999-2000; England to Zimbabwe and New Zealand
1996-97, to Sri Lanka (ICC Champions Trophy) 2002-03, to Australia 2002-03
(VB Series), to Africa (World Cup) 2002-03; England VI to Hong Kong 2002
Overseas teams played for: Technicol Natal, Durban 1992-93; Eden-Roskill,
Auckland 1993-94
Career highlights to date: 'Playing for England. Winning one-day trophies with
Essex'
Cricket moments to forget: 'Admiring lady streaker and getting caught on TV
cameras doing it!'
Cricketers particularly admired: Graham Gooch, Javed Miandad, Viv Richards,
Wasim Akram
Other sports played: Golf, pool
Other sports followed: Football (Manchester United), Muay Thai boxing
Favourite band: Manic Street Preachers, Travis, Joyce Simms, Alexander O'Neal
Relaxations: Fly fishing
Extras: Bull Man of the Series, England YC v Australia YC 1991. Appointed vice-

captain of Essex 1999. Achieved double of 1000 first-class runs and 50 first-class wickets 1999. Took over 1st XI captaincy of Essex at the start of the 2000 season, Nasser Hussain remaining as club captain until his retirement in 2004. Recorded a five-wicket innings return (5-58) and scored a century (119) for Essex v Surrey at Ilford 2001. Man of the Match v India at The Oval in the NatWest Series 2002 (53/5-26); also named 'Fans' Player of the Series'. Captained England XI v Sir Donald Bradman XI at Bowral 2002-03. Granted Freedom of the City of London in April 2003. Forced by knee injury to give up bowling 2003. Scored century (100* from 61 balls) v Sussex at Hove in the Twenty20 2006

Best batting: 207* Essex v Northamptonshire, Ilford 2002
Best bowling: 6-71 Essex v Nottinghamshire, Trent Bridge 2002

2006 Season

	M	Inn	NO	Runs	HS	Avg	100	50	Ct	St	Balls	Runs	Wkts	Avg	BB	5I	10M
Test																	
FC	16	23	5	1075	145	59.72	3	6	1	-	0	0	0		-	-	-
ODI																	
List A	15	15	2	577	132 *	44.38	2	3	4	-	0	0	0		-	-	
20/20 Int																	
20/20	10	10	2	338	100 *	42.25	1	3	7	-	0	0	0		-	-	

Career Performances

	M	Inn	NO	Runs	HS	Avg	100	50	Ct	St	Balls	Runs	Wkts	Avg	BB	5I	10M
Test	3	5	0	86	41	17.20	-	-	2	-	192	112	3	37.33	1-22	-	-
FC	228	367	47	13007	207 *	40.64	26	72	75	-	20387	10007	339	29.51	6-71	9	-
ODI	31	30	5	360	53	14.40	-	1	6	-	1283	989	24	41.20	5-26	1	
List A	310	288	42	7498	158 *	30.47	7	43	81	-	10452	7796	309	25.22	5-26	4	
20/20 Int																	
20/20	27	26	3	651	100 *	28.30	1	4	12	-	0	0	0		-	-	

JAMES, N. A.   Warwickshire

Name: Nicholas (Nick) Alexander James
Role: Left-hand bat, slow left-arm bowler, wicket-keeper 'if needed!'
Born: 17 September 1986, Sandwell, West Midlands
Height: 5ft 10in **Weight:** 11st 10lbs
Nickname: Jaymo
County debut: 2006 (one-day)
Parents: Ann and Mike
Marital status: Single
Family links with cricket: 'Dad and brother play at Aldridge CC. Dad coaches youth and Aldridge Ladies cricket team'
Education: King Edward VI, Aston

Qualifications: 10 GCSEs, 3 A-levels

Off-season: 'ECB Skills Set training at Loughborough. Training and playing abroad (possible visit to Mumbai spin academy and pre-season tour away with county)'

Overseas tours: England U19 to Bangladesh 2005-06, to Sri Lanka (U19 World Cup) 2005-06

Career highlights to date: 'Representing England U19. Reaching semi-final of 2006 U19 World Cup. Making debut for Warwickshire first team (C&G) in front of a large crowd at Edgbaston against local rivals Worcestershire'

Cricket moments to forget: 'Diving to stop the ball in C&G game against Lancs and fracturing bone in hand!'

Cricketers particularly admired: Brian Lara, Ashley Giles, Nick Knight

Young players to look out for: Andrew Miller

Other sports played: 'Recreational football, golf'

Other sports followed: Football (Aston Villa)

Injuries: 'Fractured bone in hand at the end of June – unavailable for selection for six weeks'

Favourite band: The Killers 'although enjoy most types of music'

Relaxations: 'Playing snooker; relaxing with friends'

Extras: Captain of Warwickshire U17 County Championship winning side 2004. Member of ECB U18 Development Squad 2004. Represented England U19 and captained ECB Development of Excellence XI v Sri Lanka U19 2005. Has won eight Warwickshire youth awards since the age of 12, including Tiger Smith Memorial Award for the most promising young player 2005. Acted as 12th man for England A v Sri Lankans at Worcester 2006

Opinions on cricket: 'Great game. Can't forget to enjoy yourself!'

2006 Season

	M	Inn	NO	Runs	HS	Avg	100	50	Ct	St	Balls	Runs	Wkts	Avg	BB	5I	10M
Test																	
FC																	
ODI																	
List A	3	2	0	44	30	22.00	-	-	1	-	156	96	4	24.00	2-34	-	
20/20 Int																	
20/20																	

Career Performances

	M	Inn	NO	Runs	HS	Avg	100	50	Ct	St	Balls	Runs	Wkts	Avg	BB	5I	10M
Test																	
FC																	
ODI																	
List A	3	2	0	44	30	22.00	-	-	1	-	156	96	4	24.00	2-34	-	
20/20 Int																	
20/20																	

JAQUES, P. A. Worcestershire

Name: Philip (Phil) Anthony Jaques
Role: Left-hand bat
Born: 3 May 1979, Wollongong, Australia
Height: 6ft 1in **Weight:** 14st 11lbs
Nickname: Pro, PJ
County debut: 2003 (Northamptonshire),
2004 (Yorkshire), 2006 (Worcestershire)
County cap: 2003 (Northamptonshire),
2005 (Yorkshire), 2006 (Worcestershire
colours)
Test debut: 2005-06
ODI debut: 2005-06
1000 runs in a season: 4
1st-Class 200s: 8
Place in batting averages: 2nd av. 88.30
(2005 9th av. 64.71)
Parents: Mary and Stuart
Wife and date of marriage: Danielle,
5 May 2006
Family links with cricket: 'Dad played league cricket in Sheffield, England'
Education: Figtree High School, Wollongong; Australian College of Physical
Education

Qualifications: Fitness certificate, Level II coach
Off-season: 'Playing for NSW'
Overseas tours: New South Wales to New Zealand 2000-01; Australia A to Pakistan 2005-06; Australia to South Africa 2005-06 (one-day series), to Bangladesh 2005-06, plus one-day tournament in Malaysia
Overseas teams played for: Sutherland DCC, Sydney 1997 – ; New South Wales Blues 2000-01 – 2001-02, 2003-04 –
Career highlights to date: 'Playing cricket for Australia'
Cricket moments to forget: 'Dropping an outfield catch on my first-class one-day debut and not getting a hand on it'
Cricket superstitions: 'Always put gear on same way in same order every time I bat'
Cricketers particularly admired: Steve Waugh, Mark Taylor
Young players to look out for: Moises Henriques (NSW)
Other sports played: Tennis, rugby league, golf, basketball
Other sports followed: Rugby league (St George Illawarra), football (Liverpool)
Injuries: Out for two weeks with a bulging disc in the back
Favourite band: Coldplay, Bon Jovi
Relaxations: 'Golf, beach, watching movies'
Extras: Attended Australian Cricket Academy 2000. Scored maiden first-class century (149*) v Worcestershire at Worcester 2003 and maiden first-class double century (222) in his next Championship innings v Yorkshire at Northampton 2003. Scored 1409 first-class runs in his first season of county cricket 2003. Holds a British passport and was not considered an overseas player with Northamptonshire in 2003. An overseas player with Yorkshire 2004 (having played for New South Wales 2003-04), deputising for Ian Harvey and Darren Lehmann, and in 2005. Scored 94 v South Africa at Melbourne in the VB Series 2005-06, the highest score by an Australia player on ODI debut. Named Australia's State Player of the Year at the 2006 Allan Border Medal awards; also won the Steve Waugh Medal (NSW Player of the Year) 2005-06. His wife, Danielle Small, is an Australia soccer international. An overseas player with Worcestershire since 2006. Scored century (107) on first-class debut for Worcestershire v Surrey at The Oval 2006 and another (112) on one-day debut for the county v Northamptonshire at Worcester in the C&G 2006. Australia contract 2006-07
Best batting: 244 Worcestershire v Essex, Chelmsford 2006

2006 Season

	M	Inn	NO	Runs	HS	Avg	100	50	Ct	St	Balls	Runs	Wkts	Avg	BB	5I	10M
Test																	
FC	8	15	2	1148	244	88.30	3	7	8	-	2	15	0		-	-	-
ODI																	
List A	4	4	0	163	112	40.75	1	-	-	-	18	19	0		-	-	
20/20 Int																	
20/20																	

Career Performances

	M	Inn	NO	Runs	HS	Avg	100	50	Ct	St	Balls	Runs	Wkts	Avg	BB	5I	10M
Test	2	3	0	96	66	32.00	-	1	1	-	0	0	0		-	-	-
FC	86	151	8	8357	244	58.44	24	40	71	-	68	87	0		-	-	-
ODI	4	4	0	121	94	30.25	-	1	2	-	0	0	0		-	-	
List A	92	90	7	3704	158 *	44.62	9	21	26	-	18	19	0		-	-	
20/20 Int																	
20/20	22	22	1	666	92	31.71	-	4	4	-	6	15	0		-	-	

JEFFERSON, W. I.   Nottinghamshire

Name: William (<u>Will</u>) Ingleby Jefferson
Role: Right-hand opening bat
Born: 25 October 1979, Derby ('but native of Norfolk')
Height: 6ft 10½in   **Weight:** 15st 2lbs
Nickname: Santa, Lemar, Jeffo
County debut: 2000 (Essex)
County cap: 2002 (Essex)
1000 runs in a season: 1
1st-Class 200s: 1
Place in batting averages: (2005 73rd av. 39.08)
Strike rate: (career 120.00)
Parents: Richard
Marital status: Single
Family links with cricket: Grandfather Jefferson played for the Army and Combined Services in the 1920s. Father, R. I. Jefferson, played for Cambridge University 1961 and Surrey 1961-66
Education: Oundle School, Northants; Durham University
Qualifications: 9 GCSEs, 3 A-levels, BA (Hons) Sport in the Community, Level 3 cricket coach

Off-season: 'Moving house – Essex to Nottingham; six weeks in Perth in January and February'

Overseas tours: Oundle School to South Africa 1995; England A to Bangladesh 2006-07

Overseas teams played for: Young People's Club, Paarl, South Africa 1998-99; South Perth, Western Australia 2002-03

Career highlights to date: 'Being awarded [Essex] county cap on final day of the 2002 season. Scoring 165* to help beat Notts and secure 2002 second division Championship. 222 v Hampshire at Rose Bowl [2004]'

Cricket moments to forget: 'Any dropped catch; any time bowled playing across the line'

Cricket superstitions: 'Put batting gear on in the same order'

Cricketers particularly admired: Andy Flower, Nasser Hussain

Young players to look out for: Alastair Cook, Stuart Broad

Other sports played: Golf (12 handicap), tennis ('occasionally')

Other sports followed: Rugby (British & Irish Lions, England), golf (Ryder Cup)

Injuries: Out for three months after injuring a wrist; for two weeks with a side strain

Favourite band: U2

Relaxations: 'Escaping to Norfolk, Pilates, spending time with family'

Extras: Holmwoods School Cricketer of the Year 1998. Represented British Universities 2000, 2001 and 2002. Played for Durham UCCE 2001 and 2002. NBC Denis Compton Award for the most promising young Essex player 2002. Scored century before lunch on the opening day for Essex v Cambridge UCCE at Fenner's 2003. C&G Man of the Match awards for his 97 v Scotland at Edinburgh 2004 and for his 126 v Nottinghamshire at Trent Bridge in the next round. Essex Player of the Year 2004. Essex Boundary Club Trophy for scoring most runs for Essex 1st XI 2004. Left Essex at the end of the 2006 season and has joined Nottinghamshire for 2007

Opinions on cricket: 'Agree with the two up/two down system – gives teams something to play for right up until final day of the season. One-day tournament structure not right – one too many. International cricket 50 overs and 20 overs so county cricket should mirror. One overseas player good. Need to be producing more English county captains and coaches so they are the best around.'

Best batting: 222 Essex v Hampshire, Rose Bowl 2004

Best bowling: 1-16 Essex v Yorkshire, Headingley 2005

2006 Season

	M	Inn	NO	Runs	HS	Avg	100	50	Ct	St	Balls	Runs	Wkts	Avg	BB	5I	10M
Test																	
FC	1	1	0	5	5	5.00	-	-	-	-	0	0	0		-	-	-
ODI																	
List A	1	1	0	11	11	11.00	-	-	1	-	0	0	0		-	-	
20/20 Int																	
20/20	4	4	0	91	51	22.75	-	1	2	-	0	0	0		-	-	

Career Performances

	M	Inn	NO	Runs	HS	Avg	100	50	Ct	St	Balls	Runs	Wkts	Avg	BB	5I	10M
Test																	
FC	67	120	11	4300	222	39.44	11	17	58	-	120	60	1	60.00	1-16	-	-
ODI																	
List A	65	64	4	2152	132	35.86	4	11	31	-	24	9	2	4.50	2-9	-	
20/20 Int																	
20/20	12	12	1	151	51	13.72	-	1	3	-	0	0	0		-	-	

JOHNSON, R. L.   Middlesex

Name: <u>Richard</u> Leonard Johnson
Role: Right-hand bat, right-arm
fast-medium bowler
Born: 29 December 1974, Chertsey, Surrey
Height: 6ft 2in **Weight:** 14st 3lbs
Nickname: Jono, Lenny, The Greek
County debut: 1992 (Middlesex),
2001 (Somerset)
County cap: 1995 (Middlesex),
2001 (Somerset)
Benefit: 2006 (Somerset)
Test debut: 2003
ODI debut: 2003
50 wickets in a season: 4
Place in batting averages: 214th av. 19.18
(2005 255th av. 14.53)
Place in bowling averages: 62nd av. 32.59
(2005 139th av. 52.40)
Strike rate: 53.27 (career 52.23)
Parents: Roger and Mary Anne
Wife and date of marriage: Nikki, 4 October 2003
Family links with cricket: Father and grandfather played club cricket

Education: Sunbury Manor School; Spelthorne College
Qualifications: 9 GCSEs, A-level in Physical Education, NCA senior coaching award
Overseas tours: England U18 to South Africa 1992-93; England U19 to Sri Lanka 1993-94; England A to India 1994-95; MCC to Bangladesh 1999-2000, to Canada 2000-01; England to India 2001-02, to Bangladesh and Sri Lanka 2003-04
Career highlights to date: 'Playing in a domestic final for Somerset. Making England debut'
Cricket moments to forget: 'Losing C&G final [2002]'
Cricketers particularly admired: Ian Botham, Richard Hadlee, Angus Fraser
Young players to look out for: James Hildreth
Other sports followed: Football (Tottenham), rugby (London Irish)
Relaxations: 'Eating out with wife and friends; having a few beers with Nashy'
Player website: www.winningwickets.com
Extras: Represented Middlesex at all levels from U11. Took 10 for 45 v Derbyshire at Derby 1994, becoming the first person to take ten wickets in an English first-class innings since 1964. Won Man of the Match awards in his first two Tests: for his 6-33 on debut in the second Test v Zimbabwe at Riverside 2003 and 5-49/4-44 in the second Test v Bangladesh at Chittagong 2003-04. Won Walter Lawrence Trophy 2004 (for the season's fastest hundred) for his 63-ball century v Durham at Riverside. Left Somerset at the end of the 2006 season and has rejoined Middlesex for 2007
Opinions on cricket: 'Twenty20 cricket has been fantastic for the game, bringing in a new generation of cricket followers. We still need to look at the amount of cricket being played, though!'
Best batting: 118 Somerset v Gloucestershire, Bristol 2003
Best bowling: 10-45 Middlesex v Derbyshire, Derby 1994

2006 Season

	M	Inn	NO	Runs	HS	Avg	100	50	Ct	St	Balls	Runs	Wkts	Avg	BB	5I	10M
Test																	
FC	8	12	1	211	51	19.18	-	1	2	-	1174	717	22	32.59	5-37	1	-
ODI																	
List A	14	8	3	32	12 *	6.40	-	-	4	-	610	542	12	45.16	2-27	-	
20/20 Int																	
20/20	5	2	1	14	10	14.00	-	-	-	-	114	169	6	28.16	2-23	-	

Career Performances

	M	Inn	NO	Runs	HS	Avg	100	50	Ct	St	Balls	Runs	Wkts	Avg	BB	5I	10M
Test	3	4	0	59	26	14.75	-	-	-	-	547	275	16	17.18	6-33	2	-
FC	162	223	28	3497	118	17.93	2	8	62	-	27269	14710	522	28.18	10-45	20	3
ODI	10	4	1	16	10	5.33	-	-	-	-	402	239	11	21.72	3-22	-	
List A	190	124	30	1107	53	11.77	-	1	23	-	8415	6808	207	32.88	5-50	1	
20/20 Int																	
20/20	9	5	1	24	10	6.00	-	-	1	-	198	279	14	19.92	3-21	-	

JONES, G. O.　　　　　　　　　　　　Kent

Name: <u>Geraint</u> Owen Jones
Role: Right-hand bat, wicket-keeper
Born: 14 July 1976, Kundiawa,
Papua New Guinea
Height: 5ft 10in　**Weight:** 11st
Nickname: Jonesy
County debut: 2001
County cap: 2003
Test debut: 2003-04
ODI debut: 2004
Twenty20 Int debut: 2005
50 dismissals in a season: 1
Place in batting averages: 194th av. 22.40
(2005 192nd av. 23.57)
Parents: Emrys, Carol (deceased), Maureen
(stepmother)
Marital status: Single
Family links with cricket: 'Father was star
off-spinner in local school side'

Education: Harristown State High School, Toowoomba, Queensland; MacGregor
SHS, Brisbane
Qualifications: Level 1 coach
Overseas tours: Beenleigh-Logan U19 to New Zealand 1995; Kent to Port Elizabeth
2001-02; England to Bangladesh and Sri Lanka 2003-04, to West Indies 2003-04, to
Zimbabwe (one-day series) 2004-05, to South Africa 2004-05, to Pakistan 2005-06, to
India 2005-06, to Australia 2006-07
Overseas teams played for: Beenleigh-Logan, Brisbane 1995-98, 2006-07; Valleys,
Brisbane 2001-02
Cricket superstitions: 'Left pad first'
Cricketers particularly admired: Jack Russell, Alec Stewart
Other sports played: Golf
Other sports followed: Rugby (Crickhowell RFC)
Favourite band: Matchbox Twenty
Extras: Set new competition record for a season's tally of wicket-keeping dismissals
in the one-day league (33; 27/6) 2003; also equalled record for number of wicket-
keeping catches in one match, six v Leicestershire at Canterbury 2003. Made 59 first-
class dismissals plus 985 first-class runs in his first full season of county cricket 2003.
Man of the Match in the second Test v New Zealand at Headingley 2004, in which he
scored his maiden Test century (100). His other international awards include Man of
the Match v Australia in the tied final of the NatWest Series 2005 (71 plus five
catches). Appointed MBE in 2006 New Year Honours as part of 2005 Ashes-winning

England team. Made 100th Test dismissal (Jayawardene, caught) in the first Test v Sri Lanka at Lord's 2006, becoming the fastest England wicket-keeper to the milestone (27 matches)
Best batting: 108* Kent v Essex, Chelmsford 2003

2006 Season

	M	Inn	NO	Runs	HS	Avg	100	50	Ct	St	Balls	Runs	Wkts	Avg	BB	5I	10M
Test	5	7	1	82	19	13.66	-	-	27	2	0	0	0		-	-	-
FC	12	17	2	336	60	22.40	-	3	39	3	0	0	0		-	-	-
ODI	5	5	1	74	23	18.50	-	-	6		0	0	0		-	-	
List A	12	12	3	271	49	30.11	-	-	19	3	0	0	0		-	-	
20/20 Int	1	1	1	14	14 *		-	-	1	-	0	0	0		-	-	
20/20	1	1	1	14	14 *		-	-	1	-	0	0	0		-	-	

Career Performances

	M	Inn	NO	Runs	HS	Avg	100	50	Ct	St	Balls	Runs	Wkts	Avg	BB	5I	10M
Test	31	47	4	1109	100	25.79	1	6	119	5	0	0	0		-	-	-
FC	73	107	13	2964	108 *	31.53	4	18	223	15	6	4	0		-	-	-
ODI	49	41	8	815	80	24.69	-	4	68	4	0	0	0		-	-	-
List A	103	89	16	1761	80	24.12	-	7	122	18	0	0	0		-	-	
20/20 Int	2	2	1	33	19	33.00	-	-	2	-	0	0	0		-	-	
20/20	9	8	2	104	22	17.33	-	-	9	-	0	0	0		-	-	

JONES, P. S. Somerset

Name: Philip <u>Steffan</u> Jones
Role: Right-hand bat, right-arm fast-medium bowler
Born: 9 February 1974, Llanelli
Height: 6ft 1in **Weight:** 15st 2lbs
Nickname: Jona
County debut: 1997 (Somerset), 2004 (Northamptonshire), 2006 (Derbyshire)
50 wickets in a season: 2
Place in batting averages: 243rd av. 15.13 (2005 264th av. 13.00)
Place in bowling averages: 57th av. 31.71
Strike rate: 53.30 (career 63.91)
Parents: Lyndon and Ann
Wife and date of marriage: Alex, 12 October 2002
Children: Seren, 2006

Family links with cricket: 'Father played locally in South Wales'
Education: Ysgol Gyfun y Strade, Llanelli; Loughborough University; Homerton College, Cambridge University
Qualifications: BSc Sports Science, PGCE in Physical Education
Career outside cricket: 'Sports conditioner'
Off-season: 'Training for next season'
Overseas tours: Wales Minor Counties to Barbados 1996; Somerset CCC to South Africa 1999, 2000, 2001
Overseas teams played for: Clarence CC, Tasmania 2005
Career highlights to date: 'C&G final 2001 with Somerset. 6-25 v Glamorgan for Derbyshire [at Cardiff 2006]' (*His full second innings figures were 20-14-25-6*)
Cricket moments to forget: '2003-04'
Cricket superstitions: 'Getting early to the ground'
Cricketers particularly admired: 'Pop' Welch, Brett Lee
Young players to look out for: Wayne White, Gary Ballance, Sam Spurway
Other sports played: Rugby union ('professionally for Bristol and Moseley 1997-99')
Other sports followed: Rugby union
Favourite band: Pussycat Dolls, Black Eyed Peas
Relaxations: 'Going to the cinema'
Extras: Took nine wickets (6-67/3-81) in the Varsity Match at Lord's 1997. Derbyshire's Championship Player of the Year 2006. Left Derbyshire at the end of the 2006 season and has rejoined Somerset for 2007
Opinions on cricket: 'Overkill on Twenty20! Moderation is the key to bringing the crowds in and keeping them interested. Wickets have also become too flat!'
Best batting: 105 Somerset v New Zealanders, Taunton 1999
Best bowling: 6-25 Derbyshire v Glamorgan, Cardiff 2006

2006 Season

	M	Inn	NO	Runs	HS	Avg	100	50	Ct	St	Balls	Runs	Wkts	Avg	BB	5I	10M
Test																	
FC	17	21	6	227	34 *	15.13	-	-	4	-	3145	1871	59	31.71	6-25	1	-
ODI																	
List A	8	5	1	49	24	12.25	-	-	2	-	412	362	11	32.90	5-49	1	
20/20 Int																	
20/20	7	3	0	14	7	4.66	-	-	1	-	139	201	10	20.10	3-26	-	

Career Performances

	M	Inn	NO	Runs	HS	Avg	100	50	Ct	St	Balls	Runs	Wkts	Avg	BB	5I	10M
Test																	
FC	100	120	30	1549	105	17.21	1	4	21	-	17002	10050	266	37.78	6-25	6	1
ODI																	
List A	151	79	38	472	27	11.51	-	-	28	-	6830	5905	206	28.66	6-56	3	
20/20 Int																	
20/20	19	8	3	41	24 *	8.20	-	-	3	-	386	557	23	24.21	3-26	-	

JONES, R. A.   Worcestershire

Name: <u>Richard</u> Alan Jones
Role: Right-hand bat, right-arm
medium-fast bowler
Born: 6 November 1986, Wordsley,
West Midlands
Height: 6ft 3in **Weight:** 12st 7lbs
Nickname: Jonesy, Jonah
County debut: No first-team appearance
Parents: Bob and Julie
Marital status: Single
Education: Grange High School,
Stourbridge; King Edward VI College,
Stourbridge
Qualifications: 13 GCSEs, 3 A-levels
Off-season: 'Get back to full fitness, work on
remodelling action and hopefully go away
and play somewhere after Christmas'
Overseas tours: England U19 to Bangladesh
2005-06

Career highlights to date: 'Being picked for U19 tour to Bangladesh. Signing
contract with Worcestershire'
Cricket moments to forget: 'Being injured whilst away on tour, having to come
home and not playing at all in 2006'
Cricket superstitions: 'None'
Cricketers particularly admired: Andrew Flintoff, Jacques Kallis, Brett Lee
Young players to look out for: Chris Bending, Adam Bending, Keith Bradley
Other sports played: Football (district schools U13 and U14), golf
Other sports followed: Football (West Bromwich Albion)
Injuries: Out for the whole of 2006 with a double stress fracture of the lower back
Favourite band: Arctic Monkeys
Relaxations: 'Listening to music, playing golf'
Extras: Scored first league hundred aged 17 for local side Old Hill (Birmingham &
District Premier League)
Opinions on cricket: 'I think there should be fewer overs in the day during County
Championship cricket, somewhere around 90-96 overs. I think this will bring a better
intensity to the game, and better cricket.'

JONES, S. P.   Glamorgan

Name: <u>Simon</u> Philip Jones
Role: Left-hand bat, right-arm fast bowler
Born: 25 December 1978, Morriston, Swansea
Height: 6ft 3in   **Weight:** 15st
Nickname: Horse
County debut: 1998
County cap: 2002
Test debut: 2002
ODI debut: 2004-05
Place in bowling averages: (2005 21st av. 24.48)
Strike rate: (career 51.60)
Parents: Irene and Jeff
Marital status: Single
Family links with cricket: 'Father played for England'
Education: Coedcae Comprehensive School; Millfield School

Qualifications: 12 GCSEs, 1 A-level, basic and senior coaching awards
Off-season: 'Rehab'
Overseas tours: Dyfed Schools to Zimbabwe 1994; Glamorgan to South Africa 1998; ECB National Academy to Australia 2001-02; England to Australia 2002-03, to West Indies 2003-04, to Zimbabwe (one-day series) 2004-05, to South Africa 2004-05, to India 2005-06; England A to Malaysia and India 2003-04
Career highlights to date: 'Winning Ashes series 2005'
Cricket moments to forget: 'Every injury'
Cricket superstitions: 'Right boot on first'
Cricketers particularly admired: Allan Donald
Young players to look out for: Ben Wright
Other sports played: Football (trials with Leeds United)
Injuries: Cartilage injury to the left knee
Favourite band: Eminem
Extras: NBC Denis Compton Award for the most promising young Glamorgan player 2001. Made Test debut in the first Test v India at Lord's 2002, striking a 43-ball 44 (more runs than his father scored in his 15-Test career); the Joneses are the eleventh father and son to have played in Tests for England. ECB National Academy 2003-04. Recorded maiden Test five-wicket return (5-57) in the second Test v West Indies at Port-of-Spain 2003-04; the Joneses thus became the first father and son to have taken five-wicket hauls for England. Appointed MBE in 2006 New Year Honours as part of 2005 Ashes-winning England team. Had best strike rate among Test bowlers taking 20

or more wickets in the calendar year 2005 (38.50 balls/wicket). One of *Wisden*'s Five Cricketers of the Year 2006. England 12-month central contract 2006-07

Opinions on cricket: 'Need more rest. (Not me personally. Ha, ha.)'
Best batting: 46 Glamorgan v Yorkshire, Scarborough 2001
Best bowling: 6-45 Glamorgan v Derbyshire, Cardiff 2002

2006 Season

	M	Inn	NO	Runs	HS	Avg	100	50	Ct	St	Balls	Runs	Wkts	Avg	BB	5I	10M
Test																	
FC	1	2	1	4	4 *	4.00	-	-	-	-	168	96	1	96.00	1-96	-	-
ODI																	
List A	2	1	1	5	5 *		-	-	-	-	49	28	2	14.00	2-23	-	
20/20 Int																		
20/20																		

Career Performances

	M	Inn	NO	Runs	HS	Avg	100	50	Ct	St	Balls	Runs	Wkts	Avg	BB	5I	10M
Test	18	18	5	205	44	15.76	-	-	4	-	2821	1666	59	28.23	6-53	3	-
FC	75	90	30	716	46	11.93	-	-	17	-	11199	6900	217	31.79	6-45	11	1
ODI	8	1	0	1	1	1.00	-	-	-	-	348	275	7	39.28	2-43	-	
List A	23	9	6	32	12 *	10.66	-	-	2	-	1000	844	18	46.88	3-19	-	
20/20 Int																		
20/20																		

43. Which was the first ground in Wales to stage an ODI, in 1973?

JORDAN, C. J. Surrey

Name: Christopher (<u>Chris</u>) James Jordan
Role: Right-hand bat, right-arm fast bowler; all-rounder
Born: 4 October 1988, Barbados
Height: 6ft 2in
Nickname: CJ
County debut: No first-team appearance
Parents: Robert and Rosie
Marital status: Single
Education: Dulwich College
Qualifications: 2 A-levels
Overseas tours: Barbados U15 to St Vincent 2004
Career highlights to date: 'Signing a summer contract for Surrey CCC'
Cricket superstitions: 'Have to touch my box, my thigh pad and my pads before I settle down to bat'
Cricketers particularly admired: Dwayne Bravo, Brian Lara, Brett Lee
Young players to look out for: Dwayne Smith
Other sports played: Football (Dulwich College 1st XI)
Other sports followed: Football (Manchester United)
Favourite band: Sizzla Kolongi
Extras: Scored 208 in a semi-final for school. Played for Surrey 2nd XI 2006
Opinions on cricket: 'It has become more exciting since Twenty20 has been introduced.'

---

44. Who made his ODI debut in June 2006, only to find
his brother playing for the opposition?

JOSEPH, R. H.   Kent

Name: <u>Robert</u> Hartman Joseph Jnr
Role: Right-hand bat, right-arm
fast-medium bowler
Born: 20 January 1982, Antigua
Height: 6ft 1in **Weight:** 13st 7lbs
Nickname: RJ, Blueie
County debut: 2004
Place in bowling averages: 92nd av. 37.37
Strike rate: 61.20 (career 53.98)
Education: Sutton Valence School; St Mary's
University College
Overseas tours: Antigua Young Lions to
England 1997; Antigua and Leeward Islands
U15 to Trinidad and St Lucia
Career highlights to date: 'Playing for the
ECB First-Class XI against New
Zealand A'
Cricket moments to forget: 'Losing in a
local school final – getting out on 47 needing one to win with four wickets in hand
and losing'
Cricketers particularly admired: Sir Vivian Richards, Andy Roberts
Other sports played: Golf
Other sports followed: Football (Arsenal)
Favourite band: Maroon 5
Relaxations: Listening to music
Extras: Made first-class debut for First-Class Counties XI v New Zealand A at Milton
Keynes 2000
Best batting: 29 Kent v Yorkshire, Canterbury 2006
Best bowling: 5-19 Kent v Bangladesh A, Canterbury 2005

45. Which current county captain made his first-class debut
for Bermuda in November 2006?

2006 Season

	M	Inn	NO	Runs	HS	Avg	100	50	Ct	St	Balls	Runs	Wkts	Avg	BB	5I	10M
Test																	
FC	9	12	4	63	29	7.87	-	-	1	-	1469	897	24	37.37	5-57	1	-
ODI																	
List A	3	1	1	0	0*		-	-	-	-	90	77	3	25.66	2-29	-	
20/20 Int																	
20/20																	

Career Performances

	M	Inn	NO	Runs	HS	Avg	100	50	Ct	St	Balls	Runs	Wkts	Avg	BB	5I	10M
Test																	
FC	19	25	9	152	29	9.50	-	-	5	-	2861	1780	53	33.58	5-19	2	-
ODI																	
List A	14	7	5	23	15	11.50	-	-	2	-	528	416	15	27.73	2-21	-	
20/20 Int																	
20/20																	

JOYCE, E. C. Middlesex

Name: Edmund (<u>Ed</u>) Christopher Joyce
Role: Left-hand bat, occasional right-arm medium bowler
Born: 22 September 1978, Dublin
Height: 5ft 10in **Weight:** 12st 7lbs
Nickname: Joycey, Spud, Piece
County debut: 1999
County cap: 2002
ODI debut: 2006
Twenty20 Int debut: 2006
1st-Class 200s: 1
1000 runs in a season: 5
Place in batting averages: 35th av. 52.82 (2005 12th av. 61.77)
Strike rate: (career 115.50)
Parents: Maureen and Jimmy
Marital status: Single
Family links with cricket: Two brothers and two sisters have represented Ireland

Education: Presentation College, Bray, County Wicklow; Trinity College, Dublin
Qualifications: Irish Leaving Certificate, BA (Hons) Economics and Geography, Level II coach

Overseas tours: Ireland U19 to Bermuda (International Youth Tournament) 1997, to South Africa (U19 World Cup) 1997-98; Ireland to Zimbabwe (ICC Emerging Nations Tournament) 1999-2000, to Canada (ICC Trophy) 2001; MCC to Namibia and Uganda 2004-05; England A to West Indies 2005-06; England to India (ICC Champions Trophy) 2006-07, to Australia 2006-07

Overseas teams played for: Coburg CC, Melbourne 1996-97; University CC, Perth 2001-02

Cricket superstitions: 'None'

Cricketers particularly admired: Larry Gomes, Brian Lara

Young players to look out for: Eoin Morgan, Nick Compton

Other sports played: Golf, rugby, soccer, snooker

Other sports followed: Rugby (Leinster), football (Manchester United)

Favourite band: The Mars Volta

Relaxations: Cinema, eating out, listening to music

Extras: NBC Denis Compton Award for the most promising young Middlesex player 2000. Became the first Irish-born-and-bred player to record a century in the County Championship with his 104 v Warwickshire at Lord's 2001. C&G Man of the Match award for his 72 v Northamptonshire at Northampton 2003. Vice-captain of Middlesex June 2004 to end of season, captaining the county in the absence of Andrew Strauss on international duty. First batsman to 1000 first-class runs in 2005 (18 June). Has represented Ireland in first-class and one-day cricket. Made England ODI debut in Belfast 2006 v Ireland, for whom his brother Dominick was also making his ODI debut. Has also represented England in Twenty20 International cricket. ECB National Academy 2005-06

Best batting: 211 Middlesex v Warwickshire, Edgbaston 2006

Best bowling: 2-34 Middlesex v CUCCE, Fenner's 2004

Stop press: Called up to England tour of Australia 2006-07 as replacement for Marcus Trescothick; scored maiden ODI century (107) v Australia at Sydney in the Commonwealth Bank Series 2006-07, winning Man of the Match award

46. Who took his 200th Test wicket in his 50th Test for England, v Pakistan at Lord's 2001?

2006 Season

	M	Inn	NO	Runs	HS	Avg	100	50	Ct	St	Balls	Runs	Wkts	Avg	BB	5I	10M
Test																	
FC	14	24	1	1215	211	52.82	3	6	10	-	132	132	1	132.00	1-21	-	-
ODI	2	2	0	21	13	10.50	-	-	2	-	0	0	0		-	-	
List A	11	11	0	251	95	22.81	-	1	8	-	30	29	0		-	-	
20/20 Int	1	0	0	0	0		-	-	-	-	0	0	0		-	-	
20/20	1	0	0	0	0		-	-	-	-	0	0	0		-	-	

Career Performances

	M	Inn	NO	Runs	HS	Avg	100	50	Ct	St	Balls	Runs	Wkts	Avg	BB	5I	10M
Test																	
FC	94	158	14	6815	211	47.32	17	37	79	-	1155	913	10	91.30	2-34	-	-
ODI	3	3	0	31	13	10.33	-	-	3	-	0	0	0		-	-	
List A	120	112	17	3407	115 *	35.86	3	23	45	-	162	181	2	90.50	2-10	-	
20/20 Int	1	0	0	0	0		-	-	-	-	0	0	0		-	-	
20/20	11	10	1	110	31	12.22	-	-	2	-	6	12	0		-	-	

KARTIK, M. Middlesex

Name: Murali Kartik
Role: Left-hand bat, slow left-arm bowler
Born: 11 September 1976, Chennai (Madras), India
County debut: 2005 (Lancashire)
Test debut: 1999-2000
ODI debut: 2001-02
Strike rate: (career 63.19)
Overseas tours: India A to Pakistan 1997-98, to West Indies 1999-2000, to South Africa 2001-02, to Sri Lanka 2002, to England 2003; India to Bangladesh 2000-01, to Australia 2003-04, to Pakistan 2003-04, to Bangladesh 2004-05, to Zimbabwe 2005-06 (Videocon Tri-Series), to Pakistan 2005-06 (one-day series)
Overseas teams played for: Railways 1996-97 –
Extras: Represented India U19. Man of the Match in the fourth Test v Australia at Mumbai (Bombay) 2004-05 (4-44/3-32). Was a temporary overseas player with Lancashire during the 2005 and 2006 seasons, taking 10-168 (5-93/5-75) on Championship debut v Essex at Chelmsford 2005; has joined Middlesex as an overseas player for 2007

Best batting: 96 Railways v Rest of India, Delhi 2005-06
Best bowling: 9-70 Rest of India v Mumbai, Mumbai (Bombay) 2000-01

2006 Season

	M	Inn	NO	Runs	HS	Avg	100	50	Ct	St	Balls	Runs	Wkts	Avg	BB	5I	10M
Test																	
FC	3	2	1	42	40	42.00	-	-	1	-	552	234	6	39.00	3-89	-	-
ODI																	
List A	4	2	1	10	10 *	10.00	-	-	1	-	192	138	8	17.25	3-24	-	
20/20 Int																	
20/20																	

Career Performances

	M	Inn	NO	Runs	HS	Avg	100	50	Ct	St	Balls	Runs	Wkts	Avg	BB	5I	10M
Test	8	10	1	88	43	9.77	-	-	2	-	1932	820	24	34.16	4-44	-	-
FC	94	110	13	1861	96	19.18	-	11	54	-	20350	8173	322	25.38	9-70	19	3
ODI	30	11	4	89	32 *	12.71	-	-	10	-	1530	1312	27	48.59	3-36	-	
List A	113	49	18	313	37 *	10.09	-	-	36	-	5902	4356	138	31.56	5-29	1	
20/20 Int																	
20/20																	

KATICH, S. M.   Derbyshire

Name: <u>Simon</u> Mathew Katich
Role: Left-hand bat, left-arm wrist-spin bowler, county captain
Born: 21 August 1975, Midland, Western Australia
Height: 6ft **Weight:** 12st 8lbs
Nickname: Kat
County debut: 2000 (Durham), 2002 (Yorkshire), 2003 (Hampshire)
County cap: 2000 (Durham), 2003 (Hampshire)
Test debut: 2001
ODI debut: 2000-01
Twenty20 Int debut: 2004-05
1000 runs in a season: 2
1st-Class 200s: 1
Place in batting averages: (2005 84th av. 37.52)
Strike rate: (career 63.75)
Parents: Vince and Kerry

Wife and date of marriage: Georgie, May 2006
Education: Trinity College, Perth; University of Western Australia
Qualifications: Bachelor of Commerce degree
Career outside cricket: Entrepreneur
Overseas tours: Australian Cricket Academy to South Africa 1996; Australia to Sri Lanka and Zimbabwe 1999-2000, to England 2001, to Sri Lanka 2003-04, to India 2004-05, to New Zealand 2004-05, to England 2005, to New Zealand (one-day series) 2005-06, to South Africa 2005-06 (one-day series), to Bangladesh 2005-06 (one-day series), to Malaysia (DLF Cup) 2006-07; Australia A to South Africa 2002-03 (vc)
Overseas teams played for: Western Australia 1996-97 – 2001-02; New South Wales 2002-03 – ; Randwick Petersham, Sydney
Career highlights to date: 'Making my maiden Test century v India at the SCG'
Cricket moments to forget: 'Any time I drop a catch'
Cricket superstitions: 'Like to wear old gear'
Cricketers particularly admired: Viv Richards
Other sports played: Australian Rules, hockey
Other sports followed: Australian Rules (Richmond), football (Newcastle United)
Favourite band: U2
Relaxations: 'Golf, watching movies and going to the beach in Sydney'
Extras: Attended Commonwealth Bank [Australian] Cricket Academy 1996. *Wisden Australia*'s Sheffield Shield Cricketer of the Year 1999. Became the first WA batsman to score a century against each of the other states in a single season 2000-01. His awards include Man of the Match in the Pura Cup final v Queensland at Brisbane 2002-03. Was Durham's overseas player in 2000. Was Yorkshire's overseas player during June 2002. Was an overseas player with Hampshire in 2003; from August to September 2004, deputising for Michael Clarke; and in 2005. Hampshire Cricket Society Player of the Year 2003. Named State Player of the Year at the 2004 Allan Border Medal awards. Captain of New South Wales since 2004-05. Australia contract 2006-07. Has joined Derbyshire as an overseas player and as captain for 2007
Best batting: 228* Western Australia v South Australia, Perth 2000-01
Best bowling: 7-130 New South Wales v Victoria, Melbourne 2002-03

2006 Season (did not make any first-class or one-day appearances)

Career Performances

	M	Inn	NO	Runs	HS	Avg	100	50	Ct	St	Balls	Runs	Wkts	Avg	BB	5I	10M
Test	23	38	3	1260	125	36.00	2	8	15	-	659	406	12	33.83	6-65	1	-
FC	148	253	34	10846	228 *	49.52	29	57	139	-	4973	2986	78	38.28	7-130	3	-
ODI	45	42	5	1324	107 *	35.78	1	9	13	-	0	0	0		-	-	
List A	182	175	21	5950	136 *	38.63	7	45	85	-	823	766	24	31.91	3-21	-	
20/20 Int	3	2	0	69	39	34.50	-	-	2	-	0	0	0		-	-	
20/20	8	7	2	248	59 *	49.60	-	2	3	-	0	0	0		-	-	

KEEDY, G.   Lancashire

Name: Gary Keedy
Role: Left-hand bat, left-arm spin bowler
Born: 27 November 1974, Wakefield
Height: 5ft 11in **Weight:** 13st
Nickname: Keeds, Phil Mitchell, Minty
County debut: 1994 (Yorkshire),
1995 (Lancashire)
County cap: 2000 (Lancashire)
50 wickets in a season: 3
Place in bowling averages: 27th av. 27.21
(2005 12th av. 22.81)
Strike rate: 55.70 (career 66.76)
Parents: Roy and Pat
Wife and date of marriage: Andrea,
12 October 2002
Children: Erin Grace, 8 September 2006
Education: Garforth Comprehensive; Open
University
Qualifications: 8 GCSEs, Level 2 cricket coach, Certificate in Natural Sciences
Off-season: 12-month contract
Overseas tours: England U18 to South Africa 1992-93, to Denmark 1993;
England U19 to Sri Lanka 1993-94; Lancashire to Portugal 1995, to Jamaica 1996,
to South Africa 1997; MCC to UAE and Oman 2004
Overseas teams played for: Frankston, Melbourne 1995-96
Career highlights to date: 'County cap; playing for Lancashire. Fourteen wickets in
match v Glos at Old Trafford. Five wickets v Yorks at Headingley'
Cricket superstitions: 'None'
Cricketers particularly admired: Graham Gooch, Shane Warne
Players to look out for: Karl Brown, 'Dominic Cork!'
Other sports followed: Rugby league (Leeds Rhinos), football (Leeds United)
Injuries: Out for three weeks with a bruised bone on the knee; for one week with a
back spasm
Favourite band: 'The Gunners'
Relaxations: 'Wine tasting; looking after family'
Extras: Player of the Series for England U19 v West Indies U19 1993; also played v
India U19 1994. Had match figures of 14-227 (7-95/7-132) v Gloucestershire at Old
Trafford 2004, the best return by an English spinner since Martyn Ball's 14-169 in
1993. Leading English wicket-taker (second overall) in the Championship 2004 (72 at
25.68). Lancashire Player of the Year 2004
Opinions on cricket: 'Congratulations to all the counties who have academies in
place and are hell bent on producing the next generation of England stars. I'm all for

quality overseas players coming over. I certainly have benefited by playing with and against world-class players. I won't mention Kolpak [*see page 13*] this year!'
Best batting: 57 Lancashire v Yorkshire, Headingley 2002
Best bowling: 7-95 Lancashire v Gloucestershire, Old Trafford 2004

2006 Season

	M	Inn	NO	Runs	HS	Avg	100	50	Ct	St	Balls	Runs	Wkts	Avg	BB	5I	10M
Test																	
FC	15	16	10	45	11 *	7.50	-	-	4	-	3398	1660	61	27.21	6-40	2	-
ODI																	
List A	10	1	0	2	2	2.00	-	-	1	-	412	315	9	35.00	2-30	-	
20/20 Int																	
20/20	8	3	2	15	9 *	15.00	-	-	-	-	168	184	6	30.66	2-21	-	

Career Performances

	M	Inn	NO	Runs	HS	Avg	100	50	Ct	St	Balls	Runs	Wkts	Avg	BB	5I	10M
Test																	
FC	147	167	88	861	57	10.89	-	1	41	-	30510	14300	457	31.29	7-95	22	5
ODI																	
List A	34	8	4	21	10 *	5.25	-	-	2	-	1339	1097	32	34.28	5-30	1	
20/20 Int																	
20/20	23	5	2	15	9 *	5.00	-	-	2	-	456	490	23	21.30	3-25	-	

KEEGAN, C. B. Middlesex

Name: <u>Chad</u> Blake Keegan
Role: Right-hand bat, right-arm fast-medium bowler
Born: 30 July 1979, Sandton, Johannesburg, South Africa
Height: 6ft 1in **Weight:** 12st
Nickname: Wick
County debut: 2001
County cap: 2003
50 wickets in a season: 1
Place in batting averages: 260th av. 12.33
Place in bowling averages: 97th av. 38.73
Strike rate: 63.36 (career 59.96)
Parents: Sharon and Blake
Marital status: Single
Education: Durban High School
Qualifications: YMCA fitness instructor

Overseas tours: MCC to Argentina and Chile 2001
Overseas teams played for: Durban High School Old Boys 1994-97; Crusaders, Durban 1998-99
Career highlights to date: 'Being awarded Player of the Year for Middlesex 2003'
Cricket moments to forget: 'Losing my pants diving for a ball at Lord's'
Cricket superstitions: 'Tapping the bat either side of the crease three times'
Cricketers particularly admired: Malcolm Marshall, Neil Johnson
Other sports played: 'Any extreme sports, golf'
Other sports followed: Football (Liverpool)
Favourite band: Jack Johnson
Relaxations: 'Making and listening to music (guitar); sketching'
Extras: Represented KwaZulu-Natal U13, KwaZulu-Natal Schools, KwaZulu-Natal U19, KwaZulu-Natal Academy. MCC Young Cricketer. Middlesex Player of the Year 2003. Is not considered an overseas player
Best batting: 44 Middlesex v Surrey, The Oval 2004
Best bowling: 6-114 Middlesex v Leicestershire, Southgate 2003

2006 Season

	M	Inn	NO	Runs	HS	Avg	100	50	Ct	St	Balls	Runs	Wkts	Avg	BB	5I	10M
Test																	
FC	7	10	1	111	34 *	12.33	-	-	3	-	1204	736	19	38.73	5-90	1	-
ODI																	
List A	10	6	2	64	31	16.00	-	-	2	-	450	352	19	18.52	4-24	-	
20/20 Int																	
20/20	6	5	1	29	17	7.25	-	-	-	-	108	175	2	87.50	1-19	-	

Career Performances

	M	Inn	NO	Runs	HS	Avg	100	50	Ct	St	Balls	Runs	Wkts	Avg	BB	5I	10M
Test																	
FC	47	57	6	607	44	11.90	-	-	14	-	8395	4887	140	34.90	6-114	6	-
ODI																	
List A	82	52	17	594	50	16.97	-	1	19	-	3854	3010	129	23.33	6-33	3	
20/20 Int																	
20/20	12	11	2	151	42	16.77	-	-	3	-	246	366	7	52.28	3-34	-	

KEMP, J. M.   Kent

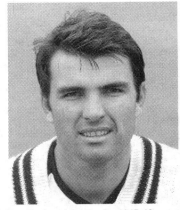

Name: <u>Justin</u> Miles Kemp
Role: Right-hand bat, right-arm
fast-medium bowler
Born: 2 October 1977, Queenstown,
Cape Province, South Africa
Nickname: Kempie
County debut: 2003 (Worcestershire),
2005 (Kent)
County cap: 2003 (Worcestershire colours),
2006 (Kent)
Test debut: 2000-01
ODI debut: 2000-01
Twenty20 Int debut: 2005-06
Place in batting averages: 16th av. 61.50
(2005 26th av. 52.70)
Place in bowling averages: 45th av. 30.27
(2005 76th av. 32.63)
Strike rate: 60.54 (career 56.98)
Family links with cricket: Grandfather (J. M. Kemp) played for Border 1947-48;
father (J. W. Kemp) played for Border 1975-76 – 1976-77; cousin of former South
Africa ODI player Dave Callaghan
Education: Queens College; University of Port Elizabeth
Overseas tours: South Africa U19 to India 1995-96; South African Academy to
Zimbabwe 1998-99; South Africa A to West Indies 2000, to Australia 2002-03, to
Zimbabwe 2004; South Africa to West Indies 2000-01, to Zimbabwe 2001-02, to
Australia 2001-02 (VB Series), to West Indies 2004-05 (one-day series), to India (one-
day series) 2005-06, to Australia 2005-06, to India (ICC Champions Trophy) 2006-07
Overseas teams played for: Eastern Province 1996-97 – 2002-03; Northerns
2003-04 – 2004-05; Titans 2004-05 –
Extras: An overseas player with Worcestershire during the 2003 season as a locum for
Andrew Hall; an overseas player with Kent 2005-06. Played for African XI v Asian
Cricket Council XI in ODI series 2005-06. Has won numerous awards in domestic and
international cricket, including Player of the [ODI] Series v New Zealand 2005-06 and
Man of the Match v England in the fifth ODI at East London 2004-05 (50-ball 80)
Best batting: 188 Eastern Province v North West, Port Elizabeth 2000-01
Best bowling: 6-56 Eastern Province v Border, Port Elizabeth 2000-01

2006 Season

	M	Inn	NO	Runs	HS	Avg	100	50	Ct	St	Balls	Runs	Wkts	Avg	BB	5I	10M
Test																	
FC	6	9	3	369	124 *	61.50	2	1	10	-	666	333	11	30.27	3-72	-	-
ODI																	
List A	6	6	2	204	57	51.00	-	2	2	-	150	161	2	80.50	1-12	-	
20/20 Int																	
20/20																	

Career Performances

	M	Inn	NO	Runs	HS	Avg	100	50	Ct	St	Balls	Runs	Wkts	Avg	BB	5I	10M
Test	4	6	0	80	55	13.33	-	1	3	-	479	222	9	24.66	3-33	-	-
FC	87	141	17	4594	188	37.04	10	22	99	-	10029	4726	176	26.85	6-56	5	-
ODI	56	44	13	976	80	31.48	-	7	24	-	1031	779	22	35.40	3-20	-	
List A	188	160	47	4091	107 *	36.20	2	28	78	-	6171	4892	165	29.64	6-20	3	
20/20 Int	1	1	0	8	8	8.00	-	-	-	-	0	0	0		-	-	
20/20	22	19	6	375	85 *	28.84	-	1	7	-	318	414	23	18.00	3-19	-	

KERVEZEE, A. N.   Worcestershire

Name: <u>Alexei</u> Nicolaas Kervezee
Role: Right-hand bat, right-arm medium bowler
Born: 11 September 1989, Walvis Bay, Namibia
County debut: No first-team appearance
ODI debut: 2006
Overseas tours: Netherlands to UAE (EurAsia Series) 2006, to Scotland (European Championship) 2006, to South Africa (ICC Associates Tri-Series) 2006-07, to Kenya (ICC World Cricket League) 2006-07, to West Indies (World Cup) 2006-07, plus various Netherlands age-group tours to Europe
Overseas teams played for: HBS, Netherlands
Extras: Made first-class debut for Netherlands v Scotland at Utrecht in the ICC Inter-Continental Cup 2005, aged 15. Made ODI debut v Sri Lanka at Amstelveen 2006, aged 16, scoring 47
Best batting: 46* Netherlands v Ireland, Belfast 2005
Stop press: Attended ICC Winter Training Camp in South Africa 2006-07

2006 Season (did not make any first-class or one-day appearances)

Career Performances

	M	Inn	NO	Runs	HS	Avg	100	50	Ct	St	Balls	Runs	Wkts	Avg	BB	5I	10M
Test																	
FC	3	3	1	88	46 *	44.00	-	-	1	-	18	11	0			-	-	-
ODI	4	4	1	94	47	31.33	-	-	3	-	0	0	0			-	-
List A	6	6	1	145	47	29.00	-	-	4	-	24	39	0			-	-
20/20 Int																	
20/20																	

KEY, R. W. T. Kent

Name: <u>Robert</u> William Trevor Key
Role: Right-hand bat, off-spin bowler, county captain
Born: 12 May 1979, Dulwich, London
Height: 6ft 1in **Weight:** 12st 7lbs
Nickname: Keysy
County debut: 1998
County cap: 2001
Test debut: 2002
ODI debut: 2003
1000 runs in a season: 4
1st-Class 200s: 1
Place in batting averages: 90th av. 36.76
(2005 14th av. 59.84)
Parents: Trevor and Lynn
Wife and date of marriage: Fleur, 2006
Children: Aaliyah, September 2006
Family links with cricket: Mother played
for Kent Ladies. Father played club cricket in Derby. Sister Elizabeth played for her junior school side
Education: Langley Park Boys' School
Qualifications: 10 GCSEs, NCA coaching award, GNVQ Business Studies
Overseas tours: Kent U13 to Netherlands; England U17 to Bermuda (International Youth Tournament) 1997 (c); England U19 to South Africa (including U19 World Cup) 1997-98; England A to Zimbabwe and South Africa 1998-99; ECB National Academy to Australia 2001-02, to Sri Lanka 2002-03; England to Australia 2002-03, to South Africa 2004-05
Overseas teams played for: Greenpoint CC, Cape Town 1996-97
Cricketers particularly admired: Min Patel, Neil Taylor, Alan Wells, Mark Ealham

Other sports played: Hockey, football, snooker, tennis (played for county)
Other sports followed: Football (Chelsea), basketball (Chicago Bulls)
Extras: Represented England U19 1997 and was England U19 Man of the Series v Pakistan U19 1998 (award shared with Graeme Swann). NBC Denis Compton Award for the most promising young Kent player 2001. Scored 221 in the first Test v West Indies 2004, in the process sharing with Andrew Strauss (137) in a record second-wicket stand for Test cricket at Lord's (291). Leading run-scorer in English first-class cricket 2004 with 1896 runs at 79.00, including nine centuries. One of *Wisden*'s Five Cricketers of the Year 2005. Scored twin centuries (112/189) v Surrey at Tunbridge Wells 2005, in the second innings sharing with Martin van Jaarsveld (168) in a new Kent record third-wicket partnership (323). ECB National Academy 2005-06, 2006-07. Captain of Kent since 2006
Best batting: 221 England v West Indies, Lord's 2004

2006 Season

	M	Inn	NO	Runs	HS	Avg	100	50	Ct	St	Balls	Runs	Wkts	Avg	BB	5I	10M
Test																	
FC	16	29	3	956	136 *	36.76	2	3	10	-	30	10	0		-	-	-
ODI																	
List A	16	15	1	447	89	31.92	-	4	3	-	0	0	0		-	-	
20/20 Int																	
20/20	7	7	1	89	41 *	14.83	-	-	2	-	0	0	0		-	-	

Career Performances

	M	Inn	NO	Runs	HS	Avg	100	50	Ct	St	Balls	Runs	Wkts	Avg	BB	5I	10M
Test	15	26	1	775	221	31.00	1	3	11	-	0	0	0		-	-	-
FC	160	278	15	10650	221	40.49	30	42	101	-	110	59	0		-	-	-
ODI	5	5	0	54	19	10.80	-	-	-	-	0	0	0		-	-	
List A	140	134	10	3638	114	29.33	1	26	21	-	0	0	0		-	-	
20/20 Int																	
20/20	16	16	3	262	66 *	20.15	-	1	4	-	0	0	0		-	-	

47. Who scored more runs in his debut Test innings in 2002 than his father did in his 15-Test career?

KHALID, S. A. Worcestershire

Name: <u>Shaftab</u> Ahmad Khalid
Role: Right-hand bat, right-arm
off-spin bowler
Born: 6 October 1982, Pakistan
Height: 5ft 11in **Weight:** 10st 6lbs
Nickname: Shafi
County debut: 2003
County colours: 2003
Strike rate: (career 91.42)
Parents: Dr Khalid Mahmood and
Mrs Nuzhat Bano
Marital status: Single
Education: Dormers Wells High School;
West Thames College
Qualifications: 11 GCSEs, 3 A-levels
Overseas tours: England A to Malaysia and
India 2003-04
Extras: ECB National Academy 2003-04.

NBC Denis Compton Award for the most promising young Worcestershire player 2003
Best batting: 20 Worcestershire v LUCCE, Kidderminster 2005
Best bowling: 4-131 Worcestershire v Northamptonshire, Northampton 2003

2006 Season (did not make any first-class or one-day appearances)

Career Performances

	M	Inn	NO	Runs	HS	Avg	100	50	Ct	St	Balls	Runs	Wkts	Avg	BB	5I	10M
Test																	
FC	10	9	2	64	20	9.14	-	-	3	-	1280	712	14	50.85	4-131	-	-
ODI																	
List A	10	6	4	13	9 *	6.50	-	-	1	-	327	284	4	71.00	2-40	-	
20/20 Int																	
20/20	1	0	0	0	0		-	-	-	-	6	13	0		-	-	

KHAN, A. Kent

Name: Amjad Khan
Role: Right-hand bat, right-arm fast bowler
Born: 14 October 1980, Copenhagen, Denmark
Height: 6ft **Weight:** 11st 6lbs
Nickname: Ammy
County debut: 2001
County cap: 2005
50 wickets in a season: 2
Place in batting averages: (2005 210th av. 21.25)
Place in bowling averages: 48th av. 30.41 (2005 52nd av. 28.27)
Strike rate: 55.08 (career 49.14)
Parents: Aslam and Raisa
Marital status: Single
Education: Skolen på Duevej, Denmark; Falkonĕrgårdens Gymnasium

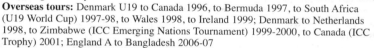

Overseas tours: Denmark U19 to Canada 1996, to Bermuda 1997, to South Africa (U19 World Cup) 1997-98, to Wales 1998, to Ireland 1999; Denmark to Netherlands 1998, to Zimbabwe (ICC Emerging Nations Tournament) 1999-2000, to Canada (ICC Trophy) 2001; England A to Bangladesh 2006-07
Overseas teams played for: Kjøbenhavns Boldklub, Denmark
Cricket moments to forget: 'I try to forget most of the games where I didn't perform as well as I would like'
Cricketers particularly admired: Wasim Akram, Dennis Lillee
Other sports followed: Football (Denmark)
Favourite band: Marvin Gaye, George Michael, Nerd (Neptunes)
Relaxations: 'Music, sleeping, reading'
Extras: Made debut for Denmark at the age of 17. Took 50 (63) first-class wickets in his first full season 2002. NBC Denis Compton Award for the most promising young Kent player 2002. Is England-qualified
Best batting: 78 Kent v Middlesex, Lord's 2003
Best bowling: 6-52 Kent v Yorkshire, Canterbury 2002

2006 Season

	M	Inn	NO	Runs	HS	Avg	100	50	Ct	St	Balls	Runs	Wkts	Avg	BB	5I	10M
Test																	
FC	9	10	7	98	38	32.66	-	-	1	-	1873	1034	34	30.41	5-100	1	-
ODI																	
List A	10	2	1	11	7 *	11.00	-	-	3	-	425	415	12	34.58	3-44		-
20/20 Int																	
20/20	9	4	2	14	12	7.00	-	-	1	-	175	266	11	24.18	3-11		-

Career Performances

	M	Inn	NO	Runs	HS	Avg	100	50	Ct	St	Balls	Runs	Wkts	Avg	BB	5I	10M
Test																	
FC	57	65	23	824	78	19.61	-	3	9	-	9338	6192	190	32.58	6-52	6	-
ODI																	
List A	51	28	6	265	65 *	12.04	-	1	13	-	2107	1818	56	32.46	4-26		-
20/20 Int																	
20/20	17	7	2	30	15	6.00	-	-	1	-	313	466	22	21.18	3-11		-

KHAN, Z.   Worcestershire

Name: Zaheer Khan
Role: Right-hand bat, left-arm fast-medium bowler
Born: 7 October 1978, Shrirampur, Maharashtra, India
County debut: 2004 (Surrey), 2006 (Worcestershire)
County colours: 2006 (Worcestershire)
Test debut: 2000-01
ODI debut: 2000-01
50 wickets in a season: 1
Place in batting averages: 267th av. 10.73
Place in bowling averages: 38th av. 29.07
Strike rate: 47.58 (career 50.77)
Overseas tours: India to Kenya (ICC Knockout Trophy) 2000-01, to Bangladesh 2000-01, to Zimbabwe 2001, to Sri Lanka 2001, to South Africa 2001-02, to West Indies 2001-02, to England 2002, to Sri Lanka (ICC Champions Trophy) 2002-03, to New Zealand 2002-03, to Africa (World Cup) 2002-03, to Australia 2003-04, to Pakistan 2003-04, to Bangladesh 2004-05, to Zimbabwe 2005-06, to Pakistan 2005-06, to South Africa 2006-07, plus other one-day tournaments in Abu Dhabi (India A), Sharjah,

Bangladesh and Sri Lanka; Asian Cricket Council XI to South Africa (Afro-Asia Cup) 2005-06

Overseas teams played for: Baroda 1999-2000 –

Extras: One of *Indian Cricket*'s five Cricketers of the Year 2002. His awards include Player of the Series in the Afro-Asia Cup 2005-06, and Man of the Match v New Zealand at Centurion in the World Cup 2002-03 (4-42) and in the Ranji Trophy final 2000-01 v Railways at Vadodara (3-92/5-43). Struck a six off each of the final four balls of the Indian innings in the third ODI v Zimbabwe at Jodhpur 2000-01. Played two games for Surrey as an amateur in May 2004 as a replacement for the injured Saqlain Mushtaq, taking a wicket (Will Jefferson) with his first ball for the county v Essex at The Oval in the totesport League. Scored 75 in the first Test v Bangladesh at Dhaka 2004-05, setting a new record highest score for a No. 11 in Tests. An overseas player with Worcestershire 2006. Had match figures of 10-140 (4-100/6-40) on Championship debut v Somerset at Worcester 2006

Best batting: 75 India v Bangladesh, Dhaka 2004-05

Best bowling: 9-138 Worcestershire v Essex, Chelmsford 2006

Stop press: Made Twenty20 International debut v South Africa at Johannesburg 2006-07

2006 Season

	M	Inn	NO	Runs	HS	Avg	100	50	Ct	St	Balls	Runs	Wkts	Avg	BB	5I	10M
Test																	
FC	16	21	6	161	30 *	10.73	-	-	4	-	3712	2268	78	29.07	9-138	5	2
ODI																	
List A	14	7	1	102	42	17.00	-	-	2	-	591	450	28	16.07	4-29	-	
20/20 Int																	
20/20	5	4	3	41	26	41.00	-	-	-	-	114	156	4	39.00	2-29	-	

Career Performances

	M	Inn	NO	Runs	HS	Avg	100	50	Ct	St	Balls	Runs	Wkts	Avg	BB	5I	10M
Test	42	54	14	508	75	12.70	-	1	10	-	7961	4398	121	36.34	5-29	3	-
FC	95	121	27	1371	75	14.58	-	2	29	-	19346	10732	381	28.16	9-138	23	7
ODI	107	58	24	453	34 *	13.32	-	-	25	-	5315	4335	155	27.96	4-19	-	
List A	156	85	32	703	42	13.26	-	-	39	-	7774	6248	226	27.64	4-19	-	
20/20 Int																	
20/20	5	4	3	41	26	41.00	-	-	-	-	114	156	4	39.00	2-29	-	

KIESWETTER, C. Somerset

Name: Craig Kieswetter
Role: Right-hand bat, wicket-keeper
Born: 28 November 1987, Johannesburg, South Africa
Nickname: Hobnob
County debut: No first-team appearance
Parents: Wayne and Belinda
Marital status: Single
Education: Diocesan College (Bishops), Cape Town; Millfield School
Off-season: 'Winter training (Somerset), tour; club cricket, Cape Town'
Overseas tours: South Africa U19 to Sri Lanka (U19 World Cup) 2005-06
Overseas teams played for: Alma Marist CC, Cape Town 2005-06
Career highlights to date: 'Being selected for South Africa for the U19 World Cup in Sri Lanka 2006'

Cricket superstitions: 'Just routine to put kit on'
Cricketers particularly admired: Justin Langer, Damien Martyn
Other sports played: Hockey
Other sports followed: Football (Aston Villa)
Injuries: Out for five days with a dislocated finger; for three weeks with a broken fifth metatarsal
Favourite band: Plan B
Relaxations: 'Snowboarding/skiing, chilling with mates, music'
Extras: PG Bison U15 Player of the Tournament (South Africa) 2002. Represented South Africa Schools 2005

48. Who scored 116* on debut for Essex 1990 and 210* on debut for Durham 1997?

KILLEEN, N.　　　　　　　　　　Durham

Name: Neil Killeen
Role: Right-hand bat, right-arm
medium-fast bowler
Born: 17 October 1975, Shotley Bridge
Height: 6ft 1in　**Weight:** 15st
Nickname: Killer, Bully, Quinny,
Squeaky, Bull
County debut: 1995
County cap: 1999
Benefit: 2006
50 wickets in a season: 1
Place in bowling averages: 82nd av. 35.31
Strike rate: 73.89 (career 64.60)
Parents: Glen and Thora
Wife and date of marriage: Clare Louise,
5 February 2000
Children: Jonathan David
Family links with cricket: 'Dad best
armchair player in the game'

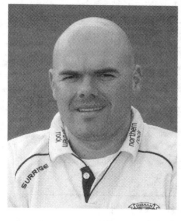

Education: Greencroft Comprehensive School; Derwentside College,
University of Teesside
Qualifications: 8 GCSEs, 2 A-levels, first year Sports Science, Level III coaching
award, Level I staff coach
Career outside cricket: Cricket coaching
Overseas tours: Durham CCC to Zimbabwe 1992; England U19 to West Indies
1994-95; MCC to Bangladesh 1999-2000
Career highlights to date: 'My county cap and first-class debut'
Cricket moments to forget: 'Injury causing me to miss most of 2001 season'
Cricketers particularly admired: Ian Botham, Curtly Ambrose, Courtney Walsh,
David Boon
Other sports played: Athletics (English Schools javelin)
Sports followed: Football (Sunderland AFC), cricket (Anfield Plain CC)
Relaxations: 'Good food, good wine; golf; spending time with wife and family'
Extras: Was first Durham bowler to take five wickets in a Sunday League game
(5-26 v Northamptonshire at Northampton 1995). Scored 35 batting at No. 10 as
Durham made 453-9 to beat Somerset at Taunton 2004. Had figures of 8.3-7-5-2 v
Derbyshire at Riverside in the totesport League 2004
Best batting: 48 Durham v Somerset, Riverside 1995
Best bowling: 7-70 Durham v Hampshire, Riverside 2003

2006 Season

	M	Inn	NO	Runs	HS	Avg	100	50	Ct	St	Balls	Runs	Wkts	Avg	BB	5I	10M
Test																	
FC	9	12	3	72	34	8.00	-	-	2	-	1404	671	19	35.31	5-29	1	-
ODI																	
List A	13	6	3	40	15 *	13.33	-	-	1	-	612	472	11	42.90	2-20	-	
20/20 Int																	
20/20	7	4	3	40	13 *	40.00	-	-	1	-	144	154	6	25.66	2-21	-	

Career Performances

	M	Inn	NO	Runs	HS	Avg	100	50	Ct	St	Balls	Runs	Wkts	Avg	BB	5I	10M
Test																	
FC	98	143	30	1297	48	11.47	-	-	25	-	16022	8033	248	32.39	7-70	8	-
ODI																	
List A	196	107	40	635	32	9.47	-	-	36	-	9283	6465	269	24.03	6-31	4	
20/20 Int																	
20/20	24	12	8	83	17 *	20.75	-	-	5	-	510	610	30	20.33	4-7	-	

KING, S. J.   Surrey

Name: <u>Simon</u> James King
Role: Right-hand bat, right-arm
off-spin bowler
Born: 4 September 1987, Lambeth, London
Height: 6ft 1in **Weight:** 11st
Nickname: Kingy
County debut: No first-team appearance
Parents: Angela Pocock and David King
Marital status: Single
Family links with cricket: 'Brother plays'
Education: Warlingham Secondary School;
John Fisher Sixth Form College
Qualifications: GCSEs, BTEC National
Diploma in Sport, ECB Level 2 coaching
Off-season: 'Coaching, training and two
proposed trips to India'
Overseas tours: Surrey Academy to South
Africa 2005; Surrey CCC to India 2006
Overseas teams played for: Mildura West CC, Victoria; Millewa CC, Victoria
(both Australia)
Career highlights to date: 'Receiving first contract at the end of the 2006 season.
First five-wicket haul, v Sussex 2nd XI 2005'

Cricket moments to forget: 'Dropping a skyer into my face in an England regional match'
Cricketers particularly admired: Alec Stewart, Shane Warne, Mark Ramprakash, Phil Matthews
Young players to look out for: Zafar Ansari, Daryl King, Harry Allen
Other sports played: Football (Warlingham FC, Hamsey Rangers FC)
Other sports followed: Football (Fulham)
Favourite band: Goo Goo Dolls, Oasis, U2, Lifehouse
Relaxations: 'Sleeping'
Extras: Surrey U15 Player of the Year 2003. Surrey Academy Player of the Year 2006

KIRBY, S. P. Gloucestershire

Name: <u>Steven</u> Paul Kirby
Role: Right-hand bat, right-arm fast bowler
Born: 4 October 1977, Bury, Lancashire
Height: 6ft 3in **Weight:** 13st 5lbs
Nickname: Tango
County debut: 2001 (Yorkshire), 2005 (Gloucestershire)
County cap: 2003 (Yorkshire), 2005 (Gloucestershire)
50 wickets in a season: 1
Place in batting averages: (2005 277th av. 10.50)
Place in bowling averages: 104th av. 39.67 (2005 30th av. 26.00)
Strike rate: 63.38 (career 49.64)
Parents: Paul and Alison
Wife and date of marriage: Sasha, 11 October 2003
Education: Elton High School, Walshaw, Bury, Lancs; Bury College
Qualifications: 10 GCSEs, BTEC/GNVQ Advanced Leisure and Tourism
Career outside cricket: 'Coaching, teaching'
Overseas tours: Yorkshire to Grenada 2001; ECB National Academy to Australia 2001-02; England A to India 2003-04
Overseas teams played for: Egmont Plains, New Zealand 1997-98
Cricket moments to forget: 'Being knocked out by Nixon McLean trying to take a return catch'
Cricketers particularly admired: Steve Waugh, Richard Hadlee, Glenn McGrath, Michael Atherton, Curtly Ambrose, Sachin Tendulkar
Other sports played: Basketball, table tennis, squash, golf – 'anything sporty and competitive'

Other sports followed: Football (Manchester United), rugby (Leicester Tigers)
Relaxations: 'Walking the dog; shooting; spending time with family; socialising with friends'
Extras: Formerly with Leicestershire but did not appear for first team. Took 14 wickets (41-18-47-14) in one day for Egmont Plains v Hawera in a New Zealand club match 1997-98. Took 7-50 in Kent's second innings at Headingley 2001, the best bowling figures by a Yorkshire player on first-class debut; Kirby had replaced Matthew Hoggard (called up by England) halfway through the match. Took 13-154 (5-74/8-80) v Somerset at Taunton 2003, the best match return by a Yorkshire bowler for 36 years
Best batting: 57 Yorkshire v Hampshire, Headingley 2002
Best bowling: 8-80 Yorkshire v Somerset, Taunton 2003

2006 Season

	M	Inn	NO	Runs	HS	Avg	100	50	Ct	St	Balls	Runs	Wkts	Avg	BB	5I	10M
Test																	
FC	15	22	11	106	19 *	9.63	-	-	3	-	3106	1944	49	39.67	5-99	1	-
ODI																	
List A	5	3	2	4	3 *	4.00	-	-	-	-	201	226	6	37.66	3-56	-	
20/20 Int																	
20/20																	

Career Performances

	M	Inn	NO	Runs	HS	Avg	100	50	Ct	St	Balls	Runs	Wkts	Avg	BB	5I	10M
Test																	
FC	76	106	36	553	57	7.90	-	1	16	-	13802	8345	278	30.01	8-80	10	3
ODI																	
List A	37	16	6	43	15	4.30	-	-	7	-	1467	1404	31	45.29	3-27	-	
20/20 Int																	
20/20	11	3	1	1	1*	.50	-	-	1	-	216	289	13	22.23	2-15	-	

KIRTLEY, R. J. — Sussex

Name: Robert James Kirtley
Role: Right-hand bat, right-arm fast-medium bowler
Born: 10 January 1975, Eastbourne
Height: 6ft **Weight:** 12st
Nickname: Ambi
County debut: 1995
County cap: 1998
Benefit: 2006
Test debut: 2003
ODI debut: 2001-02
50 wickets in a season: 7

Place in batting averages: (2005 227th av. 19.40)
Place in bowling averages: 111th av. 41.55 (2005 20th av. 24.33)
Strike rate: 78.88 (career 50.81)
Parents: Bob and Pip
Wife and date of marriage: Jenny, 26 October 2002
Family links with cricket: Brother plays league cricket
Education: St Andrews School, Eastbourne; Clifton College, Bristol
Qualifications: 9 GCSEs, 2 A-levels, NCA coaching first level
Overseas tours: Sussex YC to Barbados 1993, to Sri Lanka 1995; Sussex to Grenada 2001; England A to Bangladesh and New Zealand 1999-2000; England to Zimbabwe (one-day series) 2001-02, to Sri Lanka (ICC Champions Trophy) 2002-03, to Australia 2002-03 (VB Series), to Bangladesh and Sri Lanka 2003-04, to West Indies 2003-04 (one-day series)

Overseas teams played for: Mashonaland, Zimbabwe 1996-97; Namibian Cricket Board/Wanderers, Windhoek, Namibia 1998-99
Career highlights to date: 'My Test debut at Trent Bridge'
Cricket moments to forget: 'The three times I've bagged a pair'
Cricket superstitions: 'Put my left boot on first!'
Cricketers particularly admired: Curtly Ambrose, Jim Andrew, Darren Gough
Other sports followed: Rugby (England), football (Brighton & Hove Albion)
Relaxations: 'Inviting friends round for a braai (barbeque) and enjoying a cold beer with them'
Extras: Played in the Mashonaland side which defeated England on their 1996-97 tour of Zimbabwe, taking seven wickets in the match. Winner of an NBC Denis Compton Award for promising cricketers 1997. Leading wicket-taker in English first-class cricket 2001 with 75 wickets (av. 23.32). Sussex Player of the Year 2002. Made Test debut in the third Test v South Africa at Trent Bridge 2003, taking 6-34 in South Africa's second innings and winning Man of the Match award. C&G Man of the Match award for his 5-27 in the final v Lancashire at Lord's 2006. Vice-captain of Sussex 2001-05
Best batting: 59 Sussex v Durham, Eastbourne 1998
Best bowling: 7-21 Sussex v Hampshire, Southampton 1999

2006 Season

	M	Inn	NO	Runs	HS	Avg	100	50	Ct	St	Balls	Runs	Wkts	Avg	BB	5I	10M
Test																	
FC	8	10	5	118	36	23.60	-	-	2	-	1420	748	18	41.55	3-82	-	-
ODI																	
List A	18	5	1	8	4 *	2.00	-	-	4	-	780	597	32	18.65	5-27	2	
20/20 Int																	
20/20	7	3	2	3	1 *	3.00	-	-	2	-	144	215	2	107.50	1-22	-	

Career Performances

	M	Inn	NO	Runs	HS	Avg	100	50	Ct	St	Balls	Runs	Wkts	Avg	BB	5I	10M
Test	4	7	1	32	12	5.33	-	-	3	-	1079	561	19	29.52	6-34	1	-
FC	158	218	73	1878	59	12.95	-	3	52	-	30183	15725	594	26.47	7-21	29	4
ODI	11	2	0	2	1	1.00	-	-	5	-	549	481	9	53.44	2-33	-	
List A	200	74	35	352	30 *	9.02	-	-	57	-	8947	6783	298	22.76	5-27	5	
20/20 Int																	
20/20	21	7	2	5	2	1.00	-	-	3	-	394	502	16	31.37	2-8	-	

KLOKKER, F. A.   Warwickshire

Name: Frederik (Freddie) Andreas Klokker
Role: Left-hand bat, wicket-keeper
Born: 13 March 1983, Odense, Denmark
Height: 5ft 11in **Weight:** 14st 2lbs
Nickname: Kloks, J-Lo, The Great Dane
County debut: 2006
Parents: Peter Palle and Ingermarie
Marital status: Single
Family links with cricket: 'Dad played for Denmark for many years and is now head coach of Danish cricket. My two sisters played a bit when they were younger'
Education: Hindsholmskolen, Denmark
Qualifications: Levels 1 and 2 coaching. Levels 1 and 2 fitness instructor
Career outside cricket: Philatelist at Rock Stamp Company, West Midlands – firm in which former Warwickshire batsman Dominic Ostler is a partner
Off-season: Three months in Adelaide at the Darren Lehmann Academy
Overseas tours: Denmark U19 to South Africa (U19 World Cup) 1997-98; Denmark to Zimbabwe (ICC Emerging Nations Tournament) 1999-2000, to Canada

(ICC Trophy) 2001, to Ireland (ICC Trophy) 2005, plus various tours and tournaments in Europe and South Africa with Denmark and Denmark age-groups; MCC YC to Sri Lanka 2003-04

Overseas teams played for: Kerteminde CC, Denmark 1989-99; Skanderborg CC, Denmark 2000-01; South Perth CC 2001-02 – 2003-04; Prospect CC, South Australia 2006-07

Career highlights to date: 'Playing in the 1997 U19 World Cup in South Africa. Debut for Denmark. Debut for Warwickshire. Breaking record for most runs by an MCC Young Cricketer'

Cricket moments to forget: 'The game against the West Indies in the 1997 U19 World Cup'

Cricket superstitions: 'Not really'

Cricketers particularly admired: Waugh twins, Dominic Ostler

Young players to look out for: Michael Pedersen (MCC YC)

Other sports played: 'Played handball in the winter before I started going to Australia'

Other sports followed: Handball (GOG)

Favourite band: Live

Relaxations: 'Can't beat a good movie'

Extras: MCC Young Cricketer 2002-05, acting as substitute fielder for England in the first Test v New Zealand at Lord's 2004. Has represented Denmark in one-day cricket, including NatWest/C&G. Man of the Match v USA at Armagh in the ICC Trophy 2005 (149-ball 138*). Played for European XI v MCC at Rotterdam 2006. Played one first-class match and one C&G match for Warwickshire 2006 as injury cover in the wicket-keeping department, scoring 40 as nightwatchman v Sussex at Hove. Plays for Berkswell CC in the Birmingham & District Premier League

Best batting: 40 Warwickshire v Sussex, Hove 2006

2006 Season

	M	Inn	NO	Runs	HS	Avg	100	50	Ct	St	Balls	Runs	Wkts	Avg	BB	5I	10M
Test																	
FC	1	1	0	40	40	40.00	-	-	3	-	0	0	0		-	-	-
ODI																	
List A	1	1	0	6	6	6.00	-	-	-	-	0	0	0		-	-	
20/20 Int																	
20/20																	

Career Performances

	M	Inn	NO	Runs	HS	Avg	100	50	Ct	St	Balls	Runs	Wkts	Avg	BB	5I	10M
Test																	
FC	1	1	0	40	40	40.00	-	-	3	-	0	0	0		-	-	-
ODI																	
List A	12	10	1	241	138 *	26.77	1	1	14	3	0	0	0		-	-	
20/20 Int																	
20/20																	

KLUSENER, L.   Northamptonshire

Name: Lance Klusener
Role: Left-hand bat, right-arm
fast-medium bowler; all-rounder
Born: 4 September 1971, Durban,
South Africa
Height: 5ft 10in **Weight:** 12st 4lbs
Nickname: Zulu
County debut: 2002 (Nottinghamshire),
2004 (Middlesex), 2006 (Northamptonshire)
County cap: 2006 (Northamptonshire)
Test debut: 1996-97
ODI debut: 1995-96
1000 runs in a season: 1
Place in batting averages: 8th av. 65.84
Place in bowling averages: 89th av. 36.78
Strike rate: 65.21 (career 58.55)
Parents: Peter and Dawn
Wife and date of marriage: Isabelle,
13 May 2000
Children: Matthew, 23 January 2002; Thomas, 1 July 2006
Education: Durban High School; Technikon Natal
Career outside cricket: 'Farming – sugar'
Off-season: 'Natal Dolphins, fishing'
Overseas tours: South Africa U24 to Sri Lanka 1995; South Africa A to England
1996; South Africa to India 1996-97, to Pakistan 1997-98, to Australia 1997-98, to
England 1998, to New Zealand 1998-99, to UK, Ireland and Netherlands (World Cup)
1999, to Zimbabwe 1999-2000, to India 1999-2000, to Sri Lanka 2000, to Kenya (ICC
Knockout Trophy) 2000-01, to West Indies 2000-01, to Zimbabwe 2001-02, to
Australia 2001-02, to Sri Lanka (ICC Champions Trophy) 2002-03, to New Zealand
2003-04 (one-day series), to Sri Lanka 2004, to England (ICC Champions Trophy)
2004, plus other one-day tournaments in Kenya, Sharjah, Australia, Singapore and
Morocco; FICA World XI to New Zealand 2004-05
Overseas teams played for: Natal/KwaZulu-Natal 1993-94 – 2003-04; Dolphins
2004-05 –
Career highlights to date: 'World Cup Man of the Tournament [1999]'
Cricketers particularly admired: Malcolm Marshall, Shaun Pollock
Young players to look out for: Hashim Amla
Other sports played: Golf
Other sports followed: Rugby (Natal Sharks, Springboks)
Relaxations: 'Fishing, hunting'
Extras: Returned the best innings analysis by a South African on Test debut – 8-64 in
the second Test v India at Kolkata 1996-97. One of *South African Cricket Annual*'s

five Cricketers of the Year 1997, 1999. Scored 174 in the second Test v England at Port Elizabeth 1999-2000, winning Man of the Match award. His other Test awards include Man of the Series v Sri Lanka 2000. One of *Wisden*'s Five Cricketers of the Year 2000. Has won numerous ODI awards, including Player of the Tournament in the World Cup 1999. His domestic awards include Man of the Match in the SuperSport Series final v Western Province at Cape Town 2003-04 (7-70/5-90). An overseas player with Nottinghamshire at the start of the 2002 season; an overseas player with Middlesex 2004. Is no longer considered an overseas player. Scored 126* and 62 and had first innings figures of 4-50 on Championship debut for Northamptonshire v Essex at Chelmsford 2006; scored century (122) and followed up with first innings figures of 5-62 v Leicestershire at Oakham School 2006

Best batting: 174 South Africa v England, Port Elizabeth 1999-2000
Best bowling: 8-34 Natal v Western Province, Durban 1995-96

2006 Season

	M	Inn	NO	Runs	HS	Avg	100	50	Ct	St	Balls	Runs	Wkts	Avg	BB	5I	10M
Test																	
FC	16	26	7	1251	147 *	65.84	6	3	9	-	1239	699	19	36.78	6-69	1	-
ODI																	
List A	15	14	5	453	85 *	50.33	-	4	7	-	651	561	24	23.37	5-33	1	
20/20 Int																	
20/20	9	8	3	170	72 *	34.00	-	1	4	-	54	82	1	82.00	1-30	-	

Career Performances

	M	Inn	NO	Runs	HS	Avg	100	50	Ct	St	Balls	Runs	Wkts	Avg	BB	5I	10M
Test	49	69	11	1906	174	32.86	4	8	34	-	6887	3033	80	37.91	8-64	1	-
FC	160	225	49	6982	174	39.67	16	32	87	-	26465	12790	452	28.29	8-34	18	4
ODI	171	137	50	3576	103 *	41.10	2	19	35	-	7336	5751	192	29.95	6-49	6	
List A	289	235	85	5893	142 *	39.28	3	31	76	-	12131	9418	312	30.18	6-49	8	
20/20 Int																	
20/20	27	25	10	538	72 *	35.86	-	3	10	-	462	648	18	36.00	2-13	-	

49. Which recently retired first-class umpire became the first England player to score a century (107) at Lord's on Test debut, v West Indies 1969?

KNAPPETT, J. P. T.   Worcestershire

Name: Joshua (<u>Josh</u>) Philip
Thomas Knappett
Role: Right-hand bat, wicket-keeper
Born: 15 April 1985, Westminster, London
Height: 6ft **Weight:** 12st 4lbs
Nickname: Badger, Edwin (van der Sar)
County debut: No first-team appearance
Place in batting averages: 120th av. 32.85
Parents: Phil and Janie
Marital status: Single
Family links with cricket: Father is Youth
and Coaching Manager at Middlesex and has
played club cricket. 'Brother, Jon, plays
socially'
Education: East Barnet School; Oxford
Brookes University
Qualifications: 10 GCSEs, 3 A-levels,
Level 3 ECB tutor trained and assessor
trained cricket coach, swimming, football and rugby Level 1 coaching qualifications
Career outside cricket: Coaching and coach education
Overseas tours: MCC A to Canada 2005
Career highlights to date: 'Going on MCC A tour to Canada. Scoring 73 against
Bangladesh for BUSA. Winning *Evening Standard* Cup with Finchley CC (Middlesex
Premier League) 2004'
Cricket moments to forget: 'Being hit on the head by Jimmy Ormond on first-class
debut for OUCCE'
Cricketers particularly admired: Jack Russell, Adam Gilchrist
Young players to look out for: Eoin Morgan, Billy Godleman, Richard Jones
Other sports played: Squash, trampolining
Other sports followed: Football (Tottenham Hotspur)
Favourite band: 'Led Zeppelin, Jack Johnson, DJ Shadow, Montana, Hendrix,
Gomez etc.'
Relaxations: 'Listening to music, eating and sleeping (as well as training)'
Extras: Played for Oxford UCCE 2004-06. Represented British Universities 2005,
2006. Attended training camp in Mumbai, India 2005 (World Cricket Academy)
Opinions on cricket: 'Fast and furious – will only get better. The more interested the
public are, the more money will be around, which will improve standards.'
Best batting: 100* OUCCE v Durham, The Parks 2006

2006 Season (did not make any first-class or one-day appearances for his county)

Career Performances

	M	Inn	NO	Runs	HS	Avg	100	50	Ct	St	Balls	Runs	Wkts	Avg	BB	5I	10M
Test																	
FC	10	16	2	507	100 *	36.21	1	3	21	3	0	0	0	-	-	-	-
ODI																	
List A																	
20/20 Int																	
20/20																	

KNIGHT, N. V. Warwickshire

Name: Nicholas (Nick) Verity Knight
Role: Left-hand bat, right-arm medium-fast bowler, close fielder
Born: 28 November 1969, Watford
Height: 6ft 1in **Weight:** 13st
Nickname: Stitch, Fungus
County debut: 1991 (Essex), 1994-95 (Warwickshire)
County cap: 1994 (Essex), 1995 (Warwickshire)
Benefit: 2004 (Warwickshire)
Test debut: 1995
ODI debut: 1996
1000 runs in a season: 7
1st-Class 200s: 3
1st-Class 300s: 1
Place in batting averages: 88th av. 36.89 (2005 51st av. 45.25)
Strike rate: (career 249.00)
Parents: John and Rosemary
Wife and date of marriage: Trudie, 3 October 1998
Family links with cricket: Father played for Cambridgeshire. Brother Andy club cricketer in local Cambridge leagues
Education: Felsted School; Loughborough University
Qualifications: 9 O-levels, 3 A-levels, BSc (Hons) Sociology, coaching qualification
Overseas tours: Felsted School to Australia 1986-87; England A to India 1994-95, to Pakistan 1995-96, to Kenya and Sri Lanka 1997-98; England to Zimbabwe and New Zealand 1996-97, to Sharjah (Champions Trophy) 1997-98, to West Indies 1997-98 (one-day series), to Bangladesh (Wills International Cup) 1998-99, to Australia

1998-99 (CUB Series), to Sharjah (Coca-Cola Cup) 1998-99, to South Africa and Zimbabwe 1999-2000 (one-day series), to Sri Lanka 2000-01 (one-day series), to Zimbabwe (one-day series) 2001-02, to India and New Zealand 2001-02 (one-day series), to Sri Lanka (ICC Champions Trophy) 2002-03, to Australia 2002-03 (VB Series), to Africa (World Cup) 2002-03; FICA World XI to New Zealand 2004-05
Overseas teams played for: Northern Districts, Sydney 1991-92; East Torrens, Adelaide 1992-94
Cricketers particularly admired: David Gower, Graham Gooch
Other sports played: Rugby (Eastern Counties), hockey (Essex and Young England)
Relaxations: Eating good food, painting
Extras: Captained England YC v New Zealand YC 1989 and captained Combined Universities 1991. Gray-Nicolls Cricketer of the Year 1988, Cricket Society Most Promising Young Cricketer of the Year 1989, Essex Young Player of the Year 1991 and Essex U19 Player of the Year. Warwickshire vice-captain 1999. Leading English player (second overall) in the 2002 first-class batting averages with 1520 runs at 95.00. Warwickshire Batsman of the Year 2002. His international awards include Man of the Match in the first Test v Zimbabwe at Bulawayo 1996-97, Man of the [ODI] Series v Zimbabwe 2001-02 (302 runs; av. 100.67), and two successive ODI Man of the Match awards v West Indies 1997-98. Retired from international cricket in April 2003. Captain of Warwickshire 2004-05. Retired from county cricket at the end of the 2006 season
Best batting: 303* Warwickshire v Middlesex, Lord's 2004
Best bowling: 1-61 Essex v Middlesex, Uxbridge 1994

2006 Season

	M	Inn	NO	Runs	HS	Avg	100	50	Ct	St	Balls	Runs	Wkts	Avg	BB	5I	10M
Test																	
FC	17	30	1	1070	126	36.89	2	6	22	-	54	41	0		-	-	-
ODI																	
List A	14	13	2	441	128*	40.09	1	2	5	-	0	0	0		-	-	
20/20 Int																	
20/20	4	3	0	88	41	29.33	-	-	2	-	0	0	0		-	-	

Career Performances

	M	Inn	NO	Runs	HS	Avg	100	50	Ct	St	Balls	Runs	Wkts	Avg	BB	5I	10M
Test	17	30	0	719	113	23.96	1	4	26	-	0	0	0		-	-	-
FC	240	409	43	16172	303*	44.18	40	77	291	-	249	271	1	271.00	1-61	-	-
ODI	100	100	10	3637	125*	40.41	5	25	44	-	0	0	0		-	-	
List A	415	394	45	13478	151	38.61	30	68	174	-	90	89	2	44.50	1-14	-	
20/20 Int																	
20/20	23	22	2	584	89	29.20	-	5	9	-	5	4	0		-	-	

KRUIS, G. J. Yorkshire

Name: Gideon (<u>Deon</u>) Jacobus Kruis
Role: Right-hand bat, right-arm
fast-medium bowler
Born: 9 May 1974, Pretoria, South Africa
Height: 6ft 3in **Weight:** 12st 12lbs
Nickname: Kruisie
County debut: 2005
County cap: 2006
50 wickets in a season: 1
Place in batting averages: 268th av. 10.62
(2005 228th av. 19.33)
Place in bowling averages: 83rd av. 35.31
(2005 66th av. 30.64)
Strike rate: 60.15 (career 61.34)
Parents: Fanie and Hester
Wife and date of marriage: Marna,
29 June 2002
Children: 1
Family links with cricket: 'Brother-in-law (P. J. Kootzen) played first-class cricket
for Griquas and Free State'
Education: St Alban's College, Pretoria; University of Pretoria
Qualifications: BComm Hotel and Tourism Management
Off-season: 'Coaching cricket; commentary on local TV; property investment'
Overseas tours: MCC to Bermuda, to Denmark; South African Invitation XI
to Malawi
Overseas teams played for: Northern Transvaal 1993-97; Griqualand West
1997-2004; Goodyear Eagles 2004-05
Career highlights to date: 'Playing for Yorkshire and being Player of the Year
in 2005'
Cricket moments to forget: 'Any time I bowl badly!'
Cricket superstitions: 'Left boot on first; four knots when batting, five when bowling
on left boot'
Cricketers particularly admired: Allan Donald, Clive Rice, Richard Hadlee,
Dennis Lillee, Glenn McGrath, Steve Waugh
Young players to look out for: Steven Davies, Adil Rashid
Other sports played: Golf, squash
Other sports followed: Golf, football (Liverpool)
Injuries: Out for the first three weeks of the season with a calf strain
Favourite band: Green Day
Relaxations: 'Want to get into falconry'
Extras: Yorkshire Player of the Year 2005. Is not considered an overseas player
Opinions on cricket: 'I think the English game is healthy and that the proposed

reduction of overs in four-day cricket will be good. There could be more Twenty20 games instead of the Pro40 league. I do feel that two overseas [players] have made a difference, as long as they are available for most of the season.'

Best batting: 59 Griqualand West v Bangladeshis, Kimberley 2000-01
Best bowling: 7-58 Griqualand West v Northerns, Centurion 1997-98

2006 Season

	M	Inn	NO	Runs	HS	Avg	100	50	Ct	St	Balls	Runs	Wkts	Avg	BB	5I	10M
Test																	
FC	13	17	9	85	28 *	10.62	-	-	2	-	2286	1342	38	35.31	5-67	2	-
ODI																	
List A	9	4	2	52	31 *	26.00	-	-	2	-	342	328	7	46.85	2-38	-	
20/20 Int																	
20/20	9	1	0	1	1	1.00	-	-	2	-	175	214	8	26.75	2-19	-	

Career Performances

	M	Inn	NO	Runs	HS	Avg	100	50	Ct	St	Balls	Runs	Wkts	Avg	BB	5I	10M
Test																	
FC	105	151	45	1491	59	14.06	-	2	41	-	21716	10676	354	30.15	7-58	18	1
ODI																	
List A	103	50	17	404	31 *	12.24	-	-	26	-	4837	3793	121	31.34	4-26	-	
20/20 Int																	
20/20	13	1	0	1	1	1.00	-	-	3	-	271	286	12	23.83	2-15	-	

KUMBLE, A. Surrey

Name: Anil Kumble
Role: Right-hand bat, leg-spin bowler
Born: 17 October 1970, Bangalore, India
Height: 6ft 1in **Weight:** 12st 8lbs
County debut: 1995 (Northants), 2000 (Leics), 2006 (Surrey)
County cap: 1995 (Northants), 2000 (Leics)
Test debut: 1990
ODI debut: 1989-90
100 wickets in a season: 1
Place in bowling averages: 7th av. 22.00
Strike rate: 44.15 (career 58.51)
Education: National High School, Bangalore; National College and RV College of Engineering, Bangalore
Overseas tours: India to England 1990, to Zimbabwe and South Africa 1992-93, to Sri Lanka 1993, to New Zealand 1993-94, to England 1996, to South Africa 1996-97, to West Indies 1996-97, to Sri Lanka 1997, to Malaysia (Commonwealth Games) 1998-99, to Zimbabwe 1998-99, to Bangladesh (Wills International Cup) 1998-99,

to New Zealand 1998-99, to UK, Ireland and Netherlands (World Cup) 1999, to Australia 1999-2000, to Kenya (ICC Knockout Trophy) 2000-01, to South Africa 2001-02, to West Indies 2001-02, to England 2002, to Sri Lanka (ICC Champions Trophy) 2002-03, to Africa (World Cup) 2002-03, to Australia 2003-04, to Pakistan 2003-04, to England (ICC Champions Trophy) 2004, to Bangladesh 2004-05, to Zimbabwe 2005-06, to Pakistan 2005-06, to West Indies 2006, to South Africa 2006-07, plus other one-day tournaments and series in Sharjah, Sri Lanka, New Zealand, Singapore, Toronto, Zimbabwe, Bangladesh and Netherlands; Asian Cricket Council to Australia (Tsunami Relief) 2004-05, to South Africa (Afro-Asia Cup) 2005-06

Overseas teams played for: Karnataka, India 1989-90 –
Other sports followed: Tennis, football
Relaxations: Listening to music, watching television
Extras: Represented India U19. One of *Indian Cricket*'s five Cricketers of the Year 1993. One of *Wisden*'s Five Cricketers of the Year 1996. Took 10-74 (14-159 in the match) in the second Test v Pakistan at Delhi 1998-99, winning Man of the Match award; it was the first ten-wicket haul by a bowler in Tests since Jim Laker's 10-53 v Australia at Old Trafford 1956. Is India's all-time leading wicket-taker in Tests and ODIs; reached 500 Test wickets in second fewest matches (behind Muttiah Muralitharan) when he dismissed Steve Harmison in the second Test at Mohali 2005-06 in his 105th Test. His numerous other international awards include Man of the [Test] Series v England 1992-93 and v Sri Lanka 2005-06 and Man of the Match in the second Test v Australia at Chennai 2004-05 (7-48/6-133). Overseas player with Northamptonshire 1995; overseas player with Leicestershire 2000; an overseas player with Surrey 2006, leaving early because of a shoulder injury
Best batting: 154* Karnataka v Kerala, Bijapur 1991-92
Best bowling: 10-74 India v Pakistan, Delhi 1998-99

2006 Season

	M	Inn	NO	Runs	HS	Avg	100	50	Ct	St	Balls	Runs	Wkts	Avg	BB	5I	10M
Test																	
FC	3	2	1	14	8	14.00	-	-	4	-	840	418	19	22.00	8-100	2	1
ODI																	
List A	3	1	1	4	4 *		-	-	-	-	138	96	4	24.00	2-24	-	
20/20 Int																	
20/20	2	1	0	8	8	8.00	-	-	-	-	47	46	4	11.50	2-20	-	

Career Performances

	M	Inn	NO	Runs	HS	Avg	100	50	Ct	St	Balls	Runs	Wkts	Avg	BB	5I	10M
Test	110	140	27	2025	88	17.92	-	4	50	-	34890	15329	533	28.75	10-74	33	8
FC	216	277	56	5045	154 *	22.82	6	16	106	-	59915	25771	1024	25.16	10-74	69	19
ODI	264	131	46	930	26	10.94	-	-	84	-	14117	10122	329	30.76	6-12	2	
List A	373	198	72	1448	30 *	11.49	-	-	121	-	19868	13888	506	27.44	6-12	3	
20/20 Int																	
20/20	2	1	0	8	8	8.00	-	-	-	-	47	46	4	11.50	2-20	-	

LAMB, G. A. Hampshire

Name: Gregory (Greg) Arthur Lamb
Role: Right-hand bat, right-arm off-spin or
medium bowler; all-rounder
Born: 4 March 1981, Harare, Zimbabwe
Height: 6ft **Weight:** 12st
Nickname: Lamby
County debut: 2004
Place in batting averages: (2005 246th
av. 16.66)
Strike rate: (career 47.09)
Parents: Terry and Jackie
Marital status: Single
Children: Isabella Grace Saskia Lamb
Education: Lomagundi College; Guildford
College (both Zimbabwe)
Qualifications: School and coaching
qualifications
Overseas tours: Zimbabwe U19 to South

Africa (U19 World Cup) 1997-98, to Sri Lanka (U19 World Cup) 1999-2000;
Zimbabwe A to Sri Lanka 1999-2000
Overseas teams played for: CFX [Zimbabwe] Academy 1999-2000; Mashonaland A
2000-01

Career highlights to date: 'Playing against Australia. Making my first first-class hundred'

Cricket superstitions: 'Every time I hit a four I have to touch the other side of the pitch'

Cricketers particularly admired: Aravinda de Silva

Other sports played: 'All sports'

Favourite band: Matchbox Twenty

Relaxations: 'Fishing, playing sport'

Extras: Played for Zimbabwe U12, U15 and U19. Represented CFX [Zimbabwe] Academy, ZCU President's XI and Zimbabwe A against various touring sides. Scored 94 on Championship debut for Hampshire v Derbyshire at Derby 2004

Best batting: 100* CFX Academy v Manicaland, Mutare 1999-2000

Best bowling: 7-73 CFX Academy v Midlands, Kwekwe 1999-2000

2006 Season

	M	Inn	NO	Runs	HS	Avg	100	50	Ct	St	Balls	Runs	Wkts	Avg	BB	5I	10M
Test																	
FC	3	4	1	61	32 *	20.33	-	-	2	-	210	135	2	67.50	2-95	-	-
ODI																	
List A	13	10	0	231	64	23.10	-	2	12	-	232	223	11	20.27	4-38	-	
20/20 Int																	
20/20	8	7	2	183	55 *	36.60	-	1	3	-	58	92	4	23.00	3-23	-	

Career Performances

	M	Inn	NO	Runs	HS	Avg	100	50	Ct	St	Balls	Runs	Wkts	Avg	BB	5I	10M
Test																	
FC	29	44	5	903	100 *	23.15	1	5	24	-	1460	854	31	27.54	7-73	1	-
ODI																	
List A	44	38	4	814	100 *	23.94	1	4	26	-	494	440	17	25.88	4-38	-	
20/20 Int																	
20/20	21	18	2	372	67	23.25	-	2	7	-	106	161	8	20.12	4-28	-	

LANGER, J. L. Somerset

Name: <u>Justin</u> Lee Langer
Role: Left-hand bat, right-arm
medium bowler
Born: 21 November 1970, Subiaco,
Western Australia
Height: 5ft 8in **Weight:** 12st 4lbs
Nickname: JL
County debut: 1998 (Middlesex),
2006 (Somerset)
County cap: 1998 (Middlesex)
Test debut: 1992-93
ODI debut: 1993-94
1000 runs in a season: 3
1st-Class 200s: 10
1st-Class 300s: 1
Strike rate: (career 70.00)
Parents: Colin and Joy-Anne
Wife and date of marriage: Sue,
13 April 1996
Children: Jessica, 28 March 1997; Ali-Rose, November 1998; Sophie, April 2001;
Grace, November 2005
Family links with cricket: Uncle, Robbie Langer, played Sheffield Shield cricket for
Western Australia and World Series for Australia
Education: Liwara Catholic School; Aquinas College, Perth; University of
Western Australia
Overseas tours: Young Australia to England 1995; Australia A to South Africa
2002-03 (c); Australia to New Zealand 1992-93, to Pakistan 1994-95, to West Indies
1994-95, to South Africa 1996-97, to England 1997, to Pakistan 1998-99, to West
Indies 1998-99, to Sri Lanka and Zimbabwe 1999-2000, to New Zealand 1999-2000,
to India 2000-01, to England 2001, to South Africa 2001-02, to Sri Lanka and Sharjah
(v Pakistan) 2002-03, to West Indies 2002-03, to Sri Lanka 2003-04, to India 2004-05,
to New Zealand 2004-05, to England 2005, to South Africa 2005-06, plus other one-
day tournaments in Sharjah, Sri Lanka and Pakistan
Overseas teams played for: Western Australia 1991-92 –
Other sports played: Tennis, golf, Australian Rules, martial arts (has black belt in
zen do kai)
Other sports followed: Football (Man Utd), Australian Rules (West Coast Eagles)
Relaxations: Family, writing
Extras: Scored 54 (Australia's only 50 of the match) in the second innings of his
debut Test v West Indies at Adelaide 1992-93. Overseas player with Middlesex 1998-
2000; county vice-captain 1999 and captain 2000. Scored 166 for Middlesex v Essex

at Southgate 1998, in the process sharing with Mike Gatting (241) in a new Middlesex record partnership for the first wicket (372). Put on 238 for the sixth wicket with Adam Gilchrist as Australia successfully chased 369 to beat Pakistan in the second Test at Hobart 1999-2000; his 127 (coupled with 59 in the first innings) won him the Man of the Match award. His numerous other awards include Man of the [Test] Series v New Zealand 2001-02, and Man of the Match in the fourth Test v England at Melbourne 2002-03 (250) and in the first Test v West Indies at Georgetown 2002-03 (146/78*). One of *Wisden*'s Five Cricketers of the Year 2001. Became first Western Australian to make 100 Test appearances, in the third Test v South Africa at Johannesburg 2005-06. An overseas player with Somerset during the 2006 season as a locum for Daniel Cullen; has returned as captain for 2007. Scored 342 v Surrey at Guildford 2006, setting a new record for the highest individual first-class score by a Somerset player

Best batting: 342 Somerset v Surrey, Guildford 2006
Best bowling: 2-17 Australia A v South Africans, Brisbane 1997-98
Stop press: Retired from international cricket after the fifth Test v England at Sydney 2006-07

2006 Season

	M	Inn	NO	Runs	HS	Avg	100	50	Ct	St	Balls	Runs	Wkts	Avg	BB	5I	10M
Test																	
FC	2	3	0	390	342	130.00	1	-	1	-	0	0	0	-	-
ODI																	
List A	2	2	0	31	26	15.50	-	-	-	-	0	0	0	-	-
20/20 Int																	
20/20	8	8	1	464	97	66.28	-	4	3	-	0	0	0	-	-

Career Performances

	M	Inn	NO	Runs	HS	Avg	100	50	Ct	St	Balls	Runs	Wkts	Avg	BB	5I	10M
Test	100	173	10	7393	250	45.35	22	29	68	-	6	3	0	-	-
FC	291	511	48	23511	342	50.77	72	90	242	-	374	204	5	40.80	2-17	-	-
ODI	8	7	2	160	36	32.00	-	-	2	1	0	0	0	-	-
List A	182	175	18	6039	146	38.46	9	42	86	2	193	215	7	30.71	3-51	-
20/20 Int																	
20/20	8	8	1	464	97	66.28	-	4	3	-	0	0	0	-	-

LATOUF, K. J.   Hampshire

Name: <u>Kevin</u> John Latouf
Role: Right-hand bat, right-arm
medium bowler
Born: 7 September 1985, Pretoria,
South Africa
Height: 5ft 10in **Weight:** 12st
Nickname: Poindexter, Mushy, Latsy, Kev
County debut: 2005 (one-day),
2006 (first-class)
Parents: Colin and Josephine
Marital status: Single
Education: Millfield School; Barton Peveril
Sixth Form College
Qualifications: 11 GCSEs, 4 AS-Levels
Overseas tours: West of England U15 to
West Indies 2000, 2001
Overseas teams played for: Melville CC,
Perth ('briefly')

Cricket moments to forget: 'Golden duck in England U15 trial match'
Cricket superstitions: 'Don't believe in superstition'
Cricketers particularly admired: Ricky Ponting, Jonty Rhodes, Allan Donald
Other sports played: Tennis (county trials), rugby (Bristol and Somerset trials), golf
('fun'), surfing, snowboarding
Other sports followed: Rugby (Natal Sharks), football (Arsenal), AFL (Collingwood)
Favourite band: Coldplay
Relaxations: 'Prefer listening to R&B and hip hop; going out with mates from cricket,
Millfield and BP'
Extras: Played for West of England U13, U14 and U15. Played for ECB U17 and
ECB U19. Played in Hampshire's 2nd XI Trophy winning side 2003. Represented
England U19 2005
Best batting: 29 Hampshire v LUCCE, Rose Bowl 2006

2006 Season

	M	Inn	NO	Runs	HS	Avg	100	50	Ct	St	Balls	Runs	Wkts	Avg	BB	5I	10M
Test																	
FC	1	1	0	29	29	29.00	-	-	-	-	0	0	0		-	-	-
ODI																	
List A	1	1	0	10	10	10.00	-	-	-	-	0	0	0		-	-	
20/20 Int																	
20/20																	

Career Performances

	M	Inn	NO	Runs	HS	Avg	100	50	Ct	St	Balls	Runs	Wkts	Avg	BB	5I	10M
Test																	
FC	1	1	0	29	29	29.00	-	-	-	-	0	0	0		-	-	-
ODI																	
List A	10	9	2	76	25	10.85	-	-	6	-	0	0	0		-	-	
20/20 Int																	
20/20																	

LAW, S. G.   Lancashire

Name: <u>Stuart</u> Grant Law
Role: Right-hand bat, county vice-captain
Born: 18 October 1968, Brisbane, Australia
Height: 6ft **Weight:** 13st 7lbs
Nickname: Lawman, Judge
County debut: 1996 (Essex), 2002
(Lancashire)
County cap: 1996 (Essex), 2002
(Lancashire)
Benefit: 2007 (Lancashire)
Test debut: 1995-96
ODI debut: 1994-95
1000 runs in a season: 9
1st-Class 200s: 5
Place in batting averages: 29th av. 55.15
(2005 75th av. 39.00)
Strike rate: (career 101.31)
Parents: Grant and Pam

Wife and date of marriage: Debbie-Lee, 31 December 1998
Children: Max, 9 January 2002
Family links with cricket: 'Dad, grandad and uncles played'
Education: Craigslea State High School, Brisbane
Qualifications: Level 2 cricket coach
Career outside cricket: 'Desperately need to find one!'
Overseas tours: Australia B to Zimbabwe 1991-92; Young Australia (Australia A) to
England and Netherlands 1995 (c); Australia to India and Pakistan (World Cup) 1995-
96, to Sri Lanka (Singer World Series) 1996, to India (Titan World Series) 1996-97, to
South Africa 1996-97 (one-day series), to New Zealand (one-day series) 1997-98
Overseas teams played for: Queensland Bulls 1988-89 – 2003-04
Career highlights to date: 'Playing for Australia. Winning first Sheffield Shield for
Queensland [1994-95]'

Cricket moments to forget: 'None. There is always a funny side to things that happen. Some take longer to become funny!'
Cricket superstitions: 'None'
Cricketers particularly admired: Greg Chappell, Viv Richards
Young players to look out for: Mitchell Johnson (Queensland)
Other sports played: Golf ('very socially')
Other sports followed: Rugby league (Brisbane Broncos)
Relaxations: 'Spending time with friends/family; lying on a beach'
Extras: Sheffield Shield Player of the Year 1990-91. Captain of Queensland 1994-95 – 1996-97 and 1999-2000 – 2001-02; is the most successful captain in modern-day Australian domestic cricket, having captained his state to five Sheffield Shield/Pura Cup titles and to three one-day titles. One of *Wisden*'s Five Cricketers of the Year 1998. PCA Player of the Year 1999. Scored century (168) v Warwickshire at Edgbaston 2003, sharing with Carl Hooper (177) in a Lancashire record fifth-wicket partnership of 360 as the county scored 781. Lancashire Player of the Year 2003. Retired from Australian cricket at the end of 2003-04. Vice-captain of Lancashire since 2005. Is a UK citizen and is England-qualified
Opinions on cricket: 'There are too many players with too many wrong opinions on the game. We all love it – that's why we play it. If you don't love it, then find an office job that will give you more satisfaction.'
Best batting: 263 Essex v Somerset, Chelmsford 1999
Best bowling: 5-39 Queensland v Tasmania, Brisbane 1995-96
Stop press: Awarded Medal of the Order of Australia (OAM) in Australia Day Honours list 2007 for service to cricket as a state, national and international player

2006 Season

	M	Inn	NO	Runs	HS	Avg	100	50	Ct	St	Balls	Runs	Wkts	Avg	BB	5I	10M
Test																	
FC	16	23	3	1103	130	55.15	4	6	16	-	72	50	1	50.00	1-24	-	-
ODI																	
List A	13	11	3	411	78	51.37	-	5	3	-	0	0	0		-	-	
20/20 Int																	
20/20	8	8	1	225	62 *	32.14	-	2	2	-	0	0	0		-	-	

Career Performances

	M	Inn	NO	Runs	HS	Avg	100	50	Ct	St	Balls	Runs	Wkts	Avg	BB	5I	10M
Test	1	1	1	54	54 *		-	1	1	-	18	9	0		-	-	
FC	338	554	61	25060	263	50.83	75	115	378	-	8409	4215	83	50.78	5-39	1	-
ODI	54	51	5	1237	110	26.89	1	7	12	-	807	635	12	52.91	2-22	-	
List A	373	352	26	11301	163	34.66	20	60	149	-	3855	3166	90	35.17	5-26	1	
20/20 Int																	
20/20	25	25	2	734	101	31.91	1	5	8	-	6	10	0		-	-	

LAWSON, M. A. K.   Yorkshire

Name: <u>Mark</u> Anthony Kenneth Lawson
Role: Right-hand bat, right-arm
leg-spin bowler
Born: 24 November 1985, Leeds
Height: 5ft 8in   **Weight:** 12st ('approx')
Nickname: Sauce
County debut: 2004
Place in batting averages: 238th av. 15.50
Place in bowling averages: 78th av. 34.50
Strike rate: 47.76 (career 52.07)
Parents: Anthony and Dawn
Marital status: Single
Family links with cricket: 'Father played
local league cricket and encouraged me to
take up the game'
Education: Castle Hall Language College,
Mirfield, West Yorkshire

Qualifications: 11 GCSEs
Overseas tours: England U19 to Australia 2002-03, to Bangladesh (U19 World Cup)
2003-04, to India 2004-05
Cricketers particularly admired: Shane Warne, Gareth Batty
Other sports played: Football (school), rugby union (school, Cleckheaton 'in early
teens'), rugby league (Dewsbury Moor ARLFC 'in early teens')
Other sports followed: Rugby league (Bradford Bulls)
Relaxations: Music, dining out, cinema
Extras: Played for Yorkshire Schools U11-U16 (captain U13-U15); ESCA North of
England U14 and U15; North of England Development of Excellence U17 and U19.
Represented England U15, U17 and U19. Awarded Brian Johnston Scholarship. Voted
Yorkshire Supporters' Young Player of the Year 2003. 2nd XI cap 2006
Best batting: 44 Yorkshire v Hampshire, Rose Bowl 2006
Best bowling: 6-88 Yorkshire v Middlesex, Scarborough 2006

2006 Season

	M	Inn	NO	Runs	HS	Avg	100	50	Ct	St	Balls	Runs	Wkts	Avg	BB	5I	10M
Test																	
FC	7	10	2	124	44	15.50	-	-	5	-	1242	897	26	34.50	6-88	2	-
ODI																	
List A	2	2	0	7	6	3.50	-	-	-	-	84	88	2	44.00	2-50	-	
20/20 Int																	
20/20																	

Career Performances

	M	Inn	NO	Runs	HS	Avg	100	50	Ct	St	Balls	Runs	Wkts	Avg	BB	5I	10M
Test																	
FC	13	19	4	188	44	12.53	-	-	6	-	2187	1577	42	37.54	6-88	4	-
ODI																	
List A	4	4	0	30	20	7.50	-	-	1	-	118	141	3	47.00	2-50	-	
20/20 Int																	
20/20	2	1	1	4	4 *		-	-	1	-	48	87	3	29.00	2-34	-	

LEE, J. E. Yorkshire

Name: <u>James</u> Edward Lee
Role: Left-hand bat, right-arm medium-fast bowler; bowling all-rounder
Born: 23 December 1988, Sheffield
Height: 6ft 1in **Weight:** 11st 4lbs
Nickname: Brett, Bert, Bing
County debut: 2006
Parents: Diane and Steven
Marital status: Single
Family links with cricket: 'Dad played Yorkshire Colts when he was 18/19'
Education: Immanuel Community College
Qualifications: 8 GCSEs
Off-season: 'Studying at college'
Career highlights to date: 'First-class debut v Lancashire'
Cricketers particularly admired: Brett Lee, Darren Gough
Young players to look out for: Adam Lyth, Chris Allinson
Other sports followed: Football (Arsenal FC)
Favourite band: Razorlight
Relaxations: 'Snooker, poker (Texas Hold 'em)'

Opinions on cricket: 'More competitive; increases the entertainment from past years.'
Best batting: 21* Yorkshire v Lancashire, Old Trafford 2006

2006 Season

	M	Inn	NO	Runs	HS	Avg	100	50	Ct	St	Balls	Runs	Wkts	Avg	BB	5I	10M
Test																	
FC	1	2	1	22	21 *	22.00	-	-	-	-	54	36	0		-	-	-
ODI																	
List A																	
20/20 Int																	
20/20																	

Career Performances

	M	Inn	NO	Runs	HS	Avg	100	50	Ct	St	Balls	Runs	Wkts	Avg	BB	5I	10M
Test																	
FC	1	2	1	22	21 *	22.00	-	-	-	-	54	36	0		-	-	-
ODI																	
List A																	
20/20 Int																	
20/20																	

LEHMANN, D. S.   Yorkshire

Name: <u>Darren</u> Scott Lehmann
Role: Left-hand bat, slow left-arm bowler
Born: 5 February 1970, Gawler,
South Australia
Nickname: Boof
Height: 5ft 11in **Weight:** 14st 2lbs
County debut: 1997
County cap: 1997
Test debut: 1997-98
ODI debut: 1996
1000 runs in a season: 5
1st-Class 200s: 9
1st-Class 300s: 1
Place in batting averages: 4th av. 77.54
Strike rate: (career 75.72)
Wife: Andrea
Overseas tours: Australia to Sri Lanka
(Singer World Series) 1996-97, to New
Zealand (one-day series) 1997-98, to Sharjah (Coca-Cola Cup) 1997-98, to India
1997-98, to Pakistan 1998-99, to Bangladesh (Wills International Cup) 1998-99,

to West Indies 1998-99 (one-day series), to UK, Ireland and Netherlands (World Cup) 1999, to Sri Lanka 1999-2000 (one-day series), to Zimbabwe 1999-2000 (one-day series), to India 2000-01 (one-day series), to South Africa 2001-02, to Sri Lanka (ICC Champions Trophy) 2002-03, to Africa (World Cup) 2002-03, to West Indies 2002-03, to Sri Lanka 2003-04, to Zimbabwe (one-day series) 2004, to Netherlands (Videocon Cup) 2004, to England (ICC Champions Trophy) 2004, to India 2004-05
Overseas teams played for: Salisbury District CC (now Northern Districts), Adelaide; South Australia 1987-88 – 1989-90; Victoria 1990-91 – 1992-93; South Australia 1993-94 –
Other sports followed: Australian Football League (Adelaide Crows)
Relaxations: Golf, watching sport
Extras: Scored 1142 runs (av. 57.10) in his first full Australian season 1989-90. Pura Milk Cup Player of the Year 1999-2000. Was voted Interstate Cricketer of the Year 1999-2000 at the inaugural Allan Border Medal awards, also winning the award in 2000-01 and 2001-02. An overseas player with Yorkshire 1997-98, 2000-02, 2004 and 2006. Won the EDS Walter Lawrence Trophy for the fastest first-class century of the 2000 season – 89 balls for Yorkshire v Kent at Canterbury. One of *Wisden*'s Five Cricketers of the Year 2001. Yorkshire Player of the Year 2001. Is highest-scoring batsman in Sheffield Shield/Pura Cup history and was leading batsman in the Pura Cup 2005-06 with 1168 runs at an average of 89.84. His international awards include Man of the Match v Sri Lanka in the VB Series at Perth 2002-03 and in the third Test v Sri Lanka at Colombo 2003-04 (153 plus match figures of 6-92). Vice-captain of Yorkshire 2001; captain of Yorkshire 2002, the first overseas player to be appointed to the office. Captain of South Australia since 1998-99. *Wisden Australia*'s Cricketer of the Year 2004-05. Book *Darren Lehmann: Worth the Wait* published 2004. Scored 339 v Durham 2006 in his final innings for Yorkshire, setting several records including a new highest individual score for Headingley, eclipsing Don Bradman's 334 in 1930. Left Yorkshire at the end of the 2006 season, having scored 8871 first-class runs for the county at an average of 68.80 and been selected in the all-time Yorkshire XI by readers of the *Yorkshire Post*
Best batting: 339 Yorkshire v Durham, Headingley 2006
Best bowling: 4-35 Yorkshire v Essex, Chelmsford 2004

2006 Season

	M	Inn	NO	Runs	HS	Avg	100	50	Ct	St	Balls	Runs	Wkts	Avg	BB	5I	10M
Test																	
FC	15	23	1	1706	339	77.54	6	3	1	-	879	472	9	52.44	2-40	-	-
ODI																	
List A	11	10	3	489	118 *	69.85	1	3	1	-	366	273	5	54.60	2-38	-	
20/20 Int																	
20/20	9	9	3	252	48	42.00	-	-	4	-	162	180	8	22.50	3-19	-	

	M	Inn	NO	Runs	HS	Avg	100	50	Ct	St	Balls	Runs	Wkts	Avg	BB	5I	10M
Test	27	42	2	1798	177	44.95	5	10	11	-	974	412	15	27.46	3-42	-	-
FC	273	459	32	24865	339	58.23	80	107	139	-	8860	4219	117	36.05	4-35	-	-
ODI	117	101	22	3078	119	38.96	4	17	26	-	1793	1445	52	27.78	4-7	-	
List A	357	331	58	12620	191	46.22	18	91	104	-	5945	4461	167	26.71	4-7	-	
20/20 Int																	
20/20	11	11	3	254	48	31.75	-	-	4	-	192	214	9	23.77	3-19	-	

LETT, R. J. H. Somerset

Name: <u>Robin</u> Jonathan Hugh Lett
Role: Right-hand top/middle-order bat,
right-arm medium bowler
Born: 23 December 1986, Westminster,
London
Height: 6ft 2in **Weight:** 13st 5lbs
Nickname: Letty
County debut: 2006
Parents: Angela and Brian
Marital status: Single
Family links with cricket: 'Grandfather.
Peter Jacques, Leicestershire CCC'
Education: Millfield School; Oxford
Brookes University
Qualifications: 3 A-levels
Career outside cricket: 'Barman'
Off-season: 'Training with the Oxford
UCCE'

Overseas tours: Millfield School to South Africa 2000, 2002; West of England to
West Indies 2002
Career highlights to date: 'Championship fifty on debut v Glamorgan, August 2006'
Cricket moments to forget: 'Any time I have bowled'
Cricket superstitions: 'None'
Cricketers particularly admired: Nasser Hussain, Michael Atherton
Young players to look out for: Craig Kieswetter, Rory Hamilton-Brown
Other sports played: 'Any ball games'
Other sports followed: Football (Manchester United), rugby (Harlequins)
Favourite band: Oasis
Relaxations: 'Cards, swimming'
Extras: Somerset 2nd XI Player of the Year 2006
Opinions on cricket: 'The game is moving so fast it is difficult to know where to

start. I think it's important that we keep the traditional values of the game going – for example, more Test cricket and no technology for lbw decisions.'
Best batting: 50 Somerset v Glamorgan, Taunton 2006

2006 Season

	M	Inn	NO	Runs	HS	Avg	100	50	Ct	St	Balls	Runs	Wkts	Avg	BB	5I	10M
Test																	
FC	3	4	0	65	50	16.25	-	1	-	-	0	0	0		-	-	-
ODI																	
List A																	
20/20 Int																	
20/20																	

Career Performances

	M	Inn	NO	Runs	HS	Avg	100	50	Ct	St	Balls	Runs	Wkts	Avg	BB	5I	10M
Test																	
FC	3	4	0	65	50	16.25	-	1	-	-	0	0	0		-	-	-
ODI																	
List A																	
20/20 Int																	
20/20																	

LEVY, S. A. M.   Middlesex

Name: <u>Shaun</u> Anthony Matthew Levy
Role: Left-hand bat, right-arm medium-fast bowler
Born: 13 May 1988, Edmonton, Middlesex
Height: 5ft 7in **Weight:** 10st 4lbs
County debut: No first-team appearance
Parents: Bing and Delores
Marital status: Single
Education: Enfield Grammar School; University of Kent
Qualifications: 10 GCSEs, 2 AS-levels, ACVE Double Award Advanced Business
Career outside cricket: Student
Off-season: 'I am currently playing in the Kent Indoor League for the university and training hard for the coming season'
Career highlights to date: 'Getting 114 on my Middlesex 2nd XI debut in 2005 against Surrey'

Cricket moments to forget: 'Being dismissed on 99 for Middlesex 2nd XI against Essex'

Cricket superstitions: 'None'

Cricketers particularly admired: Andrew Strauss, Brian Lara, Shane Warne

Young players to look out for: Maurice Chambers

Other sports played: Football – Darwin College (University of Kent)

Other sports followed: Football (Arsenal)

Favourite band: Ludacris

Relaxations: 'Reading, music'

Extras: His Middlesex CCC age-group awards include Ron Gerard batting awards in 2001 and 2002. Winchmore Hill U15 Player of the Year 2002 and 1st XI Player of the Year 2005, 2006, scoring club record 987 runs (av. 75.92) in the Middlesex League 2006; scored 11 hundreds and 13 fifties in all cricket 2006. Middlesex CCC Young Player of the Year 2006

Opinions on cricket: 'The game is evolving more and more into a batsman's game and also batsmen are becoming increasingly aggressive.'

---

50. In 1994, which left-arm seamer
became only the second player to take a hat-trick
on Championship debut, for Leicestershire?

LEWIS, J.   Gloucestershire

Name: Jonathan (<u>Jon</u>) Lewis
Role: Right-hand bat, right-arm
fast-medium bowler, county captain
Born: 26 August 1975, Aylesbury
Height: 6ft 3in **Weight:** 14st
Nickname: Lewy, JJ, King Black
County debut: 1995
County cap: 1998
Benefit: 2007
Test debut: 2006
ODI debut: 2005
Twenty20 Int debut: 2005
50 wickets in a season: 6
Place in batting averages: 221st av. 17.93
(2005 181st av. 24.92)
Place in bowling averages: 6th av. 21.70
(2005 64th av. 30.44)
Strike rate: 39.43 (career 51.85)

Parents: John and Jane
Marital status: Married
Education: Churchfields School, Swindon; Swindon College
Qualifications: 9 GCSEs, BTEC in Leisure and Hospitality, Level III coach
Overseas tours: Bath Schools to New South Wales 1993; England A to West Indies
2000-01, to Sri Lanka 2004-05; England to South Africa 2004-05, to India (ICC
Champions Trophy) 2006-07, to Australia 2006-07 (C'wealth Bank series)
Overseas teams played for: Marist, Christchurch, New Zealand 1994-95; Richmond
City, Melbourne 1995-96; Wanderers, Johannesburg 1996-98; Techs CC, Cape Town
1998-99; Randwick-Petersham, Sydney 2003-04
Cricket moments to forget: 'Any injury'
Cricket superstitions: 'I always get a haircut if I go for a gallon'
Cricketers particularly admired: Courtney Walsh, Jack Russell, Jonty Rhodes
Other sports played: Golf (7 handicap), football (Bristol North West FC)
Other sports followed: Football (Swindon Town FC)
Favourite band: Brand New Heavies
Relaxations: Movies
Extras: Was on Northamptonshire staff in 1994 but made no first-team appearance.
Took Championship hat-trick (Gallian, Afzaal, Morris) v Nottinghamshire at Trent
Bridge 2000. Leading first-class wicket-taker among English bowlers in 2000 with 72
wickets (av. 20.91). Gloucestershire Player of the Year 2000. C&G Man of the Match
award for his 4-39 v Hampshire at Bristol 2004. ECB National Academy 2004-05,
2006-07. Took 4-24 v Australia at The Rose Bowl in Twenty20 International 2005.
Captain of Gloucestershire since 2006

Best batting: 62 Gloucestershire v Worcestershire, Cheltenham 1999
Best bowling: 8-95 Gloucestershire v Zimbabweans, Gloucester 2000
Stop press: Forced to return early from Australia tour 2006-07 with an Achilles injury

2006 Season

	M	Inn	NO	Runs	HS	Avg	100	50	Ct	St	Balls	Runs	Wkts	Avg	BB	5I	10M
Test	1	2	0	27	20	13.50	-	-	-	-	246	122	3	40.66	3-68	-	-
FC	13	17	2	269	57	17.93	-	1	4	-	2366	1302	60	21.70	7-38	4	2
ODI	4	2	0	9	7	4.50	-	-	-	-	222	117	7	16.71	2-11	-	
List A	13	7	1	50	26 *	8.33	-	-	2	-	678	398	17	23.41	4-14	-	
20/20 Int																	
20/20	6	4	1	81	43	27.00	-	-	2	-	132	242	6	40.33	3-44	-	

Career Performances

	M	Inn	NO	Runs	HS	Avg	100	50	Ct	St	Balls	Runs	Wkts	Avg	BB	5I	10M
Test	1	2	0	27	20	13.50	-	-	-	-	246	122	3	40.66	3-68	-	-
FC	158	222	47	2513	62	14.36	-	5	38	-	29767	15200	574	26.48	8-95	30	5
ODI	7	3	1	16	7 *	8.00	-	-	-	-	372	241	11	21.90	3-32	-	
List A	161	91	35	599	40	10.69	-	-	30	-	7557	5582	210	26.58	5-19	2	
20/20 Int	1	1	1	0	0 *		-	-	-	-	24	24	4	6.00	4-24	-	
20/20	19	8	4	116	43	29.00	-	-	2	-	391	543	26	20.88	4-24	-	

LEWIS, J. J. B.   Durham

Name: Jonathan (<u>Jon</u>) James Benjamin Lewis
Role: Right-hand bat
Born: 21 May 1970, Isleworth, Middlesex
Height: 5ft 10in   **Weight:** 12st 7lbs
Nickname: JJ, Judge
County debut: 1990 (Essex), 1997 (Durham)
County cap: 1994 (Essex), 1998 (Durham)
Benefit: 2004 (Durham)
1000 runs in a season: 4
1st-Class 200s: 1
Place in batting averages: 197th av. 22.18
(2005 136th av. 30.93)
Strike rate: (career 120.00)
Parents: Ted and Nina
Wife and date of marriage: Fiona,
6 July 1999
Children: Candice, Michael and Heather
Family links with cricket: Father played
County Schools. Uncle a lifelong Somerset supporter. Sister a right-arm
medium-fast bowler

Education: King Edward VI School, Chelmsford; Roehampton Institute of Higher Education
Qualifications: 5 O-levels, 3 A-levels, BSc (Hons) Sports Science, NCA Senior Coach
Overseas tours: Durham to Cape Town 2002, to Sharjah and Dubai 2005
Overseas teams played for: Old Hararians, Zimbabwe 1991-92; Taita District, New Zealand 1992-93; Eshowe and Zululand, South Africa 1994-95; Richards Bay, South Africa 1996-97; Empangeni, Natal 1997-98; Eshowe 1998-2002
Career highlights to date: 'Captaining Durham CCC'
Cricket moments to forget: 'Even the bad days are worth remembering: you always learn something'
Cricketers particularly admired: John Childs, Greg Matthews, Alan Walker, Shane Warne
Other sports followed: Soccer (West Ham United), rugby (Newcastle Falcons), 'most sports really'
Relaxations: Sleep
Extras: Hit century (116*) on first-class debut in Essex's final Championship match of the 1990 season, v Surrey at The Oval. Scored a double century on his debut for Durham (210* v Oxford University at The Parks 1997), placing him in a small club of players who have scored centuries on debut for two different counties. Scored 112 v Nottinghamshire at Riverside 2001, in the process sharing with Martin Love in a record second-wicket partnership for Durham (258). Became Durham's leading first-class run-scorer when he passed John Morris's record of 5670 runs during his 124 v Yorkshire at Headingley 2003. Durham Player of the Year and Batsman of the Year 2003. Captain of Durham 2000-04. Released by Durham at the end of the 2006 season
Best batting: 210* Durham v Oxford University, The Parks 1997
Best bowling: 1-73 Durham v Surrey, Riverside 1998

2006 Season

	M	Inn	NO	Runs	HS	Avg	100	50	Ct	St	Balls	Runs	Wkts	Avg	BB	5I	10M
Test																	
FC	9	16	0	355	99	22.18	-	2	5	-	0	0	0		-	-	-
ODI																	
List A	8	8	0	241	73	30.12	-	2	2	-	0	0	0		-	-	
20/20 Int																	
20/20																	

Career Performances

	M	Inn	NO	Runs	HS	Avg	100	50	Ct	St	Balls	Runs	Wkts	Avg	BB	5I	10M
Test																	
FC	205	365	26	10821	210 *	31.92	16	66	117	-	120	121	1	121.00	1-73	-	-
ODI																	
List A	237	215	42	4747	102	27.43	1	22	41	-	8	35	0		-	-	
20/20 Int																	
20/20	10	9	4	132	49 *	26.40	-	-	6	-	0	0	0		-	-	

LEWIS, M. L.   Durham

Name: Michael (<u>Mick</u>) Llewellyn Lewis
Role: Right-hand bat, right-arm fast bowler
Born: 29 June 1974, Greensborough, Victoria, Australia
Height: 6ft **Weight:** 13st 8lbs
Nickname: Billy
County debut: 2004 (Glamorgan), 2005 (Durham)
ODI debut: 2005-06
Twenty20 Int debut: 2005-06
Place in batting averages: 252nd av. 14.11
Place in bowling averages: 43rd av. 29.45 (2005 18th av. 23.61)
Strike rate: 50.14 (career 52.14)
Parents: Melva and Graeme
Marital status: 'Engaged to Christine'
Family links with cricket: 'Brother played local cricket'

Education: Parade College, Victoria
Qualifications: Horticultural Certificate III (Turf Management)
Career outside cricket: 'Golf course'
Off-season: 'Playing back in Australia'
Overseas tours: Australia A to Pakistan 2005-06; Australia to New Zealand (one-day series) 2005-06, to South Africa 2005-06 (one-day series)
Overseas teams played for: Northcote CC, Victoria; Victorian Bushrangers 1999-2000 –
Career highlights to date: 'Playing for Australia'
Cricket moments to forget: '0-113 off 10 overs in ODI' (*The most expensive figures in ODI cricket, returned in the fifth ODI v South Africa at Johannesburg 2005-06. Australia made 434-4; South Africa replied with 438-9*)
Cricket superstitions: 'None really'
Cricketers particularly admired: Rodney Hogg, Michael Holding
Young players to look out for: Dan Cullen, Cameron White
Other sports played: Aussie Rules
Other sports followed: Aussie Rules, golf, horse racing
Injuries: Out for four weeks with a hamstring injury
Favourite band: Live
Relaxations: 'Horse racing'
Extras: Victoria's leading wicket-taker in the Pura Cup 2002-03 (32; av. 28.53), 2003-04 (34; av. 27.85) and 2004-05 (38; av. 22.05). An overseas player with Glamorgan August to September 2004, deputising for Michael Kasprowicz; an overseas player

with Durham for parts of 2005, as a replacement for the injured Ashley Noffke, and in 2006
Opinions on cricket: 'Wickets are too slow and low.'
Best batting: 54* Victoria v New South Wales, Sydney 2001-02
Best bowling: 6-59 Victoria v Queensland, Melbourne 2003-04

2006 Season

	M	Inn	NO	Runs	HS	Avg	100	50	Ct	St	Balls	Runs	Wkts	Avg	BB	5I	10M
Test																	
FC	11	18	9	127	38	14.11	-	-	4	-	1755	1031	35	29.45	4-69	-	-
ODI																	
List A	11	4	2	8	4 *	4.00	-	-	1	-	472	424	8	53.00	2-26	-	
20/20 Int																	
20/20	8	3	2	20	11 *	20.00	-	-	-	-	174	199	14	14.21	4-19	-	

Career Performances

	M	Inn	NO	Runs	HS	Avg	100	50	Ct	St	Balls	Runs	Wkts	Avg	BB	5I	10M
Test																	
FC	75	104	31	672	54 *	9.20	-	1	35	-	13609	7458	261	28.57	6-59	7	-
ODI	7	1	1	4	4 *		-	-	1	-	341	391	7	55.85	3-56	-	
List A	86	25	12	109	19	8.38	-	-	21	-	4094	3319	111	29.90	5-48	1	
20/20 Int	2	0	0	0	0		-	-	1	-	45	49	4	12.25	2-18	-	
20/20	11	4	2	20	11 *	10.00	-	-	1	-	237	271	20	13.55	4-19	-	

LEWRY, J. D.   Sussex

Name: <u>Jason</u> David Lewry
Role: Left-hand bat, left-arm fast-medium bowler
Born: 2 April 1971, Worthing
Height: 6ft 3in **Weight:** 'Going up'
Nickname: Lew, Lewie
County debut: 1994
County cap: 1996
Benefit: 2002
50 wickets in a season: 5
Place in batting averages: 265th av. 11.12
Place in bowling averages: 9th av. 23.17 (2005 8th av. 21.75)
Strike rate: 52.03 (career 49.39)
Parents: David and Veronica
Wife and date of marriage: Naomi Madeleine, 18 August 1997
Children: William, 14 February 1998; Louis, 20 November 2000
Family links with cricket: Father coaches
Education: Durrington High School, Worthing; Worthing Sixth Form College

Qualifications: 6 O-levels, 3 GCSEs, City and Guilds, NCA Award
Career outside cricket: 'Still looking, but with more urgency with each passing year!'
Overseas tours: Goring CC to Isle of Wight 1992, 1993; England A to Zimbabwe and South Africa 1998-99
Career highlights to date: 'Winning County Championship 2003 and the month of debauchery that followed'
Cricket moments to forget: 'King pair, Eastbourne 1995'
Cricketers particularly admired: David Gower, Martin Andrews, Darren Lehmann
Other sports played: Golf, squash; darts, pool ('anything you can do in a pub')
Other sports followed: Football (West Ham United)
Favourite band: REM

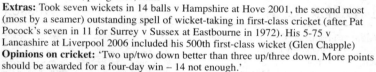

Relaxations: Golf, pub games, films
Extras: Took seven wickets in 14 balls v Hampshire at Hove 2001, the second most (most by a seamer) outstanding spell of wicket-taking in first-class cricket (after Pat Pocock's seven in 11 for Surrey v Sussex at Eastbourne in 1972). His 5-75 v Lancashire at Liverpool 2006 included his 500th first-class wicket (Glen Chapple)
Opinions on cricket: 'Two up/two down better than three up/three down. More points should be awarded for a four-day win – 14 not enough.'
Best batting: 72 Sussex v Surrey, The Oval 2004
Best bowling: 8-106 Sussex v Leicestershire, Hove 2003

---

51. Which England left-hander called time
on his international career in April 2003 after
exactly 100 ODIs (and 17 Tests)?

2006 Season

	M	Inn	NO	Runs	HS	Avg	100	50	Ct	St	Balls	Runs	Wkts	Avg	BB	5I	10M
Test																	
FC	16	19	11	89	27 *	11.12	-	-	10	-	2966	1321	57	23.17	6-68	2	-
ODI																	
List A	2	0	0	0	0		-	-	-	-	103	78	3	26.00	2-37	-	
20/20 Int																	
20/20																	

Career Performances

	M	Inn	NO	Runs	HS	Avg	100	50	Ct	St	Balls	Runs	Wkts	Avg	BB	5I	10M
Test																	
FC	152	205	53	1609	72	10.58	-	2	41	-	26524	14048	537	26.16	8-106	31	4
ODI																	
List A	76	44	15	217	16 *	7.48	-	-	13	-	3531	2712	100	27.12	4-29	-	
20/20 Int																	
20/20	11	4	1	10	8 *	3.33	-	-	4	-	197	239	14	17.07	3-34	-	

LIDDLE, C. J.   Sussex

Name: Christopher (<u>Chris</u>) John Liddle
Role: Right-hand lower-order bat,
left-arm fast bowler
Born: 1 February 1984, Middlesbrough
Height: 6ft 4in **Weight:** 12st 7lbs
Nickname: Lids, Chuck, Lido
County debut: 2005 (Leicestershire)
Place in bowling averages: 120th av. 43.45
Strike rate: 69.09 (career 76.72)
Parents: Pat and John
Marital status: Single
Family links with cricket: 'Brother plays for
Marton CC and Cleveland Schools county
team'
Education: Nunthorpe Comprehensive
School, Middlesbrough; Teesside Tertiary
College; TTE Advanced Modern
Apprenticeship
Qualifications: 9 GCSEs, qualified instrument technician, Level 1 coaching
Off-season: 'Training in Durban, South Africa'
Overseas teams played for: Balcatta CC, Perth (while attending Paul Terry Academy)
Career highlights to date: 'Making my Championship first-class debut [2006]'

Cricket superstitions: 'Right bowling boot on first for bowling; left pad on first for batting'
Cricketers particularly admired: Shaun Pollock, Brett Lee
Young players to look out for: Andrew Liddle, Mat Craven
Other sports played: Football, tennis
Other sports followed: Football (Middlesbrough)
Favourite band: Arctic Monkeys
Relaxations: 'Going to the gym or just hanging out with my mates'
Extras: Yorkshire Area Bowler of the Year 2001-02. Left Leicestershire at the end of the 2006 season and has joined Sussex for 2007
Best batting: 4* Leicestershire v West Indies A, Leicester 2006
Best bowling: 3-42 Leicestershire v Somerset, Leicester 2006

2006 Season

	M	Inn	NO	Runs	HS	Avg	100	50	Ct	St	Balls	Runs	Wkts	Avg	BB	5I	10M
Test																	
FC	6	6	3	6	4 *	2.00	-	-	2	-	760	478	11	43.45	3-42	-	-
ODI																	
List A	1	1	0	1	1	1.00	-	-	1	-	48	50	0		-	-	
20/20 Int																	
20/20																	

Career Performances

	M	Inn	NO	Runs	HS	Avg	100	50	Ct	St	Balls	Runs	Wkts	Avg	BB	5I	10M
Test																		
FC	7	6	3	6	4 *	2.00	-	-	2	-	844	523	11	47.54	3-42	-	-
ODI																	
List A	1	1	0	1	1	1.00	-	-	1	-	48	50	0		-	-	
20/20 Int																	
20/20																	

52. Which current county captain announced himself
by scoring 210* on his Championshp debut v Worcestershire
at Kidderminster in 1996 at the age of 18?

LINLEY, T. E. Sussex

Name: Timothy (<u>Tim</u>) Edward Linley
Role: Right-hand lower-order bat,
right-arm medium-fast bowler
Born: 23 March 1982, Leeds
Height: 6ft 2in **Weight:** 12st
Nickname: Joe Club, Sheephead,
Sloth, Bambi
County debut: 2006
Strike rate: (career 62.14)
Parents: Francis and Jane
Marital status: Single
Education: St Mary's RC Comprehensive;
Notre Dame Sixth Form College; Oxford
Brookes University
Qualifications: 10 GCSEs, 4 A-levels,
BSc (Hons) Geography/Theology
Career highlights to date: 'Playing for
British Universities v New Zealand in 2004.
Signing my first professional contract in 2005 for Sussex'
Cricket moments to forget: 'Being hit for six by my mate Pete "The Lumberjack"
Lawrence in a friendly held at Horsforth CC in 2005. I've never lived it down'
Cricketers particularly admired: Glenn McGrath, Shaun Pollock, Andrew Flintoff,
Jonty Rhodes
Young players to look out for: Steve Moreton
Other sports played: Pool, hockey (Leeds VIth team), badminton
Other sports followed: Football (Halifax Town FC)
Relaxations: 'Playing most other sports; historical fiction books, especially Conn
Iggulden, Bernard Cornwell, Christian Jacq; also Paulo Coelho books; watching films
or *Lost* or *Orange County* on TV'
Extras: Played for Oxford UCCE 2003-05. Represented British Universities 2004.
Won London County CC 'Search 4 A Star' bowling competition 2005. Released by
Sussex at the end of the 2006 season
Opinions on cricket: 'Lunch and tea breaks are not long enough. By the time I've
taken my size 13s off, it's time to go out again.'
Best batting: 42 OUCCE v Derbyshire, The Parks 2005
Best bowling: 3-44 OUCCE v Surrey, The Parks 2004

2006 Season

	M	Inn	NO	Runs	HS	Avg	100	50	Ct	St	Balls	Runs	Wkts	Avg	BB	5I	10M
Test																	
FC	1	1	0	0	0	0.00	-	-	-	-	162	56	1	56.00	1-56	-	-
ODI																	
List A																	
20/20 Int																	
20/20																	

Career Performances

	M	Inn	NO	Runs	HS	Avg	100	50	Ct	St	Balls	Runs	Wkts	Avg	BB	5I	10M
Test																	
FC	8	8	0	75	42	9.37	-	-	1	-	870	536	14	38.28	3-44	-	-
ODI																	
List A																	
20/20 Int																	
20/20																	

LOGAN, R. J.   Northamptonshire

Name: <u>Richard</u> James Logan
Role: Right-hand bat, right-arm fast bowler
Born: 28 January 1980, Cannock, Staffordshire
Height: 6ft 1in **Weight:** 14st
Nickname: Bungle
County debut: 1999 (Northants), 2001 (Notts), 2005 (Hants)
Strike rate: (career 57.16)
Parents: Margaret and Robert
Marital status: Single
Family links with cricket: 'Dad played local cricket for Cannock'
Education: Wolverhampton Grammar School
Qualifications: 11 GCSEs, 1 A-level
Overseas tours: England U17 to Bermuda (International Youth Tournament) 1997; England U19 to South Africa (including U19 World Cup) 1997-98, to New Zealand 1998-99
Overseas teams played for: St George, Sydney 1999-2000; Lancaster Park, New Zealand; Rovers, Durban; Northerns Goodwood, Cape Town
Career highlights to date: 'Winning junior World Cup'

Cricketers particularly admired: Malcolm Marshall, Dennis Lillee
Other sports played: Hockey
Other sports followed: Football (Wolverhampton Wanderers)
Relaxations: 'Spending time with my mates. Training'
Extras: Played for Staffordshire U11-U19 (captain U13-U17); Midlands U14 and U15 (both as captain); HMC Schools U15. 1995 *Daily Telegraph*/Lombard U15 Midlands Bowler and Batsman of the Year. Played for Northamptonshire U17 and U19 national champions 1997. Played for England U15, U17 and U19. C&G Man of the Match award for his 5-24 v Suffolk at Mildenhall 2001. Took 5-26 v Lancashire at Trent Bridge 2003, the best return by a Nottinghamshire bowler in the Twenty20 Cup. Left Hampshire at the end of the 2006 season and has rejoined Northamptonshire for 2007
Best batting: 37* Nottinghamshire v Hampshire, Trent Bridge 2001
Best bowling: 6-93 Nottinghamshire v Derbyshire, Trent Bridge 2001

2006 Season

	M	Inn	NO	Runs	HS	Avg	100	50	Ct	St	Balls	Runs	Wkts	Avg	BB	5I	10M
Test																	
FC	3	3	0	8	4	2.66	-	-	1	-	258	178	3	59.33	2-71	-	-
ODI																	
List A	1	0	0	0	0		-	-	-	-	6	16	0			-	-
20/20 Int																	
20/20																	

Career Performances

	M	Inn	NO	Runs	HS	Avg	100	50	Ct	St	Balls	Runs	Wkts	Avg	BB	5I	10M
Test																	
FC	46	64	13	494	37 *	9.68	-	-	15	-	6688	4473	117	38.23	6-93	4	-
ODI																	
List A	56	28	10	202	28 *	11.22	-	-	19	-	2260	2120	61	34.75	5-24	1	
20/20 Int																	
20/20	17	8	4	39	11 *	9.75	-	-	-	-	244	315	17	18.52	5-26	1	

LOUDON, A. G. R.   Warwickshire

Name: Alexander (<u>Alex</u>) Guy Rushworth Loudon
Role: Right-hand bat, right-arm off-spin bowler
Born: 6 September 1980, London
Height: 6ft 3in   **Weight:** 14st 8lbs
Nickname: Noisy, The Minotaur, Dolf, A-Lo, Minor
County debut: 2002 (one-day, Kent), 2003 (first-class, Kent), 2005 (Warwickshire)
County cap: 2006 (Warwickshire)
ODI debut: 2006
Place in batting averages: 170th av. 26.19 (2005 126th av. 32.07)

Place in bowling averages: 74th av. 34.28 (2005 92nd av. 36.64)

Strike rate: 67.03 (career 66.51)

Parents: Jane and James

Marital status: Single

Family links with cricket: 'Father and brother played at Hampshire CCC. Grandmother played for Hindleap Harriers CC'

Education: Eton College; Durham University

Qualifications: 9 GCSEs, 1 AO-level, 3 A-levels, 2.1 degree, ECB Level 1 coaching

Career outside cricket: 'Student. Setting up a gastropub in London called the Noisy Bear with my best friend'

Off-season: 'Studying for my CIMA exams. Training'

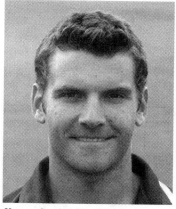

Overseas tours: England U19 to Malaysia and (U19 World Cup) Sri Lanka 1999-2000 (c); Kent to South Africa 2002; England to Pakistan 2005-06; England A to West Indies 2005-06, to Bangladesh 2006-07

Overseas teams played for: University, Western Australia 2005

Career highlights to date: 'Teaching J-Lo the doosra'

Cricket moments to forget: 'Running out the Hurricane at prep school'

Cricket superstitions: 'Not to have any!'

Cricketers particularly admired: Nick Knight

Young players to look out for: 'Tom Bristowe Jnr, Jamie Moyes III'

Other sports played: American football, golf, rackets, tennis

Other sports followed: Football (Man Utd, Brazil)

Injuries: Out for ten days with a neck injury

Favourite band: U2, The Levellers

Relaxations: 'Reading, studying, learning the guitar, TV, eating, travelling, photography, sleeping'

Extras: Captained England U15 in U15 World Cup 1996. Len Newbery Award for Best Schools Cricketer 1999. NBC Denis Compton Award for the most promising young Kent player 1999. Silk Trophy batting award 1999. Played for Durham UCCE 2001, 2002 and 2003, and was captain of Durham's BUSA winning side 2003. Represented British Universities 2003

Opinions on cricket: 'It is an exciting time for the game in England. Clever balancing is required to ensure its continued ascendancy in the public domain.'

Best batting: 172 DUCCE v Durham, Durham 2003

Best bowling: 6-47 Kent v Middlesex, Canterbury 2004

	M	Inn	NO	Runs	HS	Avg	100	50	Ct	St	Balls	Runs	Wkts	Avg	BB	5I	10M
Test																	
FC	17	26	0	681	123	26.19	1	5	12	-	2145	1097	32	34.28	5-49	2	-
ODI	1	1	0	0	0	0.00	-	-	-	-	36	36	0		-	-
List A	15	11	1	185	36	18.50	-	-	5	-	535	432	4	108.00	2-39	-
20/20 Int																	
20/20	3	2	0	39	27	19.50	-	-	1	-	72	65	8	8.12	4-20	-

Career Performances

	M	Inn	NO	Runs	HS	Avg	100	50	Ct	St	Balls	Runs	Wkts	Avg	BB	5I	10M
Test																	
FC	58	95	5	2724	172	30.26	2	17	41	-	6651	3732	100	37.32	6-47	6	-
ODI	1	1	0	0	0	0.00	-	-	-	-	36	36	0		-	-
List A	59	53	6	1031	73 *	21.93	-	7	21	-	1659	1351	35	38.60	4-48	-
20/20 Int																	
20/20	17	14	0	149	27	10.64	-	-	6	-	192	213	16	13.31	5-33	1

LOUW, J.   Middlesex

Name: Johann Louw
Role: Right-hand bat, right-arm medium-fast bowler; all-rounder
Born: 12 April 1979, Cape Town, South Africa
Height: 6ft 3in **Weight:** 14st
Nickname: J-Lo
County debut: 2004 (Northants), 2006 (Middlesex)
50 wickets in a season: 1
Place in batting averages: 249th av. 14.27 (2005 247th av. 16.29)
Place in bowling averages: 122nd av. 43.95 (2005 74th av. 32.36)
Strike rate: 74.74 (career 62.91)
Parents: Louis and Petro
Wife and date of marriage: Mardie, 17 December 2006
Overseas teams played for: Griqualand West 2000-01 – 2002-03; Eastern Province 2003-04; Dolphins 2004-05, 2006-07 – ; Eagles 2005-06
Extras: His awards include Man of the Match v Boland at Port Elizabeth in the SuperSport Series 2003-04 (124 and match figures of 5-131). Played for

Northamptonshire 2004-05 (2004 as an overseas player), in 2004 taking 60 first-class wickets at 26.51 and finishing as leading wicket-taker in Division One of the totesport League (34; av. 15.67). An overseas player with Middlesex 2006

Best batting: 124 Eastern Province v Boland, Port Elizabeth 2003-04
Best bowling: 6-51 Northamptonshire v Essex, Northampton 2005

2006 Season

	M	Inn	NO	Runs	HS	Avg	100	50	Ct	St	Balls	Runs	Wkts	Avg	BB	5I	10M
Test																	
FC	17	27	5	314	42	14.27	-	-	1	-	3214	1890	43	43.95	5-117	1	-
ODI																	
List A	16	10	2	147	39	18.37	-	-	3	-	735	582	20	29.10	2-19	-	
20/20 Int																	
20/20	8	6	1	17	13 *	3.40	-	-	1	-	177	265	12	22.08	4-18	-	

Career Performances

	M	Inn	NO	Runs	HS	Avg	100	50	Ct	St	Balls	Runs	Wkts	Avg	BB	5I	10M
Test																	
FC	77	113	17	1798	124	18.72	1	7	27	-	13716	7453	218	34.18	6-51	7	-
ODI																	
List A	81	59	12	896	72	19.06	-	3	10	-	3690	2915	123	23.69	5-27	3	
20/20 Int																	
20/20	20	11	2	49	17	5.44	-	-	4	-	412	563	23	24.47	4-18	-	

53. Which Glamorgan batsman scored 200* on first-class debut v Oxford University at The Parks in 1997?

LOWE, J. A. Durham

Name: <u>James</u> Adam Lowe
Role: Right-hand bat, right-arm
off-spin bowler
Born: 4 November 1982, Bury St Edmunds
Height: 6ft 2in **Weight:** 14st 10lbs
Nickname: Lowey, J-Lo
County debut: 2003
Place in batting averages: 258th av. 13.00
Parents: Jim and Pat
Marital status: Single
Family links with cricket: 'Dad played for
Northallerton CC and is a qualified coach'
Education: Northallerton College
Qualifications: Coaching Level 2
Overseas tours: Durham to India 2004
Overseas teams played for: Gosnells CC,
Perth 2003-04
Career highlights to date: '80 on my first-
class debut v Hampshire'
Cricketers particularly admired: Ritchie Storr, Paul Collingwood, Danny Law
Young players to look out for: Graham Onions
Other sports played: Football ('played for school and town as a youngster')
Other sports followed: Football (Middlesbrough)
Favourite band: Stone Roses
Relaxations: Eating out; watching Middlesbrough
Extras: Scored 80 on first-class debut v Hampshire at The Rose Bowl 2003. Released
by Durham at the end of the 2006 season
Best batting: 80 Durham v Hampshire, Rose Bowl 2003

2006 Season

	M	Inn	NO	Runs	HS	Avg	100	50	Ct	St	Balls	Runs	Wkts	Avg	BB	5I	10M
Test																	
FC	5	10	0	130	30	13.00	-	-	4	-	0	0	0		-	-	-
ODI																	
List A																		
20/20 Int																		
20/20																		

Career Performances

	M	Inn	NO	Runs	HS	Avg	100	50	Ct	St	Balls	Runs	Wkts	Avg	BB	5I	10M
Test																	
FC	9	18	0	341	80	18.94	-	1	6	-	0	0	0		-	-	-
ODI																	
List A	1	1	0	36	36	36.00	-	-	-	-	0	0	0		-	-	
20/20 Int																	
20/20																	

LOYE, M. B. Lancashire

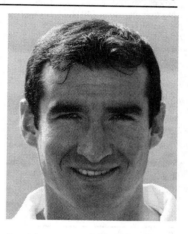

Name: Malachy (<u>Mal</u>) Bernard Loye
Role: Right-hand bat, off-spin bowler, occasional wicket-keeper
Born: 27 September 1972, Northampton
Height: 6ft 3in **Weight:** 14st
Nickname: Chairman, Jacko, Shermanator
County debut: 1991 (Northamptonshire), 2003 (Lancashire)
County cap: 1994 (Northamptonshire), 2003 (Lancashire)
1000 runs in a season: 5
1st-Class 200s: 2
1st-Class 300s: 1
Place in batting averages: 24th av. 58.90 (2005 36th av. 49.91)
Strike rate: (career 55.00)
Parents: Patrick and Anne
Marital status: Single
Family links with cricket: Father and brother played for Cogenhoe CC in Northampton
Education: Moulton Comprehensive School
Qualifications: GCSEs, 'numerous coaching certificates'
Overseas tours: England U18 to Canada (International Youth Tournament) 1991; England U19 to Pakistan 1991-92; England A to South Africa 1993-94, to Zimbabwe and South Africa 1998-99; Northamptonshire to Cape Town 1993, to Zimbabwe 1995, 1998, to Johannesburg 1996, to Grenada 2001, 2002; England VI to Hong Kong 2006; England to Australia 2006-07 (C'wealth Bank Series)
Overseas teams played for: Riccarton, Christchurch, New Zealand 1992-95; Onslow, Wellington, New Zealand 1995-96; North Perth, Australia 1997-98; Claremont, Perth 2001

Career highlights to date: 'PCA Player of the Year 1998'
Cricket moments to forget: 'Not being picked for 1995 and 1996 cup finals'
Cricket superstitions: 'None'
Cricketers particularly admired: Wayne Larkins, Gordon Greenidge, Curtly Ambrose, Devon Malcolm, Peter Carlstein, David Capel
Other sports followed: Football (Liverpool, Northampton Town), rugby union (Ireland), boxing
Relaxations: 'Playing the guitar, swimming, singing, reading. Having the odd large night out!'
Extras: Played for England YC and for England U19. PCA Young Player of the Year and Whittingdale Young Player of the Year 1993. Scored 322* v Glamorgan at Northampton 1998 (the then highest individual first-class score for the county), in the process sharing with David Ripley in a new record partnership for any wicket for Northamptonshire (401). PCA Player of the Year 1998. Scored century (126) on Championship debut for Lancashire v Surrey at The Oval 2003 and another (113) in the next match v Nottinghamshire at Old Trafford to become the first batsman to score centuries in his first two matches for the county
Best batting: 322* Northamptonshire v Glamorgan, Northampton 1998
Best bowling: 1-8 Lancashire v Kent, Blackpool 2003
Stop press: Called up to the England squad for the Commonwealth Bank Series in Australia 2006-07 as cover for the injured Michael Vaughan; made ODI debut v Australia at Brisbane, top-scoring with a 36-ball 36

2006 Season

	M	Inn	NO	Runs	HS	Avg	100	50	Ct	St	Balls	Runs	Wkts	Avg	BB	5I	10M
Test																	
FC	16	24	2	1296	148 *	58.90	6	6	6	-		0	0	0		-	-	-
ODI																	
List A	16	16	2	751	127	53.64	2	5	1	-		0	0	0		-	-
20/20 Int																	
20/20	2	2	0	25	18	12.50	-	-	-	-		0	0	0		-	-

Career Performances

	M	Inn	NO	Runs	HS	Avg	100	50	Ct	St	Balls	Runs	Wkts	Avg	BB	5I	10M
Test																	
FC	212	336	29	12839	322 *	41.82	38	52	104	-	55	61	1	61.00	1-8	-	-
ODI																	
List A	261	255	31	7904	127	35.28	10	52	61	-		0	0	0		-	-
20/20 Int																	
20/20	23	23	1	625	100	28.40	1	3	8	-		0	0	0		-	-

LUCAS, D. S. Northamptonshire

Name: <u>David</u> Scott Lucas
Role: Right-hand bat, left-arm
medium-fast bowler
Born: 19 August 1978, Nottingham
Height: 6ft 3in **Weight:** 13st 3lbs
Nickname: Muke, Lukey
County debut: 1999 (Nottinghamshire),
2005 (Yorkshire)
Strike rate: (career 55.23)
Parents: Mary and Terry
Marital status: Married
Education: Djanogly City Technology
College, Nottingham
Qualifications: 6 GCSEs, pass in Computer-
Aided Design
Overseas tours: England (Indoor) to
Australia (Indoor Cricket World Cup) 1998
Overseas teams played for: Bankstown-

Canterbury Bulldogs, Sydney 1996-97; Wanneroo, Perth 2001-02
Career highlights to date: 'Getting Man of the Match against Derbyshire in a
close fixture' (*4-27 v Derbyshire at Derby in the NUL 2000*)
Cricket superstitions: 'Always walk back to the left of my mark when bowling.
Always put left pad on first'
Cricketers particularly admired: Wasim Akram, Glenn McGrath, Steve Waugh,
Damien Martyn
Other sports played: Indoor cricket, football
Other sports followed: Football (Arsenal FC)
Relaxations: 'Food, cars, PS2, movies'
Extras: Won Yorkshire League with Rotherham in 1996. NBC Denis Compton Award
for the most promising young Nottinghamshire player 2000. Released by Yorkshire at
the end of the 2005 season; has joined Northamptonshire for 2007
Best batting: 49 Nottinghamshire v DUCCE, Trent Bridge 2002
Best bowling: 5-49 Yorkshire v Bangladesh A, Headingley 2005

Career Performances

	M	Inn	NO	Runs	HS	Avg	100	50	Ct	St	Balls	Runs	Wkts	Avg	BB	5I	10M
Test																	
FC	23	28	8	436	49	21.80	-	-	3	-	3314	1993	60	33.21	5-49	2	-
ODI																	
List A	35	13	3	109	32	10.90	-	-	4	-	1431	1386	44	31.50	4-27	-	
20/20 Int																	
20/20																	

LUMB, M. J. Hampshire

Name: Michael John Lumb
Role: Left-hand bat, right-arm medium bowler
Born: 12 February 1980, Johannesburg, South Africa
Height: 6ft **Weight:** 13st
Nickname: China, Joe
County debut: 2000 (Yorkshire)
County cap: 2003 (Yorkshire)
1000 runs in a season: 1
Place in batting averages: 69th av. 41.86 (2005 109th av. 34.35)
Strike rate: (career 49.00)
Parents: Richard and Sue
Marital status: Single
Family links with cricket: Father played for Yorkshire. Uncle played for Natal
Education: St Stithians College
Qualifications: Matriculation
Overseas tours: Transvaal U19 to Barbados; Yorkshire to Cape Town 2001, to Grenada 2002; England A to Malaysia and India 2003-04
Overseas teams played for: Pirates CC, Johannesburg; Wanderers CC, Johannesburg
Career highlights to date: 'Getting my Yorkshire cap'
Cricket moments to forget: 'Relegation in 2002'
Cricket superstitions: 'None'
Cricketers particularly admired: Graham Thorpe, Darren Lehmann, Craig White, Stephen Fleming
Other sports played: Golf
Other sports followed: Rugby union (Sharks in Super 14, Leeds Tykes)
Favourite band: Oasis

Relaxations: 'Golf, socialising with friends'
Extras: Scored maiden first-class century (122) v Leicestershire at Headingley 2001; the Lumbs thus became only the fourth father and son to have scored centuries for Yorkshire. Yorkshire Young Player of the Year 2002, 2003. ECB National Academy 2003-04. C&G Man of the Match award in the quarter-final v Northamptonshire at Headingley 2005 (89). Scored 98 v Durham at Headingley 2006, in the process sharing with Darren Lehmann (339) in a new record fourth-wicket partnership for Yorkshire (358). Left Yorkshire at the end of the 2006 season and has joined Hampshire for 2007
Best batting: 144 Yorkshire v Middlesex, Southgate 2006
Best bowling: 2-10 Yorkshire v Kent, Canterbury 2001

2006 Season

	M	Inn	NO	Runs	HS	Avg	100	50	Ct	St	Balls	Runs	Wkts	Avg	BB	5I	10M
Test																	
FC	16	25	2	963	144	41.86	2	7	10	-	6	6	0		-	-	-
ODI																	
List A	15	14	2	353	76	29.41	-	2	7	-	0	0	0		-	-	
20/20 Int																	
20/20	9	9	1	218	84 *	27.25	-	2	6	-	0	0	0		-	-	

Career Performances

	M	Inn	NO	Runs	HS	Avg	100	50	Ct	St	Balls	Runs	Wkts	Avg	BB	5I	10M
Test																	
FC	81	141	12	4286	144	33.22	8	25	48	-	294	212	6	35.33	2-10	-	-
ODI																	
List A	108	102	8	2649	92	28.18	-	18	32	-	12	28	0		-	-	
20/20 Int																	
20/20	26	26	3	442	84 *	19.21	-	4	8	-	36	65	3	21.66	3-32	-	

54. Who bowled New Zealand's Mark Richardson
to claim a wicket with his first ball in Tests on English soil
at Headingley in 2004?

LUNGLEY, T.   Derbyshire

Name: Tom Lungley
Role: Left-hand bat, right-arm
medium bowler
Born: 25 July 1979, Derby
Height: 6ft 2in **Weight:** 13st
Nickname: Lungfish, Monkfish, Sweaty,
Full Moon, Half Moon, Lungo
County debut: 2000
Strike rate: (career 51.18)
Parents: Richard and Christina
Marital status: 'Taken'
Family links with cricket: 'Dad was captain
of Derby Road CC. Grandad was bat maker
in younger days'
Education: Saint John Houghton School;
South East Derbyshire College
Qualifications: 9 GCSEs, Sport and
Recreation Levels 1 and 2, pool lifeguard

qualification, coaching qualifications in cricket, tennis, basketball, football
and volleyball
Career outside cricket: Painter and decorator
Overseas teams played for: Delacombe Park, Melbourne 1999-2000
Cricket moments to forget: 'Unable to speak when interviewed by Sybil Ruscoe on
Channel 4 Cricket Roadshow (live)'
Cricketers particularly admired: Ian Botham, Dennis Lillee, Courtney Walsh, Curtly
Ambrose, Brian Lara, Richard Hadlee, Glenn McGrath
Other sports played: 'Enjoy playing most sports, mainly football and basketball'
Other sports followed: Football (Derby County), basketball
Extras: First home-grown cricketer to become professional from Ockbrook and
Borrowash CC (for whom he struck the Derbyshire Premier League 2006 season's
best, 213 v Marehay). Took 4-13 v Nottinghamshire at Derby in the Twenty20 2003.
NBC Denis Compton Award for the most promising young Derbyshire player 2003
Best batting: 47 Derbyshire v Warwickshire, Derby 2001
Best bowling: 4-101 Derbyshire v Glamorgan, Swansea 2003

2006 Season

	M	Inn	NO	Runs	HS	Avg	100	50	Ct	St	Balls	Runs	Wkts	Avg	BB	5I	10M
Test																	
FC	1	1	1	27	27 *	-	-	1	-		96	88	2	44.00	2-59	-	-
ODI																	
List A	5	3	1	16	13	8.00	-	-	5	-	217	244	4	61.00	2-61	-	
20/20 Int																	
20/20	3	2	0	14	7	7.00	-	-	2	-	48	53	1	53.00	1-17	-	

Career Performances

	M	Inn	NO	Runs	HS	Avg	100	50	Ct	St	Balls	Runs	Wkts	Avg	BB	5I	10M
Test																	
FC	23	36	6	424	47	14.13	-	-	8	-	2508	1742	49	35.55	4-101	-	-
ODI																	
List A	57	35	9	353	45	13.57	-	-	15	-	2121	1812	61	29.70	4-28	-	
20/20 Int																	
20/20	16	10	3	97	25	13.85	-	-	5	-	264	324	15	21.60	4-13	-	

LYTH, A.   Yorkshire

Name: Adam Lyth
Role: Left-hand bat
Born: 25 September 1987, Whitby, North Yorkshire
Height: 5ft 10in **Weight:** 10st
Nickname: Pipe
County debut: 2006 (one-day)
Parents: Alistair and Christine
Marital status: Single
Family links with cricket: 'Dad and grandparents played cricket. Father Alistair played for Whitby and Scarborough cricket clubs and grandfather Peter kept wicket for Whitby'
Education: Caedmon School; Whitby Community College
Qualifications: GCSEs, Level 2 coaching certificate
Off-season: 'Practising and training ready for the next season. Hoping eventually to spend winter months abroad playing cricket'
Overseas tours: England U16 to South Africa 2004; England U19 to Malaysia 2006-07

Career highlights to date: 'Making my England U19 "Test" debut in 2006 and scoring 113. Also playing my first Pro40 game for Yorkshire against Hampshire, taking the field with Shane Warne and facing Shaun Udal when I was only 18'

Cricket superstitions: 'None'

Cricketers particularly admired: Craig White, Graham Thorpe

Young players to look out for: Adil Rashid

Other sports played: Football (played county level; plays for Scarborough FC U19; had trials with Man City and Sunderland); golf

Other sports followed: Football (Arsenal), 'any sport – sports mad'

Favourite band: 'All types of music; Jay-Z'

Relaxations: 'Golf, driving and socialising'

Extras: North Player of Tournament at Taunton at U13. Played in Bunbury Festival 2003. Led Yorkshire to U17 County Championship 2005. Represented England at all age-groups, including England U19 2006, scoring 64 and 113 on U19 "Test" debut v India U19 at Canterbury

Stop press: Called up to England U19 tour to Malaysia 2006-07 as replacement for Rory Hamilton-Brown

2006 Season

	M	Inn	NO	Runs	HS	Avg	100	50	Ct	St	Balls	Runs	Wkts	Avg	BB	5I	10M
Test																	
FC																	
ODI																	
List A	1	1	0	23	23	23.00	-	-	1	-	0	0	0		-	-	
20/20 Int																	
20/20																	

Career Performances

	M	Inn	NO	Runs	HS	Avg	100	50	Ct	St	Balls	Runs	Wkts	Avg	BB	5I	10M
Test																	
FC																	
ODI																	
List A	1	1	0	23	23	23.00	-	-	1	-	0	0	0		-	-	
20/20 Int																	
20/20																	

MADDY, D. L. — Warwickshire

Name: <u>Darren</u> Lee Maddy
Role: Right-hand bat, right-arm medium bowler
Born: 23 May 1974, Leicester
Height: 5ft 9in **Weight:** 12st 7lbs
Nickname: Roaster, Dazza, Fire Starter
County debut: 1993 (one-day, Leicestershire),
1994 (first-class, Leicestershire)
County cap: 1996 (Leicestershire)
Benefit: 2006 (Leicestershire)
Test debut: 1999
ODI debut: 1998
1000 runs in a season: 4
1st-Class 200s: 2
Place in batting averages: 146th av. 29.88 (2005 174th av. 26.40)
Place in bowling averages: 141st av. 51.27 (2005 118th av. 43.69)
Strike rate: 95.18 (career 60.41)
Parents: William Arthur and Hilary Jean
Wife and date of marriage: Justine Marie, 7 October 2000
Children: George William, 13 October 2005
Family links with cricket: Father and younger brother, Greg, play club cricket
Education: Roundhill, Thurmaston; Wreake Valley, Syston
Qualifications: 8 GCSEs, Level 1 coach
Career outside cricket: Fitness advisor
Off-season: 'Completing my benefit year and spending time with the family'
Overseas tours: Leicestershire to Bloemfontein 1995, to Western Transvaal 1996, to Durban 1997, to Barbados 1998, to Anguilla 2000, to Potchefstroom 2001; England A to Kenya and Sri Lanka 1997-98, to Zimbabwe and South Africa 1998-99; England to South Africa and Zimbabwe 1999-2000; England VI to Hong Kong 2003, 2004, 2005, 2006; Lord's Taverners to Dubai
Overseas teams played for: Wanderers, Johannesburg 1992-93; Northern Free State, South Africa 1993-95; Rhodes University, South Africa 1995-97; Sunshine CC, Grenada 2002; Perth CC, 2002-04
Career highlights to date: 'Winning two Championship medals. Playing for England. Winning Twenty20 final 2004 and 2006'
Cricket moments to forget: 'Too many to mention. I hate losing a cricket match and I hate getting out – losing two Lord's finals, finishing second in the Norwich Union League, and being relegated'

Cricket superstitions: 'Always put my left pad on first'
Cricketers particularly admired: 'Anyone who has made a success of their career'
Young players to look out for: George William Maddy
Other sports played: Touch rugby, golf
Other sports followed: Rugby (Leicester Tigers), football (Leicester City), baseball, golf, boxing – 'most sports really except for horse racing and motor racing'
Favourite band: 'Too many to mention – Two Tone Deaf, Bon Jovi, Def Leppard, Stereophonics, Aerosmith, Red Hot Chili Peppers'
Relaxations: 'Going to the gym, playing sport, spending time with my wife, Justine; listening to music, watching TV, going on holiday, scuba diving, bungee jumping, playing the drums'
Player website: www.darrenmaddy.com
Extras: Rapid Cricketline 2nd XI Championship Player of the Year 1994. Was leading run-scorer on England A's 1997-98 tour (687; av. 68.7). In 1998, broke the season record for runs scored in the B&H (629; av. 125.80), winning five Gold Awards. Scored 229* v Loughborough UCCE at Leicester 2003, in the process sharing with Brad Hodge (202*) in a record partnership for any wicket for Leicestershire (436*). Struck 60-ball 111 v Yorkshire at Headingley in the Twenty20 2004, in the process sharing with Brad Hodge (78) in a then competition record partnership for any wicket (167; still stands as first-wicket record). Scored 86* (also took a wicket and two catches) in the final of the Twenty20 Cup at Trent Bridge 2006, becoming the first player to pass 1000 career runs in the competition and winning the Man of the Match award. President of the Leicestershire School Sports Federation. Vice-captain of Leicestershire July 2004-2005. Left Leicestershire at the end of the 2006 season and has joined Warwickshire for 2007
Opinions on cricket: 'Regional cricket against touring sides. Championship cricket should be three two-hour sessions and no extra hour to be played. Two one-day competitions – Twenty20 and 50-over cricket.'
Best batting: 229* Leicestershire v LUCCE, Leicester 2003
Best bowling: 5-37 Leicestershire v Hampshire, Rose Bowl 2002

2006 Season

	M	Inn	NO	Runs	HS	Avg	100	50	Ct	St	Balls	Runs	Wkts	Avg	BB	5I	10M
Test																	
FC	11	19	1	538	97	29.88	-	4	16	-	1047	564	11	51.27	3-70	-	-
ODI																	
List A	16	16	1	565	167 *	37.66	2	2	11	-	376	292	10	29.20	3-24	-	
20/20 Int																	
20/20	11	11	3	313	86 *	39.12	-	3	12	-	162	192	7	27.42	2-10	-	

Career Performances

	M	Inn	NO	Runs	HS	Avg	100	50	Ct	St	Balls	Runs	Wkts	Avg	BB	5I	10M
Test	3	4	0	46	24	11.50	-	-	4	-	84	40	0		-	-	
FC	214	350	21	10673	229 *	32.44	19	53	228	-	10452	5734	173	33.14	5-37	4	-
ODI	8	6	0	113	53	18.83	-	1	1	-	0	0	0		-	-	
List A	295	272	29	7388	167 *	30.40	9	44	111	-	5960	5027	176	28.56	4-16	-	
20/20 Int																	
20/20	35	35	4	1111	111	35.83	1	9	21	-	470	598	19	31.47	2-10	-	

MAHER, J. P.   Durham

Name: James (Jimmy) Patrick Maher
Role: Left-hand bat, right-arm medium bowler, occasional wicket-keeper
Born: 27 February 1974, Innisfail, Queensland, Australia
Height: 6ft **Weight:** 13st 5lbs
Nickname: Rock, Mahbo
County debut: 2001 (Glamorgan), 2005 (Durham)
County cap: 2001 (Glamorgan)
ODI debut: 1997-98
1000 runs in a season: 1
1st-Class 200s: 4
Place in batting averages: 101st av. 34.92
Strike rate: (career 85.20)
Parents: Marie Ann and Warren George
Wife and date of marriage: Debbie, 6 April 2001
Children: Lily Matilda, 2002
Family links with cricket: Father and uncle played for Queensland Country
Education: St Augustine's College, Cairns; Nudgee College, Brisbane
Overseas tours: Australia U19 to New Zealand 1992-93; Queensland Academy to South Africa 1993; Australia to South Africa 2001-02 (one-day series), to Kenya (PSO Tri-Nation Tournament) 2002, to Sri Lanka (ICC Champions Trophy) 2002-03, to Africa (World Cup) 2002-03, to West Indies 2002-03 (one-day series), to India (TVS Cup) 2003-04
Overseas teams played for: Queensland 1993-94 –
Career highlights to date: 'Playing for Australia. Being part of Queensland's first ever Sheffield Shield title win at The Gabba [1994-95]'
Cricket moments to forget: 'Running out Allan Border on my debut'
Cricketers particularly admired: Allan Border, Matt Hayden, Shane Warne, Glenn McGrath

Young players to look out for: Mark Wallace, Mitchell Johnson
Other sports played: Squash ('played State titles U12-U16'), tennis ('ranked in top ten in Queensland at U14')
Other sports followed: Rugby union (Queensland Reds), rugby league (Canterbury Bulldogs)
Relaxations: 'Golf, dinner with friends, couple of lagers with mates'
Extras: Represented Australia U17 and U19. Attended Australian Cricket Academy 1993. Was Glamorgan's overseas player in 2001, returning in 2003. Pura Cup Player of the Year 2001-02 (jointly with Brad Hodge of Victoria) and *Wisden Australia*'s Pura Cup Cricketer of the Year 2002-03. Recalled to Australia's one-day squad for tour of South Africa 2001-02 and was Man of the Match in his first two ODIs since 1997-98 (95 and 43*). His other match awards include Man of the Match in the ING Cup final 2004-05 v Tasmania at The Gabba (104) and in the Pura Cup final 2005-06 at The Gabba (223 out of Queensland's 900-6 dec). Captain of Queensland since 2002-03 and has captained Australia A. Was an overseas player with Durham during the 2005 season, as a locum for Mike Hussey; and in 2006
Best batting: 223 Queensland v Victoria, Brisbane 2005-06
Best bowling: 3-11 Queensland v Western Australia, Perth 1995-96

2006 Season

	M	Inn	NO	Runs	HS	Avg	100	50	Ct	St	Balls	Runs	Wkts	Avg	BB	5I	10M
Test																	
FC	16	30	2	978	106	34.92	2	4	12	1	0	0	0		-	-	-
ODI																	
List A	15	15	1	595	125	42.50	3	1	8	-	0	0	0		-	-	
20/20 Int																	
20/20	8	8	2	177	55 *	29.50	-	2	2	-	0	0	0		-	-	

Career Performances

	M	Inn	NO	Runs	HS	Avg	100	50	Ct	St	Balls	Runs	Wkts	Avg	BB	5I	10M
Test																	
FC	178	318	30	11972	223	41.56	25	58	181	3	852	504	10	50.40	3-11	-	-
ODI	26	20	3	438	95	25.76	-	1	18	-	0	0	0		-	-	
List A	188	182	17	6662	187	40.37	14	32	95	1	163	168	6	28.00	3-29	-	
20/20 Int																	
20/20	10	10	2	244	59	30.50	-	3	2	-	0	0	0		-	-	

MAHMOOD, S. I.   Lancashire

Name: Sajid Iqbal Mahmood
Role: Right-hand bat, right-arm
fast-medium bowler
Born: 21 December 1981, Bolton
Height: 6ft 4in **Weight:** 12st 7lbs
Nickname: Saj, King
County debut: 2002
Test debut: 2006
ODI debut: 2004
Twenty20 Int debut: 2006
Place in batting averages: 266th av. 11.00
(2005 236th av. 17.70)
Place in bowling averages: 21st av. 25.69
(2005 94th av. 37.21)
Strike rate: 44.77 (career 48.80)
Parents: Shahid and Femida
Marital status: Single
Family links with cricket: Father played in
Bolton League; younger brother plays in Bolton League
Education: Smithills School; North College, Bolton (sixth form)
Qualifications: 9 GCSEs, 3 A-levels
Overseas tours: Lancashire to South Africa 2003; England A to Malaysia and India
2003-04, to Sri Lanka 2004-05, to West Indies 2005-06; England to India 2005-06
(one-day series), to India (ICC Champions Trophy) 2006-07, to Australia 2006-07
Overseas teams played for: Napier, New Zealand 2002-03
Cricket moments to forget: 'None'
Cricket superstitions: 'None'
Cricketers particularly admired: Brett Lee, Shoaib Akhtar
Favourite band: Nelly, Eminem
Relaxations: 'Music and chillin' with mates'
Extras: Took 5-62 for England A v East Zone at Amritsar 2003-04. NBC Denis
Compton Award for the most promising young Lancashire player 2003. Struck 66-ball
94 in Championship v Sussex at Old Trafford 2004. Man of the Match in the fifth ODI
v Pakistan at Edgbaston 2006 (10-2-24-2). ECB National Academy 2003-04, 2004-05,
2005-06. Is cousin of boxer Amir Khan
Best batting: 94 Lancashire v Sussex, Old Trafford 2004
Best bowling: 5-37 Lancashire v DUCCE, Durham 2003

2006 Season

	M	Inn	NO	Runs	HS	Avg	100	50	Ct	St	Balls	Runs	Wkts	Avg	BB	5I	10M
Test	5	5	1	63	34	15.75	-	-	-	-	822	498	15	33.20	4-22	-	-
FC	9	10	1	99	34	11.00	-	-	1	-	1612	925	36	25.69	5-52	1	-
ODI	7	5	1	35	22 *	8.75	-	-	-	-	288	321	7	45.85	2-24	-	
List A	12	7	2	44	22 *	8.80	-	-	3	-	476	440	16	27.50	3-16	-	
20/20 Int	2	1	1	0	0 *		-	-	-	-	42	63	1	63.00	1-34	-	
20/20	4	2	2	16	16 *		-	-	-	-	84	116	3	38.66	1-17	-	

Career Performances

	M	Inn	NO	Runs	HS	Avg	100	50	Ct	St	Balls	Runs	Wkts	Avg	BB	5I	10M
Test	5	5	1	63	34	15.75	-	-	-	-	822	498	15	33.20	4-22	-	-
FC	40	50	7	655	94	15.23	-	2	7	-	5613	3450	115	30.00	5-37	3	-
ODI	12	8	1	53	22 *	7.57	-	-	-	-	528	562	12	46.83	3-37	-	
List A	73	44	12	275	29	8.59	-	-	7	-	3149	2651	105	25.24	4-37	-	
20/20 Int	2	1	1	0	0 *		-	-	-	-	42	63	1	63.00	1-34	-	
20/20	12	6	2	38	21	9.50	-	-	-	-	252	332	6	55.33	1-17	-	

MAHOMED, U.   Durham

Name: Uzair Mahomed
Role: Right-hand middle-order bat,
right-arm off-spin bowler
Born: 20 August 1987, Johannesburg,
South Africa
Height: 5ft 9in **Weight:** 11st
Nickname: Uzi
County debut: No first-team appearance
Parents: Ishtiyak and Faghmida
Marital status: Single
Family links with cricket: Father captained
Transvaal High Schools on four occasions
and played for South African Schools twice.
Brother, Sarfaraaz, played for Yorkshire
Schools and Yorkshire Academy
Education: Bradford Grammar School;
Woodhouse Grove
Qualifications: 10 GCSEs, 3 A-levels
Off-season: 'Playing cricket in South Africa'
Overseas tours: Two school tours to West Indies
Overseas teams played for: Delfos, Gauteng 2005, 2006
Career highlights to date: '165 off 113 balls for Bradford & Bingley 2nd XI at age of

15; 118 off 114 balls for Durham 2nd XI v Lancashire 2nd XI 2006; 102 off 89 balls for Durham Academy v Sussex Academy 2006'

Cricket moments to forget: 'Any dropped catch'

Cricket superstitions: 'None'

Cricketers particularly admired: Shaun Pollock, Hansie Cronje, Jonty Rhodes

Young players to look out for: Adil Rashid, Mark Stoneman

Other sports played: Golf, table tennis (school)

Other sports followed: Football (Liverpool, England)

Favourite band: Eminem

Relaxations: 'Watching sport on TV and reading cricket autobiographies'

Extras: Youngest centurion for Bradford Grammar School (record previously held by Ashley Metcalfe). National U15 championship winner (Yorkshire Schools). Played for Northumberland in the Minor Counties Championship 2005

Extras: 'The game is becoming more professional. Fitness levels and mental strength are key to success.'

MALAN, D. J. Middlesex

Name: <u>Dawid</u> Johannes Malan

Role: Left-hand bat, right-arm leg-spin bowler

Born: 3 September 1987, Roehampton, London

Height: 6ft **Weight:** 13st

Nickname: AC ('as in AC Milan')

County debut: 2006 (one-day)

Strike rate: (career 53.00)

Parents: Dawid and Janet

Family links with cricket: 'My father played for the University of Stellenbosch and for the Western Province B cricket team. My brother (Charl) is currently at the Eric Simons Cricket Academy'

Education: Paarl Boys' High, South Africa; UNISA

Qualifications: School

Career outside cricket: 'Studying psychology through UNISA'

Off-season: 'Playing club cricket in South Africa'

Overseas teams played for: Wellington CC 2005-06 – 2006-07; Boland 2005-06; Western Province/Boland Cricket Academy 2006

Career highlights to date: 'Playing for Middlesex in a Twenty20 game against Surrey at The Oval in front of a packed house'

Cricket moments to forget: 'Getting a first-ball in my school's yearly interschool match in my final year at school'
Cricket superstitions: 'The way I pack my cricket bag'
Cricketers particularly admired: Gary Kirsten
Young players to look out for: Eoin Morgan
Other sports played: Rugby, golf
Other sports followed: Rugby (Blue Bulls)
Injuries: Stress fracture in the lower back
Favourite band: The Killers
Relaxations: 'Just started to get into fishing'
Extras: Boland U19 Provincial Player of the Year 2005. Wellington CC Player of the Year 2005-06. Western Province/Boland Academy Player of the Year 2006. Is not considered an overseas player
Opinions on cricket: 'In my opinion the game has changed dramatically in the past few years. The introduction of Twenty20 has changed the mindset of batsmen and caused them to become more attacking in all forms of the game, which in turn has made cricket more exciting.'
Best batting: 64 Boland v Border, Paarl 2005-06
Best bowling: 1-22 Boland v Eastern Province, Port Elizabeth 2005-06

2006 Season

	M	Inn	NO	Runs	HS	Avg	100	50	Ct	St	Balls	Runs	Wkts	Avg	BB	5I	10M
Test																	
FC																	
ODI																	
List A																	
20/20 Int																	
20/20	1	1	0	11	11	11.00	-	-	-	-	0	0	0			-	-

Career Performances

	M	Inn	NO	Runs	HS	Avg	100	50	Ct	St	Balls	Runs	Wkts	Avg	BB	5I	10M
Test																	
FC	4	7	0	158	64	22.57	-	1	2	-	159	152	3	50.66	1-22	-	-
ODI																	
List A	5	5	0	90	42	18.00	-	-	-	-	6	13	0			-	-
20/20 Int																	
20/20	1	1	0	11	11	11.00	-	-	-	-	0	0	0			-	-

MALIK, M. N. Worcestershire

Name: Muhammad <u>Nadeem</u> Malik
Role: Right-hand bat, right-arm
fast-medium bowler
Born: 6 October 1982, Nottingham
Height: 6ft 5in **Weight:** 14st 7lbs
Nickname: Nad, Busta, Nigel, Gerz
County debut: 2001 (Nottinghamshire),
2004 (Worcestershire)
County colours: 2004 (Worcestershire)
Place in batting averages: 264th av. 11.33
Place in bowling averages: 54th av. 31.52
(2005 49th av. 27.83)
Strike rate: 48.35 (career 49.24)
Parents: Abdul and Arshad
Marital status: Single
Family links with cricket: Brother plays
club cricket for Carrington

Education: Wilford Meadows Secondary
School; Bilborough College
Qualifications: 9 GCSEs
Career outside cricket: Personal trainer
Overseas tours: ZRK to Pakistan 2000; Nottinghamshire to South Africa 2001;
England U19 to India 2000-01, to Australia and (U19 World Cup) New Zealand
2001-02
Career highlights to date: '5-57 against Derbyshire 2001'
Cricket moments to forget: 'Norwich Union match v Yorkshire at Scarborough 2001
– Lehmann 191'
Cricketers particularly admired: Glenn McGrath, Wasim Akram, Curtly Ambrose
Young players to look out for: Steve Davies, Will Gifford
Other sports played: Football
Other sports followed: Football, boxing
Relaxations: Music, games consoles
Extras: Made Nottinghamshire 2nd XI debut in 1999, aged 16, and took 15 wickets at
an average of 19.40 for the 2nd XI 2000. Represented England U19 2001 and 2002
Best batting: 39* Worcestershire v New Zealanders, Worcester 2004
Best bowling: 5-57 Nottinghamshire v Derbyshire, Trent Bridge 2001

2006 Season

	M	Inn	NO	Runs	HS	Avg	100	50	Ct	St	Balls	Runs	Wkts	Avg	BB	5I	10M
Test																	
FC	6	9	3	68	35	11.33	-	-	-	-	822	536	17	31.52	3-49	-	-
ODI																	
List A	4	2	2	3	3 *		-	-	1	-	158	185	4	46.25	2-62	-	
20/20 Int																	
20/20																	

Career Performances

	M	Inn	NO	Runs	HS	Avg	100	50	Ct	St	Balls	Runs	Wkts	Avg	BB	5I	10M
Test																	
FC	37	48	17	276	39 *	8.90	-	-	3	-	5515	3522	112	31.44	5-57	4	-
ODI																	
List A	47	22	15	83	11	11.85	-	-	7	-	1867	1640	45	36.44	4-42	-	
20/20 Int																	
20/20	12	4	2	4	3 *	2.00	-	-	1	-	264	391	16	24.43	3-23	-	

MANSOOR AMJAD — Leicestershire

Name: Mansoor Amjad
Role: Right-hand bat, leg-spin bowler; all-rounder
Born: 14 December 1987, Sialkot, Punjab, Pakistan
County debut: 2006
Strike rate: (career 52.14)
Overseas tours: Pakistan U19 to Bangladesh (U19 World Cup) 2003-04; Pakistan A to India (Kenstar Tournament) 2003-04, to Kenya 2004, to Zimbabwe 2004-05, to UAE (EurAsia Cricket Series) 2006, to Australia (Top End Series) 2006
Overseas teams played for: Sialkot/Sialkot Stallions 2001-02 – ; Zarai Taraqiati Bank 2003-04 – 2004-05; National Bank of Pakistan 2005-06
Extras: Represented Pakistan U19, winning Man of the Match award v India U19 at Khulna in the U19 World Cup 2003-04 (4-28). Scored 81-ball 99 and had second innings figures of 6-19 for Pakistan A v Zimbabwe A at Harare 2004-05. Took 5-97 for Pakistan A v England XI at Lahore 2005-06. An overseas player with Leicestershire during the 2006 season as a locum for Dinesh Mongia; has returned for 2007

Best batting: 122* National Bank v Sialkot, Multan 2005-06
Best bowling: 6-19 Pakistan A v Zimbabwe A, Harare 2004-05

2006 Season

	M	Inn	NO	Runs	HS	Avg	100	50	Ct	St	Balls	Runs	Wkts	Avg	BB	5I	10M
Test																	
FC	1	2	0	52	27	26.00	-	-	1	-	144	102	0			-	-
ODI																	
List A	1	1	0	18	18	18.00	-	-	-	-	42	45	1	45.00	1-45		
20/20 Int																	
20/20	1	0	0	0	0		-	-	1	-	0	0	0			-	-

Career Performances

	M	Inn	NO	Runs	HS	Avg	100	50	Ct	St	Balls	Runs	Wkts	Avg	BB	5I	10M
Test																	
FC	35	51	4	1415	122 *	30.10	2	7	19	-	5471	3025	105	28.80	6-19	5	-
ODI																	
List A	54	39	6	587	52 *	17.78	-	1	15	-	2501	2109	71	29.70	5-37	1	
20/20 Int																	
20/20	9	6	0	68	23	11.33	-	-	5	-	72	98	4	24.50	2-28	-	

MARSHALL, H. J. H.   Gloucestershire

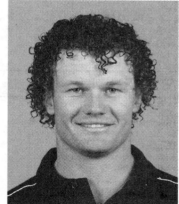

Name: <u>Hamish</u> John Hamilton Marshall
Role: Right-hand bat, right-arm
medium bowler
Born: 15 February 1979, Warkworth,
Auckland, New Zealand
County debut: 2006
County cap: 2006
Test debut: 2000-01
ODI debut: 2003-04
Twenty20 Int debut: 2004-05
1000 runs in a season: 1
Place in batting averages: 18th av. 60.90
Strike rate: (career 112.00)
Family links with cricket: Twin brother
James Marshall also plays for Northern
Districts and New Zealand
Overseas tours: New Zealand U19 to South
Africa (U19 World Cup) 1997-98; New
Zealand to South Africa 2000-01, to Pakistan (one-day series) 2003-04, to England
2004 (NatWest Series), to England (ICC Champions Trophy) 2004, to Bangladesh

2004-05, to Australia 2004-05, to Zimbabwe 2005-06, to South Africa 2005-06, to India (ICC Champions Trophy) 2006-07, to Australia (C'wealth Bank Series) 2006-07
Overseas teams played for: Northern Districts 1998-99 –
Extras: MCC Young Cricketer 1998. Attended New Zealand Cricket Academy 1999. Played for Buckinghamshire in the 2004 C&G competition. Represented New Zealand v FICA World XI 2004-05. One of *New Zealand Cricket Almanack*'s two Players of the Year 2005. His match awards include Man of the Match v West Indies at Cardiff in the NatWest Series 2004 (75*) and v Australia in the first ODI at Melbourne 2004-05 (50*). An overseas player with Gloucestershire since 2006
Best batting: 168 Gloucestershire v Leicestershire, Cheltenham 2006
Best bowling: 1-12 New Zealand A v Sri Lanka A, Christchurch 2003-04

2006 Season

	M	Inn	NO	Runs	HS	Avg	100	50	Ct	St	Balls	Runs	Wkts	Avg	BB	5I	10M
Test																	
FC	11	21	1	1218	168	60.90	5	7	6	-	156	63	1	63.00	1-16	-	-
ODI																	
List A	12	12	2	322	105 *	32.20	1	1	9	-	0	0	0		-	-	
20/20 Int																	
20/20	1	1	0	18	18	18.00	-	-	-	-	0	0	0		-	-	

Career Performances

	M	Inn	NO	Runs	HS	Avg	100	50	Ct	St	Balls	Runs	Wkts	Avg	BB	5I	10M
Test	13	19	2	652	160	38.35	2	2	1	-	6	4	0		-	-	-
FC	75	125	8	3913	168	33.44	8	19	37	-	336	176	3	58.66	1-12	-	-
ODI	55	51	8	1310	101 *	30.46	1	11	15	-	0	0	0		-	-	
List A	160	152	20	3661	111	27.73	3	24	65	-	60	72	1	72.00	1-14	-	
20/20 Int	3	3	0	12	8	4.00	-	-	1	-	0	0	0		-	-	
20/20	6	6	0	48	18	8.00	-	-	3	-	0	0	0		-	-	

MARSHALL, S. J.   Lancashire

Name: Simon James Marshall
Role: Right-hand bat, right-arm leg-spin bowler; all-rounder
Born: 20 September 1982, Arrowe Park, Wirral
Height: 6ft 3in **Weight:** 13st 2lbs
Nickname: Tron, David Dickinson
County debut: 2005
Strike rate: (career 127.35)
Parents: Jim and Dinah
Marital status: Single
Family links with cricket: Father captained Radley School and Liverpool University
Education: Birkenhead School; Cambridge University

Qualifications: 9 GCSEs, 4 A-levels, BA (Cantab) Land Economy

Off-season: 'Wintering in Manchester, working on some technical aspects of my game with the coaching staff at Lancs. Playing hockey for Bowdon'

Overseas tours: ESCA and ECB age-group tours 1996-2001; British Universities to South Africa 2004

Overseas teams played for: Adelaide Buffalos CC, Adelaide 2004-05; West Torrens Eagles, Adelaide 2005-06

Career highlights to date: 'First-class debut for Lancashire CCC'

Cricket moments to forget: 'Losing the C&G final to Sussex 2006'

Cricket superstitions: 'Like to give the bat a few spins before facing up'

Cricketers particularly admired: Carl Hooper, Brad Hodge, Mal Loye, Gary Keedy

Young players to look out for: Karl Brown, David Hurst, Adam Quail, Jack Withy

Other sports played: Hockey (Cambridge Blue)

Other sports followed: Football (Everton FC), hockey (Cambridge University HC)

Injuries: Injection in right knee early season

Favourite band: Dire Straits, Man from Michael

Relaxations: 'Loafing in coffee houses and spending time with mates; poodle-faking'

Extras: Played for Cheshire in the C&G 2002, 2003. Played for Cambridge UCCE 2002, (as captain) 2003, and 2004; took 6-128 then followed up with 99 in CUCCE's second innings v Essex at Fenner's 2002. Cambridge Blue 2002-04. Represented British Universities 2004. Cambridge University Sportsman of the Year 2004

Opinions on cricket: 'Heavy scheduling makes it very difficult to achieve and maintain an intensity of performance in all competitions throughout the season. A straight knockout format in one of the limited-over competitions would be preferable.'

Best batting: 126* Cambridge University v Oxford University, Fenner's 2003

Best bowling: 6-128 CUCCE v Essex, Fenner's 2002

2006 Season

	M	Inn	NO	Runs	HS	Avg	100	50	Ct	St	Balls	Runs	Wkts	Avg	BB	5I	10M
Test																	
FC	2	3	0	40	34	13.33	-	-	-	-	351	163	4	40.75	2-27	-	-
ODI																	
List A	12	2	0	10	9	5.00	-	-	7	-	498	429	10	42.90	3-36	-	
20/20 Int																	
20/20	8	6	2	97	47	24.25	-	-	5	-	184	186	12	15.50	4-20	-	

Career Performances

	M	Inn	NO	Runs	HS	Avg	100	50	Ct	St	Balls	Runs	Wkts	Avg	BB	5I	10M
Test																		
FC	18	29	6	773	126 *	33.60	1	3	4	-	3566	1892	28	67.57	6-128	1	-
ODI																	
List A	16	6	0	25	9	4.16	-	-	7	-	662	564	10	56.40	3-36	-	
20/20 Int																	
20/20	8	6	2	97	47	24.25	-	-	5	-	184	186	12	15.50	4-20	-	

MARTIN-JENKINS, R. S. C. — Sussex

Name: <u>Robin</u> Simon Christopher Martin-Jenkins
Role: Right-hand bat, right-arm fast-medium bowler
Born: 28 October 1975, Guildford
Height: 6ft 5in **Weight:** 14st
Nickname: Tucker
County debut: 1995
County cap: 2000
1000 runs in a season: 1
1st-Class 200s: 1
Place in batting averages: 118th av. 32.88 (2005 96th av. 36.62)
Place in bowling averages: 80th av. 34.92 (2005 109th av. 41.20)
Strike rate: 92.64 (career 67.55)
Parents: Christopher and Judy
Wife and date of marriage: Flora, 19 February 2000
Family links with cricket: Father is *The Times* chief cricket correspondent and BBC *TMS* commentator. Brother plays for the Radley Rangers
Education: Radley College, Oxon; Durham University

Qualifications: 10 GCSEs, 3 A-levels, 1 AS-level, Grade 3 bassoon (with merit), BA (Hons) Social Sciences, Don Mackenzie School of Professional Photography Certificate, SWPP (Society of Wedding and Portrait Photographers), BPPA (British Professional Photographers Associates), Wine and Spirit Education Trust Intermediate Certificate

Off-season: 'Selling wine and training'

Overseas tours: Radley College to Barbados 1992; Sussex U19 to Sri Lanka 1995; Durham University to Vienna 1995; MCC to Kenya 1999; Sussex to Grenada 2001, 2002

Overseas teams played for: Lima CC, Peru 1994; Bellville CC, Cape Town 2000-01

Career highlights to date: 'Winning National League Division Two in 1999. Scoring maiden first-class century in same match that Sussex won to take second division Championship 2001. Scoring maiden first-class 200 v Somerset at Taunton 2002. Winning first division Championship 2003. Winning C&G Trophy 2006 – whole of 2006 really'

Cricket superstitions: 'Never bowl first at Colwyn Bay'

Young players to look out for: Chris Nash

Other sports played: Golf, tennis, Rugby fives

Other sports followed: Rugby, football (Liverpool)

Relaxations: Photography, guitar, reading, TV, films

Extras: Played for ESCA U15-U19. European Player of the Year, Vienna 1995. Best Performance Award for Sussex 1998. NBC Denis Compton Award for the most promising young Sussex player 1998, 1999, 2000. Scored 205* v Somerset at Taunton 2002, in the process sharing with Mark Davis (111) in a record eighth-wicket stand for Sussex (291); the stand fell one run short of the record eighth-wicket partnership in English first-class cricket, set in 1896. BBC South Cricketer of the Year 2002

Opinions on cricket: 'Get rid of Pro40. Extend C&G throughout year (it could be league then semis and final). Keep Twenty20 as is. Keep Championship as it is. On no account should we have to play in the disastrous four-county floodlit Twenty20 competition <u>ever</u> again.'

Best batting: 205* Sussex v Somerset, Taunton 2002

Best bowling: 7-51 Sussex v Leicestershire, Horsham 2002

2006 Season

	M	Inn	NO	Runs	HS	Avg	100	50	Ct	St	Balls	Runs	Wkts	Avg	BB	5I	10M
Test																	
FC	14	21	3	592	91	32.88	-	3	1	-	1297	489	14	34.92	4-78	-	-
ODI																	
List A	18	14	6	186	34 *	23.25	-	-	3	-	738	523	9	58.11	3-15		
20/20 Int																	
20/20	6	3	1	18	9	9.00	-	-	4	-	138	152	4	38.00	2-29	-	

Career Performances

	M	Inn	NO	Runs	HS	Avg	100	50	Ct	St	Balls	Runs	Wkts	Avg	BB	5I	10M
Test																	
FC	130	201	25	5357	205 *	30.43	3	27	34	-	17767	9044	263	34.38	7-51	5	-
ODI																	
List A	181	136	23	1643	68 *	14.53	-	3	41	-	8054	5571	191	29.16	4-22	-	
20/20 Int																	
20/20	14	11	3	153	56 *	19.12	-	1	6	-	307	377	14	26.92	4-20	-	

MASCARENHAS, D. A. Hampshire

Name: <u>Dimitri</u> Adrian Mascarenhas
Role: Right-hand bat, right-arm medium bowler
Born: 30 October 1977, Chiswick, London
Height: 6ft 1in **Weight:** 12st 2lbs
Nickname: Dimi, D-Train
County debut: 1996
County cap: 1998
Benefit: 2007
50 wickets in a season: 1
Place in batting averages: 210th av. 19.75 (2005 39th av. 49.09)
Place in bowling averages: 15th av. 24.97 (2005 17th av. 23.55)
Strike rate: 59.86 (career 60.82)
Parents: Malik and Pauline
Marital status: Single
Family links with cricket: Uncle played in

Sri Lanka and brothers both play for Melville CC in Perth, Western Australia
Education: Trinity College, Perth
Qualifications: Level 2 coaching
Career outside cricket: Personal trainer

Overseas tours: England VI to Hong Kong 2004, 2005
Overseas teams played for: Melville CC, Perth 1991 –
Career highlights to date: 'Debut for Hampshire 1996 – 6-88 v Glamorgan'
Cricketers particularly admired: Sir Viv Richards, Malcolm Marshall, Shane Warne
Other sports followed: Australian Rules (Collingwood)
Favourite band: Red Hot Chili Peppers
Relaxations: Tennis, golf, Australian Rules
Extras: Played for Western Australia at U17 and U19 level as captain. Took 6-88 on first-class debut, for Hampshire v Glamorgan at Southampton 1996. Won NatWest Man of the Match awards in semi-final v Lancashire at Southampton 1998 (3-28/73) and in quarter-final v Middlesex at Lord's 2000 (4-25). Scorer of the first Championship century at The Rose Bowl (104) v Worcestershire 2001. Took Hampshire competition best 5-14 v Sussex at Hove in the Twenty20 2004, including the competition's first hat-trick (Davis, Mushtaq Ahmed, Lewry)
Best batting: 131 Hampshire v Kent, Canterbury 2006
Best bowling: 6-25 Hampshire v Derbyshire, Rose Bowl 2004

2006 Season

	M	Inn	NO	Runs	HS	Avg	100	50	Ct	St	Balls	Runs	Wkts	Avg	BB	5I	10M
Test																	
FC	16	24	0	474	131	19.75	1	-	4	-	2574	1074	43	24.97	6-65	2	-
ODI																	
List A	16	14	3	336	47 *	30.54	-	-	3	-	496	408	13	31.38	3-41	-	
20/20 Int																	
20/20	8	8	4	127	42 *	31.75	-	-	3	-	150	166	9	18.44	4-23	-	

Career Performances

	M	Inn	NO	Runs	HS	Avg	100	50	Ct	St	Balls	Runs	Wkts	Avg	BB	5I	10M
Test																	
FC	146	220	24	4769	131	24.33	7	16	58	-	21227	9742	349	27.91	6-25	14	-
ODI																	
List A	181	161	31	2991	79	23.00	-	18	46	-	7605	5361	222	24.14	5-27	1	
20/20 Int																	
20/20	20	20	8	350	52	29.16	-	1	9	-	365	449	24	18.70	5-14	1	

MASON, M. S. Worcestershire

Name: Matthew (<u>Matt</u>) Sean Mason
Role: Right-hand bat, right-arm
fast-medium bowler
Born: 20 March 1974, Perth, Western
Australia
Height: 6ft 5in **Weight:** 16st
Nickname: Mase, Moose
County debut: 2002
County colours: 2002
50 wickets in a season: 3
Place in batting averages: 250th av. 14.16
(2005 252nd av. 14.83)
Place in bowling averages: 8th av. 22.19
(2005 50th av. 28.03)
Strike rate: 43.34 (career 57.15)
Parents: Bill and Sue
Wife and date of marriage: Kellie,
8 October 2005

Family links with cricket: Brother Simon plays first-grade cricket in Perth
Education: Mazenod College, Perth; Curtin University of Technology
Qualifications: Level 1 ACB coach
Career outside cricket: 'Would like to get into sports management'
Overseas tours: Worcestershire to South Africa 2003
Overseas teams played for: Western Australia 1996-1998; Wanneroo District CC
1999-2001
Career highlights to date: 'Two Lord's finals'
Cricket moments to forget: 'Losing both Lord's finals, and 2005 season'
Cricketers particularly admired: Justin Langer, Dennis Lillee, Darren Gough
Young players to look out for: Steve Davies
Other sports played: 'Very bad golf and love Aussie Rules football'
Other sports followed: 'Follow all sports'
Favourite band: Coldplay
Relaxations: 'Spending time with my wife, friends and family'
Extras: Scored maiden first-class fifty (50) from 27 balls v Derbyshire at Worcester
2002. Dick Lygon Award for the [Worcestershire] Clubman of the Year 2003. Is
England-qualified by residency
Best batting: 63 Worcestershire v Warwickshire, Worcester 2004
Best bowling: 8-45 Worcestershire v Gloucestershire, Worcester 2006

2006 Season

	M	Inn	NO	Runs	HS	Avg	100	50	Ct	St	Balls	Runs	Wkts	Avg	BB	5I	10M
Test																	
FC	10	11	5	85	29 *	14.16	-	-	2	-	1777	910	41	22.19	8-45	3	1
ODI																	
List A	13	5	3	15	11	7.50	-	-	4	-	564	368	13	28.30	3-26	-	
20/20 Int																	
20/20	5	1	1	7	7 *		-	-	-	-	105	166	5	33.20	3-42	-	

Career Performances

	M	Inn	NO	Runs	HS	Avg	100	50	Ct	St	Balls	Runs	Wkts	Avg	BB	5I	10M
Test																	
FC	68	87	23	924	63	14.43	-	3	13	-	12859	5984	225	26.59	8-45	8	1
ODI																	
List A	70	32	12	153	25	7.65	-	-	15	-	3254	2311	84	27.51	4-34	-	
20/20 Int																	
20/20	10	4	2	18	8 *	9.00	-	-	2	-	220	290	9	32.22	3-42	-	

MASTERS, D. D. Leicestershire

Name: <u>David</u> Daniel Masters
Role: Right-hand bat, right-arm
medium-fast bowler
Born: 22 April 1978, Chatham, Kent
Height: 6ft 4ins **Weight:** 12st 5lbs
Nickname: Hod, Race Horse, Hoddy
County debut: 2000 (Kent),
2003 (Leicestershire)
Place in batting averages: 246th av. 14.60
(2005 225th av. 19.50)
Place in bowling averages: 96th av. 38.50
(2005 35th av. 26.55)
Strike rate: 87.34 (career 64.98)
Parents: Kevin and Tracey
Marital status: Single
Family links with cricket: 'Dad was on staff
at Kent 1983-86'
Education: Fort Luton High School;
Mid-Kent College
Qualifications: 8 GCSEs, GNVQ in Leisure and Tourism, qualified coach in cricket,
football and athletics, bricklayer and plasterer
Career outside cricket: Builder

Overseas teams played for: Doubleview, Perth 1998-99
Cricketers particularly admired: Ian Botham
Other sports played: Football, boxing 'and most other sports'
Other sports followed: Football (Manchester United)
Relaxations: 'Going out with mates'
Extras: Joint Kent Player of the Year 2000 (with Martin Saggers). NBC Denis Compton Award for the most promising young Kent player 2000
Best batting: 119 Leicestershire v Sussex, Hove 2003
Best bowling: 6-27 Kent v Durham, Tunbridge Wells 2000

2006 Season

	M	Inn	NO	Runs	HS	Avg	100	50	Ct	St	Balls	Runs	Wkts	Avg	BB	5I	10M
Test																	
FC	14	16	1	219	52	14.60	-	1	6	-	2795	1232	32	38.50	4-89	-	-
ODI																	
List A	12	6	1	98	39	19.60	-	-	1	-	550	349	16	21.81	3-21	-	
20/20 Int																	
20/20	11	0	0	0	0		-	-	4	-	204	264	12	22.00	3-18	-	

Career Performances

	M	Inn	NO	Runs	HS	Avg	100	50	Ct	St	Balls	Runs	Wkts	Avg	BB	5I	10M
Test																	
FC	78	94	20	953	119	12.87	1	2	26	-	12673	6553	195	33.60	6-27	5	-
ODI																	
List A	79	46	20	340	39	13.07	-	-	8	-	3187	2492	65	38.33	5-20	1	
20/20 Int																	
20/20	27	7	4	16	7	5.33	-	-	9	-	504	632	27	23.40	3-7	-	

MAUNDERS, J. K.   Leicestershire

Name: <u>John</u> Kenneth Maunders
Role: Left-hand opening bat, right-arm medium bowler
Born: 4 April 1981, Ashford, Middlesex
Height: 5ft 10in **Weight:** 13st
Nickname: Rod, Weaz
County debut: 1999 (Middlesex), 2003 (Leicestershire)
Place in batting averages: 109th av. 34.25 (2005 163rd av. 28.11)
Place in bowling averages: (2005 39th av. 27.42)
Strike rate: (career 55.72)
Parents: Lynn and Kenneth
Marital status: Single
Family links with cricket: Grandfather and two uncles club cricketers for Thames Valley Ramblers

Education: Ashford High School; Spelthorne College
Qualifications: 10 GCSEs, coaching certificates
Career outside cricket: Cricket coach
Overseas tours: England U19 to New Zealand 1998-99, to Malaysia and (U19 World Cup) Sri Lanka 1999-2000
Overseas teams played for: University CC, Perth 2001-02
Career highlights to date: 'Scoring maiden first-class hundred v Surrey at Grace Road'
Cricket moments to forget: 'Not any one in particular; getting 0 and dropping catches are not great moments!'
Cricket superstitions: 'Just a few small ones'
Cricketers particularly admired: Brad Hodge, Justin Langer
Other sports played: Football, hockey, squash
Other sports followed: Horse racing
Extras: Has been Seaxe Player of Year. Represented England U17 and U19. NBC Denis Compton Award 1999
Best batting: 180 Leicestershire v Gloucestershire, Cheltenham 2006
Best bowling: 4-15 Leicestershire v Worcestershire, Worcester 2006

2006 Season

	M	Inn	NO	Runs	HS	Avg	100	50	Ct	St	Balls	Runs	Wkts	Avg	BB	5I	10M
Test																	
FC	16	29	1	959	180	34.25	1	6	9	-	410	219	6	36.50	4-15	-	-
ODI																	
List A	7	7	1	113	38	18.83	-	-	3	-	72	48	2	24.00	2-25	-	
20/20 Int																	
20/20																	

Career Performances

	M	Inn	NO	Runs	HS	Avg	100	50	Ct	St	Balls	Runs	Wkts	Avg	BB	5I	10M
Test																	
FC	56	102	3	2969	180	29.98	5	14	26	-	1226	725	22	32.95	4-15	-	-
ODI																	
List A	22	22	1	314	49	14.95	-	-	6	-	109	82	4	20.50	2-16	-	
20/20 Int																	
20/20	9	6	2	18	10	4.50	-	-	1	-	0	0	0		-	-	

McCULLUM, B. B. Glamorgan

Name: Brendon Barrie McCullum
Role: Right-hand bat, wicket-keeper
Born: 27 September 1981, Dunedin,
New Zealand
County debut: 2006
County cap: 2006
Test debut: 2003-04
ODI debut: 2001-02
Twenty20 Int debut: 2004-05
Family links with cricket: Father Stuart
played first-class cricket for Otago; brother
Nathan plays first-class cricket for Otago
Overseas tours: New Zealand U19 to Sri
Lanka (U19 World Cup) 1999-2000; New
Zealand to Australia (VB Series) 2001-02, to
Africa (World Cup) 2002-03, to England
2004, to England (ICC Champions Trophy)
2004, to Bangladesh 2004-05, to Australia

2004-05, to Zimbabwe 2005-06, to South Africa 2005-06, to India (ICC Champions
Trophy) 2006-07, to Australia (C'wealth Bank Series) 2006-07, plus other one-day
tournaments and series in Sri Lanka, India and Pakistan
Overseas teams played for: Otago 1999-2000 – 2002-03; Canterbury 2003-04 –
Extras: Represented New Zealand U19. His awards include Man of the Match in the
first Test v Bangladesh at Dhaka 2004-05 (143). An overseas player with Glamorgan
during the 2006 season as a locum for Mark Cosgrove. His career best 160 v
Leicestershire at Cardiff 2006 set a new record for the highest score by a Glamorgan
batsman on Championship debut
Best batting: 160 Glamorgan v Leicestershire, Cardiff 2006

2006 Season

	M	Inn	NO	Runs	HS	Avg	100	50	Ct	St	Balls	Runs	Wkts	Avg	BB	5I	10M
Test																	
FC	3	6	1	306	160	61.20	1	1	3	-	0	0	0		-	-	-
ODI																	
List A	2	2	0	8	8	4.00	-	-	-	-	0	0	0		-	-	
20/20 Int																	
20/20	8	8	1	188	63	26.85	-	1	3	-	0	0	0		-	-	

Career Performances

	M	Inn	NO	Runs	HS	Avg	100	50	Ct	St	Balls	Runs	Wkts	Avg	BB	5I	10M
Test	23	35	2	1083	143	32.81	2	6	56	5	0	0	0	-	-	-	-
FC	55	90	5	2815	160	33.11	6	14	130	11	0	0	0	-	-	-	-
ODI	84	65	14	1120	56 *	21.96	-	4	104	8	0	0	0	-	-	-	
List A	120	96	17	1646	58	20.83	-	7	138	9	0	0	0	-	-	-	
20/20 Int	3	3	1	57	36	28.50	-	-	2	-	0	0	0	-	-	-	
20/20	14	14	2	346	63	28.83	-	2	7	-	0	0	0	-	-		

McGRATH, A. Yorkshire

Name: Anthony McGrath
Role: Right-hand bat, right-arm medium bowler
Born: 6 October 1975, Bradford
Height: 6ft 2in **Weight:** 14st 7lbs
Nickname: Gripper, Mags, Terry
County debut: 1995
County cap: 1999
Test debut: 2003
ODI debut: 2003
1000 runs in a season: 2
Place in batting averages: 15th av. 61.57 (2005 15th av. 59.37)
Place in bowling averages: 108th av. 40.77 (2005 126th av. 45.43)
Strike rate: 72.00 (career 66.05)
Parents: Terry and Kath
Marital status: Single
Education: Yorkshire Martyrs Collegiate School
Qualifications: 9 GCSEs, BTEC National Diploma in Leisure Studies, senior coaching award
Overseas tours: England U19 to West Indies 1994-95; England A to Pakistan 1995-96, to Australia 1996-97; MCC to Bangladesh 1999-2000; England to Bangladesh and Sri Lanka 2003-04 (one-day series), to West Indies 2003-04 (one-day series)
Overseas teams played for: Deep Dene, Melbourne 1998-99; Wanneroo, Perth 1999-2001
Cricket moments to forget: 'Losing semi-final to Lancashire 1996. Relegation to Division Two 2002'
Cricketers particularly admired: Darren Lehmann, Robin Smith
Other sports followed: 'Most sports', football (Manchester United)
Relaxations: 'Music; spending time with friends; eating out'

Extras: Captained Yorkshire Schools U13, U14, U15, U16; captained English Schools U17. Bradford League Young Cricketer of the Year 1992 and 1993. Played for England U17 and U19. Captain of Yorkshire 2003. Recorded maiden first-class five-wicket return (5-39) v Derbyshire at Derby 2004, scoring career best 174 in the same match
Best batting: 174 Yorkshire v Derbyshire, Derby 2004
Best bowling: 5-39 Yorkshire v Derbyshire, Derby 2004

2006 Season

	M	Inn	NO	Runs	HS	Avg	100	50	Ct	St	Balls	Runs	Wkts	Avg	BB	5I	10M
Test																	
FC	15	24	3	1293	140 *	61.57	4	9	18	-	1296	734	18	40.77	4-62	-	-
ODI																	
List A	13	12	1	308	148	28.00	1	1	5	-	216	213	5	42.60	2-22	-	
20/20 Int																	
20/20	9	9	2	230	58 *	32.85	-	2	2	-	66	77	2	38.50	2-18	-	

Career Performances

	M	Inn	NO	Runs	HS	Avg	100	50	Ct	St	Balls	Runs	Wkts	Avg	BB	5I	10M
Test	4	5	0	201	81	40.20	-	2	3	-	102	56	4	14.00	3-16	-	-
FC	170	290	23	9816	174	36.76	22	46	122	-	6275	3223	95	33.92	5-39	1	-
ODI	14	12	2	166	52	16.60	-	1	4	-	228	175	4	43.75	1-13	-	
List A	230	213	28	5704	148	30.83	4	32	73	-	2528	2109	61	34.57	4-41	-	
20/20 Int																	
20/20	21	20	3	384	58 *	22.58	-	2	6	-	209	314	10	31.40	3-27	-	

55. Who was summoned from Auckland
to make his ODI debut against Australia at The Gabba
on 19 January 2007?

McLAREN, R. Kent

Name: Ryan McLaren
Role: Left-hand bat, right-arm medium-fast bowler
Born: 9 February 1983, Kimberley, South Africa
County debut: No first-team appearance
Strike rate: (career 62.43)
Family links with cricket: Father (Paul McLaren) and uncle (Keith McLaren) played for Griqualand West. Cousin (Adrian McLaren) plays for Griqualand West
Overseas tours: South Africa U19 to New Zealand (U19 World Cup) 2001-02
Overseas teams played for: Free State 2003-04 – 2004-05; Eagles 2004-05 –
Extras: His awards include Man of the Match v Canada U19 at Auckland in the U19 World Cup 2001-02 (4-9; full figures 10-4-9-4) and v Warriors at Bloemfontein in the Supersport Series 2005-06 (140; 3-31/4-50). Is not considered an overseas player
Best batting: 140 Eagles v Warriors, Bloemfontein 2005-06
Best bowling: 6-96 Eagles v Dolphins, Bloemfontein 2005-06
Stop press: Man of the Match v Dolphins at Bloemfontein (53*; 5-57/4-59) and (with JP Duminy) v Cape Cobras at Stellenbosch (48*; 8-38/3-100), both in the SuperSport Series 2006-07

2006 Season (did not make any first-class or one-day appearances)

Career Performances

	M	Inn	NO	Runs	HS	Avg	100	50	Ct	St	Balls	Runs	Wkts	Avg	BB	5I	10M
Test																	
FC	23	35	4	1019	140	32.87	1	6	14	-	3746	1849	60	30.81	6-96	3	-
ODI																	
List A	26	16	5	337	55	30.63	-	1	10	-	815	632	18	35.11	4-43	-	
20/20 Int																	
20/20	12	7	4	30	10	10.00	-	-	2	-	180	204	5	40.80	2-21	-	

McLEAN, J. J.   Hampshire

Name: Jonathan (<u>Jono</u>) James McLean
Role: Right-hand bat, right-arm seam bowler
Born: 11 July 1980, Johannesburg,
South Africa
Height: 6ft 1in **Weight:** 12st 8lbs
County debut: 2005
Place in batting averages: (2005 150th
av. 30.25)
Parents: Brian and Rosey
Marital status: Single
Education: St Stithians College, Gauteng
Overseas teams played for: University of
Cape Town 2000-04; Western Province
2001-02 – 2003-04
Career highlights to date: 'Making my
first-class debut'
Cricketers particularly admired: Sachin
Tendulkar, Jacques Kallis

Other sports played: Hockey (Provincial U15), golf (social)
Other sports followed: Rugby
Relaxations: Golf, listening to music, reading
Extras: Made first-class debut for Western Province v Northerns at Centurion
2001-02. Released by Hampshire at the end of the 2006 season
Best batting: 68 Hampshire v Gloucestershire, Cheltenham 2005

2006 Season

	M	Inn	NO	Runs	HS	Avg	100	50	Ct	St	Balls	Runs	Wkts	Avg	BB	5I	10M
Test																	
FC	1	1	0	60	60	60.00	-	1	-	-	0	0	0		-	-	
ODI																	
List A	1	1	0	4	4	4.00	-	-	1	-	0	0	0		-	-	
20/20 Int																	
20/20	6	4	0	39	23	9.75	-	-	1	-	0	0	0		-	-	

Career Performances

	M	Inn	NO	Runs	HS	Avg	100	50	Ct	St	Balls	Runs	Wkts	Avg	BB	5I	10M
Test																	
FC	13	18	1	464	68	27.29	-	5	11	-	0	0	0		-	-	-
ODI																	
List A	11	6	1	60	36	12.00	-	-	7	-	0	0	0		-	-	
20/20 Int																	
20/20	6	4	0	39	23	9.75	-	-	1	-	0	0	0		-	-	

McMAHON, P. J.   Nottinghamshire

Name: <u>Paul</u> Joseph McMahon
Role: Right-hand bat, off-spin bowler
Born: 12 March 1983, Wigan
Height: 6ft 1in **Weight:** 12st
Nickname: Vince, Macca, Boffin
County debut: 2002
Place in bowling averages: (2005 42nd av. 27.66)
Strike rate: (career 73.27)
Parents: Gerry and Teresa
Marital status: Single
Family links with cricket: 'Dad was club professional in Lancashire and Cheshire leagues; now plays for Notts Over 50s and for Wollaton in Notts Premier League. Mum now an expert at finding out scores on Teletext'
Education: Trinity RC Comprehensive, Nottingham; Wadham College, Oxford University

Qualifications: 11 GCSEs, 4 A-levels, BA (Hons) Law
Career outside cricket: 'Potentially something related to the legal profession'
Overseas tours: England U19 to Australia and (U19 World Cup) New Zealand 2001-02; Nottinghamshire to South Africa 2002, 2003; WCA spin bowling camp, Mumbai 2004
Overseas teams played for: Sydney University 2005-06
Career highlights to date: 'Captaining England U19 against India U19 [2002], and taking eight wickets [4-47 and 4-58] in the victory at Northampton in the deciding final "Test"'
Cricketers particularly admired: Mike Atherton, Steve Waugh, Nasser Hussain
Young players to look out for: Michael Munday, Will Smith, Ed Cowan (NSW), Amit Suman (Delhi)
Other sports played: Football (OUAFC reserve goalkeeper in 2005 Varsity Match), darts (Wadham College 2nd VIII), tennis ('badly'), golf ('even worse')
Other sports followed: Football
Favourite band: End of Fashion
Relaxations: 'Reading, current affairs, music'
Extras: Played for Notts from U11 to 1st XI. Captained England U19 v India U19 2002; leading wicket-taker in 'Test' series with ten wickets (av. 22.20). Nottinghamshire Young Player of the Year 2003. Oxford UCCE 2003-05 (captain 2004, during which season OUCCE won the UCCE Championship and One-Day Challenge). Oxford University 2003-05 (captain 2004-05). Represented British

Universities 2004. Oxford University Sportsman of the Year 2004. Released by Nottinghamshire at the end of the 2006 season

Best batting: 99 Oxford University v Cambridge University, The Parks 2004
Best bowling: 5-30 Oxford University v Cambridge University, Fenner's 2005

2006 Season

	M	Inn	NO	Runs	HS	Avg	100	50	Ct	St	Balls	Runs	Wkts	Avg	BB	5I	10M
Test																	
FC	1	0	0	0	0	-	-	-	-	-	6	6	0			-	-	-
ODI																	
List A	3	1	0	8	8	8.00	-	-	3	-	84	80	0			-	-	-
20/20 Int																	
20/20																	

Career Performances

	M	Inn	NO	Runs	HS	Avg	100	50	Ct	St	Balls	Runs	Wkts	Avg	BB	5I	10M
Test																	
FC	18	21	3	340	99	18.88	-	2	11	-	3224	1587	44	36.06	5-30	1	-
ODI																	
List A	4	2	0	8	8	4.00	-	-	3	-	114	113	0			-	-
20/20 Int																	
20/20	1	0	0	0	0		-	-	1	-	24	22	1	22.00	1-22	-	

MIDDLEBROOK, J. D.   Essex

Name: <u>James</u> Daniel Middlebrook
Role: Right-hand bat, off-spin bowler
Born: 13 May 1977, Leeds
Height: 6ft 1in   **Weight:** 13st
Nickname: Brooky, Midi, Midders, Midhouse, Dog
County debut: 1998 (Yorkshire), 2002 (Essex)
County cap: 2003 (Essex)
50 wickets in a season: 1
Place in batting averages: 137th av. 30.87 (2005 116th av. 33.83)
Place in bowling averages: 113th av. 41.60 (2005 119th av. 44.28)
Strike rate: 82.46 (career 74.42)
Parents: Ralph and Mavis
Marital status: Single

Family links with cricket: 'Dad is a senior staff coach'
Education: Crawshaw, Pudsey
Qualifications: NVQ Level 2 in Coaching Sport and Recreation, ECB senior coach
Overseas tours: Yorkshire CCC to Guernsey
Overseas teams played for: Stokes Valley CC, New Zealand; Gold Coast Dolphins, Brisbane; Surfers Paradise CC, Brisbane
Cricket superstitions: 'Always put my batting gear on the same way'
Cricketers particularly admired: John Emburey, Ian Botham
Young players to look out for: Alastair Cook, Ravinder Bopara
Other sports played: Golf, tennis, squash, badminton
Other sports followed: Football (Leeds United), athletics
Relaxations: 'Any music – MTV – sleeping, socialising, catching up with old friends'
Extras: Played for Yorkshire from U11 to 1st XI. His 6-82 v Hampshire at Southampton 2000 included a spell of four wickets in five balls. Took Championship hat-trick (Saggers, Muralitharan, Sheriyar) v Kent at Canterbury 2003
Best batting: 115 Essex v Somerset, Taunton 2004
Best bowling: 6-82 Yorkshire v Hampshire, Southampton 2000

2006 Season

	M	Inn	NO	Runs	HS	Avg	100	50	Ct	St	Balls	Runs	Wkts	Avg	BB	5I	10M
Test																	
FC	15	17	1	494	113	30.87	1	2	6	-	3381	1706	41	41.60	5-70	1	-
ODI																	
List A	17	10	3	176	44	25.14	-	-	7	-	721	568	18	31.55	4-27	-	
20/20 Int																	
20/20	10	8	3	90	43	18.00	-	-	1	-	102	190	1	190.00	1-14	-	

Career Performances

	M	Inn	NO	Runs	HS	Avg	100	50	Ct	St	Balls	Runs	Wkts	Avg	BB	5I	10M
Test																	
FC	104	148	16	3212	115	24.33	3	12	47	-	18607	9755	250	39.02	6-82	7	1
ODI																	
List A	108	69	20	911	47	18.59	-	-	32	-	3918	2979	94	31.69	4-27	-	
20/20 Int																	
20/20	22	18	3	221	43	14.73	-	-	5	-	288	390	9	43.33	3-25	-	

Name: Joshua (<u>Josh</u>) Aleck Mierkalns
Role: Right-hand top-order bat, backward point fielder, occasional wicket-keeper
Born: 11 September 1985, Nottingham
Height: 6ft **Weight:** 12st 7lbs
Nickname: Meerkat, Cat, Dirk
County debut: 2006
Parents: Christine and Rob
Marital status: Single
Family links with cricket: 'Mum played in Australia when she was growing up. Uncle should have played for Leicestershire but Gran made him go to uni. Two younger brothers play in local league and Notts age-groups'
Education: Arnold Hill School
Qualifications: GCSEs, 3 AS-levels
Career outside cricket: 'Bricklayer's apprenticeship'
Off-season: 'Usually go to New Zealand but this year I decided to stay and do my coaching awards and do some coaching helping youngsters in schools'
Overseas teams played for: Lancaster Park, Christchurch, New Zealand ('Chris Cairns' club') 2004-06
Career highlights to date: 'Playing in front of a packed house at Trent Bridge in the Twenty20 quarter-final. It was amazing'
Cricket moments to forget: 'In Twenty20 semi-final, came on as 12th man and collided with Samit Patel on the boundary live on Sky Sports'
Cricket superstitions: 'None'
Cricketers particularly admired: Shane Warne, Ricky Ponting, Andrew Flintoff, Kevin Pietersen
Other sports played: Hockey, golf, rugby ('played for Beeston U18 in national final')
Other sports followed: Rugby (Canterbury), football (Liverpool)
Injuries: Shoulder injury – no time lost
Favourite band: 'Eclectic'
Relaxations: 'Going to the gym and spa'
Extras: Joined Caythorpe CC at age seven
Best batting: 18 Nottinghamshire v West Indies A, Trent Bridge 2006

2006 Season

	M	Inn	NO	Runs	HS	Avg	100	50	Ct	St	Balls	Runs	Wkts	Avg	BB	5I	10M
Test																	
FC	1	1	0	18	18	18.00	-	-	-	-	0	0	0		-	-	-
ODI																	
List A	1	1	0	4	4	4.00	-	-	-	-	0	0	0		-	-	
20/20 Int																	
20/20	2	1	0	4	4	4.00	-	-	1	-	0	0	0		-	-	

Career Performances

	M	Inn	NO	Runs	HS	Avg	100	50	Ct	St	Balls	Runs	Wkts	Avg	BB	5I	10M
Test																	
FC	1	1	0	18	18	18.00	-	-	-	-	0	0	0		-	-	-
ODI																	
List A	1	1	0	4	4	4.00	-	-	-	-	0	0	0		-	-	
20/20 Int																	
20/20	2	1	0	4	4	4.00	-	-	1	-	0	0	0		-	-	

MILLER, A. S.　　　　　　　　　　Warwickshire

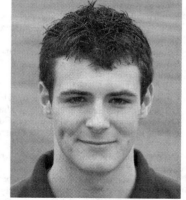

Name: <u>Andrew</u> Stephen Miller
Role: Right-hand bat, right-arm
medium-fast bowler
Born: 27 September 1987, Preston
Height: 6ft 4in **Weight:** 13st
Nickname: Millsy, Donk
County debut: No first-team appearance
Parents: Steve and Sharon
Education: St Cecilia's RC High School;
Preston College
Qualifications: 11 GCSEs, BTEC National
Diploma in Sports Development and Fitness,
coaching Levels 1 and 2
Off-season: England U19 tour to Malaysia
Overseas tours: England U16 to South
Africa 2004; England U19 to India 2004-05,
to Bangladesh 2005-06, to Sri Lanka (U19
World Cup) 2005-06, to Malaysia 2006-07
Career highlights to date: 'Playing in an U19 Cricket World Cup and getting a
contract at Warwickshire CCC'
Cricket moments to forget: 'None'
Cricketers particularly admired: Glenn McGrath

Young players to look out for: Nick James, Graeme White, Steven Finn
Other sports followed: Football (Blackburn Rovers)
Favourite band: The Fratellis
Relaxations: 'TV, music, golf'
Extras: Represented England U19 2005, 2006. NBC Denis Compton Award for the most promising young Warwickshire player 2006

MITCHELL, D. K. H. Worcestershire

Name: <u>Daryl</u> Keith Henry Mitchell
Role: Right-hand bat, right-arm medium bowler; batting all-rounder
Born: 25 November 1983, Evesham
Height: 5ft 10in **Weight:** 11st 10lbs
Nickname: Mitch, Peggy, Toucan
County debut: 2005
County colours: 2005
Place in batting averages: 52nd av. 47.00 (2005 185th av. 24.50)
Strike rate: (career 90.00)
Parents: Keith and Jane
Marital status: Single
Family links with cricket: 'Dad played club cricket and coaches WYC (Worcestershire Young Cricketers) U13'
Education: Prince Henry's High, Evesham; University of Worcester
Qualifications: 10 GCSEs, 4 A-levels, BSc (Hons) Sports Studies and Geography (2.2), ECB Level 1 coaching
Career outside cricket: 'None as yet. Hoping to become a teacher'
Off-season: 'Club cricket in Perth (Midland-Guildford CC)'
Overseas teams played for: Midland-Guildford, Perth 2005-07
Career highlights to date: '134 not out v Glamorgan – maiden first-class century [2006]'
Cricket moments to forget: 'Run out first ball by a Monty direct hit v Northants, Twenty20 2006'
Cricket superstitions: 'Put gloves on before helmet'
Cricketers particularly admired: Michael Atherton, Graeme Hick
Young players to look out for: Steve Davies, James Taylor, Keith Bradley
Other sports played: Football, golf ('badly'), pool, darts, skittles
Other sports followed: Football (Aston Villa), rugby (Worcester), AFL (West Coast Eagles)

Injuries: No bowling for four weeks after a slight intercostal strain; out for two weeks with a badly bruised knee ('fielding at short leg')
Favourite band: Oasis
Relaxations: 'Music, movies, PlayStation'
Extras: Scored 210* for Worcestershire v Bradford/Leeds UCCE at Harrogate 2006
Opinions on cricket: 'Game in this country is in good shape. Standard is high in all forms. Move to one overseas in 2008 is a good one, as it will allow the abundance of young English talent to break through.'
Best batting: 134* Worcestershire v Glamorgan, Colwyn Bay 2006
Best bowling: 1-59 Worcestershire v Essex, Worcester 2005

2006 Season

	M	Inn	NO	Runs	HS	Avg	100	50	Ct	St	Balls	Runs	Wkts	Avg	BB	5I	10M
Test																	
FC	4	8	2	282	134 *	47.00	1	2	3	-	0	0	0		-	-	-
ODI																	
List A	3	3	0	11	7	3.66	-	-	2	-	60	67	4	16.75	4-42	-	
20/20 Int																	
20/20	8	1	0	0	0	0.00	-	-	3	-	150	242	1	242.00	1-47	-	

Career Performances

	M	Inn	NO	Runs	HS	Avg	100	50	Ct	St	Balls	Runs	Wkts	Avg	BB	5I	10M
Test																	
FC	10	18	4	478	134 *	34.14	1	4	9	-	90	99	1	99.00	1-59	-	-
ODI																	
List A	4	4	0	13	7	3.25	-	-	2	-	60	67	4	16.75	4-42	-	
20/20 Int																	
20/20	14	5	2	9	4	3.00	-	-	3	-	228	350	6	58.33	2-26	-	

---

56. Who reached his 29th Test century off
the final ball of the second day of his last Ashes Test
at his home ground of Sydney in 2002-03?

MOHAMMAD AKRAM   Surrey

Name: Mohammad Akram Awan
Role: Right-hand bat, right-arm fast bowler
Born: 10 September 1974, Islamabad,
Pakistan
Height: 6ft 2in **Weight:** 13st 7lbs
Nickname: Haji, Akee
County debut: 1997 (Northamptonshire),
2003 (Essex), 2004 (Sussex), 2005 (Surrey)
County cap: 2006 (Surrey)
Test debut: 1995-96
ODI debut: 1995-96
Place in bowling averages: 51st av. 30.80
(2005 89th av. 35.86)
Strike rate: 52.14 (career 48.12)
Parents: Mohammad Akbar
Wife and date of marriage: Hamera Akram,
May 1999
Children: Imaan Akram; Amaar Akram
Education: Modern Secondary School; Gordon College, Rawalpindi
Career outside cricket: Business
Overseas tours: Pakistan to Australia 1995-96, to England 1996, to South Africa and
Zimbabwe 1997-98, to Australia 1999-2000, to West Indies 1999-2000, to New
Zealand 2000-01, plus one-day tournaments in Sharjah, Singapore, Toronto,
Bangladesh and Sri Lanka
Overseas teams played for: Rawalpindi Cricket Association 1992-93 – 2002-03;
Allied Bank 1996-97 – 2000-01
Career highlights to date: 'When I played Test cricket'
Cricket moments to forget: 'All good'
Cricket superstitions: 'None'
Cricketers particularly admired: Wasim, Waqar, Michael Holding
Other sports played: Football, gulee danda (traditional Pakistani game)
Other sports followed: Football, boxing
Favourite band: 'Not into music'
Relaxations: 'Meeting friends, swimming, eating out'
Extras: Was Northamptonshire's overseas player in 1997. Took 5-98 on
Championship debut for Essex v Sussex at Colchester 2003. Took career best 8-49 v
Surrey at The Oval 2003, including the first four wickets without conceding a run. No
longer classed as an overseas player, having qualified by residency
Opinions on cricket: 'I don't like too much technology involved in decision-making.
Leave it natural. That is the beauty of this game.'
Best batting: 35* Sussex v Warwickshire, Edgbaston 2004
Best bowling: 8-49 Essex v Surrey, The Oval 2003

2006 Season

	M	Inn	NO	Runs	HS	Avg	100	50	Ct	St	Balls	Runs	Wkts	Avg	BB	5I	10M
Test																	
FC	14	11	4	64	21 *	9.14	-	-	3	-	2190	1294	42	30.80	6-34	2	-
ODI																	
List A	7	2	0	7	4	3.50	-	-	1	-	285	248	8	31.00	3-36	-	
20/20 Int																	
20/20																	

Career Performances

	M	Inn	NO	Runs	HS	Avg	100	50	Ct	St	Balls	Runs	Wkts	Avg	BB	5I	10M
Test	9	15	6	24	10 *	2.66	-	-	4	-	1477	859	17	50.52	5-138	1	-
FC	122	149	43	927	35 *	8.74	-	-	31	-	19731	11727	410	28.60	8-49	18	1
ODI	23	9	7	14	7 *	7.00	-	-	8	-	989	790	19	41.57	2-28	-	
List A	119	55	25	231	33	7.70	-	-	23	-	5450	4199	131	32.05	4-19	-	
20/20 Int																	
20/20	3	1	1	7	7 *		-	-	2	-	66	96	3	32.00	2-22	-	

MOHAMMAD ALI   *Middlesex*

Name: Syed Mohammad Ali Bukhari
Role: Right-hand bat, left-arm
fast-medium bowler
Born: 8 November 1973, Bahawalpur,
Punjab
County debut: 2002 (Derbyshire),
2005 (one-day, Middlesex), 2006 (first-class,
Middlesex)
Place in bowling averages: 131st av. 45.30
Strike rate: 69.20 (career 52.55)
Family links with cricket: Uncle Taslim Arif
played for Pakistan 1979-80
Overseas teams played for: Numerous,
including Bahawalpur, Islamabad Cricket
Association, Lahore Cricket Association,
Railways and United Bank
Extras: Played for Glamorgan 2nd XI 2000
and 2001. Struck a 38-ball 53 on debut for
Derbyshire v Durham at Derby 2002, batting at No. 9. Is England-qualified. Released
by Middlesex at the end of the 2006 season
Best batting: 92 Bahawalpur v Lahore City, Rahimyarkhan 1998-99
Best bowling: 6-37 Railways v National Bank, Faisalabad 1993-94

2006 Season

	M	Inn	NO	Runs	HS	Avg	100	50	Ct	St	Balls	Runs	Wkts	Avg	BB	5I	10M
Test																	
FC	5	8	4	87	23 *	21.75	-	-	3	-	692	453	10	45.30	2-15	-	-
ODI																	
List A	3	1	1	15	15 *		-	-	2	-	156	138	3	46.00	3-36	-	
20/20 Int																	
20/20	4	1	1	0	0 *		-	-	-	-	72	124	3	41.33	1-10	-	

Career Performances

	M	Inn	NO	Runs	HS	Avg	100	50	Ct	St	Balls	Runs	Wkts	Avg	BB	5I	10M
Test																	
FC	89	120	30	1334	92	14.82	-	5	28	-	14392	9060	274	33.06	6-37	11	2
ODI																	
List A	52	24	11	129	19	9.92	-	-	8	-	2230	1913	60	31.88	4-34	-	
20/20 Int																	
20/20	8	1	1	0	0 *		-	-	-	-	162	219	13	16.84	3-24	-	

MOHAMMAD ASIF — Leicestershire

Name: Mohammad Asif
Role: Left-hand bat, right-arm fast-medium bowler
Born: 20 December 1982, Sheikhupura, Pakistan
County debut: 2006
Test debut: 2004-05
ODI debut: 2005-06
Twenty20 Int debut: 2006
Place in bowling averages: 67th av. 33.20
Strike rate: 59.63 (career 43.65)
Overseas tours: Pakistan A to Sri Lanka 2004-05, to Namibia and Zimbabwe 2004-05; Pakistan to Australia 2004-05, to Sri Lanka 2005-06, to UAE (DLF Cup) 2006, to England 2006, to South Africa 2006-07
Overseas teams played for: Lahore Division 1999-2000; Sheikhupura 2000-01 – 2001-02; Khan Research Laboratories 2001-02 – 2003-04; Quetta 2003-04; National Bank of Pakistan 2004-05 – 2005-06; Sialkot/Sialkot Stallions 2004-05 –
Extras: Returned match figures of 10-106 (7-62/3-44) for Pakistan A v England XI at Lahore 2005-06. Man of the [Test] Series v Sri Lanka 2005-06. An overseas player with Leicestershire 2006

Best batting: 42 KRL v Allied Bank, Karachi 2002-03
Best bowling: 7-35 Sialkot v Multan, Multan 2004-05

2006 Season

	M	Inn	NO	Runs	HS	Avg	100	50	Ct	St	Balls	Runs	Wkts	Avg	BB	5I	10M
Test	1	1	0	0	0	0.00	-	-	-	-	216	135	5	27.00	4-56	-	-
FC	9	9	2	58	21	8.28	-	-	4	-	1795	996	30	33.20	5-56	2	-
ODI	5	1	1	4	4 *		-	-	-	-	282	180	8	22.50	3-28	-	
List A	8	2	2	5	4 *		-	-	1	-	438	278	11	25.27	3-28	-	
20/20 Int	1	0	0	0	0		-	-	-	-	24	21	2	10.50	2-21	-	
20/20	1	0	0	0	0		-	-	-	-	24	21	2	10.50	2-21	-	

Career Performances

	M	Inn	NO	Runs	HS	Avg	100	50	Ct	St	Balls	Runs	Wkts	Avg	BB	5I	10M
Test	6	8	3	18	12 *	3.60	-	-	2	-	1159	635	30	21.16	6-44	2	1
FC	64	85	34	426	42	8.35	-	-	26	-	11350	6347	259	24.50	7-35	15	5
ODI	17	4	2	13	6	6.50	-	-	2	-	856	562	19	29.57	3-28	-	
List A	44	16	12	75	12 *	18.75	-	-	14	-	2161	1609	51	31.54	4-30	-	
20/20 Int	1	0	0	0	0		-	-	-	-	24	21	2	10.50	2-21	-	
20/20	9	0	0	0	0		-	-	1	-	215	235	19	12.36	5-11	1	

MONGIA, D.   Leicestershire

Name: Dinesh Mongia
Role: Left-hand bat, slow left-arm bowler
Born: 17 April 1977, Chandigarh, India
County debut: 2004 (Lancashire),
2005 (Leicestershire)
County cap: 2005 (Leicestershire)
ODI debut: 2000-01
1st-Class 200s: 3
1st-Class 300s: 1
Place in batting averages: 33rd av. 53.33
(2005 69th av. 40.23)
Strike rate: (career 83.44)
Overseas tours: India to Zimbabwe 2001
(Coca-Cola Cup), to Sri Lanka 2001, to West
Indies 2001-02, to England 2002, to Sri
Lanka (ICC Champions Trophy) 2002-03, to
New Zealand 2002-03 (one-day series), to
Africa (World Cup) 2002-03, to Bangladesh

(TVS Cup) 2003, to Bangladesh 2004-05 (one-day series), to Malaysia (DLF Cup)
2006-07, to South Africa 2006-07 (one-day series)

Overseas teams played for: Punjab (India) 1995-96 –
Extras: Represented India U19 1995-96. His awards include Man of the Match in ODI v Zimbabwe at Guwahati 2001-02 (159*; also Man of the Series) and in ODI v West Indies in Barbados 2001-02 (74). An overseas player with Lancashire June to August 2004, deputising first for Carl Hooper, then for Stuart Law; an overseas player with Leicestershire 2005-06
Best batting: 308* Punjab v Jammu & Kashmir, Jalandhar 2000-01
Best bowling: 4-34 Punjab v Kerala, Palakkad 2003-04
Stop press: Represented India in the ICC Champions Trophy 2006-07

2006 Season

	M	Inn	NO	Runs	HS	Avg	100	50	Ct	St	Balls	Runs	Wkts	Avg	BB	5I	10M
Test																	
FC	11	18	3	800	165	53.33	3	2	2	-	961	417	8	52.12	2-62	-	-
ODI																	
List A	7	7	1	51	22	8.50	-	-	2	-	240	186	10	18.60	4-25	-	
20/20 Int																	
20/20	7	7	0	93	21	13.28	-	-	2	-	67	96	1	96.00	1-5	-	

Career Performances

	M	Inn	NO	Runs	HS	Avg	100	50	Ct	St	Balls	Runs	Wkts	Avg	BB	5I	10M
Test																	
FC	118	179	19	8004	308 *	50.02	27	28	118	-	3755	1611	45	35.80	4-34	-	-
ODI	52	46	7	1136	159 *	29.12	1	4	21	-	454	413	9	45.88	3-31	-	
List A	179	167	26	4973	159 *	35.26	10	22	78	-	3332	2558	102	25.07	5-44	1	
20/20 Int																	
20/20	21	20	0	369	50	18.45	-	1	6	-	319	329	19	17.31	3-19	-	

MONTGOMERIE, R. R.   Sussex

Name: Richard Robert Montgomerie
Role: Right-hand opening bat, occasional right-arm slow bowler
Born: 3 July 1971, Rugby
Height: 5ft 10in **Weight:** 13st
Nickname: Monty
County debut: 1991 (Northamptonshire), 1999 (Sussex)
County cap: 1995 (Northamptonshire), 1999 (Sussex)
Benefit: 2007 (Sussex)
1000 runs in a season: 5
Place in batting averages: 124th av. 32.32 (2005 146th av. 30.39)
Strike rate: (career 141.00)
Parents: Robert and Gillian
Wife and date of marriage: Frances Elizabeth, 23 October 2004

Family links with cricket: Father captained Oxfordshire
Education: Rugby School; Worcester College, Oxford University
Qualifications: 12 O-levels, 4 A-levels, BA (Hons) Chemistry, Level II coaching
Career outside cricket: Teacher
Overseas tours: Oxford University to Namibia 1991; Northamptonshire to Zimbabwe and Johannesburg; Christians in Sport to South Africa 2000; Sussex to Grenada 2001, 2002
Overseas teams played for: Sydney University CC 1995-96
Cricket moments to forget: 'Running [Northants] captain Allan Lamb out on my Championship debut ... as his runner'
Other sports followed: Golf, rackets, real tennis 'and many others'
Favourite band: The Police

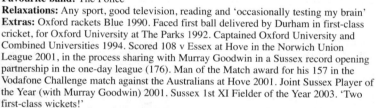

Relaxations: Any sport, good television, reading and 'occasionally testing my brain'
Extras: Oxford University Blue 1990. Faced first ball delivered by Durham in first-class cricket, for Oxford University at The Parks 1992. Captained Oxford University and Combined Universities 1994. Scored 108 v Essex at Hove in the Norwich Union League 2001, in the process sharing with Murray Goodwin in a Sussex record opening partnership in the one-day league (176). Man of the Match award for his 157 in the Vodafone Challenge match against the Australians at Hove 2001. Joint Sussex Player of the Year (with Murray Goodwin) 2001. Sussex 1st XI Fielder of the Year 2003. 'Two first-class wickets!'
Opinions on cricket: 'It's going well!'
Best batting: 196 Sussex v Hampshire, Hove 2002
Best bowling: 1-0 Sussex v Middlesex, Lord's 2001

2006 Season

	M	Inn	NO	Runs	HS	Avg	100	50	Ct	St	Balls	Runs	Wkts	Avg	BB	5I	10M
Test																	
FC	17	28	0	905	100	32.32	1	7	17	-	0	0	0		-	-	-
ODI																	
List A	17	17	2	551	127	36.73	2	3	6	-	0	0	0		-	-	
20/20 Int																	
20/20	4	3	0	45	20	15.00	-	-	3	-	0	0	0		-	-	

Career Performances

	M	Inn	NO	Runs	HS	Avg	100	50	Ct	St	Balls	Runs	Wkts	Avg	BB	5I	10M
Test																	
FC	234	404	32	13208	196	35.50	27	73	217	-	282	147	2	73.50	1-0	-	-
ODI																	
List A	189	185	21	5939	132 *	36.21	7	40	49	-	6	0	0		-	-	
20/20 Int																	
20/20	4	3	0	45	20	15.00	-	-	3	-	0	0	0		-	-	

MOORE, S. C.   Worcestershire

Name: Stephen Colin Moore
Role: Right-hand opening bat, right-arm medium bowler
Born: 4 November 1980, Johannesburg, South Africa
Height: 6ft 1in **Weight:** 13st
Nickname: Mandy, Circles, Mork
County debut: 2003
County colours: 2003
1000 runs in a season: 2
1st-Class 200s: 1
Place in batting averages: 108th av. 34.28 (2005 42nd av. 48.24)
Strike rate: (career 57.60)
Parents: Shane and Carrol
Marital status: Single
Education: St Stithians College, South Africa; Exeter University
Qualifications: MEng (Hons) Electronic Engineering
Overseas teams played for: Midland-Guildford, Perth 2002-04
Career highlights to date: 'First-class debut and Lord's final 2004'
Cricket moments to forget: 'Losing Lord's final 2004 and getting a duck!'

Cricket superstitions: 'Left pad first!'
Other sports played: Hockey, tennis (both Exeter University 1st team), golf, squash
Other sports followed: Tennis
Favourite band: Soul Jazz Collective
Relaxations: 'My music (guitar and saxophone); watersports and wildlife'
Extras: Scored 1000 first-class runs in his first full season 2004. Is not considered an overseas player
Best batting: 246 Worcestershire v Derbyshire, Worcester 2005
Best bowling: 1-13 Worcestershire v Lancashire, Worcester 2004

2006 Season

	M	Inn	NO	Runs	HS	Avg	100	50	Ct	St	Balls	Runs	Wkts	Avg	BB	5I	10M
Test																	
FC	16	30	2	960	97	34.28	-	9	6	-	60	108	1	108.00	1-61	-	-
ODI																	
List A	17	17	1	482	105 *	30.12	1	3	2	-	6	9	0			-	-
20/20 Int																	
20/20	8	6	1	115	27	23.00	-	-	2	-	0	0	0			-	-

Career Performances

	M	Inn	NO	Runs	HS	Avg	100	50	Ct	St	Balls	Runs	Wkts	Avg	BB	5I	10M
Test																	
FC	53	96	10	3460	246	40.23	5	19	26	-	288	279	5	55.80	1-13	-	-
ODI																	
List A	55	54	5	1554	105 *	31.71	2	9	12	-	35	42	1	42.00	1-1	-	
20/20 Int																	
20/20	26	22	4	370	53	20.55	-	1	11	-	0	0	0			-	-

57. Who was the first bowler to take 200 wickets in Tests?

MORGAN, E. J. G. Middlesex

Name: <u>Eoin</u> Joseph Gerard Morgan
Role: Left-hand bat, right-arm
medium bowler
Born: 10 September 1986, Dublin
Height: 5ft 10in **Weight:** 11st 11lbs
Nickname: Moggie
County debut: 2005 (one-day),
2006 (first-class)
ODI debut: 2006
Place in batting averages: 257th av. 13.09
Parents: Joseph and Olivia
Marital status: Single
Family links with cricket: 'My father, three
brothers, two sisters, grandfather and great-
grandfather all played'
Education: Catholic University School,
Dublin
Overseas tours: Ireland U19 to Bangladesh
(U19 World Cup) 2003-04, to Sri Lanka (U19 World Cup) 2005-06; Ireland to
Namibia (ICC Inter-Continental Cup) 2005, to Scotland (European Championship)
2006, plus various Ireland age-group tours to Europe
Overseas teams played for: St Henry's Marist School U19, Durban 2003
Career highlights to date: 'Winning the Inter-Continental Cup with Ireland in
Namibia'
Cricketers particularly admired: Ricky Ponting, Brian Lara
Young players to look out for: Billy Godleman
Other sports played: Rugby (Schools), Gaelic football
Other sports followed: Gaelic football (Dublin GAA – 'The Dubs'), rugby,
snooker, darts
Favourite band: Aslan
Relaxations: 'Watching sports and listening to music'
Extras: Player of the Tournament at European U15 Championships 2000, 2002 and at
European U17 Championships 2002. Became then youngest player to represent Ireland
2003. NBC Denis Compton Award for the most promising young Middlesex player
2003. C&G Man of the Match award for Ireland v Yorkshire in Belfast 2005 (59).
Made ODI debut for Ireland v Scotland at Ayr in the European Championship 2006,
winning Man of the Match award (99). Has also played first-class cricket for Ireland
Best batting: 151 Ireland v United Arab Emirates, Windhoek 2005-06

2006 Season

	M	Inn	NO	Runs	HS	Avg	100	50	Ct	St	Balls	Runs	Wkts	Avg	BB	5I	10M
Test																	
FC	6	11	0	144	38	13.09	-	-	1	1	0	0	0		-	-	-
ODI																	
List A	16	14	1	317	56	24.38	-	2	3	-	0	0	0		-	-	
20/20 Int																	
20/20	8	7	0	174	66	24.85	-	1	4	-	0	0	0		-	-	

Career Performances

	M	Inn	NO	Runs	HS	Avg	100	50	Ct	St	Balls	Runs	Wkts	Avg	BB	5I	10M
Test																	
FC	10	19	0	438	151	23.05	1	1	4	1	12	14	0		-	-	-
ODI	1	1	0	99	99	99.00	-	1	-	-	0	0	0		-	-	
List A	27	23	3	653	99	32.65	-	5	7	-	30	44	0		-	-	
20/20 Int																	
20/20	8	7	0	174	66	24.85	-	1	4	-	0	0	0		-	-	

MORRIS, R. K.　　　　　　　　Hampshire

Name: <u>Richard</u> Kyle Morris
Role: Right-hand bat, right-arm
fast bowler
Born: 26 September 1987, Newbury
Height: 6ft 2in **Weight:** 12st 6lbs
Nickname: Moz, Stipe, Moby
County debut: No first-team appearance
Strike rate: (career 62.00)
Parents: David and Debbie
Marital status: Single
Family links with cricket: 'Brother Jimmy
captains Durham UCCE. Dad played good
club cricket'
Education: Bradfield College;
Loughborough University
Qualifications: GCSEs, A-levels,
Level 1 coaching
Career outside cricket: Student
Off-season: 'At Loughborough training hard. Perth for five weeks at Christmas
to train'
Overseas tours: Hampshire U16 to Jersey 2000, 2001, 2002; Bradfield College to
Cape Town 2001, to Sri Lanka 2004

Career highlights to date: 'Signing for Hampshire. My first-class debut [for LUCCE] v Essex this year [2006]. Representing England U17'

Cricket moments to forget: 'Any "free hit"!'

Cricket superstitions: 'Touch my guard three times before I move into my stance'

Cricketers particularly admired: Shane Watson, Dimi Mascarenhas, Nic Pothas, James Tomlinson, Dwayne Bravo, Andy Bichel

Young players to look out for: Chris Benham, David Balcombe, James Vince, Liam Dawson

Other sports played: Football (Reading Academy), darts

Other sports followed: Football (Reading FC)

Injuries: Out for five weeks with an ankle ligament injury; for four weeks with a quad tear

Favourite band: Bloc Party, Dirty Pretty Things, The Young Knives, Kooks

Relaxations: 'Live music; cooking'

Extras: Represented England U17. Made Hampshire 2nd XI debut aged 16 v Bangladesh U19, taking 3-25 from ten overs. *Cricketer* Cup winner with Bradfield Waifs 2005. Is a sport scholar at Loughborough University. Played for Loughborough UCCE 2006

Opinions on cricket: 'I'd like to see a change back to the original format of the C&G Trophy. It gave the Minor Counties an opportunity on a big stage. Also the group format brought with it many "dead rubber" matches which in my opinion make for a less entertaining and exciting competition alongside increasing the amount of cricket played.'

Best batting: 7 LUCCE v Essex, Chelmsford 2006

Best bowling: 2-58 LUCCE v Hampshire, Rose Bowl 2006

2006 Season (did not make any first-class or one-day appearances for his county)

Career Performances

	M	Inn	NO	Runs	HS	Avg	100	50	Ct	St		Balls	Runs	Wkts	Avg	BB	5I	10M
Test																		
FC	2	2	0	8	7	4.00	-	-	1	-		186	166	3	55.33	2-58	-	-
ODI																		
List A																		
20/20 Int																		
20/20																		

MUCHALL, G. J.   Durham

Name: <u>Gordon</u> James Muchall
Role: Right-hand bat, right-arm
medium bowler
Born: 2 November 1982,
Newcastle upon Tyne
Height: 6ft **Weight:** 13st
Nickname: Much, Head, Pumpkin
County debut: 2002
County cap: 2005
1st-Class 200s: 1
Place in batting averages: 162nd av. 27.78
(2005 143rd av. 30.56)
Strike rate: (career 59.33)
Parents: Mary and Arthur
Marital status: Single
Family links with cricket: 'Dad and brother
Matthew play for South Shields CC; brother
Paul for Tynemouth and Durham Academy'
Education: Durham School
Qualifications: 7 GCSEs, 2 A-levels, Level 2 cricket coach
Career outside cricket: Coaching
Off-season: 'Three weeks in India. Cricket coaching (for SCK)'
Overseas tours: England U19 to India 2000-01, to Australia and (U19 World Cup)
New Zealand 2001-02; ECB National Academy to Australia and Sri Lanka 2002-03
Overseas teams played for: Fremantle 2001-02; Claremont-Nedlands, Perth 2005-06
Career highlights to date: '100 at Lord's. 200 against Kent. 250 for England U19'
Cricket moments to forget: 'With the opposition needing four off the last ball to win,
going into the long barrier position and the ball bouncing over my head for four'
Cricketers particularly admired: Dale Benkenstein, Mike Hussey, Jimmy Maher,
Paul Collingwood, Jon Lewis
Young players to look out for: Paul Muchall, Ben Harmison
Other sports played: Rugby (Durham School – played in *Daily Mail* cup final at
Twickenham)
Other sports followed: Rugby (Newcastle Falcons)
Favourite band: Green Day
Relaxations: Listening to music, socialising with friends
Extras: Represented England U19, scoring 254 in the first 'Test' v India U19 at
Cardiff 2002. Cricket Society's Most Promising Young Cricketer of the Year Award
2002. NBC Denis Compton Award for the most promising young Durham player 2002.
Durham Batsman of the Year 2004. Scored maiden first-class double century (219) v
Kent at Canterbury 2006, in the process sharing with Phil Mustard (130) in a new
Durham record partnership for the sixth wicket (249)

Opinions on cricket: 'Too many games; not enough time to prepare.'
Best batting: 219 Durham v Kent, Canterbury 2006
Best bowling: 3-26 Durham v Yorkshire, Headingley 2003

2006 Season

	M	Inn	NO	Runs	HS	Avg	100	50	Ct	St	Balls	Runs	Wkts	Avg	BB	5I	10M
Test																	
FC	15	28	0	778	219	27.78	2	3	11	-	18	26	0		-	-	-
ODI																	
List A	10	10	0	159	35	15.90	-	-	-	-	0	0	0		-	-	
20/20 Int																	
20/20	8	8	0	148	46	18.50	-	-	2	-	0	0	0		-	-	

Career Performances

	M	Inn	NO	Runs	HS	Avg	100	50	Ct	St	Balls	Runs	Wkts	Avg	BB	5I	10M
Test																	
FC	79	143	6	4009	219	29.26	7	19	51	-	890	615	15	41.00	3-26	-	-
ODI																	
List A	65	58	9	1472	101 *	30.04	1	7	12	-	162	137	1	137.00	1-15	-	
20/20 Int																	
20/20	23	21	3	463	64 *	25.72	-	1	9	-	12	8	1	8.00	1-8	-	

MULLANEY, S. J.   Lancashire

Name: Steven John Mullaney
Role: Right-hand bat, right-arm medium
bowler; all-rounder
Born: 19 November 1986, Warrington
Height: 5ft 10in **Weight:** 12st
Nickname: Mull, Mahoney
County debut: 2006
Parents: Andrew John and Elaine
Marital status: Single
Family links with cricket: 'Dad played
league cricket for 25 years'
Education: St Mary's RC High School
Qualifications: 7 GCSEs
Off-season: 'Australia (Melbourne) from
October to February'
Overseas tours: England U19 to India
2004-05, to Sri Lanka (U19 World Cup)
2005-06
Overseas teams played for: McKinnon, Melbourne 2006-07

Career highlights to date: 'Making first-team debut for Lancashire CCC and being selected for U19 World Cup'
Cricket moments to forget: 'Semi-final defeat to India in [U19] World Cup
Cricket superstitions: 'Put left pad on first'
Cricketers particularly admired: Andrew Flintoff
Young players to look out for: Karl Brown, Moeen Ali, Rory Hamilton-Brown, Tom Smith
Other sports played: Rugby league ('toured France with England U15')
Other sports followed: Football (Manchester City FC), rugby league (St Helens)
Favourite band: Kooks
Relaxations: 'Watching rugby'
Extras: Scored 208 for Lancashire U17. Represented England U19 2005, 2006
Opinions on cricket: 'The standard is getting higher and higher so you have got to work harder and harder.'
Best batting: 44 Lancashire v DUCCE, Durham 2006

2006 Season

	M	Inn	NO	Runs	HS	Avg	100	50	Ct	St	Balls	Runs	Wkts	Avg	BB	5I	10M
Test																	
FC	1	1	0	44	44	44.00	-	-	1	-	60	36	0			-	-
ODI																	
List A	1	0	0	0	0		-	-	-	-	26	23	1	23.00	1-23	-	
20/20 Int																	
20/20	1	1	0	5	5	5.00	-	-	-	-	0	0	0			-	-

Career Performances

	M	Inn	NO	Runs	HS	Avg	100	50	Ct	St	Balls	Runs	Wkts	Avg	BB	5I	10M
Test																	
FC	1	1	0	44	44	44.00	-	-	1	-	60	36	0			-	-
ODI																	
List A	1	0	0	0	0		-	-	-	-	26	23	1	23.00	1-23	-	
20/20 Int																	
20/20	1	1	0	5	5	5.00	-	-	-	-	0	0	0			-	-

MUNDAY, M. K. Somerset

Name: <u>Michael</u> Kenneth Munday
Role: Right-hand bat, leg-spin bowler
Born: 22 October 1984, Nottingham
Height: 5ft 8in **Weight:** 12st
County debut: 2005
Place in bowling averages: 65th av. 32.90
Strike rate: 53.95 (career 47.17)
Parents: John and Maureen
Marital status: Single
Family links with cricket: 'Dad, brother and
sister have played league cricket in Cornwall'
Education: Truro School; Corpus Christi
College, Oxford University
Qualifications: 10 GCSEs, 3 A-levels,
master's degree in Chemistry
Off-season: 'Playing club cricket in Adelaide
until Christmas'

Overseas tours: Cornwall Schools U13 to
South Africa 1998; ESCA West U15 to West Indies 2000
Career highlights to date: 'Any Varsity victory and Somerset and England
U19 debuts'
Cricket moments to forget: 'Being part of a Cornwall Minor Counties team that
dropped 17 catches against Dorset'
Cricket superstitions: 'None'
Cricketers particularly admired: Shane Warne, Graham Gooch
Young players to look out for: Joe Sayers, Luke Parker, Rob Woodman
Other sports played: Chess ('Yes, it is a sport')
Other sports followed: Football (Liverpool)
Favourite band: Coldplay
Relaxations: Swimming, reading
Extras: Played for Cornwall in the C&G 2001. Played for Oxford UCCE 2003-06.
Oxford Blue 2003-06, returning match figures of 11-143 v Cambridge University in
the Varsity Match at The Parks 2006. Represented England U19 2004
Best batting: 17* Oxford University v Cambridge University, The Parks 2006
Best bowling: 6-77 Oxford University v Cambridge University, The Parks 2006

2006 Season

	M	Inn	NO	Runs	HS	Avg	100	50	Ct	St	Balls	Runs	Wkts	Avg	BB	5I	10M
Test																	
FC	7	8	3	42	17 *	8.40	-	-	3	-	1073	658	20	32.90	6-77	2	1
ODI																	
List A																	
20/20 Int																	
20/20																	

Career Performances

	M	Inn	NO	Runs	HS	Avg	100	50	Ct	St	Balls	Runs	Wkts	Avg	BB	5I	10M
Test																	
FC	19	16	8	58	17 *	7.25	-	-	8	-	2453	1580	52	30.38	6-77	3	1
ODI																	
List A	1	0	0	0	0		-	-	-	-	30	39	1	39.00	1-39	-	
20/20 Int																	
20/20																	

MURALITHARAN, M.   Lancashire

Name: Muttiah Muralitharan
Role: Right-hand bat, off-spin bowler
Born: 17 April 1972, Kandy, Sri Lanka
Height: 5ft 7in **Weight:** 9st 6lbs
Nickname: Murali
County debut: 1999 (Lancashire),
2003 (Kent)
County cap: 1999 (Lancashire), 2003 (Kent)
Test debut: 1992
ODI debut: 1993
50 wickets in a season: 2
Place in batting averages: (2005 263rd
av. 13.00)
Place in bowling averages: 3rd av. 18.10
(2005 1st av. 15.00)
Strike rate: 40.57 (career 48.03)
Parents: Sinnasamy and Lakshmi
Wife and date of marriage: Madhi Malar,
21 March 2005
Children: Naren
Education: St Anthony's College, Kandy
Overseas tours: Sri Lanka U24 to South Africa 1992-93; Sri Lanka to England 1991,

to India 1993-94, to Zimbabwe 1994-95, to South Africa 1994-95, to New Zealand 1994-95, to Pakistan 1995-96, to Australia 1995-96, to India and Pakistan (World Cup) 1995-96, to New Zealand 1996-97, to West Indies 1996-97, to India 1997-98, to South Africa 1997-98, to England 1998, to Bangladesh (Wills International Cup) 1998-99, to UK, Ireland and Netherlands (World Cup) 1999, to Zimbabwe 1999-2000, to Pakistan 1999-2000, to Kenya (ICC Knockout Trophy) 2000-01, to South Africa 2000-01, to England 2002, to South Africa 2002-03, to Africa (World Cup) 2002-03, to West Indies 2003, to Zimbabwe 2004, to India 2005-06, to Bangladesh 2005-06, to England 2006, to India (ICC Champions Trophy) 2006-07, to New Zealand 2006-07, plus numerous other one-day series and tournaments in Sharjah, India, Singapore, West Indies, Kenya, Pakistan, Australia, Bangladesh, New Zealand and Morocco; Asian Cricket Council XI to Australia (Tsunami Relief) 2004-05, to South Africa (Afro-Asia Cup) 2005-06; FICA World XI to New Zealand 2004-05; ICC World XI to Australia (Super Series) 2005-06

Overseas teams played for: Tamil Union Cricket and Athletic Club 1991-92 –

Extras: One of *Wisden*'s Five Cricketers of the Year 1999. Was an overseas player with Lancashire 1999 (taking 66 wickets in the 12 Championship innings in which he bowled), 2001 and 2005; has returned for 2007. Lancashire Player of the Year 1999. Took 7-30 v India in the Champions Trophy in Sharjah 2000, at the time the best return in ODI history. Highest wicket-taker in Test cricket for the calendar year 2000 with 75 wickets in ten matches. Has won numerous international series and match awards, including Man of the Match v England at The Oval 1998 (7-155/9-65 from 113.5 overs), in the first Test at Galle 2000 in Sri Lanka's first Test win over South Africa (6-87/7-84) and in the third Test v England at Trent Bridge 2006 (3-62/8-70). Was an overseas player with Kent July to September 2003. Took 500th Test wicket (Michael Kasprowicz) in the second Test v Australia in his home town, Kandy, 2003-04, becoming the third bowler to reach the milestone. In the first Test v Bangladesh at Chittagong 2005-06 (his 100th Test), he became the first bowler to reach 1000 international wickets (589 Test/411 ODI) when he dismissed Khaled Mashud. Took 600th Test wicket (also Khaled Mashud) in the second Test v Bangladesh at Bogra 2005-06, becoming the second bowler to reach the milestone

Best batting: 67 Sri Lanka v India, Kandy 2001

Best bowling: 9-51 Sri Lanka v Zimbabwe, Kandy 2001-02

Stop press: Made Twenty20 International debut v New Zealand at Wellington 2006-07

2006 Season

	M	Inn	NO	Runs	HS	Avg	100	50	Ct	St	Balls	Runs	Wkts	Avg	BB	5I	10M
Test	3	6	3	37	33	12.33	-	-	-	-	878	405	24	16.87	8-70	2	2
FC	4	6	3	37	33	12.33	-	-	-	-	1136	507	28	18.10	8-70	2	2
ODI	2	2	2	1	1 *		-	-	2	-	118	98	2	49.00	1-47	-	
List A	2	2	2	1	1 *		-	-	2	-	118	98	2	49.00	1-47	-	
20/20 Int																	
20/20																	

Career Performances

	M	Inn	NO	Runs	HS	Avg	100	50	Ct	St	Balls	Runs	Wkts	Avg	BB	5I	10M
Test	108	140	49	1095	67	12.03	-	1	59	-	36139	14432	657	21.96	9-51	56	18
FC	164	204	63	1561	67	11.07	-	1	83	-	50691	19855	996	19.93	9-51	90	26
ODI	276	128	49	456	27	5.77	-	-	111	-	15067	9685	416	23.28	7-30	8	
List A	329	149	57	557	27	6.05	-	-	125	-	17808	11260	484	23.26	7-30	9	
20/20 Int																	
20/20	5	2	1	16	9	16.00	-	-	2	-	102	90	10	9.00	4-19	-	

MURTAGH, C. P.   Surrey

Name: Christopher (Chris) Paul Murtagh
Role: Right-hand bat
Born: 14 October 1984, Lambeth, London
Height: 5ft 11in **Weight:** 11st 9lbs
Nickname: Murts, Baby, Brow
County debut: 2005 (one-day)
Parents: Dominic and Elizabeth
Marital status: Single
Family links with cricket: Elder brother Tim played for Surrey and is now with Middlesex; Uncle Andy (A. J. Murtagh) played for Hampshire
Education: John Fisher, Purley, Surrey; Loughborough University
Qualifications: 10 GCSEs, 2 A-levels
Off-season: 'Final year at Loughborough University; studying Sports Science degree and training hard for next season'
Overseas tours: Surrey U19 to Sri Lanka 2002, to Perth 2004
Overseas teams played for: Parramatta, Sydney 2004
Cricket moments to forget: 'Dislocating finger in first training session in Australia – unable to play for two weeks'
Cricket superstitions: 'Left pad on first'
Cricketers particularly admired: Sachin Tendulkar, Andrew Flintoff, Curtly Ambrose
Young players to look out for: Tim Murtagh, Danny Miller, Neil Saker, Jade Dernbach
Other sports played: Rugby, football, golf
Other sports followed: Football (Liverpool FC)
Relaxations: 'Playing golf; watching sport'

Extras: Played for Surrey age-groups and attended Surrey Academy. Made 2nd XI Championship debut 2002. Played for Loughborough UCCE 2005, 2006
Best batting: 37* LUCCE v Nottinghamshire, Trent Bridge 2005

2006 Season (did not make any first-class or one-day appearances for his county)

Career Performances

	M	Inn	NO	Runs	HS	Avg	100	50	Ct	St	Balls	Runs	Wkts	Avg	BB	5I	10M
Test																	
FC	5	7	2	98	37 *	19.60	-	-	2	-	0	0	0		-	-	-
ODI																	
List A	2	2	2	34	30 *		-	-	2	-	0	0	0		-	-	
20/20 Int																	
20/20																	

MURTAGH, T. J. Middlesex

Name: Timothy (Tim) James Murtagh
Role: Left-hand bat, right-arm
fast-medium bowler
Born: 2 August 1981, Lambeth, London
Height: 6ft 2in **Weight:** 12st
County debut: 2000 (one-day, Surrey),
2001 (first-class, Surrey)
Place in batting averages: (2005 89th
av. 37.00)
Place in bowling averages: (2005 132nd
av. 46.91)
Strike rate: (career 61.47)
Parents: Dominic and Elizabeth
Marital status: Single
Family links with cricket: Younger brother
Chris plays for Surrey; Uncle Andy
(A. J. Murtagh) played for Hampshire
Education: John Fisher, Purley, Surrey;
St Mary's University, Twickenham

Qualifications: 10 GCSEs, 2 A-levels
Overseas tours: Surrey U17 to South Africa 1997; England U19 to Malaysia and (U19 World Cup) Sri Lanka 1999-2000; British Universities to South Africa 2002
Overseas teams played for: Eastern Suburbs, Sydney 2006-07
Cricketers particularly admired: Darren Gough, Glenn McGrath
Young players to look out for: Neil Saker, Chris Murtagh, Danny Miller
Other sports played: Rugby (was captain of John Fisher 2nd XV), skiing ('in the past')

Other sports followed: Football (Liverpool FC), rugby
Relaxations: Playing golf, watching sport, films, reading
Extras: Represented British Universities 2000, 2001, 2002 and 2003. Represented England U19 2000. NBC Denis Compton Award for the most promising young Surrey player 2001. Took 6-24 v Middlesex at Lord's 2005, the best return in the history of the Twenty20 Cup. Left Surrey at the end of the 2006 season and has joined Middlesex for 2007
Best batting: 74* Surrey v Middlesex, The Oval 2004
74* Surrey v Warwickshire, Croydon 2005
Best bowling: 6-86 British Universities v Pakistanis, Trent Bridge 2001

2006 Season

	M	Inn	NO	Runs	HS	Avg	100	50	Ct	St	Balls	Runs	Wkts	Avg	BB	5I	10M
Test																	
FC	3	3	2	82	41*	82.00	-	-	2	-	402	223	7	31.85	3-48	-	-
ODI																	
List A	16	10	3	78	14	11.14	-	-	9	-	607	592	8	74.00	1-22	-	
20/20 Int																	
20/20	10	6	3	24	7	8.00	-	-	-	-	222	323	13	24.84	3-27	-	

Career Performances

	M	Inn	NO	Runs	HS	Avg	100	50	Ct	St	Balls	Runs	Wkts	Avg	BB	5I	10M
Test																	
FC	38	53	22	933	74*	30.09	-	6	17	-	4672	2818	76	37.07	6-86	3	-
ODI																	
List A	66	45	17	350	31*	12.50	-	-	18	-	3005	2618	80	32.72	4-14	-	
20/20 Int																	
20/20	29	16	5	90	24*	8.18	-	-	4	-	579	848	37	22.91	6-24	1	

58. Who was the first bowler to take 400 wickets in Tests?

MUSHTAQ AHMED
Sussex

Name: Mushtaq Ahmed
Role: Right-hand bat, leg-spin bowler
Born: 28 June 1970, Sahiwal, Pakistan
Height: 5ft 4in
Nickname: Mushie
County debut: 1993 (Somerset),
2002 (Surrey), 2003 (Sussex)
County cap: 1993 (Somerset), 2003 (Sussex)
Test debut: 1989-90
ODI debut: 1988-89
50 wickets in a season: 5
100 wickets in a season: 2
Place in batting averages: 234th av. 15.85
(2005 231st av. 18.94)
Place in bowling averages: 4th av. 19.91
(2005 36th av. 26.73)
Strike rate: 36.69 (career 50.77)
Wife and date of marriage: Uzma,
18 December 1994
Children: Bazal, Nawal, Habiba, Sumea
Overseas tours: Pakistan YC to Australia (U19 World Cup) 1987-88; Pakistan to Sharjah (Sharjah Cup) 1988-89, to Australia 1989-90, to New Zealand and Australia (World Cup) 1991-92, to England 1992, to New Zealand 1992-93, to West Indies 1992-93, to New Zealand 1993-94, to Sri Lanka 1994-95, to Australia 1995-96, to New Zealand 1995-96, to England 1996, to Sri Lanka 1996-97, to South Africa 1997-98, to Zimbabwe 1997-98, to India 1998-99, to UK, Ireland and Netherlands (World Cup) 1999, to Australia 1999-2000, to West Indies 1999-2000, to Sri Lanka 2000, to New Zealand 2000-01, to England 2001, plus numerous other one-day tournaments in India, Sharjah, Australia, South Africa, Zimbabwe, Singapore, Toronto and Bangladesh
Overseas teams played for: Numerous, including Multan, United Bank, and National Bank of Pakistan; WAPDA 2005-06 –
Career highlights to date: 'Winning the 1992 cricket World Cup final'
Cricket moments to forget: 'Losing the 1996 World Cup quarter-final to India at Bangalore'
Cricket superstitions: 'None'
Cricketers particularly admired: Imran Khan
Other sports followed: Hockey, football (Brazil)
Relaxations: 'Spending time with family, prayer'
Extras: Somerset's overseas player 1993-95 and 1997-98; Player of the Year 1993. Had match figures of 9-198 and 9-186 in successive Tests (Man of the Match in the latter) v Australia 1995-96, following up with 10-171 in next Test v New Zealand eight

days later, winning Man of the Match award. His other international awards include Man of the [Test] Series v England 1996 and v South Africa 1997-98. One of *Wisden*'s Five Cricketers of the Year 1997. Was Surrey's overseas player during August 2002; an overseas player with Sussex since 2003. Took 103 Championship wickets (av. 24.65) 2003. Sussex Player of the Year 2003, 2006. PCA Player of the Year 2003. Took 1000th first-class wicket (Martin Bicknell) v Surrey at The Oval 2004. Took 9-48 (13-108 in the match) v Nottinghamshire at Trent Bridge 2006 to finish the season with 102 Championship wickets (av. 19.91) and as the competition's leading wicket-taker for the fourth consecutive season

Best batting: 90* Sussex v Kent, Hove 2005
Best bowling: 9-48 Sussex v Nottinghamshire, Trent Bridge 2006

2006 Season

	M	Inn	NO	Runs	HS	Avg	100	50	Ct	St	Balls	Runs	Wkts	Avg	BB	5I	10M
Test																	
FC	15	19	5	222	42 *	15.85	-	-	2	-	3743	2031	102	19.91	9-48	11	4
ODI																	
List A	13	5	2	43	14	14.33	-	-	1	-	650	425	20	21.25	5-25	1	
20/20 Int																	
20/20	4	1	0	0	0	0.00	-	-	1	-	96	87	10	8.70	4-30	-	

Career Performances

	M	Inn	NO	Runs	HS	Avg	100	50	Ct	St	Balls	Runs	Wkts	Avg	BB	5I	10M
Test	52	72	16	656	59	11.71	-	2	23	-	12532	6100	185	32.97	7-56	10	3
FC	285	357	50	4871	90 *	15.86	-	19	112	-	65040	32785	1281	25.59	9-48	93	28
ODI	144	76	34	399	34 *	9.50	-	-	30	-	7543	5361	161	33.29	5-36	1	
List A	371	214	74	1597	41	11.40	-	-	58	-	18499	12853	453	28.37	7-24	4	
20/20 Int																	
20/20	20	7	0	29	16	4.14	-	-	2	-	399	376	33	11.39	5-11	1	

59. Who scored 100* for England v Bangladesh
in his 100th ODI, at The Oval 2005?

MUSTARD, P.   Durham

Name: Philip (<u>Phil</u>) Mustard
Role: Left-hand bat, wicket-keeper
Born: 8 October 1982, Sunderland
Height: 5ft 11in   **Weight:** 13st 3lbs
Nickname: Colonel
County debut: 2002
50 dismissals in a season: 1
Place in batting averages: 123rd av. 32.64
(2005 175th av. 26.27)
Parents: Maureen
Marital status: Single
Children: Haydon Samuel, 12 July 2006
Education: Usworth Comprehensive
Off-season: 'Holiday'
Overseas teams played for: Bulleen,
Melbourne 2002; Glenorchy, Tasmania 2003;
Bankstown, Sydney 2004; Tea Tree Gully,
South Australia

Career highlights to date: 'First century 2006. Playing for England U19'
Cricket moments to forget: 'First ball against Jimmy Anderson on debut in C&G'
(Caught Flintoff, bowled Anderson)
Cricketers particularly admired: Alec Stewart
Young players to look out for: Ben Harmison
Other sports played: Golf, football
Other sports followed: Football (Newcastle)
Favourite band: Bee Gees
Relaxations: 'Socialising'
Extras: Scored 77-ball 75 on first-class debut v Sri Lankans at Riverside 2002.
Represented England U19 2002. Scored maiden first-class century (130) v Kent at
Canterbury 2006, in the process sharing with Gordon Muchall (219) in a new Durham
record partnership for the sixth wicket (249). Made 50 (54) dismissals in a season for
the first time and also scored 816 runs in first-class cricket 2006
Opinions on cricket: 'Too many overs in a day.'
Best batting: 130 Durham v Kent, Canterbury 2006

2006 Season

	M	Inn	NO	Runs	HS	Avg	100	50	Ct	St	Balls	Runs	Wkts	Avg	BB	5I	10M
Test																	
FC	16	27	2	816	130	32.64	2	3	53	1	0	0	0		-	-	-
ODI																	
List A	15	14	3	274	84	24.90	-	1	13	4	0	0	0		-	-	
20/20 Int																	
20/20	7	7	1	122	67 *	20.33	-	1	3	1	0	0	0		-	-	

Career Performances

	M	Inn	NO	Runs	HS	Avg	100	50	Ct	St	Balls	Runs	Wkts	Avg	BB	5I	10M
Test																	
FC	50	79	4	2103	130	28.04	2	9	151	7	0	0	0		-	-	-
ODI																	
List A	57	43	5	663	84	17.44	-	2	60	11	0	0	0		-	-	
20/20 Int																	
20/20	24	24	1	447	67 *	19.43	-	3	5	9	0	0	0		-	-	

NAIK, J. K. H.   Leicestershire

Name: Jigar Kumar Hakumatrai Naik
Role: Right-hand bat, right-arm off-break bowler
Born: 10 August 1984, Leicester
Height: 6ft 2in **Weight:** 14st
Nickname: Jigs, Jiggy, Jigsy
County debut: 2006
Strike rate: (career 234.00)
Parents: Hakumatrai and Daxa
Marital status: Single
Education: Rushey Mead; Gateway College; Nottingham Trent University; Loughborough University
Qualifications: BSc (Hons) Multimedia Technology, MSc Computer Science
Career outside cricket: Technical systems engineer
Off-season: 'Finishing university; going to India to develop my bowling; being part of Loughborough UCCE'
Career highlights to date: 'Making my first-class debut'
Cricketers particularly admired: Sachin Tendulkar, Shane Warne
Young players to look out for: Stuart Broad, Adil Rashid

Other sports followed: Tennis, football (Liverpool FC)
Favourite band: Nickelback
Relaxations: 'Music, movies, going to the gym'
Extras: Played for Leicestershire Board XI in the 2003 C&G. First Leicester-born player of Asian origin to represent the county
Opinions on cricket: 'The new ruling of having only one overseas player can only be better for English cricket, so long as the overseas player has enough experience and talent at the highest level to provide input to the club and be helpful to the younger members of the squad.'
Best batting: 13 Leicestershire v West Indies A, Leicester 2006
Best bowling: 1-55 Leicestershire v West Indies A, Leicester 2006

2006 Season

	M	Inn	NO	Runs	HS	Avg	100	50	Ct	St	Balls	Runs	Wkts	Avg	BB	5I	10M
Test																	
FC	3	2	0	14	13	7.00	-	-	2	-	234	181	1	181.00	1-55	-	-
ODI																	
List A																	
20/20 Int																	
20/20																	

Career Performances

	M	Inn	NO	Runs	HS	Avg	100	50	Ct	St	Balls	Runs	Wkts	Avg	BB	5I	10M
Test																	
FC	3	2	0	14	13	7.00	-	-	2	-	234	181	1	181.00	1-55	-	-
ODI																	
List A	2	1	0	1	1	1.00	-	-	-	-	114	75	0		-	-	
20/20 Int																	
20/20																	

NAPIER, G. R. Essex

Name: <u>Graham</u> Richard Napier
Role: Right-hand bat, right-arm medium bowler
Born: 6 January 1980, Colchester
Height: 5ft 10in **Weight:** 12st 7lbs
Nickname: Plank, Napes
County debut: 1997
Place in batting averages: (2005 203rd av. 21.85)
Place in bowling averages: (2005 125th av. 45.28)
Strike rate: (career 62.86)
Parents: Roger and Carol
Marital status: Single

Family links with cricket: Father played for Palmers Boys School 1st XI (1965-68), Essex Police divisional teams, and Harwich Immigration CC

Education: Gilberd School, Colchester

Qualifications: NCA coaching award

Overseas tours: England U17 to Bermuda (International Youth Tournament) 1997; England U19 to South Africa (including U19 World Cup) 1997-98; England A to Malaysia and India 2003-04; England VI to Hong Kong 2004; MCC to Namibia and Uganda 2004-05

Overseas teams played for: Campbelltown CC, Sydney 2000-01; North Perth, Western Australia 2001-02

Career highlights to date: 'Testing myself against the world's best and scoring some runs'

Other sports followed: Football ('The Tractor Boys' – Ipswich Town FC)

Extras: Represented England U19 1999. Man of the Match award for Essex Board XI v Lancashire Board XI in the NatWest 2000. ECB National Academy 2003-04. Included in preliminary England one-day squad of 30 for ICC Champions Trophy 2004

Best batting: 106* Essex v Nottinghamshire, Trent Bridge 2004

Best bowling: 5-56 Essex v Derbyshire, Derby 2004

2006 Season

	M	Inn	NO	Runs	HS	Avg	100	50	Ct	St	Balls	Runs	Wkts	Avg	BB	5I	10M
Test																	
FC	3	3	1	131	62	65.50	-	2	1	-	336	203	1	203.00	1-6	-	-
ODI																	
List A	11	5	3	23	7 *	11.50	-	-	3	-	370	356	5	71.20	2-41	-	
20/20 Int																	
20/20	7	2	0	17	10	8.50	-	-	-	-	162	197	10	19.70	3-19	-	

Career Performances

	M	Inn	NO	Runs	HS	Avg	100	50	Ct	St	Balls	Runs	Wkts	Avg	BB	5I	10M
Test																	
FC	68	98	18	2429	106 *	30.36	2	16	30	-	8298	5399	132	40.90	5-56	2	-
ODI																	
List A	124	94	15	1384	79	17.51	-	7	31	-	3296	2780	114	24.38	6-29	1	
20/20 Int																	
20/20	17	10	0	122	38	12.20	-	-	1	-	392	477	23	20.73	3-13	-	

NASH, C. D.   Sussex

Name: Christopher (<u>Chris</u>) David Nash
Role: Right-hand bat, right-arm
off-spin bowler
Born: 19 May 1983, Cuckfield
Height: 5ft 11in **Weight:** 12st 10lbs
Nickname: Knocker, Nashdog, Little Ears
County debut: 2002
Place in batting averages: 140th av. 30.66
Strike rate: (career 118.66)
Parents: Nick and Jane
Marital status: Single

Family links with cricket: 'Brother played
for Sussex 2nd XI and club team'
Education: Tanbridge House; Collyers Sixth
Form College; Loughborough University
Qualifications: 11 GCSEs, 3 A-levels, degree
in Sports Science, Level II squash and cricket
coaching
Off-season: 'Relaxing, training, going to India in February, and buying a house'
Overseas tours: England U17 to Northern Ireland (ECC Colts Festival) 1999; Sussex
U19 to Cape Town 1999; Horsham CC to Barbados 2005
Overseas teams played for: Subiaco Marist, Perth 2004-05, 2005-06
Career highlights to date: 'Winning the double with Sussex in 2006 (C&G and
Championship)'
Cricket moments to forget: 'Getting a first-baller on debut v Warwicks 2002'
Cricket superstitions: 'Honey on toast and coffee in the morning'
Cricketers particularly admired: 'Dr Dew, Ryan Leverton, Luke Marshall, Philip
Hudson, Murray Goodwin'
Young players to look out for: 'Richard Hawkes, Andrew Hodd, Milton Nash'
Other sports played: Squash (England U16), football (county)
Other sports followed: Football (Horsham, Brighton & Hove Albion)
Injuries: Out for three weeks with a broken finger
Favourite band: Razorlight
Relaxations: 'Fishing, listening to music, going out with friends, training, squash'
Extras: Represented England U15, U17, U18, U19, captaining at U17 and U18 levels.
Sussex League Young Player of the Year 2001. Played for Loughborough UCCE 2002,
2003, 2004. Represented British Universities 2004. Man of the Match in the 2nd XI
Trophy final v Nottinghamshire at Horsham 2005 (2-21/72*). Scored 82 v
Warwickshire in the Pro40 at Hove 2006, winning Man of the Match award. Sussex
Most Improved Player (Umer Rashid Memorial Award) 2006
Opinions on cricket: 'It's in pretty good shape. We shouldn't make too many
changes. Keep it simple so the public can get used to and understand it.'

Best batting: 67 Sussex v Hampshire, Hove 2006
Best bowling: 1-5 LUCCE v Sussex, Hove 2004

2006 Season

	M	Inn	NO	Runs	HS	Avg	100	50	Ct	St	Balls	Runs	Wkts	Avg	BB	5I	10M
Test																	
FC	4	6	0	184	67	30.66	-	1	-	-	150	87	1	87.00	1-63	-	-
ODI																	
List A	7	7	0	205	82	29.28	-	1	1	-	42	64	0			-	-
20/20 Int																	
20/20	5	5	1	61	20	15.25	-	-	4	-	0	0	0			-	-

Career Performances

	M	Inn	NO	Runs	HS	Avg	100	50	Ct	St	Balls	Runs	Wkts	Avg	BB	5I	10M
Test																	
FC	13	19	2	547	67	32.17	-	5	5	-	712	544	6	90.66	1-5	-	-
ODI																	
List A	7	7	0	205	82	29.28	-	1	1	-	42	64	0			-	-
20/20 Int																	
20/20	5	5	1	61	20	15.25	-	-	4	-	0	0	0			-	-

NASH, D. C.   Middlesex

Name: <u>David</u> Charles Nash
Role: Right-hand bat, wicket-keeper
Born: 19 January 1978, Chertsey, Surrey
Height: 5ft 7in **Weight:** 11st 5lbs
Nickname: Nashy, Knocker
County debut: 1995 (one-day), 1997 (first-class)
County cap: 1999
Benefit: 2007
50 dismissals in a season: 1
Place in batting averages: 60th av. 46.00
Strike rate: (career 45.00)
Parents: David and Christine
Marital status: Single
Family links with cricket: 'Father played
club cricket; brother plays now and again for
Ashford CC; mother is avid watcher and tea
lady'

Education: Sunbury Manor; Malvern College
Qualifications: 9 O-levels, 1 A-level, Levels 1 and 2 cricket coaching, qualified
football referee

Career outside cricket: Qualified cricket coach
Overseas tours: England U15 to South Africa 1993; British Airways Youth Team to West Indies 1993-94; England U19 to Zimbabwe 1995-96, to Pakistan 1996-97; England A to Kenya and Sri Lanka 1997-98
Overseas teams played for: Fremantle, Perth 2000-01, 2002-03
Career highlights to date: 'Touring with England A and scoring first hundred for Middlesex at Lord's v Somerset'
Cricket moments to forget: 'All golden ducks'
Cricket superstitions: 'Too many to mention'
Cricketers particularly admired: Angus Fraser
Other sports played: Rugby, football ('played for Millwall U15 and my district side'), 'and most other sports'
Other sports followed: Rugby (London Irish), football (Chelsea)
Relaxations: 'Listening to music, watching sport and socialising with friends'
Extras: Represented Middlesex at all ages. Played for England U14, U15, U17 and U19. Once took six wickets in six balls, aged 11 – 'when I could bowl!' Seaxe Young Player of the Year 1993
Best batting: 114 Middlesex v Somerset, Lord's 1998
Best bowling: 1-8 Middlesex v Essex, Chelmsford 1997

2006 Season

	M	Inn	NO	Runs	HS	Avg	100	50	Ct	St	Balls	Runs	Wkts	Avg	BB	5I	10M
Test																	
FC	8	14	4	460	68 *	46.00	-	4	13	2	29	53	1	53.00	1-53	-	-
ODI																	
List A																	
20/20 Int																	
20/20																	

Career Performances

	M	Inn	NO	Runs	HS	Avg	100	50	Ct	St	Balls	Runs	Wkts	Avg	BB	5I	10M
Test																	
FC	124	178	37	4755	114	33.72	7	24	252	21	90	105	2	52.50	1-8	-	-
ODI																	
List A	112	82	18	1321	67	20.64	-	5	88	15	0	0	0			-	-
20/20 Int																	
20/20																	

NAVED-UL-HASAN   Sussex

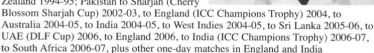

Name: Rana Naved-ul-Hasan
Role: Right-hand bat, right-arm
medium-fast bowler
Born: 28 February 1978, Sheikhupura,
Pakistan
County debut: 2005
County cap: 2005
Test debut: 2004-05
ODI debut: 2002-03
Twenty20 Int debut: 2006
50 wickets in a season: 1
Place in batting averages: 232nd av. 16.75
(2005 160th av. 28.83)
Place in bowling averages: 2nd av. 16.71
(2005 4th av. 19.92)
Strike rate: 28.34 (career 41.53)
Overseas tours: Pakistan U19 to New
Zealand 1994-95; Pakistan to Sharjah (Cherry
Blossom Sharjah Cup) 2002-03, to England (ICC Champions Trophy) 2004, to
Australia 2004-05, to India 2004-05, to West Indies 2004-05, to Sri Lanka 2005-06, to
UAE (DLF Cup) 2006, to England 2006, to India (ICC Champions Trophy) 2006-07,
to South Africa 2006-07, plus other one-day matches in England and India
Overseas teams played for: Lahore Division 1999-2000; Pakistan Customs 2000-01;
Sheikhupura 2000-01 – 2001-02; Allied Bank 2001-02; WAPDA 2002-03 – 2003-04,
2006-07 – ; Sialkot/Sialkot Stallions 2003-04 –
Extras: Played for Herefordshire in the 2003 C&G competition. Played one game for
Essex 2nd XI 2003. Has won several awards, including Player of the [ODI] Series v
India 2004-05. An overseas player with Sussex since 2005
Best batting: 139 Sussex v Middlesex, Lord's 2005
Best bowling: 7-49 Sheikhupura v Sialkot, Muridke 2001-02
Stop press: Player of [ODI] Series v West Indies 2006-07

60. Who became the first player to score 150 in each innings of
a Test match, v Pakistan at Lahore 1979-80?

2006 Season

	M	Inn	NO	Runs	HS	Avg	100	50	Ct	St	Balls	Runs	Wkts	Avg	BB	5I	10M
Test																	
FC	6	8	0	134	64	16.75	-	1	1	-	992	585	35	16.71	7-62	3	1
ODI	5	3	1	24	9 *	12.00	-	-	2	-	210	220	4	55.00	4-57	-	
List A	11	5	2	34	10 *	11.33	-	-	4	-	504	460	21	21.90	5-30	1	
20/20 Int	1	0	0	0	0		-	-	1	-	24	26	1	26.00	1-26	-	
20/20	1	0	0	0	0		-	-	1	-	24	26	1	26.00	1-26	-	

Career Performances

	M	Inn	NO	Runs	HS	Avg	100	50	Ct	St	Balls	Runs	Wkts	Avg	BB	5I	10M
Test	8	13	3	176	42 *	17.60	-	-	3	-	1421	931	16	58.18	3-30	-	-
FC	82	118	14	2452	139	23.57	2	8	44	-	16116	8870	388	22.86	7-49	23	4
ODI	50	33	13	302	29	15.10	-	-	11	-	2401	2182	81	26.93	6-27	1	
List A	111	80	26	1162	70 *	21.51	-	4	34	-	5330	4506	180	25.03	6-27	3	
20/20 Int	1	0	0	0	0		-	-	1	-	24	26	1	26.00	1-26	-	
20/20	14	7	6	127	40 *	127.00	-	-	11	-	276	342	14	24.42	3-37	-	

NEEDHAM, J. Derbyshire

Name: Jake Needham
Role: Right-hand bat, right-arm off-spin bowler; all-rounder
Born: 30 September 1986, Portsmouth, Hampshire
Height: 6ft 1in **Weight:** 11st 7lbs
County debut: 2005
Strike rate: (career 90.00)
Extras: Man of the Match playing for Ockbrook & Borrowash v Kibworth in the Cockspur Cup final at Lord's 2004 (51/4-27). Derbyshire Academy Player of the Year 2005. Represented England U19 2006
Best batting: 29 Derbyshire v Essex, Chelmsford 2006
Best bowling: 2-42 Derbyshire v Essex, Derby 2005

2006 Season

	M	Inn	NO	Runs	HS	Avg	100	50	Ct	St	Balls	Runs	Wkts	Avg	BB	5I	10M
Test																	
FC	1	2	0	29	29	14.50	-	-	-	-	90	88	0			-	-
ODI																	
List A	7	5	3	51	14	25.50	-	-	2	-	284	235	4	58.75	1-29	-	
20/20 Int																	
20/20																	

Career Performances

	M	Inn	NO	Runs	HS	Avg	100	50	Ct	St	Balls	Runs	Wkts	Avg	BB	5I	10M
Test																	
FC	2	4	1	36	29	12.00	-	-	-	-	180	156	2	78.00	2-42	-	-
ODI																	
List A	11	7	4	60	14	20.00	-	-	2	-	380	337	6	56.16	1-29	-	
20/20 Int																	
20/20																	

NEL, A. Essex

Name: Andre Nel
Role: Right-hand bat, right-arm
fast-medium bowler
Born: 15 July 1977, Germiston, Gauteng,
South Africa
County debut: 2003 (Northants),
2005 (Essex)
County cap: 2003 (Northants)
Test debut: 2001-02
ODI debut: 2000-01
Twenty20 Int debut: 2005-06
Strike rate: (career 55.79)
Education: Hoërskool Dr E.G. Jansen,
Boksburg
Overseas tours: South African Academy to
Ireland and Scotland 1999; South Africa A to
Zimbabwe 2002-03, to Australia 2002-03;
South Africa to West Indies 2000-01, to

Zimbabwe 2001-02, to England 2003 (NatWest Series), to Pakistan 2003-04, to New
Zealand 2003-04, to West Indies 2004-05, to India (one-day series) 2005-06, to
Australia 2005-06, to Sri Lanka 2006, to India (ICC Champions Trophy) 2006-07
Overseas teams played for: Easterns 1996-97 – 2005-06; Titans 2003-04 –

Extras: Was an overseas player with Northamptonshire 2003. One of *South African Cricket Annual*'s five Cricketers of the Year 2004, 2005. His match awards include Man of the Match in the fourth ODI v Pakistan at Rawalpindi 2003-04 (4-39) and in the third Test v West Indies in Barbados 2004-05 (4-56/6-32). Was an overseas player with Essex during the 2005 season as a locum for André Adams, taking a wicket (Matthew Wood) with his first ball for the county, v Somerset at Colchester; has returned for the first part of the 2007 season

Best batting: 44 Easterns v Free State, Benoni 2000-01

Best bowling: 6-25 Easterns v Gauteng, Johannesburg 2001-02

2006 Season (did not make any first-class or one-day appearances)

Career Performances

	M	Inn	NO	Runs	HS	Avg	100	50	Ct	St	Balls	Runs	Wkts	Avg	BB	5I	10M
Test	23	25	6	135	18 *	7.10	-	-	9	-	4959	2503	84	29.79	6-32	3	1
FC	83	93	32	844	44	13.83	-	-	30	-	16460	7582	295	25.70	6-25	12	1
ODI	47	7	5	12	4 *	6.00	-	-	12	-	2286	1796	62	28.96	4-39	-	
List A	146	53	31	234	21 *	10.63	-	-	34	-	7221	5014	208	24.10	6-27	3	
20/20 Int	1	1	1	0	0 *		-	-	1	-	24	19	2	9.50	2-19	-	
20/20	11	4	1	23	12	7.66	-	-	3	-	252	237	12	19.75	2-19	-	

NELSON, M. A. G.   Northamptonshire

Name: <u>Mark</u> Anthony George Nelson
Role: Left-hand bat, right-arm medium-fast bowler
Born: 24 September 1986, Milton Keynes
Height: 5ft 11in **Weight:** 11st 7lbs
Nickname: Nelo, Nelly
County debut: 2006 (one-day)
Parents: George and Janet
Marital status: Single
Education: Lord Grey School, Milton Keynes; Stowe School
Qualifications: 3 A-levels
Off-season: 'In Australia (Perth) training and playing'
Overseas tours: England U19 to Sri Lanka (U19 World Cup) 2005-06
Career highlights to date: 'Scoring unbeaten century for England U19' (*104* in the first 'Test' v India U19 at Canterbury 2006*)

Cricket moments to forget: 'Batting for U19, the ball hit my bat and a piece of bat broke off, knocked on to a stump and I was declared out'

Cricket superstitions: 'Nobody can touch my bat before I go in'

Cricketers particularly admired: Brian Lara 'for his skill'

Young players to look out for: Alex Wakely, Ben Howgego

Other sports played: Football 'for recreational purposes only'

Other sports followed: Football (Manchester United)

Injuries: No bowling for six weeks with a stress fracture in the back

Favourite band: Tupac, Notorious B.I.G.

Relaxations: 'Music and dancing'

Extras: NBC Denis Compton Award for the most promising young Northamptonshire player 2006. Represented England U19 2006

2006 Season

	M	Inn	NO	Runs	HS	Avg	100	50	Ct	St	Balls	Runs	Wkts	Avg	BB	5I	10M
Test																	
FC																	
ODI																	
List A	2	1	1	13	13 *	-	-	-	-	-	6	10	0		-	-	
20/20 Int																	
20/20																	

Career Performances

	M	Inn	NO	Runs	HS	Avg	100	50	Ct	St	Balls	Runs	Wkts	Avg	BB	5I	10M
Test																	
FC																	
ODI																	
List A	2	1	1	13	13 *	-	-	-	-	-	6	10	0		-	-	
20/20 Int																	
20/20																	

61. Who became the first batsman to pass 5000 runs in Test cricket, v Australia at Melbourne 1928-29?

NEW, T. J. Leicestershire

Name: Thomas (Tom) James New
Role: Left-hand bat, wicket-keeper
Born: 18 January 1985, Sutton-in-Ashfield
Height: 5ft 9in **Weight:** 10st
Nickname: Newy, P
County debut: 2003 (one-day),
2004 (first-class)
Place in batting averages: 106th av. 34.50
(2005 120th av. 32.90)
Parents: Martin and Louise
Marital status: Engaged
Family links with cricket: 'Dad played local
cricket'
Education: Quarrydale Comprehensive
Qualifications: GCSEs
Overseas tours: England U19 to Bangladesh
(U19 World Cup) 2003-04
Overseas teams played for: Geelong
Cement, Victoria 2001-02

Career highlights to date: 'Making first-class debut. Playing England U19'
Cricket moments to forget: 'Losing semi-final of Costcutter World Challenge 2000
to Pakistan'
Cricket superstitions: 'None'
Cricketers particularly admired: Ian Healy, Jack Russell
Other sports played: Golf, football
Other sports followed: Football (Mansfield Town)
Relaxations: 'Golf, music'
Extras: Played for Nottinghamshire U12, U13, U15, U16 and Midlands U13, U14,
U15. Captained England U15 in Costcutter World Challenge [U15 World Cup] 2000.
Sir John Hobbs Silver Jubilee Memorial Prize 2000. Represented England U19 2003
and 2004. NBC Denis Compton Award for the most promising young Leicestershire
player 2003
Best batting: 89 Leicestershire v Derbyshire, Leicester 2005

2006 Season

	M	Inn	NO	Runs	HS	Avg	100	50	Ct	St	Balls	Runs	Wkts	Avg	BB	5I	10M
Test																	
FC	6	12	0	414	85	34.50	-	5	2	-	0	0	0		-	-	-
ODI																	
List A	5	5	0	189	68	37.80	-	2	-	-	0	0	0		-	-	
20/20 Int																	
20/20																	

464

Career Performances

	M	Inn	NO	Runs	HS	Avg	100	50	Ct	St	Balls	Runs	Wkts	Avg	BB	5I	10M
Test																	
FC	18	30	4	837	89	32.19	-	8	20	2	0	0	0		-	-	-
ODI																	
List A	17	16	0	425	68	26.56	-	2	1	-	0	0	0		-	-	
20/20 Int																	
20/20																	

NEWBY, O. J. Lancashire

Name: <u>Oliver</u> James Newby
Role: Right-hand bat, right-arm
fast-medium bowler
Born: 26 August 1984, Blackburn
Height: 6ft 5in **Weight:** 13st
Nickname: Newbz, Uncle, Flipper
County debut: 2003 (*see Extras*)
Place in bowling averages: 29th av. 27.52
Strike rate: 43.73 (career 55.44)
Parents: Frank and Carol
Marital status: Single
Family links with cricket: 'Dad played
league cricket for Read CC'
Education: Ribblesdale High School;
Myerscough College
Qualifications: 10 GCSEs, ND Sports
Science, Level 1 coaching
Career highlights to date: 'First-class debut'
Other sports played: Golf

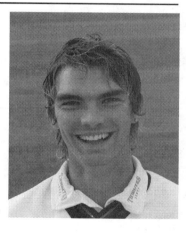

Favourite band: Eminem, Counting Crows
Relaxations: Music
Extras: Took a wicket in each of his first two overs on one-day debut for Lancashire v
India A at Blackpool 2003. Played two Championship matches for Nottinghamshire on
loan 2005
Best batting: 38* Nottinghamshire v Kent, Trent Bridge 2005
Best bowling: 4-58 Lancashire v Nottinghamshire, Old Trafford 2006

2006 Season

	M	Inn	NO	Runs	HS	Avg	100	50	Ct	St	Balls	Runs	Wkts	Avg	BB	5I	10M
Test																	
FC	7	7	2	51	19	10.20	-	-	1	-	831	523	19	27.52	4-58	-	-
ODI																	
List A	1	0	0	0	0		-	-	1	-	36	43	0			-	-
20/20 Int																	
20/20	5	3	1	8	5	4.00	-	-	2	-	84	104	3	34.66	2-34	-	

Career Performances

	M	Inn	NO	Runs	HS	Avg	100	50	Ct	St	Balls	Runs	Wkts	Avg	BB	5I	10M
Test																	
FC	11	11	4	100	38 *	14.28	-	-	1	-	1497	935	27	34.62	4-58	-	-
ODI																	
List A	7	5	4	16	7 *	16.00	-	-	2	-	290	308	6	51.33	2-37	-	
20/20 Int																	
20/20	7	3	1	8	5	4.00	-	-	2	-	108	136	4	34.00	2-34	-	

NEWMAN, S. A. Surrey

Name: Scott Alexander Newman
Role: Left-hand bat
Born: 3 November 1979, Epsom
Height: 6ft 1in **Weight:** 13st 7lbs
Nickname: Ronaldo
County debut: 2001 (one-day),
2002 (first-class)
County cap: 2005
1000 runs in a season: 3
1st-Class 200s: 1
Place in batting averages: 43rd av. 50.14
(2005 44th av. 47.62)
Parents: Ken and Sandy
Marital status: Married
Children: Lemoy, 1985; Brandon,
8 September 2002
Family links with cricket: 'Dad and brother
both played'
Education: Trinity School, Croydon; Brighton University
Qualifications: 10 GCSEs, GNVQ (Advanced) Business Studies
Overseas tours: SCB to Barbados; England A to Malaysia and India 2003-04
Overseas teams played for: Mount Lawley CC, Perth

Cricket moments to forget: 'Any time I fail'
Cricket superstitions: 'None'
Cricketers particularly admired: 'All of Surrey CCC'
Other sports played: 'Most sports'
Other sports followed: Football (Man Utd)
Favourite band: Nas
Relaxations: 'Music, relaxing with family'
Extras: Scored 99 on first-class debut v Hampshire at The Oval 2002. Scored 284 v Derbyshire 2nd XI at The Oval 2003, in the process sharing with Nadeem Shahid (266) in an opening partnership of 552, just three runs short of the English all-cricket record first-wicket stand of 555 set in 1932. Scored 117 and 219 v Glamorgan at The Oval 2005, becoming the first Surrey batsman to score a double hundred and a hundred in the same Championship match. ECB National Academy 2003-04
Best batting: 219 Surrey v Glamorgan, The Oval 2005

2006 Season

	M	Inn	NO	Runs	HS	Avg	100	50	Ct	St	Balls	Runs	Wkts	Avg	BB	5I	10M
Test																	
FC	17	29	1	1404	144 *	50.14	2	10	13	-	0	0	0		-	-	-
ODI																	
List A	10	10	1	155	53	17.22	-	1	2	-	0	0	0		-	-	
20/20 Int																	
20/20	4	3	2	54	24	54.00	-	-	2	-	0	0	0		-	-	

Career Performances

	M	Inn	NO	Runs	HS	Avg	100	50	Ct	St	Balls	Runs	Wkts	Avg	BB	5I	10M
Test																	
FC	58	101	3	4449	219	45.39	10	25	45	-	24	22	0		-	-	-
ODI																	
List A	47	46	2	929	106	21.11	1	3	10	-	0	0	0		-	-	
20/20 Int																	
20/20	21	19	3	352	59	22.00	-	2	8	-	0	0	0		-	-	

NICHOLSON, M. J. Surrey

Name: <u>Matthew</u> James Nicholson
Role: Right-hand bat, right-arm
fast-medium bowler
Born: 2 October 1974, Sydney, Australia
Height: 6ft 6in
Nickname: Nicho
County debut: 2006 (Northamptonshire)
Test debut: 1998-99
Place in batting averages: 157th av. 28.37
Place in bowling averages: 59th av. 31.97
Strike rate: 61.93 (career 55.96)
Overseas tours: Australia U19 to New
Zealand 1992-93, to India 1993-94; Australia
to Zimbabwe 1999-2000
Overseas teams played for: Western
Australia 1996-97 – 2002-03; New South
Wales 2003-04 –
Extras: Australia U19 Player of the Year
1992-93. Attended Commonwealth Bank [Australian] Cricket Academy 1994-95. Had
first innings figures of 7-77 (and scored 58*) for Western Australia v England XI at
Perth 1998-99; it was his first first-class match after 18 months out with glandular
fever and chronic fatigue syndrome (CFS). Man of the Match v South Australia at
Adelaide in the Pura Cup 2001-02 (4-58/4-60). Had second innings figures of 5-60 v
Queensland at Brisbane in the final of the Pura Cup 2004-05. Has played for Australia
A against touring sides. An overseas player with Northamptonshire 2006; has joined
Surrey as an overseas player for 2007
Best batting: 106* Northamptonshire v Derbyshire, Northampton 2006
Best bowling: 7-62 Northamptonshire v Gloucestershire, Northampton 2006

2006 Season

	M	Inn	NO	Runs	HS	Avg	100	50	Ct	St	Balls	Runs	Wkts	Avg	BB	5I	10M
Test																	
FC	15	20	4	454	106*	28.37	1	1	6	-	2849	1471	46	31.97	7-62	2	-
ODI																	
List A	16	9	3	63	23	10.50	-	-	3	-	747	672	17	39.52	3-23	-	
20/20 Int																	
20/20	9	2	0	10	8	5.00	-	-	3	-	189	280	10	28.00	3-12	-	

Career Performances

	M	Inn	NO	Runs	HS	Avg	100	50	Ct	St	Balls	Runs	Wkts	Avg	BB	5I	10M
Test	1	2	0	14	9	7.00	-	-	-	-	150	115	4	28.75	3-56	-	-
FC	86	125	24	2114	106 *	20.93	2	4	46	-	16900	8783	302	29.08	7-62	10	-
ODI																	
List A	51	31	8	244	25	10.60	-	-	15	-	2301	2030	54	37.59	3-23	-	
20/20 Int																	
20/20	12	3	1	12	8	6.00	-	-	4	-	249	359	14	25.64	3-12	-	

NIXON, P. A. Leicestershire

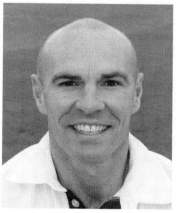

Name: <u>Paul</u> Andrew Nixon
Role: Left-hand bat, wicket-keeper
Born: 21 October 1970, Carlisle
Height: 6ft **Weight:** 12st 10lbs
Nickname: Badger, Nico, Nobby
County debut: 1989 (Leicestershire),
2000 (Kent)
County cap: 1994 (Leicestershire),
2000 (Kent)
Benefit: 2007 (Leicestershire)
1000 runs in a season: 1
50 dismissals in a season: 7
Place in batting averages: 20th av. 59.66
(2005 100th av. 35.40)
Parents: Brian and Sylvia
Wife and date of marriage: Jen,
9 October 1999
Family links with cricket: 'Grandad and
father played local league cricket. Mum made the teas for Edenhall CC, Penrith'
Education: Ullswater High
Qualifications: 2 O-levels, 6 GCSEs, coaching certificates
Overseas tours: Cumbria Schools U15 to Denmark 1985; Leicestershire to Barbados,
to Jamaica, to Netherlands, to Johannesburg, to Bloemfontein; MCC to Bangladesh
1999-2000; England A to India and Bangladesh 1994-95; England to Pakistan and Sri
Lanka 2000-01, to Australia 2006-07 (C'wealth Bank Series)
Overseas teams played for: Melville, Western Australia; North Fremantle, Western
Australia; Mitchells Plain, Cape Town 1993; Primrose CC, Cape Town 1995-96
Career highlights to date: 'Winning the Championship in 1996 with Leicestershire.
Receiving phone call from David Graveney advising me of England [tour] selection'
Cricket moments to forget: 'Losing Lord's one-day finals'
Cricketers particularly admired: David Gower, Ian Botham, Ian Healy, Viv Richards

Other sports played: Golf, football (played for Carlisle United)
Other sports followed: Football (Leicester City, Carlisle United, Liverpool), rugby (Leicester Tigers)
Relaxations: Watching England rugby
Extras: Played for England U15. Played in Minor Counties Championship for Cumberland at 16. MCC Young Pro 1988. Took eight catches in debut match v Warwickshire at Hinckley 1989. Leicestershire Young Player of the Year two years running. In 1994 became only second Leicestershire wicket-keeper to score 1000 (1046) first-class runs in a season; also made 62 first-class dismissals to achieve double. Voted Cumbria Sports Personality of the Year 1994-95. Captained First-Class Counties Select XI v New Zealand A at Milton Keynes 2000. Released by Kent at the end of the 2002 season and rejoined Leicestershire for 2003
Best batting: 144* Leicestershire v Northamptonshire, Northampton 2006
Stop press: Made Twenty20 International debut v Australia at Sydney and ODI debut v Australia at Melbourne 2006-07

2006 Season

	M	Inn	NO	Runs	HS	Avg	100	50	Ct	St	Balls	Runs	Wkts	Avg	BB	5I	10M
Test																	
FC	16	23	8	895	144 *	59.66	2	6	43	3	30	69	0		-	-	-
ODI																	
List A	16	13	4	389	69	43.22	-	3	17	7	0	0	0		-	-	
20/20 Int																	
20/20	11	10	3	271	57 *	38.71	-	2	8	1	0	0	0		-	-	

Career Performances

	M	Inn	NO	Runs	HS	Avg	100	50	Ct	St	Balls	Runs	Wkts	Avg	BB	5I	10M
Test																	
FC	297	437	99	11122	144 *	32.90	16	52	786	65	63	91	0		-	-	-
ODI																	
List A	341	290	61	5722	101	24.98	1	24	359	85	3	1	0		-	-	
20/20 Int																	
20/20	35	32	8	586	57 *	24.41	-	2	19	8	0	0	0		-	-	

NOFFKE, A. A.   Gloucestershire

Name: <u>Ashley</u> Allan Noffke
Role: Right-hand bat, right-arm fast bowler; all-rounder
Born: 30 April 1977, Sunshine Coast, Queensland, Australia
Height: 6ft 3in **Weight:** 14st
Nickname: Noffers, Wombat
County debut: 2002 (Middlesex), 2005 (Durham)
County cap: 2003 (Middlesex)
Place in batting averages: (2005 197th av. 23.00)
Place in bowling averages: (2005 65th av. 30.56)
Strike rate: (career 59.08)
Parents: Rob and Lesley Simpson, and Allan Noffke
Wife and date of marriage: Michelle, 8 April 2000

Family links with cricket: Father played club cricket
Education: Immanuel Lutheran College; Sunshine Coast University
Qualifications: Bachelor of Business, ACB Level 2 coaching certificate
Overseas tours: Commonwealth Bank [Australian] Cricket Academy to Zimbabwe 1998-99; Australia to England 2001, to West Indies 2002-03
Overseas teams played for: Queensland 1999-2000 –
Career highlights to date: 'Man of the Match in a winning Pura Cup final for Queensland. Being selected for Australia for 2001 Ashes tour'
Cricket moments to forget: 'Rolling my ankle playing for Australia v Sussex, forcing me home from the [2001] Ashes tour'
Cricket superstitions: 'None'
Cricketers particularly admired: Steve Waugh
Other sports played: Golf
Other sports followed: Rugby league, rugby union, 'enjoy all sports'
Favourite band: Powderfinger
Relaxations: Fishing
Extras: Queensland Academy of Sport Player of the Year 1998-99. Awarded an ACB contract 2001-02 after just six first-class matches. Has represented Australia A. Sunshine Coast Sportstar of the Year 2001. His awards include Man of the Match in the Pura Cup final v Victoria 2000-01 for his 7-120 match return and 43 runs batting as nightwatchman and v South Australia at Brisbane in the Pura Cup 2003-04 (4-48/2-37; 114*). Was Middlesex overseas player for two periods during the 2002

season; returned as an overseas player for 2003. Was an overseas player with Durham in 2005 but was ruled out with a back injury from late July. Has joined Gloucestershire as an overseas player for the first part of the 2007 season as a locum for Umar Gul
Best batting: 114* Queensland v South Australia, Brisbane 2003-04
Best bowling: 8-24 Middlesex v Derbyshire, Derby 2002

2006 Season (did not make any first-class or one-day appearances)

Career Performances

	M	Inn	NO	Runs	HS	Avg	100	50	Ct	St	Balls	Runs	Wkts	Avg	BB	5I	10M
Test																	
FC	77	96	19	1893	114 *	24.58	1	6	31	-	14594	7657	247	31.00	8-24	9	1
ODI																	
List A	76	38	13	348	58	13.92	-	1	20	-	3714	2811	81	34.70	4-32	-	
20/20 Int																	
20/20	4	2	0	10	7	5.00	-	-	2	-	90	123	8	15.37	3-22	-	

NORTH, M. J.   Gloucestershire

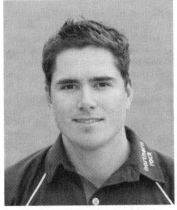

Name: <u>Marcus</u> James North
Role: Left-hand bat, right-arm off-spin bowler
Born: 28 July 1979, Pakenham, Melbourne, Australia
Height: 6ft 1in **Weight:** 12st 10lbs
County debut: 2004 (Durham), 2005 (Lancashire), 2006 (Derbyshire)
1st-Class 200s: 2
Strike rate: (career 84.79)
Wife: Joanne
Overseas tours: Australia U19 to Pakistan 1996-97, to South Africa (U19 World Cup) 1997-98; Commonwealth Bank [Australian] Cricket Academy to Zimbabwe 1998-99; Australia A to Pakistan 2005-06
Overseas teams played for: Western Australia 1999-2000 –
Extras: Commonwealth Bank [Australian] Cricket Academy 1998. Won President's Silver Trophy (season's best individual performance for Western Australia) for his 200* v Victoria at Melbourne in the Pura Cup 2001-02. Scored 200* and 132 in the second 'Test' v Pakistan U19 at Sheikhupura 1996-97, winning Man of the Match award (also Australia's Man of the 'Test' Series). Other awards include Man of the Match for Australia A v Zimbabweans at Adelaide 2003-04 (115). An overseas player

with Durham 2004; an overseas player with Lancashire during the 2005 season as a locum for Brad Hodge; an overseas player with Derbyshire during the 2006 season as a locum for Travis Birt; has joined Gloucestershire as an overseas player for the first part of the 2007 season as a locum for Hamish Marshall
Best batting: 219 Durham v Glamorgan, Cardiff 2004
Best bowling: 4-16 Durham v DUCCE, Riverside 2004

2006 Season

	M	Inn	NO	Runs	HS	Avg	100	50	Ct	St	Balls	Runs	Wkts	Avg	BB	5I	10M
Test																	
FC	3	6	1	465	161	93.00	2	2	6	-	252	91	1	91.00	1-43	-	-
ODI																	
List A	1	1	0	8	8	8.00	-	-	-	-	6	10	0			-	-
20/20 Int																	
20/20	8	7	0	112	45	16.00	-	-	3	-	120	132	2	66.00	1-23	-	

Career Performances

	M	Inn	NO	Runs	HS	Avg	100	50	Ct	St	Balls	Runs	Wkts	Avg	BB	5I	10M
Test																	
FC	85	150	16	5801	219	43.29	14	33	60	-	3646	1977	43	45.97	4-16	-	-
ODI																	
List A	86	82	9	2340	134 *	32.05	4	16	27	-	1219	1053	36	29.25	4-26	-	
20/20 Int																	
20/20	13	12	1	150	45	13.63	-	-	5	-	132	142	2	71.00	1-23	-	

62. Who was the first player to score a century
in both his first and his last ODIs?

NORTHEAST, S. A.   Kent

Name: <u>Sam</u> Alexander Northeast
Role Right-hand top-order bat,
off-spin bowler
Born: 16 October 1989, Ashford, Kent
Height: 5ft 11in **Weight:** 11st
Nickname: North, Bam, Nick Knight
County debut: No first-team appearance
Parents: Allan and Diane
Marital status: Single
Family links with cricket: 'My brother
played Kent age-group as a kid'
Education: Harrow School
Qualifications: 10 GCSEs
Off-season: 'On tour with England U19 to
Malaysia and pre-season with Kent'
Overseas tours: Harrow School to Sri Lanka
2004; England U16 to South Africa; England
U19 to Malaysia 2006-07

Career highlights to date: 'Playing against Sri Lanka first team with players like
Muralitharan and Sangakkara playing and then to go and get 62*'
Cricket moments to forget: 'Not scoring many runs in first two appearances at
Lord's in the Eton v Harrow match'
Cricket superstitions: 'Right pad on first'
Cricketers particularly admired: Graham Thorpe, Steve Waugh
Young players to look out for: Alex Blake, Paul Dixey, Glen Querl
Other sports played: Football, squash and rackets
Other sports followed: Football (Spurs), rugby (Bath)
Favourite band: Starsailor, Snow Patrol
Relaxations: 'Fishing, gardening; playing rackets releases stress'
Extras: Broke Graham Cowdrey's run record at Wellesley House (prep school).
Captained England U15. *Daily Telegraph* Bunbury Scholarship 2005. BBC *Test Match
Special* Young Cricketer of the Year 2005. Sir John Hobbs Silver Jubilee Memorial
Prize for the outstanding U16 schoolboy cricketer 2005. Scored 96 on debut for Kent
2nd XI v Derbyshire 2nd XI at Beckenham 2005. Scored 62* for Sir JP Getty's XI v
Sri Lankans in a 50-over game at Wormsley 2006. Top ten nominee for BBC Young
Sports Personality of the Year 2006. Kent Academy scholar
Opinions on cricket: 'Young players are getting more of a chance to shine in the
game. Hopefully that will help me.'

NORTON, G. Yorkshire

Name: Greg Norton
Role: Right-hand bat, right-arm
fast-medium bowler
Born: 25 January 1988, Rotherham
Height: 6ft **Weight:** 12st 7lbs
Nickname: Norts
County debut: No first-team appearance
Parents: Karen and Dean
Marital status: Single
Education: Swinton Comprehensive School
Qualifications: 'Sport and Recreation'
Off-season: 'Part-time work and doing my
coaching levels'
Career highlights to date: 'Taking five
wickets in the second-team final' (*5-54 v
Warwickshire 2nd XI in the final of the 2nd
XI Trophy 2006 at Headingley*)
Cricket moments to forget: 'Needing two to
win and getting bowled first ball against Doncaster in the Yorkshire League'
Cricket superstitions: 'None'
Cricketers particularly admired: Darren Gough, Ricky Ponting
Young players to look out for: Adil Rashid, Adam Lyth
Other sports played: Golf (3 handicap)
Other sports followed: Football (Liverpool) 'and I love to watch Tiger Woods play on
the TV'
Favourite band: 'Dance and R&B'
Relaxations: 'Playing poker and going swimming'
Extras: Topped Yorkshire League junior bowling averages. Played for Yorkshire
Academy 2005-06
Opinions on cricket: 'It is becoming quicker and more exciting, especially with the
introduction of the Twenty20.'

O'BRIEN, N. J.
Northamptonshire

Name: Niall John O'Brien
Role: Left-hand bat, leg-spin bowler, wicket-keeper
Born: 8 November 1981, Dublin
Height: 5ft 7in **Weight:** 10st 7lbs
Nickname: Nobby, Spud, Paddy, Irish
County debut: 2004 (Kent)
ODI debut: 2006
50 dismissals in a season: 1
Place in batting averages: 209th av. 20.08 (2005 184th av. 24.55)
Strike rate: (career 3.00)
Parents: Brendan and Camilla
Marital status: Single
Family links with cricket: Father a past captain of Ireland; brother Kevin an U19 international and an MCC Young Cricketer
Education: Marian College, Ballsbridge, Dublin
Qualifications: Cricket coach
Overseas tours: Ireland U19 to Sri Lanka (U19 World Cup) 1999-2000; Ireland to Namibia (ICC Inter-Continental Cup) 2005, to Scotland (European Championship) 2006, plus various Ireland age-group and A tours to Europe
Overseas teams played for: Railway Union CC, Dublin; Mosman DCC, Sydney 2000-02; University of Port Elizabeth Academy, South Africa 2002; North Sydney DCC 2003-04
Career highlights to date: 'Gaining first international cap for Ireland; first hundred for Ireland (111 v MCC); making first-class debut for Kent'
Cricket moments to forget: 'Getting a duck on Sky, bowled Warne'
Cricket superstitions: 'None'
Cricketers particularly admired: Steve Waugh, Brett Lee
Young players to look out for: Kevin O'Brien ('brother')
Other sports played: Hockey (Railway Union, Dublin), football
Other sports followed: Football (Everton), rugby (Ireland)
Favourite band: Oasis
Relaxations: 'Music; walking dog; going to my local in the winter with mates'
Extras: Made Ireland senior debut v Denmark 2002 and has played first-class and one-day cricket for Ireland, including ODI (debut v Scotland at Ayr 2006) and C&G. Ireland Cricketer of the Year 2002. Scored 58* as Ireland defeated West Indians in 50-over game in Belfast 2004, winning Man of the Match award. Released by Kent at the end of the 2006 season and has joined Northamptonshire for 2007

Best batting: 176 Ireland v United Arab Emirates, Windhoek 2005-06
Best bowling: 1-4 Kent v CUCCE, Fenner's 2006

2006 Season

	M	Inn	NO	Runs	HS	Avg	100	50	Ct	St	Balls	Runs	Wkts	Avg	BB	5I	10M
Test																	
FC	10	13	1	241	62	20.08	-	1	19	8	3	4	1	4.00	1-4	-	-
ODI																	
List A	9	1	1	11	11 *		-	-	7	5	0	0	0			-	-
20/20 Int																	
20/20	9	5	3	27	11 *	13.50	-	-	4	2	0	0	0			-	-

Career Performances

	M	Inn	NO	Runs	HS	Avg	100	50	Ct	St	Balls	Runs	Wkts	Avg	BB	5I	10M
Test																	
FC	41	59	10	1461	176	29.81	2	7	111	19	3	4	1	4.00	1-4	-	-
ODI	2	2	0	85	53	42.50	-	1	3	1	0	0	0			-	-
List A	38	20	3	318	53	18.70	-	1	29	13	0	0	0			-	-
20/20 Int																	
20/20	20	11	6	59	12	11.80	-	-	5	5	0	0	0			-	-

O'SHEA, M. P.   Glamorgan

Name: <u>Michael</u> Peter O'Shea
Role: Right-hand middle/top-order bat, right-arm off-spin bowler; all-rounder
Born: 4 September 1987, Cardiff
Height: 5ft 11in **Weight:** 12st 6lbs
Nickname: Rik, O'Sh, Mosh
County debut: 2005
Parents: Paul and June
Marital status: Single
Education: Barry Comprehensive School; Millfield School
Qualifications: 13 GCSEs
Overseas tours: England U19 to India 2004-05, to Bangladesh 2005-06
Career highlights to date: 'Championship debut v Kent'
Cricket moments to forget: 'Getting 0 on Championship debut'
Cricket superstitions: 'Put left pad on first'
Cricketers particularly admired: Damien Martyn, Andrew Flintoff

Young players to look out for: Chris Thompson, Rory Hamilton-Brown, Karl Brown, Andy Miller, Ben Wright, Greg Wood
Other sports played: Rugby (Millfield 1st XV – won national XVs competition)
Other sports followed: Rugby (Cardiff Blues, Wales)
Favourite band: Oasis, Westlife
Extras: Has represented England U15, U16, U17, U19. Played for Wales Minor Counties in the C&G 2005 and in Minor Counties competitions 2005-06
Opinions on cricket: 'Improving every year, with great forward thinking, drawing bigger crowds – e.g. Twenty20.'
Best batting: 24 Glamorgan v Kent, Canterbury 2005

2006 Season

	M	Inn	NO	Runs	HS	Avg	100	50	Ct	St	Balls	Runs	Wkts	Avg	BB	5I	10M
Test																	
FC																	
ODI																	
List A	1	1	1	7	7 *		-	-	1	-	12	14	0		-	-	
20/20 Int																	
20/20																	

Career Performances

	M	Inn	NO	Runs	HS	Avg	100	50	Ct	St	Balls	Runs	Wkts	Avg	BB	5I	10M
Test																	
FC	3	5	0	52	24	10.40	-	-	1	-	0	0	0		-	-	-
ODI																	
List A	2	2	1	7	7 *	7.00	-	-	2	-	12	14	0		-	-	
20/20 Int																	
20/20																	

ONIONS, G.   Durham

Name: Graham Onions
Role: Right-hand bat, right-arm medium bowler
Born: 9 September 1982, Gateshead
Height: 6ft 2in **Weight:** 11st 2lbs
Nickname: Wills
County debut: 2004
50 wickets in a season: 1
Place in batting averages: 263rd av. 11.60
Place in bowling averages: 55th av. 31.55
Strike rate: 48.92 (career 58.56)
Parents: Maureen and Richard

Marital status: Single
Education: St Thomas More RC Comprehensive School, Blaydon
Qualifications: 10 GCSEs, GNVQ Advanced Science (Distinction), Level 2 coach
Career outside cricket: Mortgage advisor
Off-season: 'Time at Loughborough training for Academy tour to Perth'
Overseas tours: Durham to Dubai 2005, 2006; England A to Bangladesh 2006-07
Overseas teams played for: South Perth CC 2004

Career highlights to date: 'Being selected in squad for England's NatWest Series against Pakistan [2006]. National Academy'
Cricket moments to forget: 'Getting out to my dad in a charity game!'
Cricket superstitions: 'Lick my fingers before I run in to bowl'
Cricketers particularly admired: Darren Gough, Paul Collingwood
Young players to look out for: Ben Harmison, Mark Turner
Other sports played: Badminton (England U17; plays for Durham County)
Other sports followed: Football (Newcastle United)
Favourite band: 'No favourite – prefer R&B'
Relaxations: 'Sleep, music, the pub with mates'
Extras: Attended UPE International Cricket Academy, Port Elizabeth 2005. Durham Young Player of the Year and Bowler of the Year 2006. ECB National Academy 2006-07
Opinions on cricket: 'Days are too long in Championship cricket – should relate more to Test match cricket. Cricket balls in 2006 have been poor – lose shape easily.'
Best batting: 40 Durham v Warwickshire, Edgbaston 2006
Best bowling: 5-45 Durham v Middlesex, Lord's 2006

63. Which all-rounder scored the first Championship century to be recorded at The Rose Bowl?

2006 Season

	M	Inn	NO	Runs	HS	Avg	100	50	Ct	St	Balls	Runs	Wkts	Avg	BB	5I	10M
Test																	
FC	16	26	6	232	40	11.60	-	-	3	-	2642	1704	54	31.55	5-45	1	-
ODI																	
List A	6	4	1	17	11	5.66	-	-	-	-	222	215	4	53.75	2-38	-	
20/20 Int																	
20/20	4	3	0	37	31	12.33	-	-	1	-	90	99	4	24.75	3-25	-	

Career Performances

	M	Inn	NO	Runs	HS	Avg	100	50	Ct	St	Balls	Runs	Wkts	Avg	BB	5I	10M
Test																	
FC	28	42	13	321	40	11.06	-	-	6	-	3924	2606	67	38.89	5-45	1	-
ODI																	
List A	21	8	3	28	11	5.60	-	-	1	-	782	670	20	33.50	3-39	-	
20/20 Int																	
20/20	11	4	0	37	31	9.25	-	-	3	-	258	254	11	23.09	3-25	-	

ORMOND, J.

Surrey

Name: James Ormond
Role: Right-hand bat, right-arm fast'ish'
bowler, can also bowl off spin
Born: 20 August 1977, Walsgrave, Coventry
Height: 6ft 3in **Weight:** 15st
Nickname: Jimmy, Horse
County debut: 1995 (Leicestershire),
2002 (Surrey)
County cap: 1999 (Leicestershire),
2003 (Surrey)
Test debut: 2001
50 wickets in a season: 4
Place in batting averages: (2005 256th
av. 14.33)
Place in bowling averages: (2005 47th
av. 27.80)
Strike rate: (career 54.26)
Parents: Richard and Margaret
Marital status: Single
Family links with cricket: 'Dad played years of cricket in Warwickshire'
Education: St Thomas More, Nuneaton; North Warwickshire College of Further
Education

Qualifications: 6 GCSEs
Overseas tours: England U19 to Zimbabwe 1995-96; England A to Kenya and Sri Lanka 1997-98; England to India and New Zealand 2001-02
Overseas teams played for: Sydney University CC 1996, 1998, 1999
Cricketers particularly admired: Curtly Ambrose, Courtney Walsh, Allan Donald, Sachin Tendulkar, Brian Lara, Steve Griffin
Other sports played: Football, mountain biking, 'anything'
Other sports followed: Football (Coventry City)
Relaxations: Spending time with friends and family
Extras: Played for the Development of Excellence side and England U19. NBC Denis Compton Award for the most promising young Leicestershire player 1998, 1999, 2000. Took 5-26 v Middlesex at The Oval in the Twenty20 2003 and was Man of the Match (4-11) at Trent Bridge in the inaugural final. Took four wickets in an over, all left-handers and including hat-trick (Hutton, Joyce, Weekes), in the Championship v Middlesex at Guildford 2003
Best batting: 57 Surrey v Gloucestershire, Bristol 2004
Best bowling: 7-63 Surrey v Glamorgan, Cardiff 2005

2006 Season

	M	Inn	NO	Runs	HS	Avg	100	50	Ct	St	Balls	Runs	Wkts	Avg	BB	5I	10M
Test																	
FC	4	4	2	62	41*	31.00	-	-	-	-	558	229	6	38.16	3-39	-	-
ODI																	
List A																	
20/20 Int																	
20/20																	

Career Performances

	M	Inn	NO	Runs	HS	Avg	100	50	Ct	St	Balls	Runs	Wkts	Avg	BB	5I	10M
Test	2	4	1	38	18	12.66	-	-	-	-	372	185	2	92.50	1-70	-	-
FC	123	148	36	1744	57	15.57	-	2	26	-	22956	12278	423	29.02	7-63	20	1
ODI																	
List A	115	71	32	356	32	9.12	-	-	23	-	5202	3825	142	26.93	4-12	-	
20/20 Int																	
20/20	12	5	3	17	6	8.50	-	-	2	-	264	259	16	16.18	5-26	1	

PAGET, C. D. — Derbyshire

Name: Christopher (<u>Chris</u>) David Paget
Role: Right-hand bat, right-arm
off-spin bowler
Born: 2 November 1987, Stafford
Height: 6ft **Weight:** 11st 8lbs
Nickname: Padge, Pooch, Noodles,
Sheephead
County debut: 2004
Strike rate: (career 112.00)
Parents: Anne and Andy
Marital status: Single
Family links with cricket: 'Brother (Alex)
plays for Milford Hall CC and the Old Man
has played in several Lads v Dads games'
Education: Repton School; Durham
University
Qualifications: 9 GCSEs, 3 A-levels
Career outside cricket: 'Student'

Off-season: 'At university, on Derbyshire Academy tour to South Africa, and working
on my game'
Overseas tours: Staffordshire to Barbados 2003; Repton School to Goa 2004, to Sri
Lanka 2005-06; Derbyshire Academy to South Africa 2006-07
Career highlights to date: 'First-class debut'
Cricket moments to forget: 'Bagging my first pair v Durham 2nd XI 2006 – first
duck being caught at deep fine leg; second, run out'
Cricket superstitions: 'Always run on to pitch when going out to bat'
Cricketers particularly admired: Damien Martyn
Other sports played: Tennis ('used to represent Staffs'); rugby, hockey, football
(school); golf
Other sports followed: Football (Everton)
Favourite band: Snow Patrol, David Gray, Jack Johnson, The Rolling Stones
Relaxations: 'Spending time with mates; having fun'
Extras: Played Staffordshire age-group cricket for six years. Took 3-63 (Joseph,
Bravo, Dwayne Smith) on first-class debut v West Indians at Derby 2004. Became
youngest player to represent Derbyshire in the Championship, v Yorkshire at
Headingley 2004, aged 16 years 283 days
Opinions on cricket: 'The diversification of the game, which is bringing a greater
appeal to all ages, has to be a good thing.'
Best batting: 7 Derbyshire v Yorkshire, Headingley 2004
Best bowling: 3-63 Derbyshire v West Indians, Derby 2004

2006 Season

	M	Inn	NO	Runs	HS	Avg	100	50	Ct	St	Balls	Runs	Wkts	Avg	BB	5I	10M
Test																	
FC																	
ODI																	
List A	1	0	0	0	0	-	-	-	-		60	61	1	61.00	1-61	-	
20/20 Int																	
20/20																	

Career Performances

	M	Inn	NO	Runs	HS	Avg	100	50	Ct	St	Balls	Runs	Wkts	Avg	BB	5I	10M
Test																	
FC	4	4	2	7	7	3.50	-	-	-	-	336	206	3	68.66	3-63	-	-
ODI																	
List A	1	0	0	0	0	-	-	-	-		60	61	1	61.00	1-61	-	
20/20 Int																	
20/20																	

PALLADINO, A. P.   Essex

Name: Antonio (Tony) Paul Palladino
Role: Right-hand bat, right-arm medium-fast bowler; all-rounder
Born: 29 June 1983, Whitechapel, London
Height: 6ft **Weight:** 12st 8lbs
Nickname: Dino, TP, Freddie, Italian Stallion
County debut: 2003
Place in batting averages: (2005 237th av. 17.66)
Place in bowling averages: 115th av. 42.07 (2005 124th av. 44.92)
Strike rate: 76.46 (career 82.75)
Parents: Antonio and Kathleen
Marital status: 'Attached'
Family links with cricket: 'Dad played cricket in the Kent League'
Education: Cardinal Pole Secondary School; Anglia Polytechnic University
Qualifications: 9 GCSEs, Advanced GNVQ Leisure and Tourism
Career outside cricket: 'Travel and tourism industry'
Off-season: 'Coaching work and training hard for a big season; possible trip to Dennis Lillee Pace Academy'

Overseas teams played for: Mount Lawley CC, Perth 2005-06
Career highlights to date: '6-41 v Kent 2003; 6-68 v Leics 2006; 111 v Hampshire 2nd XI 2006'
Cricket moments to forget: 'Losing to Sussex 2006 in the C&G Trophy when defending nearly 300 and they were 30-4. Felt sick for about a week' (*Just for the record, the fourth Sussex wicket fell at 56 at Chelmsford 2006, but ... – Ed*)
Cricket superstitions: 'Try and get a corner spot in changing room. Don't let Chris Swainland change near me'
Cricketers particularly admired: Ian Botham, Andy and Grant Flower, Kevin Brooks
Young players to look out for: Adam Wheater, Tom Huggins, Craig Estlea, Chris Liddle, Dave Balcombe, Gareth James, Julian Goodall (Australia)
Other sports played: Football, golf, snooker
Other sports followed: Football (Chelsea), baseball (Boston Red Sox)
Injuries: 'Minor niggles here and there'
Favourite band: 'Various artists'
Relaxations: 'Computer games, cinema, going out with the lads'
Extras: Represented England U17. Represented ECB U19 2000 and 2001. Played for Cambridge UCCE 2003, 2004, 2005. Recorded maiden first-class five-wicket return (6-41) v Kent at Canterbury 2003 in only his second Championship match. Represented British Universities 2005. His 6-68 v Leicestershire at Chelmsford 2006 included a spell of 5-9 in seven overs
Opinions on cricket: 'Twenty20 is the daddy – great game, big crowds and big buzz. County Championship is right with two up/two down – should be 96 overs a day, making lunch and tea longer. Don't like C&G format – should be old-style regional groups into knockout stage.'
Best batting: 41 Essex v Nottinghamshire, Trent Bridge 2004
Best bowling: 6-41 Essex v Kent, Canterbury 2003

2006 Season

	M	Inn	NO	Runs	HS	Avg	100	50	Ct	St	Balls	Runs	Wkts	Avg	BB	5I	10M
Test																	
FC	6	6	2	7	7	1.75	-	-	5	-	994	547	13	42.07	6-68	1	-
ODI																	
List A	3	0	0	0	0		-	-	-	-	138	118	4	29.50	2-21	-	
20/20 Int																	
20/20																	

Career Performances

	M	Inn	NO	Runs	HS	Avg	100	50	Ct	St	Balls	Runs	Wkts	Avg	BB	5I	10M
Test																	
FC	23	24	10	178	41	12.71	-	-	10	-	3310	1992	40	49.80	6-41	2	-
ODI																	
List A	14	4	1	17	16	5.66	-	-	1	-	582	464	18	25.77	3-32	-	
20/20 Int																	
20/20	6	0	0	0	0		-	-	-	-	102	123	6	20.50	2-3	-	

PANESAR, M. S.   Northamptonshire

Name: <u>Mudhsuden</u> Singh Panesar
Role: Left-hand bat, slow left-arm bowler
Born: 25 April 1982, Luton
Height: 6ft 1in   **Weight:** 12st 7lbs
Nickname: Monty
County debut: 2001
County cap: 2006
Test debut: 2005-06
50 wickets in a season: 2
Place in batting averages: 270th av. 10.46
Place in bowling averages: 33rd av. 28.57
(2005 9th av. 22.47)
Strike rate: 64.14 (career 63.06)
Parents: Paramjit and Gursharan
Marital status: Single
Family links with cricket: 'Father used to
play cricket'
Education: Stopsley High School, Luton;
Bedford Modern School; Loughborough University
Qualifications: 10 GCSEs, 3 A-levels, Computer Science degree
Overseas tours: Bedford Modern School to Barbados 1999; England U19 to India
2000-01; Northamptonshire to Grenada 2001-02; British Universities to South Africa
2002; ECB National Academy to Australia and Sri Lanka 2002-03; England to India
2005-06, to Australia 2006-07
Career highlights to date: 'Playing for England'
Cricketers particularly admired: Sachin Tendulkar
Other sports followed: Football (Luton, Arsenal)
Relaxations: 'Reading'
Player website: www.monty-panesar.com
Extras: Represented England U19. Had match figures of 8-131 on first-class debut v
Leicestershire at Northampton 2001, including 4-11 in the second innings. NBC Denis
Compton Award for the most promising young Northamptonshire player 2001. Played
for Loughborough UCCE 2002, 2004. Represented British Universities 2002, 2004,
2005. Recorded maiden Test five-wicket return (5-78) in the third Test v Sri Lanka at
Trent Bridge 2006. England 12-month central contract 2006-07
Best batting: 39* Northamptonshire v Worcestershire, Northampton 2005
Best bowling: 7-181 Northamptonshire v Essex, Chelmsford 2005
Stop press: Had first innings figures of 5-92 in the third Test v Australia 2006-07,
becoming the first England spinner to record a five-wicket innings return in a Test at
Perth. Made Twenty20 International debut v Australia at Sydney 2006-07 and ODI
debut v Australia at Melbourne 2006-07

2006 Season

	M	Inn	NO	Runs	HS	Avg	100	50	Ct	St	Balls	Runs	Wkts	Avg	BB	5I	10M
Test	7	8	5	39	26	13.00	-	-	1	-	1700	725	27	26.85	5-72	2	-
FC	17	21	8	136	34	10.46	-	-	3	-	4554	2029	71	28.57	5-32	6	1
ODI																	
List A	6	3	1	26	14 *	13.00	-	-	2	-	258	199	5	39.80	2-24	-	
20/20 Int																	
20/20	6	1	0	2	2	2.00	-	-	-	-	144	195	8	24.37	2-22	-	

Career Performances

	M	Inn	NO	Runs	HS	Avg	100	50	Ct	St	Balls	Runs	Wkts	Avg	BB	5I	10M
Test	10	13	8	51	26	10.20	-	-	2	-	2408	1037	32	32.40	5-72	2	-
FC	49	62	26	304	39 *	8.44	-	-	13	-	11667	5428	185	29.34	7-181	11	2
ODI																	
List A	11	7	4	50	16 *	16.66	-	-	3	-	486	337	11	30.63	5-20	1	
20/20 Int																	
20/20	6	1	0	2	2	2.00	-	-	-	-	144	195	8	24.37	2-22	-	

PARK, G. T.   Durham

Name: <u>Garry</u> Terence Park
Role: Right-hand bat, wicket-keeper
Born: 19 April 1983, Empangeni, South Africa
Height: 5ft 7in **Weight:** 10st 8lbs
Nickname: Parkie
County debut: 2005 (one-day), 2006 (first-class)
Parents: Michael Park and Christine Reeves
Marital status: Single
Family links with cricket: 'Father played competitive level in Rhodesia (Zimbabwe)'
Education: Eshowe High School, South Africa; Anglia Ruskin University, Cambridge
Qualifications: Matric Exemption (South Africa), Levels 1 and 2 cricket coaching
Career outside cricket: 'Cricket coaching (South Africa)'
Off-season: 'Four months playing and coaching cricket in South Africa'
Overseas teams played for: Crusaders CC, Durban 2005
Career highlights to date: 'Hitting Tino Best for 20 off the over'
Cricket superstitions: 'None'

Cricketers particularly admired: Jonty Rhodes, Dale Benkenstein
Other sports played: Hockey (KwaZulu-Natal U15 and U19), rugby (Natal U14), golf
Other sports followed: Rugby (Natal Sharks)
Injuries: Out for four weeks with a broken finger
Favourite band: Watershed, Daler Mehndi
Relaxations: 'Deep-sea fishing, golf'
Extras: Played for Cambridge UCCE 2003-05
Opinions on cricket: 'I believe cricket is heading in the right direction in terms of the popularity of the game.'
Best batting: 100* Durham v Yorkshire, Headingley 2006

2006 Season

	M	Inn	NO	Runs	HS	Avg	100	50	Ct	St	Balls	Runs	Wkts	Avg	BB	5I	10M
Test																	
FC	4	8	4	316	100 *	79.00	1	1	4	-	0	0	0		-	-	-
ODI																	
List A	2	1	0	7	7	7.00	-	-	2	-	0	0	0		-	-	
20/20 Int																	
20/20																	

Career Performances

	M	Inn	NO	Runs	HS	Avg	100	50	Ct	St	Balls	Runs	Wkts	Avg	BB	5I	10M
Test																	
FC	13	21	6	647	100 *	43.13	1	2	19	-	300	261	0		-	-	-
ODI																	
List A	3	2	0	39	32	19.50	-	-	3	-	0	0	0		-	-	
20/20 Int																	
20/20																	

> 64. Who was the first batsman to score a century in each innings of a Championship match for Durham?

PARKER, L. C. Warwickshire

Name: <u>Luke</u> Charles Parker
Role: Right-hand bat, right-arm
medium bowler
Born: 27 September 1983, Coventry
Height: 6ft **Weight:** 13st
Nickname: Parks
County debut: 2005
Place in batting averages: 154th av. 28.73
(2005 94th av. 36.66)
Strike rate: (career 70.66)
Parents: Linda and Neil
Marital status: Single
Family links with cricket: 'Dad played for
Lincolnshire'
Education: Finham Park; Oxford Brookes
University
Qualifications: 8 GCSEs, 3 A-levels, ECB
Level 1 coach
Overseas teams played for: United, Cape Town 2002-03
Career highlights to date: 'Making first-class debut for Warwickshire CCC in 2005.
Captaining Oxford UCCE 2005'
Cricket moments to forget: 'Dropping Matt Windows three times in an innings of
200-plus'
Cricket superstitions: 'Not really'
Cricketers particularly admired: Nick Knight, Damien Martyn
Young players to look out for: Thomas Beaney, Josh Knappett, Mike Munday,
Navdeep Poonia
Other sports played: Football (Coventry City Academy U10-15)
Other sports followed: Football (Coventry City)
Favourite band: Mylo
Extras: Played for Warwickshire Board XI in the 2002 C&G. Played for Oxford
UCCE 2004-06 (captain 2005). Represented British Universities 2005 and as captain v
Sri Lankans at Fenner's 2006
Opinions on cricket: 'Tea break is not long enough.'
Best batting: 140 OUCCE v Durham, The Parks 2006
Best bowling: 2-37 OUCCE v Gloucestershire, The Parks 2005

2006 Season

	M	Inn	NO	Runs	HS	Avg	100	50	Ct	St	Balls	Runs	Wkts	Avg	BB	5I	10M
Test																	
FC	8	15	0	431	140	28.73	1	2	4	-	202	114	2	57.00	1-21	-	-
ODI																	
List A	2	2	0	17	15	8.50	-	-	1	-	0	0	0			-	-
20/20 Int																	
20/20																	

Career Performances

	M	Inn	NO	Runs	HS	Avg	100	50	Ct	St	Balls	Runs	Wkts	Avg	BB	5I	10M
Test																	
FC	20	33	3	903	140	30.10	1	4	10	-	424	258	6	43.00	2-37	-	-
ODI																	
List A	4	4	1	40	17	13.33	-	-	2	-	12	11	0			-	-
20/20 Int																	
20/20																	

PARSONS, K. A.   Somerset

Name: <u>Keith</u> Alan Parsons
Role: Right-hand bat, right-arm medium bowler; all-rounder
Born: 2 May 1973, Taunton
Height: 6ft 1in   **Weight:** 14st 7lbs
Nickname: Pilot, Pars, Orv
County debut: 1992
County cap: 1999
Benefit: 2004
Place in batting averages: 77th av. 39.30 (2005 54th av. 44.55)
Place in bowling averages: 64th av. 32.72
Strike rate: 53.27 (career 75.50)
Parents: Alan and Lynne
Wife and date of marriage: Sharon, 12 January 2002
Children: Joseph Luke, 17 October 2002; Alex Mathew, 23 March 2005
Family links with cricket: Identical twin brother, Kevin, was on the Somerset staff 1992-94 and then captained the Somerset Board XI. Father played six seasons for Somerset 2nd XI and captained National Civil Service XI
Education: The Castle School, Taunton; Richard Huish Sixth Form College, Taunton

Qualifications: 8 GCSEs, 3 A-levels, NCA senior coach
Career outside cricket: 'Working for Sporting Spectrum Ltd, a corporate hospitality company [based in Taunton] specialising in sporting events throughout England'
Off-season: 'Working for my company, Sporting Spectrum Ltd'
Overseas tours: Castle School to Barbados 1989; Somerset CCC to Cape Town 1999, 2000, 2001
Overseas teams played for: Kapiti Old Boys, Horowhenua, New Zealand 1992-93; Taita District, Wellington, New Zealand 1993-96; Wembley Downs CC, Perth 1998
Career highlights to date: 'C&G final 2001 v Leicestershire – great to win a trophy, and Man of the Match capped a dream day'
Cricket moments to forget: 'Any bad days at Taunton'
Cricket superstitions: 'None'
Cricketers particularly admired: Andy Caddick, Marcus Trescothick, Glenn McGrath, Saqlain Mushtaq
Other sports followed: Rugby union (Bath RFC), football (Nottingham Forest FC), golf, horse racing
Injuries: Out for four weeks with a broken hand
Relaxations: Playing golf, watching movies, listening to music 'and the odd social pint of beer'
Extras: Captained two National Cup winning sides – Taunton St Andrews in National U15 Club Championship and Richard Huish College in National U17 School Championship. Represented English Schools at U15 and U19 level. Somerset Young Player of the Year 1993. C&G Man of the Match award for his 52-ball 60* (including sixes from the last two balls of the innings) and 2-40 in the final v Leicestershire at Lord's 2001
Best batting: 193* Somerset v West Indians, Taunton 2000
Best bowling: 5-13 Somerset v Lancashire, Taunton 2000

2006 Season

	M	Inn	NO	Runs	HS	Avg	100	50	Ct	St	Balls	Runs	Wkts	Avg	BB	5I	10M
Test																	
FC	10	15	2	511	153	39.30	1	2	9	-	586	360	11	32.72	3-33	-	-
ODI																	
List A	14	12	4	287	65	35.87	-	1	7	-	353	314	10	31.40	3-24	-	
20/20 Int																	
20/20	7	7	1	114	40	19.00	-	-	3	-	122	175	6	29.16	2-27	-	

Career Performances

	M	Inn	NO	Runs	HS	Avg	100	50	Ct	St	Balls	Runs	Wkts	Avg	BB	5I	10M
Test																	
FC	130	209	23	5324	193 *	28.62	6	28	115	-	8004	4646	106	43.83	5-13	2	-
ODI																	
List A	239	209	40	5099	121	30.17	2	28	98	-	6081	5087	143	35.57	5-39	1	
20/20 Int																	
20/20	30	29	7	455	57 *	20.68	-	1	9	-	338	467	18	25.94	3-12	-	

PATEL, M. M.   Kent

Name: Minal (<u>Min</u>) Mahesh Patel
Role: Right-hand bat, slow left-arm
orthodox bowler, county vice-captain
Born: 7 July 1970, Mumbai, India
Height: 5ft 7in **Weight:** 10st
Nickname: Ho Chi, Diamond, Geez
County debut: 1989
County cap: 1994
Benefit: 2004
Test debut: 1996
50 wickets in a season: 4
Place in batting averages: 259th av. 12.78
(2005 161st av. 28.64)
Place in bowling averages: 88th av. 36.59
(2005 41st av. 27.55)
Strike rate: 73.03 (career 70.90)
Parents: Mahesh and Aruna
Wife and date of marriage: Karuna,
8 October 1995
Family links with cricket: Father played good club cricket in India,
Africa and England
Education: Dartford Grammar School; Manchester Polytechnic
Qualifications: 6 O-levels, 3 A-levels, BA (Hons) Economics
Overseas tours: Dartford GS to Barbados 1988; England A to India and Bangladesh
1994-95; MCC to Malta 1997, 1999, to Fiji, Sydney and Hong Kong 1998, to East and
Central Africa 1999, to Bangladesh 1999-2000 (c), to Argentina and Chile 2001, to
Namibia and Uganda 2004-05 (c); Kent to Port Elizabeth 2001; Club Cricket
Conference to Australia 2002
Overseas teams played for: St Augustine's, Cape Town 1993-94; Alberton,
Johannesburg 1997-98
Career highlights to date: 'Winning 2001 Norwich Union League at Edgbaston. First
Test cap. Any match-winning performance for Kent'
Cricket moments to forget: 'Being left out of the final XI for the Lord's Test
v India 1996'
Cricketers particularly admired: Derek Underwood, Aravinda de Silva
Other sports played: Golf, snooker
Other sports followed: Football (Tottenham Hotspur), 'most sports that you
can name'
Favourite band: 'A lot of 1970s/80s soul – Phyllis Hyman, Loose Ends,
Keni Burke etc.'
Extras: Played for English Schools 1988, 1989 and NCA England South 1989. Was
voted Kent League Young Player of the Year 1987 while playing for Blackheath.

Whittingdale Young Player of the Year 1994. Vice-captain of Kent since 2006
Best batting: 87 Kent v Glamorgan, Cardiff 2005
Best bowling: 8-96 Kent v Lancashire, Canterbury 1994

2006 Season

	M	Inn	NO	Runs	HS	Avg	100	50	Ct	St	Balls	Runs	Wkts	Avg	BB	5I	10M
Test																	
FC	13	16	2	179	61	12.78	-	1	4	-	2337	1171	32	36.59	4-83	-	-
ODI																	
List A	6	2	1	14	13 *	14.00	-	-	1	-	252	206	10	20.60	3-20	-	
20/20 Int																	
20/20	9	4	1	18	8	6.00	-	-	-	-	196	257	15	17.13	4-26	-	

Career Performances

	M	Inn	NO	Runs	HS	Avg	100	50	Ct	St	Balls	Runs	Wkts	Avg	BB	5I	10M
Test	2	2	0	45	27	22.50	-	-	2	-	276	180	1	180.00	1-101	-	-
FC	207	276	51	3878	87	17.23	-	16	101	-	44601	19202	629	30.52	8-96	30	9
ODI																	
List A	84	43	16	269	27 *	9.96	-	-	24	-	3648	2701	88	30.69	3-20	-	
20/20 Int																	
20/20	9	4	1	18	8	6.00	-	-	-	-	196	257	15	17.13	4-26	-	

PATEL, S. R. Nottinghamshire

Name: <u>Samit</u> Rohit Patel
Role: Right-hand bat, left-arm orthodox spin bowler; all-rounder
Born: 30 November 1984, Leicester
Height: 5ft 8in **Weight:** 12st
Nickname: Pilchy Patel
County debut: 2002
Place in batting averages: 17th av. 61.20
Strike rate: (career 100.75)
Parents: Rohit and Sejal
Marital status: Single
Family links with cricket: Father local league cricketer and brother has played for Nottinghamshire U15
Education: Worksop College
Qualifications: 7 GCSEs, 2 A-levels
Career outside cricket: 'Want to be a coach'
Overseas tours: England U17 to Australia 2001; England U19 to Australia and (U19 World Cup) New Zealand 2001-02, to Australia 2002-03, to Bangladesh (U19 World Cup) 2003-04

Career highlights to date: 'Scoring 122 against South Africa U19 at Arundel [2003], because we were 90-6 at the time'

Cricket moments to forget: 'Playing at Headingley in the Twenty20 Cup against Yorkshire, where I got hit for 28 in an over by Michael Lumb'

Cricket superstitions: 'Put my right pad on first'

Cricketers particularly admired: Sachin Tendulkar, Brian Lara

Young players to look out for: Akhil Patel, Bilal Shafayat, Ravinder Bopara

Other sports played: Rugby, hockey (both for Worksop College 1st XI)

Other sports followed: Football (Nottingham Forest)

Favourite band: G-Unit

Relaxations: 'Listening to music; playing snooker; just generally relaxing'

Extras: Made Nottinghamshire 2nd XI debut in 1999, aged 14. Winner of inaugural BBC *Test Match Special* U15 Young Cricketer of the Year Award 2000. Represented England U19 2002, 2003 (captain in one-day series 2003) and 2004. Scored maiden Championship hundred (156) v Middlesex at Lord's 2006, progressing from century to 150 in 17 balls

Best batting: 173 Nottinghamshire v DUCCE, Durham 2006

Best bowling: 3-73 Nottinghamshire v Kent, Trent Bridge 2005

2006 Season

	M	Inn	NO	Runs	HS	Avg	100	50	Ct	St	Balls	Runs	Wkts	Avg	BB	5I	10M
Test																	
FC	8	12	2	612	173	61.20	2	2	3	-	295	158	2	79.00	1-22	-	-
ODI																	
List A	14	13	2	387	93 *	35.18	-	2	-	-	374	336	13	25.84	3-40		
20/20 Int																	
20/20	11	10	1	239	65	26.55	-	2	5	-	128	174	6	29.00	3-11	-	

Career Performances

	M	Inn	NO	Runs	HS	Avg	100	50	Ct	St	Balls	Runs	Wkts	Avg	BB	5I	10M
Test																	
FC	13	19	2	738	173	43.41	2	3	4	-	806	386	8	48.25	3-73	-	-
ODI																	
List A	42	34	8	834	93 *	32.07	-	4	4	-	878	729	25	29.16	3-40		
20/20 Int																	
20/20	25	24	5	431	65	22.68	-	2	9	-	325	433	18	24.05	3-11	-	

PATTERSON, S. A.   Yorkshire

Name: <u>Steven</u> Andrew Patterson
Role: Right-hand bat, right-arm
medium-fast bowler
Born: 3 October 1983, Hull
Height: 6ft 4in **Weight:** 14st
Nickname: Dead
County debut: 2005
Place in batting averages: 251st av. 14.16
Strike rate: (career 242.00)
Parents: Sue and Alan
Marital status: Single
Education: Malet Lambert School; St Mary's
Sixth Form College; Leeds University
Qualifications: 11 GCSEs, 3 A-levels,
BSc Maths, Level 2 cricket coach
Off-season: 'Travelling'
Overseas tours: MCC A to UAE and Oman
2004
Overseas teams played for: Suburbs New Lynn CC, Auckland 2005-06
Career highlights to date: 'Making my first-class debut for Yorkshire'
Cricket moments to forget: 'Going in as nightwatchman and getting a
first-ball duck!'
Cricket superstitions: 'Not really'
Cricketers particularly admired: Glenn McGrath, Allan Donald
Young players to look out for: Adam Lyth, James Lee
Other sports played: Football, golf, badminton, skiing, scuba diving
Injuries: Shin splints
Favourite band: Coldplay
Relaxations: 'Playing guitar, travelling, reading'
Extras: Played for Yorkshire Board XI in the 2003 C&G. 2nd XI cap 2006
Best batting: 46 Yorkshire v Lancashire, Old Trafford 2006
Best bowling: 1-25 Yorkshire v Warwickshire, Scarborough 2006

2006 Season

	M	Inn	NO	Runs	HS	Avg	100	50	Ct	St	Balls	Runs	Wkts	Avg	BB	5I	10M
Test																	
FC	5	7	1	85	46	14.16	-	-	1	-	376	203	2	101.50	1-25	-	
ODI																	
List A	8	7	7	50	25 *		-	-	2	-	342	330	8	41.25	3-59	-	
20/20 Int																	
20/20																	

494

Career Performances

	M	Inn	NO	Runs	HS	Avg	100	50	Ct	St	Balls	Runs	Wkts	Avg	BB	5I	10M
Test																	
FC	6	7	1	85	46	14.16	-	-	2	-	484	256	2	128.00	1-25	-	-
ODI																	
List A	14	11	10	69	25 *	69.00	-	-	3	-	620	543	13	41.76	3-11	-	
20/20 Int																	
20/20																	

PENG, N. Glamorgan

Name: Nicky Peng
Role: Right-hand bat
Born: 18 September 1982, Newcastle upon Tyne
Height: 6ft 3in **Weight:** 14st 5lbs
Nickname: Pengy
County debut: 2000 (Durham), 2006 (Glamorgan)
County cap: 2001 (Durham)
Place in batting averages: 187th av. 23.80 (2005 234th av. 18.80)
Parents: Linda and Wilf
Marital status: Single
Education: Royal Grammar School, Newcastle upon Tyne
Qualifications: 10 GCSEs
Overseas tours: England U19 to India 2000-01, to Australia and (U19 World Cup) New Zealand 2001-02 (c); ECB National Academy to Australia 2001-02; Durham to South Africa 2002
Overseas teams played for: Subiaco-Floreat, Perth
Career highlights to date: 'Double promotion at Durham. Signing for Glamorgan. PCA Young Player of the Year 2001'
Cricketers particularly admired: Steve Waugh, Jacques Kallis, Paul Collingwood
Young players to look out for: Gordon Muchall, Ben Harmison, Mark Turner
Other sports followed: Football (Newcastle United), rugby (Newcastle Falcons)
Extras: Full name Nicky Peng Gillender. Has represented England at U14, U15, U17 and U19 levels. Represented Minor Counties at age 15. Sir John Hobbs Silver Jubilee Memorial Prize 1998. Scored 98 on Championship debut, v Surrey at Riverside 2000. NBC Denis Compton Award for the most promising young Durham player 2000, 2001. Durham CCC Young Player of the Year 2001. PCA Young Player of the Year 2001
Best batting: 158 Durham v DUCCE, Durham 2003

2006 Season

	M	Inn	NO	Runs	HS	Avg	100	50	Ct	St	Balls	Runs	Wkts	Avg	BB	5I	10M
Test																	
FC	8	15	0	357	59	23.80	-	2	10	-	0	0	0		-	-	-
ODI																	
List A	6	6	0	95	46	15.83	-	-	1	-	0	0	0		-	-	
20/20 Int																	
20/20	7	5	1	89	24	22.25	-	-	2	-	0	0	0		-	-	

Career Performances

	M	Inn	NO	Runs	HS	Avg	100	50	Ct	St	Balls	Runs	Wkts	Avg	BB	5I	10M
Test																	
FC	76	131	2	3089	158	23.94	4	14	45	-	6	2	0		-	-	-
ODI																	
List A	99	98	5	2340	121	25.16	3	12	20	-	0	0	0		-	-	
20/20 Int																	
20/20	19	17	1	296	49	18.50	-	-	10	-	0	0	0		-	-	

PEPLOE, C. T. — Middlesex

Name: Christopher (Chris) Thomas Peploe
Role: Left-hand lower-order bat,
slow left-arm bowler
Born: 26 April 1981, Hammersmith, London
Height: 6ft 4in **Weight:** 13st 7lbs
Nickname: Peps, Pepsy
County debut: 2003
Place in batting averages: 235th av. 15.69
(2005 235th av. 18.37)
Place in bowling averages: 148th av. 78.66
(2005 122nd av. 44.50)
Strike rate: 141.16 (career 102.69)
Parents: Trevor and Margaret
Marital status: Single
Education: Twyford C of E High School;
University of Surrey, Roehampton
Qualifications: 9 GCSEs, 3 A-levels, Sports
Science degree, ECB Level 2 coach, YMCA
gym instructor
Career outside cricket: Cricket coach
Overseas tours: MCC Young Cricketers to South Africa 2002, to Sri Lanka 2003;
Middlesex to India 2004

Overseas teams played for: Northern Districts CC, Sydney
Career highlights to date: 'Making my debut at Lord's for Middlesex'
Cricket moments to forget: 'Bowling at Nick Knight and Craig Spearman when they both scored 300-plus in 2004'
Cricket superstitions: 'None'
Cricketers particularly admired: Daniel Vettori, Andrew Strauss, Phil Tufnell
Young players to look out for: Ed Joyce
Other sports played: Golf
Other sports followed: English rugby
Favourite band: Linkin Park
Relaxations: 'Music, movies, golf'
Extras: MCC Young Cricketer 2002-03
Best batting: 46 Middlesex v Lancashire, Lord's 2006
Best bowling: 4-31 Middlesex v Yorkshire, Southgate 2006

2006 Season

	M	Inn	NO	Runs	HS	Avg	100	50	Ct	St	Balls	Runs	Wkts	Avg	BB	5I	10M
Test																	
FC	10	14	1	204	46	15.69	-	-	2	-	1694	944	12	78.66	4-31	-	-
ODI																	
List A	8	5	1	13	5	3.25	-	-	4	-	354	259	15	17.26	4-41	-	
20/20 Int																	
20/20	6	3	1	8	7	4.00	-	-	-	-	65	149	2	74.50	1-27	-	

Career Performances

	M	Inn	NO	Runs	HS	Avg	100	50	Ct	St	Balls	Runs	Wkts	Avg	BB	5I	10M
Test																	
FC	27	38	6	504	46	15.75	-	-	9	-	5032	2729	49	55.69	4-31	-	-
ODI																	
List A	16	9	2	30	14 *	4.28	-	-	6	-	732	519	26	19.96	4-38	-	
20/20 Int																	
20/20	15	6	4	12	7	6.00	-	-	4	-	221	378	10	37.80	3-35	-	

65. Who was the first player to score twin centuries in his 100th Test?

PETERS, S. D.   Northamptonshire

Name: <u>Stephen</u> David Peters
Role: Right-hand bat, leg-break bowler
Born: 10 December 1978, Harold Wood, Essex
Height: 5ft 11in   **Weight:** 11st 4lbs
Nickname: Pedro, Geezer
County debut: 1996 (Essex), 2002 (Worcestershire), 2006 (Northamptonshire)
County colours: 2002 (Worcestershire)
1000 runs in a season: 2
Place in batting averages: 74th av. 40.07 (2005 233rd av. 18.80)
Strike rate: (career 35.00)
Parents: Lesley and Brian
Marital status: Single
Family links with cricket: 'All family is linked with Upminster CC'

Education: Coopers Company and Coborn School
Qualifications: 9 GCSEs, Level 2 coaching
Off-season: 'Training; travelling'
Overseas tours: Essex U14 to Barbados; Essex U15 to Hong Kong; England U19 to Pakistan 1996-97, to South Africa (including U19 World Cup) 1997-98
Overseas teams played for: Cornwall CC, Auckland 2001-02; Willetton CC, Perth 2002-03
Career highlights to date: 'Winning B&H Cup in 1998 with Essex'
Cricket moments to forget: 'Running myself out for a pair against Durham in 2003'
Cricketers particularly admired: 'Anyone who has played at the top level'
Other sports played: Football, golf
Other sports followed: Football (West Ham United)
Favourite band: Rooster
Relaxations: 'My sofa'
Extras: Sir John Hobbs Silver Jubilee Memorial Prize 1994. Represented England at U14, U15, U17 and U19. Scored century (110) on Essex first-class debut v Cambridge University at Fenner's 1996, aged 17 years 194 days. Essex Young Player of the Year 1996. Man of the Match in the U19 World Cup final in South Africa 1997-98 (107)
Best batting: 178 Northamptonshire v Essex, Northampton 2006
Best bowling: 1-19 Essex v Oxford University, Chelmsford 1999

2006 Season

	M	Inn	NO	Runs	HS	Avg	100	50	Ct	St	Balls	Runs	Wkts	Avg	BB	5I	10M
Test																	
FC	16	30	2	1122	178	40.07	3	5	11	-	0	0	0		-	-	-
ODI																	
List A	7	7	1	173	84 *	28.83	-	1	3	-	0	0	0		-	-	
20/20 Int																	
20/20	1	1	0	0	0	0.00	-	-	-	-	-	0	0	0		-	-

Career Performances

	M	Inn	NO	Runs	HS	Avg	100	50	Ct	St	Balls	Runs	Wkts	Avg	BB	5I	10M
Test																	
FC	132	223	19	6400	178	31.37	12	32	97	-	35	31	1	31.00	1-19	-	-
ODI																	
List A	122	111	6	2026	84 *	19.29	-	10	33	-	0	0	0		-	-	
20/20 Int																	
20/20	11	10	1	82	26 *	9.11	-	-	3	-	0	0	0		-	-

PETTINI, M. L. Essex

Name: <u>Mark</u> Lewis Pettini
Role: Right-hand bat, occasional wicket-keeper
Born: 7 August 1983, Brighton
Height: 5ft 11in **Weight:** 11st 7lbs
Nickname: Swampy, Michelle
County debut: 2001
County cap: 2006
1000 runs in a season: 1
1st-Class 200s: 1
Place in batting averages: 56th av. 46.84
Parents: Pauline and Max
Marital status: Single
Family links with cricket: 'Brother Tom plays. Mum and Dad watch'
Education: Comberton Village College and Hills Road Sixth Form College, Cambridge; Cardiff University

Qualifications: 10 GCSEs, 3 A-levels, Level 1 cricket coaching award
Overseas tours: England U19 to Australia and (U19 World Cup) New Zealand 2001-02; MCC to Sierra Leone and Nigeria; Essex to Cape Town
Cricket moments to forget: 'Losing three U19 ODIs to India [2002]'

Cricketers particularly admired: 'All the Essex first team', Graham Gooch, Damien West

Extras: Captained Cambridgeshire U11-U16. Played for Development of Excellence XI (South) 2001. Represented England U19 2002. Essex 2nd XI Player of the Year 2002. Represented British Universities 2003 and 2004. Scored maiden first-class double century (208*) v Derbyshire at Chelmsford 2006, in the process passing 1000 first-class runs in a season for the first time

Best batting: 208* Essex v Derbyshire, Chelmsford 2006

2006 Season

	M	Inn	NO	Runs	HS	Avg	100	50	Ct	St	Balls	Runs	Wkts	Avg	BB	5I	10M
Test																	
FC	17	29	3	1218	208 *	46.84	3	3	15	-	0	0	0		-	-	
ODI																	
List A	14	12	1	388	80	35.27	-	5	7	-	0	0	0		-	-	
20/20 Int																	
20/20	10	10	0	275	57	27.50	-	1	3	-	0	0	0		-	-	

Career Performances

	M	Inn	NO	Runs	HS	Avg	100	50	Ct	St	Balls	Runs	Wkts	Avg	BB	5I	10M
Test																	
FC	28	48	5	1734	208 *	40.32	3	8	24	-	0	0	0		-	-	-
ODI																	
List A	53	45	4	1023	92 *	24.95	-	9	16	-	0	0	0		-	-	
20/20 Int																	
20/20	22	20	3	471	60	27.70	-	2	7	-	0	0	0		-	-	

PHILLIPS, B. J.   Somerset

Name: Ben James Phillips
Role: Right-hand bat, right-arm fast-medium bowler
Born: 30 September 1975, Lewisham, London
Height: 6ft 6in **Weight:** 15st
Nickname: Bennyphil, Bus
County debut: 1996 (Kent), 2002 (Northamptonshire)
County cap: 2005 (Northamptonshire)
Place in batting averages: 195th av. 22.39 (2005 128th av. 31.92)
Place in bowling averages: 58th av. 31.79 (2005 86th av. 34.66)
Strike rate: 66.05 (career 62.01)
Parents: Glynis and Trevor
Wife and date of marriage: Sarah Jane, 20 January 2003
Family links with cricket: Father and brother both keen club cricketers for Hayes CC (Kent)

Education: Langley Park School for Boys, Beckenham

Qualifications: 9 GCSEs, 3 A-levels

Overseas tours: Northamptonshire to Grenada 2002

Overseas teams played for: University of Queensland, Australia 1993-94; Cape Technikon Green Point, Cape Town 1994-95, 1996-98; University of Western Australia, Perth 1998-99; Valley, Brisbane 2001-02

Career highlights to date: '100* v Lancashire, Old Trafford 1997'

Cricket moments to forget: 'Having to leave the field in a televised game against Worcestershire with a shoulder injury that kept me out for most of [2002] season – that would be up there'

Cricket superstitions: 'Arrive at the ground early – hate rushing!'

Cricketers particularly admired: Glenn McGrath, Jason Gillespie

Other sports followed: Football (West Ham United), rugby (Northampton Saints)

Relaxations: 'Enjoy swimming, watching a good movie, and just generally like spending time with family and friends'

Extras: Set Langley Park School record for the fastest half-century, off 11 balls. Represented England U19 Schools 1993-94. Left Northamptonshire at the end of the 2006 season and has joined Somerset for 2007

Best batting: 100* Kent v Lancashire, Old Trafford 1997

Best bowling: 6-29 Northamptonshire v CUCCE, Fenner's 2006

66. Who was the first batsman to reach 10,000 runs in Tests?

2006 Season

	M	Inn	NO	Runs	HS	Avg	100	50	Ct	St	Balls	Runs	Wkts	Avg	BB	5I	10M
Test																	
FC	17	25	2	515	75	22.39	-	4	6	-	2246	1081	34	31.79	6-29	1	-
ODI																	
List A	15	14	7	247	38 *	35.28	-	-	2	-	652	531	16	33.18	3-48	-	
20/20 Int																	
20/20	9	6	1	119	38 *	23.80	-	-	4	-	204	253	10	25.30	3-12	-	

Career Performances

	M	Inn	NO	Runs	HS	Avg	100	50	Ct	St	Balls	Runs	Wkts	Avg	BB	5I	10M
Test																	
FC	80	114	17	2009	100 *	20.71	1	11	19	-	10914	5339	176	30.33	6-29	4	-
ODI																	
List A	92	62	19	802	44 *	18.65	-	-	23	-	3774	3008	99	30.38	4-25	-	
20/20 Int																	
20/20	25	20	7	335	41 *	25.76	-	-	10	-	540	727	30	24.23	4-18	-	

PHILLIPS, T. J.   Essex

Name: Timothy (<u>Tim</u>) James Phillips
Role: Left-hand bat, slow left-arm bowler
Born: 13 March 1981, Cambridge
Height: 6ft 1in   **Weight:** 13st
Nickname: Pips
County debut: 1999
County cap: 2006
Place in batting averages: 193rd av. 22.40
Place in bowling averages: 121st av. 43.64
Strike rate: 69.67 (career 75.24)
Parents: Carolyn and Martin (deceased)
Marital status: Single
Family links with cricket: 'Father played in Lancashire League then village cricket in Essex. Brother Nick plays for local village, Lindsell'
Education: Felsted School; Durham University
Qualifications: 10 GCSEs, 3 A-levels, BA (Hons) Sport in the Community
Overseas tours: Felsted School to Australia 1995-96; England U19 to Malaysia and (U19 World Cup) Sri Lanka 1999-2000
Cricket moments to forget: '2003 season' (*Out for the whole of the season with cartilage and ligament damage to a knee*)

Cricketers particularly admired: Phil Tufnell
Other sports played: Golf, hockey (Essex Schools U14, U15; East of England U21 trials)
Other sports followed: Rugby union
Favourite band: The Libertines, Coldplay, The White Stripes
Relaxations: 'Music, gigs, socialising, fishing'
Extras: Holmwoods School Cricketer of the Year runner-up 1997 and 1998. Broke Nick Knight's and Elliott Wilson's record for runs in a season for Felsted School, scoring 1213 in 1999. NBC Denis Compton Award 1999. Played for Durham UCCE 2001 and 2002
Best batting: 89 Essex v Worcestershire, Worcester 2005
Best bowling: 5-41 Essex v Derbyshire, Chelmsford 2006

2006 Season

	M	Inn	NO	Runs	HS	Avg	100	50	Ct	St	Balls	Runs	Wkts	Avg	BB	5I	10M
Test																	
FC	14	17	2	336	49	22.40	-	-	16	-	2578	1615	37	43.64	5-41	1	-
ODI																	
List A	11	4	2	48	22 *	24.00	-	-	5	-	418	290	16	18.12	5-34	1	
20/20 Int																	
20/20	8	3	2	10	5 *	10.00	-	-	3	-	147	171	7	24.42	2-11	-	

Career Performances

	M	Inn	NO	Runs	HS	Avg	100	50	Ct	St	Balls	Runs	Wkts	Avg	BB	5I	10M
Test																	
FC	34	46	7	840	89	21.53	-	2	23	-	5643	3641	75	48.54	5-41	1	-
ODI																	
List A	23	13	7	101	24 *	16.83	-	-	8	-	862	674	31	21.74	5-34	1	
20/20 Int																	
20/20	8	3	2	10	5 *	10.00	-	-	3	-	147	171	7	24.42	2-11	-	

67. Who was the first batsman to reach 10,000 runs in ODIs?

PIETERSEN, C.   Northamptonshire

Name: Charl Pietersen
Role: Left-hand bat, left-arm medium-fast opening bowler
Born: 6 January 1983, Kimberley, South Africa
Height: 6ft **Weight:** 13st
County debut: 2005
Strike rate: (career 72.50)
Parents: Thinus and Dalena
Marital status: Single
Family links with cricket: Younger brother was selected for SA Schools in 2005 and has played first-class cricket for Griqualand West
Education: Northern Cape High School, Kimberley
Qualifications: Grade 12 (Matriculation)
Overseas teams played for: Griqualand West 2001-02 – 2003-04, 2006-07

Cricket moments to forget: 'When in 2004 there was no longer a place for me in SA cricket'
Cricket superstitions: 'None'
Cricketers particularly admired: Allan Donald, Steve Harmison, Gary Kirsten, Steve Waugh, Shane Warne
Other sports played: Indoor cricket (Griqualand West)
Other sports followed: Rugby (Blue Bulls)
Favourite band: The Rolling Stones, Blink-182
Relaxations: 'Play a little bit of golf'
Extras: South African indoor cricketer of 1999. Represented South African Schools 2001. Man of the Match v KwaZulu-Natal at Pietermaritzburg in the Standard Bank Cup 2002-03 (4-32). C&G Man of the Match award on county debut for his 7-10 (8-3-10-7) v Denmark at Brøndby 2005; it was the best one-day return by a Northamptonshire bowler. Is not considered an overseas player. Released by Northamptonshire at the end of the 2006 season
Best batting: 45 Griqualand West v North West, Kimberley 2003-04
Best bowling: 6-43 Griqualand West v Boland, Kimberley 2002-03

2006 Season

	M	Inn	NO	Runs	HS	Avg	100	50	Ct	St	Balls	Runs	Wkts	Avg	BB	5I	10M
Test																	
FC	3	4	2	91	39 *	45.50	-	-	-	-	310	212	2	106.00	1-39	-	-
ODI																	
List A	3	2	1	13	12	13.00	-	-	1	-	63	73	0			-	-
20/20 Int																	
20/20	2	1	1	3	3 *		-	-	3	-	36	57	3	19.00	3-35	-	

Career Performances

	M	Inn	NO	Runs	HS	Avg	100	50	Ct	St	Balls	Runs	Wkts	Avg	BB	5I	10M
Test																	
FC	21	32	9	418	45	18.17	-	-	4	-	3045	1816	42	43.23	6-43	1	-
ODI																	
List A	23	11	7	51	14 *	12.75	-	-	4	-	999	856	27	31.70	7-10	1	
20/20 Int																	
20/20	2	1	1	3	3 *		-	-	3	-	36	57	3	19.00	3-35	-	

PIETERSEN, K. P.   Hampshire

Name: <u>Kevin</u> Peter Pietersen
Role: Right-hand bat, right-arm
off-spin bowler
Born: 27 June 1980, Pietermaritzburg,
South Africa
Height: 6ft 4in **Weight:** 14st 9lbs
Nickname: KP, Kelv, Kapes
County debut: 2001 (Nottinghamshire),
2005 (Hampshire)
County cap: 2002 (Nottinghamshire),
2005 (Hampshire)
Test debut: 2005
ODI debut: 2004-05
Twenty20 Int debut: 2005
1000 runs in a season: 3
1st-Class 200s: 3
Place in batting averages: 23rd av. 58.91
(2005 53rd av. 44.85)
Strike rate: (career 84.92)
Parents: Jannie and Penny
Marital status: Engaged to Jessica
Education: Maritzburg College; University of South Africa

Qualifications: 3 A-levels

Overseas tours: Natal to Zimbabwe 1999-2000, to Australia 2000-01; Nottinghamshire to South Africa 2001, 2002; England A to Malaysia and India 2003-04; England to Zimbabwe (one-day series) 2004-05, to South Africa 2004-05 (one-day series), to Pakistan 2005-06, to India 2005-06, to India (ICC Champions Trophy) 2006-07, to Australia 2006-07; ICC World XI to Australia (Super Series) 2005-06

Overseas teams played for: Berea Rovers, Durban 1997 – 2001-02; KwaZulu-Natal 1997-98 – 2000-01; Sydney University 2002-03

Career highlights to date: 'Scoring the three centuries in South Africa for England 2005'

Cricket moments to forget: 'Breaking my leg against Glamorgan in August 2002 in an NUL game'

Cricket superstitions: 'Left pad first'

Cricketers particularly admired: Shaun Pollock, Errol Stewart

Other sports played: Golf, swimming ('represented my state in 1992-93'), running

Other sports followed: Formula One (Ferrari), rugby (Natal Sharks)

Player website: www.kevinpietersen.com

Extras: Played for South African Schools B 1997. Scored 61* and had figures of 4-141 from 56 overs for KwaZulu-Natal v England XI 1999-2000. Scored 1275 first-class runs in first season of county cricket 2001. Player of the [ODI] Series v South Africa 2004-05 (454 runs at 151.33, including the fastest hundred for England in ODIs, from 69 balls). Scored maiden Test century (158, including an Ashes record seven sixes) in the fifth Test v Australia at The Oval 2005, winning Man of the Match award. His other international awards include Man of the Match v Australia at Bristol in the NatWest Series 2005 (65-ball 91*) and England's Man of the [Test] Series v Sri Lanka 2006. ECB National Academy 2003-04, 2004-05. ICC Emerging Player of the Year and ICC ODI Player of the Year awards 2005. Appointed MBE in 2006 New Year Honours as part of 2005 Ashes-winning England team. One of *Wisden*'s Five Cricketers of the Year 2006. Autobiography *Crossing the Boundary: The Early Years in My Cricketing Life* published 2006. England 12-month central contract 2006-07. Is engaged to Liberty X singer Jessica Taylor

Best batting: 254* Nottinghamshire v Middlesex, Trent Bridge 2002

Best bowling: 4-31 Nottinghamshire v DUCCE, Trent Bridge 2003

Stop press: Scored 158 in the second Test v Australia at Adelaide 2006-07, in the process sharing with Paul Collingwood (206) in a record fourth-wicket partnership for England in Tests v Australia (310). Forced to return home early from the England tour to Australia 2006-07 with a fractured rib

2006 Season

	M	Inn	NO	Runs	HS	Avg	100	50	Ct	St	Balls	Runs	Wkts	Avg	BB	5I	10M
Test	7	12	0	707	158	58.91	3	1	7	-	84	76	1	76.00	1-11	-	-
FC	7	12	0	707	158	58.91	3	1	7	-	84	76	1	76.00	1-11	-	-
ODI	8	8	1	203	73	29.00	-	1	3	-	66	65	0		-	-	
List A	10	10	1	344	98	38.22	-	2	3	-	66	65	0		-	-	
20/20 Int	2	2	0	17	17	8.50	-	-	1	-	0	0	0		-	-	
20/20	2	2	0	17	17	8.50	-	-	1	-	0	0	0		-	-	

Career Performances

	M	Inn	NO	Runs	HS	Avg	100	50	Ct	St	Balls	Runs	Wkts	Avg	BB	5I	10M
Test	18	34	1	1597	158	48.39	5	6	11	-	84	76	1	76.00	1-11	-	-
FC	98	161	13	7584	254 *	51.24	26	31	91	-	4756	2681	56	47.87	4-31	-	-
ODI	38	32	7	1382	116	55.28	3	9	19	-	84	91	1	91.00	1-4	-	-
List A	140	125	23	4597	147	45.06	8	28	61	-	1996	1754	35	50.11	3-14	-	-
20/20 Int	3	3	0	51	34	17.00	-	-	4	-	0	0	0		-	-	
20/20	13	13	0	307	67	23.61	-	2	4	-	108	136	6	22.66	2-9	-	

PIPE, D. J. — Derbyshire

Name: David <u>James</u> Pipe
Role: Right-hand bat, wicket-keeper
Born: 16 December 1977, Bradford
Height: 5ft 11in **Weight:** 13st
Nickname: Pipey
County debut: 1998 (Worcestershire), 2006 (Derbyshire)
County colours: 2002 (Worcestershire)
50 dismissals in a season: 1
Place in batting averages: 127th av. 32.18 (2005 229th av. 19.17)
Parents: David and Dorothy
Marital status: Single
Family links with cricket: 'My dad and uncle played in the local league'
Education: Queensbury Upper School; BICC
Qualifications: 8 GCSEs, BTEC National in Business and Finance, HND Leisure Management, senior coaching award, Diploma in Personal Training, Diploma in Sports Therapy
Career outside cricket: Student physiotherapist
Off-season: 'Training, working and studying'

Overseas teams played for: Leeming Spartans CC/South Metropolitan Cricket Association, Perth 1998-99; Manly CC, Australia 1999-2004
Career highlights to date: 'Getting first hundred'
Cricket moments to forget: 'Any game we lose'
Cricket superstitions: 'None'
Cricketers particularly admired: Adam Gilchrist, Ian Healy
Young players to look out for: Brett D'Oliveira (Worcestershire Academy), Gary Ballance, Dan Redfern
Other sports followed: Rugby league (Bradford Bulls, Manly Sea Eagles), boxing ('all British fighters'), AFL (West Coast Eagles)
Injuries: Out for six weeks with a broken thumb
Relaxations: Training
Extras: MCC School of Merit Wilf Slack Memorial Trophy winner 1995. Took eight catches v Hertfordshire at Hertford in the C&G 2001 to set a new NatWest/C&G record for most dismissals in a match by a wicket-keeper. Dick Lygon Award 2002 (Worcestershire Club Man of the Year). Derbyshire Club Man of the Year 2006
Best batting: 104* Worcestershire v Hampshire, Rose Bowl 2003

2006 Season

	M	Inn	NO	Runs	HS	Avg	100	50	Ct	St	Balls	Runs	Wkts	Avg	BB	5I	10M
Test																	
FC	14	20	4	515	89	32.18	-	3	43	7	0	0	0		-	-	-
ODI																	
List A	13	10	2	89	19	11.12	-	-	10	1	0	0	0		-	-	
20/20 Int																	
20/20	8	6	1	80	29 *	16.00	-	-	4	3	0	0	0		-	-	

Career Performances

	M	Inn	NO	Runs	HS	Avg	100	50	Ct	St	Balls	Runs	Wkts	Avg	BB	5I	10M
Test																	
FC	45	67	9	1296	104 *	22.34	1	5	124	14	0	0	0		-	-	-
ODI																	
List A	43	33	8	479	56	19.16	-	2	36	13	0	0	0		-	-	
20/20 Int																	
20/20	21	16	4	131	29 *	10.91	-	-	10	5	0	0	0		-	-	

PLUNKETT, L. E.   Durham

Name: <u>Liam</u> Edward Plunkett
Role: Right-hand bat, right-arm fast bowler
Born: 6 April 1985, Middlesbrough
Height: 6ft 4in **Weight:** 13st
Nickname: Pudsey
County debut: 2003
Test debut: 2005-06
ODI debut: 2005-06
Twenty20 Int debut: 2006
50 wickets in a season: 1
Place in batting averages: 228th av. 17.16
(2005 243rd av. 17.06)
Place in bowling averages: 26th av. 27.15
(2005 68th av. 30.84)
Strike rate: 51.26 (career 50.67)
Parents: Alan and Marie
Marital status: Engaged to Lisa
Family links with cricket: 'Father played
local cricket'

Education: Nunthorpe Comprehensive
Qualifications: 9 GCSEs, volleyball coaching badge
Off-season: 'Tours'
Overseas tours: England U19 to Australia 2002-03, to Bangladesh (U19 World Cup)
2003-04; England to Pakistan 2005-06, to India 2005-06, to Australia 2006-07
Overseas teams played for: Adelaide University 2005
Career highlights to date: 'England debut'
Cricket moments to forget: 'This injury (oblique)' (*see **Injuries***)
Cricket superstitions: 'None'
Cricketers particularly admired: Glenn McGrath
Young players to look out for: Ben Harmison
Other sports played: Golf, swimming
Other sports followed: Football (Middlesbrough, Arsenal)
Injuries: Out from July to September 2006 with a damaged oblique muscle
Favourite band: 'R&B'
Relaxations: 'Travelling to different countries with Lisa'
Extras: Became only the second bowler to record a five-wicket innings return on
Championship debut for Durham, 5-53 v Yorkshire at Headingley 2003. Represented
England U19 2003. NBC Denis Compton Award for the most promising young
Durham player 2003. ECB National Academy 2004-05 (part-time), 2005-06
Opinions on cricket: 'Twenty20 game loaded towards batsmen.'
Best batting: 74* Durham v Somerset, Stockton 2005
Best bowling: 6-74 Durham v Hampshire, Riverside 2004

2006 Season

	M	Inn	NO	Runs	HS	Avg	100	50	Ct	St	Balls	Runs	Wkts	Avg	BB	5I	10M
Test	4	5	1	59	28	14.75	-	-	1	-	766	417	13	32.07	3-17	-	-
FC	6	7	1	103	28	17.16	-	-	2	-	974	516	19	27.15	3-17	-	-
ODI	5	5	3	61	29	30.50	-	-	-	-	206	242	3	80.66	2-60	-	
List A	7	5	3	61	29	30.50	-	-	-	-	297	337	6	56.16	2-44	-	
20/20 Int	1	0	0	0	0		-	-	-	-	24	37	1	37.00	1-37	-	
20/20	1	0	0	0	0		-	-	-	-	24	37	1	37.00	1-37	-	

Career Performances

	M	Inn	NO	Runs	HS	Avg	100	50	Ct	St	Balls	Runs	Wkts	Avg	BB	5I	10M
Test	6	9	1	69	28	8.62	-	-	2	-	1004	601	16	37.56	3-17	-	-
FC	40	60	14	887	74 *	19.28	-	2	13	-	6233	3917	123	31.84	6-74	4	-
ODI	16	15	5	200	56	20.00	-	1	4	-	734	727	16	45.43	3-51	-	
List A	45	31	12	354	56	18.63	-	1	9	-	2055	1797	52	34.55	4-28	-	
20/20 Int	1	0	0	0	0		-	-	-	-	24	37	1	37.00	1-37	-	
20/20	10	6	4	29	8	14.50	-	-	4	-	184	242	6	40.33	2-18	-	

POONIA, N. S.   Warwickshire

Name: Navdeep (<u>Navi</u>) Singh Poonia
Role: Right-hand bat, right-arm medium bowler
Born: 11 May 1986, Glasgow
Height: 6ft 3in **Weight:** 14st
Nickname: Nav, Sat Nav
County debut: 2006
ODI debut: 2006
Parents: Jaipal and Bindy Poonia
Marital status: Single
Family links with cricket: 'Dad played club cricket at Walsall CC'
Education: Moseley Park School; Wolverhampton University
Qualifications: 10 GCSEs, 2 A-levels, Levels 1 and 2 coaching
Overseas tours: Warwickshire Academy to South Africa 2005; Scotland to Bangladesh (one-day series) 2006-07, to Kenya (ICC Associates Tri-Series) 2006-07, to West Indies (World Cup) 2006-07
Cricket superstitions: 'None'
Cricketers particularly admired: Sachin Tendulkar, Brian Lara, Allan Donald

Young players to look out for: Jasbir Poonia
Other sports played: Football, badminton
Other sports followed: Football (Man Utd and Glasgow Rangers)
Favourite band: 112, Jagged Edge
Relaxations: 'Playing snooker with mates and cousins'
Extras: Played for Warwickshire Board XI in the 2003 C&G. Cyril Goodway (Warwickshire Old County Cricketers' Association) Trophy U17. Top-scored with 59 on county one-day debut v Nottinghamshire at Edgbaston in the C&G 2006. Made ODI debut for Scotland v Ireland at Ayr in the European Championship 2006
Opinions on cricket: 'Better cricketing wickets for both batters and bowlers.'
Best batting: 35 Warwickshire v West Indies A, Edgbaston 2006

2006 Season

	M	Inn	NO	Runs	HS	Avg	100	50	Ct	St	Balls	Runs	Wkts	Avg	BB	5I	10M
Test																	
FC	1	1	0	35	35	35.00	-	-	-	-	0	0	0		-	-	-
ODI																	
List A	9	9	0	234	59	26.00	-	1	1	-	0	0	0		-	-	
20/20 Int																	
20/20	3	3	0	32	19	10.66	-	-	-	-	0	0	0		-	-	

Career Performances

	M	Inn	NO	Runs	HS	Avg	100	50	Ct	St	Balls	Runs	Wkts	Avg	BB	5I	10M
Test																	
FC	1	1	0	35	35	35.00	-	-	-	-	0	0	0		-	-	-
ODI	1	1	0	26	26	26.00	-	-	1	-	0	0	0		-	-	
List A	11	11	0	277	59	25.18	-	1	2	-	0	0	0		-	-	
20/20 Int																	
20/20	3	3	0	32	19	10.66	-	-	-	-	0	0	0		-	-	

68. Who was the first bowler to take 1000 international wickets?

POPE, S. P.

Name: <u>Stephen</u> Patrick Pope
Role: Right-hand bat, wicket-keeper
Born: 25 January 1983, Cheltenham
Height: 5ft 8in **Weight:** 12st
Nickame: Bod
County debut: 2003 (Gloucestershire),
2006 (one-day, Surrey)
Parents: John and Patricia
Marital status: Single
Education: Cheltenham Bournside
Comprehensive
Qualifications: 11 GCSEs, 2 A-levels
Overseas tours: ESCA South West U15 to
West Indies 1998; England U19 to Australia
and (U19 World Cup) New Zealand 2001-02;
Gloucestershire to South Africa 2002
Overseas teams played for: St Kilda,
Melbourne 2001-02
Career highlights to date: 'Playing for England U19 in the World Cup 2002'
Cricketers particularly admired: Jack Russell, David Partridge
Other sports played: Rugby union (scrum half for England U16 v Portugal and
Wales; England U18 Development Squad)
Other sports followed: Football (Arsenal FC)
Relaxations: 'Going out with my friends'
Extras: Represented England at U14, U15, U17 and U19 levels. Played for
Gloucestershire Board XI in the NatWest 1999 and 2000 and in the C&G 2001 and
2002. NBC Denis Compton Award for the most promising young Gloucestershire
player 2001. Released by Gloucestershire at the end of the 2003 season; played one
C&G match for Surrey 2006
Best batting: 17* Gloucestershire v Worcestershire, Cheltenham 2003

2006 Season

	M	Inn	NO	Runs	HS	Avg	100	50	Ct	St	Balls	Runs	Wkts	Avg	BB	5I	10M
Test																	
FC																	
ODI																	
List A	1	1	0	5	5	5.00	-	-	1	-	0	0	0		-	-	
20/20 Int																	
20/20																	

Career Performances

	M	Inn	NO	Runs	HS	Avg	100	50	Ct	St	Balls	Runs	Wkts	Avg	BB	5I	10M
Test																	
FC	5	8	3	65	17 *	13.00	-	-	10	1	0	0	0		-	-	-
ODI																	
List A	6	5	0	27	15	5.40	-	-	11	1	0	0	0		-	-	
20/20 Int																	
20/20	3	1	1	4	4 *		-	-	1	2	0	0	0		-	-	

POTHAS, N.   Hampshire

Name: Nicolas (<u>Nic</u>) Pothas
Role: Right-hand bat, wicket-keeper
Born: 18 November 1973, Johannesburg, South Africa
Height: 6ft 1in **Weight:** 13st 7lbs
Nickname: Skeg
County debut: 2002
County cap: 2003
ODI debut: 2000
50 dismissals in a season: 3
Place in batting averages: 10th av. 64.86 (2005 31st av. 51.21)
Strike rate: (career 120.00)
Parents: Emmanuel and Penelope
Marital status: 'Very single'
Family links with cricket: 'Greek by nationality, therefore clearly none'
Education: King Edward VII High School; Rand Afrikaans University

Overseas tours: South Africa A to England 1996, to Sri Lanka 1998-99, to West Indies 2000-01; Gauteng to Australia 1997; South Africa to Singapore (Singapore Challenge) 2000-01
Overseas teams played for: Transvaal/Gauteng 1993-94 – 2001-02
Career highlights to date: 'First tour for South Africa A. Playing for South Africa'
Cricket superstitions: 'Too many to mention'
Cricketers particularly admired: Ray Jennings, Jimmy Cook, Robin Smith
Other sports played: Hockey (South Africa U21, Transvaal)
Other sports followed: Football (Manchester United)
Favourite band: Counting Crows, Gin Blossoms, Just Jinger
Relaxations: 'Shopping; designing clothes; sleeping; gym'
Extras: Scored maiden first-class century (147) for South African Students v England

tourists at Pietermaritzburg 1995-96. Benson and Hedges Young Player of the Year 1996. Transvaal Player of the Year 1996, 1998. C&G Man of the Match award v Glamorgan at Cardiff 2005 (114*). Scored 139 v Gloucestershire at Cheltenham 2005, in the process sharing with Andy Bichel (138) in a new Hampshire record partnership for the eighth wicket (257). Took seven catches in an innings v Lancashire at Old Trafford 2006, becoming the first Hampshire wicket-keeper to achieve the feat in a first-class match. Made 51 dismissals and scored 973 runs in first-class cricket 2005; 58 dismissals and 973 runs in first-class cricket 2006. Is now England-qualified
Best batting: 165 Gauteng v KwaZulu-Natal, Johannesburg 1998-99
Best bowling: 1-16 Hampshire v Middlesex, Lord's 2006

2006 Season

	M	Inn	NO	Runs	HS	Avg	100	50	Ct	St	Balls	Runs	Wkts	Avg	BB	5I	10M
Test																	
FC	15	22	7	973	122 *	64.86	4	5	56	2	114	58	1	58.00	1-16	-	-
ODI																	
List A	16	14	4	241	69	24.10	-	2	11	4	0	0	0		-	-	
20/20 Int																	
20/20	8	5	2	64	30	21.33	-	-	1	3	0	0	0		-	-	

Career Performances

	M	Inn	NO	Runs	HS	Avg	100	50	Ct	St	Balls	Runs	Wkts	Avg	BB	5I	10M
Test																		
FC	161	249	43	8075	165	39.19	19	40	454	38	120	63	1	63.00	1-16	-	-
ODI	3	1	0	24	24	24.00	-	-	4	1	0	0	0		-	-	
List A	191	162	57	3741	114 *	35.62	2	21	176	42	0	0	0		-	-	
20/20 Int																	
20/20	26	19	7	282	59	23.50	-	2	13	4	0	0	0		-	-	

POWELL, M. J. Warwickshire

Name: <u>Michael</u> James Powell
Role: Right-hand opening/middle-order bat, right-arm medium bowler
Born: 5 April 1975, Bolton
Height: 5ft 10in **Weight:** 12st 2lbs
Nickname: Arthur, Powelly
County debut: 1996
County cap: 1999
1000 runs in a season: 1
1st-Class 200s: 1
Place in batting averages: 174th av. 25.60 (2005 145th av. 30.40)
Strike rate: (career 119.45)
Parents: Terry and Pat

Marital status: Single
Family links with cricket: 'Father loves the game. Brother John played for Warwickshire youth teams'
Education: Lawrence Sheriff Grammar School, Rugby
Qualifications: 6 GCSEs, 2 A-levels, Levels I-III ECB coaching awards
Career outside cricket: Coaching
Overseas tours: England U18 to South Africa 1992-93 (c), to Denmark 1993 (c); England U19 to Sri Lanka 1993-94; England A to West Indies 2000-01
Overseas teams played for: Avendale CC, Cape Town 1994-95, 1996-97, 2000-01; Griqualand West, South Africa 2001-02
Career highlights to date: 'B&H Cup winners 2002. Frizzell County Champions 2004'

Cricket moments to forget: 'My first pair against my old friend Gary Keedy v Lancs 2004'
Cricket superstitions: 'None'
Cricketers particularly admired: Dermot Reeve, Shaun Pollock, Allan Donald
Young players to look out for: Moeen Ali
Other sports played: Golf, rugby (Warwickshire U16-U18)
Other sports followed: Football
Favourite band: 'No band, just Robbie!! (Williams, that is)'
Extras: Captained Warwickshire U14-U19 and England U17 and U18. Became first uncapped Warwickshire player for 49 years to carry his bat, for 70* out of 130 v Nottinghamshire at Edgbaston 1998. Captain of Warwickshire 2001-03
Best batting: 236 Warwickshire v OUCCE, The Parks 2001
Best bowling: 2-16 Warwickshire v Oxford University, The Parks 1998

2006 Season

	M	Inn	NO	Runs	HS	Avg	100	50	Ct	St	Balls	Runs	Wkts	Avg	BB	5I	10M
Test																	
FC	6	11	1	256	56	25.60	-	1	4	-	114	80	0			-	-	-
ODI																	
List A	9	8	0	152	43	19.00	-	-	7	-	0	0	0			-	-	
20/20 Int																	
20/20	8	7	2	133	44 *	26.60	-	-	2	-	0	0	0			-	-	

Career Performances

	M	Inn	NO	Runs	HS	Avg	100	50	Ct	St	Balls	Runs	Wkts	Avg	BB	5I	10M
Test																	
FC	134	224	11	6857	236	32.19	12	37	97	-	1314	744	11	67.63	2-16	-	-
ODI																	
List A	109	92	15	1961	101 *	25.46	1	5	53	-	824	727	25	29.08	5-40	1	
20/20 Int																	
20/20	11	10	3	194	44 *	27.71	-	-	5	-	0	0	0			-	-	

POWELL, M. J. Glamorgan

Name: Michael John Powell
Role: Right-hand bat
Born: 3 February 1977, Abergavenny
Height: 6ft 1in **Weight:** 14st 8lbs
Nickname: Powelly
County debut: 1997
County cap: 2000
1000 runs in a season: 5
1st-Class 200s: 3
Place in batting averages: 38th av. 51.03
(2005 105th av. 34.80)
Strike rate: (career 82.00)
Parents: Linda and John
Marital status: Single
Family links with cricket: 'Dad John and Uncle Mike both played for Abergavenny'
Education: Crickhowell Secondary School; Pontypool College
Qualifications: 5 GCSEs, BTEC National Diploma in Sports Science, Level 1 coaching award
Overseas tours: Glamorgan to Cape Town 1999, 2002; England A to Sri Lanka 2004-05

Overseas teams played for: Wests, Brisbane 1996-97; Cornwall CC, Auckland 1998-99, 2000-01

Cricket moments to forget: 'You wouldn't want to forget any of it'

Cricket superstitions: 'None'

Other sports played: Rugby (Crickhowell RFC)

Other sports followed: Rugby (Cardiff)

Relaxations: Eating and sleeping

Extras: Scored 200* on first-class debut v Oxford University at The Parks 1997. Second XI Championship Player of the Year 1997 (1210 runs at 75.63). NBC Denis Compton Award for the most promising young Glamorgan player 2000. Acted as 12th man in the third Test v Sri Lanka at Old Trafford 2002, taking the catch that ended Sri Lanka's second innings. Included in England one-day squad for NatWest Series 2004. ECB National Academy 2004-05

Best batting: 299 Glamorgan v Gloucestershire, Cheltenham 2006

Best bowling: 2-39 Glamorgan v Oxford University, The Parks 1999

2006 Season

	M	Inn	NO	Runs	HS	Avg	100	50	Ct	St	Balls	Runs	Wkts	Avg	BB	5I	10M
Test																	
FC	16	29	3	1327	299	51.03	4	2	7	-	0	0	0		-	-	-
ODI																	
List A	17	16	0	411	81	25.68	-	2	8	-	0	0	0		-	-	
20/20 Int																	
20/20	8	8	0	207	54	25.87	-	2	2	-	0	0	0		-	-	

Career Performances

	M	Inn	NO	Runs	HS	Avg	100	50	Ct	St	Balls	Runs	Wkts	Avg	BB	5I	10M
Test																	
FC	154	262	23	9445	299	39.51	21	44	95	-	164	132	2	66.00	2-39	-	-
ODI																	
List A	175	165	19	4094	91 *	28.04	-	23	70	-	24	26	1	26.00	1-26	-	
20/20 Int																	
20/20	25	24	2	534	68 *	24.27	-	5	9	-	0	0	0		-	-	

PRATT, G. J.   Durham

Name: <u>Gary</u> Joseph Pratt
Role: Left-hand bat, right-arm spin bowler,
wicket-keeper ('if I need to')
Born: 22 December 1981, Bishop Auckland
Height: 5ft 10in **Weight:** 10st 7lbs
Nickname: Gonzo, Gazza, Gates
County debut: 2000
1000 runs in a season: 1
Place in batting averages: 213th av. 19.30
Parents: Gordon and Brenda
Marital status: Single
Family links with cricket: Father played for
many years in Durham and one brother was
on Lord's groundstaff (MCC Young
Cricketers). Brother Andrew also played
for Durham
Education: Parkside Comprehensive
Qualifications: 9 GCSEs
Overseas tours: England U19 to Malaysia and (U19 World Cup) Sri Lanka
1999-2000, to India 2000-01
Overseas teams played for: Melville, Perth 2001-02
Cricket moments to forget: 'Getting my first pair in my cricket career v
Gloucestershire'
Cricket superstitions: 'Right pad first'
Cricketers particularly admired: Steve Waugh, Graham Thorpe, David Gower
Young players to look out for: Mark Turner
Other sports played: Golf (14 handicap)
Other sports followed: Football ('all northern teams')
Favourite band: Stereophonics
Relaxations: 'Golf, TV, singing, socialising'
Extras: Represented England U17 and U19. NBC Denis Compton Award 1999. On
his first-class debut, against Lancashire at Old Trafford 2000, he and brother Andrew
became the first brothers to play in a Championship match for Durham. Durham
Player of the Year 2002. Durham Fielder of the Year 2002, 2003. Durham Young
Player of the Year 2003. Ran out Australia captain Ricky Ponting with a direct hit
while fielding as a substitute for England in the fourth Test at Trent Bridge 2005.
Released by Durham at the end of the 2006 season
Best batting: 150 Durham v Northamptonshire, Riverside 2003

2006 Season

	M	Inn	NO	Runs	HS	Avg	100	50	Ct	St	Balls	Runs	Wkts	Avg	BB	5I	10M
Test																	
FC	6	10	0	193	52	19.30	-	1	7	-	0	0	0		-	-	-
ODI																	
List A	8	8	2	132	43	22.00	-	-	1	-	0	0	0		-	-	
20/20 Int																	
20/20	8	8	1	73	25	10.42	-	-	2	-	0	0	0		-	-	

Career Performances

	M	Inn	NO	Runs	HS	Avg	100	50	Ct	St	Balls	Runs	Wkts	Avg	BB	5I	10M
Test																	
FC	53	94	1	2410	150	25.91	1	15	39	-	33	19	0		-	-	-
ODI																	
List A	78	73	18	1749	101 *	31.80	1	11	31	-	0	0	0		-	-	
20/20 Int																	
20/20	25	25	3	321	62 *	14.59	-	1	8	-	0	0	0		-	-	

PRICE, R. W. Worcestershire

Name: Raymond (<u>Ray</u>) William Price
Role: Right-hand bat, slow left-arm bowler
Born: 12 June 1976, Harare, Zimbabwe
Height: 6ft 2in **Weight:** 13st 4lbs
Nickname: Razor
County debut: 2004
County colours: 2004
Test debut: 1999-2000
ODI debut: 2002-03
Place in batting averages: 242nd av. 15.14
Place in bowling averages: 143rd av. 54.20
(2005 73rd av. 32.13)
Strike rate: 111.86 (career 72.36)
Parents: Tim and Pam
Wife and date of marriage: Julie, 13 July 2003
Children: Ashleigh Rayne
Family links with cricket: Father captained Zimbabwe Schools team
Education: Watershed College, Zimbabwe; Delta Engineering Training Centre
Qualifications: 7 O-levels, 2 A-levels, refrigeration and air conditioning technician
Career outside cricket: 'Small business'

Off-season: 'Fitness, fishing, coaching'

Overseas tours: Zimbabwe A to Sri Lanka 1999-2000, to Kenya 2001-02; Zimbabwe to India 2001-02, to Sri Lanka (ICC Champions Trophy) 2002-03, to Sharjah (Cherry Blossom Sharjah Cup) 2002-03, to England 2003, to Australia 2003-04

Overseas teams played for: Midlands, Zimbabwe 1999-2000 – 2003-04; Old Hararians

Career highlights to date: 'Six wickets v Australia at Sydney 2003-04. Tendulkar twice in same Test' (*In the second Test v India at Delhi 2001-02*)

Cricket moments to forget: 'Missed stumping off first ball in Test cricket'

Cricket superstitions: 'None'

Cricketers particularly admired: Steve Waugh, Heath Streak, Andy Flower, Sachin Tendulkar, Shane Warne

Young players to look out for: Steve Davies

Other sports played: Tennis, squash, golf

Other sports followed: BASS League USA (Jerry Joost)

Favourite band: Dire Straits

Relaxations: Fishing, walking

Extras: Took 33 wickets in six Tests 2003-04, including 6-121 in Australia's first innings of the second Test at Sydney and 19 wickets (av. 20.84) in two-Test home series v West Indies. Zimbabwe Cricketer of the Year. Worcestershire One-Day Player of the Year 2005. Is nephew of golfer Nick Price. Is not considered an overseas player

Opinions on cricket: 'More Twenty20!'

Best batting: 117* Midlands v Manicaland, Mutare 2003-04

Best bowling: 8-35 Midlands v CFX Academy, Kwekwe 2001-02

2006 Season

	M	Inn	NO	Runs	HS	Avg	100	50	Ct	St	Balls	Runs	Wkts	Avg	BB	5I	10M
Test																	
FC	8	10	3	106	56	15.14	-	1	3	-	1678	813	15	54.20	4-38	-	-
ODI																	
List A	17	8	3	74	47	14.80	-	-	7	-	804	523	18	29.05	2-16	-	
20/20 Int																	
20/20	5	1	0	10	10	10.00	-	-	3	-	114	124	6	20.66	2-13	-	

Career Performances

	M	Inn	NO	Runs	HS	Avg	100	50	Ct	St	Balls	Runs	Wkts	Avg	BB	5I	10M
Test	18	30	7	224	36	9.73	-	-	3	-	5135	2475	69	35.86	6-73	5	1
FC	79	124	23	1608	117*	15.92	1	7	28	-	19539	8983	270	33.27	8-35	15	3
ODI	26	12	5	90	20*	12.85	-	-	1	-	1328	917	15	61.13	2-16	-	
List A	92	48	13	326	47	9.31	-	-	19	-	4428	2985	89	33.53	4-21	-	
20/20 Int																	
20/20	8	1	0	10	10	10.00	-	-	4	-	162	213	7	30.42	2-13	-	

PRIOR, M. J.   Sussex

Name: Matthew (<u>Matt</u>) James Prior
Role: Right-hand bat, wicket-keeper
Born: 26 February 1982, Johannesburg,
South Africa
Height: 5ft 11in **Weight:** 13st
Nickname: MP, Cheese
County debut: 2001
County cap: 2003
ODI debut: 2004-05
1000 runs in a season: 2
1st-Class 200s: 1
Place in batting averages: 57th av. 46.70
(2005 117th av. 33.61)
Parents: Michael and Teresa
Marital status: Engaged
Education: Brighton College, East Sussex
Qualifications: 9 GCSEs, 3 A-levels, Level 1
coaching certificate

Overseas tours: Brighton College to India 1997-98; Sussex Academy to Cape Town
1999; Sussex to Grenada 2001, 2002; England A to Malaysia and India 2003-04, to Sri
Lanka 2004-05, to Bangladesh 2006-07; England to Zimbabwe (one-day series) 2004-
05, to Pakistan 2005-06, to India 2005-06
Cricket moments to forget: 'Falling on to stumps at The Rose Bowl on Sky TV!'
Cricket superstitions: 'Too many to name all of them'
Cricketers particularly admired: Steve Waugh, Alec Stewart, Mushtaq Ahmed,
Murray Goodwin
Other sports played: Golf
Other sports followed: Football (Arsenal), golf, rugby
Favourite band: Red Hot Chili Peppers
Relaxations: 'Gym, listening to music'
Extras: Has played for Sussex since U12. Represented England U14-U19, captaining
England U17. NBC Denis Compton Award for the most promising young Sussex
player 2001, 2002, 2003. Umer Rashid Award for Most Improved [Sussex] Player
2003. ECB National Academy 2003-04, 2004-05, 2006-07
Best batting: 201* Sussex v LUCCE, Hove 2004

2006 Season

	M	Inn	NO	Runs	HS	Avg	100	50	Ct	St	Balls	Runs	Wkts	Avg	BB	5I	10M
Test																	
FC	14	22	2	934	124	46.70	3	4	34	11	0	0	0		-	-	-
ODI																	
List A	18	18	0	457	141	25.38	1	2	12	5	0	0	0		-	-	
20/20 Int																	
20/20	8	8	0	179	73	22.37	-	1	11	-	0	0	0		-	-	

Career Performances

	M	Inn	NO	Runs	HS	Avg	100	50	Ct	St	Balls	Runs	Wkts	Avg	BB	5I	10M
Test																	
FC	102	160	15	5676	201 *	39.14	14	29	224	18	0	0	0		-	-	-
ODI	12	12	0	240	45	20.00	-	-	4	1	0	0	0		-	-	
List A	130	120	6	2756	144	24.17	3	14	93	21	0	0	0		-	-	
20/20 Int																	
20/20	23	21	2	542	73	28.52	-	4	22	1	0	0	0		-	-	

PYRAH, R. M. Yorkshire

Name: Richard (<u>Rich</u>) Michael Pyrah
Role: Right-hand bat, right-arm medium bowler
Born: 1 November 1982, Dewsbury
Height: 6ft **Weight:** 12st
Nickname: RP, Pyro
County debut: 2004
Strike rate: (career 32.00)
Parents: Mick and Lesley
Marital status: Single
Family links with cricket: 'Dad and Grandad both played for Ossett CC'
Education: Ossett High School; Wakefield College
Qualifications: 10 GCSEs, Level 1 coaching
Overseas teams played for: Kaponga, New Zealand 2000-02; Taranaki, New Zealand 2003-04
Career highlights to date: 'Making my debut for Yorkshire on Sky. Man of the Match in my second NCL game at Scarborough'
Cricket moments to forget: 'First ever pair!'
Cricket superstitions: 'Left pad on first. Bat in some whites'

Cricketers particularly admired: Michael Vaughan, Matthew Wood
Other sports played: Golf
Other sports followed: Football (Leeds United)
Favourite band: Oasis, Evanescence
Relaxations: Xbox
Extras: C&G Man of the Match award for his 5-50 (plus 26 runs) for Yorkshire Board XI v Somerset at Scarborough in the third round 2002
Best batting: 78 Yorkshire v Worcestershire, Worcester 2005
Best bowling: 1-4 Yorkshire v Bangladesh A, Headingley 2005

2006 Season

	M	Inn	NO	Runs	HS	Avg	100	50	Ct	St	Balls	Runs	Wkts	Avg	BB	5I	10M
Test																	
FC																	
ODI																	
List A	3	3	0	88	32	29.33	-	-	2	-	84	97	2	48.50	2-51	-	
20/20 Int																	
20/20																	

Career Performances

	M	Inn	NO	Runs	HS	Avg	100	50	Ct	St	Balls	Runs	Wkts	Avg	BB	5I	10M
Test																	
FC	6	10	1	236	78	26.22	-	1	1	-	96	36	3	12.00	1-4	-	-
ODI																	
List A	19	19	2	328	42	19.29	-	-	7	-	288	319	12	26.58	5-50	1	
20/20 Int																	
20/20	8	7	3	100	33 *	25.00	-	-	3	-	18	26	0			-	-

69. Who was the first batsman in the post-war era to average more than 100 in an English first-class season?

RAMPRAKASH, M. R. Surrey

Name: <u>Mark</u> Ravindra Ramprakash
Role: Right-hand bat, right-arm
off-spin bowler
Born: 5 September 1969, Bushey, Herts
Height: 5ft 10in **Weight:** 12st 4lbs
Nickname: Ramps, Bloodaxe
County debut: 1987 (Middlesex),
2001 (Surrey)
County cap: 1990 (Middlesex),
2002 (Surrey)
Benefit: 2000 (Middlesex)
Test debut: 1991
ODI debut: 1991
1000 runs in a season: 16
1st-Class 200s: 11
1st-Class 300s: 1
Place in batting averages: 1st av. 103.54

(2005 3rd av. 74.66)
Strike rate: (career 122.50)
Parents: Deonarine and Jennifer
Wife and date of marriage: Van, 24 September 1993
Children: Cara, 1997; Anya, 2002
Family links with cricket: Father played club cricket in Guyana
Education: Gayton High School; Harrow Weald Sixth Form College
Qualifications: 6 O-levels, 2 A-levels, Level 3 cricket coach, Level 2 FA
football coach
Overseas tours: England YC to Sri Lanka 1986-87, to Australia (U19 World Cup)
1987-88; England A to Pakistan 1990-91, to West Indies 1991-92, to India 1994-95
(vc); Lion Cubs to Barbados 1993; England to New Zealand 1991-92, to West Indies
1993-94, to Australia 1994-95, to South Africa 1995-96, to West Indies 1997-98, to
Australia 1998-99, to South Africa 1999-2000, to Zimbabwe (one-day series) 2001-02,
to India and New Zealand 2001-02
Overseas teams played for: Nairobi Jafferys, Kenya 1988; North Melbourne 1989;
University of Perth 1996-97; Clico-Preysal, Trinidad 2004
Career highlights to date: 'My two Test hundreds, v West Indies and Australia'
Cricket moments to forget: 'There are so many bad days!'
Cricket superstitions: 'Same piece of chewing gum in innings'
Cricketers particularly admired: 'All the great all-rounders'; Alec Stewart
Young players to look out for: Arun Harinath
Other sports played: Football (Corinthian Casuals FC, Arsenal Pro-Celeb XI)
Other sports followed: Football (Arsenal FC)

Favourite band: 'Have lost touch!'

Extras: Voted Best U15 Schoolboy of 1985 by Cricket Society (Sir John Hobbs Silver Jubilee Memorial Prize) and Cricket Society's Most Promising Young Cricketer of the Year 1988. Man of the Match for his 56 in Middlesex's NatWest Trophy final win in 1988, on his debut in the competition. Represented England YC. Cricket Writers' Young Cricketer of the Year 1991. Middlesex captain May 1997 to the end of the 1999 season. Man of the Match in the fifth Test v West Indies at Bridgetown 1997-98 (154). Leading run-scorer in the single-division four-day era of the County Championship with 8392 runs (av. 56.32) 1993-99. Became first player to score a Championship century against all 18 first-class counties with his 110 v Middlesex at Lord's 2003. Scored century in each innings of a Championship match (130/100*) for the fifth time, v Worcestershire at The Oval 2004. Surrey Players' Player of the Year 2003, 2004, 2005, 2006; Surrey Supporters' Player of the Year 2003, 2004. First batsman to 1000 first-class runs 2006 (22 June). In 2006 became the first English batsman to score 2000 first-class runs in a season since the start of the two-division Championship in 2000, reaching the landmark in a record 20 innings and finishing the season with 2278 runs at an average of 103.54. PCA Player of the Year 2006. Vice-captain of Surrey 2004-05

Best batting: 301* Surrey v Northamptonshire, The Oval 2006

Best bowling: 3-32 Middlesex v Glamorgan, Lord's 1998

Stop press: Winner, with Karen Hardy, of *Strictly Come Dancing*, December 2006

2006 Season

	M	Inn	NO	Runs	HS	Avg	100	50	Ct	St	Balls	Runs	Wkts	Avg	BB	5I	10M
Test																	
FC	15	24	2	2278	301 *	103.54	8	9	13	-	0	0	0		-	-	-
ODI																	
List A	11	11	3	403	106 *	50.37	1	2	3	-	0	0	0		-	-	
20/20 Int																	
20/20	10	10	0	312	85	31.20	-	3	1	-	0	0	0		-	-	

Career Performances

	M	Inn	NO	Runs	HS	Avg	100	50	Ct	St	Balls	Runs	Wkts	Avg	BB	5I	10M
Test	52	92	6	2350	154	27.32	2	12	39	-	895	477	4	119.25	1-2	-	-
FC	386	636	79	28633	301 *	51.40	87	130	222	-	4165	2178	34	64.05	3-32	-	-
ODI	18	18	4	376	51	26.85	-	1	8	-	132	108	4	27.00	3-28	-	
List A	368	357	57	11739	147 *	39.13	12	77	124	-	1734	1354	46	29.43	5-38	1	
20/20 Int																	
20/20	26	26	5	712	85	33.90	-	5	8	-	0	0	0		-	-	

RANKIN, W. B.　　　　　　　　Derbyshire

Name: William <u>Boyd</u> Rankin
Role: Left-hand lower-order bat, right-arm
fast-medium bowler
Born: 5 July 1984, Londonderry
Height: 6ft 8in　**Weight:** 16st 7lbs
Nickname: Boydo
County debut: 2006 (one-day)
Parents: Robert and Dawn
Marital status: Single
Family links with cricket: Both brothers
(Robert and David) have played in Ireland
age-group teams
Education: Strabane Grammar School;
Harper Adams University College
Qualifications: 10 GCSEs, 3 A-levels, Level
1 cricket coaching
Career outside cricket: 'Student and work
on home farm'
Off-season: 'Work and train at home up to Christmas, then three-month tour with
Ireland cricket team to South Africa, Kenya, UAE and West Indies (World Cup)'
Overseas tours: Ireland U19 to Bangladesh (U19 World Cup) 2003-04; Ireland to
Scotland (European Championship) 2006, to Kenya (ICC World Cricket League)
2006-07, to West Indies (World Cup) 2006-07, plus various Ireland age-group and A
tours to Europe and UAE
Career highlights to date: 'Making debut for Ireland and Derbyshire CCC. Selection
for squad to Cricket World Cup (West Indies 2007)'
Cricket moments to forget: 'U19 World Cup match against West Indies (2004)'
(*Ireland U19 lost by just six runs*)
Cricket superstitions: 'None'
Cricketers particularly admired: Glenn McGrath, Curtly Ambrose
Young players to look out for: Gary Ballance, Daniel Redfern, Eoin Morgan
Other sports played: Rugby, football, badminton, snooker
Other sports followed: Football (Liverpool FC), rugby (Ulster)
Injuries: Out for two weeks with a side strain
Favourite band: Coldplay, Oasis
Relaxations: 'Shooting'
Extras: Attended European Cricket Academy in Spain. Formerly with Middlesex but
made no first-team appearances; joined Derbyshire 2006. Has represented Ireland A in
one-day (List A) cricket
Opinions on cricket: 'Twenty20 cricket brings good crowds to games, which is good
for cricket and clubs. I feel all 2nd XI cricket one-day matches should be coloured

clothing and white ball, as this will help get young players used to playing in these conditions; otherwise it's completely new to them when they play first-team cricket.'

2006 Season

	M	Inn	NO	Runs	HS	Avg	100	50	Ct	St	Balls	Runs	Wkts	Avg	BB	5I	10M
Test																	
FC																	
ODI																	
List A	1	0	0	0	0		-	-	-	-	24	25	1	25.00	1-25	-	
20/20 Int																	
20/20																	

Career Performances

	M	Inn	NO	Runs	HS	Avg	100	50	Ct	St	Balls	Runs	Wkts	Avg	BB	5I	10M
Test																	
FC																	
ODI																	
List A	3	2	1	5	5 *	5.00	-	-	-	-	90	77	2	38.50	1-25	-	
20/20 Int																	
20/20																	

RASHID, A.   Yorkshire

Name: Adil Rashid
Role: Right-hand bat, right-arm leg-break bowler; all-rounder
Born: 17 February 1988, Bradford
Nickname: Dilly
County debut: 2006
Place in batting averages: 215th av. 19.16
Place in bowling averages: 16th av. 25.16
Strike rate: 43.28 (career 43.28)
Family links with cricket: Brothers Amar and Haroon have both played for Bradford/Leeds UCCE
Overseas tours: England A to Bangladesh 2006-07
Extras: Has twice attended Terry Jenner spin-bowling courses in Australia. Played for Yorkshire Academy 2005. Recorded maiden first-class five-wicket return (6-67 from 28 successive overs) on debut v Warwickshire at Scarborough 2006. Scored 114 then took 8-157 in India U19's first innings in the second 'Test' at Taunton 2006 to become the

first England player to score a century and record a five-wicket innings return in an U19 international. 2nd XI cap 2006
Best batting: 63 Yorkshire v Nottinghamshire, Headingley 2006
Best bowling: 6-67 Yorkshire v Warwickshire, Scarborough 2006

2006 Season

	M	Inn	NO	Runs	HS	Avg	100	50	Ct	St	Balls	Runs	Wkts	Avg	BB	5I	10M
Test																	
FC	5	6	0	115	63	19.16	-	1	2	-	1082	629	25	25.16	6-67	1	-
ODI																	
List A	2	2	0	28	28	14.00	-	-	-	-	96	97	3	32.33	2-63	-	
20/20 Int																	
20/20																	

Career Performances

	M	Inn	NO	Runs	HS	Avg	100	50	Ct	St	Balls	Runs	Wkts	Avg	BB	5I	10M
Test																	
FC	5	6	0	115	63	19.16	-	1	2	-	1082	629	25	25.16	6-67	1	-
ODI																	
List A	2	2	0	28	28	14.00	-	-	-	-	96	97	3	32.33	2-63	-	
20/20 Int																	
20/20																	

RAYNER, O. P. Sussex

Name: Oliver (<u>Ollie</u>) Philip Rayner
Role: Right-hand bat, right-arm
off-spin bowler
Born: 1 November 1985, Walsrode, Germany
Height: 6ft 5¼in **Weight:** 16st
Nickname: Mervin, Rocket, Rain-cakes, KP
('Kelvin Pietersen, not Kevin!')
County debut: 2006
Strike rate: (career 98.00)
Parents: Mark and Penny
Marital status: Single
Education: St Bede's, The Dicker,
East Sussex
Qualifications: 7 GCSEs, 2 A-levels,
Level 1 coaching
Overseas tours: Sussex Academy to Sri
Lanka 2001, to South Africa 2003
Overseas teams played for: University of
Cape Town; Western Province

Cricket moments to forget: 'Chirping at Somerset, then getting a pair!'
Cricketers particularly admired: Andrew Flintoff, Shane Warne, Chris Gayle
Young players to look out for: Tom Smith, Krishna Singh
Other sports played: Football (Eastbourne Town Reserves; Eastbourne United 1st XI)
Other sports followed: Football (Brighton & Hove Albion)
Favourite band: Kanye West, Common, Talib Kwali
Relaxations: 'Body-boarding, skiing, chilling with mates'
Extras: South of England U15. England Development Squad U19. Sussex 2nd XI Player of the Year 2005. Scored century (101) on first-class debut v Sri Lankans at Hove 2006, batting at No. 8
Opinions on cricket: 'Progressing. Twenty20 good idea – exciting, appealing to audience.'
Best batting: 101 Sussex v Sri Lankans, Hove 2006
Best bowling: 3-89 Sussex v Kent, Hove 2006

2006 Season

	M	Inn	NO	Runs	HS	Avg	100	50	Ct	St	Balls	Runs	Wkts	Avg	BB	5I	10M
Test																	
FC	5	6	1	133	101	26.60	1	-	6	-	588	348	6	58.00	3-89	-	-
ODI																	
List A	5	4	2	94	61	47.00	-	1	-	-	138	169	3	56.33	1-25	-	
20/20 Int																	
20/20	2	1	0	11	11	11.00	-	-	-	-	24	46	0			-	-

Career Performances

	M	Inn	NO	Runs	HS	Avg	100	50	Ct	St	Balls	Runs	Wkts	Avg	BB	5I	10M
Test																	
FC	5	6	1	133	101	26.60	1	-	6	-	588	348	6	58.00	3-89	-	-
ODI																	
List A	5	4	2	94	61	47.00	-	1	-	-	138	169	3	56.33	1-25	-	
20/20 Int																	
20/20	2	1	0	11	11	11.00	-	-	-	-	24	46	0			-	-

---

70. Who was the first wicket-keeper to make 300 dismissals in Tests?

READ, C. M. W.   Nottinghamshire

Name: Christopher (<u>Chris</u>) Mark Wells Read
Role: Right-hand bat, wicket-keeper
Born: 10 August 1978, Paignton, Devon
Height: 5ft 8in **Weight:** 11st
Nickname: Readie, Reados
County debut: 1997 (one-day, Glos), 1998 (Notts)
County cap: 1999 (Notts)
Test debut: 1999
ODI debut: 1999-2000
Twenty20 Int debut: 2006
50 dismissals in a season: 3
Place in batting averages: 66th av. 42.76 (2005 55th av. 44.47)
Parents: Geoffrey and Carolyn
Wife and date of marriage: Louise, 2 October 2004
Education: Torquay Boys' Grammar School; University of Bath; Loughborough University
Qualifications: 9 GCSEs, 4 A-levels, senior coaching award
Overseas tours: West of England U13 to Netherlands 1991; West of England U15 to West Indies 1992-93; England U17 to Netherlands (International Youth Tournament) 1995; England U19 to Pakistan 1996-97; England A to Kenya and Sri Lanka 1997-98, to Zimbabwe and South Africa 1998-99, to West Indies 2000-01, to West Indies 2005-06; England to South Africa and Zimbabwe 1999-2000, to Australia 2002-03 (VB Series), to Bangladesh and Sri Lanka 2003-04, to West Indies 2003-04, to South Africa 2004-05, to India (ICC Champions Trophy) 2006-07, to Australia 2006-07; British Universities to South Africa 2002; ECB National Academy to Australia and Sri Lanka 2002-03; England VI to Hong Kong 2005
Career highlights to date: 'Winning Test series v West Indies 2004'
Cricket moments to forget: 'Ducking a slower ball from Chris Cairns in second Test v New Zealand at Lord's 1999'
Cricketers particularly admired: Adam Gilchrist, Bruce French, Alan Knott, Bob Taylor, Jack Russell, Ian Healy
Young players to look out for: James Hildreth
Other sports played: Hockey (Devon U18, U21; West of England U17; South Nottingham)
Other sports followed: Football (Torquay United)
Favourite band: Stereophonics
Relaxations: 'Reading, listening to music, keeping fit and going out with friends'
Extras: Played for Devon 1995-97. Represented England U18 1996 and England U19 1997. Was selected for the England A tour to Kenya and Sri Lanka 1997-98 aged 18

and without having played a first-class game. Recorded eight dismissals on Test debut in the first Test v New Zealand at Edgbaston 1999. Man of the Match in the first ODI v West Indies at Georgetown 2003-04 after striking a match-winning 15-ball 27 including three sixes and a four. ECB National Academy 2005-06

Best batting: 160 Nottinghamshire v Warwickshire, Trent Bridge 1999

2006 Season

	M	Inn	NO	Runs	HS	Avg	100	50	Ct	St	Balls	Runs	Wkts	Avg	BB	5I	10M
Test	2	3	0	126	55	42.00	-	1	6	1	0	0	0	-	-	-	-
FC	14	21	4	727	150 *	42.76	3	3	44	1	18	8	0	-	-	-	-
ODI	5	4	1	55	30	18.33	-	-	4	-	0	0	0	-	-		
List A	14	10	2	356	135	44.50	1	2	9	-	0	0	0	-	-		
20/20 Int	1	1	0	13	13	13.00	-	-	1	-	0	0	0	-	-		
20/20	9	8	1	121	48 *	17.28	-	-	7	1	0	0	0	-	-		

Career Performances

	M	Inn	NO	Runs	HS	Avg	100	50	Ct	St	Balls	Runs	Wkts	Avg	BB	5I	10M
Test	13	19	3	325	55	20.31	-	1	37	5	0	0	0	-	-		
FC	171	258	40	6790	160	31.14	9	37	495	23	36	33	0	-	-	-	-
ODI	33	21	7	294	30 *	21.00	-	-	40	2	0	0	0	-	-		
List A	205	161	40	3333	135	27.54	2	8	214	46	0	0	0	-	-		
20/20 Int	1	1	0	13	13	13.00	-	-	1	-	0	0	0	-	-		
20/20	22	21	4	460	48 *	27.05	-	-	18	3	0	0	0	-	-		

> 71. Who became the first player to score a
> double century in an English domestic one-day competition,
> v Oxfordshire in the NatWest 1984?

REDFERN, D. J.   Derbyshire

Name: Daniel (<u>Dan</u>) James Redfern
Role: Left-hand bat, occasional
off-spin bowler
Born: 18 April 1990, Shrewsbury
Height: 5ft 9in **Weight:** 10st
Nickname: Redders, Panda
County debut: 2006 (one-day)
Parents: Mike and Shirley
Marital status: Single
Family links with cricket: 'Grandfathers,
father and brother all played for Leycett CC,
Staffs. Brother also plays Shropshire U21'
Education: Adams' Grammar School,
Newport, Shropshire
Qualifications: 10 GCSEs
Off-season: 'Academy winter programme; 3
December – academy tour to Port Elizabeth,
South Africa'
Overseas tours: England U16 to South Africa 2005-06
Career highlights to date: 'First-team debut for Derbyshire (Pro40 game against
Worcestershire)'
Cricket moments to forget: 'Run out by Lou Vincent on Sky (in above game)'
Cricket superstitions: 'None'
Cricketers particularly admired: Rob Heath (Leycett CC), Brian Lara
Young players to look out for: Tom Poynton, Billy Godleman
Other sports played: Rugby, basketball, golf
Other sports followed: Football (Stoke City)
Favourite band: The Kooks
Relaxations: 'Reading'
Extras: Has represented England U15, U16, U17. Neil Lloyd Memorial Trophy for
Best Batsman at Bunbury Festival 2005. Made one-day debut for Derbyshire v
Worcestershire at Worcester in Pro40 2006, aged 16
Opinions on cricket: 'Best game there is!'

2006 Season

	M	Inn	NO	Runs	HS	Avg	100	50	Ct	St	Balls	Runs	Wkts	Avg	BB	5I	10M
Test																	
FC																	
ODI																	
List A	1	1	0	6	6	6.00	-	-	-	-	0	0	0			-	-
20/20 Int																	
20/20																	

Career Performances

	M	Inn	NO	Runs	HS	Avg	100	50	Ct	St	Balls	Runs	Wkts	Avg	BB	5I	10M
Test																	
FC																	
ODI																	
List A	1	1	0	6	6	6.00	-	-	-	-	0	0	0			-	-
20/20 Int																	
20/20																	

REES, G. P.   Glamorgan

Name: <u>Gareth</u> Peter Rees
Role: Left-hand opening bat, right-arm medium-fast 'utility bowler'
Born: 8 April 1985, Swansea
Height: 6ft 1in   **Weight:** 14st 2lbs
Nickname: Gums, Nasser, Albert
County debut: 2006
Parents: Peter and Diane
Marital status: Single
Education: Coedcae Comprehensive, Llanelli; Coleg Sir Gar; Bath University
Qualifications: 10 GCSEs, 3 A-levels, Maths and Physics degree (1st class)
Career outside cricket: 'Inventor'
Off-season: 'Inventing and becoming an athlete'
Career highlights to date: 'Making first-class debut'
Cricket moments to forget: 'Getting run out by Ryan Watkins'
Cricket superstitions: 'Left pad on first'
Cricketers particularly admired: Brian Lara
Young players to look out for: James Harris

Other sports played: Rugby (Wales U17, Llanelli Scarlets U21)
Other sports followed: Rugby (Scarlets, Felinfoel RFC)
Favourite band: Oasis
Relaxations: 'Golf'
Extras: Played for Wales Minor Counties in the 2004 and 2005 C&G and in Minor Counties competitions 2002-06
Opinions on cricket: 'The game today is becoming much more entertaining.'
Best batting: 57 Glamorgan v Northamptonshire, Cardiff 2006

2006 Season

	M	Inn	NO	Runs	HS	Avg	100	50	Ct	St	Balls	Runs	Wkts	Avg	BB	5I	10M
Test																	
FC	3	5	1	84	57	21.00	-	1	1	-	0	0	0		-	-	-
ODI																	
List A																	
20/20 Int																	
20/20																	

Career Performances

	M	Inn	NO	Runs	HS	Avg	100	50	Ct	St	Balls	Runs	Wkts	Avg	BB	5I	10M
Test																	
FC	3	5	1	84	57	21.00	-	1	1	-	0	0	0		-	-	-
ODI																	
List A	3	3	0	38	15	12.66	-	-	1	-	0	0	0		-	-	
20/20 Int																	
20/20																	

RICHARDSON, A.   Middlesex

Name: Alan Richardson
Role: Right-hand bat, right-arm medium bowler
Born: 6 May 1975, Newcastle-under-Lyme, Staffs
Height: 6ft 2in **Weight:** 13st
Nickname: Richo
County debut: 1995 (Derbyshire), 1999 (Warwickshire), 2005 (Middlesex)
County cap: 2002 (Warwickshire), 2005 (Middlesex)
50 wickets in a season: 1
Place in batting averages: (2005 266th av. 12.45)
Place in bowling averages: (2005 23rd av. 25.22)
Strike rate: (career 62.97)
Parents: Roy and Sandra
Marital status: Single

Family links with cricket: 'Dad captained Little Stoke 3rd XI and now patrols the boundary with pint in hand at the Sid Jenkins Cricket Ground'

Education: Alleyne's High School, Stone; Stafford College of Further Education

Qualifications: 8 GCSEs, 2 A-levels, 2 AS-levels, Level 2 cricket coach

Career outside cricket: Landscape gardener

Off-season: 'Coaching in Sydney for Northern Districts CC. Starting journalism course'

Overseas tours: Derbyshire to Malaga 1995; Warwickshire to Bloemfontein 2000, to Cape Town 2001, 2002, to Portugal 2003

Overseas teams played for: Northern Natal, South Africa 1994-96; Hawkesbury CC, Sydney 1997-99; Northern Districts, Sydney 1999-2000, 2001-03; Avendale, Cape Town 2000-01; Kyriang Mountains, Australia 2003-04

Career highlights to date: 'Getting capped by both Warwickshire and Middlesex. Doing well on my home debuts'

Cricket moments to forget: 'The whole 2006 season!'

Cricket superstitions: 'None'

Cricketers particularly admired: Ian Carr, Ali Natkiel, Jason Fellows ('their retirements are only temporary, I'm sure')

Young players to look out for: Ryan Nelson, Chris Monk ('more Test match wickets to come!')

Other sports played: Football, golf, tennis ('all very badly')

Other sports followed: Football (Stoke City)

Injuries: Out for four weeks with a broken thumb; for the rest of the season with a floating bone in the elbow

Favourite band: Josh Rouse, Jeff Buckley, The Housemartins

Extras: *Cricket World* award for best bowling performance in Oxford U19 Festival (8-60 v Devon). Topped Minor Counties bowling averages with Staffordshire 1998 and won Minor Counties bowling award. Most Improved 2nd XI Player 1999. Outstanding Performance of the Year 1999 for his 8-51 v Gloucestershire on home debut. Scored 91 v Hampshire at Edgbaston 2002, in the process sharing with Nick Knight (255*) in a Warwickshire record tenth-wicket stand of 214. Had first innings figures of 7-113 on first-class debut for Middlesex v Nottinghamshire at Lord's 2005

Opinions on cricket: 'Being a cricketer is almost fashionable now, and so attracting young kids into the game shouldn't be a problem. Still think we need longer tea breaks.'

Best batting: 91 Warwickshire v Hampshire, Edgbaston 2002

Best bowling: 8-46 Warwickshire v Sussex, Edgbaston 2002

2006 Season

	M	Inn	NO	Runs	HS	Avg	100	50	Ct	St	Balls	Runs	Wkts	Avg	BB	5I	10M
Test																	
FC	1	2	1	9	9	9.00	-	-	-	-	240	121	4	30.25	4-50	-	-
ODI																	
List A																	
20/20 Int																	
20/20																	

Career Performances

	M	Inn	NO	Runs	HS	Avg	100	50	Ct	St	Balls	Runs	Wkts	Avg	BB	5I	10M
Test																	
FC	78	80	31	538	91	10.97	-	1	20	-	14296	6978	227	30.74	8-46	7	1
ODI																	
List A	57	26	16	102	21 *	10.20	-	-	11	-	2488	1928	53	36.37	5-35	1	
20/20 Int																	
20/20	5	1	1	6	6 *		-	-	1	-	102	120	4	30.00	3-13	-	

ROBINSON, D. D. J.   Leicestershire

Name: <u>Darren</u> David John Robinson
Role: Right-hand bat, leg-spin bowler
Born: 2 March 1973, Braintree, Essex
Height: 5ft 11in **Weight:** 14st
Nickname: Pies, Pie Shop, Robbo
County debut: 1993 (Essex),
2004 (Leicestershire)
County cap: 1997 (Essex)
1000 runs in a season: 3
1st-Class 200s: 1
Place in batting averages: 138th av. 30.75
(2005 63rd av. 42.61)
Strike rate: (career 300.00)
Parents: Dorothy (deceased) and David
Wife and date of marriage: Alyssa,
2 December 2001
Children: Kalli, 20 July 1998; Cameron, 20
May 2000; Evie, 30 October 2002

Family links with cricket: Father club cricketer for Halstead
Education: Tabor High School, Braintree; Chelmsford College of Further Education
Qualifications: 5 GCSEs, BTEC National Diploma in Building and Construction
Career outside cricket: Site investigation and surveying

Overseas tours: England U18 to Canada (International Youth Tournament) 1991; England U19 to Pakistan 1991-92

Overseas teams played for: Waverley, Sydney 1992-94; Eden Roskill CC, Auckland 1995-96

Career highlights to date: 'Every trophy won'

Cricket moments to forget: 'Being bowled out for 57 against Lancashire in the NatWest final [1996]'

Cricket superstitions: 'None'

Cricketers particularly admired: Steve Hale, David Denny

Other sports played: Football, golf, squash

Other sports followed: Golf, football, rugby, swimming

Relaxations: Reading, music

Extras: International Youth Tournament in Canada batting award 1991. Scored two centuries (102/118*) in match v Leicestershire at Chelmsford 2001. Essex Player of the Year 2002. Scored 81 v Australians at Leicester 2005, in the process sharing with Chris Rogers (209) in a record opening partnership for a county against an Australian touring side (247)

Best batting: 200 Essex v New Zealanders, Chelmsford 1999

Best bowling: 1-7 Essex v Middlesex, Chelmsford 2003

2006 Season

	M	Inn	NO	Runs	HS	Avg	100	50	Ct	St	Balls	Runs	Wkts	Avg	BB	5I	10M
Test																	
FC	13	25	1	738	106	30.75	1	3	10	-	28	117	0		-	-	-
ODI																	
List A	11	11	0	321	85	29.18	-	1	5	-	0	0	0		-	-	
20/20 Int																	
20/20	4	4	0	58	41	14.50	-	-	2	-	0	0	0		-	-	

Career Performances

	M	Inn	NO	Runs	HS	Avg	100	50	Ct	St	Balls	Runs	Wkts	Avg	BB	5I	10M
Test																	
FC	181	320	15	10082	200	33.05	21	49	152	-	300	399	1	399.00	1-7	-	-
ODI																	
List A	190	181	14	4399	137 *	26.34	4	21	51	-	17	26	1	26.00	1-7	-	
20/20 Int																	
20/20	8	8	1	82	41	11.71	-	-	3	-	0	0	0		-	-	

ROGERS, C. J. L.   Northamptonshire

Name: Christopher (<u>Chris</u>) John
Llewellyn Rogers
Role: Left-hand bat, leg-spin/right-arm
medium bowler
Born: 31 August 1977, Sydney, Australia
Height: 5ft 11in **Weight:** 12st 8lbs
County debut: 2004 (Derbyshire),
2005 (Leicestershire), 2006
(Northamptonshire)
1000 runs in a season: 1
1st-Class 200s: 1
1st-Class 300s: 1
Place in batting averages: 13th av. 61.81
(2005 4th av. 73.50)
Strike rate: (career 184.00)
Family links with cricket: Father played for
New South Wales and became cricket
administrator

Overseas teams played for: Western Australia 1998-99 –
Extras: Represented Australia U19 1995-96. Has represented Australia A. Scored two
centuries (101*/102*) in Pura Cup match v South Australia at Perth 2001-02, winning
Man of the Match award. Won three Western Australia awards 2002-03 – Lawrie
Sawle Medal (leading first-class and one-day player), President's Silver Trophy
(season's best individual performance – for his 194 v NSW in the Pura Cup), and
Excalibur Award (spirit of WA cricket). An overseas player with Derbyshire 2004 but
forced to return home early injured; an overseas player with Leicestershire during the
2005 season as a locum for Dinesh Mongia. Scored 209 v Australians at Leicester
2005, in the process sharing with Darren Robinson (81) in a record opening
partnership for a county against an Australian touring side (247). An overseas player
with Northamptonshire since 2006. Scored maiden first-class triple century v
Gloucestershire at Northampton 2006. Scored century and double century (128/222*)
in the same match, v Somerset at Taunton 2006, becoming the first Northants batsman
to achieve the feat since Allan Lamb in 1992
Best batting: 319 Northamptonshire v Gloucestershire, Northampton 2006
Best bowling: 1-16 Northamptonshire v Leicestershire, Northampton 2006
Stop press: Named State Player of the Year at the 2007 Allan Border Medal awards

2006 Season

	M	Inn	NO	Runs	HS	Avg	100	50	Ct	St	Balls	Runs	Wkts	Avg	BB	5I	10M
Test																	
FC	14	24	2	1360	319	61.81	4	5	12	-	126	71	1	71.00	1-16	-	-
ODI																	
List A	14	14	0	426	85	30.42	-	4	14	-	24	26	2	13.00	2-22	-	
20/20 Int																	
20/20																	

Career Performances

	M	Inn	NO	Runs	HS	Avg	100	50	Ct	St	Balls	Runs	Wkts	Avg	BB	5I	10M
Test																	
FC	79	143	9	6360	319	47.46	17	30	75	-	184	106	1	106.00	1-16	-	-
ODI																	
List A	61	60	6	1725	117 *	31.94	1	11	33	-	24	26	2	13.00	2-22	-	
20/20 Int																	
20/20	3	3	0	53	35	17.66	-	-	1	-	0	0	0			-	-

ROSENBERG, M. C.   Leicestershire

Name: <u>Marc</u> Christopher Rosenberg
Role: Right-hand bat, right-arm medium-fast bowler; all-rounder
Born: 10 February 1982, Johannesburg, South Africa
Height: 6ft **Weight:** 12st 10lbs
Nickname: Rosie, Goz
County debut: 2006
Strike rate: (career 36.50)
Parents: Terry and Carol
Marital status: Single
Education: Kearsney College; Loughborough University
Qualifications: BSc (Hons) Sports Science and Management
Career outside cricket: 'Doral Properties Pty Ltd – property development'
Off-season: 'Club cricket in Durban; tours to India'
Overseas teams played for: North West, South Africa 2004-05
Career highlights to date: 'Debut for Leicestershire'
Cricket moments to forget: 'Whenever I play with James Allenby'

Cricket superstitions: 'Too many to mention'
Cricketers particularly admired: Errol Stewart, Jonty Rhodes, Michael Vaughan, HD Ackerman
Young players to look out for: James Allenby
Other sports played: Golf, rugby, surfing
Other sports followed: Rugby (Natal Sharks, Leicester Tigers)
Favourite band: Two Tone Deaf, Jack Johnson
Relaxations: 'Surfing'
Extras: Played for Loughborough UCCE 2003-04. Is not considered an overseas player
Best batting: 86 North West v Griqualand West, Potchefstroom 2004-05
Best bowling: 1-27 LUCCE v Somerset, Taunton 2004

2006 Season

	M	Inn	NO	Runs	HS	Avg	100	50	Ct	St	Balls	Runs	Wkts	Avg	BB	5I	10M
Test																	
FC	1	2	1	48	33 *	48.00	-	-	1	-	0	0	0		-	-	-
ODI																	
List A																	
20/20 Int																	
20/20																	

Career Performances

	M	Inn	NO	Runs	HS	Avg	100	50	Ct	St	Balls	Runs	Wkts	Avg	BB	5I	10M
Test																	
FC	6	10	1	255	86	28.33	-	1	1	-	73	69	2	34.50	1-27	-	-
ODI																	
List A	3	3	0	29	26	9.66	-	-	1	-	18	17	3	5.66	3-17	-	
20/20 Int																	
20/20																	

72. Who was the first wicket-keeper to make 400 dismissals in ODIs?

ROWE, D. T.   Leicestershire

Name: <u>Daniel</u> Thomas Rowe
Role: Right-hand bat, right-arm fast bowler
Born: 22 March 1984, Bridgend,
South Wales
Height: 6ft **Weight:** 14st 7lbs
Nickname: Rowster
County debut: 2006
Strike rate: (career 54.00)
Parents: Paul and Barbara
Marital status: Single
Education: Archbishop McGrath Roman
Catholic School; University of Glamorgan,
Cardiff
Qualifications: 10 GCSEs, 2 A-levels,
BSc Sports Science
Career outside cricket: 'Coaching, teaching'
Off-season: 'Training – fitness, bowling'
Career highlights to date: 'Achieving pro
contract'

Cricket superstitions: 'Kissing the cricket bat medallion on my chain before
I bat and bowl'
Cricketers particularly admired: Darren Gough, Chris Cairns
Young players to look out for: Matt Boyce
Other sports played: Golf
Other sports followed: Rugby (Ospreys)
Favourite band: Blink-182
Relaxations: 'Going to the beach'
Extras: Played for Glamorgan U17 and U19. Played for Cardiff UCCE 2004-06
Opinions on cricket: 'A game which is moving very fast towards one-day mode in all
aspects of the game. I believe it's a very exciting time for the game.'
Best bowling: 1-22 Leicestershire v West Indies A, Leicester 2006

2006 Season

	M	Inn	NO	Runs	HS	Avg	100	50	Ct	St	Balls	Runs	Wkts	Avg	BB	5I	10M
Test																	
FC	1	1	0	0	0	0.00	-	-	1	-	54	22	1	22.00	1-22	-	-
ODI																	
List A	1	0	0	0	0		-	-	1	-	30	26	1	26.00	1-26	-	
20/20 Int																	
20/20																	

Career Performances

	M	Inn	NO	Runs	HS	Avg	100	50	Ct	St	Balls	Runs	Wkts	Avg	BB	5I	10M
Test																	
FC	1	1	0	0	0	0.00	-	-	1	-	54	22	1	22.00	1-22	-	-
ODI																	
List A	1	0	0	0	0		-	-	1	-	30	26	1	26.00	1-26	-	
20/20 Int																	
20/20																	

RUDGE, W. D. — Gloucestershire

Name: William (Will) Douglas Rudge
Role: Right-hand lower-order bat, right-arm medium-fast bowler
Born: 15 July 1983, Bristol
Height: 6ft 4in **Weight:** 14st 6lbs
Nickname: Rudgey, Glasseye, Sloth
County debut: 2005
County cap: 2005
Place in bowling averages: (2005 91st av. 36.07)
Strike rate: (career 63.43)
Parents: Barry and Susan
Marital status: Single
Family links with cricket: 'Dad played club cricket for Timsbury'
Education: Clifton College
Qualifications: 10 GCSEs, 3 A-levels
Off-season: 'Training in Bristol'
Overseas tours: Clifton College to Australia 1997, to Barbados 1999
Overseas teams played for: Albion CC, Tauranga, New Zealand 2001-02; Greeton CC, Tauranga, New Zealand 2002-03; Central CC, Rotorua, New Zealand 2004-05
Career highlights to date: 'Debut v Sussex 2005 at Cheltenham'

Cricket moments to forget: 'Twenty20 v Somerset 2006. They set a new record 250 off their 20 overs'

Cricketers particularly admired: Glenn McGrath, Ian Botham, Curtly Ambrose

Young players to look out for: Rich Morrison, Mike Chappell

Other sports played: Rugby (at school), football (Bristol North West), golf

Other sports followed: Rugby (Bristol), football (Tottenham Hotspur)

Injuries: Out for two months after a knee operation (cartilage) in March 2006

Favourite band: The Stone Roses

Relaxations: 'Eating out, golf'

Extras: Played for Gloucestershire Board XI in the C&G 2002, 2003. NBC Denis Compton Award for the most promising young Gloucestershire player 2004

Opinions on cricket: 'Too many Kolpak players [*see page 13*].'

Best batting: 15 Gloucestershire v Surrey, The Oval 2005

Best bowling: 3-46 Gloucestershire v Bangladesh A, Bristol 2005

2006 Season

	M	Inn	NO	Runs	HS	Avg	100	50	Ct	St	Balls	Runs	Wkts	Avg	BB	5I	10M
Test																	
FC	4	2	1	9	8 *	9.00	-	-	1	-	354	311	2	155.50	1-99	-	-
ODI																	
List A	2	1	0	4	4	4.00	-	-	-	-	59	56	3	18.66	2-1	-	
20/20 Int																	
20/20	3	1	0	1	1	1.00	-	-	-	-	58	105	4	26.25	3-37	-	

Career Performances

	M	Inn	NO	Runs	HS	Avg	100	50	Ct	St	Balls	Runs	Wkts	Avg	BB	5I	10M
Test																	
FC	9	10	2	44	15	5.50	-	-	3	-	1015	816	16	51.00	3-46	-	-
ODI																	
List A	4	3	1	8	4	4.00	-	-	-	-	131	131	3	43.66	2-1	-	
20/20 Int																	
20/20	3	1	0	1	1	1.00	-	-	-	-	58	105	4	26.25	3-37	-	

RUDOLPH, J. A.   Yorkshire

Name: Jacobus (<u>Jacques</u>) Andries Rudolph
Role: Left-hand bat, right-arm
leg-spin bowler
Born: 4 May 1981, Springs, South Africa
County debut: No first-team appearance
Test debut: 2003
ODI debut: 2003
Twenty20 Int debut: 2005-06
1st-Class 200s: 1
Strike rate: (career 73.81)
Overseas tours: South Africa U19 to
Pakistan 1998-99, to Sri Lanka (U19 World
Cup) 1999-2000; South Africa A to
Zimbabwe 2002-03, to Sri Lanka 2005-06;
South Africa to Australia 2001-02, to
Bangladesh 2003, to England 2003, to
Pakistan 2003-04, to New Zealand 2003-04,
to Sri Lanka 2004, to England (ICC
Champions Trophy) 2004, to India 2004-05, to West Indies 2004-05, to Australia
2005-06, to Sri Lanka 2006
Overseas teams played for: Northerns B/Northerns 1997-98 – 2003-04;
Titans 2003-04 – 2004-05; Eagles 2005-06 –
Extras: Was twice on verge of Test debut – selected for the third Test v India at
Centurion 2001-02, only for the match to be stripped of Test status due to the Denness
Affair; chosen for the third Test v Australia in Sydney 2001-02, only for his selection
to be overruled in favour of Justin Ontong. Man of the Match for his 222* on Test
debut in the first Test v Bangladesh in Chittagong 2003; in the process shared with
Boeta Dippenaar (177*) in the highest partnership for any wicket for South Africa in
Tests (429*). One of *South African Cricket Annual*'s five Cricketers of the Year 2003.
Scored second innings 102* to help save the first Test v Australia at Perth 2005-06.
Was due to join Derbyshire as an overseas player in 2006 but withdrew with a
shoulder problem. Has joined Yorkshire for 2007; is not considered an overseas player
Best batting: 222* South Africa v Bangladesh, Chittagong 2003
Best bowling: 5-87 Northerns B v Griqualand West B, Centurion 1998-99

2006 Season (did not make any first-class or one-day appearances)

Career Performances

	M	Inn	NO	Runs	HS	Avg	100	50	Ct	St	Balls	Runs	Wkts	Avg	BB	5I	10M
Test	35	63	7	2028	222 *	36.21	5	8	22	-	664	432	4	108.00	1-1	-	-
FC	93	167	10	6521	222 *	41.53	18	30	66	-	3248	1833	44	41.65	5-87	2	-
ODI	45	39	6	1174	81	35.57	-	7	11	-	24	26	0		-	-	
List A	100	92	17	3445	134 *	45.93	3	23	29	-	238	230	6	38.33	4-40	-	-
20/20 Int	1	1	1	6	6 *		-	-	-	-	0	0	0		-	-	
20/20	10	10	2	209	71	26.12	-	1	4	-	1	1	0		-	-	

SADLER, J. L. Leicestershire

Name: <u>John</u> Leonard Sadler
Role: Left-hand top-order bat,
right-arm off-spin bowler
Born: 19 November 1981, Dewsbury
Height: 5ft 11in **Weight:** 12st 7lbs
Nickname: Sads, Chrome, Super
County debut: 2002 (one-day, Yorkshire),
2003 (Leicestershire)
1000 runs in a season: 1
Place in batting averages: 46th av. 48.76
(2005 35th av. 50.33)
Strike rate: (career 87.00)
Parents: Sue and Mike ('Baz')
Marital status: Single
Family links with cricket: 'Dad played
league cricket for 30 years, fielding round the
corner with his sun hat on; now coaches.

Brothers Dave and Jamie represented
Yorkshire Schools and now play local league in Yorkshire CYCL'
Education: St Thomas à Becket RC Comprehensive School, Wakefield
Qualifications: 9 GCSEs, Levels I and II coaching awards
Off-season: 'Training, dog walking, working till Christmas, golf'
Overseas tours: England U19 to Malaysia and (U19 World Cup) Sri Lanka
1999-2000, to India 2000-01; Yorkshire to Grenada 2002
Overseas teams played for: Tuart Hill, Perth 2001-04
Career highlights to date: 'First first-class century. Winning Twenty20 2004, 2006'
Cricket moments to forget: 'Getting released by Yorkshire. Breaking collarbone,
July 2005'
Cricket superstitions: 'None'

Cricketers particularly admired: Robin Smith, Brian Lara, Sachin Tendulkar
Other sports played: Five-a-side football, squash, golf
Other sports followed: Football (Leeds United)
Favourite band: Oasis, Green Day, Michael Jackson
Relaxations: 'Dog walking (Max), training, eating out, quiet pint in the Bakers Arms'
Extras: Played for Yorkshire Schools at all levels; attended Yorkshire Academy; awarded Yorkshire 2nd XI cap. Yorkshire Supporters' Club Young Player of the Year 1998. Represented England U14, U15, U17, U18 and U19
Opinions on cricket: 'The game seems to be getting quicker and more exciting every year, which is great. Twenty20 has helped the longer form, and is no longer a lottery, but shouldn't be overdone. Still the best game in the world but the hardest at times.'
Best batting: 145 Leicestershire v Surrey, Leicester 2003
               145 Leicestershire v Sussex, Hove 2003
Best bowling: 1-22 Leicestershire v New Zealanders, Leicester 2004

2006 Season

	M	Inn	NO	Runs	HS	Avg	100	50	Ct	St	Balls	Runs	Wkts	Avg	BB	5I	10M
Test																	
FC	15	26	5	1024	128 *	48.76	1	8	15	-	0	0	0	-	-	-	
ODI																	
List A	14	14	2	247	68	20.58	-	1	6	-	0	0	0		-	-	
20/20 Int																	
20/20	11	8	1	136	33	19.42	-	-	2	-	0	0	0		-	-	

Career Performances

	M	Inn	NO	Runs	HS	Avg	100	50	Ct	St	Balls	Runs	Wkts	Avg	BB	5I	10M
Test																	
FC	42	72	12	2326	145	38.76	3	15	31	-	87	98	1	98.00	1-22	-	-
ODI																	
List A	59	54	6	997	88	20.77	-	3	13	-	0	0	0		-	-	
20/20 Int																	
20/20	32	28	6	444	73	20.18	-	1	10	-	0	0	0		-	-	

SAGGERS, M. J. Kent

Name: <u>Martin</u> John Saggers
Role: Right-hand bat, right-arm
fast-medium bowler
Born: 23 May 1972, King's Lynn
Height: 6ft 2in **Weight:** 14st 2lbs
Nickname: Saggs, Saggy Bits, Bits of Aloo,
Jurgen Burgen
County debut: 1996 (Durham), 1999 (Kent)
County cap: 2001 (Kent)
Test debut: 2003-04
50 wickets in a season: 4
Place in batting averages: (2005 168th
av. 27.00)
Place in bowling averages: (2005 114th
av. 42.70)
Strike rate: (career 48.11)
Parents: Brian and Edna
Wife and date of marriage: Samantha,
27 February 2004
Children: Ethan, 9 October 2005
Family links with cricket: Grandfather played in the Essex League
Education: Springwood High School; University of Huddersfield
Qualifications: BA (Hons) Architectural Studies International
Career outside cricket: Runs a website (www.africanwildlife.co.uk) devoted to
African wildlife photography
Overseas tours: Kent to South Africa 2001; England VI to Hong Kong 2002; England
to Bangladesh 2003-04
Overseas teams played for: Randburg CC, Johannesburg 1996-98, 2000-04; Southern
Suburbs CC, Johannesburg 1998-99
Career highlights to date: 'Winning the Norwich Union League 2001. Making my
Test debut in Bangladesh. Taking a wicket with my first delivery in Test cricket on
English soil'
Cricket moments to forget: 'Any form of injury'
Cricket superstitions: 'Getting a corner spot in the changing room'
Cricketers particularly admired: Neil Foster, Graham Dilley, Allan Donald,
Richard Ellison
Young players to look out for: Neil Dexter, Samuel Jordan
Other sports played: Golf (10 handicap), 'base jumping, snail racing'
Other sports followed: Football (Spurs), 'any form of motor sport'
Injuries: Out for three months with plantar fasciitis; for three months with a post-tib
tendon problem

Favourite band: Nickelback
Relaxations: 'Going on safari in the Kruger National Park in South Africa. Wildlife photography'
Extras: Won Most Promising Uncapped Player Award 2000. Joint Kent Player of the Year 2000 (with David Masters). Underwood Award (Kent leading wicket-taker) 2001, 2002, 2003. *Kent Messenger* Group Readers' Player of the Season 2002. Shepherd Neame Award for Best Bowler 2002. Cowdrey Award (Kent Player of the Year) 2002. Scored career best 64 as nightwatchman as Kent scored a then county record fourth-innings 429-5 to beat Worcestershire at Canterbury 2004. Took wicket (Mark Richardson) with his first delivery in Test cricket on English soil, in the second Test v New Zealand at Headingley 2004
Best batting: 64 Kent v Worcestershire, Canterbury 2004
Best bowling: 7-79 Kent v Durham, Riverside 2000

2006 Season

	M	Inn	NO	Runs	HS	Avg	100	50	Ct	St	Balls	Runs	Wkts	Avg	BB	5I	10M
Test																	
FC	2	2	1	2	2 *	2.00	-	-	-	-	259	149	5	29.80	3-38	-	-
ODI																	
List A	2	1	1	4	4 *		-	-	1	-	108	128	3	42.66	2-78	-	
20/20 Int																	
20/20																	

Career Performances

	M	Inn	NO	Runs	HS	Avg	100	50	Ct	St	Balls	Runs	Wkts	Avg	BB	5I	10M
Test	3	3	0	1	1	.33	-	-	1	-	493	247	7	35.28	2-29	-	-
FC	95	119	32	1010	64	11.60	-	2	26	-	16936	8669	352	24.62	7-79	16	-
ODI																	
List A	112	61	30	293	34 *	9.45	-	-	22	-	5097	3881	149	26.04	5-22	2	
20/20 Int																	
20/20	5	1	0	5	5	5.00	-	-	2	-	84	93	3	31.00	2-14	-	

SAKER, N. C.   Surrey

Name: <u>Neil</u> Clifford Saker
Role: Right-hand bat, right-arm fast bowler
Born: 20 September 1984, Tooting, London
Height: 6ft 4in **Weight:** 12st 7lbs
Nickname: Bulby, Sakes
County debut: 2003
Place in batting averages: 205th av. 21.33
Place in bowling averages: 134th av. 46.92
Strike rate: 62.85 (career 76.43)

Parents: Pauline and Steve
Marital status: Single
Family links with cricket: 'Dad played league cricket in Surrey'
Education: Raynes Park High School; Nescot College, Ewell
Qualifications: ECB Level 1 coach, City & Guilds Carpentry
Overseas tours: Guildford CC to Trinidad and Tobago 2001; Surrey U19 to Sri Lanka 2002
Overseas teams played for: Randwick Petersham, Sydney 2003-04; Blacktown CC, Sydney
Career highlights to date: 'Maiden first-class fifty'
Cricket moments to forget: 'Haven't had that bad a moment as yet!'
Cricket superstitions: 'Bowling marker has to be lying on the grass, not pushed in'
Cricketers particularly admired: Brett Lee, Allan Donald
Young players to look out for: Jade Dernbach, Rory Hamilton-Brown, Danny Miller
Other sports played: Snooker, golf
Other sports followed: Football (Tottenham)
Favourite band: Queen
Relaxations: 'Music, sleeping and eating!'
Extras: First academy player at Surrey to sign full-time professional contract. Attended University of Port Elizabeth International Cricket Academy 2002-03
Opinions on cricket: 'County Championship [should be] three two-hour sessions a day – 96 overs.'
Best batting: 58* Surrey v Essex, Colchester 2006
Best bowling: 4-79 Surrey v Somerset, Bath 2006

> 73. Who scored the first Twenty20 Cup century,
> v Warwickshire at Edgbaston 2003?

2006 Season

	M	Inn	NO	Runs	HS	Avg	100	50	Ct	St	Balls	Runs	Wkts	Avg	BB	5I	10M
Test																	
FC	7	10	1	192	58 *	21.33	-	1	4	-	880	657	14	46.92	4-79	-	-
ODI																	
List A	3	3	1	42	22	21.00	-	-	-	-	117	144	2	72.00	2-47	-	
20/20 Int																	
20/20																	

Career Performances

	M	Inn	NO	Runs	HS	Avg	100	50	Ct	St	Balls	Runs	Wkts	Avg	BB	5I	10M
Test																	
FC	10	14	1	198	58 *	15.23	-	1	4	-	1223	929	16	58.06	4-79	-	-
ODI																	
List A	15	7	4	48	22	16.00	-	-	2	-	585	610	14	43.57	4-43	-	
20/20 Int																	
20/20																	

SALES, D. J. G. Northamptonshire

Name: <u>David</u> John Grimwood Sales
Role: Right-hand bat, right-arm medium bowler, county captain
Born: 3 December 1977, Carshalton, Surrey
Height: 6ft **Weight:** 14st 7lbs
Nickname: Jumble
County debut: 1994 (one-day), 1996 (first-class)
County cap: 1999
Benefit: 2007
1000 runs in a season: 4
1st-Class 200s: 5
1st-Class 300s: 1
Place in batting averages: 55th av. 46.88 (2005 47th av. 46.84)
Strike rate: (career 37.00)
Parents: Daphne and John
Wife and date of marriage: Abigail, 22 September 2001
Children: James, 11 February 2003
Family links with cricket: Father played club cricket
Education: Caterham Boys' School

Qualifications: 7 GCSEs, cricket coach

Overseas tours: England U15 to South Africa 1993; England U19 to West Indies 1994-95, to Zimbabwe 1995-96, to Pakistan 1996-97; England A to Kenya and Sri Lanka 1997-98, to Bangladesh and New Zealand 1999-2000, to West Indies 2000-01; Northamptonshire to Grenada 2000

Overseas teams played for: Wellington Firebirds, New Zealand 2001-02

Career highlights to date: '303 not out v Essex; 104 v Pakistan 2003'

Cricket moments to forget: 'Watching White and Powell for five hours, then getting 0' (*Rob White and Mark Powell shared in a new record Northamptonshire opening partnership of 375 v Gloucestershire at Northampton 2002*)

Cricket superstitions: 'None'

Cricketers particularly admired: Graham Gooch, Steve Waugh

Other sports followed: Rugby (Northampton Saints), football (Crystal Palace), golf

Favourite band: Coldplay

Relaxations: Fishing and golf

Extras: Sir John Hobbs Silver Jubilee Memorial Prize 1993. Scored 56-ball 70* v Essex at Chelmsford in the Sunday League 1994, aged 16 years 289 days. Scored 210* on Championship debut v Worcs at Kidderminster 1996, aged 18 years 237 days. Became the youngest Englishman to score a first-class triple century (303*) v Essex at Northampton 1999, aged 21 years 240 days. PCA/CGU Young Player of the Year 1999. Man of the Match for Wellington v Canterbury in the final of New Zealand's State Shield at Wellington 2001-02 (62). Captain of Northamptonshire since 2004

Best batting: 303* Northamptonshire v Essex, Northampton 1999

Best bowling: 4-25 Northamptonshire v Sri Lanka A, Northampton 1999

2006 Season

	M	Inn	NO	Runs	HS	Avg	100	50	Ct	St	Balls	Runs	Wkts	Avg	BB	5I	10M
Test																	
FC	17	27	1	1219	225	46.88	2	5	13	-	12	2	0		-	-	-
ODI																	
List A	16	15	0	468	161	31.20	1	1	7	-	0	0	0		-	-	
20/20 Int																	
20/20	9	9	4	274	68*	54.80	-	3	6	-	0	0	0		-	-	

Career Performances

	M	Inn	NO	Runs	HS	Avg	100	50	Ct	St	Balls	Runs	Wkts	Avg	BB	5I	10M
Test																	
FC	155	243	20	8937	303*	40.07	17	46	130	-	333	171	9	19.00	4-25	-	-
ODI																	
List A	203	191	25	5265	161	31.71	3	33	91	-	84	67	0		-	-	
20/20 Int																	
20/20	26	26	6	677	78*	33.85	-	6	16	-	12	23	1	23.00	1-10	-	

SALISBURY, I. D. K.   Surrey

Name: <u>Ian</u> David Kenneth Salisbury
Role: Right-hand bat, leg-break bowler
Born: 21 January 1970, Moulton,
Northampton
Height: 5ft 11in **Weight:** 12st 7lbs
Nickname: Solly, Dingle, Sals
County debut: 1989 (Sussex), 1997 (Surrey)
County cap: 1991 (Sussex), 1998 (Surrey)
Benefit: 2007 (Surrey)
Test debut: 1992
ODI debut: 1992-93
50 wickets in a season: 7
Place in batting averages: 183rd av. 24.20
Place in bowling averages: 30th av. 27.93
Strike rate: 55.88 (career 63.65)
Parents: Dave and Margaret
Wife and date of marriage: Emma Louise,
25 September 1993

Children: Anya-Rose, 10 August 2002
Family links with cricket: 'Dad is vice-president of my first club, Brixworth. He also re-lays cricket squares (e.g. Lord's, Northampton, Leicester)'
Education: Moulton Comprehensive, Northampton
Qualifications: 7 O-levels, NCA coaching certificate
Overseas tours: England A to Pakistan 1990-91, to Bermuda and West Indies 1991-92, to India 1994-95, to Pakistan 1995-96; England to India and Sri Lanka 1992-93, to West Indies 1993-94, to Pakistan 2000-01; World Masters XI v Indian Masters XI November 1996 ('Masters aged 26?')
Overseas teams played for: University of New South Wales, Sydney 1997-2000
Cricketers particularly admired: 'Any that keep performing day in, day out, for both country and county'
Other sports played: 'Most sports'
Other sports followed: Football (Southampton FC, Northampton Town FC), rugby union (Northampton Saints), 'any England team'
Relaxations: 'Spending time with wife Emma; meeting friends and relaxing with them and eating out with good wine'
Extras: In 1992 was named Young Player of the Year by both the Wombwell Cricket Lovers and the Cricket Writers. One of *Wisden*'s Five Cricketers of the Year 1993. Won Bill O'Reilly Medal for Sydney first-grade player of the year 1999-2000. Took 800th first-class wicket (Tim Phillips) v Essex at Croydon 2006
Best batting: 101* Surrey v Leicestershire, The Oval 2003
Best bowling: 8-60 Surrey v Somerset, The Oval 2000

2006 Season

	M	Inn	NO	Runs	HS	Avg	100	50	Ct	St	Balls	Runs	Wkts	Avg	BB	5I	10M
Test																	
FC	16	19	4	363	74	24.20	-	2	11	-	3465	1732	62	27.93	5-46	1	-
ODI																	
List A	5	3	0	48	22	16.00	-	-	3	-	186	137	8	17.12	3-28	-	
20/20 Int																	
20/20	7	3	0	17	15	5.66	-	-	2	-	148	183	9	20.33	2-6	-	

Career Performances

	M	Inn	NO	Runs	HS	Avg	100	50	Ct	St	Balls	Runs	Wkts	Avg	BB	5I	10M
Test	15	25	3	368	50	16.72	-	1	5	-	2492	1539	20	76.95	4-163	-	-
FC	305	391	79	6445	101 *	20.65	2	23	195	-	53601	27255	842	32.36	8-60	35	6
ODI	4	2	1	7	5	7.00	-	-	1	-	186	177	5	35.40	3-41	-	
List A	249	162	46	1569	59 *	13.52	-	1	89	-	10574	8102	247	32.80	5-30	1	
20/20 Int																	
20/20	22	14	3	94	20	8.54	-	-	7	-	286	361	12	30.08	2-6	-	

SANGAKKARA, K. C.   Warwickshire

Name: Kumar Chokshanada Sangakkara
Role: Left-hand bat, wicket-keeper, occasional off-break bowler
Born: 27 October 1977, Matale, Sri Lanka
County debut: No first-team appearance
Test debut: 2000
ODI debut: 2000
Twenty20 Int debut: 2006
1st-Class 200s: 4
Strike rate: (career 108.00)
Career outside cricket: Is training to be a lawyer
Overseas tours: Sri Lanka A to South Africa 1999-2000; Sri Lanka to Kenya (ICC Knockout Trophy) 2000-01, to South Africa 2000-01, to England 2002, to South Africa 2002-03, to Africa (World Cup) 2002-03, to West Indies 2003, to Zimbabwe 2004, to Australia 2004, to England (ICC Champions Trophy) 2004, to Pakistan 2004-05, to New Zealand 2004-05, to India 2005-06, to Bangladesh 2005-06, to England 2006, to India (ICC Champions Trophy) 2006-07, to New Zealand 2006-07, plus other one-day series and tournaments in Sharjah, New Zealand, Morocco, Australia and Netherlands; Asian Cricket Council XI to Australia (Tsunami Relief) 2004-05, to South Africa

(Afro-Asia Cup) 2005-06; FICA World XI to New Zealand 2004-05; ICC World XI to Australia (Super Series) 2005-06
Overseas teams played for: Nondescripts CC, Colombo 1997-98 –
Extras: Represented Sri Lanka U19. Scored 287 in the first Test v South Africa at Colombo 2006, in the process sharing with Mahela Jayawardene (374) in a record partnership for any wicket in Tests (624). His numerous awards include Man of the [ODI] Series v South Africa 2004 and v Bangladesh 2005-06. Has joined Warwickshire as an overseas player for 2007
Best batting: 287 Sri Lanka v South Africa, Colombo 2006
Best bowling: 1-13 Sri Lankans v Zimbabwe A, Harare 2003-04

2006 Season

	M	Inn	NO	Runs	HS	Avg	100	50	Ct	St	Balls	Runs	Wkts	Avg	BB	5I	10M
Test	3	6	0	231	66	38.50	-	2	3	1	0	0	0	-	-	-	-
FC	6	12	1	347	66	31.54	-	2	9	1	30	20	0	-	-	-	-
ODI	5	5	2	154	58 *	51.33	-	2	6	3	0	0	0	-	-	-	
List A	6	6	2	206	58 *	51.50	-	3	6	3	0	0	0	-	-	-	
20/20 Int	1	1	0	21	21	21.00	-	-	1	-	0	0	0	-	-		
20/20	1	1	0	21	21	21.00	-	-	1	-	0	0	0	-	-		

Career Performances

	M	Inn	NO	Runs	HS	Avg	100	50	Ct	St	Balls	Runs	Wkts	Avg	BB	5I	10M
Test	62	103	5	4796	287	48.93	10	22	142	20	6	4	0	-	-	-	-
FC	135	214	14	8098	287	40.49	14	43	289	33	108	66	1	66.00	1-13	-	-
ODI	174	160	21	4974	138 *	35.78	5	33	146	45	0	0	0	-	-	-	
List A	226	209	28	6951	156 *	38.40	7	47	199	61	0	0	0	-	-	-	
20/20 Int	1	1	0	21	21	21.00	-	-	1	-	0	0	0	-	-	-	
20/20	4	4	0	192	93	48.00	-	1	4	-	0	0	0	-	-	-	

SAYERS, J. J.   Yorkshire

Name: Joseph (Joe) John Sayers
Role: Left-hand bat, right-arm off-spin bowler
Born: 5 November 1983, Leeds
Height: 6ft **Weight:** 13st
Nickname: Squirrel
County debut: 2003 (one-day), 2004 (first-class)
Place in batting averages: 121st av. 32.77 (2005 90th av. 37.00)
Parents: Geraldine and Roger
Marital status: Single
Family links with cricket: 'Father played at school, but otherwise none'
Education: St Mary's RC Comprehensive School, Menston; Worcester College, Oxford University

Qualifications: 12 GCSEs, 4 A-levels, BA Physics (Oxon)

Off-season: 'I will be teaching at St Aidan's School, Harrogate, through the autumn. I also intend to do some painting and drawing whilst at home in Yorkshire'

Overseas tours: Leeds Schools to South Africa 1998; Yorkshire U17 to South Africa 2001; England U17 to Australia 2001

Overseas teams played for: Manly-Warringah, Sydney 2004-05

Career highlights to date: 'Carrying my bat for 122* v Middlesex at Scarborough 2006'

Cricket superstitions: 'None. I am not a superstitious person'

Cricketers particularly admired: Anthony McGrath, Mark Ramprakash, Darren Lehmann, Dale Benkenstein

Young players to look out for: Adam Lyth

Other sports played: Football ('played as goalkeeper for Bradford City AFC for three years'), rowing (Worcester College)

Other sports followed: Rugby league (Leeds Rhinos, 'our neighbours at Headingley Carnegie')

Favourite band: Coldplay

Relaxations: 'Drawing, painting, writing, watching movies'

Extras: Captained England U17 v Australia U17 at Adelaide 2001. Played for Oxford UCCE 2002, 2003, 2004 (captain 2003). Oxford Blue 2002, 2003, 2004. Represented England U19 2002, 2003 (captain in the third 'Test' 2003). Wrote weekly column 'View from the Balcony' for *Yorkshire Post* during the 2006 season

Opinions on cricket: 'Promotion and relegation between two divisions in the Championship continues to produce competitive cricket and focus for the players right to the last day of the season.'

Best batting: 147 Oxford University v Cambridge University, The Parks 2004

2006 Season

	M	Inn	NO	Runs	HS	Avg	100	50	Ct	St	Balls	Runs	Wkts	Avg	BB	5I	10M
Test																	
FC	13	21	3	590	122 *	32.77	1	3	7	-	12	7	0		-	-	-
ODI																	
List A	3	3	0	33	13	11.00	-	-	-	-	0	0	0		-	-	
20/20 Int																	
20/20																	

Career Performances

	M	Inn	NO	Runs	HS	Avg	100	50	Ct	St	Balls	Runs	Wkts	Avg	BB	5I	10M
Test																	
FC	39	65	5	2095	147	34.91	5	11	21	-	72	54	0		-	-	-
ODI																	
List A	12	12	2	232	62	23.20	-	2	-	-	54	71	1	71.00	1-31	-
20/20 Int																	
20/20	3	1	0	12	12	12.00	-	-	2	-	0	0	0		-	-

SCHOFIELD, C. P.   Surrey

Name: Christopher (<u>Chris</u>) Paul Schofield
Role: Left-hand bat, leg-break bowler
Born: 6 October 1978, Rochdale
Height: 6ft 1in **Weight:** 11st 5lbs
Nickname: Scoey, Junior, Scoffer
County debut: 1998 (Lancashire),
2006 (Surrey)
County cap: 2002 (Lancashire)
Test debut: 2000
Strike rate: (career 61.76)
Parents: David and Judith
Marital status: Single
Family links with cricket: Father played
with local club team Whittles and brother
with local team Littleborough
Education: Wardle High School
Qualifications: 4 GCSEs, NVQ Levels 2 and
3 in Information Technology
Overseas tours: England U17 to Bermuda 1997; England U19 to South Africa
(including U19 World Cup) 1997-98; England A to Bangladesh and New Zealand 1999-
2000, to West Indies 2000-01; ECB National Academy to Australia 2001-02
Other sports played: Football (Littleborough FC, Whittles FC), snooker (Wardle
Con Club)

Other sports followed: Football ('like watching Liverpool FC')
Relaxations: Listening to music, playing snooker, socialising
Extras: Was part of England U19 World Cup winning squad 1997-98. Won double twice in two years with Littleborough CC (Wood Cup and Lancashire Cup 1997; League and Wood Cup 1998). Won Sir Ron Brierley/Crusaders Scholarship 1998. NBC Denis Compton Award for the most promising young Lancashire player 1998, 1999, 2000. Was the only uncapped player to be contracted to England in 2000. Leading first-class wicket-taker on England A tour to West Indies 2000-01 (22 wickets; av. 26.27). Released by Lancashire at the end of the 2004 season; joined Surrey in August 2006
Best batting: 99 Lancashire v Warwickshire, Old Trafford 2004
Best bowling: 6-120 England A v Bangladesh, Chittagong 1999-2000

2006 Season

	M	Inn	NO	Runs	HS	Avg	100	50	Ct	St	Balls	Runs	Wkts	Avg	BB	5I	10M
Test																	
FC	2	3	0	114	95	38.00	-	1	2	-	440	296	8	37.00	3-78	-	-
ODI																	
List A	4	3	2	11	7	11.00	-	-	1	-	150	144	6	24.00	3-34	-	
20/20 Int																	
20/20																	

Career Performances

	M	Inn	NO	Runs	HS	Avg	100	50	Ct	St	Balls	Runs	Wkts	Avg	BB	5I	10M
Test	2	3	0	67	57	22.33	-	1	-	-	108	73	0		-	-	-
FC	70	98	14	2537	99	30.20	-	21	42	-	11056	5643	179	31.52	6-120	4	-
ODI																	
List A	93	66	17	1078	69 *	22.00	-	3	24	-	2658	2260	88	25.68	5-31	1	
20/20 Int																	
20/20	11	9	2	84	27	12.00	-	-	2	-	54	49	4	12.25	2-9	-	

---

74. Who became the first batsman to score a
century in each innings of a Test match for Zimbabwe,
v New Zealand at Harare 1997-98?

SCOTT, B. J. M.　　　　　　　　　　Middlesex

Name: Benjamin (<u>Ben</u>) James Matthew Scott
Role: Right-hand bat, wicket-keeper
Born: 4 August 1981, Isleworth
Height: 'Small' (5ft 9in)　**Weight:** 11st 7lbs
Nickname: Scotty
County debut: 2002 (one-day, Surrey), 2003
(first-class, Surrey), 2004 (Middlesex)
50 dismissals in a season: 1
Place in batting averages: 216th av. 19.07
(2005 183rd av. 24.55)
Parents: Terry and Edna
Marital status: Single
Family links with cricket: Father played for
the Primitives; brother played local cricket
Education: Whitton School, Richmond;
Richmond College
Qualifications: 9 GCSEs, 3 A-levels studied,
ECB Level 1 coach, YMCA Fitness
Instructor's Award

Overseas tours: MCC YC to Cape Town 1999-2000; Middlesex to Mumbai, India
2005, 2006
Overseas teams played for: Portland CC, Victoria 1999-2000; Mt Gambia, South
Australia 2001-02; South Melbourne CC 2006
Career highlights to date: 'Scoring 101* at Lord's v Northants; just getting there
with Nantie Hayward down the other end'
Cricket moments to forget: 'Being the hat-trick for Billy Taylor v Hampshire' (*At
The Rose Bowl 2006*)
Cricket superstitions: 'None'
Cricketers particularly admired: Alec Stewart, Jack Russell, Nad Shahid
Young players to look out for: Eoin Morgan, Joel Pope
Other sports played: Golf
Favourite band: Michael Jackson, The Jacksons, Usher
Relaxations: Music, golf, TV
Extras: Middlesex YC cap. Represented ESCA U14 and U15. Played for
Development of Excellence XI 1999. Finchley CC Player of the Season 2000
Best batting: 101* Middlesex v Northamptonshire, Lord's 2004

2006 Season

	M	Inn	NO	Runs	HS	Avg	100	50	Ct	St	Balls	Runs	Wkts	Avg	BB	5I	10M
Test																	
FC	9	15	2	248	49	19.07	-	-	28	2	0	0	0		-	-	-
ODI																	
List A	16	11	4	186	73 *	26.57	-	1	12	4	0	0	0		-	-	
20/20 Int																	
20/20	8	7	4	116	32 *	38.66	-	-	3	2	0	0	0		-	-	

Career Performances

	M	Inn	NO	Runs	HS	Avg	100	50	Ct	St	Balls	Runs	Wkts	Avg	BB	5I	10M
Test																	
FC	34	54	12	1005	101 *	23.92	1	4	86	11	0	0	0		-	-	-
ODI																	
List A	56	30	9	400	73 *	19.04	-	2	48	16	0	0	0		-	-	
20/20 Int																	
20/20	21	15	8	138	32 *	19.71	-	-	8	6	0	0	0		-	-	

SCOTT, G. M.   Durham

Name: <u>Gary</u> Michael Scott
Role: Right-hand bat, right-arm
off-spin/seam bowler; all-rounder
Born: 21 July 1984, Sunderland
Height: 6ft **Weight:** 14st
Nickname: Diggler
County debut: 2001
Place in batting averages: 141st av. 30.61
(2005 164th av. 27.90)
Strike rate: (career 114.33)
Parents: Mary and Michael
Marital status: Single
Family links with cricket: 'Dad and uncle
played club cricket. Older brother played at
same club (Hetton Lyons CC)'
Education: Hetton Comprehensive
Qualifications: 7 GCSEs
Off-season: 'Passing driving test and
coaching badges (1 and 2)'
Overseas tours: England U17 to Australia 2000-01; Durham to Sharjah and Dubai
2005, to India and Sharjah 2006; Durham Development Team to India 2005
Overseas teams played for: Northern Districts, Adelaide 2002-03

Career highlights to date: 'First-class debut v Derbyshire at Riverside 2001'
Cricket moments to forget: 'Pair on same day on second-team debut v Warwickshire'
Cricketers particularly admired: Shane Warne, Jacques Kallis, Steve Waugh
Young players to look out for: Mark Turner, Graham Onions
Other sports played: Football (represented Sunderland Schools U14 and U15 as goalkeeper)
Other sports followed: Football (Newcastle Utd)
Favourite band: U2
Relaxations: 'Socialising'
Extras: Sir John Hobbs Silver Jubilee Memorial Prize 1999. C&G Man of the Match award (for Durham Board XI) for his 100 v Herefordshire at Darlington in the 2003 competition. Became youngest to play first-class cricket for Durham, v Derbyshire at Riverside 2001 aged 17 years and 19 days
Opinions on cricket: 'Not enough rest and preparation time in between games in general.'
Best batting: 133 Durham v OUCCE, The Parks 2006
Best bowling: 2-39 Durham v Warwickshire, Riverside 2006

2006 Season

	M	Inn	NO	Runs	HS	Avg	100	50	Ct	St	Balls	Runs	Wkts	Avg	BB	5I	10M
Test																	
FC	9	18	0	551	133	30.61	1	3	7	-	265	237	3	79.00	2-39	-	-
ODI																	
List A	10	10	2	294	57	36.75	-	2	1	-	68	65	3	21.66	2-24	-	
20/20 Int																	
20/20	8	8	0	77	30	9.62	-	-	2	-	48	77	1	77.00	1-44	-	

Career Performances

	M	Inn	NO	Runs	HS	Avg	100	50	Ct	St	Balls	Runs	Wkts	Avg	BB	5I	10M
Test																	
FC	17	33	2	891	133	28.74	1	4	10	-	343	296	3	98.66	2-39	-	-
ODI																	
List A	14	13	2	424	100	38.54	1	2	4	-	242	172	7	24.57	2-24	-	
20/20 Int																	
20/20	15	13	2	129	31	11.72	-	-	8	-	96	157	8	19.62	3-27	-	

SHAFAYAT, B. M.　　Nottinghamshire

Name: <u>Bilal</u> Mustafa Shafayat
Role: Right-hand bat, right-arm medium-fast
bowler, occasional wicket-keeper
Born: 10 July 1984, Nottingham
Height: 5ft 7in **Weight:** 10st 7lbs
Nickname: Billy, Muzzy, Our Kid
County debut: 2001 (Nottinghamshire),
2005 (Northamptonshire)
1000 runs in a season: 1
Place in batting averages: 130th av. 31.67
(2005 82nd av. 37.78)
Strike rate: (career 157.00)
Parents: Mohammad Shafayat and
Mahfooza Begum
Marital status: Single
Family links with cricket: 'Brother Rashid
played for Notts up to 2nd XI and is now
playing in Staffordshire Premier (took ten

wickets in a game 2003). Uncle Nadeem played for PCC. Father just loves it!'
Education: Greenwood Dale; Nottingham Bluecoat School and Sixth Form College
Qualifications: 9 GCSEs, 2 A-levels, Level 1 coaching
Overseas tours: ZRK to Pakistan 2000; Sparkhill ('Kadeer Ali's dad's academy') to
Pakistan; England U17 to Australia 2000-01; England U19 to Australia and (U19
World Cup) New Zealand 2001-02, to Australia 2002-03 (c); Nottinghamshire to South
Africa 2002, 2003; England A to Malaysia and India 2003-04
Overseas teams played for: National Bank of Pakistan 2004-05
Career highlights to date: 'Making my first-class debut for Notts v Middlesex
(scoring 72). Scoring a hundred and double hundred v India in final U19 "Test" 2002.
Scoring crucial hundred v Worcestershire for promotion in Championship. Beating
Australia U19 in first "Test" 2002-03, scoring 66, 108 and taking six wickets'
Cricket moments to forget: 'Losing U19 "Test" series to Australia'
Cricketers particularly admired: Sachin Tendulkar, Carl Hooper, Andrew Jackman
Other sports played: Football, badminton, squash, pool
Other sports followed: Football (Liverpool), boxing, snooker
Favourite band: Sean Paul, 50 Cent, Tupac, Nusrat Fateh Ali Khan
Relaxations: 'Praying Namaz; chilling with loved ones'
Extras: Scored 72 on Championship debut v Middlesex at Trent Bridge 2001, aged 16
years 360 days. NBC Denis Compton Award for the most promising young
Nottinghamshire player 2001, 2002. Scored record-equalling four 'Test' centuries for
England U19. BBC East Midlands Junior Sportsman of the Year 2003. ECB National
Academy 2003-04. Left Northamptonshire at the end of the 2006 season and has
rejoined Nottinghamshire for 2007

Best batting: 161 Northamptonshire v Derbyshire, Derby 2005
Best bowling: 2-25 Northamptonshire v Pakistanis, Northampton 2006

2006 Season

	M	Inn	NO	Runs	HS	Avg	100	50	Ct	St	Balls	Runs	Wkts	Avg	BB	5I	10M
Test																	
FC	17	30	2	887	118	31.67	2	5	20	3	104	86	2	43.00	2-25	-	-
ODI																	
List A	16	14	1	268	55	20.61	-	2	7	1	138	159	3	53.00	2-32	-	
20/20 Int																	
20/20	9	5	1	54	25	13.50	-	-	1	-	0	0	0		-	-	

Career Performances

	M	Inn	NO	Runs	HS	Avg	100	50	Ct	St	Balls	Runs	Wkts	Avg	BB	5I	10M
Test																		
FC	61	106	3	3277	161	31.81	6	18	51	4	471	339	3	113.00	2-25	-	-
ODI																	
List A	78	72	5	1466	97 *	21.88	-	6	29	2	718	660	20	33.00	4-33	-	
20/20 Int																	
20/20	23	19	2	272	40	16.00	-	-	5	1	90	150	3	50.00	2-13	-	

SHAH, O. A.   Middlesex

Name: <u>Owais</u> Alam Shah
Role: Right-hand bat, off-spin bowler
Born: 22 October 1978, Karachi, Pakistan
Height: 6ft 1in **Weight:** 13st 7lbs
Nickname: Ace, The Mauler
County debut: 1995 (one-day),
1996 (first-class)
County cap: 1999
Test debut: 2005-06
ODI debut: 2001
1000 runs in a season: 6
1st-Class 200s: 1
Place in batting averages: 96th av. 35.96
(2005 8th av. 66.46)
Strike rate: (career 77.76)
Parents: Jamshed and Mehjabeen
Wife and date of marriage: Gemma,
25 September 2004
Family links with cricket: Father played for his college side
Education: Isleworth and Syon School; Lampton School; Westminster
University, Harrow

Qualifications: 7 GCSEs, 2 A-levels
Off-season: 'England Academy based in Perth'
Overseas tours: England U19 to Zimbabwe 1995-96, to South Africa (including U19 World Cup) 1997-98 (c); England A to Australia 1996-97, to Kenya and Sri Lanka 1997-98, to Sri Lanka 2004-05, to West Indies 2005-06; ECB National Academy to Australia 2001-02; England to Zimbabwe (one-day series) 2001-02, to India and New Zealand 2001-02 (one-day series), to Sri Lanka (ICC Champions Trophy) 2002-03, to Australia 2002-03 (VB Series), to India 2005-06
Overseas teams played for: University of Western Australia, Perth
Career highlights to date: '[Debut] Test match against India in Mumbai'
Cricket moments to forget: 'Getting a pair in first-class cricket'
Cricketers particularly admired: Viv Richards, Sachin Tendulkar, Mark Waugh
Young players to look out for: Graham Onions, Nick Compton, Eoin Morgan
Other sports played: Snooker
Other sports followed: Football ('like to watch Man Utd play')
Favourite band: 'Too many to mention'
Relaxations: 'Movies, eating out'
Extras: Man of the U17 'Test' series v India 1994. Captained England U19 to success in the 1997-98 U19 World Cup in South Africa, scoring 54* in the final; captain of England U19 v Pakistan U19 1998. Cricket Writers' Young Player of the Year 2001. Middlesex Player of the Year 2002. *Evening Standard* Player of the Month August 2004. Vice-captain of Middlesex 2002 to June 2004. Leading run-scorer in English first-class cricket 2005 (1728; av. 66.46). Made Test debut in the third Test v India at Mumbai 2005-06, scoring 88. ECB National Academy 2004-05, 2005-06, 2006-07
Best batting: 203 Middlesex v Derbyshire, Southgate 2001
Best bowling: 3-33 Middlesex v Gloucestershire, Bristol 1999

2006 Season

	M	Inn	NO	Runs	HS	Avg	100	50	Ct	St	Balls	Runs	Wkts	Avg	BB	5I	10M
Test																	
FC	17	30	0	1079	126	35.96	2	7	14	-	124	106	0		-	-	-
ODI																	
List A	16	16	4	732	125 *	61.00	3	4	12	-	72	59	2	29.50	1-10	-	
20/20 Int																	
20/20	5	5	0	70	33	14.00	-	-	-	-	12	10	1	10.00	1-10	-	

Career Performances

	M	Inn	NO	Runs	HS	Avg	100	50	Ct	St	Balls	Runs	Wkts	Avg	BB	5I	10M
Test	1	2	0	126	88	63.00	-	1	1	-	0	0	0		-	-	-
FC	168	284	23	10778	203	41.29	28	58	129	-	1633	1098	21	52.28	3-33	-	-
ODI	18	18	2	294	62	18.37	-	2	6	-	0	0	0		-	-	-
List A	223	211	27	5995	134	32.58	10	34	79	-	375	373	11	33.90	2-2	-	
20/20 Int																	
20/20	23	23	5	636	79	35.33	-	5	6	-	13	11	1	11.00	1-10	-	

SHAHZAD, A.   Yorkshire

Name: Ajmal Shahzad
Role: Right-hand bat, right-arm fast bowler; all-rounder
Born: 27 July 1985, Bradford
Height: 6ft **Weight:** 13st 8lbs
Nickname: The Dark Destroyer, AJ
County debut: 2004 (one-day), 2006 (first-class)
Parents: Parveen and Mohammed
Marital status: Single
Family links with cricket: 'Father played in Bradford League'
Education: Bradford Grammar School, Woodhouse Grove School; Leeds Metropolitan University (BSc Sports Performance Coaching – second year)
Qualifications: 9 GCSEs, 4 A-levels
Career outside cricket: University and coaching

Off-season: 'Training hard in the gym; studying'
Overseas tours: Schools tours to Scotland and Grenada; England U18 to Netherlands 2003
Career highlights to date: 'Making my debut for Yorkshire and being the first British-born Asian to play for YCCC'
Cricket moments to forget: 'Playing against Ireland in Holland – enough said. Also ripping my side (getting a side strain) in Twenty20 quarter-final in Essex'
Cricket superstitions: 'Put right pad on before left'
Cricketers particularly admired: Wasim Akram, Waqar Younis, Craig White, Anthony McGrath
Young players to look out for: 'Me', Adam Lyth, Moeen Ali
Other sports played: Badminton (Yorkshire U15-U17), rugby (school), squash (school)
Other sports followed: Rugby league (Bradford Bulls)
Injuries: Out for four weeks with a side strain; for two weeks with a hamstring strain
Favourite band: Danny Bond, DJ Veteran, Jamie Duggan, DJ Leverton
Relaxations: 'Socialising, gym, study and Islam'
Extras: First British-born Asian to play for Yorkshire first team. Man of the Match in first match representing England – century and 3-22
Opinions on cricket: 'Too much to think about – if we get a cold or illness we can't just take medication; it's got to be passed and approved by WADA [World Anti-Doping Agency]!? Love the new games – Twenty20 and Pro40. Brings crowds in and love the hit!'

Best batting: 2 Yorkshire v Middlesex, Scarborough 2006

2006 Season

	M	Inn	NO	Runs	HS	Avg	100	50	Ct	St	Balls	Runs	Wkts	Avg	BB	5I	10M
Test																	
FC	1	1	0	2	2	2.00	-	-	-	-	72	45	0			-	-
ODI																	
List A	3	3	1	13	11 *	6.50	-	-	-	-	138	101	5	20.20	3-30	-	
20/20 Int																	
20/20	1	1	1	2	2 *		-	-	-	-	18	22	2	11.00	2-22	-	

Career Performances

	M	Inn	NO	Runs	HS	Avg	100	50	Ct	St	Balls	Runs	Wkts	Avg	BB	5I	10M
Test																	
FC	1	1	0	2	2	2.00	-	-	-	-	72	45	0			-	-
ODI																	
List A	4	4	1	18	11 *	6.00	-	-	-	-	174	136	5	27.20	3-30	-	
20/20 Int																	
20/20	1	1	1	2	2 *		-	-	-	-	18	22	2	11.00	2-22	-	

SHANTRY, A. J.   Warwickshire

Name: <u>Adam</u> John Shantry
Role: Left-hand bat, left-arm
swing bowler
Born: 13 November 1982, Bristol
Height: 6ft 2in **Weight:** 13st 8lbs
Nickname: Shants
County debut: 2003 (Northamptonshire),
2005 (one-day, Warwickshire),
2006 (first-class, Warwickshire)
Strike rate: (career 37.29)
Parents: Brian and Josephine
Marital status: Single
Family links with cricket: 'Father Brian
played for Gloucestershire. Brother Jack will
be better than me'
Education: The Priory School, Shrewsbury;
Shrewsbury Sixth Form College
Qualifications: 11 GCSEs, 4 A-levels,
Level 2 coaching
Career outside cricket: 'In development'

Off-season: 'Training, going to Oz and following the mighty Bristol City all over the country'
Overseas teams played for: Balwyn, Melbourne 2001-02; Subiaco-Floreat, Perth 2004-05 – 2006-07
Career highlights to date: 'Five-fors against New Zealand and West Indies A'
Cricket moments to forget: 'Giving Tino Best a send-off, forgetting that I still had to bat'
Cricket superstitions: 'Try not to bowl up the hill into the wind on a flat one'
Cricketers particularly admired: Brian Shantry, Mike Smith
Young players to look out for: Jack Shantry, Moeen Ali
Other sports played: Football ('Bears football team – solid centre back')
Other sports followed: Football (Bristol City)
Injuries: Out for the last month of the season with a stress fracture of the shin
Favourite band: Feeder, Aiden, The Wurzels
Relaxations: 'Fishing, music'
Extras: England U17 squad. Represented ESCA U18 2001. Radio Shropshire Young Player of the Year 2001. Took 3-8 (including spell of three wickets in five balls before conceding a run) on Championship debut v Somerset at Northampton 2003. Took 5-37 v New Zealanders in 50-over match at Northampton 2004, winning Carlsberg Man of the Match award. His 5-15 v Warwickshire 2nd XI at Kenilworth 2004 included four wickets in four balls (bowled, bowled, lbw, bowled). Took 5-49 on first-class debut for Warwickshire v West Indies A at Edgbaston 2006
Opinions on cricket: 'Good game.'
Best batting: 38* Northamptonshire v Somerset, Northampton 2003
Best bowling: 5-49 Warwickshire v West Indies A, Edgbaston 2006

2006 Season

	M	Inn	NO	Runs	HS	Avg	100	50	Ct	St	Balls	Runs	Wkts	Avg	BB	5I	10M
Test																	
FC	1	1	1	4	4*		-	-	-	-	144	65	7	9.28	5-49	1	-
ODI																	
List A	3	0	0	0	0		-	-	1	-	66	48	3	16.00	3-30	-	
20/20 Int																	
20/20																	

Career Performances

	M	Inn	NO	Runs	HS	Avg	100	50	Ct	St	Balls	Runs	Wkts	Avg	BB	5I	10M
Test																	
FC	6	7	5	66	38*	33.00	-	-	2	-	634	328	17	19.29	5-49	1	-
ODI																	
List A	7	3	0	25	15	8.33	-	-	5	-	222	167	10	16.70	5-37	1	
20/20 Int																	
20/20	1	0	0	0	0		-	-	-	-	12	31	0		-	-	

SHEIKH, M. A. Derbyshire

Name: <u>Mohamed</u> Avez Sheikh
Role: Left-hand bat, right-arm
medium bowler
Born: 2 July 1973, Birmingham
Height: 6ft
Nickname: Sheikhy
County debut: 1997 (Warwickshire),
2004 (Derbyshire)
Place in batting averages: 168th av. 27.00
(2005 242nd av. 17.12)
Place in bowling averages: 119th av. 43.33
(2005 100th av. 38.30)
Strike rate: 87.53 (career 79.30)
Education: Broadway School
Overseas teams played for: Western
Province CC 1997-98
Extras: Played for Warwickshire U19.

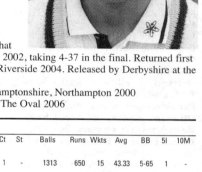

Played for the Warwickshire Board side that
won the last ECB 38-County competition 2002, taking 4-37 in the final. Returned first
innings figures of 11-7-9-4 v Durham at Riverside 2004. Released by Derbyshire at the
end of the 2006 season
Best batting: 58* Warwickshire v Northamptonshire, Northampton 2000
Best bowling: 5-65 Derbyshire v Surrey, The Oval 2006

2006 Season

	M	Inn	NO	Runs	HS	Avg	100	50	Ct	St	Balls	Runs	Wkts	Avg	BB	5I	10M
Test																	
FC	9	13	3	270	51 *	27.00	-	1	1	-	1313	650	15	43.33	5-65	1	-
ODI																	
List A	6	3	0	40	15	13.33	-	-	2	-	277	179	7	25.57	2-30	-	
20/20 Int																	
20/20																	

Career Performances

	M	Inn	NO	Runs	HS	Avg	100	50	Ct	St	Balls	Runs	Wkts	Avg	BB	5I	10M
Test																	
FC	47	66	16	1238	58 *	24.76	-	4	5	-	7137	3484	90	38.71	5-65	1	-
ODI																	
List A	109	60	20	470	50 *	11.72	-	1	18	-	4871	3268	110	29.70	4-17	-	
20/20 Int																	
20/20	10	5	2	29	20	9.66	-	-	3	-	157	217	8	27.12	2-20	-	

SHERIYAR, A. Leicestershire

Name: Alamgir Sheriyar
Role: Right-hand bat, left-arm fast bowler
Born: 15 November 1973, Birmingham
Height: 6ft 1in **Weight:** 13st
Nickname: Sheri
County debut: 1993 (one-day, Leics),
1994 (first-class, Leics), 1996 (Worcs),
2003 (Kent)
County cap: 1997; colours, 2002 (both
Worcs)
50 wickets in a season: 4
Strike rate: (career 51.47)
Parents: Mohammed Zaman (deceased) and
Safia Sultana
Marital status: Single
Education: George Dixon Secondary School,
Birmingham; Joseph Chamberlain Sixth Form
College, Birmingham; Oxford Brookes
University
Qualifications: 6 O-levels
Overseas tours: Leicestershire to South Africa 1995; Worcestershire to Barbados
1996; England A to Bangladesh and New Zealand 1999-2000
Cricketers particularly admired: Wasim Akram
Other sports followed: Football, basketball
Relaxations: Time at home, music
Extras: Played for English Schools U17. Became only the second player to take a hat-
trick on his Championship debut, for Leicestershire v Durham at Durham University
1994. First bowler to reach 50 first-class wickets in 1999 and ended season as leading
wicket-taker with 92 wickets (av. 24.70). Took second first-class hat-trick of his career
v Kent at Worcester 1999. Played for Worcestershire on loan from Kent 2005.
Released by Kent at the end of the 2005 season, rejoining Leicestershire in 2006;
released at the end of the 2006 season
Best batting: 21 Worcestershire v Nottinghamshire, Trent Bridge 1997
21 Worcestershire v Pakistan A, Worcester 1997
Best bowling: 7-130 Worcestershire v Hampshire, Southampton 1999

2006 Season

	M	Inn	NO	Runs	HS	Avg	100	50	Ct	St	Balls	Runs	Wkts	Avg	BB	5I	10M
Test																	
FC																	
ODI																	
List A	4	1	1	8	8 *	-	-	-	-	-	186	153	6	25.50	3-35	-	
20/20 Int																	
20/20																	

Career Performances

	M	Inn	NO	Runs	HS	Avg	100	50	Ct	St	Balls	Runs	Wkts	Avg	BB	5I	10M
Test																	
FC	152	165	65	829	21	8.29	-	-	22	-	25890	15085	503	29.99	7-130	23	3
ODI																	
List A	122	40	23	156	19	9.17	-	-	7	-	4682	3856	133	28.99	4-18	-	
20/20 Int																	
20/20	3	2	2	13	9 *	-	-	-	-	-	60	64	2	32.00	1-18	-	

SHINGLER, A. C.   Glamorgan

Name: <u>Aaron</u> Craig Shingler
Role: Right-hand bat, right-arm fast-medium bowler
Born: 7 August 1987, Aldershot, Hampshire
Height: 6ft 5in   **Weight:** 13st 7lbs
Nickname: Ron, Long
County debut: No first-team appearance
Parents: Craig and Jeanette
Marital status: Single
Education: Pontarddulais Comprehensive; Gorseinon College
Qualifications: 7 GCSEs, 3 A-levels
Off-season: 'Working, uni, training'
Overseas tours: England U19 to Bangladesh 2005-06
Career highlights to date: 'Pro contract'
Cricket moments to forget: 'Am sure there's plenty'
Cricket superstitions: 'None'
Cricketers particularly admired: Shane Warne, Brett Lee ('enjoy watching them')
Other sports played: Golf, rugby
Other sports followed: Rugby (Llanelli Scarlets)

Favourite band: 50 Cent
Relaxations: 'Sauna, steam room'
Extras: Played for Wales Minor Counties 2004-06. Played for Cardiff UCCE 2006

SHRECK, C. E. Nottinghamshire

Name: Charles (<u>Charlie</u>) Edward Shreck
Role: Right-hand bat, right-arm
fast-medium bowler
Born: 6 January 1978, Truro
Height: 6ft 7in **Weight:** 15st 7lbs
Nickname: Shrecker, Ogre, Stoat, Chough
County debut: 2002 (one-day),
2003 (first-class)
County cap: 2006
50 wickets in a season: 1
Place in bowling averages: 12th av. 24.78
Strike rate: 41.90 (career 47.13)
Parents: Peter and Sheila
Marital status: Single
Family links with cricket: 'Grandfather
watched Southampton'
Education: Truro School
Qualifications: Level 1 coaching
Career outside cricket: 'Sleeping'

Overseas tours: Cornwall U17 to South Africa 1997
Overseas teams played for: Merewether District CC, NSW 1997-98;
Hutt District CC, New Zealand 2000-03; Wellington, New Zealand 2005-06
Cricket moments to forget: 'Being run out off the last ball of the game against
Shropshire, walking off – we lost!'
Cricket superstitions: 'None'
Cricketers particularly admired: Viv Richards, Michael Holding, Ian Botham
Young players to look out for: Michael Munday, Carl Gazzard
Relaxations: 'Swimming, music'
Extras: C&G Man of the Match award for his 5-19 for Cornwall v Worcestershire at
Truro 2002. Took wicket (Vikram Solanki) with his third ball in county cricket v
Worcestershire at Trent Bridge in the NUL 2002, going on to record maiden one-day
league five-wicket return (5-35). Took four wickets in six balls, including hat-trick
(Smith, Morgan, Weekes), v Middlesex at Lord's 2006. Took 61 first-class wickets in
2006 (including 12-129 v Middlesex at Trent Bridge), having missed the entire 2005
season after undergoing back surgery. Nottinghamshire Player of the Year 2006
Best batting: 19 Nottinghamshire v Essex, Chelmsford 2003
Best bowling: 8-31 Nottinghamshire v Middlesex, Trent Bridge 2006

2006 Season

	M	Inn	NO	Runs	HS	Avg	100	50	Ct	St	Balls	Runs	Wkts	Avg	BB	5I	10M
Test																	
FC	12	16	10	11	5 *	1.83	-	-	4	-	2556	1512	61	24.78	8-31	5	2
ODI																	
List A	10	3	3	5	2 *		-	-	-	-	363	327	10	32.70	3-40	-	
20/20 Int																	
20/20	10	1	1	0	0 *		-	-	3	-	228	291	12	24.25	3-33	-	

Career Performances

	M	Inn	NO	Runs	HS	Avg	100	50	Ct	St	Balls	Runs	Wkts	Avg	BB	5I	10M
Test																	
FC	34	40	21	78	19	4.10	-	-	8	-	6127	3657	130	28.13	8-31	10	2
ODI																	
List A	21	9	7	28	9 *	14.00	-	-	5	-	933	805	31	25.96	5-19	2	
20/20 Int																	
20/20	12	2	2	1	1 *		-	-	3	-	276	332	15	22.13	3-33	-	

SIDEBOTTOM, R. J.   Nottinghamshire

Name: <u>Ryan</u> Jay Sidebottom
Role: Left-hand bat, left-arm fast bowler
Born: 15 January 1978, Huddersfield
Height: 6ft 4in **Weight:** 14st 7lbs
Nickname: Siddy, Sexual, Jazz
County debut: 1997 (Yorkshire), 2004 (Nottinghamshire)
County cap: 2000 (Yorkshire), 2004 (Nottinghamshire)
Test debut: 2001
ODI debut: 2001-02
50 wickets in a season: 2
Place in batting averages: 256th av. 13.87 (2005 271st av. 11.72)
Place in bowling averages: 22nd av. 26.14 (2005 11th av. 22.64)
Strike rate: 58.30 (career 52.70)
Parents: Arnie and Gillian
Marital status: Single
Family links with cricket: Father played cricket for Yorkshire and England and football for Manchester United and Huddersfield Town
Education: King James Grammar School, Almondbury

Qualifications: 5 GCSEs
Overseas tours: England U17 to Netherlands 1995; MCC to Bangladesh 1999-2000; England A to West Indies 2000-01; England to Zimbabwe (one-day series) 2001-02; ECB National Academy to Australia 2001-02
Overseas teams played for: Ringwood, Melbourne 1998
Cricketers particularly admired: Darren Gough, Chris Silverwood, Glenn McGrath
Young players to look out for: Joe Sayers
Other sports played: Football (once with Sheffield United), 'all sports'
Other sports followed: 'Love rugby league (any team)', football (Man Utd)
Relaxations: 'Music (R&B), films, clubbing, going out with my team-mates'
Extras: NBC Denis Compton Award for the most promising young Yorkshire player 1999, 2000. Took 5-31 (8-65 in match) for England A v Jamaica at Kingston in the Busta Cup 2000-01, winning the Man of the Match award; topped tour first-class bowling averages (16 wickets; av. 16.81). Made Test debut in the first Test v Pakistan at Lord's 2001 (England's 100th Test at the ground), becoming the tenth player to follow his father into the England Test team
Best batting: 54 Yorkshire v Glamorgan, Cardiff 1998
Best bowling: 7-97 Yorkshire v Derbyshire, Headingley 2003

2006 Season

	M	Inn	NO	Runs	HS	Avg	100	50	Ct	St	Balls	Runs	Wkts	Avg	BB	5I	10M
Test																	
FC	15	22	6	222	33	13.87	-	-	7	-	2915	1307	50	26.14	5-22	1	-
ODI																	
List A	8	5	2	21	7	7.00	-	-	3	-	395	229	8	28.62	2-15	-	
20/20 Int																	
20/20	5	2	2	12	12*		-	-	1	-	108	73	5	14.60	2-16	-	

Career Performances

	M	Inn	NO	Runs	HS	Avg	100	50	Ct	St	Balls	Runs	Wkts	Avg	BB	5I	10M
Test	1	1	0	4	4	4.00	-	-	-	-	120	64	0		-	-	
FC	100	126	36	1024	54	11.37	-	1	39	-	16286	7727	309	25.00	7-97	11	1
ODI	2	1	1	2	2*		-	-	-	-	84	84	2	42.00	1-42	-	
List A	134	58	27	341	32	11.00	-	-	30	-	5755	4094	138	29.66	6-40	2	
20/20 Int																	
20/20	15	5	4	23	12*	23.00	-	-	4	-	313	343	17	20.17	3-20	-	

SILLENCE, R. J. Worcestershire

Name: <u>Roger</u> John Sillence
Role: Right-hand bat, right-arm
fast-medium bowler
Born: 29 June 1977, Salisbury, Wiltshire
Height: 6ft 3in **Weight:** 13st 7lbs
Nickname: Sillo
County debut: 2001 (Gloucestershire),
2006 (Worcestershire)
County cap: 2004 (Gloucestershire),
2006 (Worcestershire colours)
Place in batting averages: 167th av. 27.05
Place in bowling averages: 75th av. 34.43
Strike rate: 57.56 (career 56.14)
Parents: Angela
Marital status: Single
Family links with cricket: Father played
cricket
Education: Highbury, Salisbury; Salisbury
Art College

Qualifications: 7 GCSEs, ND and HND Graphic Design, ECB Level 2 coach
Career outside cricket: Graphic designer
Overseas teams played for: Napier Old Boys, New Zealand 1997-98; St Augustine's,
Cape Town 1998-99; East Keilor, Melbourne 2000-01; Hamersley Carine, Perth
2001-02; South Melbourne 2002-03, 2005-06
Career highlights to date: 'Getting five wickets on debut v Sussex at Hove and then
getting 100 on home debut v Derby'
Cricket moments to forget: 'Whenever I drop a catch'
Cricket superstitions: 'Always bowl in a short-sleeved shirt'
Cricketers particularly admired: Mike Smith, Jack Russell
Young players to look out for: Steve Davies
Other sports followed: 'Follow football but not really one team, and look out for my
mate who plays AFL for St Kilda'
Favourite band: Jamiroquai, Razorlight, Coldplay
Relaxations: 'Enjoy a good coffee with a slice of carrot cake. Other interests such as
design, photography, fashion design, music – the normal same old same old'
Extras: Wiltshire Player of the Year 2000. Recorded maiden first-class five-wicket
return (5-97) on debut v Sussex at Hove 2001. Scored maiden first-class century (101)
v Derbyshire at Bristol 2002 on home debut, batting at No. 9
Best batting: 101 Gloucestershire v Derbyshire, Bristol 2002
Best bowling: 7-96 Worcestershire v Somerset, Taunton 2006

2006 Season

	M	Inn	NO	Runs	HS	Avg	100	50	Ct	St	Balls	Runs	Wkts	Avg	BB	5I	10M
Test																	
FC	13	19	1	487	64	27.05	-	3	5	-	1324	792	23	34.43	7-96	1	-
ODI																	
List A	13	11	5	257	94	42.83	-	1	5	-	330	368	9	40.88	2-46		-
20/20 Int																	
20/20	8	8	2	94	22 *	15.66	-	-	2	-	157	225	8	28.12	2-27		-

Career Performances

	M	Inn	NO	Runs	HS	Avg	100	50	Ct	St	Balls	Runs	Wkts	Avg	BB	5I	10M
Test																	
FC	26	37	1	866	101	24.05	1	4	8	-	3200	2028	57	35.57	7-96	3	-
ODI																	
List A	20	17	5	359	94	29.91	-	2	6	-	496	504	19	26.52	4-35		-
20/20 Int																	
20/20	8	8	2	94	22 *	15.66	-	-	2	-	157	225	8	28.12	2-27		-

SILVERWOOD, C. E. W.   Middlesex

Name: Christopher (<u>Chris</u>) Eric
Wilfred Silverwood
Role: Right-hand bat, right-arm
fast bowler
Born: 5 March 1975, Pontefract
Height: 6ft 1in **Weight:** 12st 9lbs
Nickname: Spoons, Silvers, Chubby
County debut: 1993 (Yorkshire),
2006 (Middlesex)
County cap: 1996 (Yorkshire),
2006 (Middlesex)
Benefit: 2004
Test debut: 1996-97
ODI debut: 1996-97
50 wickets in a season: 2
Place in batting averages: 244th av. 15.05
(2005 171st av. 26.57)
Place in bowling averages: 17th av. 25.25
Strike rate: 48.03 (career 50.94)
Parents: Brenda
Marital status: Single
Family links with cricket: 'Dad played a bit'

Education: Garforth Comprehensive
Qualifications: 8 GCSEs, City and Guilds in Leisure and Recreation
Overseas tours: England A to Kenya and Sri Lanka 1997-98, to Bangladesh and New Zealand 1999-2000, to West Indies 2000-01; England to Zimbabwe and New Zealand 1996-97, to West Indies 1997-98, to Bangladesh (Wills International Cup) 1998-99, to South Africa 1999-2000, to Zimbabwe (one-day series) 2001-02, to Australia 2002-03; England VI to Hong Kong 2002, 2003
Overseas teams played for: Wellington, Cape Town 1993-94, 1995-96
Career highlights to date: 'Making Test debut. Winning the Championship [2001]'
Cricketers particularly admired: Ian Botham, Allan Donald
Other sports played: Karate (black belt), rugby league (Kippax Welfare), athletics (represented Yorkshire)
Other sports followed: Rugby league (Castleford)
Extras: Attended Yorkshire Academy. Represented England U19. C&G Man of the Match awards v Northamptonshire at Northampton 2002 (61/2-35) and v Dorset at Dean Park 2004 (4-18). Took 500th first-class wicket (Andrew Gale) against his old county, Yorkshire, at Southgate 2006, finishing with match figures of 8-64
Best batting: 80 Yorkshire v Durham, Riverside 2005
Best bowling: 7-93 Yorkshire v Kent, Headingley 1997

2006 Season

	M	Inn	NO	Runs	HS	Avg	100	50	Ct	St	Balls	Runs	Wkts	Avg	BB	5I	10M
Test																	
FC	16	24	6	271	50	15.05	-	1	4	-	3026	1591	63	25.25	6-51	4	-
ODI																	
List A	10	8	2	25	10	4.16	-	-	2	-	446	356	7	50.85	2-36	-	
20/20 Int																	
20/20	5	3	2	12	9 *	12.00	-	-	-	-	102	134	5	26.80	2-26	-	

Career Performances

	M	Inn	NO	Runs	HS	Avg	100	50	Ct	St	Balls	Runs	Wkts	Avg	BB	5I	10M
Test	6	7	3	29	10	7.25	-	-	2	-	828	444	11	40.36	5-91	1	-
FC	164	221	44	2782	80	15.71	-	9	38	-	27155	14359	533	26.94	7-93	24	1
ODI	7	4	0	17	12	4.25	-	-	-	-	306	244	6	40.66	3-43	-	
List A	190	109	37	979	61	13.59	-	4	29	-	8542	6045	248	24.37	5-28	1	
20/20 Int																	
20/20	14	8	4	44	13 *	11.00	-	-	4	-	306	398	12	33.16	2-22	-	

SINGH, A. Nottinghamshire

Name: Anurag Singh
Role: Right-hand bat, right-arm 'all sorts'
Born: 9 September 1975, Kanpur, India
Height: 5ft 11½in **Weight:** 11st
Nickname: Ragi
County debut: 1995 (Warwickshire), 2001 (Worcestershire), 2004 (Nottinghamshire)
County colours: 2002 (Worcestershire)
1000 runs in a season: 2
Place in batting averages: (2005 152nd av. 30.10)
Parents: Vijay and Rajul
Marital status: Single
Family links with cricket: 'Brother (Rudi) has played first-class cricket for Cambridge Uni and has a Cambridge Blue'
Education: King Edward's School, Birmingham; Gonville and Caius College, Cambridge; College of Law, London
Qualifications: 12 GCSEs, 1 AO-level, 4 A-levels, passed Law School exams
Career outside cricket: Solicitor
Overseas tours: England U19 to West Indies 1994-95; Warwickshire U21 to South Africa; Warwickshire CCC to South Africa; Quidnuncs to South Africa 2002; Worcestershire to South Africa 2003
Overseas teams played for: Gordon CC, Sydney; Avendale CC, Cape Town
Cricket moments to forget: 'Losing two cup finals to Gloucestershire'
Cricket superstitions: 'None'
Cricketers particularly admired: Steve Waugh, Sachin Tendulkar, Michael Atherton, Brian Lara
Young players to look out for: Samit Patel, Mark Footitt
Other sports played: Hockey ('college and school'), football ('college and firm')
Other sports followed: Football (Aston Villa FC)
Favourite band: 'Too many to mention'
Relaxations: Reading, socialising with friends
Extras: Cambridge Blue 1996-98; captain of Cambridge University 1997-98. Scored 1000 first-class runs in each of his first two full seasons of county cricket (2001 and 2002). C&G Man of the Match award for his 74 v Leicestershire in the quarter-final at Leicester 2003. Released by Nottinghamshire at the end of the 2006 season
Best batting: 187 Worcestershire v Gloucestershire, Bristol 2002

2006 Season

	M	Inn	NO	Runs	HS	Avg	100	50	Ct	St	Balls	Runs	Wkts	Avg	BB	5I	10M
Test																	
FC	1	1	0	0	0	0.00	-	-	-	-	0	0	0		-	-	-
ODI																	
List A	3	3	1	90	78 *	45.00	-	1	1	-	0	0	0		-	-	
20/20 Int																	
20/20	3	3	0	59	35	19.66	-	-	-	-	0	0	0		-	-	

Career Performances

	M	Inn	NO	Runs	HS	Avg	100	50	Ct	St	Balls	Runs	Wkts	Avg	BB	5I	10M
Test																	
FC	108	176	7	5437	187	32.17	11	24	42	-	101	124	0		-	-	-
ODI																	
List A	116	114	6	3031	123	28.06	1	20	29	-	0	0	0		-	-	
20/20 Int																	
20/20	3	3	0	59	35	19.66	-	-	-	-	0	0	0		-	-	

SMITH, B. F.   Worcestershire

Name: Benjamin (<u>Ben</u>) Francis Smith
Role: Right-hand bat, right-arm
medium bowler
Born: 3 April 1972, Corby
Height: 5ft 9in **Weight:** 11st
Nickname: Turnip, Sven
County debut: 1990 (Leicestershire),
2002 (Worcestershire)
County cap: 1995 (Leicestershire),
2002 (Worcestershire colours)
1000 runs in a season: 7
1st-Class 200s: 3
Place in batting averages: 91st av. 36.60
(2005 19th av. 57.25)
Strike rate: (career 152.75)
Parents: Keith and Janet
Wife and date of marriage: Lisa,
10 October 1998
Children: Ruby, 6 November 2005
Family links with cricket: Father, grandfather and uncles all played club and
representative cricket
Education: Kibworth High School; Robert Smyth, Market Harborough

Qualifications: 5 O-levels, 8 GCSEs, NCA coaching certificate
Off-season: 'Being a dad; keeping fit'
Overseas tours: England YC to New Zealand 1990-91; MCC to Bangladesh 1999-2000; 'numerous pre-season tours to South Africa, Caribbean and Sri Lanka'
Overseas teams played for: Alexandria, Zimbabwe 1990; Bankstown-Canterbury, Sydney 1993-96; Central Hawke's Bay CC, New Zealand 1997-98; Central Districts, New Zealand 2000-02
Career highlights to date: 'Winning 1996 County Championship'
Cricket moments to forget: 'Lord's finals'
Cricketers particularly admired: Viv Richards, David Gower, Steve Waugh
Young players to look out for: Steve Davies
Other sports played: Tennis (Leicestershire aged 12), golf, touch rugby
Other sports followed: Rugby union (Leicester Tigers)
Favourite band: Coldplay
Relaxations: 'Music, DIY, good wine'
Extras: Cricket Society Young Player of the Year 1991. Vice-captain of Leicestershire 2001. Scored century (137) on first-class debut for Worcestershire v OUCCE at The Parks and another (129) on Championship debut for the county v Gloucestershire at Worcester 2002 to become the first player to achieve this 'double' for Worcestershire. Worcestershire Supporters' Player of the Year 2002. Worcestershire Player of the Year 2003. Scored 187 v Gloucestershire at Worcester 2004, in the process sharing with Graeme Hick (262) in the highest first-class partnership ever made at New Road (417). Scored 203 v Somerset at Taunton 2006, in the process sharing with Graeme Hick (182) in a Worcestershire record partnership for the fourth wicket (330). Captain of Worcestershire 2003 until standing down in August 2004
Best batting: 204 Leicestershire v Surrey, The Oval 1998
Best bowling: 1-5 Leicestershire v Essex, Ilford 1991

2006 Season

	M	Inn	NO	Runs	HS	Avg	100	50	Ct	St	Balls	Runs	Wkts	Avg	BB	5I	10M
Test																	
FC	16	27	2	915	203	36.60	2	3	23	-	30	48	1	48.00	1-39	-	-
ODI																	
List A	16	16	2	487	76	34.78	-	3	14	-	0	0	0		-	-	
20/20 Int																	
20/20	8	8	1	120	69 *	17.14	-	1	5	-	0	0	0		-	-	

Career Performances

	M	Inn	NO	Runs	HS	Avg	100	50	Ct	St	Balls	Runs	Wkts	Avg	BB	5I	10M
Test																	
FC	282	441	50	16235	204	41.52	40	77	173	-	611	439	4	109.75	1-5	-	-
ODI																	
List A	350	337	46	8788	115	30.19	2	56	125	-	115	105	2	52.50	1-2	-	
20/20 Int																	
20/20	25	25	2	450	105	19.56	1	1	13	-	0	0	0		-	-	

SMITH, E. T.   Middlesex

Name: Edward (<u>Ed</u>) Thomas Smith
Role: Right-hand bat, right-arm
medium bowler, county captain
Born: 19 July 1977, Pembury, Kent
Height: 6ft 2in **Weight:** 13st
Nickname: Smudge
County debut: 1996 (Kent),
2005 (Middlesex)
County cap: 2001 (Kent), 2005 (Middlesex)
Test debut: 2003
1000 runs in a season: 7
1st-Class 200s: 2
Place in batting averages: 72nd av. 40.30
(2005 71st av. 39.81)
Strike rate: (career 102.00)
Parents: Jonathan and Gillie
Marital status: Single
Family links with cricket: 'Dad wrote *Good*

Enough? with Chris Cowdrey'
Education: Tonbridge School; Peterhouse, Cambridge University
Qualifications: 11 GCSEs, 3 A-levels, degree in History
Career outside cricket: Journalism; broadcasting
Overseas tours: England A to Malaysia and India 2003-04
Overseas teams played for: University CC, Perth, Western Australia
Career highlights to date: 'My Test debut'
Cricket moments to forget: 'Getting a pair at Chelmsford 2003'
Cricket superstitions: 'Left pad on first'
Cricketers particularly admired: Steve Waugh, Rahul Dravid
Other sports played: Squash, golf
Other sports followed: Football (Arsenal FC), baseball (New York Mets)
Favourite band: Bob Dylan
Relaxations: 'Listening to music, reading, going to concerts'
Extras: Scored century (101) on first-class debut v Glamorgan 1996; was also the first person to score 50 or more in each of his first six first-class games. Cambridge Blue 1996. Represented England U19. Equalled Kent record of four consecutive first-class centuries with his 108 v Essex at Canterbury 2003. *Kent Messenger* Readers Player of the Year 2003. Denness Award (Kent leading run-scorer) 2003. Cowdrey Award (Kent Player of the Season) 2003. Slazenger 'Sheer Instinct' award for 2003. Books *Playing Hard Ball* (about baseball) published 2001 and *On and Off the Field* published 2004; series *Peak Performance* (comparing sporting and musical performance) broadcast on Radio 3 2005. Appointed captain of Middlesex for 2007

Best batting: 213 Kent v Warwickshire, Canterbury 2003
Best bowling: 1-60 Middlesex v Sussex, Southgate 2006

2006 Season

	M	Inn	NO	Runs	HS	Avg	100	50	Ct	St	Balls	Runs	Wkts	Avg	BB	5I	10M
Test																	
FC	17	31	1	1209	166	40.30	5	2	12	-	30	60	1	60.00	1-60	-	-
ODI																	
List A	15	15	1	374	88	26.71	-	3	5	-	0	0	0			-	-
20/20 Int																	
20/20	6	6	0	58	34	9.66	-	-	2	-	0	0	0			-	-

Career Performances

	M	Inn	NO	Runs	HS	Avg	100	50	Ct	St	Balls	Runs	Wkts	Avg	BB	5I	10M
Test	3	5	0	87	64	17.40	-	1	5	-	0	0	0			-	-
FC	168	290	15	11173	213	40.62	29	46	73	-	102	119	1	119.00	1-60	-	-
ODI																	
List A	112	109	9	3146	122	31.46	2	22	24	-	0	0	0			-	-
20/20 Int																	
20/20	17	17	0	388	85	22.82	-	2	4	-	0	0	0			-	-

SMITH, G. J.   Nottinghamshire

Name: Gregory (<u>Greg</u>) James Smith
Role: Right-hand bat, left-arm fast bowler
Born: 30 October 1971, Pretoria,
South Africa
Height: 6ft 4in **Weight:** 15st
Nickname: Claw, Smudge, G
County debut: 2001
County cap: 2001
50 wickets in a season: 3
Place in batting averages: (2005 276th
av. 10.53)
Place in bowling averages: 100th av. 38.91
(2005 26th av. 25.76)
Strike rate: 67.66 (career 54.14)
Parents: Fred and Nellie
Wife and date of marriage: Thea,
5 September 1999
Children: Rob, 1989; Keeghan, 1999
Education: Pretoria BHS
Overseas tours: South Africa A to England 1996

Overseas teams played for: Northern Transvaal/Northerns Titans 1993-94 – 2001-02

Career highlights to date: 'Playing for South Africa A. Being capped by Notts'

Cricket moments to forget: 'Losing to Surrey in semi-final of B&H Cup [2001]. Losing to Natal in final of Standard Bank Cup [2000-01]'

Cricketers particularly admired: Wasim Akram, Fanie de Villiers, Kepler Wessels

Other sports played: Golf

Other sports followed: Football (Arsenal), South African rugby

Relaxations: 'Spending time with my family and friends'

Extras: Attended National Academy in South Africa. Took hat-trick (Mitchell, Drakes, Henderson) v Border at East London in semi-final (second leg) of Standard Bank Cup 2000-01; took 3-15 in deciding leg at East London, winning Man of the Match award. Nottinghamshire Player of the Year 2001. Holds a British passport and is not considered an overseas player. Released by Nottinghamshire at the end of the 2006 season

Best batting: 68 Northern Transvaal v Western Province, Centurion 1995-96

Best bowling: 8-53 Nottinghamshire v Essex, Trent Bridge 2002

2006 Season

	M	Inn	NO	Runs	HS	Avg	100	50	Ct	St	Balls	Runs	Wkts	Avg	BB	5I	10M
Test																	
FC	6	6	0	21	17	3.50	-	-	1	-	812	467	12	38.91	4-75	-	-
ODI																	
List A	5	4	3	27	20	27.00	-	-	2	-	225	180	3	60.00	1-23	-	
20/20 Int																	
20/20																	

Career Performances

	M	Inn	NO	Runs	HS	Avg	100	50	Ct	St	Balls	Runs	Wkts	Avg	BB	5I	10M
Test																	
FC	147	179	56	1619	68	13.16	-	2	30	-	24742	12700	457	27.78	8-53	17	2
ODI																	
List A	134	49	23	231	20	8.88	-	-	20	-	6319	4586	186	24.65	5-11	3	
20/20 Int																	
20/20	9	4	3	18	11 *	18.00	-	-	2	-	202	269	5	53.80	1-17	-	

SMITH, G. M. Derbyshire

Name: Gregory (Greg) Marc Smith
Role: Right-hand bat, right-arm off-spin/medium bowler; all-rounder
Born: 20 April 1983, Johannesburg, South Africa
Height: 5ft 8in **Weight:** 11st 5lbs
Nickname: Smithy, Smudge
County debut: 2006
Place in batting averages: 158th av. 28.37
Strike rate: (career 90.62)
Parents: Ian and Nadine
Marital status: Single

Family links with cricket: 'Father was financial adviser for UCBSA [United Cricket Board of South Africa]'
Education: St Stithians College; UNISA (University of South Africa)
Qualifications: Level 2 coaching certificate
Off-season: 'Relaxing and training for next season'
Overseas tours: South Africa U19 to New Zealand (U19 World Cup) 2001-02
Overseas teams played for: Griqualand West 2003-04
Career highlights to date: 'Scoring half-century in U19 World Cup final v Australia'
Cricketers particularly admired: Jacques Kallis, Kevin Pietersen
Young players to look out for: Gary Ballance, Dan Redfern
Other sports played: Tennis, golf
Other sports followed: Football (Arsenal)
Favourite band: U2
Relaxations: 'Spending time with my girlfriend Nicole'
Extras: Represented Gauteng U13–U19. South Africa Academy 2003-04
Opinions on cricket: 'Getting stronger and stronger each year.'
Best batting: 86 Derbyshire v Gloucestershire, Derby 2006
Best bowling: 2-60 Griqualand West v Border, East London 2003-04

2006 Season

	M	Inn	NO	Runs	HS	Avg	100	50	Ct	St	Balls	Runs	Wkts	Avg	BB	5I	10M
Test																	
FC	5	9	1	227	86	28.37	-	1	4	-	281	182	2	91.00	1-18	-	-
ODI																	
List A	7	7	0	182	57	26.00	-	1	5	-	144	165	4	41.25	2-44	-	
20/20 Int																	
20/20																	

Career Performances

	M	Inn	NO	Runs	HS	Avg	100	50	Ct	St	Balls	Runs	Wkts	Avg	BB	5I	10M
Test																	
FC	14	27	2	538	86	21.52	-	3	5	-	725	433	8	54.12	2-60	-	-
ODI																	
List A	14	14	1	281	57	21.61	-	2	8	-	234	286	5	57.20	2-44	-	
20/20 Int																	
20/20																	

SMITH, T. C. P.   Lancashire

Name: Thomas (Tom) Christopher Pascoe Smith
Role: Left-hand bat, right-arm medium-fast bowler; all-rounder
Born: 26 December 1985, Liverpool
Height: 6ft 3in   **Weight:** 14st
Nickname: Smudger, Yeti
County debut: 2005
Place in batting averages: 219th av. 18.00
Place in bowling averages: 50th av. 30.65
Strike rate: 65.65 (career 67.16)
Parents: Mark and Jacqui
Marital status: Single
Family links with cricket: Brother Lancashire U19. Father and stepfather play for local village teams
Education: Parklands High School; Runshaw College
Qualifications: 10 GCSEs, 4 A-levels
Off-season: National Academy
Overseas tours: England U19 to India 2004-05; England A to Bangladesh 2006-07
Career highlights to date: 'Contract with Lancs and being picked for National Academy 2005-06'

Cricket moments to forget: 'First-ball duck on my first-class debut'
Cricket superstitions: 'Right pad on first'
Cricketers particularly admired: Andrew Flintoff, Ricky Ponting
Young players to look out for: Karl Brown
Other sports played: Football, golf, swimming
Other sports followed: Football (Liverpool FC)
Favourite band: Oasis, Goo Goo Dolls, Kelly Clarkson
Relaxations: 'Watching films and socialising with friends'
Extras: Represented England U19 2005. ECB National Academy 2005-06, 2006-07
Opinions on cricket: 'The game today has improved in all areas – technically, tactically and physically – making it a more exciting game to be involved in.'
Best batting: 49 Lancashire v Hampshire, Rose Bowl 2006
Best bowling: 4-57 Lancashire v Yorkshire, Headingley 2006

2006 Season

	M	Inn	NO	Runs	HS	Avg	100	50	Ct	St	Balls	Runs	Wkts	Avg	BB	5I	10M
Test																	
FC	15	18	5	234	49	18.00	-	-	14	-	2298	1073	35	30.65	4-57	-	-
ODI																	
List A	11	4	2	28	14 *	14.00	-	-	3	-	428	290	13	22.30	3-8	-	
20/20 Int																	
20/20	8	7	3	71	21	17.75	-	-	3	-	152	175	5	35.00	2-17	-	

Career Performances

	M	Inn	NO	Runs	HS	Avg	100	50	Ct	St	Balls	Runs	Wkts	Avg	BB	5I	10M
Test																	
FC	16	19	5	234	49	16.71	-	-	15	-	2418	1119	36	31.08	4-57	-	-
ODI																	
List A	12	5	2	36	14 *	12.00	-	-	3	-	458	332	13	25.53	3-8	-	
20/20 Int																	
20/20	8	7	3	71	21	17.75	-	-	3	-	152	175	5	35.00	2-17	-	

75. What was significant about Yorkshire's B&H clash with
Kent at Headingley at the end of April 1992?

SMITH, T. M. J.   Sussex

Name: <u>Thomas</u> Michael John Smith
Role: Right-hand bat, slow left-arm
orthodox bowler
Born: 29 August 1987, Eastbourne, Sussex
Height: 5ft 9in **Weight:** 11st 7lbs
Nickname: Smudge
County debut: 2006 (one-day)
Parents: Michael and Claudine
Marital status: Single
Education: Seaford Head Community
College; Sussex Downs College
Qualifications: NVQ Level 2 in Plumbing
Off-season: 'Training in the indoor school
in Hove'
Overseas tours: Sussex Academy to Cape
Town 2003, 2005
Career highlights to date: 'Pro40 debut
v Durham 2006'

Cricket moments to forget: 'Semi-dislocating my shoulder in a net a week before I
went to Cape Town on a cricket tour'
Cricket superstitions: 'None'
Cricketers particularly admired: Daniel Vettori, Monty Panesar, Mike Yardy
Young players to look out for: Andrew Hodd, Ollie Rayner, Ben Brown
Other sports played: Football (Seaford Town FC), golf
Favourite band: The Subways
Extras: Sussex 2nd XI Player of the Year 2006. Sussex League Young Player of the
Year 2006
Opinions on cricket: 'Good that younger players are getting more opportunity and
also Twenty20 great competition.'

---

76. Which limited-overs competition first got under way on 29 April 1972?
    a) John Player League b) Gillette Cup c) B&H Cup

2006 Season

	M	Inn	NO	Runs	HS	Avg	100	50	Ct	St	Balls	Runs	Wkts	Avg	BB	5I	10M
Test																	
FC																	
ODI																	
List A	1	0	0	0	0	-	-	-	1	-	48	45	2	22.50	2-45	-	
20/20 Int																	
20/20																	

Career Performances

	M	Inn	NO	Runs	HS	Avg	100	50	Ct	St	Balls	Runs	Wkts	Avg	BB	5I	10M
Test																	
FC																	
ODI																	
List A	1	0	0	0	0	-	-	-	1	-	48	45	2	22.50	2-45	-	
20/20 Int																	
20/20																	

SMITH, W. R.   Durham

Name: William (<u>Will</u>) Rew Smith
Role: Right-hand opening bat, occasional right-arm off-spin bowler, occasional wicket-keeper
Born: 28 September 1982, Luton
Height: 5ft 10in **Weight:** 12st
Nickname: Smudge, Jiggy, Posh Kid
County debut: 2002 (Nottinghamshire)
Place in batting averages: 165th av. 27.38 (2005 92nd av. 36.88)
Strike rate: (career 95.50)
Parents: Jim and Barbara
Marital status: Single
Family links with cricket: 'Brother played a lot of county age group; Dad an avid follower and statistician!'
Education: Bedford School; Durham University
Qualifications: 11 GCSEs, 3 A-levels, BSc Molecular Biology and Biochemistry
Overseas tours: Bedford School to Barbados (Sir Garfield Sobers International Tournament) 1998; British Universities to South Africa 2004
Overseas teams played for: Gordon DCC, Sydney 2001-02

Career highlights to date: 'Being part of Notts CCC Championship winning side 2005'
Cricket moments to forget: 'Still bagging pair at Rose Bowl for Notts 2nd XI 2001'
Cricket superstitions: 'None'
Cricketers particularly admired: Ian Botham, Steve Waugh, Graeme Fowler
Young players to look out for: Billy Godleman, Josh Mierkalns
Other sports played: 'Used to play everything; now concentrate on cricket as keep getting injured'
Other sports followed: Horse racing, football (Rushden & Diamonds, Luton Town), rugby union
Favourite band: Athlete
Relaxations: 'Watching horse racing, music, film etc'
Extras: Represented England U16-U18. Played for Durham UCCE 2003-05 (captain 2004-05). Represented British Universities 2004, 2005 (captain 2005). Nottinghamshire 2nd XI Player of the Year 2005. Left Nottinghamshire at the end of the 2006 season and has joined Durham for 2007
Best batting: 156 DUCCE v Somerset, Taunton 2005
Best bowling: 3-34 DUCCE v Leicestershire, Leicester 2005

2006 Season

	M	Inn	NO	Runs	HS	Avg	100	50	Ct	St	Balls	Runs	Wkts	Avg	BB	5I	10M
Test																	
FC	14	21	0	575	141	27.38	1	2	8	-	0	0	0		-	-	-
ODI																	
List A	15	14	1	456	95 *	35.07	-	5	6	-	0	0	0		-	-	
20/20 Int																	
20/20	11	7	3	75	31	18.75	-	-	9	-	0	0	0		-	-	

Career Performances

	M	Inn	NO	Runs	HS	Avg	100	50	Ct	St	Balls	Runs	Wkts	Avg	BB	5I	10M
Test																	
FC	29	44	3	1123	156	27.39	2	3	18	-	573	448	6	74.66	3-34	-	-
ODI																	
List A	29	25	1	584	95 *	24.33	-	5	8	-	0	0	0		-	-	
20/20 Int																	
20/20	21	15	3	234	55	19.50	-	2	13	-	0	0	0		-	-	

SNAPE, J. N. Leicestershire

Name: <u>Jeremy</u> Nicholas Snape
Role: Right-hand bat, off-spin bowler,
county captain; all-rounder
Born: 27 April 1973, Stoke-on-Trent
Height: 5ft 8in **Weight:** 12st
Nickname: Snapper
County debut: 1992 (Northamptonshire),
1999 (Gloucestershire),
2003 (Leicestershire)
County cap: 1999 (Gloucestershire),
2003 (Leicestershire)
ODI debut: 2001-02
Place in batting averages: 200th av. 21.90
Strike rate: (career 94.93)
Parents: Keith and Barbara
Wife and date of marriage: Joanne,
4 October 2003
Children: Tamsin, 26 September 2005
Family links with cricket: 'Brother Jonathan plays at Rode Park in Cheshire'
Education: Denstone College, Staffordshire; Durham University; Loughborough
University
Qualifications: 8 GCSEs, 3 A-levels, BSc Natural Science, MSc Sport Psychology
Career outside cricket: Sport psychology
Off-season: 'Working as a sport psychologist, helping players and teams in sport and
business reach their potential'
Overseas tours: England U18 to Canada (International Youth Tournament) 1991 (c);
England U19 to Pakistan 1991-92; Durham University to South Africa 1993, to Vienna
(European Indoor Championships) 1994; Northamptonshire to Cape Town 1993;
Christians in Sport to Zimbabwe 1994-95; Troubadours to South Africa 1997;
Gloucestershire to South Africa 1999; England to Zimbabwe (one-day series) 2001-02,
to India and New Zealand 2001-02 (one-day series), to Sri Lanka (ICC Champions
Trophy) 2002-03, to Australia 2002-03 (VB Series)
Overseas teams played for: Petone, Wellington, New Zealand 1994-95; Wainuiamata,
Wellington, New Zealand 1995-96; Techs CC, Cape Town 1996-99
Career highlights to date: 'England debut. England ODI in Calcutta – 120,000
people. Twenty20 Cup wins'
Cricket moments to forget: 'Breaking my thumb in Australia 2003 and being ruled
out of World Cup'
Cricketers particularly admired: Allan Lamb, Jack Russell
Other sports followed: Rugby (Leicester Tigers)
Injuries: Out for one month with a broken thumb
Relaxations: Travelling, music, cooking, good food and wine

Player website: www.sportingedgesolutions.co.uk

Extras: Sir John Hobbs Silver Jubilee Memorial Prize 1988. B&H Gold Award for his 3-34 for Combined Universities v Worcestershire at The Parks 1992. Player of the Tournament at European Indoor 6-a-side Championships 1994. Made ODI debut in first ODI v Zimbabwe at Harare 2001-02, winning Man of the Match award for his 2-39 and brilliant catch. BBC West Country Sports Cricketer of the Year for 2001. Struck 16-ball 34*, including winning runs, in the Twenty20 Cup final at Edgbaston 2004. Captain of Leicestershire since 2006

Opinions on cricket: 'A balance must be struck between a commercially viable amount of cricket and the preparation, rest and motivation needed to provide top-class competition in every game.'

Best batting: 131 Gloucestershire v Sussex, Cheltenham 2001

Best bowling: 5-65 Northamptonshire v Durham, Northampton 1995

2006 Season

	M	Inn	NO	Runs	HS	Avg	100	50	Ct	St	Balls	Runs	Wkts	Avg	BB	5I	10M
Test																	
FC	8	11	1	219	90	21.90	-	1	3	-	319	183	3	61.00	2-27	-	-
ODI																	
List A	12	10	1	161	45 *	17.88	-	-	6	-	341	285	11	25.90	3-28		
20/20 Int																	
20/20	11	9	3	237	47 *	39.50	-	-	3	-	160	166	12	13.83	4-22	-	

Career Performances

	M	Inn	NO	Runs	HS	Avg	100	50	Ct	St	Balls	Runs	Wkts	Avg	BB	5I	10M
Test																	
FC	121	180	31	4194	131	28.14	3	23	74	-	10728	5583	113	49.40	5-65	1	-
ODI	10	7	3	118	38	29.50	-	-	5	-	529	403	13	31.00	3-43	-	
List A	259	209	55	3559	104 *	23.11	1	11	91	-	7979	6123	210	29.15	5-32	1	
20/20 Int																	
20/20	35	32	12	518	47 *	25.90	-	-	13	-	586	634	33	19.21	4-22	-	

77. Which limited-overs competition first got under way on 22 May 1979?
a) World Cup b) ICC Trophy c) ICC Champions Trophy

SNELL, S. D.   Gloucestershire

Name: <u>Steven</u> David Snell
Role: Right-hand bat, wicket-keeper
Born: 27 February 1983, Winchester
Height: 6ft   **Weight:** 11st 7lbs
Nickname: Snelly, Glove Monkey,
Gonzo, Jaws
County debut: 2005
County cap: 2005
Parents: Jonathan and Sandra
Marital status: Single
Family links with cricket: 'Grandad and
Dad both keen amateur cricketers. Brothers
Rob and Peter both play at Ventnor Cricket
Club (the real home of cricket!) on the Isle
of Wight'
Education: Sandown High School
Qualifications: 10 GCSEs, 2 A-levels, ECB
Level 2 cricket coach, FA Level 1 football

coach, EBA basketball coach, YMCA fitness instructor
Overseas tours: MCC Young Cricketers to Cape Town 2002, to Lanzarote 2003, to
Sri Lanka 2004; MCC B to USA 2004
Overseas teams played for: Hermanus, Cape Town 2001-02; Brighton, Melbourne
2003-05
Career highlights to date: '83* on first-class debut against Bangladesh A'
Cricket moments to forget: 'Breaking my jaw in three places during nets at Lord's'
Cricket superstitions: 'Always have to ask somebody if I have the right shirt on.
Bordering on obsessive-compulsive…'
Cricketers particularly admired: Jack Russell, Ian Healy, Jonty Rhodes
Young players to look out for: Will Rudge, Tom Stayt, Ben Woodhouse, Peter Snell
Other sports played: Football, squash ('thought I was half-decent till I played
Matt Windows')
Other sports followed: Football (Portsmouth FC)
Favourite band: John Mayer, The Killers
Relaxations: 'Enjoy writing about the game; meals out; lying on Sandown beach on
the Isle of Wight'
Extras: Played for Hampshire Board XI in the 2002 C&G. Attended World Cricket
Academy, Mumbai 2003; International Cricket Academy, Port Elizabeth 2005
Opinions on cricket: 'Controversial decisions are an interesting part of the game!
Leave the decisions to the guys in the middle and only use the third umpire for run-
outs/stumpings. Creates some great talking points. It should be compulsory for wicket-
keepers to bowl an over in every match in every competition.'
Best batting: 83* Gloucestershire v Bangladesh A, Bristol 2005

2006 Season

	M	Inn	NO	Runs	HS	Avg	100	50	Ct	St	Balls	Runs	Wkts	Avg	BB	5I	10M
Test																	
FC																	
ODI																	
List A	2	2	0	2	2	1.00	-	-	7	-	0	0	0			-	-
20/20 Int																	
20/20																	

Career Performances

	M	Inn	NO	Runs	HS	Avg	100	50	Ct	St	Balls	Runs	Wkts	Avg	BB	5I	10M
Test																	
FC	2	4	1	141	83 *	47.00	-	1	4	-	0	0	0		-	-	-
ODI																	
List A	10	8	0	31	17	3.87	-	-	16	-	0	0	0			-	-
20/20 Int																	
20/20																	

SOLANKI, V. S. — Worcestershire

Name: <u>Vikram</u> Singh Solanki
Role: Right-hand bat, right-arm off-spin bowler, county captain
Born: 1 April 1976, Udaipur, India
Height: 6ft **Weight:** 12st
Nickname: Vik
County debut: 1993 (one-day), 1995 (first-class)
County cap: 1998; colours, 2002
Benefit: 2007
ODI debut: 1999-2000
Twenty20 Int debut: 2005
1000 runs in a season: 3
1st-Class 200s: 1
Place in batting averages: 59th av. 46.37 (2005 138th av. 30.78)
Strike rate: (career 78.01)
Parents: Mr Vijay Singh and Mrs Florabel Solanki
Marital status: Single
Family links with cricket: 'Father played in India. Brother Vishal is a keen cricketer'
Education: Regis School, Wolverhampton; Open University

Qualifications: 9 GCSEs, 3 A-levels
Overseas tours: England U18 to South Africa 1992-93, to Denmark (ICC Youth Tournament) 1994; England U19 to West Indies 1994-95; Worcestershire CCC to Barbados 1996, to Zimbabwe 1997; England A to Zimbabwe and South Africa 1998-99, to Bangladesh and New Zealand 1999-2000, to West Indies 2000-01, to Sri Lanka 2004-05, to West Indies 2005-06 (c); England to South Africa and Zimbabwe 1999-2000 (one-day series), to Kenya (ICC Knockout Trophy) 2000-01, to Pakistan 2000-01 (one-day series), to Bangladesh and Sri Lanka 2003-04 (one-day series), to Zimbabwe (one-day series) 2004-05, to South Africa 2004-05 (one-day series), to Pakistan 2005-06 (one-day series), to India 2005-06 (one-day series)
Overseas teams played for: Midland-Guildford, Perth, Western Australia; Rajasthan, India 2006-07
Career highlights to date: 'Playing for England'
Cricket moments to forget: 'Losing to Scotland (NatWest 1998)'
Cricketers particularly admired: Sachin Tendulkar, Graeme Hick
Other sports played: 'Enjoy most sports'
Relaxations: 'Reading; spending time with family and friends'
Extras: Scored more first-class runs (1339) in 1999 season than any other English player. Scored 106 v South Africa at The Oval in the NatWest Series 2003, winning the Man of the Match award and sharing with Marcus Trescothick (114*) in a record England opening partnership in ODIs (200). Man of the Match in the third ODI v Zimbabwe at Bulawayo 2004-05 (100*). C&G Man of the Match awards for his 127 (plus three catches and a run-out) in the semi-final v Warwickshire at Edgbaston 2004 and for his 115 in the final v Gloucestershire at Lord's 2004. Captain of Worcestershire since 2005
Best batting: 222 Worcestershire v Gloucestershire, Bristol 2006
Best bowling: 5-40 Worcestershire v Middlesex, Lord's 2004

2006 Season

	M	Inn	NO	Runs	HS	Avg	100	50	Ct	St	Balls	Runs	Wkts	Avg	BB	5I	10M
Test																	
FC	16	29	2	1252	222	46.37	4	4	12	-	315	165	5	33.00	2-16	-	-
ODI	2	2	1	54	44 *	54.00	-	-	1	-	27	26	1	26.00	1-17	-	-
List A	18	18	1	571	61	33.58	-	4	4	-	287	224	11	20.36	4-14	-	-
20/20 Int																	
20/20	6	6	0	307	92	51.16	-	2	6	-	18	36	1	36.00	1-25	-	

Career Performances

	M	Inn	NO	Runs	HS	Avg	100	50	Ct	St	Balls	Runs	Wkts	Avg	BB	5I	10M
Test																	
FC	202	332	23	11260	222	36.44	20	61	231	-	6475	3771	83	45.43	5-40	4	1
ODI	51	46	5	1097	106	26.75	2	5	16	-	111	105	1	105.00	1-17	-	
List A	302	275	23	7541	164 *	29.92	11	41	114	-	926	803	24	33.45	4-14	-	
20/20 Int	1	1	0	9	9	9.00	-	-	1	-	0	0	0		-	-	
20/20	13	13	0	454	92	34.92	-	3	11	-	18	36	1	36.00	1-25		

SPEARMAN, C. M.   Gloucestershire

Name: <u>Craig</u> Murray Spearman
Role: Right-hand opening bat
Born: 4 July 1972, Auckland, New Zealand
Height: 6ft **Weight:** 13st 7lbs
Nickname: Spears
County debut: 2002
County cap: 2002
Test debut: 1995-96
ODI debut: 1995-96
1000 runs in a season: 3
1st-Class 200s: 2
1st-Class 300s: 1
Place in batting averages: 64th av. 44.19
(2005 108th av. 34.44)
Strike rate: (career 78.00)
Parents: Murray and Sandra
Wife and date of marriage: Maree,
4 March 2004

Education: Kelston Boys High School, Auckland; Massey University, Palmerston North, New Zealand
Qualifications: Bachelor of Business Studies (BBS; Finance major)
Overseas tours: New Zealand to India and Pakistan (World Cup) 1995-96, to West Indies 1995-96, to Sharjah (Singer Champions Trophy) 1996-97, to Pakistan 1996-97, to Zimbabwe 1997-98, to Australia 1997-98 (CUB Series), to Sri Lanka 1998, to India 1999-2000, to Zimbabwe 2000-01, to Kenya (ICC Knockout Trophy) 2000-01, to South Africa 2000-01; FICA World XI to New Zealand 2004-05
Overseas teams played for: Auckland 1993-96; Central Districts 1996-97 – 2000-01, 2002-03 – 2004-05
Career highlights to date: 'Playing international cricket; Test century; winning ICC Knockout Trophy [2000-01] with New Zealand; winning two C&G finals with Gloucestershire; scoring 341 for Gloucestershire v Middlesex (highest score for Gloucestershire)'
Cricket moments to forget: 'Misfielding on the boundary at the SCG in the fifth over and hearing about it for the next 45 overs'
Cricket superstitions: 'None'
Cricketers particularly admired: Gordon Greenidge
Other sports played: Golf, tennis
Other sports followed: Rugby, golf, football
Favourite band: U2
Relaxations: 'Sleeping'
Extras: Gloucestershire Players' Player of the Year 2002. Scored 123-ball 153 v

Warwickshire at Gloucester in the NCL 2003 to set a new individual record score for Gloucestershire in the one-day league. Vice-captain of Gloucestershire 2003. Scored 341, the highest individual score for Gloucestershire in first-class cricket, v Middlesex at Gloucester 2004. C&G Man of the Match award for his 122-ball 143* in the semi-final v Yorkshire at Bristol 2004. Struck century (100) before lunch on first day v Surrey at Bristol 2006. Is England-qualified

Best batting: 341 Gloucestershire v Middlesex, Gloucester 2004
Best bowling: 1-37 Central Districts v Wellington, New Plymouth 1999-2000

2006 Season

	M	Inn	NO	Runs	HS	Avg	100	50	Ct	St	Balls	Runs	Wkts	Avg	BB	5I	10M
Test																	
FC	16	31	0	1370	192	44.19	6	2	18	-	0	0	0		-	-	-
ODI																	
List A	15	15	0	266	44	17.73	-	-	5	-	0	0	0		-	-	
20/20 Int																	
20/20	8	8	0	193	63	24.12	-	2	4	-	0	0	0		-	-	

Career Performances

	M	Inn	NO	Runs	HS	Avg	100	50	Ct	St	Balls	Runs	Wkts	Avg	BB	5I	10M
Test	19	37	2	922	112	26.34	1	3	21	-	0	0	0		-	-	-
FC	179	325	15	11954	341	38.56	28	51	171	-	78	55	1	55.00	1-37	-	-
ODI	51	50	0	936	86	18.72	-	5	15	-	3	6	0		-	-	
List A	258	256	7	7078	153	28.42	7	43	96	-	33	43	0		-	-	
20/20 Int																	
20/20	29	25	2	511	88	22.21	-	3	8	-	0	0	0		-	-	

78. Who captained West Indies when they won the World Cup for the first time?
a) Clive Lloyd b) Viv Richards c) Rohan Kanhai

SPENCER, D. J. Sussex

Name: <u>Duncan</u> John Spencer
Role: Right-hand bat, right-arm fast bowler
Born: 5 April 1972, Nelson, Lancashire
Height: 5ft 8in
County debut: 1993 (Kent), 2006 (Sussex)
Education: Gosnells High School,
Western Australia
Career outside cricket: Personal fitness
instructor
Overseas teams played for: Western
Australia 1993-94, 2000-01
Strike rate: (career 58.16)
Extras: Family moved to Western Australia
when he was five years old. Appearances in
senior cricket severely limited by chronic
back trouble during 1990s. Played two first-
class matches for Sussex 2006
Best batting: 75 Kent v Zimbabweans,
Canterbury 1993
Best bowling: 4-31 Kent v Leicestershire, Leicester 1994

2006 Season

	M	Inn	NO	Runs	HS	Avg	100	50	Ct	St	Balls	Runs	Wkts	Avg	BB	5I	10M
Test																	
FC	2	2	0	33	17	16.50	-	-	1	-	228	155	2	77.50	1-70	-	-
ODI																	
List A																	
20/20 Int																	
20/20																	

Career Performances

	M	Inn	NO	Runs	HS	Avg	100	50	Ct	St	Balls	Runs	Wkts	Avg	BB	5I	10M
Test																	
FC	16	18	2	233	75	14.56	-	1	10	-	2094	1412	36	39.22	4-31	-	-
ODI																	
List A	20	11	3	79	17*	9.87	-	-	5	-	843	680	23	29.56	4-35	-	
20/20 Int																	
20/20																	

SPRIEGEL, M. N. W. Surrey

Name: <u>Matthew</u> Neil William Spriegel
Role: Left-hand bat, right-arm
off-spin bowler
Born: 4 March 1987, Epsom, Surrey
Height: 6ft 3in **Weight:** 13st 3lbs
Nickname: Spriegs
County debut: No first-team appearance
Parents: Geoff and Julie
Marital status: Single
Education: Whitgift School; Loughborough
University ('currently in first year')
Qualifications: 11 GCSEs, 3 A-levels,
1 AS-level, Level 1 ECB coach
Career outside cricket: Student
Off-season: 'Studying Sports and Exercise
Sciences at Loughborough University'
Overseas tours: Surrey U19 to Perth 2004,
to Cape Town 2005, 2006

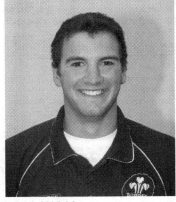

Overseas teams played for: Subiaco Marist CC, Perth 2005-06
Career highlights to date: 'Taking 7-85 and scoring 96 in the same game for Surrey against Kent in the 2nd XI Championship last season'
Cricket moments to forget: 'Scoring three ducks in six innings on tour in Perth in 2004'
Cricket superstitions: 'Always put my right pad on before my left pad'
Cricketers particularly admired: Steve Waugh, Alec Stewart, Mark Ramprakash
Young players to look out for: Richard Morris, Dan Newton, Zafar Ansari
Other sports played: Golf, football
Other sports followed: Football, rugby, golf
Favourite band: Pete Murray
Opinions on cricket: 'It is a very exciting time for domestic cricket, with the success of Twenty20 and introduction of new one-day competitions attracting bigger crowds. The success of the England team in the last few years has raised the profile of the sport and this has filtered down into the county game. It is a great time to be involved in cricket.'

SPURWAY, S. H. P.   Somerset

Name: Samuel (<u>Sam</u>) Harold
Patrick Spurway
Role: Left-hand bat, wicket-keeper
Born: 13 March 1987, Taunton
Height: 6ft 1in **Weight:** 12st 7lbs
Nickname: Spurs, Speedy
County debut: 2005 (one-day),
2006 (first-class)
Parents: Susan and Colin
Marital status: Single
Family links with cricket: 'Dad and older
brother Tom play local cricket'
Education: Wadham Community School;
Richard Huish College
Qualifications: 11 GCSEs, 3 A-levels
Overseas tours: West Region to West Indies
2001; Somerset to Cape Town 2006
Career highlights to date: 'Making my
debut for Somerset in the International 20:20 v Leicestershire'
Cricket moments to forget: 'Getting my three front teeth knocked out whilst playing
for my local club side, Ilminster'
Cricket superstitions: 'None'
Cricketers particularly admired: Adam Gilchrist, Tim Crawley
Young players to look out for: Jack Cooper, William Spurway
Other sports played: Football, skittles
Other sports followed: Football (Yeovil and Man Utd)
Injuries: Out for 12 weeks with a broken thumb
Favourite band: 'Tick in the Box'
Best batting: 83 Somerset v Northamptonshire, Taunton 2006

79. Who was on the receiving end of the first
official 100mph delivery, bowled by Shoaib Akhtar
in Cape Town in February 2003?

2006 Season

	M	Inn	NO	Runs	HS	Avg	100	50	Ct	St	Balls	Runs	Wkts	Avg	BB	5I	10M
Test																	
FC	3	4	0	164	83	41.00	-	1	7	-	0	0	0		-	-	-
ODI																	
List A	4	2	0	31	31	15.50	-	-	4	2	0	0	0		-	-	
20/20 Int																	
20/20																	

Career Performances

	M	Inn	NO	Runs	HS	Avg	100	50	Ct	St	Balls	Runs	Wkts	Avg	BB	5I	10M
Test																	
FC	3	4	0	164	83	41.00	-	1	7	-	0	0	0		-	-	-
ODI																	
List A	4	2	0	31	31	15.50	-	-	4	2	0	0	0		-	-	
20/20 Int																	
20/20	1	1	1	15	15 *		-	-	-	-	0	0	0		-	-	

STEVENS, D. I.   Kent

Name: <u>Darren</u> Ian Stevens
Role: Right-hand top-order bat, right-arm
medium bowler
Born: 30 April 1976, Leicester
Height: 5ft 11in **Weight:** 13st
Nickname: Stevo, Hover
County debut: 1997 (Leicestershire),
2005 (Kent)
County cap: 2002 (Leicestershire),
2005 (Kent)
1000 runs in a season: 1
1st-Class 200s: 1
Place in batting averages: 79th av. 39.00
(2005 38th av. 49.11)
Place in bowling averages: 87th av. 36.21
(2005 101st av. 38.52)
Strike rate: 74.47 (career 78.14)
Parents: Maddy and Bob
Marital status: Single

Family links with cricket: Father and grandfather played league cricket in
Leicestershire
Education: Mount Grace High School; John Cleveland College, Hinckley;
Hinckley Tech; Charles Klein College

Qualifications: 5 GCSEs, BTEC National in Sports Studies
Off-season: 'Trip to India (academy)'
Overseas tours: Leicestershire U19 to South Africa 1994-95; Leicestershire to Barbados 1998, to Sri Lanka 1999, to Potchefstroom 2001; ECB National Academy to Australia and Sri Lanka 2002-03
Overseas teams played for: Wanderers CC, Johannesburg, South Africa 1996-97; Rhodes University, Grahamstown, South Africa 1997-98; Fairfield CC, Sydney 1998-99; Hawthorn-Waverley, Melbourne 1999-2000; Taita CC, Wellington, New Zealand 2000-01; Ringwood CC, Melbourne 2001-02
Career highlights to date: 'The build-up to my first final at Lord's'
Cricket moments to forget: 'Losing in my first final in the C&G against Somerset 2001'
Cricketers particularly admired: Steve Waugh, Viv Richards, Ian Botham
Young players to look out for: Neil Dexter, Warren Lee
Other sports played: Squash, golf
Other sports followed: Football (Leicester City), rugby union (Leicester Tigers)
Favourite band: U2, Snow Patrol
Relaxations: 'Music, spending time with close friends'
Extras: Received painting from Sir Colin Cowdrey on day of maiden first-class 100 (130 in fourth Championship match), v Sussex at Arundel 1999. Won Sir Ron Brierley/Crusaders Scholarship 1999. Included in provisional England squad of 30 for the 2002-03 World Cup. Kent Player of the Year 2005
Best batting: 208 Kent v Glamorgan, Canterbury 2005
Best bowling: 4-36 Kent v Yorkshire, Canterbury 2006

2006 Season

	M	Inn	NO	Runs	HS	Avg	100	50	Ct	St	Balls	Runs	Wkts	Avg	BB	5I	10M
Test																	
FC	17	27	4	897	126 *	39.00	2	6	18	-	1415	688	19	36.21	4-36	-	-
ODI																	
List A	16	16	0	647	82	40.43	-	7	6	-	180	179	5	35.80	2-10	-	
20/20 Int																	
20/20	9	9	0	201	69	22.33	-	1	3	-	0	0	0		-	-	

Career Performances

	M	Inn	NO	Runs	HS	Avg	100	50	Ct	St	Balls	Runs	Wkts	Avg	BB	5I	10M
Test																	
FC	113	188	13	5716	208	32.66	10	35	95	-	3282	1756	42	41.80	4-36	-	-
ODI																	
List A	162	153	11	4062	133	28.60	3	27	68	-	1235	1033	30	34.43	5-32	1	
20/20 Int																	
20/20	30	29	1	525	69	18.75	-	1	10	-	54	91	3	30.33	1-13	-	

STEYN, D. W. — Warwickshire

Name: <u>Dale</u> Willem Steyn
Role: Right-hand bat, right-arm fast bowler
Born: 27 June 1983, Phalaborwa, South Africa
County debut: 2005 (Essex)
Test debut: 2004-05
ODI debut: 2005-06
Place in bowling averages: (2005 144th av. 59.85)
Strike rate: (career 51.84)
Overseas tours: South Africa A to Sri Lanka 2005-06; South Africa to Australia 2005-06 (VB Series), to Sri Lanka 2006
Overseas teams played for: Northerns 2003-04; Titans 2004-05 –
Extras: One of *South African Cricket Annual*'s five Cricketers of the Year 2006.

Made ODI debut for African XI v Asian Cricket Council XI at Centurion 2005-06; has also played in ODIs for South Africa. His match awards include Man of the Match v Warriors at East London in the SuperSport Series 2004-05 (5-30/4-66) and v Warriors at Benoni in the SuperSport Series 2005-06 (5-44/5-27). Joint leading wicket-taker (with Paul Harris) in the SuperSport Series 2005-06 with 49 at 18.22. Was an overseas player with Essex during the 2005 season as a locum for Danish Kaneria; has joined Warwickshire as an overseas player for the first part of the 2007 season
Best batting: 82 Essex v Durham, Riverside 2005
Best bowling: 5-27 Titans v Warriors, Benoni 2005-06

2006 Season (did not make any first-class or one-day appearances)

Career Performances

	M	Inn	NO	Runs	HS	Avg	100	50	Ct	St	Balls	Runs	Wkts	Avg	BB	5I	10M
Test	8	13	4	70	13	7.77	-	-	2	-	1631	1124	32	35.12	5-47	2	-
FC	35	44	12	317	82	9.90	-	1	7	-	6844	3997	132	30.28	5-27	6	1
ODI	4	2	0	4	3	2.00	-	-	-	-	109	132	3	44.00	1-2	-	
List A	27	8	3	14	6 *	2.80	-	-	4	-	1189	901	37	24.35	5-20	1	
20/20 Int																	
20/20	7	0	0	0	0		-	-	1	-	132	98	4	24.50	2-10	-	

STIFF, D. A.   Leicestershire

Name: <u>David</u> Alexander Stiff
Role: Right-hand bat, right-arm fast bowler
Born: 20 October 1984, Dewsbury
Height: 6ft 6in   **Weight:** 14st 10lbs
Nickname: Stiffy, Stiffmeister, Light Bulb
County debut: 2004 (Kent)
Strike rate: (career 72.30)
Parents: Christine and Ian
Marital status: Single
Family links with cricket: 'Eldest and
youngest brothers as well as one of my sisters
have all played cricket at various levels'
Education: Batley Grammar School
Qualifications: 9 GCSEs, Level 2 coach
Off-season: 'Getting fitter, stronger and
generally better at all aspects of my game'
Overseas tours: England U17 to Australia

2001; Yorkshire to Grenada 2002; England
U19 to Australia 2002-03, to Bangladesh (U19 World Cup) 2003-04
Overseas teams played for: Adelaide University 2006
Career highlights to date: 'Five wickets in the third U19 "Test" v Australia 2003'
Cricket moments to forget: 'Being booed at Canterbury for no-balling, Kent v
Middlesex, September 2004'
Cricketers particularly admired: Allan Donald, Brett Lee, Courtney Walsh
Young players to look out for: Mark Lawson, Greg Wood, Harry Gurney
Other sports played: 'Dabble in most sports; represented West Yorkshire Schools at
high jump'
Injuries: Out for eight weeks with a twisted knee
Favourite band: Radiohead, Guns N' Roses
Relaxations: 'Music, sleeping, going home to see family/friends'
Extras: Yorkshire Cricket Academy 1999-2003. Took 5-35 for England U19 in the
third 'Test' v Australia U19 at Bankstown Oval, Sydney 2002-03. Represented
England U19 2004. ECB National Academy 2004-05 (part-time). Released by Kent at
the end of the 2006 season and has joined Leicestershire for 2007
Best batting: 18 Kent v Lancashire, Tunbridge Wells 2004
Best bowling: 3-88 Kent v New Zealanders, Canterbury 2004

2006 Season

	M	Inn	NO	Runs	HS	Avg	100	50	Ct	St	Balls	Runs	Wkts	Avg	BB	5I	10M
Test																	
FC	1	0	0	0	0		-	-	-	-	93	75	1	75.00	1-53	-	-
ODI																	
List A																	
20/20 Int																	
20/20																	

Career Performances

	M	Inn	NO	Runs	HS	Avg	100	50	Ct	St	Balls	Runs	Wkts	Avg	BB	5I	10M
Test																	
FC	8	6	3	57	18	19.00	-	-	1	-	723	579	10	57.90	3-88	-	-
ODI																	
List A	1	0	0	0	0		-	-	-	-	30	27	1	27.00	1-27	-	
20/20 Int																	
20/20																	

STOKES, M. S. T.   Hampshire

Name: <u>Mitchell</u> Sam Thomas Stokes
Role: Right-hand bat, right-arm
off-spin bowler
Born: 27 March 1987, Basingstoke
Height: 5ft 8in **Weight:** 10st
Nickname: Bram Stoker, Stokesy,
Chuckavati
County debut: 2005 (one-day)
Parents: Paul and Janice
Marital status: Single
Education: Cranbourne School; Basingstoke
College of Technology
Qualifications: Level 1 cricket coaching
Off-season: 'Off to Perth for six months'
Overseas tours: West of England U15 to
West Indies 2002; England U19 to India
2004-05
Career highlights to date: 'Making 62

against Middlesex in Twenty20 2006. Making debut in both Twenty20 2005 and Pro40
2006 for Hampshire'
Young players to look out for: David Griffiths, Liam Dawson, Adil Rashid
Other sports played: Football (Crystal Palace younger age-groups)

Other sports followed: Football (Tottenham Hotspur)
Favourite band: 'Don't have a favourite band but listen to all types of music – R&B, hip hop, indie, old school music'
Relaxations: 'Football, going out with mates, music, poker with the lads'
Extras: Bunbury U15 Festival Bowler of the Tournament 2002. Basingstoke Sportsman of the Year 2005

2006 Season

	M	Inn	NO	Runs	HS	Avg	100	50	Ct	St	Balls	Runs	Wkts	Avg	BB	5I	10M
Test																	
FC																	
ODI																	
List A	4	3	0	49	36	16.33	-	-	2	-	24	26	0		-	-	
20/20 Int																	
20/20	8	8	0	125	62	15.62	-	1	3	-	0	0	0		-	-	

Career Performances

	M	Inn	NO	Runs	HS	Avg	100	50	Ct	St	Balls	Runs	Wkts	Avg	BB	5I	10M
Test																	
FC																	
ODI																	
List A	4	3	0	49	36	16.33	-	-	2	-	24	26	0		-	-	
20/20 Int																	
20/20	14	12	0	179	62	14.91	-	1	4	-	6	14	0		-	-	

80. Who captained New Zealand to their first Test series victory in England?
a) Martin Crowe b) Stephen Fleming c) Jeremy Coney

STONEMAN, M. D.   Durham

Name: <u>Mark</u> Daniel Stoneman
Role: Left-hand top-order bat,
'right-arm variations'
Born: 26 June 1987, Newcastle upon Tyne
Height: 5ft 11in **Weight:** 12st 5lbs
Nickname: Rocky, Doug
County debut: No first-team appearance
Parents: Ian and Pauline
Marital status: Single
Family links with cricket: 'Father played.
Grandfather played and was also an umpire'
Education: Whickham Comprehensive
School
Qualifications: 11 GCSEs, 3 A-levels
Overseas tours: Durham Development
Squad to Mumbai 2004-05; England U19 to
Sri Lanka (U19 World Cup) 2005-06

Career highlights to date: 'Making 155 for
North Region in U19 trials; 46 on 2nd XI debut'
Cricket moments to forget: 'None. All experiences can provide positives and
lessons learned'
Cricket superstitions: 'Right pad on first'
Cricketers particularly admired: Brian Lara
Young players to look out for: Mark Turner, Ben Harmison, Karl Turner
Other sports followed: Football (Newcastle United FC)
Favourite band: 'None in particular. Like dance, R&B music'
Relaxations: 'Watching films, socialising with friends'
Extras: Attended Darren Lehmann Talent Squad, Adelaide, January-March 2006.
Represented England U19 2006

---

81. Who captained India to their first Test series victory in England?
a) Ajit Wadekar b) Sunil Gavaskar c) Kapil Dev

STRAUSS, A. J.   Middlesex

Name: <u>Andrew</u> John Strauss
Role: Left-hand bat, left-arm medium bowler
Born: 2 March 1977, Johannesburg,
South Africa
Height: 5ft 11in **Weight:** 13st
Nickname: Straussy, Johann, Levi,
Mareman, Muppet, Lord Brocket
County debut: 1997 (one-day),
1998 (first-class)
County cap: 2001
Test debut: 2004
ODI debut: 2003-04
Twenty20 Int debut: 2005
1000 runs in a season: 3
Place in batting averages: 34th av. 52.92
(2005 156th av. 29.40)
Strike rate: (career 48.00)
Parents: David and Dawn

Wife and date of marriage: Ruth, 18 October 2003
Children: Samuel David, December 2005
Education: Radley College; Durham University
Qualifications: 4 A-levels, BA (Hons) Economics
Overseas tours: Durham University to Zimbabwe 1997-98; Middlesex to South
Africa 2000; ECB National Academy to Australia 2001-02; England to Bangladesh
and Sri Lanka 2003-04 (one-day series), to West Indies 2003-04, to Zimbabwe (one-day
series) 2004-05, to South Africa 2004-05, to Pakistan 2005-06, to India 2005-06, to India
(ICC Champions Trophy) 2006-07, to Australia 2006-07
Overseas teams played for: Sydney University 1998-99; Mosman, Sydney 1999-2001
Cricket moments to forget: 'Getting out second ball of the season 2001'
Cricketers particularly admired: Allan Donald, Brian Lara, Saqlain Mushtaq
Other sports played: Golf (Durham University 1998), rugby (Durham University 1996-97)
Other sports followed: 'Anything with a ball'
Extras: Middlesex Player of the Year 2001. Scored century (112) plus 83 in second
innings on Test debut in the first Test v New Zealand at Lord's (his home ground)
2004, winning Man of the Match award. Scored century (100) v West Indies, also at
Lord's, in the NatWest Series 2004, in the process sharing with Andrew Flintoff (123)
in a new record partnership for England in ODIs (226). Wombwell Cricket Lovers'
Society George Spofforth Cricketer of the Year 2004. Captain of Middlesex 2002-04.
Scored 126 in the first Test v South Africa at Port Elizabeth 2004-05, achieving feat of
scoring a Test century on home and away debuts and becoming first player to score a
Test century in his first innings against each of first three opponents. His other

international awards include Man of the [Test] Series v South Africa 2004-05 (656 runs at 72.88) and England's Man of the [Test] Series v Pakistan 2006. Vodafone England Cricketer of the Year 2004-05. One of *Wisden*'s Five Cricketers of the Year 2005. Appointed MBE in 2006 New Year Honours as part of 2005 Ashes-winning England team. Captain of England in series v Sri Lanka (ODIs) and Pakistan 2006 in the absence of Michael Vaughan and Andrew Flintoff, having deputised for Flintoff in India 2005-06. England 12-month central contract 2006-07

Best batting: 176 Middlesex v Durham, Lord's 2001
Best bowling: 1-27 Middlesex v Nottinghamshire, Lord's 2003

2006 Season

	M	Inn	NO	Runs	HS	Avg	100	50	Ct	St	Balls	Runs	Wkts	Avg	BB	5I	10M
Test	7	12	0	600	128	50.00	2	2	9	-	0	0	0		-	-	-
FC	8	14	0	741	141	52.92	3	2	11	-	0	0	0		-	-	-
ODI	10	10	0	298	78	29.80	-	2	8	-	0	0	0		-	-	
List A	10	10	0	298	78	29.80	-	2	8	-	0	0	0		-	-	
20/20 Int	2	2	0	33	33	16.50	-	-	1	-	0	0	0		-	-	
20/20	2	2	0	33	33	16.50	-	-	1	-	0	0	0		-	-	

Career Performances

	M	Inn	NO	Runs	HS	Avg	100	50	Ct	St	Balls	Runs	Wkts	Avg	BB	5I	10M
Test	31	58	2	2597	147	46.37	10	7	39	-	0	0	0		-	-	-
FC	121	215	12	8544	176	42.08	22	37	89	-	48	58	1	58.00	1-27	-	-
ODI	61	60	7	1847	152	34.84	2	11	19	-	6	3	0		-	-	
List A	162	155	12	4353	152	30.44	4	29	39	-	6	3	0		-	-	
20/20 Int	3	3	0	51	33	17.00	-	-	1	-	0	0	0		-	-	
20/20	10	10	0	245	60	24.50	-	2	5	-	0	0	0		-	-	

STREAK, H. H.   Warwickshire

Name: Heath Hilton Streak
Role: Right-hand bat, right-arm fast-medium bowler, county captain
Born: 16 March 1974, Bulawayo, Zimbabwe
Height: 6ft 1in **Weight:** 15st 5lbs
Nickname: Streaky
County debut: 1995 (Hampshire), 2004 (Warwickshire)
County cap: 2005 (Warwickshire)
Test debut: 1993-94
ODI debut: 1993-94
50 wickets in a season: 1
Place in batting averages: 156th av. 28.50 (2005 206th av. 21.55)
Place in bowling averages: 70th av. 33.51 (2005 38th av. 27.23)
Strike rate: 65.36 (career 60.87)

Parents: Denis and Sheona
Wife and date of marriage: Nadine, 18 August 2000
Children: Holly, 23 December 1992; Charlotte, 14 August 2002; Harry, 5 January 2005
Family links with cricket: 'Father played for Rhodesia and Zimbabwe'
Education: Falcon College, Zimbabwe
Qualifications: 3 A-levels, professional safari guide
Career outside cricket: Safari guide, farming
Off-season: 'Ranch and family holidays'
Overseas tours: Zimbabwe to England 1993, to India (Hero Cup) 1993-94, to Pakistan 1993-94, to New Zealand 1995-96, to India and Pakistan (World Cup) 1995-96, to Sri

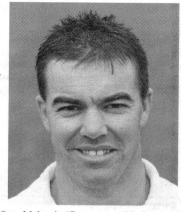

Lanka 1996, 1997-98, to New Zealand 1997-98, to Malaysia (Commonwealth Games) 1998-99, to Bangladesh (Wills International Cup) 1998-99, to Pakistan 1998-99, to UK, Ireland and Netherlands (World Cup) 1999, to West Indies 1999-2000, to England 2000, to Kenya (ICC Knockout Trophy) 2000-01 (c), to India 2000-01 (c), to New Zealand 2000-01 (c), to Bangladesh 2001-02, to Sri Lanka 2001-02, to India 2001-02, to Sri Lanka (ICC Champions Trophy) 2002-03 (c), to England 2003 (c), to Australia 2003-04 (c), to South Africa 2004-05, plus other one-day tournaments in Australia, South Africa, Sharjah, India and Bangladesh; FICA World XI to New Zealand 2004-05
Overseas teams played for: Matabeleland 1993-94 – 2003-04
Career highlights to date: 'First Test win v Pakistan for Zimbabwe [1994-95]'
Cricket moments to forget: 'Being bowled out for 38 as a team by Sri Lanka [2001-02]'
Cricket superstitions: 'Nelson – 111'
Cricketers particularly admired: Dennis Lillee, Richard Hadlee, Malcolm Marshall
Young players to look out for: Ian Bell, Alastair Cook
Other sports played: Rugby (Zimbabwe U19)
Other sports followed: Football (Liverpool), rugby (Natal Sharks)
Injuries: Out for three weeks with a back injury
Favourite band: Bon Jovi
Relaxations: 'Fishing'
Extras: First Zimbabwe player to 100 and 200 wickets in both Tests and ODIs. Has won several ODI awards, including Man of the Match v West Indies at Sydney in the CUB Series 2000-01 (45/4-8) and Man of the Series v Bangladesh 2003-04. His Test awards include Zimbabwe's Man of the Series v England in 2000 and 2003. Captain of Zimbabwe 2000-01 and 2002-04, including the 2002-03 World Cup. An overseas player with Hampshire 1995; an overseas player with Warwickshire 2004-06; is no longer considered an overseas player. Had match figures of 13-158 (7-80/6-78) in his

first game for Warwickshire, v Northamptonshire at Edgbaston 2004. Announced retirement from international cricket in October 2005. Captain of Warwicks since 2006
Opinions on cricket: 'More Twenty20 cricket – exciting and fun for players and spectators.'
Best batting: 131 Matabeleland v Mashonaland CD, Bulawayo 1995-96
131 Matabeleland v Midlands, Bulawayo 2003-04
Best bowling: 7-55 Matabeleland v Mashonaland, Bulawayo 2003-04

2006 Season

	M	Inn	NO	Runs	HS	Avg	100	50	Ct	St	Balls	Runs	Wkts	Avg	BB	5I	10M
Test																	
FC	15	24	6	513	68 *	28.50	-	2	5	-	2680	1374	41	33.51	6-73	2	-
ODI																	
List A	14	11	6	168	46	33.60	-	-	-	-	464	394	12	32.83	3-13	-	
20/20 Int																	
20/20	8	6	2	149	40	37.25	-	-	4	-	164	239	9	26.55	2-23	-	

Career Performances

	M	Inn	NO	Runs	HS	Avg	100	50	Ct	St	Balls	Runs	Wkts	Avg	BB	5I	10M
Test	65	107	18	1990	127 *	22.35	1	11	17	-	13559	6079	216	28.14	6-73	7	-
FC	164	249	45	5406	131	26.50	6	25	58	-	29585	13563	486	27.90	7-55	17	2
ODI	189	159	55	2943	79 *	28.29	-	13	46	-	9468	7129	239	29.82	5-32	1	
List A	294	236	82	4008	90 *	26.02	-	14	72	-	14192	10535	369	28.55	5-32	1	
20/20 Int																	
20/20	15	11	3	256	59	32.00	-	1	6	-	266	386	13	29.69	3-21	-	

STUBBINGS, S. D.   Derbyshire

Name: Stephen David Stubbings
Role: Left-hand bat, right-arm bowler 'all disciplines', occasional wicket-keeper
Born: 31 March 1978, Huddersfield
Height: 6ft 4in **Weight:** 15st
Nickname: Stubbo, Hollywood, Wilton Shagpile, The Plank
County debut: 1997
County cap: 2001
1000 runs in a season: 4
Place in batting averages: 112th av. 34.06 (2005 70th av. 40.21)
Parents: Marie and David
Marital status: Single
Family links with cricket: 'Father and brother both played, as I did, for Delacombe Park Cricket Club in Melbourne, Australia'
Education: Frankston High School; Swinburne University – both Melbourne, Australia

Qualifications: Victorian Certificate of Education (VCE), Level 2 coaching
Career outside cricket: 'Coach/journalist/labourer'
Off-season: 'Trying to keep warm, possibly by renovating my house'
Overseas tours: Derbyshire to Portugal 2000
Overseas teams played for: Delacombe Park CC, Melbourne 1989-90 – 1993-94; Frankston Peninsula CC, Victoria 1994-95 – 1999-2000, 2002-03 – 2005-06; Kingborough CC, Tasmania 2000-01 – 2001-02
Career highlights to date: '2006 Championship season at Derbyshire'
Cricket moments to forget: '2005 Championship season at Derbyshire'
Cricket superstitions: 'No shaving on first day of a game'
Cricketers particularly admired: Michael DiVenuto
Young players to look out for: Chris Taylor, Jake Needham, Wayne White
Other sports played: Golf, Aussie Rules, football
Other sports followed: AFL (Essendon Bombers), football (Cambridge United FC)
Favourite band: Powderfinger
Relaxations: 'Spending time with my girlfriend Claire and anything else that involves lying on the couch with either a laptop or Sky remote!'
Extras: Represented Victoria at all junior levels. Spent two years on the cricket programme at the Victorian Institute of Sport. Scored 135* v Kent at Canterbury 2000, taking part in an unbroken opening partnership of 293 with Steve Titchard (141*); it was the first occasion on which Derbyshire had batted all day without losing a wicket. Derbyshire Player of the Year 2001 and 2006
Best batting: 151 Derbyshire v Somerset, Taunton 2005

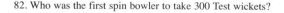

82. Who was the first spin bowler to take 300 Test wickets?

2006 Season

	M	Inn	NO	Runs	HS	Avg	100	50	Ct	St	Balls	Runs	Wkts	Avg	BB	5I	10M
Test																	
FC	18	32	1	1056	124	34.06	2	6	12	-	6	2	0		-	-	-
ODI																	
List A	17	17	0	583	110	34.29	1	4	6	-	0	0	0		-	-	
20/20 Int																	
20/20	8	8	1	178	57	25.42	-	2	3	-	0	0	0		-	-	

Career Performances

	M	Inn	NO	Runs	HS	Avg	100	50	Ct	St	Balls	Runs	Wkts	Avg	BB	5I	10M
Test																	
FC	106	191	8	5879	151	32.12	10	33	48	-	60	79	0		-	-	-
ODI																	
List A	102	95	5	2326	110	25.84	1	12	16	-	0	0	0		-	-	
20/20 Int																	
20/20	9	9	1	186	57	23.25	-	2	4	-	0	0	0		-	-	

STYRIS, S. B. Middlesex

Name: <u>Scott</u> Bernard Styris
Role: Right-hand bat, right-arm
medium-fast bowler; all-rounder
Born: 10 July 1975, Brisbane, Australia
Height: 5ft 10in **Weight:** 11st 4lbs
Nickname: Billy Ray
County debut: 2005
County cap: 2006
Test debut: 2002
ODI debut: 1999-2000
Twenty20 Int debut: 2004-05
1st-Class 200s: 1
Place in batting averages: 68th av. 42.31
(2005 149th av. 30.25)
Place in bowling averages: 91st av. 37.22
(2005 16th av. 23.54)
Strike rate: 66.16 (career 60.92)
Parents: Bernie and Heather
Marital status: Partner Nicky

Children: Emison (<u>Emi</u>), 29 May 2006
Family links with cricket: 'Brother/father played club cricket'
Education: Hamilton Boys High School

Off-season: 'Hopefully playing for NZ'

Overseas tours: New Zealand A to England 2002; New Zealand to India 1999-2000 (one-day series), to Zimbabwe and South Africa 2000-01, to Kenya (ICC Knockout Trophy) 2000-01, to Australia 2001-02 (VB Series), to Pakistan 2002, to West Indies 2002, to Sri Lanka (ICC Champions Trophy) 2002-03, to Africa (World Cup) 2002-03, to Sri Lanka 2003, to India 2003-04, to England 2004, to England (ICC Champions Trophy) 2004, to Bangladesh 2004-05, to Australia 2004-05, to Zimbabwe 2005-06, to South Africa 2005-06, to India (ICC Champions Trophy) 2006-07, plus one-day tournaments in Singapore and Sharjah

Overseas teams played for: Northern Districts 1994-95 – 2004-05; Auckland 2005-06 –

Career highlights to date: 'Test century on debut'

Cricket moments to forget: 'Any duck, dropped catch'

Cricket superstitions: 'None'

Cricketers particularly admired: Jacques Kallis, Ricky Ponting

Young players to look out for: Kane Williamson (New Zealand)

Other sports played: Golf

Other sports followed: Rugby (Chiefs), baseball (Oakland), football (Man U)

Injuries: Out for the last four games of the season with a back injury

Favourite band: Green Day, Metallica

Extras: Made Test debut in the second Test v West Indies in Grenada 2002, scoring 107 and 69*. His ODI awards include Man of the Series v Bangladesh 2004-05 and Man of the Match in the fourth ODI v West Indies at Port of Spain 2002 (63*/6-25) and in the third ODI v Australia at Christchurch 2005-06 (101). An overseas player with Middlesex 2005-06

Best batting: 212* Northern Districts v Otago, Hamilton 2001-02

Best bowling: 6-32 Northern Districts v Otago, Gisborne 1999-2000

2006 Season

	M	Inn	NO	Runs	HS	Avg	100	50	Ct	St	Balls	Runs	Wkts	Avg	BB	5I	10M
Test																	
FC	10	17	1	677	133	42.31	1	5	14	-	1191	670	18	37.22	6-71	1	-
ODI																	
List A	11	10	3	245	74 *	35.00	-	2	1	-	366	284	12	23.66	3-36	-	
20/20 Int																	
20/20	8	8	1	226	56	32.28	-	2	3	-	158	190	9	21.11	3-25	-	

Career Performances

	M	Inn	NO	Runs	HS	Avg	100	50	Ct	St	Balls	Runs	Wkts	Avg	BB	5I	10M
Test	27	44	4	1527	170	38.17	5	6	23	-	1900	973	20	48.65	3-28	-	-
FC	109	179	18	5181	212 *	32.18	9	26	88	-	12124	5998	199	30.14	6-32	9	1
ODI	116	99	12	2503	141	28.77	3	14	45	-	4287	3365	106	31.74	6-25	1	
List A	232	203	32	5178	141	30.28	4	33	87	-	9162	6985	247	28.27	6-25	1	
20/20 Int	3	3	0	109	66	36.33	-	1	-	-	24	33	2	16.50	2-33	-	
20/20	22	21	2	614	73 *	32.31	-	5	4	-	418	499	23	21.69	3-25	-	

SUPPIAH, A. V.   Somerset

Name: <u>Arul</u> Vivasvan Suppiah
Role: Right-hand bat, left-arm orthodox
spin bowler
Born: 30 August 1983, Kuala Lumpur,
Malaysia
Height: 6ft **Weight:** 12st 7lbs
Nickname: Ruley, Ja Rule
County debut: 2002
Place in batting averages: 150th av. 29.63
(2005 124th av. 32.23)
Strike rate: (career 92.58)
Parents: Suppiah and Baanumathi
Marital status: Single
Family links with cricket: Brother Rohan
Vishnu Suppiah has played cricket for
Malaysia
Education: Millfield School; Exeter
University
Qualifications: 9 GCSEs, 4 A-levels, BA (Hons) in Accounting and Finance, Level 1
coaching qualification
Overseas tours: Millfield School to South Africa 1997, to Sri Lanka 1999; West of
England U15 to West Indies 1998; Malaysia to Sharjah (Asian Cricket Council
Trophy) 2000-01
Overseas teams played for: Doubleview Carine CC, Perth 2005-06
Career highlights to date: 'Making my first-class debut v West Indies A for Somerset
2002; making my debut in the NUL for Somerset v Durham 2002; being the youngest
ever cricketer to play for Malaysia; playing for England through the age groups;
maiden first-class hundred for Somerset against Derbyshire 2005'
Cricket moments to forget: 'Being bowled out for a golden duck off the seventh ball
of the over'
Cricket superstitions: 'Right pad first'
Cricketers particularly admired: Sachin Tendulkar, Wasim Akram,
Marcus Trescothick
Young players to look out for: Eoin Morgan
Other sports played: Hockey (Somerset U16), badminton (Millfield School 1st team)
Other sports followed: Football (Manchester United)
Favourite band: Red Hot Chili Peppers
Relaxations: 'Starbucks'
Extras: Made debut for Malaysia aged 15. Has represented England U14, U15, U17
and U18. Somerset U15 Player of the Year 1998. West of England U15 Player of the
Year 1998. Most Promising Sportsman for Malaysia 2000. NBC Denis Compton
Award for the most promising young Somerset player 2002

Best batting: 123 Somerset v Derbyshire, Derby 2005
Best bowling: 3-46 Somerset v West Indies A, Taunton 2002

2006 Season

	M	Inn	NO	Runs	HS	Avg	100	50	Ct	St	Balls	Runs	Wkts	Avg	BB	5I	10M
Test																	
FC	12	19	0	563	99	29.63	-	4	6	-	546	385	2	192.50	1-13	-	-
ODI																	
List A	15	14	0	383	72	27.35	-	3	7	-	434	386	14	27.57	4-39	-	
20/20 Int																	
20/20	7	3	0	21	10	7.00	-	-	5	-	102	150	7	21.42	2-14	-	

Career Performances

	M	Inn	NO	Runs	HS	Avg	100	50	Ct	St	Balls	Runs	Wkts	Avg	BB	5I	10M
Test																	
FC	24	40	0	1069	123	26.72	1	6	9	-	1111	780	12	65.00	3-46	-	-
ODI																	
List A	34	33	1	821	79	25.65	-	5	13	-	861	765	25	30.60	4-39	-	
20/20 Int																	
20/20	15	8	1	66	18 *	9.42	-	-	7	-	108	155	8	19.37	2-14	-	

SUTCLIFFE, I. J.   Lancashire

Name: <u>Iain</u> John Sutcliffe
Role: Left-hand bat, leg-spin bowler
Born: 20 December 1974, Leeds
Height: 6ft 2in **Weight:** 13st
Nickname: Sutty
County debut: 1995 (Leicestershire),
2003 (Lancashire)
County cap: 1997 (Leicestershire),
2003 (Lancashire)
1000 runs in a season: 3
1st-Class 200s: 1
Place in batting averages: 89th av. 36.82
(2005 45th av. 47.54)
Strike rate: (career 49.66)
Parents: John and Valerie
Marital status: Single
Education: Leeds Grammar School;
Oxford University
Qualifications: 10 GCSEs, 4 A-levels, 2.1 PPE degree

Overseas tours: Leeds GS to Kenya; Leicestershire to South Africa, to West Indies, to Sri Lanka

Career highlights to date: 'Championship winner's medal 1998'

Cricketers particularly admired: Brian Lara, David Gower

Other sports played: Boxing (Oxford Blue 1994, 1995; British Universities Light-middleweight Champion 1993)

Other sports followed: Football (Liverpool)

Relaxations: Socialising, cinema

Extras: Played NCA England U14 and NCA Development Team U18/U19. Scored 55 of Leicestershire's first innings total of 96 v Pakistanis at Leicester 2001. Leicestershire vice-captain 2002. Leicestershire Player of the Year 2002. Scored century (102*) v Surrey at Whitgift School in the totesport League 2004, in the process sharing with Mark Chilton (115) in a new Lancashire record opening stand in one-day cricket (223)

Best batting: 203 Leicestershire v Glamorgan, Cardiff 2001

Best bowling: 2-21 Oxford University v Cambridge University, Lord's 1996

2006 Season

	M	Inn	NO	Runs	HS	Avg	100	50	Ct	St	Balls	Runs	Wkts	Avg	BB	5I	10M
Test																	
FC	17	27	4	847	159	36.82	2	3	11	-	6	1	0		-	-	-
ODI																	
List A																		
20/20 Int																		
20/20																		

Career Performances

	M	Inn	NO	Runs	HS	Avg	100	50	Ct	St	Balls	Runs	Wkts	Avg	BB	5I	10M
Test																		
FC	179	285	26	9097	203	35.12	15	49	102	-	447	330	9	36.66	2-21	-	-
ODI																		
List A	122	120	11	3220	105 *	29.54	4	20	27	-	0	0	0		-	-	
20/20 Int																		
20/20	4	3	0	4	4	1.33	-	-	-	-	0	0	0		-	-	

SUTTON, L. D. Lancashire

Name: Luke David Sutton
Role: Right-hand bat, wicket-keeper,
'right-arm rubbish'
Born: 4 October 1976, Keynsham
Height: 5ft 11in **Weight:** 12st 13lbs
Nickname: Sutts
County debut: 1997 (Somerset),
2000 (Derbyshire), 2006 (Lancashire)
County cap: 2002 (Derbyshire)
50 dismissals in a season: 1
Place in batting averages: 37th av. 51.23
(2005 119th av. 33.32)
Parents: David and Molly
Wife and date of marriage: Jude,
7 October 2006
Education: Millfield School; Durham
University
Qualifications: 9 GCSEs, 4 A-levels,
2.1 degree in Economics, CeMAP 1, 2 and 3, Level 1 coaching
Career outside cricket: 'Running Activate Sport camps. Maybe coaching if
opportunities came about'
Off-season: 'Relaxing, training, working with Activate Sport, doing Level 2 coaching'
Overseas tours: Various Somerset Schools tours to Netherlands; West of England U15
to West Indies 1991; Millfield School to Zimbabwe 1993, to Sri Lanka 1994; Durham
University to Zimbabwe 1997
Overseas teams played for: UNSW, Sydney 1998-99; Northville, Port Elizabeth,
South Africa 1999-2000; Subiaco Marist, Perth 2000-01
Career highlights to date: 'Scoring my highest first-class score to date of 151* in the
Roses match at Old Trafford in 2006'
Cricket moments to forget: 'Losing the C&G final and the Championship to Sussex
in 2006'
Cricket superstitions: 'Plenty!'
Cricketers particularly admired: Ian Healy, Jack Russell, Alec Stewart, Steve Waugh
Young players to look out for: Tom Smith, Karl Brown, Steven Croft
Other sports followed: Football (Derby County), rugby (Bath)
Injuries: Out for six weeks with a broken right thumb
Relaxations: 'Quality time with family and friends'
Extras: Captained England U15 and also represented England U18 and U19. Won Sir
John Hobbs Silver Jubilee Memorial Prize for the U16 Cricketer of the Year in 1992
and the Gray-Nicolls Award for the English Schools Cricketer of the Year in 1995.
Voted Derbyshire 2nd XI Player of the Year 2000. NBC Denis Compton Award for the

most promising young Derbyshire player 2000, 2001, 2002. Captain of Derbyshire 2004-05. Scored 151* v Yorkshire at Old Trafford 2006, setting a new record for the highest Championship score by a Lancashire wicket-keeper. 'Set up a charity with my brother Noel called Freddie Fright, which raises money for CAH research; CAH is a condition suffered by my nephew Freddie'

Opinions on cricket: 'Didn't like the formats of C&G and Pro40 this year. They should make the two competitions into one.'

Best batting: 151* Lancashire v Yorkshire, Old Trafford 2006

2006 Season

	M	Inn	NO	Runs	HS	Avg	100	50	Ct	St	Balls	Runs	Wkts	Avg	BB	5I	10M
Test																	
FC	13	16	3	666	151 *	51.23	2	2	38	3	0	0	0		-	-	-
ODI																	
List A	13	9	3	192	53 *	32.00	-	1	26	4	0	0	0		-	-	
20/20 Int																	
20/20																	

Career Performances

	M	Inn	NO	Runs	HS	Avg	100	50	Ct	St	Balls	Runs	Wkts	Avg	BB	5I	10M
Test																	
FC	100	170	23	4764	151 *	32.40	7	16	219	10	0	0	0		-	-	-
ODI																	
List A	121	106	22	1698	83	20.21	-	6	134	14	0	0	0		-	-	
20/20 Int																	
20/20	16	14	4	306	61 *	30.60	-	1	9	7	0	0	0		-	-	

SWANN, G. P. Nottinghamshire

Name: Graeme Peter Swann
Role: Right-hand bat, right-arm off-spin bowler
Born: 24 March 1979, Northampton
Height: 6ft **Weight:** 13st
Nickname: G-spot, Besty
County debut: 1997 (one-day, Northants), 1998 (first-class, Northants), 2005 (Notts)
County cap: 1999 (Northants)
ODI debut: 1999-2000
50 wickets in a season: 1
Place in batting averages: 166th av. 27.30 (2005 209th av. 21.46)
Place in bowling averages: 125th av. 44.53 (2005 105th av. 39.60)
Strike rate: 94.25 (career 65.80)
Parents: Ray and Mavis
Marital status: Single ('for now')

Family links with cricket: Father played Minor Counties cricket for Bedfordshire and Northumberland and also for England Amateurs. Brother was contracted to Northamptonshire and Lancashire. 'Cat is named after Gus Logie'

Education: Sponne School, Towcester
Qualifications: 10 GCSEs, 4 A-levels, Levels 1 and 2 coaching awards, 'London Marathon sub 2hr 45min certificate'
Career outside cricket: 'After-dinner speaking, journalism'
Off-season: 'Fixing elbow. See above'
Overseas tours: England U19 to South Africa (including U19 World Cup) 1997-98; England A to Zimbabwe and South Africa 1998-99, to West Indies 2000-01, to Sri Lanka 2004-05; England to South Africa 1999-2000; ECB National Academy to Australia 2001-02
Overseas teams played for: Old Colts, Christchurch 2002-03
Career highlights to date: 'Winning County Championship'
Cricket moments to forget: 'Being hit for an enormous six by Peter Such'
Cricketers particularly admired: Neil Foster, Devon Malcolm
Young players to look out for: 'George and Tommy Ealham'
Other sports played: Golf, rugby (Northants U14, U15, U16), football (Old Northamptonians Chenecks FC)
Other sports followed: Football (Newcastle United)
Injuries: 'Right elbow problems – September 2006'
Favourite band: Oasis, Fratellis, Stone Roses, Charlatans
Relaxations: 'Playing guitar, writing, playing with my dog'
Extras: Played for England U14, U15, U17 and U19. Gray-Nicolls Len Newbery Schools Cricketer of the Year 1996. Took 8-118 for England U19 in second 'Test' v Pakistan U19 1998, the best ever figures for England in an U19 'Test'. Cricket Society's Leading Young All-rounder award 1999, 2002. Man of the Match for England A v Windward Islands in St Lucia in the Busta Cup 2000-01. ECB National Academy 2004-05
Opinions on cricket: 'Twenty20 is great. Championship should be 96 overs a day. Food should be better around the circuit.'
Best batting: 183 Northamptonshire v Gloucestershire, Bristol 2002
Best bowling: 7-33 Northamptonshire v Derbyshire, Northampton 2003

2006 Season

	M	Inn	NO	Runs	HS	Avg	100	50	Ct	St	Balls	Runs	Wkts	Avg	BB	5I	10M
Test																	
FC	15	21	1	546	85	27.30	-	3	9	-	2639	1247	28	44.53	4-54	-	-
ODI																	
List A	12	8	2	120	42	20.00	-	-	3	-	398	296	11	26.90	3-35	-	
20/20 Int																	
20/20	11	11	0	170	40	15.45	-	-	5	-	246	270	13	20.76	3-16	-	

Career Performances

	M	Inn	NO	Runs	HS	Avg	100	50	Ct	St	Balls	Runs	Wkts	Avg	BB	5I	10M
Test																	
FC	141	202	11	4932	183	25.82	4	23	94	-	23360	11751	355	33.10	7-33	14	2
ODI	1	0	0	0	0		-	-	-	-	30	24	0		-	-	
List A	158	125	13	2194	83	19.58	-	11	44	-	5801	4368	152	28.73	5-35	1	
20/20 Int																	
20/20	29	28	3	448	62	17.92	-	1	9	-	630	711	30	23.70	3-16	-	

TAHIR, N.   Warwickshire

Name: Naqaash Tahir
Role: Right-hand bat, right-arm fast bowler
Born: 14 November 1983, Birmingham
Height: 5ft 10in **Weight:** 11st
Nickname: Naq, Naqy
County debut: 2004
Place in bowling averages: 34th av. 28.84
(2005 53rd av. 28.45)
Strike rate: 45.23 (career 44.84)
Parents: Mohammed Amin and
Ishrat Nasreen
Marital status: Single
Family links with cricket: 'Dad played club
cricket and brother played for Worcestershire
and Warwickshire'

Education: Moseley School; Spring Hill
College
Qualifications: 3 GCSEs, Level 1 coaching
Overseas tours: Warwickshire U15 to South Africa 1999
Overseas teams played for: Mirpur, Pakistan; Subiaco-Floreat, Perth
Cricket superstitions: 'Putting my pads on in a certain way'
Cricketers particularly admired: Waqar Younis, Wasim Akram, Darren Gough,
Brett Lee

Young players to look out for: Moeen Ali
Other sports played: Football
Other sports followed: Football (Man Utd)
Relaxations: 'Watching TV; PlayStation 2'
Extras: Has been Moseley Ashfield U15 Player of the Year, Warwickshire U15 Youth Player of the Year, Warwickshire U19 Players' Player of the Year and Warwickshire U19 Player of the Year (Coney Edmonds Trophy). Had match figures of 8-90 (4-47/4-43) on Championship debut v Worcestershire at Edgbaston 2004
Best batting: 49 Warwickshire v Worcestershire, Worcester 2004
Best bowling: 7-107 Warwickshire v Lancashire, Blackpool 2006

2006 Season

	M	Inn	NO	Runs	HS	Avg	100	50	Ct	St	Balls	Runs	Wkts	Avg	BB	5I	10M
Test																	
FC	3	3	1	36	21	18.00	-	-	1	-	588	375	13	28.84	7-107	1	-
ODI																	
List A	1	0	0	0	0		-	-	-	-	42	30	1	30.00	1-30	-	
20/20 Int																	
20/20																	

Career Performances

	M	Inn	NO	Runs	HS	Avg	100	50	Ct	St	Balls	Runs	Wkts	Avg	BB	5I	10M
Test																		
FC	20	22	9	281	49	21.61	-	-	2	-	2332	1479	52	28.44	7-107	1	-
ODI																	
List A	7	3	2	2	1 *	2.00	-	-	1	-	216	169	2	84.50	1-23	-	
20/20 Int																	
20/20																	

83. Who became only the second bowler to take all ten wickets in a Test innings, v Pakistan in 1998-99?

Name: <u>Billy</u> Victor Taylor
Role: Left-hand bat, right-arm medium-fast bowler
Born: 11 January 1977, Southampton
Height: 6ft 3in **Weight:** 14st
Nickname: Tav
County debut: 1999 (Sussex), 2004 (Hampshire)
County cap: 2006 (Hampshire)
Place in bowling averages: 47th av. 30.33 (2005 69th av. 30.89)
Strike rate: 58.25 (career 61.37)
Parents: Jackie and Victor
Marital status: Single
Family links with cricket: 'Learnt from and played cricket with both my brothers, Martin and James'
Education: Bitterne Park; Southampton Tech College; Sparsholt Agricultural College, Hampshire
Qualifications: 5 GCSEs, NVQ Level 2 Carpentry and Joinery, NTPC Tree Surgery, Level 2 coaching
Career outside cricket: 'Tree surgery'
Overseas tours: Sussex/Hampshire to Cyprus 1999; Sussex to Grenada 2002
Overseas teams played for: Central Hawke's Bay, New Zealand 1996-97; Manawatu Foxton CC and Horowhenua rep team, New Zealand 1998-99, 2000-01; Te Puke 2002
Career highlights to date: 'Winning the County Championship in 2003 [with Sussex]. Playing for Hampshire'
Cricket moments to forget: 'Don't want to forget any moments as it's such a great career and too short a one'
Cricket superstitions: 'Have a towel hanging out of back of trousers'
Cricketers particularly admired: Malcolm Marshall, Robin Smith, Mushtaq Ahmed
Other sports played: Golf
Other sports followed: Football (Havant & Waterlooville)
Favourite band: Dido, Black Eyed Peas
Extras: Took 98 wickets in New Zealand club cricket in 1998-99. Sussex 2nd XI Player of the Year 1999, 2000. Took hat-trick (Ormond, Sampson, Giddins) v Surrey at Hove in the B&H and another (G. Flower, Maddy, Malcolm) v Leicestershire at Leicester in the C&G, both in 2002. Took Championship hat-trick (Compton, Weekes, Scott) v Middlesex at The Rose Bowl 2006, finishing with 6-32
Best batting: 40 Hampshire v Essex, Rose Bowl 2004
Best bowling: 6-32 Hampshire v Middlesex, Rose Bowl 2006

2006 Season

	M	Inn	NO	Runs	HS	Avg	100	50	Ct	St	Balls	Runs	Wkts	Avg	BB	5I	10M
Test																	
FC	6	6	3	5	3	1.66	-	-	1	-	699	364	12	30.33	6-32	1	-
ODI																	
List A	15	7	5	21	10 *	10.50	-	-	3	-	620	408	15	27.20	2-21	-	
20/20 Int																	
20/20	8	3	2	2	2 *	2.00	-	-	1	-	151	175	8	21.87	2-9	-	

Career Performances

	M	Inn	NO	Runs	HS	Avg	100	50	Ct	St	Balls	Runs	Wkts	Avg	BB	5I	10M
Test																	
FC	53	68	26	431	40	10.26	-	-	6	-	8286	4483	135	33.20	6-32	4	-
ODI																	
List A	111	51	24	177	21 *	6.55	-	-	20	-	4887	3542	142	24.94	5-28	1	
20/20 Int																	
20/20	14	6	5	17	12 *	17.00	-	-	3	-	277	318	12	26.50	2-9	-	

TAYLOR, C. G.   Gloucestershire

Name: Christopher (<u>Chris</u>) Glyn Taylor
Role: Right-hand bat, right-arm
off-spin bowler
Born: 27 September 1976, Bristol
Height: 5ft 8in **Weight:** 10st
Nickname: Tales, Tootsie
County debut: 2000
County cap: 2001
1000 runs in a season: 1
Place in batting averages: 171st av. 26.11
(2005 102nd av. 35.18)
Strike rate: (career 138.50)
Parents: Chris and Maggie
Wife and date of marriage: Sarah,
8 December 2001
Family links with cricket: Father and
grandfather both played local club cricket
Education: Colston's Collegiate School
Qualifications: GCSEs and A-levels
Overseas teams played for: Harbord CC, Manly, Australia 2000
Cricket moments to forget: 'B&H loss to Surrey at Lord's [2001]'
Cricketers particularly admired: Jonty Rhodes, Mark Waugh

Other sports played: Rugby, hockey (both county level); squash, tennis
Other sports followed: Rugby
Relaxations: Fishing
Extras: Represented England Schools U18. In 1995 won the Cricket Society's A. A. Thomson Fielding Prize and Wetherell Award for Leading All-rounder in English Schools Cricket. Scored maiden first-class century (104) v Middlesex 2000, becoming the first player to score a century at Lord's on Championship debut; also the first player to score a century for Gloucestershire in match that was both first-class and Championship debut. NBC Denis Compton Award for the most promising young Gloucestershire player 2000. Four-day captain of Gloucestershire 2004-05
Best batting: 196 Gloucestershire v Nottinghamshire, Trent Bridge 2001
Best bowling: 3-126 Gloucestershire v Northamptonshire, Cheltenham 2000

2006 Season

	M	Inn	NO	Runs	HS	Avg	100	50	Ct	St	Balls	Runs	Wkts	Avg	BB	5I	10M
Test																	
FC	14	27	0	705	121	26.11	1	4	12	-	456	267	2	133.50	2-75	-	-
ODI																	
List A	15	15	2	527	93	40.53	-	5	8	-	60	55	2	27.50	1-17	-	
20/20 Int																	
20/20	9	9	1	287	83	35.87	-	3	4	-	0	0	0		-	-	

Career Performances

	M	Inn	NO	Runs	HS	Avg	100	50	Ct	St	Balls	Runs	Wkts	Avg	BB	5I	10M
Test																	
FC	82	148	7	4602	196	32.63	11	16	55	-	831	532	6	88.66	3-126	-	-
ODI																	
List A	113	102	16	1976	93	22.97	-	11	40	1	158	129	6	21.50	2-5	-	
20/20 Int																	
20/20	27	23	5	533	83	29.61	-	3	11	-	6	11	0		-	-	

84. Against whom did Zimbabwe record their first Test win, in February 1995?

TAYLOR, C. R. Derbyshire

Name: Christopher (<u>Chris</u>) Robert Taylor
Role: Right-hand top-order bat, right-arm fast bowler
Born: 21 February 1981, Leeds
Height: 6ft 3in **Weight:** 15st
Nickname: CT
County debut: 2001 (Yorkshire), 2006 (Derbyshire)
Place in batting averages: 102nd av. 34.92
Parents: Phil and Elaine
Wife and date of marriage: Charlotte, 10 February 2007
Family links with cricket: 'Father slogged a few in Bradford League and Dales Council League. Brother has had more clubs in Bradford League than Jack Nicklaus! Mum used to give good throw-downs but shoulder has gone!'
Education: Benton Park High School, Leeds
Qualifications: 9 GCSEs, 4 A-levels
Career outside cricket: 'Opened own business called Pro Cricket Coaching Academy to coach kids in Derbyshire during off-season'
Off-season: 'Running coaching business. Going to Indian Cricket Academy at Mumbai. Getting married and honeymooning in the Maldives'
Overseas tours: Yorkshire to Grenada 2002
Overseas teams played for: Western Suburbs Magpies, Sydney 1999-2003; Fairfield-Liverpool Lions, Sydney 2003-05
Career highlights to date: 'Becoming the only Derbyshire player in history to score a century on my first-class and one-day debut for the club. Scoring 100 in my first game back at Yorkshire for Derbyshire'
Cricket moments to forget: 'Bagging 'em live on Sky in a Roses match six years ago!'
Cricket superstitions: 'Loads – keeping them to myself!'
Cricketers particularly admired: Geoffrey Boycott, Michael DiVenuto, Steve Stubbings
Young players to look out for: Wayne White, Jake Needham, Andy Gale, Mark Lawson
Other sports played: Football (goalkeeper), scuba diving
Other sports followed: Football (Everton), rugby league (Leeds Rhinos)
Injuries: Out for three weeks with a broken finger
Relaxations: 'Love a punt on the football!'

Extras: Represented Yorkshire U10-U17. Neil Lloyd Trophy for top run-scorer at Bunbury Festival 1996. Represented England U15, U17 and U19. Yorkshire CCC Supporters' Club Young Player of the Year 1999. Became first Derbyshire player to score a hundred on both first-class debut (102 v Oxford UCCE at The Parks 2006) and one-day debut (100 v Yorkshire at Headingley in the C&G 2006) for the county. Scored 564 List A runs at 62.66 in 2006 and was named Derbyshire One-Day Player of the Season. Derbyshire Supporters' Player of the Year 2006

Opinions on cricket: 'Too many Kolpaks [*see page 13*] are getting into our game through back doors! There are too many in our game and it is seriously limiting the chances of our home-grown talent. Great game. "Let your bat do the talking!"'

Best batting: 121 Derbyshire v Glamorgan, Cardiff 2006

2006 Season

	M	Inn	NO	Runs	HS	Avg	100	50	Ct	St	Balls	Runs	Wkts	Avg	BB	5I	10M
Test																	
FC	15	26	0	908	121	34.92	3	4	10	-	0	0	0		-	-	-
ODI																	
List A	13	13	4	564	111 *	62.66	2	2	7	-	0	0	0		-	-	
20/20 Int																	
20/20	8	7	3	92	25	23.00	-	-	-	-	0	0	0		-	-	

Career Performances

	M	Inn	NO	Runs	HS	Avg	100	50	Ct	St	Balls	Runs	Wkts	Avg	BB	5I	10M
Test																	
FC	31	53	3	1324	121	26.48	3	6	18	-	0	0	0		-	-	-
ODI																	
List A	17	16	4	621	111 *	51.75	2	2	7	-	0	0	0		-	-	
20/20 Int																	
20/20	8	7	3	92	25	23.00	-	-	-	-	0	0	0		-	-	

TEN DOESCHATE, R. N.   Essex

Name: <u>Ryan</u> Neil ten Doeschate
Role: Right-hand bat, right-arm medium-fast bowler
Born: 30 June 1980, Port Elizabeth, South Africa
Height: 5ft 11in **Weight:** 13st 5lbs
Nickname: Tendo
County debut: 2003
County cap: 2006
ODI debut: 2006
Place in batting averages: 73rd av. 40.30
Place in bowling averages: 105th av. 39.82
Strike rate: 53.39 (career 55.80)

Parents: Boudewyn and Ingrid
Marital status: Single
Education: Fairbairn College; University of Cape Town
Qualifications: Business science degree
Overseas tours: Netherlands to Ireland (ICC Trophy) 2005, to Scotland (European Championship) 2006, to South Africa (ICC Associates Tri-Series) 2006-07
Overseas teams played for: Western Province, South Africa; Bloemendaal, Netherlands; Rockingham Mandura, Australia
Career highlights to date: 'Winning totesport in 2005. Getting county cap this year [2006]'
Cricket moments to forget: 'My county debut at Chelmsford'
Cricketers particularly admired: Jacques Kallis, Kepler Wessels

Young players to look out for: Tom Westley, Mervyn Westfield
Other sports played: Rugby
Other sports followed: Football (Arsenal), rugby (Stormers)
Favourite band: Phil Collins
Relaxations: Golf, tennis, reading
Extras: Has played first-class and one-day cricket for Netherlands; made ODI debut for Netherlands v Sri Lanka in Amstelveen 2006. Is not considered an overseas player
Best batting: 158 Netherlands v Kenya, Nairobi 2006
Best bowling: 5-143 Essex v Surrey, Croydon 2006
Stop press: Scored century in each innings (138/100) for Netherlands v Bermuda, and competition record 259* (plus match figures of 6-20/3-92) v Canada, both in ICC Inter-Continental Cup 2006 in Pretoria

85. Who was the first player to score 5000 runs
and take 300 wickets in Tests?

2006 Season

	M	Inn	NO	Runs	HS	Avg	100	50	Ct	St	Balls	Runs	Wkts	Avg	BB	5I	10M
Test																	
FC	9	12	2	403	105 *	40.30	2	1	4	-	1495	1115	28	39.82	5-143	1	-
ODI																	
List A	17	13	4	300	63 *	33.33	-	1	5	-	187	202	8	25.25	4-49	-	
20/20 Int																	
20/20	10	9	5	174	49 *	43.50	-	-	5	-	0	0	0		-	-	

Career Performances

	M	Inn	NO	Runs	HS	Avg	100	50	Ct	St	Balls	Runs	Wkts	Avg	BB	5I	10M
Test																	
FC	18	20	2	798	158	44.33	3	3	8	-	2232	1621	40	40.52	5-143	1	-
ODI	2	2	1	95	56 *	95.00	-	1	-	-	60	86	3	28.66	2-51	-	
List A	40	29	13	826	89 *	51.62	-	5	14	-	627	622	30	20.73	4-18	-	
20/20 Int																	
20/20	21	16	7	267	49 *	29.66	-	-	7	-	121	167	5	33.40	2-27	-	

THOMAS, S. D.   Essex

Name: Stuart Darren Thomas
Role: Left-hand bat, right-arm fast-medium bowler; all-rounder
Born: 25 January 1975, Morriston, Swansea
Height: 6ft **Weight:** 13st
Nickname: Ted, Stu
County debut: 1992 (Glamorgan)
County cap: 1997 (Glamorgan)
Benefit: 2006 (Glamorgan)
50 wickets in a season: 5
Place in batting averages: (2005 224th av. 19.57)
Strike rate: (career 52.61)
Parents: Stu and Ann
Wife and date of marriage: Claire, 30 September 2000
Children: Ellie Sofia, 20 August 2002
Family links with cricket: 'Father was a good striker of the ball for Llanelli CC'
Education: Graig Comprehensive, Llanelli; Neath Tertiary College
Qualifications: 5 GCSEs, BTEC National Diploma in Sports Studies, Level 2 coaching award
Overseas tours: Glamorgan to Cape Town 1993, 1999, 2002, to Zimbabwe 1994,

to Pretoria 1995, to Portugal 1996, to Jersey 1998; England U18 to South Africa 1992-93; England U19 to Sri Lanka 1993-94; England A to Zimbabwe and South Africa 1998-99, to Bangladesh and New Zealand 1999-2000

Overseas teams played for: Rovers CC, Welkom, Free State 1994; Burnside West University CC, Christchurch, New Zealand 2003

Career highlights to date: 'Winning County Championship 1997 by far, followed by my two England A tours'

Cricket moments to forget: 'There are too many to mention'

Cricket superstitions: 'None'

Cricketers particularly admired: Allan Donald, Malcolm Marshall, Ian Botham, Andrew Flintoff

Young players to look out for: Gareth Rees, Alastair Cook

Other sports followed: 'All kinds on Sky Sports'

Favourite band: 'Don't have [favourite] band but Robbie Williams is quality'

Relaxations: 'Spending time with family; training; enjoy seeing the globe; eating out'

Extras: Took 5-80 on debut v Derbyshire 1992, aged 17 years 217 days, and finished eighth in national bowling averages. BBC Welsh Young Sports Personality 1992. Represented England U19. Returned Glamorgan best B&H bowling figures (6-20) on competition debut v Combined Universities at Cardiff 1995. Took 7-16 v Surrey at Swansea in the Sunday League 1998, a competition best by a Glamorgan bowler. Glamorgan Player of the Year 1998. Took 8-50 for England A v Zimbabwe A at Harare 1998-99 – the first eight-wicket haul by an England A tourist. Became the second 12th man to score a century (105*) in a first-class match, v Hampshire at The Rose Bowl 2004. Released by Glamorgan at the end of the 2006 season and has joined Essex for 2007

Best batting: 138 Glamorgan v Essex, Chelmsford 2001
Best bowling: 8-50 England A v Zimbabwe A, Harare 1998-99

2006 Season

	M	Inn	NO	Runs	HS	Avg	100	50	Ct	St	Balls	Runs	Wkts	Avg	BB	5I	10M
Test																	
FC																	
ODI																	
List A	2	1	1	17	17*	-	-	-	-	-	42	65	0		-	-	
20/20 Int																	
20/20																	

Career Performances

	M	Inn	NO	Runs	HS	Avg	100	50	Ct	St	Balls	Runs	Wkts	Avg	BB	5I	10M
Test																	
FC	169	234	44	3977	138	20.93	2	18	55	-	26518	16023	504	31.79	8-50	18	1
ODI																	
List A	140	104	27	1273	71*	16.53	-	1	25	-	5381	4668	171	27.29	7-16	3	
20/20 Int																	
20/20	14	13	3	169	43*	16.90	-	-	2	-	234	394	11	35.81	3-32	-	

THORNELY, D. J. Hampshire

Name: Dominic (<u>Dom</u>) John Thornely
Role: Right-hand bat, right-arm
medium-fast bowler
Born: 1 October 1978, Albury, New South
Wales, Australia
Height: 6ft 2in **Weight:** 14st
County debut: 2005 (Surrey),
2006 (Hampshire)
County cap: 2006 (Hampshire)
1st-Class 200s: 1
Place in batting averages: 105th av. 34.50
Place in bowling averages: 23rd av. 26.27
Strike rate: 54.27 (career 78.38)
Parents: John and Leonie
Marital status: Single
Education: James Fallon High School,
Albury, NSW
Off-season: 'NSW season'

Overseas tours: Australia U19 to Pakistan 1996-97, to South Africa (U19 World Cup) 1997-98; Australia A to Pakistan 2005-06
Overseas teams played for: Northern District CC, NSW 1995 – ; New South Wales 2001-02 –
Career highlights to date: 'Pura Cup champions 2004-05'
Cricket moments to forget: 'Running out Steve Waugh searching for my first first-class hundred'
Cricket superstitions: 'Left foot on field first'
Cricketers particularly admired: Mark Waugh
Young players to look out for: Moises Henriques (NSW)
Other sports played: Australian Rules football
Other sports followed: Australian Rules football (Sydney Swans)
Favourite band: Bon Jovi
Relaxations: 'Fishing'
Extras: Represented Australia U19. Has represented Australia A. Scored 261* v Western Australia in the Pura Cup at Sydney 2004-05, in the process sharing with Stuart MacGill (27) in a last-wicket stand of 219 and winning the Man of the Match award (innings also included an Australian first-class record 11 sixes). His other match awards include Man of the Match v Queensland at Brisbane in the ING Cup final 2001-02 (20*/3-36) and v South Australia at Adelaide in the Pura Cup 2004-05 (74/102). Was an overseas player with Surrey during the 2005 season as a locum for Azhar Mahmood; an overseas player with Hampshire 2006
Best batting: 261* New South Wales v Western Australia, Sydney 2004-05
Best bowling: 3-38 Hampshire v Sussex, Rose Bowl 2006

2006 Season

	M	Inn	NO	Runs	HS	Avg	100	50	Ct	St	Balls	Runs	Wkts	Avg	BB	5I	10M
Test																	
FC	15	25	3	759	76	34.50	-	6	12	-	1194	578	22	26.27	3-38	-	-
ODI																	
List A	16	16	5	485	107 *	44.09	1	4	3	-	207	213	6	35.50	3-17	-	
20/20 Int																	
20/20	8	8	1	150	50 *	21.42	-	1	5	-	122	161	9	17.88	4-22	-	

Career Performances

	M	Inn	NO	Runs	HS	Avg	100	50	Ct	St	Balls	Runs	Wkts	Avg	BB	5I	10M
Test																	
FC	47	78	7	3038	261 *	42.78	6	19	28	-	2430	1246	31	40.19	3-38	-	-
ODI																	
List A	65	61	9	1497	107 *	28.78	1	11	21	-	1411	1225	35	35.00	3-17	-	
20/20 Int																	
20/20	15	14	3	305	67 *	27.72	-	3	7	-	197	269	15	17.93	4-22	-	

THORNICROFT, N. D.   Yorkshire

Name: Nicholas (Nick) David Thornicroft
Role: Left-hand bat, right-arm fast bowler
Born: 23 January 1985, York
Height: 5ft 11in **Weight:** 12st 8lbs
Nickname: Thorny, Mad Dog, Harry Potter
County debut: 2002 (*see Extras*)
Strike rate: (career 77.18)
Parents: Lyn and David
Marital status: Single
Education: Easingwold
Overseas tours: Yorkshire U16 to Cape Town, to Jersey; England U19 to Australia 2002-03
Career highlights to date: 'Getting Neil Fairbrother as my first first-class wicket'
Cricketers particularly admired: Darren Gough, Brett Lee, Ian Botham, Craig White, Andrew Flintoff
Other sports played: Athletics, football, basketball
Other sports followed: Football (York City FC), horse racing
Relaxations: 'Spending time with family; music; shooting'
Extras: Made first-class debut in Roses match v Lancashire at Old Trafford 2002,

aged 17. Represented England U19 2002 and 2003. Played for Essex on loan 2005. Yorkshire 2nd XI cap 2006

Best batting: 30 Yorkshire v Nottinghamshire, Headingley 2004

Best bowling: 2-27 Yorkshire v Durham, Riverside 2004

2006 Season

	M	Inn	NO	Runs	HS	Avg	100	50	Ct	St	Balls	Runs	Wkts	Avg	BB	5I	10M
Test																	
FC																	
ODI																	
List A	6	4	1	44	20	14.66	-	-	1	-	247	292	5	58.40	3-35	-	
20/20 Int																	
20/20																	

Career Performances

	M	Inn	NO	Runs	HS	Avg	100	50	Ct	St	Balls	Runs	Wkts	Avg	BB	5I	10M
Test																	
FC	7	12	5	54	30	7.71	-	-	1	-	849	543	11	49.36	2-27	-	-
ODI																	
List A	14	7	4	52	20	17.33	-	-	2	-	535	563	16	35.18	5-42	1	
20/20 Int																	
20/20	1	1	1	0	0 *		-	-	-	-	6	20	0		-	-	

THORP, C. D. Durham

Name: <u>Callum</u> David Thorp

Role: Right-hand bat, right-arm fast-medium bowler

Born: 11 January 1975, Perth, Western Australia

Height: 6ft 3in **Weight:** 13st 5lbs

County debut: 2005

Place in batting averages: 229th av. 17.15

Place in bowling averages: 13th av. 24.82

Strike rate: 50.38 (career 62.77)

Parents: Annette and David

Marital status: Single

Education: Servite College

Off-season: 'Returning to Perth and enjoying the summer'

Overseas teams played for: Western Warriors 2002-03 – 2003-04; Wanneroo DCC

Career highlights to date: 'Winning the one-day title with Wanneroo'
Cricket superstitions: 'Left shoe on first'
Cricketers particularly admired: Mike Hussey
Young players to look out for: Graham Onions, Luke Evans
Other sports followed: AFL (West Coast Eagles), football (West Ham United)
Relaxations: 'Golf'
Extras: Took 4-58 for Western Australia v England XI in two-day match at Perth 2002-03. Attended Commonwealth Bank [Australian] Cricket Academy 2003. Took 6-17 v Scotland at The Grange in the C&G 2006, the best one-day figures for Durham since the county gained first-class status, following up with 100 runs (75/28) and ten wickets (6-55/5-42) in the Championship match v Hampshire at The Rose Bowl later that week. Has British parents and is not considered an overseas player
Best batting: 75 Durham v Hampshire, Rose Bowl 2006
Best bowling: 6-55 Durham v Hampshire, Rose Bowl 2006

2006 Season

	M	Inn	NO	Runs	HS	Avg	100	50	Ct	St	Balls	Runs	Wkts	Avg	BB	5I	10M
Test																	
FC	12	21	2	326	75	17.15	-	2	4	-	1965	968	39	24.82	6-55	2	1
ODI																	
List A	12	11	4	142	28	20.28	-	-	1	-	480	393	14	28.07	6-17	1	
20/20 Int																	
20/20	6	5	0	51	13	10.20	-	-	1	-	114	178	3	59.33	2-32	-	

Career Performances

	M	Inn	NO	Runs	HS	Avg	100	50	Ct	St	Balls	Runs	Wkts	Avg	BB	5I	10M
Test																	
FC	23	35	2	441	75	13.36	-	2	9	-	3327	1726	53	32.56	6-55	2	1
ODI																	
List A	27	17	6	215	52	19.54	-	1	3	-	1242	949	33	28.75	6-17	1	
20/20 Int																	
20/20	9	6	0	63	13	10.50	-	-	1	-	162	266	3	88.66	2-32	-	

TOMLINSON, J. A. Hampshire

Name: <u>James</u> Andrew Tomlinson
Role: Left-hand lower-order bat, left-arm fast-medium bowler
Born: 12 June 1982, Appleshaw, Hampshire
Height: 6ft 1½in **Weight:** 13st
Nickname: Tommo, T, Dangerous Dave
County debut: 2002
Strike rate: (career 70.47)
Parents: Ian and Janet
Marital status: Single
Family links with cricket: 'Brothers Hugh and Ralph play at South Wilts and Dulwich respectively'
Education: Harrow Way Community School, Andover; Cricklade College, Andover; Cardiff University
Qualifications: 3 A-levels, 2.1 degree in Education and Psychology
Career outside cricket: 'Patient!'
Off-season: 'Operation on ankle. Few weeks in Perth maybe'
Overseas teams played for: South Perth 2004-05
Career highlights to date: '6-63 v Derbyshire 2003; 44 wickets in eight games for 2nd XI'
Cricket moments to forget: 'Any dropped catch!'
Cricket superstitions: 'None'
Cricketers particularly admired: Dimi Mascarenhas, Nic Pothas, Wasim Akram
Young players to look out for: Liam Dawson, Hamza Riazuddin, Richard Dawson
Other sports played: Golf, darts
Other sports followed: Football (West Ham)
Favourite band: The Killers
Relaxations: 'Birdwatching (raptors in particular)'
Extras: Played for Development of Excellence XI (South) 2001. Played for Cardiff UCCE 2002-03. Represented British Universities 2002-03. NBC Denis Compton Award for the most promising young Hampshire player 2003. Cardiff University Sportsperson of the Year award 2003
Opinions on cricket: 'One-day competition (C&G) should be knockout. Too many Kolpak players [*see page 13*].'
Best batting: 23 Hampshire v Indians, Rose Bowl 2002
Best bowling: 6-63 Hampshire v Derbyshire, Derby 2003

2006 Season

	M	Inn	NO	Runs	HS	Avg	100	50	Ct	St	Balls	Runs	Wkts	Avg	BB	5I	10M
Test																	
FC	2	2	0	3	3	1.50	-	-	-	-	234	146	4	36.50	2-54	-	-
ODI																	
List A	4	3	1	1	1*	.50	-	-	1	-	156	129	4	32.25	4-47	-	
20/20 Int																	
20/20	2	1	0	5	5	5.00	-	-	-	-	42	48	1	48.00	1-20	-	

Career Performances

	M	Inn	NO	Runs	HS	Avg	100	50	Ct	St	Balls	Runs	Wkts	Avg	BB	5I	10M
Test																	
FC	17	26	11	76	23	5.06	-	-	5	-	2396	1731	34	50.91	6-63	1	-
ODI																	
List A	18	11	4	15	6	2.14	-	-	2	-	758	588	16	36.75	4-47	-	
20/20 Int																	
20/20	2	1	0	5	5	5.00	-	-	-	-	42	48	1	48.00	1-20	-	

TREDWELL, J. C.   Kent

Name: <u>James</u> Cullum Tredwell
Role: Left-hand bat, right-arm
off-spin bowler
Born: 27 February 1982, Ashford, Kent
Height: 5ft 11in **Weight:** 14st 2lbs
Nickname: Tredders, Pingu, Chad
County debut: 2001
Place in batting averages: 255th av. 14.00
Place in bowling averages: 85th av. 35.65
Strike rate: 62.26 (career 70.53)
Parents: John and Rosemary
Marital status: Single
Family links with cricket: Father played for
Ashford and Folkestone in Kent League
Education: Southlands Community
Comprehensive
Qualifications: 10 GCSEs, 2 A-levels, ECB
Level 1 coach
Overseas tours: Kent U17 to Sri Lanka 1998-99; Kent to Port Elizabeth 2002;
England A to Malaysia and India 2003-04
Overseas teams played for: Redlands Tigers, Brisbane 2000-02
Cricket moments to forget: 'Being hit for six in a crucial B&H Cup match v Essex,
which probably cost Kent's qualification to next stage'

Cricketers particularly admired: 'All the great spinners'
Extras: Represented England U19 2001 (captain in second 'Test'). Kent Most Improved Player Award 2003. ECB National Academy 2003-04. Took over captaincy of England A in India 2003-04 after Alex Gidman was forced to return home with a hand injury. NBC Denis Compton Award for the most promising young Kent player 2003
Best batting: 61 Kent v Yorkshire, Headingley 2002
Best bowling: 6-81 Kent v Sussex, Canterbury 2006

2006 Season

	M	Inn	NO	Runs	HS	Avg	100	50	Ct	St	Balls	Runs	Wkts	Avg	BB	5I	10M
Test																	
FC	7	10	1	126	47	14.00	-	-	7	-	1619	927	26	35.65	6-81	1	1
ODI																	
List A	15	11	8	123	28	41.00	-	-	8	-	672	552	17	32.47	3-35	-	
20/20 Int																	
20/20	9	7	0	47	28	6.71	-	-	4	-	174	243	10	24.30	4-21	-	

Career Performances

	M	Inn	NO	Runs	HS	Avg	100	50	Ct	St	Balls	Runs	Wkts	Avg	BB	5I	10M
Test																	
FC	39	55	7	953	61	19.85	-	3	41	-	6419	3752	91	41.23	6-81	2	1
ODI																	
List A	87	68	22	808	71	17.56	-	2	42	-	3455	2625	82	32.01	4-16	-	
20/20 Int																	
20/20	26	20	2	233	34	12.94	-	-	7	-	438	595	22	27.04	4-21	-	

TREGO, P. D.   Somerset

Name: Peter David Trego
Role: Right-hand bat, right-arm fast-medium bowler
Born: 12 June 1981, Weston-super-Mare
Height: 6ft **Weight:** 13st 2lbs
Nickname: Steve the Pirate, Pikey, Tregs
County debut: 2000 (Somerset), 2003 (Kent), 2005 (Middlesex)
Place in batting averages: 148th av. 29.80 (2005 177th av. 26.00)
Place in bowling averages: 140th av. 50.78 (2005 90th av. 36.00)
Strike rate: 76.68 (career 63.09)
Parents: Carol and Paul
Wife and date of marriage: Claire, 8 May 2000
Children: Amelia, 9 July 2001; Davis, 8 February 2005
Family links with cricket: 'Brother on Somerset staff for a year; good player – pretty unlucky not to get a better go'

Education: Wyvern Comprehensive
Qualifications: 'Spare-time general builder/carpenter, so none to speak of'
Career outside cricket: 'Building and football semi-pro'
Off-season: 'Recovering and keeping fit along with enjoying my babies'
Career highlights to date: 'Scoring a hundred in my first game back at Taunton for Somerset'
Cricket moments to forget: 'Most things involving 2003'
Cricketers particularly admired: Graham Rose ('what a player and bloke')
Other sports played: Football (Weston-super-Mare, Margate FC), golf (4 handicap)
Injuries: 'Broken forearm – that was fun, but at least it was in September'

Favourite band: Oasis, Green Day, Elvis, Ray Charles
Relaxations: 'I'm interested in poker and other money-making games'
Extras: Represented England U19. NBC Denis Compton Award for the most promising young Somerset player 2000. Scored 140 at Taunton 2002 as Somerset, chasing 454 to win, tied with West Indies A. 'I'm very proud of being the first player ever to incur a five-run penalty for replacing Jamie Cox and nobody thinking to tell Mr Dudleston.' 'Played football in the FA Cup on *Match of the Day* – that was cool up until the part where I was 'megged to let in the goal to send us out; but still got Star Man in the paper.' Left Middlesex at the end of the 2005 season and rejoined Somerset for 2006
Opinions on cricket: 'Too much emphasis put on speed of bowling. The vast majority of great/good seam bowlers move the ball sideways. I'm not sure why we always seem to go for 85mph and straight rather than 78-80mph and clever. Why we feel that unless you're rapid you won't cut it at the highest level, I don't know.'
Best batting: 140 Somerset v West Indies A, Taunton 2002
Best bowling: 6-59 Middlesex v Nottinghamshire, Trent Bridge 2005

2006 Season

	M	Inn	NO	Runs	HS	Avg	100	50	Ct	St	Balls	Runs	Wkts	Avg	BB	5I	10M
Test																	
FC	12	20	0	596	135	29.80	3	2	5	-	1457	965	19	50.78	3-87	-	-
ODI																	
List A	10	8	1	76	20 *	10.85	-	-	1	-	185	172	4	43.00	2-32	-	
20/20 Int																	
20/20	5	5	2	97	47	32.33	-	-	2	-	80	142	3	47.33	2-20	-	

Career Performances

	M	Inn	NO	Runs	HS	Avg	100	50	Ct	St	Balls	Runs	Wkts	Avg	BB	5I	10M
Test																	
FC	34	52	4	1364	140	28.41	4	5	13	-	4038	2813	64	43.95	6-59	1	-
ODI																	
List A	45	37	7	351	31 *	11.70	-	-	8	-	1280	1192	38	31.36	4-39	-	
20/20 Int																	
20/20	9	9	2	112	47	16.00	-	-	2	-	98	176	7	25.14	2-17	-	

TREMLETT, C. T.   Hampshire

Name: Christopher (Chris) Timothy Tremlett
Role: Right-hand bat, right-arm
fast-medium bowler
Born: 2 September 1981, Southampton
Height: 6ft 7in   **Weight:** 16st 1lb
Nickname: Twiggy, Goober
County debut: 2000
County cap: 2004
ODI debut: 2005
Place in batting averages: (2005 187th
av. 24.33)
Place in bowling averages: 11th av. 24.55
(2005 37th av. 26.78)
Strike rate: 46.64 (career 46.85)
Parents: Timothy and Carolyn
Marital status: Single
Family links with cricket: Grandfather
[Maurice] played for Somerset and in three
Tests for England. Father played for Hampshire and is now director of cricket
at the county
Education: Thornden School, Chandlers Ford; Taunton's College, Southampton
Qualifications: 5 GCSEs, BTEC National Diploma in Sports Science, Level 2 coach

Overseas tours: West of England U15 to West Indies 1997; Hampshire U16 to Jersey; England U17 to Northern Ireland (ECC Colts Festival) 1999; England U19 to India 2000-01; ECB National Academy to Australia 2001-02, to Australia and Sri Lanka 2002-03; England VI to Hong Kong 2004; England to Australia 2006-07 (C'wealth Bank Series)

Cricketers particularly admired: Glenn McGrath, Mark Waugh, Shane Warne

Other sports played: Basketball, volleyball

Other sports followed: Football (Arsenal)

Relaxations: 'Socialising with friends; cinema'

Extras: Took wicket (Mark Richardson) with first ball in first-class cricket v New Zealand A at Portsmouth 2000; finished with debut match figures of 6-91. Represented England U19. NBC Denis Compton Award for the most promising young Hampshire player 2000, 2001. Hampshire Young Player of the Year 2001. Took Championship hat-trick (Ealham, Swann, G. Smith) v Nottinghamshire at Trent Bridge 2005. ECB National Academy 2006-07

Best batting: 64 Hampshire v Gloucestershire, Rose Bowl 2005

Best bowling: 6-44 Hampshire v Sussex, Hove 2005

Stop press: Forced to return early from Australia tour 2006-07 with a back injury

2006 Season

	M	Inn	NO	Runs	HS	Avg	100	50	Ct	St	Balls	Runs	Wkts	Avg	BB	5I	10M
Test																	
FC	9	10	1	76	23	8.44	-	-	-	-	1586	835	34	24.55	6-89	1	-
ODI																	
List A	5	2	0	0	0	0.00	-	-	1	-	190	155	8	19.37	4-35	-	
20/20 Int																	
20/20	7	4	1	15	9	5.00	-	-	-	-	150	190	6	31.66	2-18	-	

Career Performances

	M	Inn	NO	Runs	HS	Avg	100	50	Ct	St	Balls	Runs	Wkts	Avg	BB	5I	10M
Test																	
FC	61	80	22	1015	64	17.50	-	2	16	-	10028	5601	214	26.17	6-44	6	-
ODI	3	1	0	8	8	8.00	-	-	-	-	146	111	5	22.20	4-32	-	
List A	81	48	14	328	38 *	9.64	-	-	16	-	3614	2727	124	21.99	4-25	-	
20/20 Int																	
20/20	12	7	2	46	13	9.20	-	-	3	-	252	300	14	21.42	3-20	-	

Name: <u>Marcus</u> Edward Trescothick
Role: Left-hand bat, right-arm swing bowler, reserve wicket-keeper
Born: 25 December 1975, Keynsham, Bristol
Height: 6ft 3in **Weight:** 14st 7lbs
Nickname: Banger, Tres
County debut: 1993
County cap: 1999
Test debut: 2000
ODI debut: 2000
Twenty20 Int debut: 2005
1st-Class 200s: 1
Place in batting averages: 159th av. 28.33 (2005 41st av. 48.44)
Strike rate: (career 74.27)
Parents: Martyn and Lin
Wife and date of marriage: Hayley, 24 January 2004
Children: Ellie, April 2005
Family links with cricket: Father played for Somerset 2nd XI; uncle played club cricket
Education: Sir Bernard Lovell School
Qualifications: 7 GCSEs
Overseas tours: England U18 to South Africa 1992-93; England U19 to Sri Lanka 1993-94, to West Indies 1994-95 (c); England A to Bangladesh and New Zealand 1999-2000; England to Kenya (ICC Knockout Trophy) 2000-01, to Pakistan and Sri Lanka 2000-01, to Zimbabwe (one-day series) 2001-02, to India and New Zealand 2001-02, to Sri Lanka (ICC Champions Trophy) 2002-03, to Australia 2002-03, to Africa (World Cup) 2002-03, to Bangladesh and Sri Lanka 2003-04, to West Indies 2003-04, to South Africa 2004-05, to Pakistan 2005-06, to India 2005-06, to Australia 2006-07
Overseas teams played for: Melville CC, Perth 1997-99
Cricketers particularly admired: Adam Gilchrist, Andy Caddick
Other sports followed: Golf, football (Bristol City FC)
Relaxations: 'Spending time at home (it's such a rare thing), playing golf'
Extras: Scored more than 1000 runs for England U19. Took hat-trick (Gilchrist, Angel, McIntyre) for Somerset v Young Australia at Taunton 1995. PCA Player of the Year 2000. Sports.com Cricketer of the Year 2001. BBC West Country Sports Sportsman of the Year 2001. One of *Indian Cricket*'s five Cricketers of the Year 2002. Scored 114* v South Africa at The Oval in the NatWest Series 2003, sharing with Vikram Solanki (106) in a record England opening partnership in ODIs (200). Scored

century in each innings (105/107) in the second Test v West Indies at Edgbaston 2004. Man of the Match in his 100th ODI v Bangladesh at The Oval in the NatWest Series 2005 (100*). His Test awards include England's Man of the Series v Bangladesh 2005 and Man of the Match in the fifth Test v South Africa at The Oval 2003 (219/69*). His other ODI awards include Man of the Series v West Indies 2003-04 and Man of the Match v Australia at Headingley in the NatWest Challenge 2005 (104*). One of *Wisden*'s Five Cricketers of the Year 2005. Appointed MBE in 2006 New Year Honours as part of 2005 Ashes-winning England team. Returned home from England tour to India 2005-06 with a stress-related illness. England 12-month central contract 2006-07

Best batting: 219 England v South Africa, The Oval 2003
Best bowling: 4-36 Somerset v Young Australia, Taunton 1995
Stop press: Returned home in mid-November from England tour to Australia 2006-07 with a recurrence of a stress-related illness

2006 Season

	M	Inn	NO	Runs	HS	Avg	100	50	Ct	St	Balls	Runs	Wkts	Avg	BB	5I	10M
Test	7	12	0	323	106	26.91	1	1	14	-	0	0	0		-	-	-
FC	10	18	0	510	154	28.33	2	1	19	-	0	0	0		-	-	-
ODI	8	8	0	299	121	37.37	1	1	2	-	0	0	0		-	-	
List A	10	10	0	485	158	48.50	2	1	3	-	0	0	0		-	-	
20/20 Int	2	2	0	125	72	62.50	-	2	-	-	0	0	0		-	-	
20/20	2	2	0	125	72	62.50	-	2	-	-	0	0	0		-	-	

Career Performances

	M	Inn	NO	Runs	HS	Avg	100	50	Ct	St	Balls	Runs	Wkts	Avg	BB	5I	10M
Test	76	143	10	5825	219	43.79	14	29	95	-	300	155	1	155.00	1-34	-	-
FC	207	360	18	12227	219	35.75	24	63	240	-	2674	1541	36	42.80	4-36	-	-
ODI	123	122	6	4335	137	37.37	12	21	49	-	232	219	4	54.75	2-7	-	
List A	273	261	23	8856	158	37.21	23	39	104	-	2004	1636	57	28.70	4-50	-	
20/20 Int	3	3	0	166	72	55.33	-	2	2	-	0	0	0		-	-	
20/20	6	6	0	257	72	42.83	-	3	5	-	0	0	0		-	-	

TROTT, I. J. L. — Warwickshire

Name: Ian <u>Jonathan</u> Leonard Trott
Role: Right-hand bat, right-arm medium bowler; all-rounder
Born: 22 April 1981, Cape Town, South Africa
Height: 6ft **Weight:** 13st 5lbs
Nickname: Booger
County debut: 2003
County cap: 2005
1000 runs in a season: 3
1st-Class 200s: 1
Place in batting averages: 71st av. 41.77 (2005 65th av. 41.46)
Strike rate: (career 59.84)
Parents: Ian and Donna
Marital status: Single
Family links with cricket: Father a professional cricket coach. Brother (Kenny

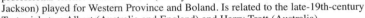

Jackson) played for Western Province and Boland. Is related to the late-19th-century Test cricketers Albert (Australia and England) and Harry Trott (Australia)
Education: Rondebosch Boys' High School; Stellenbosch University
Qualifications: Level 2 coaching
Overseas tours: South Africa U15 to England (U15 World Cup) 1996; South Africa U19 to Pakistan 1998-99, to Sri Lanka (U19 World Cup) 1999-2000
Overseas teams played for: Boland 1999-2000 – 2000-01; Western Province 2001-02; Otago 2005-06
Cricket moments to forget: 'Losing in the final of the Standard Bank Cup 2002'
Cricket superstitions: 'Personal'
Cricketers particularly admired: Sachin Tendulkar, Adam Hollioake, Steve Waugh
Other sports played: Hockey (Western Province U16, U18, U21), golf
Other sports followed: Football (Tottenham Hotspur)
Favourite band: Roxette, Robbie Williams
Relaxations: 'Music, watching sport'
Extras: Represented South Africa A. Struck 245 on debut for Warwickshire 2nd XI v Somerset 2nd XI at Knowle & Dorridge 2002. Scored century (134) on Championship debut for Warwickshire v Sussex at Edgbaston 2003. Became the first player to bat for the full 20 overs in the Twenty20, for a 54-ball 65* v Gloucestershire at Edgbaston 2003. Is England-qualified
Best batting: 210 Warwickshire v Sussex, Edgbaston 2005
Best bowling: 7-39 Warwickshire v Kent, Canterbury 2003

2006 Season

	M	Inn	NO	Runs	HS	Avg	100	50	Ct	St	Balls	Runs	Wkts	Avg	BB	5I	10M
Test																	
FC	17	29	2	1128	177 *	41.77	3	4	20	-	18	28	1	28.00	1-22	-	-
ODI																	
List A	17	15	3	348	76 *	29.00	-	2	10	-	0	0	0			-	-
20/20 Int																	
20/20	8	7	2	275	75 *	55.00	-	2	2	-	0	0	0			-	-

Career Performances

	M	Inn	NO	Runs	HS	Avg	100	50	Ct	St	Balls	Runs	Wkts	Avg	BB	5I	10M
Test																	
FC	83	145	14	5297	210	40.43	11	29	84	-	1915	1173	32	36.65	7-39	1	-
ODI																	
List A	102	94	19	2924	112 *	38.98	4	19	34	-	869	818	34	24.05	4-55	-	
20/20 Int																	
20/20	29	25	7	670	75 *	37.22	-	3	9	-	132	200	7	28.57	2-19	-	

TROUGHTON, J. O.   Warwickshire

Name: Jamie (<u>Jim</u>) Oliver Troughton
Role: Left-hand bat, slow left-arm bowler
Born: 2 March 1979, London
Height: 5ft 11in **Weight:** 12st 12lbs
Nickname: Troughts
County debut: 2001
County cap: 2002
ODI debut: 2003
1000 runs in a season: 1
Place in batting averages: 191st av. 22.94
(2005 123rd av. 32.38)
Strike rate: (career 90.65)
Parents: Ali and David
Wife and date of marriage: Naomi,
28 September 2002
Family links with cricket: Father was a
Middlesex Colt. Great-grandfather Henry
Crichton played for Warwickshire. 'Young
brother Wigsy plays for Stratford CC'
Education: Trinity School, Leamington Spa; Birmingham University
Qualifications: 8 GCSEs, 3 A-levels, BSc Sport & Exercise Psychology
Overseas tours: Warwickshire Development of Excellence squad to Cape Town 1998;

MCC to Australia and Singapore 2001; ECB National Academy to Australia and Sri Lanka 2002-03

Overseas teams played for: Harvinia CC, Free State, South Africa 2000; Avendale CC, Cape Town 2001-02; Belville CC, Cape Town 2003-04; Claremont-Nedlands CC, Perth 2004-05

Career highlights to date: 'Winning the Championship 2004'

Cricket moments to forget: 'Being relegated in one-day league [2004]'

Cricket superstitions: 'None'

Cricketers particularly admired: Graham Thorpe, Steve Waugh, Allan Donald, Ashley Giles

Young players to look out for: Jonathan Trott, Ian Westwood, Naqaash Tahir, Moeen Ali

Other sports played: Football (Stoke City youth player)

Other sports followed: 'Hooked on Manchester United since going to their soccer school aged five'

Favourite band: Red Hot Chili Peppers, Coldplay, Stone Roses

Relaxations: 'Music, films, playing my guitar, spending time with Naomi, going abroad'

Extras: Is grandson of *Dr Who* actor Patrick Troughton; father also an actor. County colours U12-U19. Has represented England U15, U16 and U17. Represented ECB Midlands U19 1998. Has won the Alec Hastilow Trophy and the Coney Edmonds Trophy (Warwickshire awards). Warwickshire 2nd XI Player of the Year 2001. Scored 1067 first-class runs in his first full season 2002. NBC Denis Compton Award for the most promising young Warwickshire player 2002. Warwickshire Young Player and Most Improved Player of the Year 2002

Best batting: 131* Warwickshire v Hampshire, Rose Bowl 2002

Best bowling: 3-1 Warwickshire v CUCCE, Fenner's 2004

2006 Season

	M	Inn	NO	Runs	HS	Avg	100	50	Ct	St	Balls	Runs	Wkts	Avg	BB	5I	10M
Test																	
FC	10	18	1	390	103	22.94	1	2	4	-	585	351	9	39.00	2-15	-	-
ODI																	
List A	10	8	0	207	58	25.87	-	2	6	-	168	149	8	18.62	4-39	-	
20/20 Int																	
20/20	6	5	0	58	25	11.60	-	-	1	-	24	43	0		-	-	

Career Performances

	M	Inn	NO	Runs	HS	Avg	100	50	Ct	St	Balls	Runs	Wkts	Avg	BB	5I	10M
Test																	
FC	65	104	8	3567	131 *	37.15	10	20	29	-	1813	1115	20	55.75	3-1	-	-
ODI	6	5	1	36	20	9.00	-	-	1	-	0	0	0		-	-	
List A	86	76	7	1977	115 *	28.65	2	10	32	-	676	570	23	24.78	4-23	-	
20/20 Int																	
20/20	21	17	1	278	51	17.37	-	1	5	-	84	112	6	18.66	2-10	-	

TUDGE, K. D. Glamorgan

Name: <u>Kyle</u> Daniel Tudge
Role: Right-hand bat, slow left-arm
orthodox bowler
Born: 19 March 1987, Newport, Wales
Height: 5ft 10in **Weight:** 13st 2lbs
Nickname: Tudgy
County debut: 2006
Parents: Gerald and Sheila
Marital status: Single
Education: Blackwood Comprehensive
(GCSEs), Monmouth Boys School (A-levels);
UWIC (University of Wales Institute Cardiff)
Qualifications: 10 GCSEs, 4 AS-levels,
1 A-level, Level 1 cricket coaching
Off-season: 'University student'
Career highlights to date: 'First-class debut

– August 2006, Glamorgan v Worcestershire,
Liverpool Victoria Championship'
Cricket moments to forget: 'Duck in first game at Lord's (MCC Young
Cricketers 2006)'
Cricket superstitions: 'None'
Cricketers particularly admired: Daniel Vettori, Mike Hussey
Young players to look out for: James Harris
Other sports played: Golf
Other sports followed: Rugby (Neath-Swansea Ospreys), football
(Manchester United)
Favourite band: Eminem
Relaxations: 'Films (*Lord of the Rings*, *Star Wars*)'
Extras: Played for Wales Minor Counties in the C&G 2005 and in Minor Counties
competitions 2004-06. MCC Young Cricketers 2004-06 (leading wicket-taker 2006)
Best batting: 4 Glamorgan v Worcestershire, Colwyn Bay 2006

2006 Season

	M	Inn	NO	Runs	HS	Avg	100	50	Ct	St	Balls	Runs	Wkts	Avg	BB	5I	10M
Test																	
FC	1	2	1	7	4	7.00	-	-	-	-	78	58	0		-	-	-
ODI																	
List A																		
20/20 Int																		
20/20																		

Career Performances

	M	Inn	NO	Runs	HS	Avg	100	50	Ct	St	Balls	Runs	Wkts	Avg	BB	5I	10M
Test																		
FC	1	2	1	7	4	7.00	-	-	-	-	78	58	0		-	-	-
ODI																		
List A	1	1	0	4	4	4.00	-	-	-	-	30	31	0		-	-	
20/20 Int																		
20/20																		

TUDOR, A. J.   Essex

Name: Alexander (<u>Alex</u>) Jeremy Tudor
Role: Right-hand bat, right-arm fast bowler
Born: 23 October 1977, West Brompton, London
Height: 6ft 4in **Weight:** 13st 7lbs
Nickname: Big Al, Bambi, Tudes
County debut: 1995 (Surrey), 2005 (Essex)
County cap: 1999 (Surrey)
Test debut: 1998-99
ODI debut: 2002
Place in batting averages: 145th av. 30.16
Place in bowling averages: 116th av. 42.67
Strike rate: 62.92 (career 48.54)
Parents: Daryll and Jennifer
Marital status: Engaged to Francesca
Children: Sienna
Family links with cricket: Brother was on the staff at The Oval

Education: St Mark's C of E, Fulham; City of Westminster College
Overseas tours: England U15 to South Africa 1992-93; England U19 to Zimbabwe 1995-96, to Pakistan 1996-97; England to Australia 1998-99, to South Africa 1999-2000, to Pakistan 2000-01, to Australia 2002-03; England A to West Indies 2000-01; ECB National Academy to Australia 2001-02, 2002-03

Cricketers particularly admired: Curtly Ambrose, Brian Lara
Other sports followed: Basketball, football (QPR)
Relaxations: Listening to music
Extras: Played for London Schools at all ages from U8. Represented England U17. MCC Young Cricketer. Took 4-89 in Australia's first innings on Test debut at Perth 1998-99; his victims included both Waugh twins. Scored 99* in second innings of the first Test v New Zealand at Edgbaston 1999, bettering the highest score by a nightwatchman for England (Harold Larwood's 98 v Australia at Sydney 1932-33) and winning Man of the Match award. Cricket Writers' Club Young Cricketer of the Year 1999. Recorded match figures of 7-109 in the third Test v Sri Lanka at Old Trafford 2002, winning Man of the Match award
Best batting: 144 Essex v Derbyshire, Chelmsford 2006
Best bowling: 7-48 Surrey v Lancashire, The Oval 2000

2006 Season

	M	Inn	NO	Runs	HS	Avg	100	50	Ct	St	Balls	Runs	Wkts	Avg	BB	5I	10M
Test																	
FC	11	13	1	362	144	30.16	1	1	2	-	1762	1195	28	42.67	5-67	1	-
ODI																	
List A	1	0	0	0	0		-	-	-	-	42	25	0		-	-	
20/20 Int																	
20/20																	

Career Performances

	M	Inn	NO	Runs	HS	Avg	100	50	Ct	St	Balls	Runs	Wkts	Avg	BB	5I	10M
Test	10	16	4	229	99 *	19.08	-	1	3	-	1512	963	28	34.39	5-44	1	-
FC	106	135	28	2489	144	23.26	2	8	31	-	15339	9268	316	29.32	7-48	14	-
ODI	3	2	1	9	6	9.00	-	-	1	-	127	136	4	34.00	2-30	-	
List A	72	48	14	428	56	12.58	-	1	21	-	3103	2435	103	23.64	4-26	-	
20/20 Int																	
20/20																	

86. Which overseas player took a wicket with his first ball
for Essex, v Somerset at Colchester 2005?

TURK, N. R. K.   Sussex

Name: <u>Neil</u> Richard Keith Turk
Role: Left-hand bat, right-arm
medium bowler
Born: 28 April 1983, Cuckfield
Height: 6ft **Weight:** 11st 8lbs
Nickname: Turkish, Neilo
County debut: 2002 (one-day),
2006 (first-class)
Parents: Keith and Lorraine
Marital status: Single
Family links with cricket: 'Father PE
teacher and grade coach. Brother county
junior. Mother junior cricket coach/manager'
Education: Sackville Community College,
East Grinstead; Exeter University
Qualifications: 9 GCSEs, 1 AS-level,
3 A-levels, FIFA-approved referee

Career highlights to date: 'County debut
2002 v Essex Eagles. Maiden 2nd XI Championship century (123) v Hampshire'
Cricket moments to forget: 'Being dismissed by Hampshire's wicket-keeper in a
match for Sussex 2nd XI, having scored a century in the first innings; his only wicket
to date'
Cricket superstitions: 'I don't believe you need superstitions to help you'
Cricketers particularly admired: Brian Lara, Jacques Kallis
Young players to look out for: Arul Suppiah
Other sports played: Hockey (West of England U21, Exeter University, ISCA HC),
golf, football
Other sports followed: Football (Liverpool FC), rugby league (Wigan Warriors),
hockey (East Grinstead HC)
Favourite band: Usher
Relaxations: 'I enjoy most sports; I also like to spend time on the golf course when
I'm not playing cricket'
Extras: Sussex U17 Player of the Year. Played for Sussex Board XI in the C&G 2003.
Attended Sussex Academy. Released by Sussex at the end of the 2006 season
Best batting: 24 Sussex v Sri Lankans, Hove 2006

2006 Season

	M	Inn	NO	Runs	HS	Avg	100	50	Ct	St	Balls	Runs	Wkts	Avg	BB	5I	10M
Test																	
FC	1	1	0	24	24	24.00	-	-	-	-	18	9	0		-	-	-
ODI																	
List A																	
20/20 Int																	
20/20																	

Career Performances

	M	Inn	NO	Runs	HS	Avg	100	50	Ct	St	Balls	Runs	Wkts	Avg	BB	5I	10M
Test																	
FC	1	1	0	24	24	24.00	-	-	-	-	18	9	0		-	-	-
ODI																	
List A	3	3	0	64	36	21.33	-	-	-	-	12	21	0		-	-	
20/20 Int																	
20/20																	

TURNER, M. L.   Somerset

Name: <u>Mark</u> Leif Turner
Role: Right-hand bat, right-arm
fast-medium bowler
Born: 23 October 1984, Sunderland
Height: 6ft **Weight:** 12st 12lbs
Nickname: Tina
County debut: 2005 (Durham)
Strike rate: (career 108.00)
Parents: Kenny and Eileen
Marital status: Single
Family links with cricket: 'Brother Ian
played county juniors and was a well-
respected local player'
Education: Thornhill Comprehensive School
Qualifications: 7 GCSEs, Level 2 coaching
Career outside cricket: 'Work wherever
possible – call centres, coaching etc'
Off-season: 'Getting myself settled in
Somerset and training hard'
Overseas tours: England U19 to Bangladesh (U19 World Cup) 2003-04; Durham to
India 2004, to South Africa 2005, to Dubai 2005
Career highlights to date: 'Signing three-year contract for Somerset'

Cricket moments to forget: 'Dropping a dolly on Sky for England U19'
Cricket superstitions: 'Before I bowl a spell I bowl two balls and always throw my last one (to mid-on/off)'
Cricketers particularly admired: Allan Donald, Sachin Tendulkar, Virender Sehwag, Dale Benkenstein
Young players to look out for: Luke Evans, Luke Anderson, Ben Harmison, Mark Stoneman
Other sports played: Football (junior with Manchester Utd and Sunderland), golf, fishing
Other sports followed: Football (Sunderland AFC)
Injuries: 'A few niggles but nothing too serious. No more than two weeks off with toe infection'
Favourite band: Maxwell, Keith Sweat, 'any neo-soul'
Relaxations: 'Golf, iPod, socialising with anyone who's interested, and Pro Evolution 5'
Extras: Represented England U19 2003 and 2004, returning match figures of 9-104 (5-57/4-47) in the second 'Test' v Bangladesh U19 at Taunton 2004. Left Durham at the end of the 2006 season and has joined Somerset for 2007
Opinions on cricket: 'Should go back to one division in the Championship; two divisions in Pro40. Keep giving the young England players a chance. More day/night cricket.'
Best batting: 18 Durham v Essex, Riverside 2005
Best bowling: 2-51 Durham v OUCCE, The Parks 2006

2006 Season

	M	Inn	NO	Runs	HS	Avg	100	50	Ct	St	Balls	Runs	Wkts	Avg	BB	5I	10M
Test																	
FC	1	0	0	0	0		-	-	-	-	138	86	2	43.00	2-51	-	-
ODI																	
List A																	
20/20 Int																	
20/20																	

Career Performances

	M	Inn	NO	Runs	HS	Avg	100	50	Ct	St	Balls	Runs	Wkts	Avg	BB	5I	10M
Test																	
FC	3	2	1	19	18	19.00	-	-	-	-	432	252	4	63.00	2-51	-	-
ODI																	
List A																	
20/20 Int																	
20/20	1	0	0	0	0		-	-	-	-	12	25	0		-	-	

UDAL, S. D. Hampshire

Name: <u>Shaun</u> David Udal
Role: Right-hand bat, off-spin bowler
Born: 18 March 1969, Farnborough, Hampshire
Height: 6ft 2in **Weight:** 14st
Nickname: Shaggy
County debut: 1989
County cap: 1992
Benefit: 2002
Test debut: 2005-06
ODI debut: 1994
50 wickets in a season: 7
Place in batting averages: 245th av. 14.75 (2005 223rd av. 19.60)
Place in bowling averages: 117th av. 43.06 (2005 3rd av. 18.90)
Strike rate: 83.60 (career 66.04)
Parents: Robin and Mary
Wife and date of marriage: Emma, 5 October 1991
Children: Katherine Mary, 26 August 1992; Rebecca Jane, 17 November 1995; Jack David, 23 August 2004
Family links with cricket: 'Great-grandfather – MCC; grandfather [G. F. Udal] – Middlesex and Leicestershire; father – Camberley CC for 40 years; brother – captain Camberley CC'
Education: Cove Comprehensive
Qualifications: 8 CSEs, print finisher, company director
Career outside cricket: 'Media – printing company'
Off-season: 'Family holiday, work, golf tour, work and training for 2007 season'
Overseas tours: England to Australia 1994-95, to Pakistan 2005-06, to India 2005-06; England A to Pakistan 1995-96; England XI to New Zealand (Cricket Max) 1997; Hampshire to Anguilla 1998, to Cape Town 2001
Overseas teams played for: Hamilton Wickham, Newcastle, NSW 1989-90
Career highlights to date: 'Captain of Hants in C&G final 2005. Being picked for England again aged 36'
Cricket moments to forget: 'Getting out twice as nightwatchman hooking'
Cricket superstitions: 'Left everything on first'
Cricketers particularly admired: Ian Botham, Shane Warne, Robin Smith
Young players to look out for: Chris Benham
Other sports played: Golf (14 handicap), football
Other sports followed: Football (West Ham Utd, Aldershot Town, Eastleigh FC)
Favourite band: Robbie Williams

Relaxations: 'Good food and wine; the odd beer with Peter Ebdon at the snooker club'

Extras: Scored double hundred for Camberley CC in 40-over game. Man of the Match on NatWest debut against Berkshire 1991. Hampshire Cricket Association Player of the Year 1993. Vice-captain of Hampshire 1998-2000. Hampshire Players' Player of the Year 2001, 2002. Skipper of Hampshire in C&G final at Lord's 2005, becoming the first Hampshire-born captain to lift silverware for the county. Had second innings figures of 4-14 as England defeated India in the third Test at Mumbai 2005-06. Leading wicket-taker for Hampshire in one-day cricket. President of Camberley CC

Opinions on cricket: 'It really is a great game. Keep agents out of affecting young players' attitudes – some get a higher opinion of their abilities and can cause friction between the player and club unnecessarily.'

Best batting: 117* Hampshire v Warwickshire, Southampton 1997
Best bowling: 8-50 Hampshire v Sussex, Southampton 1992

2006 Season

	M	Inn	NO	Runs	HS	Avg	100	50	Ct	St	Balls	Runs	Wkts	Avg	BB	5I	10M
Test																	
FC	10	9	1	118	28	14.75	-	-	3	-	1254	646	15	43.06	2-12	-	-
ODI																	
List A	18	13	2	174	34	15.81	-	-	6	-	677	513	18	28.50	3-42		
20/20 Int																	
20/20	8	4	1	35	15	11.66	-	-	4	-	192	209	8	26.12	3-21		

Career Performances

	M	Inn	NO	Runs	HS	Avg	100	50	Ct	St	Balls	Runs	Wkts	Avg	BB	5I	10M
Test	4	7	1	109	33 *	18.16	-	-	1	-	596	344	8	43.00	4-14	-	-
FC	255	359	67	6727	117 *	23.03	1	28	116	-	46890	23180	710	32.64	8-50	33	4
ODI	11	7	4	35	11 *	11.66	-	-	1	-	612	400	9	44.44	2-37	-	
List A	357	231	71	2504	78	15.65	-	8	117	-	16531	12083	405	29.83	5-43	1	
20/20 Int																	
20/20	25	18	7	188	37	17.09	-	-	7	-	465	557	25	22.28	3-21	-	

UMAR GUL   Gloucestershire

Name: Umar Gul
Role: Right-hand bat, right-arm fast-medium bowler
Born: 15 October 1982, Peshawar, Pakistan
County debut: No first-team appearance
Test debut: 2003-04
ODI debut: 2002-03
Place in bowling averages: 73rd av. 34.00
Strike rate: 53.83 (career 44.38)

Overseas tours: Pakistan U19 to New Zealand (U19 World Cup) 2001-02; Pakistan A to UAE (EurAsia Cricket Series) 2006; Pakistan to Sharjah (Cherry Blossom Sharjah Cup) 2002-03, to Sri Lanka (Bank Alfalah Cup) 2003, to England (NatWest Challenge) 2003, to New Zealand 2003-04, to Sri Lanka 2005-06, to England 2006, to India (ICC Champions Trophy) 2006-07
Overseas teams played for: PIA 2001-02 – 2005-06; Peshawar 2003-04 – 2005-06; Habib Bank 2006-07
Extras: His awards include Man of the Match in the third ODI v Bangladesh at Lahore 2003-04 (5-17) and in the second Test v India at Lahore 2003-04 (5-31). Pakistan's top wicket-taker in Test series v England 2006 with 18 (av. 34.11). Has joined Gloucestershire as an overseas player for 2007

Best batting: 46 Peshawar v Multan, Peshawar 2005-06
Best bowling: 8-78 Peshawar v Karachi Urban, Peshawar 2005-06
Stop press: Man of the Match in the first Test v West Indies at Lahore 2006-07 (5-65/4-99)

2006 Season

	M	Inn	NO	Runs	HS	Avg	100	50	Ct	St	Balls	Runs	Wkts	Avg	BB	5I	10M
Test	4	6	1	34	13	6.80	-	-	1	-	950	614	18	34.11	5-123	1	-
FC	6	7	1	34	13	5.66	-	-	2	-	1292	816	24	34.00	5-123	1	-
ODI																	
List A																		
20/20 Int																		
20/20																		

Career Performances

	M	Inn	NO	Runs	HS	Avg	100	50	Ct	St	Balls	Runs	Wkts	Avg	BB	5I	10M
Test	11	14	1	67	14	5.15	-	-	4	-	2390	1440	45	32.00	5-31	2	-
FC	35	38	6	349	46	10.90	-	-	10	-	7073	4102	162	25.32	8-78	11	1
ODI	19	2	1	19	17 *	19.00	-	-	1	-	848	664	22	30.18	5-17	1	
List A	52	17	9	70	17 *	8.75	-	-	6	-	2483	1996	67	29.79	5-17	1	
20/20 Int																	
20/20	5	3	0	20	11	6.66	-	-	3	-	118	140	10	14.00	4-21	-	

VAAS, W. P. U. J. C.   Middlesex

Name: Warnakulasuriya Patabendige
Ushantha Joseph <u>Chaminda</u> Vaas
Role: Left-hand bat, left-arm
fast-medium bowler
Born: 27 January 1974, Mattumagala,
Sri Lanka
County debut: 2003 (Hampshire),
2005 (Worcestershire)
County colours: 2005 (Worcestershire)
Test debut: 1994
ODI debut: 1993-94
Place in batting averages: (2005 151st
av. 30.11)
Place in bowling averages: 42nd av. 29.33
(2005 48th av. 27.82)
Strike rate: 71.00 (career 54.38)
Overseas tours: Sri Lanka U19 to England

1992; Sri Lanka to India 1993-94, to
Zimbabwe 1994-95, to South Africa 1994-95, to New Zealand 1994-95, to Pakistan
1995-96, to Australia 1995-96, to India and Pakistan (World Cup) 1995-96, to New
Zealand 1996-97, to India 1997-98, to South Africa 1997-98, to Bangladesh (Wills
International Cup) 1998-99, to UK, Ireland and Netherlands (World Cup) 1999, to
Zimbabwe 1999-2000, to Pakistan 1999-2000, to Kenya (ICC Knockout Trophy)
2000-01, to South Africa 2000-01, to England 2002, to South Africa 2002-03, to Africa
(World Cup) 2002-03, to West Indies 2003, to Zimbabwe 2004, to Australia 2004, to
England (ICC Champions Trophy) 2004, to Pakistan 2004-05, to New Zealand 2004-
05, to India 2005-06, to England 2006, to India (ICC Champions Trophy) 2006-07, to
New Zealand 2006-07, plus numerous other one-day series and tournaments in
Sharjah, Singapore, West Indies, Kenya, India, Pakistan, Australia, Bangladesh, New
Zealand and Morocco; ICC World XI to Australia (Tsunami Relief) 2004-05; FICA
World XI to New Zealand 2004-05
Overseas teams played for: Colts CC, Sri Lanka 1990-91 –
Extras: Man of the Match for his 8-19 v Zimbabwe in the LG Abans Triangular Series
at Colombo 2001-02, a new world's best analysis for ODIs; his figures included a hat-
trick (Carlisle, Wishart, Taibu) as Zimbabwe were bowled out for 38. Took hat-trick
(Hannan Sarkar, Mohammad Ashraful, Ehsanul Haque) with the first three balls of the
match (four wickets in first over) v Bangladesh at Pietermaritzburg in the World Cup
2002-03, finishing with 6-25 and winning Man of the Match award. His other
international awards include Man of the [Test] Series v South Africa 2004 and Man of
the Match (jointly with Brian Lara) in the third Test v West Indies at Colombo 2001-
02 (7-120/7-71). An overseas player with Hampshire in the latter part of the 2003

season; an overseas player with Worcestershire for the early part of the 2005 season; has joined Middlesex as an overseas player for 2007
Best batting: 134 Colts v Burgher, Colombo 2004-05
Best bowling: 7-54 Western Province v Southern Province, Colombo 2004-05

2006 Season

	M	Inn	NO	Runs	HS	Avg	100	50	Ct	St	Balls	Runs	Wkts	Avg	BB	5I	10M
Test	3	6	4	184	50 *	92.00	-	1	-	-	564	265	5	53.00	2-71	-	-
FC	5	10	5	248	50 *	49.60	-	1	-	-	852	352	12	29.33	4-34	-	-
ODI	5	3	0	30	13	10.00	-	-	-	-	246	203	2	101.50	2-38	-	
List A	5	3	0	30	13	10.00	-	-	-	-	246	203	2	101.50	2-38	-	
20/20 Int																	
20/20																	

Career Performances

	M	Inn	NO	Runs	HS	Avg	100	50	Ct	St	Balls	Runs	Wkts	Avg	BB	5I	10M
Test	94	136	26	2503	74 *	22.75	-	11	28	-	20374	9062	307	29.51	7-71	11	2
FC	163	219	44	4064	134	23.22	3	16	49	-	31707	14378	583	24.66	7-54	25	3
ODI	281	194	62	1814	50 *	13.74	-	1	55	-	13791	9698	354	27.39	8-19	4	
List A	325	223	73	2300	62 *	15.33	-	3	68	-	15746	10999	415	26.50	8-19	4	
20/20 Int																	
20/20	1	1	0	12	12	12.00	-	-	-	-	0	0	0			-	-

VAN DER WATH, J. J.   Northamptonshire

Name: <u>Johannes</u> Jacobus van der Wath
Role: Right-hand bat, right-arm fast-medium bowler; all-rounder
Born: 10 January 1978, Newcastle, Natal, South Africa
County debut: 2005 (Sussex)
ODI debut: 2005-06
Twenty20 Int debut: 2005-06
Place in bowling averages: (2005 106th av. 39.90)
Strike rate: (career 59.69)
Education: Ermelo High School
Overseas tours: South Africa A to Sri Lanka 2005-06; South Africa to Australia 2005-06 (VB Series), to Sri Lanka 2006
Overseas teams played for: Easterns 1995-96 – 1996-97; Free State 1997-98 – 2003-04; Eagles 2004-05 –

Extras: Represented South Africa U19 1996-97. Scored century (100) and recorded five-wicket innings return (5-30) v Titans at Bloemfontein in the SuperSport Series 2004-05, winning the Man of the Match award. His other match awards include Man of the Match v Dolphins at Durban in the Standard Bank Cup 2004-05 (2-38/91) and v Titans at Centurion in the final of the Standard Bank Cup 2005-06 (3-25/20). Was an overseas player with Sussex during the 2005 season as a locum for Naved-ul-Hasan; has joined Northamptonshire as an overseas player for 2007

Best batting: 113* Free State v KwaZulu-Natal, Bloemfontein 2001-02
Best bowling: 6-37 Free State v Boland, Bloemfontein 2001-02

2006 Season (did not make any first-class or one-day appearances)

Career Performances

	M	Inn	NO	Runs	HS	Avg	100	50	Ct	St	Balls	Runs	Wkts	Avg	BB	5I	10M
Test																	
FC	53	83	14	1734	113*	25.13	2	10	20	-	9134	4413	153	28.84	6-37	8	-
ODI	8	7	2	85	37*	17.00	-	-	2	-	424	442	10	44.20	2-21	-	
List A	97	78	21	1472	91	25.82	-	9	23	-	4087	3300	123	26.82	4-31	-	
20/20 Int	1	1	0	14	14	14.00	-	-	-	-	24	40	1	40.00	1-40	-	
20/20	19	14	3	118	28*	10.72	-	-	1	-	349	446	19	23.47	2-11	-	

VAN JAARSVELD, M.   Kent

Name: Martin van Jaarsveld
Role: Right-hand top-order bat, right-arm off-spin bowler
Born: 18 June 1974, Klerksdorp, South Africa
Height: 6ft 2in **Weight:** 12st 12lbs
Nickname: Jarre
County debut: 2004 (Northamptonshire), 2005 (Kent)
County cap: 2005 (Kent)
Test debut: 2002-03
ODI debut: 2002-03
1000 runs in a season: 2
1st-Class 200s: 3
Place in batting averages: 48th av. 48.68 (2005 56th av. 44.37)
Strike rate: (career 89.64)
Parents: Leon and Isobel
Wife and date of marriage: Jill, 6 May 2005

Education: Warmbads High School; University of Pretoria
Qualifications: BComm (Financial Management)
Off-season: 'Captaining the Titans in South Africa'
Overseas tours: South Africa A to Sri Lanka 1998, to Zimbabwe 2002-03, to Australia 2002-03; South African Academy to Zimbabwe 1998-99; South Africa to England 2003, to New Zealand 2003-04, to Sri Lanka 2004, to England (ICC Champions Trophy) 2004, to India 2004-05
Overseas teams played for: Northern Transvaal/Northerns Titans 1994-95 – 2003-04; Titans 2004-05 –
Career highlights to date: 'Playing for South Africa. Being chosen as one of the five Cricketers of the Year in South Africa 2002'
Cricket moments to forget: 'Losing the NatWest Series final [with South Africa] at Lord's, July 2003'
Cricket superstitions: 'Left pad first when padding up'
Cricketers particularly admired: Gary Kirsten, Michael Atherton
Young players to look out for: Neil Dexter, Joe Denly
Other sports played: Golf, tennis
Other sports followed: Rugby (Blue Bulls), football (Blackburn Rovers)
Favourite band: Snow Patrol
Relaxations: 'Having throw-downs; going to the cinema'
Extras: Scored 182* and 158* v Griqualand West at Centurion 2001-02, becoming only the second batsman to record two 150s in the same match in South Africa. Player of the SuperSport Series 2001-02 (934 runs at 84.90); also topped South African first-class averages 2001-02 (1268 runs at 74.58). One of *South African Cricket Annual*'s five Cricketers of the Year 2002. Was an overseas player with Northamptonshire 2004. Scored a century in each innings (118/111) on first-class debut for Kent, v Warwickshire at Canterbury 2005, becoming the first Kent debutant to achieve the feat. Scored 168 v Surrey at Tunbridge Wells 2005, in the process sharing with Robert Key (189) in a new Kent record third-wicket partnership (323). Retired from international cricket in February 2005. Is no longer considered an overseas player
Opinions on cricket: 'I think the standard of county cricket, with the inclusion of two overseas players and the odd Kolpak player [*see page 13*], is very strong and although there is a lot of resistance I do think the English game has benefited from it.'
Best batting: 262* Kent v Glamorgan, Cardiff 2005
Best bowling: 2-30 South Africa A v Sri Lanka A, Potchefstroom 2003-04

2006 Season

	M	Inn	NO	Runs	HS	Avg	100	50	Ct	St	Balls	Runs	Wkts	Avg	BB	5I	10M
Test																	
FC	16	27	2	1217	116	48.68	3	10	36	-	174	114	1	114.00	1-37	-	-
ODI																	
List A	16	15	2	430	75 *	33.07	-	3	11	-	216	189	5	37.80	1-22	-	
20/20 Int																	
20/20	9	9	1	229	75	28.62	-	1	9	-	0	0	0			-	-

Career Performances

	M	Inn	NO	Runs	HS	Avg	100	50	Ct	St	Balls	Runs	Wkts	Avg	BB	5I	10M
Test	9	15	2	397	73	30.53	-	3	11	-	42	28	0		-	-	-
FC	152	259	24	10453	262 *	44.48	28	50	203	-	1255	664	14	47.42	2-30	-	-
ODI	11	7	1	124	45	20.66	-	-	4	-	31	18	2	9.00	1-0	-	
List A	192	177	26	5861	123	38.81	8	38	107	-	758	658	14	47.00	1-0	-	
20/20 Int																	
20/20	35	32	4	786	75	28.07	-	6	25	-	42	52	3	17.33	2-19	-	

VAUGHAN, M. P.   Yorkshire

Name: <u>Michael</u> Paul Vaughan
Role: Right-hand bat, off-spin bowler
Born: 29 October 1974, Eccles, Manchester
Height: 6ft 2in **Weight:** 11st 7lbs
Nickname: Frankie, Virgil
County debut: 1993
County cap: 1995
Benefit: 2005
Test debut: 1999-2000
ODI debut: 2000-01
Twenty20 Int debut: 2005
1000 runs in a season: 4
Place in batting averages: 149th av. 29.66
(2005 83rd av. 37.60)
Strike rate: (career 80.78)
Parents: Graham John and Dee
Wife and date of marriage: Nichola,
September 2003
Children: Tallulah Grace, 4 June 2004; Archie, December 2005
Family links with cricket: Father played league cricket for Worsley CC. Brother
plays for Sheffield Collegiate. Mother is related to the famous Tyldesley family
(Lancashire and England)

Education: Silverdale Comprehensive, Sheffield
Qualifications: 7 GCSEs
Overseas tours: Yorkshire to West Indies 1994, to South Africa 1995, to Zimbabwe 1996; England U19 to India 1992-93, to Sri Lanka 1993-94 (c); England A to India 1994-95, to Australia 1996-97, to Zimbabwe and South Africa 1998-99 (c); England to South Africa 1999-2000, to Pakistan and Sri Lanka 2000-01, to India and New Zealand 2001-02, to Australia 2002-03, to Africa (World Cup) 2002-03, to Bangladesh and Sri Lanka 2003-04 (c), to West Indies 2003-04 (c), to Zimbabwe (one-day series) 2004-05 (c), to South Africa 2004-05 (c), to Pakistan 2005-06 (c), to India 2005-06 (c), to Australia 2006-07 (C'wealth Bank Series; c)
Cricketers particularly admired: Darren Lehmann, 'all the Yorkshire and England squads'
Other sports played: Football (Baslow FC), golf (10 handicap)
Other sports followed: Football (Sheffield Wednesday), all golf
Relaxations: Most sports. 'Enjoy a good meal with friends'
Extras: Maurice Leyland Batting Award 1990; Cricket Society's Most Promising Young Cricketer 1993; A. A. Thompson Memorial Trophy 1993. Scored 1066 runs in first full season of first-class cricket 1994. Captained England U19. PCA Player of the Year 2002. Highest-scoring batsman in Test cricket for the calendar year 2002 (1481 runs). One of *Wisden*'s Five Cricketers of the Year 2003. Topped Pricewaterhouse Coopers rankings for Test batsmen in early summer 2003. Vodafone Cricketer of the Year 2002-03. Scored century in each innings (103/101*) in the first Test v West Indies at Lord's 2004. His international awards include England's Man of the [Test] Series v India 2002 (615 runs at 102.50) and Man of the [Test] Series v Australia 2002-03 (633 runs at 63.30), as well as Man of the Match v Australia at Edgbaston in the ICC Champions Trophy 2004 (86/2-42 plus run-out). England one-day captain since May 2003 and England Test captain since July 2003; led England to a Test series win over Australia in 2005, their first Ashes success for 18 years, and was appointed OBE in 2006 New Year Honours. Book *A Year in the Sun* published 2003. England 12-month central contract 2006-07
Best batting: 197 England v India, Trent Bridge 2002
Best bowling: 4-39 Yorkshire v Oxford University, The Parks 1994
Stop press: Forced to return early from Australia tour 2006-07 with a hamstring injury

2006 Season

	M	Inn	NO	Runs	HS	Avg	100	50	Ct	St	Balls	Runs	Wkts	Avg	BB	5I	10M
Test																	
FC	3	6	0	178	99	29.66	-	2	-	-	0	0	0		-	-	-
ODI																	
List A	2	2	0	103	67	51.50	-	1	1	-	0	0	0		-	-	
20/20 Int																	
20/20																	

Career Performances

	M	Inn	NO	Runs	HS	Avg	100	50	Ct	St	Balls	Runs	Wkts	Avg	BB	5I	10M
Test	64	115	8	4595	197	42.94	15	14	37	-	936	537	6	89.50	2-71	-	-
FC	230	407	25	14549	197	38.08	39	61	106	-	9210	5142	114	45.10	4-39	-	-
ODI	74	71	10	1730	90 *	28.36	-	15	20	-	664	562	12	46.83	4-22	-	
List A	258	249	25	6527	125 *	29.13	3	41	77	-	3075	2370	73	32.46	4-22	-	
20/20 Int	1	1	0	0	0	0.00	-	-	-	-	0	0	0		-	-	
20/20	1	1	0	0	0	0.00	-	-	-	-	0	0	0		-	-	

VETTORI, D. L.   Warwickshire

Name: <u>Daniel</u> Luca Vettori
Role: Left-hand bat, slow left-arm bowler
Born: 27 January 1979, Auckland, New Zealand
County debut: 2003 (Nottinghamshire), 2006 (Warwickshire)
County cap: 2003 (Nottinghamshire)
Test debut: 1996-97
ODI debut: 1996-97
Strike rate: (career 72.99)
Family links with cricket: Cousin (J. V. Hill) and uncle (A. J. Hill) played for Central Districts in New Zealand
Overseas tours: New Zealand U19 to England 1996; New Zealand Academy to South Africa 1997; New Zealand to Zimbabwe 1997-98, to Australia 1997-98, to Sri Lanka 1998, to Malaysia (Commonwealth Games) 1998-99, to Bangladesh (Wills International Cup) 1998-99, to UK, Ireland and Netherlands (World Cup) 1999, to England 1999, to India 1999-2000, to Zimbabwe 2000-01, to Australia 2001-02, to Pakistan 2002, to West Indies 2002, to Sri Lanka (ICC Champions Trophy) 2002-03, to Africa (World Cup) 2002-03, to Sri Lanka 2003,

to India 2003-04, to England 2004, to England (ICC Champions Trophy) 2004, to Bangladesh 2004-05, to Australia 2004-05, to Zimbabwe 2005-06, to South Africa 2005-06, to India (ICC Champions Trophy) 2006-07, to Australia (C'wealth Bank Series) 2006-07, plus other one-day series and tournaments in Singapore, Sri Lanka, India and Pakistan; ICC World XI to Australia (Tsunami Relief) 2004-05, to Australia (Super Series) 2005-06

Overseas teams played for: Northern Districts 1996-97 –

Extras: Became youngest player to play Test cricket for New Zealand when he made his debut in the second Test v England at Wellington 1996-97 aged 18 years 10 days. One of *New Zealand Cricket Almanack*'s two Cricketers of the Year 2000, 2005. His awards include Player of the [ODI] Series v Australia 2004-05, Player of the [Test] Series v Bangladesh 2004-05 (20 wickets; av. 11.20) and Man of the Match in the first Test v Australia at Auckland 1999-2000 (5-62/7-87). Was an overseas player with Nottinghamshire during July 2003 as a locum for Stuart MacGill; an overseas player with Warwickshire 2006, leaving after two matches with a stress fracture of the back

Best batting: 137* New Zealand v Pakistan, Hamilton 2003-04

Best bowling: 7-87 New Zealand v Australia, Auckland 1999-2000

2006 Season

	M	Inn	NO	Runs	HS	Avg	100	50	Ct	St	Balls	Runs	Wkts	Avg	BB	5I	10M
Test																	
FC	1	1	0	27	27	27.00	-	-	-	-	186	92	0		-	-	-
ODI																	
List A	1	0	0	0	0		-	-	-	-	0	0	0		-	-	
20/20 Int																	
20/20																	

Career Performances

	M	Inn	NO	Runs	HS	Avg	100	50	Ct	St	Balls	Runs	Wkts	Avg	BB	5I	10M
Test	71	102	16	2136	137 *	24.83	2	11	35	-	17234	7658	219	34.96	7-87	12	2
FC	115	157	22	3289	137 *	24.36	3	17	53	-	26642	11963	365	32.77	7-87	22	2
ODI	173	108	34	1043	83	14.09	-	2	43	-	7979	5608	167	33.58	5-30	1	
List A	239	158	42	2287	138	19.71	2	8	74	-	11337	7739	244	31.71	5-30	1	
20/20 Int																	
20/20	1	1	0	5	5	5.00	-	-	-	-	18	13	0		-	-	

VINCENT, L.   Worcestershire

Name: Lou Vincent
Role: Right-hand bat, right-arm medium bowler
Born: 11 November 1978, Warkworth, New Zealand
Height: 5ft 10in **Weight:** 12st 7lbs
Nickname: Flusher
County debut: 2006
County colours: 2006
Test debut: 2001-02
ODI debut: 2000-01
Twenty20 Int debut: 2005-06
1st-Class 200s: 1
Place in batting averages: 54th av. 46.90
Strike rate: (career 150.50)
Parents: Mike and Kathy
Wife and date of marriage: Elly, August 2006
Children: Molly, April 2006
Family links with cricket: 'Great-grandma used to make cookies for the great Eddie Paynter'
Qualifications: 'Level III lawn bowls coach'
Off-season: 'NZ tours/season'
Overseas tours: New Zealand U19 to South Africa (U19 World Cup) 1997-98; New Zealand Academy to Australia 1999-2000; New Zealand A to South Africa 2004-05; New Zealand to Sharjah (ARY Gold Cup) 2000-01, to Australia 2001-02, to Pakistan 2002, to West Indies 2002, to Sri Lanka (ICC Champions Trophy) 2002-03, to Africa (World Cup) 2002-03, to India 2003-04, to Zimbabwe 2005-06, to South Africa 2005-06 (one-day series), to India (ICC Champions Trophy) 2006-07, to Australia (C'wealth Bank Series) 2006-07, plus other one-day tournaments in Sri Lanka and India
Overseas teams played for: Auckland 1997-98 – ; Chin Hill CC, Kaukapakapa, New Zealand 2004 –
Career highlights to date: 'Places it takes me around the world'
Cricket moments to forget: 'Pair on debut for Worcestershire'
Cricketers particularly admired: Zaheer Khan
Young players to look out for: 'G. Hick'
Other sports followed: Poker
Player website: www.louvincent.com
Extras: Played for Suffolk in the C&G 2005. Scored century (104) on Test debut in the third Test v Australia at Perth 2001-02. Set record for highest individual score for New Zealand in ODI cricket (172) v Zimbabwe at Bulawayo in the Videocon Tri-Series 2005-06, winning Man of the Match award. His other awards include Man of

the Match in the fourth ODI v West Indies at Napier 2005-06 (102). An overseas player with Worcestershire during the 2006 season as a locum for Phil Jaques. Scored 114 v Essex at Worcester 2006, becoming the first Worcestershire player to score a century before lunch since Glenn Turner in 1982

Opinions on cricket: 'Twenty20 has increased the skill and we will see more higher scores.'

Best batting: 224 New Zealand v Sri Lanka, Wellington 2004-05

Best bowling: 2-37 Auckland v Wellington, Auckland 1999-2000

Stop press: Called up to the New Zealand squad for the Commonwealth Bank Series in Australia 2006-07 on the retirement of Nathan Astle, winning Man of the Match v England at Perth (76)

2006 Season

	M	Inn	NO	Runs	HS	Avg	100	50	Ct	St	Balls	Runs	Wkts	Avg	BB	5I	10M
Test																	
FC	6	11	1	469	141	46.90	2	1	5	-	132	76	1	76.00	1-12	-	-
ODI																	
List A	8	8	0	427	106	53.37	1	4	4	-	12	13	0		-	-	
20/20 Int																	
20/20	8	8	0	138	40	17.25	-	-	4	-	50	73	4	18.25	3-28	-	

Career Performances

	M	Inn	NO	Runs	HS	Avg	100	50	Ct	St	Balls	Runs	Wkts	Avg	BB	5I	10M
Test	22	38	1	1295	224	35.00	3	9	19	-	6	2	0		-	-	
FC	80	128	9	4442	224	37.32	10	27	100	-	903	456	6	76.00	2-37	-	-
ODI	83	80	9	1867	172	26.29	2	7	33	-	2	3	0		-	-	
List A	159	153	12	4016	172	28.48	5	20	96	3	121	132	1	132.00	1-8	-	
20/20 Int	1	1	0	42	42	42.00	-	-	-	-	0	0	0		-	-	
20/20	11	11	0	235	42	21.36	-	-	4	-	50	73	4	18.25	3-28	-	

87. Which player took a wicket with his fourth ball on Test debut 1984-85, causing his famous cricketing father to drive the wrong way down a one-way street as he listened on the radio?

WAGG, G. G.   Derbyshire

Name: <u>Graham</u> Grant Wagg
Role: Right-hand bat, left-arm
fast-medium bowler
Born: 28 April 1983, Rugby
Height: 6ft **Weight:** 12st 5lbs
Nickname: Waggy, DC, Caveman
County debut: 2002 (Warwickshire),
2006 (Derbyshire)
Place in batting averages: 181st av. 24.38
Place in bowling averages: 95th av. 37.66
Strike rate: 53.37 (career 49.55)
Parents: John and Dawn
Marital status: Engaged to Natalie
Family links with cricket: 'Dad played and
coached in local leagues in Rugby'
Education: Ashlawn School, Rugby;
Warwickshire College (Sports Science)
Qualifications: Level 1 cricket coach
('coached in South Africa and Holland')

Off-season: 'Cape Town, playing and coaching'
Overseas tours: Warwickshire Development tour to South Africa 1998, to West Indies
2000; England A to Malaysia and India 2003-04
Overseas teams played for: Hams Tech, East London, South Africa 1999;
HBS, Netherlands
Career highlights to date: 'Winning our first match for Derby at Derby for four
years. Getting 6-38 against Somerset [at Taunton 2006] to win us the game'
Cricket moments to forget: 'Bowling at Cameron White at Derby when he made 260
in no time, but they still lost (ha, ha)'
Cricketers particularly admired: Cameron White, Andy Flower
Young players to look out for: Travis Birt
Other sports played: Snooker, fishing, football, rugby
Other sports followed: Football (Man United), snooker (Ronnie O'Sullivan)
Injuries: Shoulder and ankle injuries
Relaxations: 'Casino, snooker, partying'
Extras: Represented England U16, U17, U18, U19 as well as Development of
Excellence (Midlands) XI. Scored 42* from 50 balls, 51 from 57 balls and took 4-43
on first-class debut v Somerset at Edgbaston 2002. NBC Denis Compton Award for the
most promising young Warwickshire player 2003. ECB National Academy 2003-04
Opinions on cricket: 'Is getting a very aggressive game and the standard and the pace
it's played is brill.'
Best batting: 94 Derbyshire v Surrey, Derby 2006
Best bowling: 6-38 Derbyshire v Somerset, Taunton 2006

2006 Season

	M	Inn	NO	Runs	HS	Avg	100	50	Ct	St	Balls	Runs	Wkts	Avg	BB	5I	10M
Test																	
FC	9	14	1	317	94	24.38	-	1	3	-	1280	904	24	37.66	6-38	1	-
ODI																	
List A	10	7	1	73	36	12.16	-	-	2	-	425	488	14	34.85	4-59	-	
20/20 Int																	
20/20	8	7	1	109	27	18.16	-	-	1	-	138	219	6	36.50	3-24	-	

Career Performances

	M	Inn	NO	Runs	HS	Avg	100	50	Ct	St	Balls	Runs	Wkts	Avg	BB	5I	10M
Test																	
FC	19	29	3	601	94	23.11	-	3	5	-	2329	1630	47	34.68	6-38	1	-
ODI																	
List A	37	27	2	396	45	15.84	-	-	10	-	1157	1135	33	34.39	4-50	-	
20/20 Int																	
20/20	19	16	2	220	27	15.71	-	-	3	-	240	353	14	25.21	3-24	-	

WAGH, M. A.   Nottinghamshire

Name: <u>Mark</u> Anant Wagh
Role: Right-hand bat, off-spin bowler
Born: 20 October 1976, Birmingham
Height: 6ft 2in **Weight:** 13st
Nickname: Waggy
County debut: 1997 (Warwickshire)
County cap: 2000 (Warwickshire)
1000 runs in a season: 3
1st-Class 200s: 1
1st-Class 300s: 1
Place in batting averages: 151st av. 29.45
Strike rate: (career 87.45)
Parents: Mohan and Rita
Marital status: Single
Education: King Edward's School, Birmingham; Keble College, Oxford
Qualifications: BA degree, Level 2 coaching award
Overseas tours: Warwickshire U19 to South Africa 1992; ECB National Academy to Australia 2001-02
Career highlights to date: '315 at Lord's 2001'
Cricket moments to forget: 'Too many to mention'

Cricketers particularly admired: Andy Flower
Young players to look out for: Moeen Ali
Favourite band: Dido
Extras: Oxford Blue 1996-98; Oxford University captain 1997. Scored maiden first-class century (116) for Oxford University v Glamorgan at The Parks 1997, following up with another hundred (101) in the second innings. Attended Zimbabwe Cricket Academy 1999. His 315 v Middlesex at Lord's 2001 is the equal second highest individual Championship score made at Lord's (behind Jack Hobbs's 316 in 1926). C&G Man of the Match award for his 102* v Kent at Edgbaston 2004. Included in preliminary England one-day squad of 30 for ICC Champions Trophy 2004. Left Warwickshire at the end of the 2006 season and has joined Nottinghamshire for 2007
Best batting: 315 Warwickshire v Middlesex, Lord's 2001
Best bowling: 7-222 Warwickshire v Lancashire, Edgbaston 2003

2006 Season

	M	Inn	NO	Runs	HS	Avg	100	50	Ct	St	Balls	Runs	Wkts	Avg	BB	5I	10M
Test																	
FC	13	24	2	648	128	29.45	2	1	2	-	18	14	0		-	-	-
ODI																	
List A	1	1	0	51	51	51.00	-	1	-	-	0	0	0		-	-	
20/20 Int																	
20/20	8	7	0	175	56	25.00	-	1	3	-	0	0	0		-	-	

Career Performances

	M	Inn	NO	Runs	HS	Avg	100	50	Ct	St	Balls	Runs	Wkts	Avg	BB	5I	10M
Test																	
FC	140	234	20	8077	315	37.74	20	34	71	-	8571	4567	98	46.60	7-222	2	-
ODI																	
List A	69	65	5	1500	102 *	25.00	1	9	12	-	1096	862	25	34.48	4-35	-	
20/20 Int																	
20/20	15	13	0	249	56	19.15	-	1	5	-	75	106	5	21.20	2-16	-	

WAINWRIGHT, D. J.   Yorkshire

Name: <u>David</u> John Wainwright
Role: Left-hand bat, left-arm orthodox spin bowler
Born: 21 March 1985, Pontefract
Height: 5ft 9in **Weight:** 9st 3lbs
Nickname: Wainers
County debut: 2004
Place in bowling averages: (2005 13th av. 23.11)
Strike rate: (career 63.25)
Parents: Paul and Debbie

Marital status: Single
Family links with cricket: 'Grandfather (Harry Heritage) represented Yorkshire Schoolboys 1950-51'
Education: Hemsworth High School; Hemsworth Arts and Community College; Loughborough University
Qualifications: 10 GCSEs, 3 A-levels, Sports Science and Physics degree, Level 1 coaching
Off-season: 'Playing cricket in Australia'
Overseas tours: Yorkshire U15 to South Africa 2000
Career highlights to date: 'Winning at Lord's in BUSA final for Loughborough'
Cricketers particularly admired: Brian Lara, Monty Panesar
Young players to look out for: Paul Harrison, Chris Murtagh, Greg Norton
Other sports played: Football, golf
Other sports followed: Football (Liverpool FC)
Favourite band: Big Will, Snoop Dogg
Relaxations: Listening to music
Extras: Best bowling award at Bunbury Festival for North of England U15. Played for Loughborough UCCE 2005-06. Represented British Universities 2005-06
Best batting: 62 Yorkshire v Bangladesh A, Headingley 2005
Best bowling: 4-48 LUCCE v Worcestershire, Kidderminster 2005

2006 Season (did not make any first-class or one-day appearances for his county)

Career Performances

	M	Inn	NO	Runs	HS	Avg	100	50	Ct	St	Balls	Runs	Wkts	Avg	BB	5I	10M
Test																	
FC	9	11	2	228	62	25.33	-	1	6	-	1265	692	20	34.60	4-48	-	-
ODI																	
List A	2	0	0	0	0		-	-	-	-	66	59	0		-	-	
20/20 Int																	
20/20																	

WALKER, M. J. Kent

Name: Matthew (<u>Matt</u>) Jonathan Walker
Role: Left-hand bat
Born: 2 January 1974, Gravesend
Height: 5ft 6in **Weight:** 13st
Nickname: Walks, Pumba
County debut: 1992-93
County cap: 2000
1000 runs in a season: 3
1st-Class 200s: 1
Place in batting averages: 14th av. 61.69
(2005 72nd av. 39.72)
Strike rate: (career 90.50)
Parents: Richard and June
Wife and date of marriage: Claudia,
25 September 1999
Children: Charlie Jack, 20 November 2002;
Lexie, 19 January 2007
Family links with cricket: 'Dad played Kent
and Middlesex 2nd XIs and was on Lord's groundstaff. Grandfather kept wicket for
Kent. Mum was women's cricket coach'
Education: King's School, Rochester
Qualifications: 9 GCSEs, 2 A-levels, advanced cricket coaching certificate
Career outside cricket: PE teacher
Off-season: 'A couple of holidays; teaching at St Edmund's School; having
another baby'
Overseas tours: Kent U17 to New Zealand 1990-91; England U19 to Pakistan
1991-92, to India 1992-93 (c); Kent to Zimbabwe 1993
Career highlights to date: 'Captaining England U19. Winning Norwich Union
League 2001'
Cricket moments to forget: 'Losing Lord's B&H final v Surrey 1997'
Cricket superstitions: 'None'
Cricketers particularly admired: Darren Lehmann, Nick Knight, Mark Ramprakash
Young players to look out for: Alex Blake, Neil Dexter
Other sports played: Hockey (England U14-U21 [captain U15-U17]), rugby
(Kent U18)
Other sports followed: Football (Charlton Athletic), hockey (Gore Court HC)
Favourite band: Razorlight, Arctic Monkeys, Jeff Buckley
Relaxations: 'Music and films'
Extras: Captained England U16 cricket and hockey teams in same year. Sir John
Hobbs Silver Jubilee Memorial Prize for outstanding U16 cricketer 1989. Captained
England U19 1993. Woolwich Kent League's Young Cricketer of the Year 1994.

Scored 275* against Somerset in 1996 – the highest ever individual score by a Kent batsman at Canterbury. Ealham Award for Fielding Excellence 2003, 2004, 2005. Cowdrey Award (Kent Player of the Year) 2004, 2006. Vice-captain of Kent 2005. Denness Award (Kent leading run-scorer) 2006. Became an Eminent Roffensian 1995
Opinions on cricket: 'The game is in great shape and domestic cricket is as competitive as ever.'
Best batting: 275* Kent v Somerset, Canterbury 1996
Best bowling: 2-21 Kent v Middlesex, Canterbury 2004

2006 Season

	M	Inn	NO	Runs	HS	Avg	100	50	Ct	St	Balls	Runs	Wkts	Avg	BB	5I	10M
Test																	
FC	16	26	3	1419	197	61.69	5	8	9	-	198	116	1	116.00	1-18	-	-
ODI																	
List A	16	13	5	288	74 *	36.00	-	2	4	-	0	0	0			-	-
20/20 Int																	
20/20	9	9	4	203	58 *	40.60	-	1	1	-	0	0	0			-	-

Career Performances

	M	Inn	NO	Runs	HS	Avg	100	50	Ct	St	Balls	Runs	Wkts	Avg	BB	5I	10M
Test																	
FC	165	273	31	8941	275 *	36.94	22	38	115	-	1810	1071	20	53.55	2-21	-	-
ODI																	
List A	235	216	33	5221	117	28.53	3	32	63	-	886	740	30	24.66	4-24	-	
20/20 Int																	
20/20	27	27	6	584	58 *	27.80	-	1	2	-	0	0	0			-	-

88. Who became the first Lancashire player to score a Test hundred for England at Old Trafford, v India in 1959?

Name: <u>Nicholas</u> Guy Eades Walker
Role: Right-hand bat, right-arm fast-medium bowler
Born: 7 August 1984, Enfield
Height: 6ft 2in **Weight:** 13st 6lbs
Nickname: Walks
County debut: 2004 (Derbyshire), 2006 (Leicestershire)
Place in batting averages: (2005 257th av. 14.18)
Place in bowling averages: 84th av. 35.57 (2005 140th av. 52.47)
Strike rate: 65.21 (career 62.85)
Parents: Amanda and Martin
Marital status: Single
Family links with cricket: 'Brother Duncan plays for the Hyde Park New Zealand Lions 4th XI. Other brother, Robbie, same club 7th XI; bats 10, doesn't bowl'
Education: Haileybury Imperial Service College
Qualifications: Level 2 coach
Career outside cricket: 'DHL delivery driver'
Off-season: 'Training in the indoor centre with Lloyd (bowling coach)'
Overseas tours: Haileybury School to South Africa 2000
Overseas teams played for: South Perth, Western Australia 2001-02; Macquarie University, Sydney 2004-05
Career highlights to date: 'Man of the Match on Sky v Somerset [Pro40] and part of Twenty20 winning squad 2006'
Cricket moments to forget: 'Dropping P. Collingwood on 25; he went on to make 225' (*For info, Collingwood was actually dropped on 51 and made 190 at Derby 2005, but point taken – Ed*)
Cricket superstitions: 'Millions'
Cricketers particularly admired: Jimmy Adams (West Indies), Brett Lee
Young players to look out for: Lee Goddard, Harry Gurney
Other sports played: Golf (9 handicap)
Other sports followed: Rugby
Injuries: Broken talus (ankle)
Favourite band: Ne-Yo
Relaxations: 'PSP [PlayStation Portable]'
Extras: Struck 57-ball 80 (highest first-class score by a Derbyshire No. 11) in his third Championship innings, then recorded maiden first-class five-wicket return (5-68), both

v Somerset at Derby 2004. Struck 24-ball fifty (ending with 63*), batting at No. 11 v Leicestershire at Oakham School 2004. NBC Denis Compton Award for the most promising young Derbyshire player 2004

Opinions on cricket: 'Two up/two down good. Ninety-six overs in the day should be adopted. New ball 80 overs. Too many formats – get rid of Pro40.'

Best batting: 80 Derbyshire v Somerset, Derby 2004
Best bowling: 5-59 Leicestershire v Somerset, Leicester 2006

2006 Season

	M	Inn	NO	Runs	HS	Avg	100	50	Ct	St	Balls	Runs	Wkts	Avg	BB	5I	10M
Test																	
FC	5	6	0	38	21	6.33	-	-	2	-	913	498	14	35.57	5-59	1	-
ODI																	
List A	4	2	1	9	8 *	9.00	-	-	1	-	150	122	7	17.42	4-26	-	
20/20 Int																	
20/20	3	1	1	16	16*		-	-	-	-	60	57	4	14.25	3-19	-	

Career Performances

	M	Inn	NO	Runs	HS	Avg	100	50	Ct	St	Balls	Runs	Wkts	Avg	BB	5I	10M
Test																	
FC	23	29	6	415	80	18.04	-	3	9	-	3080	2057	49	41.97	5-59	2	
ODI																	
List A	20	15	2	118	43	9.07	-	-	8	-	420	388	16	24.25	4-26	-	
20/20 Int																	
20/20	4	2	1	24	16 *	24.00	-	-	-	-	60	57	4	14.25	3-19	-	

89. Which current commentator celebrated his Test debut v Australia in 1981 with his maiden first-class fifty?

WALLACE, M. A.   Glamorgan

Name: <u>Mark</u> Alexander Wallace
Role: Left-hand bat, wicket-keeper,
right-arm leg-spin bowler
Born: 19 November 1981, Abergavenny
Height: 5ft 9in **Weight:** 11st 13lbs
Nickname: Wally, Gromit, Marcellus, Wash,
Screech, Kyle, Curly
County debut: 1999
County cap: 2003
50 dismissals in a season: 2
Place in batting averages: 143rd av. 30.34
(2005 170th av. 26.64)
Parents: Ryland and Alvine
Marital status: Single
Family links with cricket: 'Father plays for
Abergavenny and Wales Over 50s'
Education: Crickhowell High School;
Glamorgan University

Qualifications: 10 GCSEs, 2 A-levels, Level 2 coach
Career outside cricket: Student
Off-season: 'Studying journalism at Glamorgan University'
Overseas tours: England U19 to New Zealand 1998-99, to Malaysia and (U19 World
Cup) Sri Lanka 1999-2000, to India 2000-01; ECB National Academy to Australia
2001-02, to Australia and Sri Lanka 2002-03; Glamorgan to Guernsey 2006
Overseas teams played for: Port Adelaide Magpies, South Australia 2002-03;
Redlands Tigers, Brisbane 2004-06
Career highlights to date: 'Winning National League 2002. Academy selections
2001-02, 2002-03'
Cricket superstitions: 'Too many to mention. Trying to cut down'
Cricketers particularly admired: Ian Healy, Jimmy Maher, Mike Kasprowicz,
Chris Read, Andy Flower, Brendan McCullum
Young players to look out for: Mark Cosgrove, Samit Patel, Will Bragg,
James Harris, Ryan Watkins
Other sports played: Rugby ('Glamorgan Most Improved Touch Player of Year 2003;
Young Player of Year 2004-06'), boxing, golf, football
Other sports followed: Football (Merthyr Tydfil FC), rugby (Cardiff Blues)
Injuries: Out for one Twenty20 game with a sprained thumb
Favourite band: Shania Twain
Relaxations: 'Golf, TV'
Extras: Represented England U17. Represented England U19 1998, 1999 and 2000
(captain for second 'Test' 2000). Made first-class debut v Somerset at Taunton 1999

aged 17 years 287 days – youngest ever Glamorgan wicket-keeper. NBC Denis Compton Award 1999. Captained ECB National Academy to innings victory over Commonwealth Bank [Australian] Cricket Academy at Adelaide 2001-02. Byron Denning Glamorgan Clubman of the Year Award 2003

Opinions on cricket: 'Too many overs in a day. First-class should mirror Test cricket. How does 40-over cricket help produce players for ODIs? Second XIs don't play enough games. Put a salary cap on overseas players. The exchange rate is so good they will still come.'

Best batting: 121 Glamorgan v Durham, Riverside 2003

2006 Season

	M	Inn	NO	Runs	HS	Avg	100	50	Ct	St	Balls	Runs	Wkts	Avg	BB	5I	10M
Test																	
FC	16	27	4	698	72	30.34	-	5	41	3	0	0	0		-	-	-
ODI																	
List A	17	16	1	236	48	15.73	-	-	16	4	0	0	0		-	-	
20/20 Int																	
20/20	8	4	2	67	35	33.50	-	-	2	3	0	0	0		-	-	

Career Performances

	M	Inn	NO	Runs	HS	Avg	100	50	Ct	St	Balls	Runs	Wkts	Avg	BB	5I	10M
Test																	
FC	102	168	16	4240	121	27.89	4	23	273	16	0	0	0		-	-	-
ODI																	
List A	99	75	15	973	48	16.21	-	-	105	23	0	0	0		-	-	
20/20 Int																	
20/20	27	20	8	261	35	21.75	-	-	10	5	0	0	0		-	-	

90. Which Sri Lanka batsman, now the proud owner of six Test double centuries, made a pair on Test debut v India at Chandigarh in 1990-91?

WALTERS, S. J. Surrey

Name: <u>Stewart</u> Jonathan Walters
Role: Right-hand bat, right-arm medium bowler
Born: 25 June 1983, Mornington, Victoria, Australia
Height: 6ft 1in
Nickname: Forrest
County debut: 2005 (one-day), 2006 (first-class)
Place in batting averages: 163rd av. 27.66
Strike rate: (career 78.00)
Parents: Stewart and Sue
Wife and date of marriage: Jacki, 24 February 2006
Education: Guildford Grammar School, Perth, Western Australia
Overseas teams played for: Midland-Guildford CC, Perth

Career highlights to date: 'First-team debut 2005'
Cricket moments to forget: 'The ducks!'
Cricket superstitions: 'Right pad first'
Cricketers particularly admired: Steve Waugh
Young players to look out for: Rory Hamilton-Brown
Other sports played: Australian Rules football (AFL)
Other sports followed: Football (Man U)
Favourite band: U2
Relaxations: 'Running; spending time with friends'
Extras: Captain of Western Australia U17 for two years
Opinions on cricket: 'Love the tempo of the one-day game; also the temperament of the four-day game and seeing players adjust.'
Best batting: 67 Surrey v Gloucestershire, Bristol 2006
Best bowling: 1-9 Surrey v Derbyshire, Derby 2006

2006 Season

	M	Inn	NO	Runs	HS	Avg	100	50	Ct	St	Balls	Runs	Wkts	Avg	BB	5I	10M
Test																	
FC	3	6	0	166	67	27.66	-	1	3	-	156	69	2	34.50	1-9	-	-
ODI																	
List A	9	7	2	57	18	11.40	-	-	1	-	84	83	1	83.00	1-38	-	
20/20 Int																	
20/20	7	4	1	21	9 *	7.00	-	-	5	-	12	17	0		-	-	

Career Performances

	M	Inn	NO	Runs	HS	Avg	100	50	Ct	St	Balls	Runs	Wkts	Avg	BB	5I	10M
Test																	
FC	3	6	0	166	67	27.66	-	1	3	-	156	69	2	34.50	1-9	-	-
ODI																	
List A	15	13	4	191	32 *	21.22	-	-	5	-	84	83	1	83.00	1-38	-	
20/20 Int																	
20/20	7	4	1	21	9 *	7.00	-	-	5	-	12	17	0		-	-	

WARNE, S. K. Hampshire

Name: <u>Shane</u> Keith Warne
Role: Right-hand bat, leg-spin bowler, county captain
Born: 13 September 1969, Ferntree Gully, Victoria, Australia
Height: 6ft **Weight:** 13st 12lbs
Nickname: Warney
County debut: 2000
County cap: 2000
Test debut: 1991-92
ODI debut: 1992-93
50 wickets in a season: 4
Place in batting averages: 135th av. 30.91 (2005 137th av. 30.91)
Place in bowling averages: 25th av. 27.08 (2005 10th av. 22.50)
Strike rate: 54.17 (career 56.58)
Parents: Keith and Brigite
Marital status: Single
Children: Brooke, 9; Jackson, 7; Summer, 5
Education: Mentone Grammar School; Hampton High School
Off-season: Playing for Australia

Overseas tours: Australia YC to West Indies 1990; Australia B to Zimbabwe 1991-92; Australia to Sri Lanka 1992, to New Zealand 1992-93, to England 1993, to South Africa 1993-94, to Pakistan 1994-95, to West Indies 1994-95, to India, Pakistan and Sri Lanka (World Cup) 1995-96, to South Africa 1996-97, to England 1997, to India 1997-98, to West Indies 1998-99, to UK, Ireland and Netherlands (World Cup) 1999, to Sri Lanka 1999, to Zimbabwe 1999-2000, to New Zealand 1999-2000, to India 2000-01, to England 2001, to South Africa 2001-02, to Sri Lanka (ICC Champions Trophy) 2002-03, to Sri Lanka and Sharjah (v Pakistan) 2002-03, to Sri Lanka 2003-04, to India 2004-05, to New Zealand 2004-05, to England 2005, to South Africa 2005-06, to Bangladesh 2005-06, plus other one-day series and tournaments in Sharjah, Sri Lanka, Pakistan, New Zealand, India, South Africa and Kenya; FICA World XI to New Zealand 2004-05

Overseas teams played for: St Kilda, Victoria; Victoria 1990-91 –

Career highlights to date: '1999 World Cup and being selected for Australia'

Cricket moments to forget: 'Losing to the West Indies by one run in 1992-93 season in Adelaide'

Cricket superstitions: 'I eat pizza the night before I bowl'

Cricketers particularly admired: Sachin Tendulkar, Brian Lara, Ian Chappell, Glenn McGrath

Young players to look out for: Jimmy Adams, Sean Ervine, Michael Clarke

Other sports played: AFL, golf, tennis

Other sports followed: AFL (St Kilda), football (Chelsea)

Favourite band: Rogue Traders, Bruce Springsteen

Relaxations: 'Yoga and kids'

Extras: One of *Wisden*'s Five Cricketers of the Year 1994, one of *South African Cricket Annual*'s five Cricketers of the Year 1994, and one of *Indian Cricket*'s five Cricketers of the Year 1996; voted one of *Wisden*'s Five Cricketers of the Century 2000. Voted Australia's ODI Player of the Year at the inaugural Allan Border Medal awards January 2000. Took hat-trick (DeFreitas, Gough, Malcolm) in the second Test v England at Melbourne 1994-95. Man of the Match in his 100th Test, v South Africa at Cape Town 2001-02 (2-70/6-161). Has won numerous other Test awards, among them Man of the Series v England 1993 (34 wickets; av. 25.79), v Pakistan in Colombo and Sharjah 2002-03 (27 wickets; av. 12.66) and Australia's Man of the Series v England 2005 (40 wickets; av. 19.92). Has also won numerous ODI awards, including Man of the Match in the 1999 World Cup semi-final v South Africa at Edgbaston (4-29) and final v Pakistan at Lord's (4-33). Has captained Australia in ODIs; has now retired from ODI cricket. Took 1000th first-class wicket (Hamish Marshall) in the first Test v New Zealand at Christchurch 2004-05. Was Hampshire's overseas player in 2000; rejoined Hampshire as an overseas player and as captain in 2004. Took 600th Test wicket (Marcus Trescothick) in the third Test v England at Old Trafford 2005. Leading wicket-taker in English first-class cricket 2005 (87; av. 22.50). BBC Overseas Sports Personality of the Year 2005. Leading Test wicket-taker for the calendar year 2005 (96; av. 22.02). Named Australia's Test Player of the Year at the 2006 Allan Border Medal awards. Awarded honorary doctorate for services to cricket by Southampton Solent University at The Rose Bowl 2006 on his 37th birthday

Opinions on cricket: 'Over rates are appalling.'
Best batting: 107* Hampshire v Kent, Canterbury 2005
Best bowling: 8-71 Australia v England, Brisbane 1994-95
Stop press: His 5-39 in England's first innings of the fourth Test at Melbourne 2006-07 included his 700th Test wicket (Andrew Strauss). Retired from Test cricket after the fifth Test v England at Sydney 2006-07

2006 Season

	M	Inn	NO	Runs	HS	Avg	100	50	Ct	St	Balls	Runs	Wkts	Avg	BB	5I	10M
Test																	
FC	13	17	5	371	61*	30.91	-	2	16	-	3142	1571	58	27.08	7-99	4	-
ODI																	
List A	12	10	0	97	30	9.70	-	-	5	-	455	327	23	14.21	6-42	1	
20/20 Int																	
20/20																	

Career Performances

	M	Inn	NO	Runs	HS	Avg	100	50	Ct	St	Balls	Runs	Wkts	Avg	BB	5I	10M
Test	140	194	16	2958	99	16.61	-	11	120	-	39257	17297	685	25.25	8-71	36	10
FC	278	379	47	6342	107*	19.10	2	24	239	-	69934	31855	1236	25.77	8-71	62	11
ODI	194	107	29	1018	55	13.05	-	1	80	-	10642	7541	293	25.73	5-33	1	
List A	297	189	35	1819	55	11.81	-	1	119	-	15699	11088	452	24.53	6-42	3	
20/20 Int																	
20/20	2	2	0	12	12	6.00	-	-	-	-	48	51	1	51.00	1-29	-	

91. Who became the first Hong Kong-born Test cricketer when he made his England debut against New Zealand in 1991-92?

WARREN, R. J.   Nottinghamshire

Name: <u>Russell</u> John Warren
Role: Right-hand bat, wicket-keeper
Born: 10 September 1971, Northampton
Height: 6ft 2in **Weight:** 13st 4lbs
Nickname: Rab C, Rabbit
County debut: 1992 (Northamptonshire),
2003 (Nottinghamshire)
County cap: 1995 (Northamptonshire),
2004 (Nottinghamshire)
1000 runs in a season: 1
1st-Class 200s: 1
Place in batting averages: 225th av. 17.50
(2005 158th av. 29.25)
Parents: John and Sally
Wife and date of marriage: Kate,
November 2004
Education: Kingsthorpe Middle and Upper
Schools

Qualifications: 8 O-levels, 2 A-levels
Overseas tours: England YC to New Zealand 1990-91; Northamptonshire to Cape
Town 1993, to Zimbabwe 1995, to Johannesburg 1996, to Grenada 2000;
Nottinghamshire to Pretoria 2003
Overseas teams played for: Lancaster Park, Christchurch, and Canterbury B, New
Zealand 1991-93; Riverside CC, Lower Hutt, New Zealand 1994-95; Petone CC,
Wellington, New Zealand 1995-96; Alma Marist CC, Cape Town, South Africa
1997-98
Cricketers particularly admired: Allan Lamb, Wayne Larkins
Other sports played: Golf, snooker
Other sports followed: Football (Manchester United, Northampton Town,
Nottingham Forest), rugby (Northampton Saints), golf, snooker and horse racing
Favourite band: The Thrills
Relaxations: 'Music, watching golf'
Extras: Scored 144 v Somerset at Taunton 2001, in the process sharing with Mike
Hussey (208) in a record third-wicket partnership for Northamptonshire in matches
against Somerset (287). Scored century in each innings (123/113*) v Middlesex at
Lord's 2003. Released by Nottinghamshire at the end of the 2006 season
Best batting: 201* Northamptonshire v Glamorgan, Northampton 1996

2006 Season

	M	Inn	NO	Runs	HS	Avg	100	50	Ct	St	Balls	Runs	Wkts	Avg	BB	5I	10M
Test																	
FC	5	8	0	140	93	17.50	-	1	3	-	0	0	0		-	-	-
ODI																	
List A	1	1	0	4	4	4.00	-	-	2	-	0	0	0		-	-	
20/20 Int																	
20/20																	

Career Performances

	M	Inn	NO	Runs	HS	Avg	100	50	Ct	St	Balls	Runs	Wkts	Avg	BB	5I	10M
Test																	
FC	146	238	26	7776	201 *	36.67	15	41	128	5	6	0	0		-	-	-
ODI																	
List A	177	162	25	3363	100 *	24.54	1	15	135	11	0	0	0		-	-	
20/20 Int																	
20/20	2	1	0	26	26	26.00	-	-	-	-	0	0	0		-	-	

WATERS, H. T.   Glamorgan

Name: <u>Huw</u> Thomas Waters
Role: Right-hand bat, right-arm
medium-fast bowler
Born: 26 September 1986, Cardiff
Height: 6ft 2in **Weight:** 13st 5lbs
Nickname: Muddy
County debut: 2005
Place in bowling averages: 56th av. 31.66
(2005 59th av. 30.18)
Strike rate: 55.75 (career 55.17)
Parents: Valerie and Donald
Marital status: Single
Family links with cricket: 'Long line of
club cricketers, most notably Big Don, a
stalwart of the old 3 Counties League'
Education: Llantarnam CS; Monmouth
School

Qualifications: 8 GCSEs, 'a couple of
A-levels – somehow!', Level 2 cricket coach
Off-season: 'Getting fitter and stronger. Home learning business course with ICS'
Overseas tours: West Region to West Indies 2002; Wales U16 to Jersey 2002;
Monmouth School to St Lucia 2003; England U19 to Bangladesh 2005-06, to Sri
Lanka (U19 World Cup) 2005-06

Career highlights to date: 'Making debut. Taking my first "five-for"'
Cricketers particularly admired: Glenn McGrath
Young players to look out for: 'Our academy boys'
Other sports played: Football ('mainly during warm-ups')
Other sports followed: Football (Man United)
Injuries: Shin splints
Favourite band: Coldplay, 'any indie rock'
Relaxations: 'Pro Evo Soccer, listening to music, watching films, chilling out with friends'
Extras: Played for Wales Minor Counties in the C&G 2005 and in Minor Counties competitions 2004-06
Opinions on cricket: 'Gaining more interest due to Twenty20. Should just have one one-day competition. Glad only one overseas – means youngsters get more of a chance.'
Best batting: 34 Glamorgan v Kent, Canterbury 2005
Best bowling: 5-86 Glamorgan v Somerset, Taunton 2006

2006 Season

	M	Inn	NO	Runs	HS	Avg	100	50	Ct	St	Balls	Runs	Wkts	Avg	BB	5I	10M
Test																	
FC	5	7	2	7	5 *	1.40	-	-	1	-	669	380	12	31.66	5-86	1	-
ODI																	
List A	1	0	0	0	0		-	-	-	-	60	47	0		-	-	
20/20 Int																	
20/20																	

Career Performances

	M	Inn	NO	Runs	HS	Avg	100	50	Ct	St	Balls	Runs	Wkts	Avg	BB	5I	10M
Test																		
FC	12	20	9	48	34	4.36	-	-	1	-	1269	712	23	30.95	5-86	1	-
ODI																	
List A	2	1	0	8	8	8.00	-	-	-	-	90	60	0		-	-	
20/20 Int																	
20/20																	

WATKINS, R. E.   Glamorgan

Name: Ryan Edward Watkins
Role: Left-hand bat, right-arm fast-medium bowler; all-rounder
Born: 9 June 1983, Abergavenny, Monmouthshire
Height: 6ft **Weight:** 14st
Nickname: Tetanus, Maverick, Hannibal, Big Red, Commando, Pete, Ting
County debut: 2003 (one-day), 2005 (first-class)
Place in batting averages: 185th av. 24.08 (2005 253rd av. 14.55)
Place in bowling averages: 138th av. 48.52
Strike rate: 72.89 (career 73.04)
Parents: Huw and Gaynor
Wife and date of marriage: Lisa, 16 October 2005
Pets: Missy (dog), 11 February 2004
Family links with cricket: 'Father and brother club cricketers'
Education: Pontllanfraith Comprehensive School; Crosskeys College
Qualifications: Level 2 coach, qualified tyre and exhaust fitter
Career outside cricket: 'Private investigator'
Off-season: 'Working on my game and my fitness'
Overseas tours: Glamorgan to Guernsey 2006
Overseas teams played for: North Balwyn CC, Victoria, Australia 2003
Career highlights to date: 'Playing at Lord's. Glamorgan debut. Beating Gareth Rees in a sprint race at Cheltenham 2006'
Cricket moments to forget: 'Getting a first-ball duck live on Sky against Durham, needing one to win off the last ball'
Cricket superstitions: 'Right pad on first'
Cricketers particularly admired: 'All the Glammy boys'
Young players to look out for: Tom Baker
Other sports played: Football ('recently retired from Ynysddu Welfare FC'), golf
Other sports followed: Football (Tottenham Hotspur), rugby (Cardiff Blues)
Injuries: Out for six months with an osteochondrial defect in the left knee
Favourite band: Pharrell Williams, N.E.R.D., Busta Rhymes
Relaxations: 'Walking my boxer dog, Missy'
Extras: Made 2nd XI Championship debut 2001. Played for Wales Minor Counties in Minor Counties competitions 2003-06
Opinions on cricket: 'More overs in a day's play, PLEASE.'
Best batting: 87 Glamorgan v Essex, Cardiff 2006
Best bowling: 4-40 Glamorgan v Worcestershire, Worcester 2006

2006 Season

	M	Inn	NO	Runs	HS	Avg	100	50	Ct	St	Balls	Runs	Wkts	Avg	BB	5I	10M
Test																	
FC	14	25	2	554	87	24.08	-	2	12	-	1385	922	19	48.52	4-40	-	-
ODI																	
List A	10	7	2	68	28 *	13.60	-	-	1	-	319	341	8	42.62	2-25	-	
20/20 Int																	
20/20																	

Career Performances

	M	Inn	NO	Runs	HS	Avg	100	50	Ct	St	Balls	Runs	Wkts	Avg	BB	5I	10M
Test																	
FC	19	34	2	685	87	21.40	-	2	12	-	1607	1047	22	47.59	4-40	-	-
ODI																	
List A	14	11	2	120	28 *	13.33	-	-	1	-	429	464	11	42.18	2-25	-	
20/20 Int																	
20/20	3	1	1	6	6 *		-	-	2	-	30	49	2	24.50	2-8	-	

WATKINSON, M.   Lancashire

Name: Michael Watkinson
Role: Right-hand bat, right-arm medium or off-spin bowler
Born: 1 August 1961, Westhoughton, Greater Manchester
Height: 6ft 1½in **Weight:** 13st
Nickname: Winker
County debut: 1982
County cap: 1987
Benefit: 1996 (£209,000)
Test debut: 1995
ODI debut: 1995-96
1000 runs in a season: 1
50 wickets in a season: 7
Strike rate: (career 64.68)
Parents: Albert and Marian
Wife and date of marriage: Susan, 12 April 1986
Children: Charlotte, 24 February 1989; Liam, 27 July 1991
Education: Rivington and Blackrod High School, Horwich
Qualifications: 8 O-levels, HTC Civil Engineering
Career outside cricket: Draughtsman

Overseas tours: England to South Africa 1995-96
Cricketers particularly admired: Clive Lloyd, Imran Khan
Other sports followed: Football
Relaxations: Watching Bolton Wanderers
Extras: Played for Cheshire in Minor Counties Championship and in NatWest Trophy (v Middlesex) 1982. Man of the Match in the first Refuge Assurance Cup final 1988 and for his 50 plus 2-37 in B&H Cup final 1990. Lancashire captain 1994-97, leading the county to one NatWest and two B&H titles. Lancashire Player of the Year 1995. 2nd XI captain and coach 2000-01. Cricket manager since 2002; retired as player but registration retained
Best batting: 161 Lancashire v Essex, Old Trafford 1995
Best bowling: 8-30 Lancashire v Hampshire, Old Trafford 1994

2006 Season (did not make any first-class or one-day appearances)

Career Performances

	M	Inn	NO	Runs	HS	Avg	100	50	Ct	St	Balls	Runs	Wkts	Avg	BB	5I	10M
Test	4	6	1	167	82 *	33.40	-	1	1	-	672	348	10	34.80	3-64	-	-
FC	308	459	49	10939	161	26.68	11	50	156	-	47805	24960	739	33.77	8-30	27	3
ODI	1	0	0	0	0		-	-	-	-	54	43	0		-	-	
List A	376	296	61	5398	130	22.97	2	20	98	-	16057	12152	381	31.89	5-44	3	
20/20 Int																	
20/20																	

92. Who became the first British-born Asian
to play first-team cricket for Yorkshire when he made his
one-day debut v Worcestershire in 2004?

WEDGE, S. A.   Worcestershire

Name: Stuart (<u>Stu</u>) Andrew Wedge
Role: Left-hand bat, left-arm medium bowler
Born: 24 October 1985, Wolverhampton
Height: 5ft 11in **Weight:** 11st 2lbs
Nickname: Wedgey
County debut: 2005
County colours: 2005
Strike rate: (career 54.22)
Parents: Barrie and Ann
Marital status: Single
Education: Codsall High School;
Rodbaston College
Qualifications: 9 GCSEs, 1 A-level
Career highlights to date: 'Taking five
wickets on my County Championship debut'
Cricket superstitions: 'Have four paces
before I hit my bowling mark'
Cricketers particularly admired: Courtney
Walsh, Brian Lara
Other sports played: Golf
Other sports followed: Rugby, football
Favourite band: 'No one in particular'
Relaxations: 'Golf, rugby, music, PlayStation, eating, snooker/pool'
Extras: Took 5-112 in first innings of Championship debut v Essex at Worcester 2005
Opinions on cricket: 'I think that cricket in this country is on the way up... There are
a lot of young English cricketers coming through the ranks, which can only be a
positive thing. The majority of our county teams to be made up of home-grown talent,
with the excitement of the overseas players to give it that extra. In the end the players
need to provide entertainment to the public, without sacrificing the young players who
will provide and make up the England team of the future.'
Best bowling: 5-112 Worcestershire v Essex, Worcester 2005

2006 Season

	M	Inn	NO	Runs	HS	Avg	100	50	Ct	St	Balls	Runs	Wkts	Avg	BB	5I	10M
Test																	
FC	2	0	0	0	0	-	-	-	-	-	162	108	4	27.00	3-11	-	-
ODI																	
List A	1	0	0	0	0	-	-	1	-		31	31	2	15.50	2-31	-	
20/20 Int																	
20/20	1	0	0	0	0	-	-	-	-	-	12	27	0		-	-	

Career Performances

	M	Inn	NO	Runs	HS	Avg	100	50	Ct	St	Balls	Runs	Wkts	Avg	BB	5I	10M
Test																	
FC	4	2	2	0	0*	-	-	-	-	-	488	319	9	35.44	5-112	1	-
ODI																	
List A	1	0	0	0	0			-	1	-	31	31	2	15.50	2-31	-	
20/20 Int																	
20/20	1	0	0	0	0	-	-	-	-	-	12	27	0			-	-

WEEKES, P. N.   Middlesex

Name: <u>Paul</u> Nicholas Weekes
Role: Left-hand bat, right-arm
off-spin bowler; all-rounder
Born: 8 July 1969, Hackney, London
Height: 5ft 10½in **Weight:** 12st 2lbs
Nickname: Twidds, Weekesy
County debut: 1990
County cap: 1993
Benefit: 2002
1000 runs in a season: 2
Place in batting averages: 132nd av. 31.63
(2005 57th av. 44.31)
Place in bowling averages: (2005 142nd
av. 54.64)
Strike rate: (career 85.23)
Parents: Robert
Marital status: Single
Children: Cherie, 4 September 1993;
Shyann, 3 May 1998

Family links with cricket: Father played club cricket
Education: Homerton House, Hackney; Hackney College
Qualifications: Level 2 coaching award
Career outside cricket: Cricket coach – Middlesex Youth squads and Hackney
Cricket Academy
Overseas tours: England A to India and Bangladesh 1994-95; Middlesex to
Johannesburg; three tours with BWIA to the West Indies
Overseas teams played for: Newcastle University, NSW 1988-89; Sunrise CC,
Harare 1990-91
Career highlights: 'Scoring 171* and 160 in the same match, v Somerset at Uxbridge
1996'
Cricket moments to forget: 'Getting a pair against Essex'

Cricketers particularly admired: Viv Richards, Courtney Walsh, Brian Lara
Favourite band: Burning Flames, Jay-Z
Relaxations: DIY
Extras: Scored fifty in debut innings for both second and first teams. Took two catches whilst appearing as 12th man for England in the second Test against West Indies at Lord's in 1995. Middlesex Player of the Year 1999, 2004. First Englishman to score more than 150 in both innings of a first-class game. Won seven one-day Man of the Match awards (three NatWest/C&G; four B&H). Captained Middlesex to their one-day victory over the Australians at Lord's 2001. Retired at the end of the 2006 season
Best batting: 171* Middlesex v Somerset, Uxbridge 1996
Best bowling: 8-39 Middlesex v Glamorgan, Lord's 1996

2006 Season

	M	Inn	NO	Runs	HS	Avg	100	50	Ct	St	Balls	Runs	Wkts	Avg	BB	5I	10M
Test																	
FC	8	15	4	348	128 *	31.63	1	-	-	-	651	338	5	67.60	1-19	-	-
ODI																	
List A	12	12	0	169	50	14.08	-	1	3	-	282	262	5	52.40	3-12	-	
20/20 Int																	
20/20	8	8	1	175	49	25.00	-	-	1	-	120	175	4	43.75	3-29	-	

Career Performances

	M	Inn	NO	Runs	HS	Avg	100	50	Ct	St	Balls	Runs	Wkts	Avg	BB	5I	10M
Test																	
FC	236	372	55	11060	171 *	34.88	20	55	210	-	25911	12759	304	41.97	8-39	5	-
ODI																	
List A	323	289	41	7632	143 *	30.77	9	46	138	-	11968	9618	329	29.23	4-17	-	
20/20 Int																	
20/20	23	21	4	516	56	30.35	-	2	5	-	390	527	10	52.70	3-29	-	

WELCH, G.   Derbyshire

Name: Graeme Welch
Role: Right-hand bat, right-arm medium-fast bowler
Born: 21 March 1972, Durham
Height: 6ft **Weight:** 13st
Nickname: Pop
County debut: 1992 (one-day, Warwickshire), 1994 (first-class, Warwickshire), 2001 (Derbyshire)
County cap: 1997 (Warwickshire), 2001 (Derbyshire)
Benefit: 2007 (Derbyshire)
50 wickets in a season: 4
Place in batting averages: 212th av. 19.61 (2005 132nd av. 31.46)

Place in bowling averages: 68th av. 33.27
(2005 28th av. 25.98)
Strike rate: 65.25 (career 59.64)
Parents: Jean and Robert
Wife and date of marriage: Emma,
4 October 1997
Children: Ethan, 4 April 2000
Family links with cricket: Brother and
father club cricketers in Leeds and
Durham respectively
Education: Hetton Comprehensive
Qualifications: 9 GCSEs, City and
Guilds in Sports and Leisure, senior
coaching award
Career outside cricket: Coaching
Overseas tours: Warwickshire to Cape Town
1992-97; England XI to New Zealand
(Cricket Max) 1997

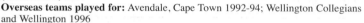

Overseas teams played for: Avendale, Cape Town 1992-94; Wellington Collegians
and Wellington 1996
Career highlights to date: 'Winning the treble with Warwickshire in 1994'
Cricket moments to forget: 'Benson and Hedges game against Lancashire in 1995'
Cricketers particularly admired: Brian Lara, Allan Donald, Sachin Tendulkar
Other sports played: Football
Other sports followed: Football (Newcastle United)
Relaxations: 'A beer at The Brook; spending time with Emma and Ethan'
Extras: Represented England YC. Warwickshire's Most Improved Player 1994. Won
seven trophies with Warwickshire 1994-97. Derbyshire Player of the Year 2005.
Captain of Derbyshire 2006
Best batting: 115* Derbyshire v Leicestershire, Oakham School 2004
Best bowling: 6-30 Derbyshire v Durham, Riverside 2001

93. Which current county captain scored his side's only fifty
of the match on Test debut v West Indies in 1992-93?

2006 Season

	M	Inn	NO	Runs	HS	Avg	100	50	Ct	St	Balls	Runs	Wkts	Avg	BB	5I	10M
Test																	
FC	15	23	5	353	94	19.61	-	2	8	-	2349	1198	36	33.27	4-33	-	-
ODI																	
List A	10	9	2	178	50	25.42	-	1	1	-	416	287	0		-	-	
20/20 Int																	
20/20	8	5	0	39	17	7.80	-	-	-	-	143	220	6	36.66	3-31	-	

Career Performances

	M	Inn	NO	Runs	HS	Avg	100	50	Ct	St	Balls	Runs	Wkts	Avg	BB	5I	10M
Test																	
FC	171	265	43	5075	115 *	22.86	2	21	73	-	28450	15034	477	31.51	6-30	17	1
ODI																	
List A	224	176	46	2582	82	19.86	-	8	32	-	9600	7009	197	35.57	6-31	3	
20/20 Int																	
20/20	24	18	2	152	20	9.50	-	-	3	-	401	613	11	55.72	3-31	-	

WESSELS, M. H.　　　　　　　　Northamptonshire

Name: Mattheus Hendrik (<u>Riki</u>) Wessels
Role: Right-hand bat, wicket-keeper
Born: 12 November 1985, Nambour, Australia
Height: 5ft 11in **Weight:** 10st 10lbs
Nickname: Blood, Moose
County debut: 2005
Place in batting averages: 189th av. 23.53 (2005 141st av. 30.65)
Parents: Kepler and Sally
Marital status: Single
Family links with cricket: 'My dad played a little bit' (*Kepler Wessels played Test and ODI cricket for Australia and South Africa between 1982-83 and 1994-95*)
Education: Woodridge College, Port Elizabeth; University College of Northampton
Qualifications: Coach
Cricket moments to forget: 'Losing in the 2nd XI [Trophy] semi-final by nine wickets [2004]'
Cricket superstitions: 'Lucky shirt'
Cricketers particularly admired: 'My dad and Justin Langer'
Young players to look out for: Alex Wakely

Other sports played: Hockey
Other sports followed: Rugby (Queensland Reds)
Favourite band: Linkin Park
Relaxations: 'Reading autobiographies'
Extras: Northamptonshire Academy Players' Player of the Year 2004. Northamptonshire Young Player of the Year (Frank Rudd Trophy) 2004. Made first-class debut for MCC v West Indians at Arundel 2004. Scored maiden first-class century (102) v Somerset at Northampton 2005 after coming to the wicket on a hat-trick ball
Best batting: 107 Northamptonshire v Durham, Riverside 2005

2006 Season

	M	Inn	NO	Runs	HS	Avg	100	50	Ct	St	Balls	Runs	Wkts	Avg	BB	5I	10M
Test																	
FC	10	17	2	353	62	23.53	-	2	27	1	0	0	0		-	-	-
ODI																	
List A	10	10	1	153	39	17.00	-	-	6	-	0	0	0		-	-	
20/20 Int																	
20/20	9	6	2	119	44	29.75	-	-	3	5	0	0	0		-	-	

Career Performances

	M	Inn	NO	Runs	HS	Avg	100	50	Ct	St	Balls	Runs	Wkts	Avg	BB	5I	10M
Test																	
FC	25	42	5	1001	107	27.05	3	4	54	6	0	0	0		-	-	-
ODI																	
List A	26	22	4	404	80	22.44	-	1	23	-	0	0	0		-	-	
20/20 Int																	
20/20	16	13	4	210	49 *	23.33	-	-	6	6	0	0	0		-	-	

94. Which England batsman scored a century on Test debut
v Australia at Trent Bridge in 1993?

WESTFIELD, M. S.   Essex

Name: Mervyn (<u>Merv</u>) Simon Westfield
Role: Right-hand bat, right-arm fast bowler
Born: 5 May 1988, Romford
Height: 6ft 1in **Weight:** 12st
Nickname: Swerve
County debut: 2005
Strike rate: (career 52.28)
Parents: Pamela and Mervyn
Marital status: Single
Family links with cricket: 'Dad used to play
cricket and my older brother played for Essex
for a couple of years'
Education: The Chafford School; Havering
College

Qualifications: 8 GCSEs, Level 1 coaching
Career outside cricket: 'College'
Off-season: 'Working with my top-drawer
bowling coach Ian Pont'
Overseas tours: England U16 to South Africa 2004-05; England U19 to Malaysia
2006-07
Career highlights to date: 'Taking four wickets against Somerset and scoring 32 runs
as well in 2006'
Cricketers particularly admired: Andy Flower, Andy Bichel
Young players to look out for: Maurice Chambers, Tom Westley, Adil Rashid
Other sports followed: Football (Manchester United)
Favourite band: TOK
Relaxations: 'Socialising with friends, listening to music'
Extras: Wanstead U11 Young Player of the Year 1997. Wanstead U11 All-Rounder of
1998. Havering District U13 Best Innings 2000. MCC Cricketer of the Year 2003,
2004. *Daily Telegraph* Bunbury Scholar 2003 (Best Fast Bowler; scholarship entailed
a week's training with England A)
Best batting: 32 Essex v Somerset, Southend 2006
Best bowling: 4-72 Essex v Somerset, Southend 2006

2006 Season

	M	Inn	NO	Runs	HS	Avg	100	50	Ct	St	Balls	Runs	Wkts	Avg	BB	5I	10M
Test																	
FC	3	4	2	41	32	20.50	-	-	1	-	258	180	6	30.00	4-72	-	-
ODI																	
List A	2	2	2	6	4 *		-	-	1	-	36	38	0			-	-
20/20 Int																	
20/20																	

Career Performances

	M	Inn	NO	Runs	HS	Avg	100	50	Ct	St	Balls	Runs	Wkts	Avg	BB	5I	10M
Test																	
FC	4	6	2	41	32	10.25	-	-	1	-	366	270	7	38.57	4-72	-	-
ODI																	
List A	2	2	2	6	4 *		-	-	1	-	36	38	0			-	-
20/20 Int																	
20/20																	

WESTLEY, T.   Essex

Name: Thomas (<u>Tom</u>) Westley
Role: Right-hand top-order bat, right-arm off-spin bowler
Born: 13 March 1989, Cambridge
Height: 6ft 2in
Nickname: Spongebob, Pup
County debut: 2006 (one-day)
Parents: Ade and Mags
Family links with cricket: 'Dad has played village club cricket in Cambridgeshire, along with uncle and brother'
Education: Linton Village College; Hills Road Sixth Form College
Off-season: 'Trying to do some college work. Two-week tour to World Cricket Academy in Mumbai with Essex'
Overseas tours: England U16 to South Africa 2004-05
Career highlights to date: 'Selection for England U15, U16 and U17. First-team debut for Essex v Sri Lanka 2006'
Cricket moments to forget: 'King pair against Surrey 2nd XI 2005'
Cricket superstitions: 'Mark my crease three times before every over and after every boundary'

Cricketers particularly admired: Steve Waugh, Sachin Tendulkar, Andy Flower, Alastair Cook
Young players to look out for: Mervyn Westfield, Adam Wheater
Other sports followed: Football (Newcastle United)
Extras: Is Essex Academy pro

2006 Season

	M	Inn	NO	Runs	HS	Avg	100	50	Ct	St	Balls	Runs	Wkts	Avg	BB	5I	10M
Test																	
FC																	
ODI																	
List A	1	0	0	0	0		-	-	-	-	0	0	0		-	-	
20/20 Int																	
20/20																	

Career Performances

	M	Inn	NO	Runs	HS	Avg	100	50	Ct	St	Balls	Runs	Wkts	Avg	BB	5I	10M
Test																	
FC																	
ODI																	
List A	1	0	0	0	0		-	-	-	-	0	0	0		-	-	
20/20 Int																	
20/20																	

WESTON, W. P. C. — Derbyshire

Name: William Philip Christopher Weston
Role: Left-hand bat, left-arm medium bowler
Born: 16 June 1973, Durham City
Height: 6ft 4in **Weight:** 14st
Nickname: Tickle, Weso
County debut: 1991 (Worcestershire), 2003 (Gloucestershire)
County cap: 1995; colours, 2002 (both Worcestershire), 2004 (Gloucestershire)
1000 runs in a season: 4
1st-Class 200s: 1
Place in batting averages: 76th av. 39.60 (2005 155th av. 29.58)
Strike rate: (career 200.20)
Parents: Michael and Kate (deceased)
Wife and date of marriage: Sarah, 30 September 2000
Family links with cricket: Brother Robin played for Durham, Derbyshire and Middlesex. Father played Minor Counties cricket for Durham (and rugby union for England)
Education: Durham School

Qualifications: 9 GCSEs, 4 A-levels, Diploma in Business and Management

Career outside cricket: 'Hoping to pursue a career in property'

Overseas tours: England U18 to Canada (International Youth Tournament) 1991 (vc); England YC to New Zealand 1990-91; England U19 to Pakistan 1991-92 (c); Worcestershire to Zimbabwe 1996

Overseas teams played for: Melville, Perth 1992-94, 1996-97; Swanbourne, Perth 1995-96

Career highlights to date: '2004 C&G final'

Cricket superstitions: 'Not really'

Cricketers particularly admired: Ian Botham

Other sports played: 'Have a go at most sports'

Other sports followed: Rugby union, football (Sunderland AFC)

Favourite band: U2

Relaxations: 'Spending time with my lovely wife; travelling, films, hanging out with friends'

Extras: Represented England YC 1991 and England U19 1992 (Man of the Series). Cricket Society's Most Promising Young Cricketer 1992. Worcestershire Uncapped Player of the Year 1992. C&G Man of the Match award for his 106 v Netherlands at Amstelveen 2004. Scored century (110*) in the C&G final v Worcestershire at Lord's 2004. Left Gloucestershire at the end of the 2006 season and has joined Derbyshire for 2007

Best batting: 205 Worcestershire v Northamptonshire, Northampton 1997

Best bowling: 2-39 Worcestershire v Pakistanis, Worcester 1992

---

95. Who returned match figures of 13-135 in his first Test as captain of his country, v Zimbabwe in 1993-94?

2006 Season

	M	Inn	NO	Runs	HS	Avg	100	50	Ct	St	Balls	Runs	Wkts	Avg	BB	5I	10M
Test																	
FC	13	24	1	911	130	39.60	2	6	7	-	0	0	0		-	-	-
ODI																	
List A	11	11	0	206	54	18.72	-	1	1	-	0	0	0		-	-	
20/20 Int																	
20/20																	

Career Performances

	M	Inn	NO	Runs	HS	Avg	100	50	Ct	St	Balls	Runs	Wkts	Avg	BB	5I	10M
Test																	
FC	228	402	34	12591	205	34.21	24	64	128	-	1001	658	5	131.60	2-39	-	-
ODI																	
List A	192	177	13	4116	134	25.09	4	21	44	-	6	2	1	2.00	1-2	-	
20/20 Int																	
20/20	7	5	2	167	73 *	55.66	-	1	3	-	0	0	0		-	-	

WESTWOOD, I. J.　　Warwickshire

Name: <u>Ian</u> James Westwood
Role: Left-hand opening bat, right-arm off-spinner
Born: 13 July 1982, Birmingham
Height: 5ft 7½in　**Weight:** 11st
Nickname: Westy, Tomato Head, Wezzo, Sammy Lee, Tot
County debut: 2003
Place in batting averages: 67th av. 42.50 (2005 106th av. 34.66)
Strike rate: (career 68.00)
Parents: Ann and David
Marital status: Single
Family links with cricket: 'Brother represented Warwickshire Schools from 11 to 16'
Education: Wheelers Lane; Solihull Sixth Form College
Qualifications: 8 GCSEs, BTEC Sports Science
Overseas tours: Warwickshire Development squad to Cape Town 1998
Overseas teams played for: Hawkesbury CC, Sydney 2001-02; Subiaco Marist CC, Perth 2002-03
Cricket superstitions: 'Put right pad on first'

Cricketers particularly admired: Brian Lara, Nick Knight
Other sports played: Football (Coleshill Town FC 2001; Moseley Mariners FC)
Other sports followed: Football (Birmingham City)
Favourite band: Fleetwood Mac
Relaxations: 'Music, films, fruit machines, socialising'
Extras: Scored 250* v Worcestershire 2nd XI at Barnt Green 2003, sharing with Jonathan Trott (248) in an opening partnership of 429; also took 6-104 in Worcestershire 2nd XI's only innings
Best batting: 178 Warwickshire v West Indies A, Edgbaston 2006
Best bowling: 2-46 Warwickshire v Kent, Edgbaston 2006

2006 Season

	M	Inn	NO	Runs	HS	Avg	100	50	Ct	St	Balls	Runs	Wkts	Avg	BB	5I	10M
Test																	
FC	13	23	3	850	178	42.50	2	4	5	-	138	58	2	29.00	2-46	-	-
ODI																	
List A	3	3	1	74	48	37.00	-	-	-	-	0	0	0			-	-
20/20 Int																	
20/20	5	2	2	27	19 *		-	-	1	-	48	78	5	15.60	3-29	-	

Career Performances

	M	Inn	NO	Runs	HS	Avg	100	50	Ct	St	Balls	Runs	Wkts	Avg	BB	5I	10M
Test																	
FC	26	48	7	1534	178	37.41	3	7	11	-	204	145	3	48.33	2-46	-	-
ODI																	
List A	13	10	4	186	55	31.00	-	1	2	-	180	139	2	69.50	1-28	-	
20/20 Int																	
20/20	7	4	4	32	19 *		-	-	1	-	48	78	5	15.60	3-29	-	

96. Who was the first England batsman to score a century
in each innings of a Test v West Indies?

WHARF, A. G. B. Glamorgan

Name: Alexander (<u>Alex</u>) George Busfield Wharf
Role: Right-hand bat, right-arm fast-medium bowler; all-rounder
Born: 4 June 1975, Bradford
Height: 6ft 4in **Weight:** 15st
Nickname: Gangster
County debut: 1994 (Yorks), 1998 (Notts), 2000 (Glamorgan)
County cap: 2000 (Glamorgan)
ODI debut: 2004
50 wickets in a season: 1
Place in batting averages: 142nd av. 30.53 (2005 218th av. 20.47)
Place in bowling averages: 142nd av. 51.73 (2005 121st av. 44.46)
Strike rate: 83.00 (career 58.53)
Parents: Jane and Derek
Wife and date of marriage: Shelley Jane, 1 December 2001
Children: Tristan Jack Busfield Wharf, 15 November 1997; Alf Alexander Busfield Wharf, 30 June 2001
Family links with cricket: Father played local cricket and brother Simon plays local cricket
Education: Buttershaw Upper School; Thomas Danby College
Qualifications: 6 GCSEs, City & Guilds in Sports Management, NCA coaching award, junior football coaching award
Overseas tours: England to Zimbabwe (one-day series) 2004-05, to South Africa 2004-05 (one-day series); England VI to Hong Kong 2005; England A to West Indies 2005-06; various pre-season tours with Yorkshire, Nottinghamshire and Glamorgan
Overseas teams played for: Somerset West, Cape Town 1993-95; Johnsonville CC, Wellington, New Zealand 1996-97; Universities, Wellington 1998-99
Cricket moments to forget: 'Too many to mention'
Cricket superstitions: 'None'
Cricketers particularly admired: Ian Botham
Other sports played: Football
Other sports followed: Football (Manchester United, Bradford City)
Relaxations: 'Spending time with family and friends, movies, PlayStation 2, eating (too much), TV, gym, football'
Extras: Took hat-trick (Wagg, Knight, Pretorius) v Warwickshire at Edgbaston in the totesport League 2004. Had figures of 6-5 v Kent at Cardiff in the totesport League 2004 (match reduced to 25 overs a side). Made ODI debut v India at Trent Bridge in

the NatWest Challenge 2004, taking a wicket in each of his first three overs, finishing with 3-30 and winning Man of the Match award
Best batting: 113 Glamorgan v Nottinghamshire, Cardiff 2005
Best bowling: 6-59 Glamorgan v Gloucestershire, Bristol 2005

2006 Season

	M	Inn	NO	Runs	HS	Avg	100	50	Ct	St	Balls	Runs	Wkts	Avg	BB	5I	10M
Test																	
FC	10	15	2	397	86	30.53	-	3	9	-	1577	983	19	51.73	4-67	-	-
ODI																	
List A	8	8	0	109	23	13.62	-	-	5	-	324	316	11	28.72	3-43		
20/20 Int																	
20/20	8	5	3	57	19	28.50	-	-	-	-	168	280	11	25.45	4-39		

Career Performances

	M	Inn	NO	Runs	HS	Avg	100	50	Ct	St	Balls	Runs	Wkts	Avg	BB	5I	10M
Test																	
FC	96	144	22	2607	113	21.36	3	12	53	-	13815	8783	236	37.21	6-59	5	1
ODI	13	5	3	19	9	9.50	-	-	1	-	584	428	18	23.77	4-24	-	
List A	129	88	19	1207	72	17.49	-	1	37	-	5496	4581	151	30.33	6-5	1	
20/20 Int																	
20/20	18	12	4	112	19	14.00	-	-	2	-	385	594	27	22.00	4-39	-	

WHELAN, C. D. Middlesex

Name: Christopher (Chris) David Whelan
Role: Right-hand bat, right-arm fast bowler
Born: 8 May 1986, Liverpool
Height: 6ft 2in **Weight:** 13st
Nickname: R-Kid, Wheelo, Scouse
County debut: 2004 (one-day), 2005 (first-class)
Strike rate: (career 35.71)
Parents: Sue and Dave
Marital status: Single
Family links with cricket: 'Dad was an accomplished left-hand opening bat'
Education: St Margaret's High School
Qualifications: 11 GCSEs, 3 A-levels, Level 1 coaching
Off-season: 'Attending Dennis Lillee fast bowling camp'

Overseas tours: Middlesex to Mumbai 2004-05, 2005-06
Overseas teams played for: Randwick-Petersham, Sydney 2005-06
Career highlights to date: 'Playing at Lord's – Pro40 debut'
Cricket superstitions: 'Clean socks every session'
Cricketers particularly admired: Brett Lee
Young players to look out for: Chris Wright, Eoin Morgan
Other sports played: Football, golf
Other sports followed: Football (Everton)
Favourite band: G. Love & Special Sauce
Relaxations: 'Internet poker; DVDs'
Extras: Merseyside Young Sports Personality of the Year 2004-05
Opinions on cricket: 'Too many Kolpaks [*see page 13*] getting in the way of young English players. The gulf between the standard of cricket played in the two divisions is becoming greater.'
Best batting: 9* Middlesex v Hampshire, Rose Bowl 2005
Best bowling: 2-34 Middlesex v CUCCE, Fenner's 2005

2006 Season

	M	Inn	NO	Runs	HS	Avg	100	50	Ct	St	Balls	Runs	Wkts	Avg	BB	5I	10M
Test																	
FC																	
ODI																	
List A	1	1	0	0	0	0.00	-	-	-	-	36	43	1	43.00	1-43	-	
20/20 Int																	
20/20																	

Career Performances

	M	Inn	NO	Runs	HS	Avg	100	50	Ct	St	Balls	Runs	Wkts	Avg	BB	5I	10M
Test																	
FC	2	2	1	10	9*	10.00	-	-	-	-	250	182	7	26.00	2-34	-	-
ODI																	
List A	2	2	0	6	6	3.00	-	-	-	-	78	83	1	83.00	1-43	-	
20/20 Int																	
20/20																	

WHITE, A. R. — Northamptonshire

Name: <u>Andrew</u> Rowland White
Role: Right-hand bat, right-arm off-spin bowler; all-rounder
Born: 3 July 1980, Newtownards, Northern Ireland
Height: 6ft **Weight:** 12st
Nickname: Whitey, Spud
County debut: 2004
ODI debut: 2006
Strike rate: (career 71.87)
Parents: Rowland and Elizabeth
Marital status: Single
Family links with cricket: 'Brother Richard and cousins play league cricket in Ulster. Uncle Andrew and sons, Ben and Rory, play for Cookham Dean, Berkshire'
Education: Regent House Grammar School; University of Ulster
Qualifications: 9 GCSEs, 2 A-levels, honours degree in Sport, Exercise and Leisure, Level 2 cricket coach
Career outside cricket: PE teacher
Overseas tours: Ireland U19 to Sri Lanka (U19 World Cup) 1999-2000; Ireland to South Africa 2001, to Canada (ICC Trophy) 2001, to Namibia (ICC Inter-Continental Cup) 2005, to Scotland (European Championship) 2006, plus other Ireland tours to Europe
Overseas teams played for: UPE International Cricket Academy, South Africa 2002
Career highlights to date: 'Qualifying for the 2007 World Cup and winning the ICC Inter-Continental Cup with Ireland in 2005. Scoring the winning runs for Ireland in their famous victory over the West Indies in 2004'
Cricket moments to forget: 'Losing the ICC Trophy final in 2005 to Scotland'
Cricket superstitions: 'None'
Cricketers particularly admired: Jonty Rhodes, Steve Waugh
Young players to look out for: Eoin Morgan
Other sports played: Football, golf
Other sports followed: Rugby (Ulster), football (Northern Ireland)
Favourite band: U2
Relaxations: 'Snooker; eating out'
Extras: Man of the Match for Ireland v Surrey at Clontarf in the C&G 2004. Scored 152* on first-class debut for Ireland v Netherlands at Deventer in the ICC Inter-Continental Cup 2004. Ireland Player of the Year 2004. Northamptonshire Young Player of the Year 2005. Man of the Match (jointly with Kyle McCallan) in the final of

the ICC Inter-Continental Cup v Kenya at Windhoek 2005. Made ODI debut for Ireland v England in Belfast 2006. Released by Northamptonshire at the end of the 2006 season

Opinions on cricket: 'Real shame to lose cricket from free-to-view television. There is a possibility of a young generation missing out on the game.'

Best batting: 152* Ireland v Netherlands, Deventer 2004

Best bowling: 3-24 Ireland v Kenya, Windhoek 2005-06

2006 Season

	M	Inn	NO	Runs	HS	Avg	100	50	Ct	St	Balls	Runs	Wkts	Avg	BB	5I	10M
Test																	
FC																	
ODI																	
List A	4	4	0	62	26	15.50	-	-	-	-	42	35	0			-	-
20/20 Int																	
20/20	3	1	1	27	27 *		-	-	2	-	30	58	0			-	-

Career Performances

	M	Inn	NO	Runs	HS	Avg	100	50	Ct	St	Balls	Runs	Wkts	Avg	BB	5I	10M
Test																	
FC	8	10	3	334	152 *	47.71	1	1	5	-	575	327	8	40.87	3-24	-	-
ODI	3	3	0	76	40	25.33	-	-	-	-	33	31	2	15.50	2-31	-	
List A	20	18	3	311	45	20.73	-	-	5	-	444	363	10	36.30	3-17	-	
20/20 Int																	
20/20	3	1	1	27	27 *		-	-	2	-	30	58	0			-	-

WHITE, C.   Yorkshire

Name: Craig White
Role: Right-hand bat, right-arm fast-medium bowler
Born: 16 December 1969, Morley, Yorkshire
Height: 6ft 1in **Weight:** 11st 11lbs
Nickname: Chalky, Bassey
County debut: 1990
County cap: 1993
Benefit: 2002
Test debut: 1994
ODI debut: 1994-95
Place in batting averages: 78th av. 39.04 (2005 40th av. 48.50)
Strike rate: (career 53.79)
Parents: Fred Emsley and Cynthia Anne
Wife and date of marriage: Elizabeth Anne, 19 September 1992
Family links with cricket: Father played for Pudsey St Lawrence

Education: Flora Hill High School; Bendigo Senior High School (both Victoria, Australia)

Overseas tours: Australia YC to West Indies 1989-90; England A to Pakistan 1995-96, to Australia 1996-97; England to Australia 1994-95, to India and Pakistan (World Cup) 1995-96, to Zimbabwe and New Zealand 1996-97, to South Africa and Zimbabwe 1999-2000 (one-day series), to Kenya (ICC Knockout Trophy) 2000-01, to Pakistan and Sri Lanka 2000-01, to India and New Zealand 2001-02, to Australia 2002-03, to Africa (World Cup) 2002-03

Overseas teams played for: Victoria, Australia 1990-91; Central Districts, New Zealand 1999-2000

Cricketers particularly admired: Graeme Hick, Mark Waugh, Brian Lara

Other sports followed: Leeds RFC, motocross, golf, tennis

Relaxations: Playing guitar, reading, gardening and socialising

Extras: Man of the Match in the second ODI v Zimbabwe at Bulawayo 1999-2000 (5-21/26). Took National League hat-trick (Fleming, Patel, Masters) v Kent at Headingley 2000. Scored 93 in the first Test at Lahore 2000-01, in the process sharing with Graham Thorpe (118) in a new record sixth-wicket partnership for England in Tests v Pakistan (166). Scored maiden Test century (121) in the second Test v India at Ahmedabad 2001-02, winning Man of the Match award. C&G Man of the Match award for his 4-35 and 78-ball 100* in the semi-final v Surrey at Headingley 2002. Captain of Yorkshire 2004-06

Best batting: 186 Yorkshire v Lancashire, Old Trafford 2001

Best bowling: 8-55 Yorkshire v Gloucestershire, Gloucester 1998

97. Who became the first overseas umpire for almost 90 years to stand in a Test in England, at Trent Bridge in 1994?

2006 Season

	M	Inn	NO	Runs	HS	Avg	100	50	Ct	St	Balls	Runs	Wkts	Avg	BB	5I	10M
Test																	
FC	15	23	1	859	147	39.04	3	3	5	-	194	75	4	18.75	2-11	-	-
ODI																	
List A	14	14	3	520	112	47.27	2	4	3	-	18	42	0			-	-
20/20 Int																	
20/20	9	9	0	185	54	20.55	-	1	4	-	0	0	0			-	-

Career Performances

	M	Inn	NO	Runs	HS	Avg	100	50	Ct	St	Balls	Runs	Wkts	Avg	BB	5I	10M
Test	30	50	7	1052	121	24.46	1	5	14	-	3959	2220	59	37.62	5-32	3	-
FC	265	420	57	11949	186	32.91	20	60	163	-	21250	11249	395	28.47	8-55	11	
ODI	51	41	5	568	57 *	15.77	-	1	12	-	2364	1726	65	26.55	5-21	1	
List A	341	304	43	6933	148	26.56	5	28	95	-	11551	8434	337	25.02	5-19	3	
20/20 Int																	
20/20	23	21	0	363	55	17.28	-	2	7	-	70	132	1	132.00	1-22	-	

WHITE, C. L. — Somerset

Name: <u>Cameron</u> Leon White
Role: Right-hand bat, leg-spin bowler
Born: 18 August 1983, Bairnsdale, Victoria, Australia
Height: 6ft 1½in **Weight:** 14st 2lbs
Nickname: Whitey
County debut: 2006
ODI debut: 2005-06
1000 runs in a season: 1
1st-Class 200s: 1
Place in batting averages: 21st av. 59.50
Place in bowling averages: 137th av. 48.20
Strike rate: 74.73 (career 64.61)
Overseas tours: Australia U19 to New Zealand (U19 World Cup) 2001-02; Australia A to Pakistan 2005-06; Australia to Zimbabwe (one-day series) 2003-04, to India 2004-05, to New Zealand (one-day series) 2005-06
Overseas teams played for: Victoria 2000-01 –
Extras: Appointed captain of Victoria one-day side 2003-04 (and deputy in Pura Cup) at age 20, becoming the youngest captain in the state's cricket history; overall captain

of Victoria since 2004-05. Has won several match awards, including Man of the Match v Queensland at Brisbane in the Pura Cup 2003-04 and v Tasmania at Devonport in the ING Cup 2003-04. Scored 53-ball 116* v Gloucestershire at Taunton 2006, in the process sharing with Justin Langer (90) in a Twenty20 world-record any-wicket partnership of 186 as Somerset reached 250-3 (also a Twenty20 world record). Scored a Twenty20 world record individual score of 141* (out of 198) from 70 balls v Worcestershire at Worcester 2006. An overseas player with Somerset since 2006; acting captain of Somerset late May to mid-August 2006 in the absence of the injured Ian Blackwell

Best batting: 260* Somerset v Derbyshire, Derby 2006
Best bowling: 6-66 Victoria v Western Australia, Melbourne 2002-03
Stop press: Made Twenty20 International debut v England at Sydney 2006-07, winning Man of the Match award

2006 Season

	M	Inn	NO	Runs	HS	Avg	100	50	Ct	St	Balls	Runs	Wkts	Avg	BB	5I	10M
Test																	
FC	12	22	2	1190	260 *	59.50	5	3	6	-	1121	723	15	48.20	5-148	1	-
ODI																	
List A	14	13	1	494	109 *	41.16	1	1	9	-	414	368	11	33.45	3-38	-	
20/20 Int																	
20/20	8	8	2	403	141 *	67.16	2	1	1	-	70	122	3	40.66	1-18	-	

Career Performances

	M	Inn	NO	Runs	HS	Avg	100	50	Ct	St	Balls	Runs	Wkts	Avg	BB	5I	10M
Test																	
FC	62	102	11	3249	260 *	35.70	6	14	63	-	8012	4683	124	37.76	6-66	2	1
ODI	5	1	0	0	0	0.00	-	-	4	-	48	60	1	60.00	1-34	-	
List A	66	52	7	1401	109 *	31.13	2	7	28	-	2083	1841	52	35.40	4-15	-	
20/20 Int																	
20/20	12	12	4	560	141 *	70.00	2	2	3	-	148	216	10	21.60	3-8	-	

WHITE, G. G.   Northamptonshire

Name: <u>Graeme</u> Geoffrey White
Role: Right-hand bat, slow left-arm bowler; all-rounder
Born: 18 April 1987, Milton Keynes
Height: 5ft 11in **Weight:** 10st
Nickname: Whitey, Chalky, Pony
County debut: 2006
Parents: David and Sophie
Marital status: Single
Family links with cricket: Sister Rachel played England Women U17. Father played good standard club cricket and is also a Level 2 coach. Brother Russell played county U11
Education: Stowe School
Qualifications: 9 GCSEs, 1 AS-level, 3 A-levels, coaching Level 2
Overseas tours: Stowe School to India 2004; England U19 to Sri Lanka (U19 World Cup) 2005-06
Career highlights to date: 'Representing my country at the U19 World Cup in Sri Lanka in 2006 and reaching the semi-finals'
Cricket moments to forget: 'Getting hit for five sixes in one over playing for Stowe School (they kept going further!)'
Cricket superstitions: 'Putting pads on from the top down'
Cricketers particularly admired: Bishan Bedi, Phil Tufnell, Daniel Vettori
Young players to look out for: Russell White, Moeen Ali, Andy Miller
Other sports played: Badminton, hockey, football
Other sports followed: Football ('big Manchester United fan')
Favourite band: Kings of Leon, Bloc Party
Relaxations: 'Like listening to music. Playing PS2'
Extras: Represented England U15, U17 and U19. Dorothy Radd Shield (Northamptonshire) 2003. Colin Shillington Award (Stowe School) 2005
Best batting: 37 Northamptonshire v Derbyshire, Northampton 2006

2006 Season

	M	Inn	NO	Runs	HS	Avg	100	50	Ct	St	Balls	Runs	Wkts	Avg	BB	5I	10M
Test																	
FC	2	3	0	37	37	12.33	-	-	-	-	156	79	0		-	-	-
ODI																	
List A																	
20/20 Int																	
20/20																	

Career Performances

	M	Inn	NO	Runs	HS	Avg	100	50	Ct	St	Balls	Runs	Wkts	Avg	BB	5I	10M
Test																	
FC	2	3	0	37	37	12.33	-	-	-	-	156	79	0		-	-	-
ODI																	
List A																	
20/20 Int																	
20/20																	

WHITE, R. A.   Northamptonshire

Name: Robert (<u>Rob</u>) Allan White
Role: Right-hand bat, leg-spin bowler
Born: 15 October 1979, Chelmsford, Essex
Height: 5ft 11in **Weight:** 11st 7lbs
Nickname: Chalky, Toff, Zorro,
Whitey, Lamb
County debut: 2000
1st-Class 200s: 1
Place in batting averages: 198th av. 22.15
(2005 157th av. 29.27)
Strike rate: (career 73.83)
Parents: Dennis and Ann
Marital status: Single
Family links with cricket: 'Grandfather on
Essex committee for many years. Dad flailed
the willow and brother travels the local
leagues high and low'
Education: Stowe School; St John's College,
Durham University; Loughborough University
Qualifications: 9 GCSEs, 3 A-levels
Cricket moments to forget: 'Franklyn Rose telling me my mates had bet £10 that he
couldn't injure me, as I walked out to play Lashings'
Cricketers particularly admired: Ian Botham, Viv Richards, Steve Waugh
Other sports played: Badminton, squash, golf, kabaddi
Other sports followed: Football (West Ham), rugby (Northampton Saints)
Extras: Northamptonshire League Young Player of the Year and Youth Cricketer of
the Year 1999. Northamptonshire Young Player of the Year (Frank Rudd Trophy) 2001.
Played for Loughborough UCCE 2001, 2002 and 2003. Recorded the highest maiden
century in the history of English first-class cricket (277, including a hundred before
lunch on the first day), v Gloucestershire at Northampton 2002 in his fifth first-class
match. NBC Denis Compton Award for the most promising young Northamptonshire
player 2002. Represented British Universities 2003

Best batting: 277 Northamptonshire v Gloucestershire, Northampton 2002
Best bowling: 2-30 Northamptonshire v Gloucestershire, Northampton 2002

2006 Season

	M	Inn	NO	Runs	HS	Avg	100	50	Ct	St	Balls	Runs	Wkts	Avg	BB	5I	10M
Test																	
FC	9	14	1	288	141	22.15	1	-	4	-	288	227	3	75.66	2-57	-	-
ODI																	
List A	12	12	0	223	77	18.58	-	2	2	-	0	0	0			-	-
20/20 Int																	
20/20	6	6	0	198	66	33.00	-	2	1	-	0	0	0			-	-

Career Performances

	M	Inn	NO	Runs	HS	Avg	100	50	Ct	St	Balls	Runs	Wkts	Avg	BB	5I	10M
Test																	
FC	42	72	4	1944	277	28.58	2	8	24	-	886	612	12	51.00	2-30	-	-
ODI																	
List A	40	38	1	719	101	19.43	1	3	8	-	48	46	2	23.00	2-18	-	
20/20 Int																	
20/20	13	13	0	279	66	21.46	-	2	3	-	0	0	0			-	-

WHITE, W. A.　　　　Derbyshire

Name: Wayne Andrew White
Role: Right-hand bat, right-arm fast-medium bowler
Born: 22 April 1985, Derby
Height: 6ft 2in **Weight:** 12st 2lbs
Nickname: Chalky, Player
County debut: 2005
Strike rate: (career 43.54)
Parents: John and Sharon
Marital status: 'Long-term relationship – Elaina Parker'
Family links with cricket: 'Brother plays in Derbyshire age-groups and same club side – Swarkestone CC'
Education: John Port School; Nottingham University
Qualifications: 11 GCSEs, 4 A-levels, BA Politics
Career outside cricket: 'Semi-professional footballer'
Career highlights to date: 'First wicket for Derbyshire – Anthony McGrath'

Cricket moments to forget: '0-107 in the first innings of my debut against Yorkshire'
Cricketers particularly admired: Graeme Welch, Mike Hendrick
Young players to look out for: Jake Needham, Dan Redfern, Harry White
Other sports played: Football (Gresley Rovers, Burton Albion, Mickleover Sports, Derby County), golf; 'darts and pool at The Bridge'
Other sports followed: Football (Derby County)
Favourite band: Faithless, Prodigy, Texas
Relaxations: 'Round of golf; night in with the "missus"; PlayStation/PC; funky house in Susumi'
Extras: Scored 76 and took 7-18 on club cricket debut for Swarkestone
Opinions on cricket: 'More four-day cricket in 2nd XI.'
Best batting: 19* Derbyshire v Surrey, Derby 2006
Best bowling: 4-35 Derbyshire v Surrey, Derby 2006

2006 Season

	M	Inn	NO	Runs	HS	Avg	100	50	Ct	St	Balls	Runs	Wkts	Avg	BB	5I	10M
Test																	
FC	1	2	2	37	19 *	-	-	-	-	-	126	83	6	13.83	4-35	-	-
ODI																	
List A	2	0	0	0	0	-	-	-	-	-	90	101	2	50.50	1-38	-	
20/20 Int																	
20/20																	

Career Performances

	M	Inn	NO	Runs	HS	Avg	100	50	Ct	St	Balls	Runs	Wkts	Avg	BB	5I	10M
Test																	
FC	3	4	2	45	19 *	22.50	-	-	-	-	479	363	11	33.00	4-35	-	-
ODI																	
List A	2	0	0	0	0	-	-	-	-	-	90	101	2	50.50	1-38	-	
20/20 Int																	
20/20																	

WIGLEY, D. H.   Northamptonshire

Name: <u>David</u> Harry Wigley
Role: Right-hand bat, right-arm fast-medium bowler
Born: 26 October 1981, Bradford, Yorkshire
Height: 6ft 3in **Weight:** 14st
Nickname: Wiggers, Wigs
County debut: 2002 (Yorkshire), 2003 (Worcestershire), 2006 (Northamptonshire)
County colours: 2003 (Worcestershire)
Place in bowling averages: 124th av. 44.22 (2005 56th av. 29.23)
Strike rate: 61.66 (career 59.60)
Parents: Max and Judith
Marital status: Single
Family links with cricket: Father played league cricket in Liverpool Competition, Bradford League and Durham Senior League

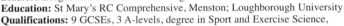

Education: St Mary's RC Comprehensive, Menston; Loughborough University
Qualifications: 9 GCSEs, 3 A-levels, degree in Sport and Exercise Science, ECB Level I coaching
Off-season: 'Training in Northampton'
Overseas tours: British Universities to Cape Town 2004
Overseas teams played for: Gormandale CC, Victoria 2001; Mount Lawley CC, Perth 2004-05
Career highlights to date: 'Taking my first five-for in first-class cricket against Pakistan'
Cricket moments to forget: 'Losing Uni final at Lord's 2004 in last over'
Cricket superstitions: 'Must turn to left to run in and bowl'
Cricketers particularly admired: Darren Gough, Andrew Flintoff
Young players to look out for: Steve Davies
Other sports played: Golf, rugby ('used to play to decent standard; gave up at 16')
Other sports followed: Football (Leeds United), rugby (Llanelli Scarlets)
Relaxations: 'Music, films, golf'
Extras: Played for ECB Schools v Sri Lanka U19 2000. Yorkshire U19 Bowling Award 2000. Played for Loughborough UCCE 2002-04 (captain 2004), taking 5-52 v Oxford in the UCCE One-Day Challenge at Lord's and 5-71 v Hampshire at The Rose Bowl 2002. Represented British Universities 2003 and (as captain) 2004
Opinions on cricket: 'Probably play too much county cricket, not allowing enough time for recovery and practice.'
Best batting: 28 Northamptonshire v Surrey, The Oval 2006
Best bowling: 5-77 Northamptonshire v Pakistanis, Northampton 2006

2006 Season

	M	Inn	NO	Runs	HS	Avg	100	50	Ct	St	Balls	Runs	Wkts	Avg	BB	5I	10M
Test																	
FC	8	10	2	73	28	9.12	-	-	5	-	1110	796	18	44.22	5-77	1	-
ODI																	
List A	5	2	0	9	9	4.50	-	-	1	-	174	213	0			-	-
20/20 Int																	
20/20																	

Career Performances

	M	Inn	NO	Runs	HS	Avg	100	50	Ct	St	Balls	Runs	Wkts	Avg	BB	5I	10M
Test																	
FC	19	23	7	175	28	10.93	-	-	9	-	2742	1922	46	41.78	5-77	1	-
ODI																	
List A	14	7	0	14	9	2.00	-	-	2	-	528	534	10	53.40	4-37	-	
20/20 Int																	
20/20	2	1	0	1	1	1.00	-	-	-	-	30	33	1	33.00	1-8	-	

WILLIAMS, R. E. M.   Middlesex

Name: Robert (<u>Robbie</u>) Edward Morgan Williams
Role: Right-hand bat, right-arm fast-medium bowler
Born: 19 January 1987, Pembury, Kent
Height: 6ft **Weight:** 13st 2lbs
County debut: No first-team appearance
Parents: Gail and Tim
Marital status: Single
Education: Marlborough College; Durham University
Qualifications: 3 A-levels
Overseas tours: Marlborough College to South Africa 2003
Overseas teams played for: Corrimal, Wollongong 2005-06
Career highlights to date: 'Being signed by Middlesex'
Cricket moments to forget: 'Leaving a ball and getting stumped at the Bunbury Festival when nine down and three balls from a draw'
Cricket superstitions: 'Batsmen can be jinxed'
Cricketers particularly admired: Brett Lee

Other sports played: Rugby (Marlborough College 1st XV), hockey (Marlborough College 1st XI)
Other sports followed: Rugby union (Leicester Tigers)
Favourite band: The Killers, Coldplay, Tenacious D
Relaxations: Sudoku
Extras: Made 2nd XI Championship debut 2005

WILLOUGHBY, C. M. Somerset

Name: <u>Charl</u> Myles Willoughby
Role: Left-hand bat, left-arm
fast-medium bowler
Born: 3 December 1974, Cape Town,
South Africa
Height: 6ft 3in **Weight:** 12st 12lbs
Nickname: Puppy, Harry
County debut: 2005 (Leicestershire),
2006 (Somerset)
County cap: 2005 (Leicestershire)
Test debut: 2003
ODI debut: 1999-2000
50 wickets in a season: 1
Place in bowling averages: 20th av. 25.56
(2005 111th av. 41.96)
Strike rate: 45.31 (career 54.86)
Parents: David and Belinda
Wife and date of marriage: Nicky,
17 April 2004
Children: Cole Spencer, 18 October 2006
Family links with cricket: 'Father played club cricket'
Education: Wynberg Boys' High School; Stellenbosch University and UNISA
Off-season: 'Playing in South Africa for Cape Cobras'
Overseas tours: South African Academy to Zimbabwe 1998-99; South Africa A to
West Indies 2000, to Zimbabwe 2004; South Africa to Sharjah (Coca-Cola Sharjah
Cup) 1999-2000, to Bangladesh 2003, to England 2003
Overseas teams played for: Boland 1994-95 – 1999-2000; Western Province 2000-01
– 2003-04; Western Province Boland 2003-04 – 2004-05; Cape Cobras 2005-06 –
Career highlights to date: 'Test and ODI debuts. Four wickets in four balls in first-
class match v Dolphins'
Cricket moments to forget: 'Dislocating my shoulder diving on boundary'
Cricketers particularly admired: Graeme Smith, Freddie Flintoff, Wasim Akram
Young players to look out for: JP Duminy, Stuart Broad
Other sports followed: Rugby (Stormers)

Favourite band: Coldplay

Relaxations: 'Movies and time with my wife'

Extras: Played for Berkshire in the NatWest 2000. Took four wickets in four balls v Dolphins at Durban in the Supersport Series 2005-06; the feat was spread over two innings and consisted of a hat-trick (Mhlongo, Gobind, Hayward) plus the wicket of Watson with his first ball of the second innings. Has won several match awards, including Man of the Match for South Africa A v Barbados at Bridgetown 2000 (6-24) and for Leicestershire v Somerset at Leicester in the C&G 2005 (6-16; the best one-day return by a Leicestershire bowler). An overseas player with Leicestershire 2005. Is no longer considered an overseas player

Best batting: 47 Somerset v Worcestershire, Taunton 2006

Best bowling: 7-44 Somerset v Gloucestershire, Taunton 2006

2006 Season

	M	Inn	NO	Runs	HS	Avg	100	50	Ct	St	Balls	Runs	Wkts	Avg	BB	5I	10M
Test																	
FC	15	22	9	127	47	9.76	-	-	2	-	2991	1687	66	25.56	7-44	3	-
ODI																	
List A	17	6	4	24	12 *	12.00	-	-	3	-	777	637	23	27.69	6-43	1	
20/20 Int																	
20/20	8	2	2	2	2 *		-	-	-	-	186	265	12	22.08	4-30	-	

Career Performances

	M	Inn	NO	Runs	HS	Avg	100	50	Ct	St	Balls	Runs	Wkts	Avg	BB	5I	10M
Test	2	0	0	0	0		-	-	-	-	300	125	1	125.00	1-47	-	-
FC	135	159	65	481	47	5.11	-	-	32	-	27979	12739	510	24.97	7-44	20	3
ODI	3	2	0	0	0	0.00	-	-	-	-	168	148	2	74.00	2-39	-	
List A	165	48	26	112	12 *	5.09	-	-	23	-	8077	5552	206	26.95	6-16	4	
20/20 Int																	
20/20	34	8	6	17	11	8.50	-	-	4	-	737	818	37	22.10	4-9	-	

98. Who scored 65 and had first innings figures of 4-47
on Test debut at Old Trafford in 1994?

WILSON, G. C.   Surrey

Name: <u>Gary</u> Craig Wilson
Role: Right-hand bat, wicket-keeper, very occasional right-arm medium bowler
Born: 5 February 1986, Belfast
Height: 5ft 10in **Weight:** 13st 2lbs
Nickname: Gaz, Wils
County debut: No first-team appearance
Parents: George and Iris
Marital status: 'Unmarried'
Family links with cricket: 'Dad played league cricket in Ireland'
Education: Methodist College, Belfast
Qualifications: 10 GCSEs, 3 A-levels, gym instructor Level 2, FA Level 1
Career outside cricket: 'Bit of coaching'
Off-season: 'Playing for a club side abroad'
Overseas tours: Ireland U19 to Bangladesh (U19 World Cup) 2003-04, to Sri Lanka (U19 World Cup) 2005-06; Ireland A to UAE (EurAsia Series) 2006, plus various Ireland age-group and Ireland A tours to Europe
Overseas teams played for: Portland Colts CC, Melbourne 2004-05; Durbanville CC, Cape Town 2006-07
Career highlights to date: 'Playing first game of U19 World Cup in Bangladesh; beating Scotland in the Inter-Continental Cup by three runs; being signed by Surrey'
Cricket moments to forget: 'Being beaten by three wickets by New Zealand in U19 World Cup 2005-06 after scoring 304; being beaten by four runs by England in the same World Cup; pair on debut for Surrey 2nd XI'
Cricket superstitions: 'Left pad first'
Cricketers particularly admired: Alec Stewart, Brian Lara, Mark Boucher
Young players to look out for: Gary Kidd, William Porterfield, Paul Stirling
Other sports played: Rugby, football, golf ('badly')
Other sports followed: Football (Man United), rugby (Ireland)
Favourite band: 'Any really'
Extras: Player of the Tournament at European U19 Championship 2003 and 2004. MCC Young Cricketer 2005-06. Has represented Ireland in first-class cricket and in the 2006 C&G and has also represented Ireland A in one-day (List A) cricket
Opinions on cricket: 'A lot of cricket being played in England – good for the advertising of the game; wouldn't fancy being a quick bowler, though.'
Best batting: 11 Ireland v Scotland, Aberdeen 2005

Career Performances

	M	Inn	NO	Runs	HS	Avg	100	50	Ct	St	Balls	Runs	Wkts	Avg	BB	5I	10M
Test																	
FC	3	4	1	24	11	8.00	-	-	4	-	0	0	0		-	-	-
ODI																	
List A	5	5	0	136	58	27.20	-	2	7	1	0	0	0		-	-	
20/20 Int																	
20/20																	

WINDOWS, M. G. N. Gloucestershire

Name: <u>Matthew</u> Guy Newman Windows
Role: Right-hand bat, left-arm
medium bowler
Born: 5 April 1973, Bristol
Height: 5ft 7in **Weight:** 11st 7lbs
Nickname: Steamy, Bedos, Boat
County debut: 1992
County cap: 1998
Benefit: 2006
1000 runs in a season: 3
Place in batting averages: 233rd av. 15.87
(2005 200th av. 22.80)
Strike rate: (career 68.50)
Parents: Tony and Carolyn
Wife and date of marriage: Emma,
12 October 2002
Family links with cricket: 'Father (A.R.)
played for Gloucestershire (1960-69) and was
Cambridge cricket Blue'
Education: Clifton College; Durham University
Qualifications: 9 GCSEs, 3 A-levels, BA (Hons) Sociology (Dunelm), SFA securities
representative of the London Stock Exchange
Overseas tours: Clifton College to Barbados 1991; England U19 to Pakistan 1991-92;
Durham University to South Africa 1992-93; England A to Zimbabwe and South
Africa 1998-99; Gloucestershire's annual pre-season tour to South Africa
Overseas teams played for: Gold Coast Dolphins, Queensland 1996-97
Career highlights: 'Winning all the Lord's finals, but [especially] being not out
against Glamorgan in the 2000 [B&H] final'
Cricketers particularly admired: David Boon, Courtney Walsh

Other sports played: Rackets (British Open runner-up 1997)
Relaxations: 'Travelling and understanding financial jargon'
Extras: Represented England U19. Gloucestershire Young Player of the Year 1994. Scored 218* for Durham University v Hull University in the BUSA Championships 1995. Gloucestershire Player of the Year 1998. Retired at the end of the 2006 season
Best batting: 184 Gloucestershire v Warwickshire, Cheltenham 1996
Best bowling: 1-6 Combined Universities v West Indians, The Parks 1995

2006 Season

	M	Inn	NO	Runs	HS	Avg	100	50	Ct	St	Balls	Runs	Wkts	Avg	BB	5I	10M
Test																	
FC	5	9	1	127	48	15.87	-	-	2	-	0	0	0		-	-	-
ODI																	
List A	8	6	1	86	30 *	17.20	-	-	5	-	0	0	0		-	-	
20/20 Int																	
20/20	2	2	1	30	29	30.00	-	-	-	-	0	0	0		-	-	

Career Performances

	M	Inn	NO	Runs	HS	Avg	100	50	Ct	St	Balls	Runs	Wkts	Avg	BB	5I	10M
Test																	
FC	170	302	21	9103	184	32.39	16	47	92	-	137	131	2	65.50	1-6	-	-
ODI																	
List A	225	211	28	4936	117	26.97	3	25	74	-	48	49	0		-	-	
20/20 Int																	
20/20	10	7	1	69	29	11.50	-	-	6	-	0	0	0		-	-	

99. Who captained New Zealand on Test debut
v India at Bangalore in 1995-96?

WISEMAN, P. J.   Durham

Name: <u>Paul</u> John Wiseman
Role: Right-hand bat, right-arm
off-spin bowler
Born: 4 May 1970, Auckland, New Zealand
Nickname: Whiz
County debut: 2006
Test debut: 1998
ODI debut: 1997-98
Strike rate: (career 75.24)
Overseas tours: New Zealand Academy to
South Africa 1997; New Zealand A to India
2001-02, to South Africa 2004-05, to Sri
Lanka 2005-06; New Zealand to Zimbabwe
1997-98, to Sri Lanka 1998, to Malaysia
(Commonwealth Games) 1998-99, to
Bangladesh (Wills International Cup) 1998-
99, to India 1999-2000, to Zimbabwe 2000-
01, to Kenya (ICC Knockout Trophy) 2000-
01, to South Africa 2000-01, to Australia 2001-02, to Sri Lanka 2003, to India 2003-
04, to Bangladesh 2004-05, to Australia 2004-05, plus other one-day tournaments and
series in Sharjah, Singapore and Namibia
Overseas teams played for: Auckland 1991-92 – 1993-94; Otago 1994-95 – 2000-01;
Canterbury 2001-02 – 2005-06
Extras: Has played cricket in the Lancashire Leagues for Rishton (1999), Haslingden
(2005) and Milnrow (2005); and for Walkden in the Bolton League (2006). Man of the
Match in the first Test v Zimbabwe at Bulawayo 2000-01 (5-90/3-54). His 9-13
(16.4-9-13-9) for Canterbury v Central Districts in the State Championship at
Christchurch 2004-05 is the second best innings return in New Zealand first-class
cricket history. Joined Durham towards the end of the 2006 season. Holds a British
passport and is not considered an overseas player
Best batting: 130 Canterbury v Northern Districts, Hamilton 2005-06
Best bowling: 9-13 Canterbury v Central Districts, Christchurch 2004-05

	M	Inn	NO	Runs	HS	Avg	100	50	Ct	St	Balls	Runs	Wkts	Avg	BB	5I	10M
Test																	
FC	2	2	1	10	6*	10.00	-	-	-	-	336	230	1	230.00	1-127	-	-
ODI																	
List A																	
20/20 Int																	
20/20																	

Career Performances

	M	Inn	NO	Runs	HS	Avg	100	50	Ct	St	Balls	Runs	Wkts	Avg	BB	5I	10M
Test	25	34	8	366	36	14.07	-	-	11	-	5660	2903	61	47.59	5-82	2	-
FC	157	213	44	3487	130	20.63	2	13	72	-	31379	14158	417	33.95	9-13	17	4
ODI	15	7	5	45	16	22.50	-	-	2	-	450	368	12	30.66	4-45	-	
List A	113	80	18	953	65*	15.37	-	2	28	-	4514	3179	72	44.15	4-45	-	
20/20 Int																	
20/20	3	0	0	0	0		-	-	2	-	54	76	5	15.20	2-20	-	

WOAKES, C. R.   Warwickshire

Name: Christopher (<u>Chris</u>) Roger Woakes
Role: Right-hand bat, right-arm medium bowler
Born: 2 March 1989, Birmingham
County debut: 2006
Strike rate: (career 46.00)
Extras: Made 2nd XI Championship debut for Warwickshire 2005. Played for Herefordshire in Minor Counties competitions 2006. England U17 squad 2006
Best batting: 4 Warwickshire v West Indies A, Edgbaston 2006
Best bowling: 2-64 Warwickshire v West Indies A, Edgbaston 2006

2006 Season

	M	Inn	NO	Runs	HS	Avg	100	50	Ct	St	Balls	Runs	Wkts	Avg	BB	5I	10M
Test																	
FC	1	1	0	4	4	4.00	-	-	3	-	138	102	3	34.00	2-64	-	-
ODI																	
List A																	
20/20 Int																	
20/20																	

Career Performances

	M	Inn	NO	Runs	HS	Avg	100	50	Ct	St	Balls	Runs	Wkts	Avg	BB	5I	10M
Test																		
FC	1	1	0	4	4	4.00	-	-	3	-	138	102	3	34.00	2-64	-	-
ODI																	
List A																	
20/20 Int																	
20/20																	

WOOD, G. L. Yorkshire

Name: Gregory (Greg) Luke Wood
Role: Left-hand bat, wicket-keeper
Born: 2 December 1988, Dewsbury, West Yorkshire
County debut: No first-team appearance
Parents: Shaun Christopher and Joan
Marital status: Single
Education: Queen Elizabeth's Grammar School (QEGS), Wakefield
Qualifications: A-levels
Off-season: 'Hopefully touring with England U19'
Overseas tours: England U16 to South Africa 2005; England U19 to Bangladesh 2005-06, to Sri Lanka (U19 World Cup) 2005-06, to Malaysia 2006-07 (c)
Career highlights to date: 'Captaining England U19 on tour a year out of age'
Cricket moments to forget: 'Dropping Herschelle Gibbs in a charity match and him then scoring 186*!'
Cricketers particularly admired: Stephen Fleming, Jack Russell
Young players to look out for: Azeem Rafiq

Other sports played: Rugby (captained school to national finals)
Other sports followed: Football (Leeds United)
Injuries: Out for several World Cup matches with a broken toe
Favourite band: The Calling
Extras: Scored 139* for QEGS v Leeds Grammar 2005, sharing with brother Daniel (also 139*) in ECB schools record first-wicket partnership (300*). Played for Yorkshire Academy 2005-06. Represented England U19 and captained ECB Development of Excellence XI 2006. Made 2nd XI Championship debut 2006
Opinions on cricket: 'As I have not been in the professional game that long it would be premature for me to say; however, I have enjoyed everything I have experienced so far.'

WOOD, M. J. Somerset

Name: <u>Matthew</u> James Wood
Role: Right-hand bat, right-arm off-spin bowler
Born: 30 September 1980, Exeter
Height: 5ft 11in **Weight:** 12st 6lbs
Nickname: Woody, Gran, Moo
County debut: 2001
County cap: 2005
1000 runs in a season: 1
1st-Class 200s: 1
Place in batting averages: 190th av. 23.03 (2005 43rd av. 48.09)
Parents: James and Trina
Marital status: Single
Family links with cricket: Father is chairman of Devon Cricket Board
Education: Exmouth College; Exeter University
Qualifications: 10 GCSEs, 2 A-levels, ECB Level 3 coach
Career outside cricket: Coach
Overseas tours: West of England U15 to West Indies 1995
Overseas teams played for: Doubleview CC, Perth 2001, 2002
Career highlights to date: 'Winning the Twenty20 Cup and scoring 297 v Yorkshire'
Cricket moments to forget: 'Getting a pair v Essex 2005'
Cricket superstitions: 'None'
Cricketers particularly admired: Marcus Trescothick
Young players to look out for: James Hildreth, Arul Suppiah, John Francis
Other sports followed: Football (Liverpool FC), horse racing
Relaxations: Golf

Extras: NBC Denis Compton Award for the most promising young Somerset player 2001. Scored century in each innings (106/131) v Surrey at Taunton 2002. Somerset Player of the Year 2002. Scored 297 v Yorkshire at Taunton 2005, the fifth highest individual score in Somerset's history. Vice-captain of Somerset July 2005-2006
Best batting: 297 Somerset v Yorkshire, Taunton 2005

2006 Season

	M	Inn	NO	Runs	HS	Avg	100	50	Ct	St	Balls	Runs	Wkts	Avg	BB	5I	10M
Test																	
FC	16	27	0	622	73	23.03	-	5	8	-	0	0	0		-	-	-
ODI																	
List A	18	17	1	690	116	43.12	1	6	2	-	0	0	0		-	-	
20/20 Int																	
20/20	8	8	0	234	43	29.25	-	-	1	-	0	0	0		-	-	

Career Performances

	M	Inn	NO	Runs	HS	Avg	100	50	Ct	St	Balls	Runs	Wkts	Avg	BB	5I	10M
Test																	
FC	74	129	6	4320	297	35.12	9	27	25	-	85	68	0		-	-	-
ODI																	
List A	73	69	4	1935	129	29.76	2	13	12	-	0	0	0		-	-	
20/20 Int																	
20/20	23	23	0	675	94	29.34	-	4	3	-	0	0	0		-	-	

100. Who appeared in his 62nd and final Test at his English home ground of Trent Bridge in 2004?

WOOD, M. J.　　　　　　　　　　　Yorkshire

Name: <u>Matthew</u> James Wood
Role: Right-hand opening bat,
off-spin bowler
Born: 6 April 1977, Huddersfield
Height: 5ft 9in **Weight:** 12st
Nickname: Ronnie, Chuddy
County debut: 1997
County cap: 2001
1000 runs in a season: 4
1st-Class 200s: 3
Place in batting averages: 223rd av. 17.70
(2005 97th av. 35.89)
Strike rate: (career 36.00)
Parents: Roger and Kathryn
Marital status: Single
Family links with cricket: 'Father played for
local team Emley. Mum made the teas and
sister Caroline scored'

Education: Shelley High School and Sixth Form Centre
Qualifications: 9 GCSEs, 2 A-levels, NCA coaching award
Overseas tours: England U19 to Zimbabwe 1995-96; Yorkshire CCC to West Indies
1996-97, to Cape Town 1997, 1998; MCC to Kenya 1999, to Bangladesh 1999-2000;
ECB National Academy to Australia 2001-02
Overseas teams played for: Somerset West CC, Cape Town 1994-95; Upper Hutt
United CC, New Zealand 1997-98; Mosman Park, Western Australia 2000-01;
Mosman CC, Sydney 2004-05
Career highlights to date: 'Being on the pitch as fielding 12th man for England
series win v South Africa at Headingley [1998]. Winning the Championship in 2001
and winning the C&G 2002 at Lord's'
Cricket moments to forget: 'Most of the 2002 season'
Cricket superstitions: 'Not any more'
Cricketers particularly admired: Darren Lehmann, Matthew Maynard,
Stephen Fleming, Michael Vaughan
Other sports played: Football (Kirkburton FC)
Other sports followed: Football (Liverpool FC)
Favourite band: Atomic Kitten
Relaxations: 'Socialising, eating out, golf, DIY'
Extras: Represented England U17. Attended Yorkshire Academy. Scored 1000 first-
class runs in first full season 1998. Yorkshire Coach's Player of the Year, Yorkshire
Club Player of the Year and Yorkshire Players' Player of the Year 2003. Set a new
Yorkshire record individual score in the NatWest/C&G (160 from 124 balls) v Devon

at Exmouth 2004, winning Man of the Match award. Vice-captain of Yorkshire 2003-04

Best batting: 207 Yorkshire v Somerset, Taunton 2003
Best bowling: 1-4 Yorkshire v Somerset, Headingley 2003

2006 Season

	M	Inn	NO	Runs	HS	Avg	100	50	Ct	St	Balls	Runs	Wkts	Avg	BB	5I	10M
Test																	
FC	6	10	0	177	92	17.70	-	1	6	-	0	0	0		-	-	-
ODI																	
List A	10	10	1	175	49	19.44	-	-	6	-	0	0	0		-	-	
20/20 Int																	
20/20	1	1	1	6	6 *		-	-	-	-	0	0	0		-	-	

Career Performances

	M	Inn	NO	Runs	HS	Avg	100	50	Ct	St	Balls	Runs	Wkts	Avg	BB	5I	10M
Test																	
FC	128	223	20	6797	207	33.48	16	30	113	-	72	39	2	19.50	1-4	-	-
ODI																	
List A	145	134	14	3271	160	27.25	5	14	57	-	66	76	3	25.33	3-45	-	
20/20 Int																	
20/20	15	15	3	328	96 *	27.33	-	2	11	-	18	32	2	16.00	1-11	-	

WOODMAN, R. J. Somerset

Name: <u>Robert</u> James Woodman
Role: Left-hand bat, left-arm medium bowler
Born: 12 October 1986, Taunton
Height: 5ft 11in
Nickname: Woody
County debut: 2005
Strike rate: (career 198.00)
Parents: Janet and Keith
Marital status: Single
Family links with cricket: 'Dad runs youth section at local club (Taunton Deane CC)'
Education: The Castle School; Richard Huish College, Taunton
Qualifications: 10 GCSEs, 2 A-levels
Overseas tours: West of England U15 to West Indies; The Castle School to Barbados 2002; England U19 to Bangladesh 2005-06, to Sri Lanka (U19 World Cup) 2005-06

Career highlights to date: '46* on debut against Worcestershire. Selection for England U19 World Cup squad'
Cricket moments to forget: 'Bowling at Neil Carter on Sky Sports and getting hit to all parts'
Cricket superstitions: 'None'
Cricketers particularly admired: Keith Parsons, Jacques Kallis, Ian Botham, Wasim Akram, Tony Keitch
Young players to look out for: Moeen Ali, Sam Spurway
Other sports played: Football (Bristol City Academy and Somerset U19), basketball (Taunton Tigers Academy)
Other sports followed: Football (Tottenham Hotspur)
Favourite band: U2, Kanye West
Relaxations: 'Watching DVDs; meeting up with mates'
Extras: Played for Somerset in the International 20:20 Club Championship 2005
Best batting: 46* Somerset v Worcestershire, Worcester 2005
Best bowling: 1-78 Somerset v Essex, Colchester 2005

2006 Season (did not make any first-class or one-day appearances)

Career Performances

	M	Inn	NO	Runs	HS	Avg	100	50	Ct	St	Balls	Runs	Wkts	Avg	BB	5I	10M
Test																	
FC	3	4	1	54	46 *	18.00	-	-	-	-	396	268	2	134.00	1-78	-	-
ODI																	
List A	4	0	0	0	0		-	-	2	-	132	136	1	136.00	1-38	-	
20/20 Int																	
20/20	2	2	2	1	1 *		-	-	-	-	42	63	2	31.50	2-37	-	

WRIGHT, B. J.   Glamorgan

Name: <u>Ben</u> James Wright
Role: Right-hand bat, right-arm medium bowler
Born: 5 December 1987, Fulwood, Preston
Height: 5ft 8in **Weight:** 11st
Nickname: Kevin, Space, Bej
County debut: 2006
Parents: Julia and Peter
Marital status: Single
Education: Cowbridge Comprehensive
Qualifications: 11 GCSEs
Overseas tours: West of England U15 to West Indies 2003; England U16 to South Africa 2004; England U19 to Bangladesh 2005-06, to Sri Lanka (U19 World Cup) 2005-06, to Malaysia 2006-07

Career highlights to date: 'County Championship debut'
Cricket moments to forget: 'Watching my dad bat and get a not out'
Cricket superstitions: 'All left kit goes on before right'
Cricketers particularly admired: Matthew Maynard
Young players to look out for: 'All the Glamorgan youngsters'
Other sports played: Rugby (Wales U16)
Other sports followed: Football (Man Utd), rugby (Leicester Tigers)
Favourite band: 'All R&B'
Relaxations: 'Spending time with girlfriend and watching TV'
Extras: Sir John Hobbs Memorial Prize 2003. A.A. Thomson Fielding Prize 2003.

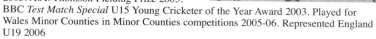

BBC *Test Match Special* U15 Young Cricketer of the Year Award 2003. Played for Wales Minor Counties in Minor Counties competitions 2005-06. Represented England U19 2006
Opinions on cricket: 'Just enjoy watching and playing.'
Best batting: 72 Glamorgan v Gloucestershire, Cardiff 2006

2006 Season

	M	Inn	NO	Runs	HS	Avg	100	50	Ct	St	Balls	Runs	Wkts	Avg	BB	5I	10M
Test																	
FC	1	1	0	72	72	72.00	-	1	2	-	0	0	0		-	-	-
ODI																	
List A	1	1	0	37	37	37.00	-	-	-	-	0	0	0		-	-	
20/20 Int																	
20/20																	

Career Performances

	M	Inn	NO	Runs	HS	Avg	100	50	Ct	St	Balls	Runs	Wkts	Avg	BB	5I	10M
Test																		
FC	1	1	0	72	72	72.00	-	1	2	-	0	0	0		-	-	-
ODI																	
List A	1	1	0	37	37	37.00	-	-	-	-	0	0	0		-	-	
20/20 Int																	
20/20																	

WRIGHT, C. J. C. Middlesex

Name: Christopher (<u>Chris</u>) Julian Clement Wright
Role: Right-hand bat, right-arm fast-medium bowler
Born: 14 July 1985, Chipping Norton, Oxfordshire
Height: 6ft 3in **Weight:** 12st
Nickname: Wrighty, Baron
County debut: 2004
Place in batting averages: (2005 169th av. 26.83)
Strike rate: (career 102.84)
Parents: Alan and Nikki
Marital status: Single
Family links with cricket: 'Dad plays for Hampshire Over 50s'
Education: Eggars School, Alton; Alton College; Anglia Polytechnic University

Qualifications: 11 GCSEs, 4 A-levels
Career outside cricket: 'Family business – Hygienics Limited'
Off-season: 'Working and in the gym'
Overseas tours: Cambridge UCCE to Grenada 2004
Overseas teams played for: Tamil Union C&AC, Colombo 2005-06
Career highlights to date: 'Middlesex debut v Yorkshire. First match at Lord's'
Cricket moments to forget: 'Relegation for Middlesex'
Cricket superstitions: 'Not really; they make people crazy'
Cricketers particularly admired: 'All my team-mates. Mark Ramprakash and Darren Gough purely for their footwork'
Young players to look out for: Chris Whelan, Eoin Morgan, Billy Godleman, Steve Finn
Other sports played: Basketball
Other sports followed: Football (Arsenal), basketball (Dallas Mavericks)
Favourite band: 'Rage Against The Machine or Weezer'
Relaxations: 'Table football, poker, eating out, films'
Extras: Played for Cambridge UCCE 2004-05. Represented British Universities 2005. 'Beat Johann Louw in a six-hitting contest this year'
Opinions on cricket: 'Game needs to avoid too much tampering – ie super subs etc.'
Best batting: 76 CUCCE v Essex, Fenner's 2005
Best bowling: 2-33 Middlesex v OUCCE, The Parks 2006

2006 Season

	M	Inn	NO	Runs	HS	Avg	100	50	Ct	St	Balls	Runs	Wkts	Avg	BB	5I	10M
Test																	
FC	5	8	3	133	42	26.60	-	-	-	-	618	506	7	72.28	2-33	-	-
ODI																	
List A	5	4	2	11	8 *	5.50	-	-	-	-	132	121	0			-	-
20/20 Int																	
20/20																	

Career Performances

	M	Inn	NO	Runs	HS	Avg	100	50	Ct	St	Balls	Runs	Wkts	Avg	BB	5I	10M
Test																	
FC	16	23	3	429	76	21.45	-	2	5	-	2056	1517	20	75.85	2-33	-	-
ODI																	
List A	16	11	5	44	18	7.33	-	-	3	-	618	522	11	47.45	3-21	-	
20/20 Int																	
20/20	4	1	1	1	1 *		-	-	2	-	78	109	3	36.33	2-24	-	

WRIGHT, L. J.   Sussex

Name: <u>Luke</u> James Wright
Role: Right-hand bat, right-arm medium-fast bowler; all-rounder
Born: 7 March 1985, Grantham
Height: 6ft **Weight:** 13st
Nickname: Wrighty
County debut: 2003 (Leicestershire), 2004 (Sussex)
Place in batting averages: 206th av. 20.86 (2005 249th av. 15.75)
Place in bowling averages: 99th av. 38.80 (2005 24th av. 25.30)
Strike rate: 71.20 (career 70.72)
Parents: Keith and Anna
Marital status: Single
Family links with cricket: 'Father very keen cricketer (Level 2 coach).' Brother Ashley played for Leicestershire
Education: Belvoir High School, Bottesford; Ratcliffe College; Loughborough University
Qualifications: 8 GCSEs, National Diploma in Sports Science and Sports Massage, ECB Level 1 coaching

Overseas tours: Leicestershire U13 to South Africa; Leicestershire U15 to South Africa; England U19 to Australia 2002-03, to Bangladesh (U19 World Cup) 2003-04; England A to West Indies 2005-06
Cricket superstitions: 'Too many to name'
Cricketers particularly admired: Andrew Flintoff, Jacques Kallis
Young players to look out for: Stuart Broad, Tim Ambrose, Chris Nash
Other sports played: Football, hockey, squash, tennis
Other sports followed: Football (Newcastle United)
Favourite band: Kelly Clarkson
Relaxations: Music, cinema, going out
Extras: NBC Denis Compton Award for the most promising young Leicestershire player 2002. Took the first ever hat-trick for England U19 in one-day cricket, v South Africa U19 at Hove 2003. Scored maiden first-class century (100) on Sussex debut v Loughborough UCCE at Hove 2004. ECB National Academy 2004-05 (part-time), 2005-06
Opinions on cricket: 'Must back home-grown English talent as much as possible.'
Best batting: 100 Sussex v LUCCE, Hove 2004
Best bowling: 3-33 Sussex v Surrey, Hove 2005

2006 Season

	M	Inn	NO	Runs	HS	Avg	100	50	Ct	St	Balls	Runs	Wkts	Avg	BB	5I	10M
Test																	
FC	11	17	2	313	59	20.86	-	3	7	-	1068	582	15	38.80	3-39	-	-
ODI																	
List A	17	10	2	134	32 *	16.75	-	-	8	-	645	601	14	42.92	4-56	-	
20/20 Int																	
20/20	8	5	1	64	26 *	16.00	-	-	7	-	180	189	13	14.53	3-17	-	

Career Performances

	M	Inn	NO	Runs	HS	Avg	100	50	Ct	St	Balls	Runs	Wkts	Avg	BB	5I	10M
Test																	
FC	21	30	3	568	100	21.03	1	3	13	-	2051	1110	29	38.27	3-33	-	-
ODI																	
List A	57	39	9	439	35	14.63	-	-	18	-	2071	1717	50	34.34	4-12	-	
20/20 Int																	
20/20	20	11	2	87	26 *	9.66	-	-	9	-	348	420	24	17.50	3-17	-	

YARDY, M. H.   Sussex

Name: Michael (<u>Mike</u>) Howard Yardy
Role: Left-hand bat, left-arm
medium/spin bowler
Born: 27 November 1980, Pembury, Kent
Height: 6ft **Weight:** 14st 2lbs
Nickname: Yards, Paolo
County debut: 1999 (one-day),
2000 (first-class)
County cap: 2005
ODI debut: 2006
Twenty20 Int debut: 2006
1000 runs in a season: 1
1st-Class 200s: 1
Place in batting averages: 39th av. 50.77
(2005 21st av. 56.29)
Strike rate: (career 117.80)
Parents: Beverly and Howard
Wife and date of marriage: Karin,
October 2005
Children: Syenna Lucienne, 24 December 2006
Family links with cricket: 'Brother plays for local team'
Education: William Parker School, Hastings
Qualifications: 5 GCSEs, 2 A-levels, ECB Level 1 coach, Sports Psychology diploma
Overseas tours: Sussex Academy to Barbados 1997; Sussex to Grenada 2001, 2002;
England A to West Indies 2005-06, to Bangladesh 2006-07 (c); England to India (ICC
Champions Trophy) 2006-07
Overseas teams played for: Cape Town CC 1999
Cricket superstitions: 'Loads – all secret'
Cricketers particularly admired: 'All those who have reached the pinnacle of
their careers'
Other sports followed: Football (West Ham)
Favourite band: Bluetones
Relaxations: 'Watching West Ham; relaxing with my wife'
Extras: Played for Sussex U15, U16 and U19. Represented England U17. Attended
Sussex Academy. Sussex Most Improved Player 2001. His 257 v Bangladeshis at Hove
2005 is the highest individual score for Sussex against a touring side; also took 5-83 in
Bangladeshis' second innings. Scored 159* v Warwickshire at Hove 2006, in the
process sharing with Murray Goodwin (214*) in a new Sussex record partnership for
the third wicket (385*). ECB National Academy 2005-06, 2006-07
Best batting: 257 Sussex v Bangladeshis, Hove 2005
Best bowling: 5-83 Sussex v Bangladeshis, Hove 2005

2006 Season

	M	Inn	NO	Runs	HS	Avg	100	50	Ct	St	Balls	Runs	Wkts	Avg	BB	5I	10M
Test																	
FC	12	20	2	914	159 *	50.77	3	4	9	-	276	159	2	79.50	1-37	-	-
ODI	2	1	1	12	12 *		-	-	1	-	102	46	4	11.50	3-24	-	
List A	16	12	3	335	98 *	37.22	-	2	7	-	579	465	17	27.35	3-20	-	
20/20 Int	1	1	1	24	24 *		-	-	1	-	18	20	1	20.00	1-20	-	
20/20	9	8	4	194	68 *	48.50	-	1	2	-	162	168	7	24.00	2-15	-	

Career Performances

	M	Inn	NO	Runs	HS	Avg	100	50	Ct	St	Balls	Runs	Wkts	Avg	BB	5I	10M
Test																	
FC	70	120	13	4184	257	39.10	9	18	54	-	1767	1056	15	70.40	5-83	1	-
ODI	2	1	1	12	12 *		-	-	1	-	102	46	4	11.50	3-24	-	
List A	101	89	13	1562	98 *	20.55	-	8	41	-	2281	1853	59	31.40	6-27	1	
20/20 Int	1	1	1	24	24 *		-	-	1	-	18	20	1	20.00	1-20	-	
20/20	18	14	6	277	68 *	34.62	-	1	7	-	204	231	7	33.00	2-15	-	

YASIR ARAFAT Kent

Name: Yasir Arafat Satti
Role: Right-hand bat, right-arm fast bowler
Born: 12 March 1982, Rawalpindi, Punjab, Pakistan
Height: 5ft 9½in **Weight:** 11st 11lbs
Nickname: Yas
County debut: 2006 (Sussex)
County cap: 2006 (Sussex)
ODI debut: 1999-2000
Place in batting averages: 65th av. 43.33
Place in bowling averages: 14th av. 24.85
Strike rate: 39.68 (career 39.42)
Parents: M. Idrees (father)
Marital status: Single
Family links with cricket: 'Father plays club cricket'
Education: Gordon College, Rawalpindi
Overseas tours: Pakistan U15 to England (U15 World Cup) 1996; Pakistan U19 to Australia 1997-98, to Sri Lanka (U19 World Cup) 1999-2000; Pakistan A to UAE (UAE National Day Tournament) 1999-2000, to Kenya 2000, to Sri Lanka 2001, 2004-05, to UAE (EurAsia Cricket Series) 2006; Pakistan to Sharjah (ARY Gold Cup) 2000-01, to India (ICC Champions Trophy) 2006-07

Overseas teams played for: Rawalpindi 1997-98, 2000-01 – 2001-02, 2003-04 – 2005-06; Pakistan Reserves 1999-2000; Khan Research Laboratories 1999-2000 – 2004-05, 2006-07; REDCO 1999-2000; National Bank of Pakistan 2005-06

Career highlights to date: 'Playing for Pakistan'

Cricket moments to forget: 'Nil'

Cricket superstitions: 'Nil'

Cricketers particularly admired: Imran Khan

Young players to look out for: Shahid Yousuf

Other sports played: Football

Other sports followed: Football (Real Madrid)

Relaxations: 'Watching movies and music'

Extras: Pakistan domestic Player of the Year 2003-04. Played for Clydesdale CC, Scotland 2001-06 and for Scotland in the totesport and C&G 2004-05. Became fourth bowler in history of first-class cricket to take five wickets in six balls, for Rawalpindi v Faisalabad at Rawalpindi in the Quaid-e-Azam Trophy 2004-05; his feat, spread across two innings, included a hat-trick. Was an overseas player with Sussex during the 2006 season as a locum for Naved-ul-Hasan; has joined Kent as an overseas player for 2007

Best batting: 100 KRL v Defence Housing Authority, Karachi 2003-04

Best bowling: 7-102 Rawalpindi v Sialkot, Sialkot 2001-02

2006 Season

	M	Inn	NO	Runs	HS	Avg	100	50	Ct	St	Balls	Runs	Wkts	Avg	BB	5I	10M
Test																	
FC	8	12	3	390	86	43.33	-	2	1	-	1627	1019	41	24.85	5-84	2	-
ODI																	
List A	10	7	4	107	37	35.66	-	-	2	-	456	363	15	24.20	4-29	-	
20/20 Int																	
20/20	8	7	1	64	34	10.66	-	-	1	-	178	223	16	13.93	4-21	-	

Career Performances

	M	Inn	NO	Runs	HS	Avg	100	50	Ct	St	Balls	Runs	Wkts	Avg	BB	5I	10M
Test																	
FC	98	152	22	3485	100	26.80	1	20	33	-	16244	9305	412	22.58	7-102	23	2
ODI	6	4	1	21	10	7.00	-	-	1	-	204	200	3	66.66	1-28	-	
List A	141	106	27	1701	87	21.53	-	6	29	-	6765	5357	219	24.46	6-24	3	
20/20 Int																	
20/20	14	13	1	152	49	12.66	-	-	1	-	286	406	18	22.55	4-21	-	

YATES, G.　　　　　　　　　　Lancashire

Name: Gary Yates
Role: Right-hand bat, right-arm
off-spin bowler
Born: 20 September 1967,
Ashton-under-Lyne
Height: 6ft 1in **Weight:** 13st 1lb
Nickname: Sweaty, Yugo, Pearly,
Backyard, Zippy
County debut: 1990
County cap: 1994
Benefit: 2005
Strike rate: (career 74.73)
Parents: Alan and Patricia
Wife and date of marriage: Christine,
20 February 2004
Children: Francis Leonard George,
1 May 1999

Family links with cricket: 'Father played for
Denton St Lawrence and other teams in the Lancashire League'
Education: Manchester Grammar School
Qualifications: 6 O-levels, ECB Level III coach, Australian Cricket Coaching
Council coach
Career outside cricket: 'Sales rep with family business (Digical Ltd), selling diaries,
calendars and business gifts'
Overseas tours: Lancashire to Tasmania and Western Australia 1990, to Western
Australia 1991, to Johannesburg 1992, to Barbados and St Lucia 1992, to Calcutta
1997, to Cape Town 1997-98, to Grenada 2003; MCC to Bangladesh 1999-2000
Overseas teams played for: South Barwon, Geelong, Australia 1987-88; Johnsonville,
Wellington, New Zealand 1989-90; Western Suburbs, Brisbane 1991-92; Old
Selbornian, East London, South Africa 1992-93; Hermanus CC, South Africa 1995-96
Career highlights to date: 'All trophies won while playing with Lancashire'
Cricket moments to forget: 'Not being selected for a 2nd XI Bain Hogg final after
playing all ten round matches and semi-final'
Cricket superstitions: 'They vary'
Cricketers particularly admired: Michael Atherton, Ian Botham, John Emburey
Other sports played: Golf ('represented Lancashire CCC at National *Times* Corporate
Golf Challenge, La Manga, Spain, December 2001')
Other sports followed: 'All sports, especially football (Manchester City), golf,
motor rallying'
Relaxations: 'Playing golf, watching football and good films, eating; spending time
with my son'

Extras: Scored century (106) on Championship debut v Nottinghamshire at Trent Bridge 1990. Rapid Cricketline Player of the Month April/May 1992. Assistant Coach at Lancashire; Lancashire 2nd XI captain/coach since 2002
Best batting: 134* Lancashire v Northamptonshire, Old Trafford 1993
Best bowling: 6-64 Lancashire v Kent, Old Trafford 1999

2006 Season (did not make any first-class or one-day appearances)

Career Performances

	M	Inn	NO	Runs	HS	Avg	100	50	Ct	St	Balls	Runs	Wkts	Avg	BB	5I	10M
Test																	
FC	82	107	36	1789	134 *	25.19	3	5	38	-	13752	7025	184	38.17	6-64	5	-
ODI																	
List A	172	78	33	661	38	14.68	-	-	39	-	6954	5114	159	32.16	4-34	-	
20/20 Int																	
20/20																	

YOUNUS KHAN   Yorkshire

Name: Mohammad Younus Khan
Role: Right-hand bat, leg-break bowler, occasional wicket-keeper
Born: 29 November 1977, Mardan, Pakistan
County debut: 2005 (Nottinghamshire)
Test debut: 1999-2000
ODI debut: 1999-2000
Twenty20 Int debut: 2006
1st-Class 200s: 5
Place in batting averages: 9th av. 65.57 (2005 204th av. 21.83)
Strike rate: (career 90.18)
Overseas tours: Pakistan to Sharjah (Coca-Cola Sharjah Cup) 1999-2000, to West Indies 1999-2000, to Sri Lanka 2000, to New Zealand 2000-01, to England 2001, to Bangladesh 2001-02, to Sharjah (v West Indies) 2001-02, to Sri Lanka (ICC

Champions Trophy) 2002-03, to Sri Lanka and Sharjah (v Australia) 2002-03, to Zimbabwe and South Africa 2002-03, to Africa (World Cup) 2002-03, to New Zealand 2003-04, to Australia 2004-05, to India 2004-05, to West Indies 2004-05, to Sri Lanka 2005-06, to England 2006, to India (ICC Champions Trophy) 2006-07 (c), to South Africa 2006-07, plus other one-day tournaments in Abu Dhabi, Singapore, Sharjah, Australia, Morocco, Kenya, Sri Lanka, England, Netherlands and India

Overseas teams played for: Peshawar/Peshawar Panthers 1998-99 – ; Habib Bank 1999-2000 –

Extras: Took a Test innings record for a substitute of four catches v Bangladesh in the Asian Test Championship 2001-02. His awards include Man of the Match in the third Test v India at Bangalore 2004-05 (267/84*), Man of the [Test] Series v India 2005-06 and Man of the [ODI] Series v England 2006. Vice-captain of Pakistan since the tour to India of 2004-05. Was an overseas player with Nottinghamshire during the 2005 season as a locum for Stephen Fleming; has joined Yorkshire as an overseas player for 2007

Best batting: 267 Pakistan v India, Bangalore 2004-05
Best bowling: 3-24 Habib Bank v Faisalabad, Faisalabad 1999-2000

2006 Season

	M	Inn	NO	Runs	HS	Avg	100	50	Ct	St	Balls	Runs	Wkts	Avg	BB	5I	10M
Test	3	5	0	329	173	65.80	1	1	2	-	0	0	0		-	-	-
FC	5	9	2	459	173	65.57	1	3	6	-	0	0	0		-	-	-
ODI	5	5	1	215	101	53.75	1	1	1	-	0	0	0		-	-	
List A	5	5	1	215	101	53.75	1	1	1	-	0	0	0		-	-	
20/20 Int	1	1	0	0	0	0.00	-	-	1	-	0	0	0		-	-	
20/20	1	1	0	0	0	0.00	-	-	1	-	0	0	0		-	-	

Career Performances

	M	Inn	NO	Runs	HS	Avg	100	50	Ct	St	Balls	Runs	Wkts	Avg	BB	5I	10M
Test	47	83	4	3884	267	49.16	12	15	49	-	264	169	2	84.50	1-24	-	-
FC	101	163	17	7465	267	51.13	24	31	106	-	1064	662	12	55.16	3-24	-	-
ODI	139	134	18	3756	144	32.37	2	25	71	-	91	101	1	101.00	1-24	-	
List A	167	161	24	4529	144	33.05	3	31	88	-	427	386	16	24.12	3-5	-	
20/20 Int	1	1	0	0	0	0.00	-	-	1	-	0	0	0		-	-	
20/20	5	5	2	120	35	40.00	-	-	2	-	12	33	0		-	-	

STOP PRESS

BOLLINGER, D. E.   Worcestershire

Name: Douglas (Doug) Erwin Bollinger
Role: Left-hand bat, left-arm fast bowler
Born: 24 July 1981, Sydney, New South Wales
Extras: Has represented Australia A. Has joined Worcestershire as an overseas player for 2007

THE UMPIRES

BAILEY, R. J.

Name: Robert (Rob) John Bailey
Born: 28 October 1963, Biddulph,
Stoke-on-Trent
Height: 6ft 3in
Nickname: Bailers
Wife and date of marriage: Rachel,
11 April 1987
Children: Harry, 7 March 1991; Alexandra,
13 November 1993
Family links with cricket: 'Son Harry plays
for Northampton Saints CC'
Education: Biddulph High School
Career outside cricket: Rob Bailey
Ceramics ('promotional mugs etc.')
Off-season: 'Working for Rob Bailey
Ceramics, supplying mugs, plates etc. to
sports clubs, businesses'
Other sports played: Badminton (county
schools)
Other sports followed: 'All football clubs that I supply mugs to!'
Appointed to 1st-Class list: 2006
Counties as player: Northamptonshire, Derbyshire
Role: Right-hand bat, off-spin bowler
County debut: 1982 (Northamptonshire), 2000 (Derbyshire)
County cap: 1985 (Northamptonshire), 2000 (Derbyshire)
Benefit: 1993 (Northamptonshire)
Test debut: 1988
ODI debut (matches): 1984-85 (4)
1000 runs in a season: 13
1st-Class 200s: 4
One-Day 100s: 9
One-Day 5 w. in innings: 1
Overseas tours: England to Sharjah 1984-85, 1986-87, to India 1988-89 (cancelled),
to West Indies 1989-90
Overseas teams played for: Rhodes University, Grahamstown, South Africa 1982-83;
Uitenhage CC, South Africa 1983-85; Fitzroy CC, Melbourne 1985-86; Gosnells CC,
Perth 1987-88
Highlights of playing career: 'Loved all of it'
Extras: Won three consecutive NatWest Man of the Match awards 1995 and three
consecutive B&H Gold Awards 1996. Northamptonshire captain 1996-97. In 1999
became sixth player to pass 20,000 first-class runs for Northamptonshire

Best batting: 224* Northamptonshire v Glamorgan, Swansea 1986
Best bowling: 5-54 Northamptonshire v Nottinghamshire, Northampton 1993

First-Class Career Performances

	M	Inn	NO	Runs	HS	Avg	100	Ct	St	Runs	Wkts	Avg	BB	5I	10M
Test	4	8	0	119	43	14.87	-	-	-						
FC	374	628	89	21844	224*	40.52	47	272	-	5144	121	42.51	5-54	2	-

BAINTON, N. L.

Name: <u>Neil</u> Laurence Bainton
Born: 2 October 1970, Romford, Essex
Height: 5ft 8in
Wife and date of marriage: Kay,
25 October 1997
Family links with cricket: Father played and
umpired club cricket
Education: Ilford County High School
Career outside cricket: 'Postman during
winter months'
Off-season: 'Postman in Braintree, Essex'
Other sports followed: Football (West Ham,
White Notley Ladies)
Appointed to 1st-Class list: 2006
Highlights of umpiring career: 'Being
appointed to first-class list'
Players to watch for the future: Billy
Godleman
County as player: Did not play first-class cricket

Did not play first-class cricket

BENSON, M. R.

Name: <u>Mark</u> Richard Benson
Born: 6 July 1958, Shoreham, Sussex
Height: 5ft 10in
Nickname: Benny
Wife and date of marriage: Sarah Patricia, 20 September 1986
Children: Laurence, 16 October 1987; Edward, 23 June 1990
Education: Sutton Valence School
Other sports played: Bridge, golf, swimming, cycling
Relaxations: Bridge, golf
Appointed to 1st-Class list: 2000
International panel: 2004-2006
Elite panel: 2006 –
Tests umpired: 15 (plus 6 as TV umpire)
ODIs umpired: 38 (plus 17 as TV umpire)
Twenty20 Ints umpired: 1 as TV umpire
Other umpiring honours: Stood in the C&G Trophy final 2003
County as player: Kent
Role: Left-hand bat
County debut: 1980
County cap: 1981
Benefit: 1991
Test debut: 1986
ODI debut (matches): 1986 (1)
1000 runs in a season: 11
1st-Class 200s: 1
One-Day 100s: 5
Overseas tours: None
Highlights of playing career: '257 v Hampshire. Winning Sunday League as captain of Kent. Two 90s to win a game against Hampshire with Malcolm Marshall bowling. One of only four cricketers in the history of Kent to have scored more than 10,000 runs and have an average in excess of 40'
Extras: Scored 1000 runs in first full season. Kent captain 1991-95
Opinions on cricket: 'Teams should be permitted a certain number of appeals against poor decisions. As an umpire I would be quite happy for a decision to be overturned if a mistake has been made. If the umpire has been proved to be correct, the team that has appealed loses one of their appeals. This occurs in American football and works very well.'
Best batting: 257 Kent v Hampshire, Southampton 1991
Best bowling: 2-55 Kent v Surrey, Dartford 1986

	M	Inn	NO	Runs	HS	Avg	100	Ct	St	Runs	Wkts	Avg	BB	5I	10M
Test	1	2	0	51	30	25.50	-	-	-						
FC	292	491	34	18387	257	40.23	48	140	-	493	5	98.60	2-55	-	-

BURGESS, G. I.

Name: Graham Iefvion Burgess
Born: 5 May 1943, Glastonbury, Somerset
Education: Millfield School
Appointed to 1st-Class list: 1991
ODIs umpired: 2 as
TV umpire
County as player: Somerset
Role: Right-hand bat, right-arm
medium bowler
County debut: 1966
County cap: 1968
Testimonial: 1977
One-Day 5 w. in innings: 2
Extras: Played Minor Counties cricket for
Wiltshire 1981-82 and for Cambridgeshire
1983-84
Best batting: 129 Somerset v
Gloucestershire, Taunton 1973
Best bowling: 7-43 Somerset v Oxford University, The Parks 1975

First-Class Career Performances

	M	Inn	NO	Runs	HS	Avg	100	Ct	St	Runs	Wkts	Avg	BB	5I	10M
Test															
FC	252	414	37	7129	129	18.90	2	120	-	13543	474	28.57	7-43	18	2

COWLEY, N. G.

Name: <u>Nigel</u> Geoffrey Cowley
Born: 1 March 1953, Shaftesbury, Dorset
Height: 5ft 6½in
Marital status: Divorced
Children: Mark Antony, 14 June 1973;
Darren James, 30 October 1976
Family links with cricket: Darren played
Hampshire Schools U11, U12, U13; Natal
Schools 1993, 1994, 1995; and toured India
with South Africa U19 1996
Education: Duchy Manor, Mere, Wiltshire
Other sports played: Golf (8 handicap)
Other sports followed: Football
(Liverpool FC)
Appointed to 1st-Class list: 2000
Counties as player: Hampshire, Glamorgan
Role: Right-hand bat, off-spin bowler
County debut: 1974 (Hampshire),
1990 (Glamorgan)
County cap: 1978 (Hampshire)

Benefit: 1988 (Hampshire)
1000 runs in a season: 1
50 wickets in a season: 2
One-Day 5 w. in innings: 1
Overseas tours: Hampshire to Barbados 1985, 1986, 1987, to Dubai 1989
Overseas teams played for: Paarl CC 1982-83; Amanzimtoti 1984-96
(both South Africa)
Extras: Played for Dorset 1972. NatWest Man of the Match award
Best batting: 109* Hampshire v Somerset, Taunton 1977
Best bowling: 6-48 Hampshire v Leicestershire, Southampton 1982

First-Class Career Performances

	M	Inn	NO	Runs	HS	Avg	100	Ct	St	Runs	Wkts	Avg	BB	5I	10M
Test															
FC	271	375	62	7309	109*	23.35	2	105	-	14879	437	34.04	6-48	5	-

DUDLESTON, B.

Name: Barry Dudleston
Born: 16 July 1945, Bebington, Cheshire
Height: 5ft 9in
Nickname: Danny
Wife and date of marriage: Louise Wendy, 19 October 1994
Children: Sharon Louise, 29 October 1968; Matthew Barry, 12 September 1988; Jack Nicholas, 29 April 1998
Family links with cricket: 'Dad was a league cricketer'
Education: Stockport School
Career outside cricket: Managing director of Sunsport Ltd
Other sports played: Golf
Other sports followed: All sports
Relaxations: Bridge, red wine
Appointed to 1st-Class list: 1984
First appointed to Test panel: 1991
Tests umpired: 2 (plus 4 as TV umpire)
ODIs umpired: 4 (plus 6 as TV umpire)
Other umpiring honours: Stood in C&G final 2001 and B&H final 2002; also officiated at the inaugural Twenty20 finals day at Trent Bridge 2003, including standing in the final, and at Twenty20 finals day 2006 at Trent Bridge
Players to watch for the future: Stuart Broad
Counties as player: Leicestershire, Gloucestershire
Role: Right-hand opening bat, slow left-arm bowler, occasional wicket-keeper
County debut: 1966 (Leicestershire), 1981 (Gloucestershire)
County cap: 1969 (Leicestershire)
Benefit: 1980 (Leicestershire)
1000 runs in a season: 8
1st-Class 200s: 1
One-Day 100s: 4
Overseas tours: Kent (as guest player) to West Indies 1972; D.H. Robins' XI to West Indies 1973; Wisden XI to West Indies 1984; MCC to Kenya 1993
Overseas teams played for: Rhodesia 1976-80
Highlights of playing career: 'Winning County Championship [with Leicestershire]'
Extras: Played for England U25. Holder with John Steele of the highest first-wicket partnership for Leicestershire, 390 v Derbyshire at Leicester in 1979. Fastest player in Rhodesian cricket history to 1000 first-class runs in Currie Cup; second fastest ever in Currie Cup

Best batting: 202 Leicestershire v Derbyshire, Leicester 1979
Best bowling: 4-6 Leicestershire v Surrey, Leicester 1972

First-Class Career Performances

	M	Inn	NO	Runs	HS	Avg	100	Ct	St	Runs	Wkts	Avg	BB	5I	10M
Test															
FC	295	501	47	14747	202	32.48	32	234	7	1365	47	29.04	4-6	-	-

EVANS, J. H.

Name: Jeffrey (Jeff) Howard Evans
Born: 7 August 1954, Llanelli
Height: 5ft 8in
Marital status: Single
Education: Llanelli Boys Grammar School; Dudley College of Education
Career outside cricket: 'Supply teaching. Driving for Interski'
Off-season: 'Skiing in Aosta Valley. Supply teaching. Training umpires'
Other sports followed: Rugby union
Relaxations: Keeping fit
Appointed to 1st-Class list: 2001
Other umpiring honours: Toured Namibia and Uganda 2004-05 with MCC (as umpire)
Highlights of umpiring career: 'First Championship match – Yorkshire v Somerset at Headingley 2001'
Players to watch for the future: Adil Rashid, Ravi Bopara
Cricket moments to forget: 'Any error of judgement!'
County as player: Did not play first-class cricket. Played league cricket in South Wales as a right-hand bat
Extras: Coach to Welsh Schools Cricket Association team on tour to Australia 1993. Taught in the Gwendraeth Grammar School – 'the old "outside-half factory"'
Opinions on cricket: 'Would like to see more honesty throughout the game!'

Did not play first-class cricket

GOULD, I. J.

Name: <u>Ian</u> James Gould
Born: 19 August 1957, Taplow, Bucks
Height: 5ft 7in
Nickname: Gunner
Wife and date of marriage: Joanne, 27 September 1986
Children: Gemma; Michael; George
Education: Westgate Secondary Modern, Slough
Other sports played: Golf
Other sports followed: Football (Arsenal), racing
Appointed to 1st-Class list: 2002
International panel: 2006 –
Tests umpired: 2 as TV umpire
ODIs umpired: 8 (plus 3 as TV umpire)
Twenty20 Ints umpired: 1 (plus 1 as TV umpire)
Other umpiring honours: Officiated at the Twenty20 finals days at Edgbaston 2004 and at The Oval 2005, including standing in both finals. PCA Umpire of the Year 2005
Players to watch for the future: Ollie Rayner
Counties as player: Middlesex, Sussex
Role: Left-hand bat, wicket-keeper
County debut: 1975 (Middlesex), 1981 (Sussex)
County cap: 1977 (Middlesex), 1981 (Sussex)
Benefit: 1990 (Sussex)
ODI debut (matches): 1982-83 (18)
Overseas tours: England YC to West Indies 1976; D.H. Robins' XI to Canada 1978-79; International XI to Pakistan 1980-81; England to Australia and New Zealand 1982-83; MCC to Namibia
Overseas teams played for: Auckland 1979-80
Highlights of playing career: 'Playing in the World Cup'
Extras: Represented England in the 1983 World Cup. Retired from county cricket in 1991
Best batting: 128 Middlesex v Worcestershire, Worcester 1978
Best bowling: 3-10 Sussex v Surrey, The Oval 1989

First-Class Career Performances

	M	Inn	NO	Runs	HS	Avg	100	Ct	St	Runs	Wkts	Avg	Best	5I	10M
Test															
FC	297	399	63	8756	128	26.06	4	536	67	365	7	52.14	3-10	-	-

HARRIS, M. J.

Name: <u>Michael</u> John Harris
Born: 25 May 1944, St Just-in-Roseland, Cornwall
Height: 6ft 1in
Nickname: Pasty
Wife and date of marriage: Danielle Ruth, 10 September 1969
Children: Jodie; Richard
Education: Gerrans Comprehensive
Career outside cricket: Sports teacher
Other sports followed: Squash, golf
Appointed to 1st-Class list: 1998
Counties as player: Middlesex, Nottinghamshire
Role: Right-hand bat, leg-break bowler, wicket-keeper
County debut: 1964 (Middlesex), 1969 (Nottinghamshire)
County cap: 1967 (Middlesex), 1970 (Nottinghamshire)
1000 runs in a season: 11
1st-Class 200s: 1
One-Day 100s: 3
Overseas teams played for: Eastern Province 1971-72; Wellington 1975-76
Extras: Shared Middlesex then record first-wicket partnership of 312 with Eric Russell v Pakistanis at Lord's 1967. Scored nine centuries in 1971 to equal Nottinghamshire county record for a season, scoring two centuries in a match twice and totalling 2238 runs at an average of 50.86
Best batting: 201* Nottinghamshire v Glamorgan, Trent Bridge 1973
Best bowling: 4-16 Nottinghamshire v Warwickshire, Trent Bridge 1969

First-Class Career Performances

	M	Inn	NO	Runs	HS	Avg	100	Ct	St	Runs	Wkts	Avg	BB	5I	10M
Test															
FC	344	581	58	19196	201*	36.70	41	288	14	3459	79	43.78	4-16	-	-

HARTLEY, P. J.

Name: <u>Peter</u> John Hartley
Born: 18 April 1960, Keighley, Yorkshire
Height: 6ft
Nickname: Jack
Wife and date of marriage: Sharon,
12 March 1988
Children: Megan, 25 April 1992;
Courtney, 25 July 1995
Family links with cricket: Father played
local league cricket
Education: Greenhead Grammar School,
Keighley; Bradford College
Career outside cricket: Sports footwear
agent
Off-season: 'Skiing when possible'
Other sports played: Golf, skiing
Other sports followed: Football (Chelsea)
Relaxations: 'Gardening, walking the hound'
Appointed to 1st-Class list: 2003

International panel: 2006 – (as TV umpire)
Tests umpired: 3 as TV umpire
ODIs umpired: 2 as TV umpire
Twenty20 Ints umpired: 1 (plus 1 as TV umpire)
Other umpiring honours: Officated at Twenty20 finals day 2006 at Trent Bridge,
including in the final
Counties as player: Warwickshire, Yorkshire, Hampshire
Role: Right-hand bat, right-arm fast-medium bowler
County debut: 1982 (Warwickshire), 1985 (Yorkshire), 1998 (Hampshire)
County cap: 1987 (Yorkshire), 1998 (Hampshire)
Benefit: 1996 (Yorkshire)
50 wickets in a season: 7
One-Day 5 w. in innings: 5
Overseas tours: Yorkshire pre-season tours to Barbados 1986-87, to South Africa
1991-92, 1992-93, to Zimbabwe
Overseas teams played for: Melville, New Zealand 1983-84; Adelaide, Australia
1985-86; Harmony and Orange Free State, South Africa 1988-89
Extras: Returned 8-65, his best figures for Hampshire, against Yorkshire, his former
county, at Basingstoke 1999. Recorded his highest B&H score (32*) and best one-day
analysis (5-20) v Sussex at Hove 2000. Retired at the end of the 2000 season
Best batting: 127* Yorkshire v Lancashire, Old Trafford 1988
Best bowling: 9-41 Yorkshire v Derbyshire, Chesterfield 1995

First-Class Career Performances

	M	Inn	NO	Runs	HS	Avg	100	Ct	St	Runs	Wkts	Avg	BB	5I	10M
Test															
FC	232	283	66	4321	127*	19.91	2	68	-	20635	683	30.21	9-41	23	3

HOLDER, J. W.

Name: <u>John</u> Wakefield Holder
Born: 19 March 1945, Barbados
Height: 5ft 11in
Nickname: Benson
Wife's name: Glenda
Children: Christopher, 1968; Nigel, 1970
Education: Combermere High School, Barbados; Rochdale College
Off-season: 'Relaxing initially, then working part-time for the European Cricket Council; keeping fit'
Other sports followed: Football (Manchester United)
Relaxations: 'Regular visits to the gym trying to keep fit. Love watching wildlife programmes on TV and travel'
Appointed to 1st-Class list: 1983
First appointed to Test panel: 1988
Tests umpired: 11 (plus 5 as TV umpire)
ODIs umpired: 19 (plus 3 as TV umpire)
Other umpiring honours: Umpired in Nehru Cup in India and in Pakistan v India Test series 1989-90. Umpired in Pepsi Champions Trophy, Sharjah 1993-94 and Masters Cup, Sharjah 1995-96. MCC tours to Kenya 1999, 2002 and to Greece 2003 (as umpire). Has stood in Refuge Assurance Cup, B&H Cup and NatWest Trophy finals and in C&G Trophy final 2002. Officiated at the inaugural Twenty20 finals day at Trent Bridge 2003, including standing in the final, and at finals day at The Oval 2005
Highlights of umpiring career: 'Ashes Test at Lord's in 2001'
County as player: Hampshire
Role: Right-hand bat, right-arm fast bowler
County debut: 1968
50 wickets in a season: 1
Highlights of playing career: 'Taking 6-7 against International Cavaliers in 1968'
Extras: Championship hat-trick v Kent at Southampton 1972. Retired from county cricket in 1972

Opinions on cricket: 'A few years ago at Headingley, about two hours before the start of a National League game, the entire Yorkshire playing staff sat at a row of tables signing autographs for fans. This is an excellent idea which I believe every county should copy for two matches every year. This would help foster better relations between players and the public.'

Best batting: 33 Hampshire v Sussex, Hove 1971
Best bowling: 7-79 Hampshire v Gloucestershire, Gloucester 1972

First-Class Career Performances

	M	Inn	NO	Runs	HS	Avg	100	Ct	St	Runs	Wkts	Avg	BB	5l	10M
Test															
FC	47	49	14	374	33	10.68	-	12	-	3415	139	24.56	7-79	5	1

HOLDER, V. A.

Name: <u>Vanburn</u> Alonza Holder
Born: 8 October 1945, St Michael, Barbados
Height: 6ft 3in
Nickname: Van
Wife's name: Christine
Children: James Vanburn, 2 September 1981
Education: St Leonard's Secondary Modern; Community High
Other sports followed: Football (Liverpool)
Relaxations: Music, doing crosswords
Appointed to 1st-Class list: 1992
ODIs umpired: 2 as TV umpire
County as player: Worcestershire
Role: Right-hand bat, right-arm fast-medium bowler
County debut: 1968
County cap: 1970
Benefit: 1979
Test debut: 1969
ODI debut (matches): 1973 (12)
50 wickets in a season: 9
One-Day 5 w. in innings: 3

Overseas tours: West Indies to England 1969, 1973, 1975 (World Cup), 1976, to India, Sri Lanka and Pakistan 1974-75, to Australia 1975-76, to India and Sri Lanka 1978-79 (vc); Rest of the World to Pakistan 1973-74
Overseas teams played for: Barbados 1966-78
Extras: Made his debut for Barbados in the Shell Shield competition in 1966-67. Won John Player League 1973 and County Championship 1974 with Worcestershire. Played in West Indies 1975 World Cup winning side

Best batting: 122 Barbados v Trinidad, Bridgetown 1973-74
Best bowling: 7-40 Worcestershire v Glamorgan, Cardiff 1974

First-Class Career Performances

	M	Inn	NO	Runs	HS	Avg	100	Ct	St	Runs	Wkts	Avg	BB	5I	10M
Test	40	59	11	682	42	14.20	-	16	-	3627	109	33.27	6-28	3	-
FC	311	354	81	3559	122	13.03	1	98	-	23183	948	24.45	7-40	38	3

ILLINGWORTH, R. K.

Name: <u>Richard</u> Keith Illingworth
Born: 23 August 1963, Greengates,
near Bradford, Yorkshire
Height: 5ft 11in
Nickname: Harry, Lucy, Illy
Wife and date of marriage: Anne Louise,
20 September 1985
Children: Miles, 28 August 1987; Thomas,
20 April 1989
Family links with cricket: Father played
Bradford League
Education: Salts GS
Off-season: 'Coaching'
Other sports played: Golf
Other sports followed: Football (Leeds),
rugby league (Bradford Bulls), rugby union
(Worcester)
Relaxations: 'Watching my two sons playing
sport; cooking; wine tasting'
Appointed to 1st-Class list: 2006
Counties as player: Worcestershire, Derbyshire
Role: Right-hand bat, left-arm orthodox spin bowler
County debut: 1982 (Worcestershire), 2001 (Derbyshire)
County cap: 1986 (Worcestershire)
Benefit: 1997 (Worcestershire)
Test debut: 1991
ODI debut (matches): 1991 (25)
50 wickets in a season: 5
One-Day 5 w. in innings: 2
Overseas tours: England A to Kenya and Zimbabwe 1989-90, to Pakistan and Sri
Lanka 1990-91; England to New Zealand and Australia (World Cup) 1991-92, to South
Africa 1995-96, to India and Pakistan (World Cup) 1995-96
Overseas teams played for: Brisbane Colts 1982-83; Zingari, Pietermaritzburg, South

Africa 1984-85, 1988-89; University/St Heliers, New Zealand 1986-88; Natal 1988-89; Abahani, Bangladesh 1994
Highlights of playing career: 'Playing for England. Being part of many Worcestershire trophy wins. Wicket [Phil Simmons of West Indies] with first ball in Test cricket'
Cricket moments to forget: 'None, apart from getting out for nought or dropping catches (of which there were a few)'
Extras: Scored three centuries batting as a nightwatchman. First Worcestershire bowler to take a one-day hat-trick, v Sussex at Hove in the Sunday League 1993. Retired at the end of the 2001 season
Best batting: 120* Worcestershire v Warwickshire, Worcester 1987
Best bowling: 7-50 Worcestershire v Oxford University, The Parks 1985

First-Class Career Performances

	M	Inn	NO	Runs	HS	Avg	100	Ct	St	Runs	Wkts	Avg	BB	5I	10M
Test	9	14	7	128	28	18.28	-	5	-	615	19	32.36	4-96	-	-
FC	376	435	122	7027	120*	22.45	4	161	-	26213	831	31.54	7-50	27	6

JESTY, T. E.

Name: <u>Trevor</u> Edward Jesty
Born: 2 June 1948, Gosport, Hampshire
Height: 5ft 9in
Nickname: Jets
Wife and date of marriage: Jacqueline, 12 September 1970
Children: Graeme Barry, 27 September 1972; Lorna Samantha, 7 November 1976
Family links with cricket: Daughter played for England XI 2000
Education: Privett County Secondary Modern, Gosport
Off-season: Cricket coaching
Other sports followed: Football (Arsenal)
Relaxations: Gardening, reading
Appointed to 1st-Class list: 1994
ODIs umpired: 3 as TV umpire
Counties as player: Hampshire, Surrey, Lancashire

Role: Right-hand bat, right-arm medium bowler
County debut: 1966 (Hampshire), 1985 (Surrey), 1988 (Lancashire)
County cap: 1971 (Hampshire), 1985 (Surrey), 1990 (Lancashire)
Benefit: 1982 (Hampshire)

ODI debut (matches): 1982-83 (10)
1000 runs in a season: 10
50 wickets in a season: 2
1st-Class 200s: 2
One-Day 100s: 7
Overseas tours: International XI to West Indies 1982; joined England tour to Australia 1982-83; Lancashire to Zimbabwe 1989
Overseas teams played for: Border, South Africa 1973-74; Griqualand West 1974-76, 1980-81; Canterbury, New Zealand 1979-80
Highlights of playing career: 'Winning Championship with Hampshire in 1973. Playing against Australia for England in one-day match on 1982-83 tour'
Extras: One of *Wisden*'s Five Cricketers of the Year 1983
Best batting: 248 Hampshire v Cambridge University, Fenner's 1984
Best bowling: 7-75 Hampshire v Worcestershire, Southampton 1976

First-Class Career Performances

	M	Inn	NO	Runs	HS	Avg	100	Ct	St	Runs	Wkts	Avg	BB	5I	10M
Test															
FC	490	777	107	21916	248	32.71	35	265	1	16075	585	27.47	7-75	19	-

JONES, A. A.

Name: <u>Allan</u> Arthur Jones
Born: 9 December 1947, Three Bridges, Sussex
Height: 6ft 3in
Nickname: Jonah
Wife and date of marriage: Stephanie, 11 December 2004
Children: Clare, 4 July 1979
Education: St John's College, Horsham
Career outside cricket: 'Selling golf holidays and villas in Spain'
Off-season: 'Enjoying life'
Other sports played: Golf
Other sports followed: Football (Arsenal)
Relaxations: 'Reading, visiting castles etc.'
Appointed to 1st-Class list: 1985
First appointed to Test panel: 1996
Tests umpired: 3 as TV umpire
ODIs umpired: 1 (plus 4 as TV umpire)

Other umpiring honours: Has umpired at Hong Kong Sixes. Stood in the C&G final

2005 at Lord's; also at Twenty20 finals day 2006 at Trent Bridge, including in the final. Former chairman of the First-Class Umpires' Association

Highlights of umpiring career: 'C&G final 2005'
Counties as player: Sussex, Somerset, Middlesex, Glamorgan
Role: Right-hand bat, right-arm fast bowler
County debut: 1964 (Sussex), 1970 (Somerset), 1976 (Middlesex), 1980 (Glamorgan)
County cap: 1972 (Somerset), 1976 (Middlesex)
50 wickets in a season: 4
One-Day 5 w. in innings: 5
Overseas teams played for: Northern Transvaal 1971-72; Orange Free State 1976-77
Highlights of playing career: '9-51 v Sussex 1972'
Cricket moments to forget: 'Being hit by Norman McVicker of Leicestershire for two sixes off last two balls of the match to lose the game'
Extras: Won two Championship medals with Middlesex (1976 and 1977). Was on stand-by for England tour of India 1976-77. Represented MCC v Australians 1977. Was the first person to play for four counties
Opinions on cricket: 'Too many technicalities used for bowling, instead of teaching basics.'
Best batting: 33 Middlesex v Kent, Canterbury 1978
Best bowling: 9-51 Somerset v Sussex, Hove 1972

First-Class Career Performances

	M	Inn	NO	Runs	HS	Avg	100	Ct	St	Runs	Wkts	Avg	BB	5I	10M
Test															
FC	214	216	68	799	33	5.39	-	50	-	15414	549	28.07	9-51	23	3

KETTLEBOROUGH, R. A.

Name: <u>Richard</u> Allan Kettleborough
Born: 15 March 1973, Sheffield
Height: 5ft 11in
Nickname: Ketts
Marital status: Engaged
Family links with cricket: 'Dad played for
Yorkshire 2nd XI and in league cricket'
Education: Worksop College; Airedale and
Wharfdale College
Career outside cricket: Groundsman
Off-season: 'Working on the grounds'
Other sports played: Football
Other sports followed: Football (Sheffield
Wednesday FC)
Relaxations: 'Spending time with fiancée
Lucy, socialising with friends and walking
the dogs'
Appointed to 1st-Class list: 2006
Highlights of umpiring career: 'All the first-class matches in which I have stood and
the international club 20/20 tournament in 2005'
Players to watch for the future: Alastair Cook, Tom Smith, Stuart Broad,
Adil Rashid
Counties as player: Yorkshire, Middlesex
Role: Left-hand bat
County debut: 1994 (Yorkshire), 1998 (Middlesex)
Overseas tours: England U18 to Canada 1991; Yorkshire to South Africa 1994, to
Zimbabwe 1995, to West Indies 1996; MCC to Hong Kong 2000, to Kenya 2001, to
Australia 2002-03, to UAE 2004, to Namibia and Uganda 2005, to India 2006
Overseas teams played for: Somerset West, Cape Town 1993-94; Constantia,
Cape Town 2003
Highlights of playing career: 'Yorkshire debut 1994. Maiden first-class hundred v
Essex 1996. Winning National Club Knockout with Sheffield Collegiate 2000'
Cricket moments to forget: '1998 and 1999 spent in London'
Extras: MCC Young Cricketer of the Year 1988. Yorkshire Young Player of the
Year 1996
Opinions on cricket: 'Reduce the number of non-English-qualified players in
county cricket.'
Best batting: 108 Yorkshire v Essex, Headingley 1996
Best bowling: 2-26 Yorkshire v Nottinghamshire, Scarborough 1996

First-Class Career Performances

	M	Inn	NO	Runs	HS	Avg	100	Ct	St	Runs	Wkts	Avg	BB	5I	10M
Test															
FC	33	56	6	1258	108	25.16	1	20	-	243	3	81.00	2-26	-	-

LEADBEATER, B.

Name: Barrie Leadbeater
Born: 14 August 1943, Leeds
Height: 6ft
Nickname: Leady
Wife and date of marriage: Penny,
8 April 2006
Children: Richard, 23 November 1972;
Michael, 21 March 1975; Daniel, 19 June
1981
Education: Harehills County Secondary,
Leeds
Career outside cricket: HGV Class A driver
Off-season: 'Driving'
Other sports played: Golf
Other sports followed: Football, rugby
league and union, snooker
Relaxations: 'Keeping fit, running'
Appointed to 1st-Class list: 1981
Tests umpired: 2 as TV umpire
ODIs umpired: 5 (plus 2 as TV umpire)

Other umpiring honours: Stood in 1983 World Cup. MCC tours to New Zealand
1999 and to Argentina and Chile 2001. Has stood in several domestic semi-finals.
Former chairman of the First-Class Umpires' Association
County as player: Yorkshire
Role: Right-hand bat, right-arm medium bowler
County debut: 1966
County cap: 1969
Benefit: 1980 (joint benefit with G.A. Cope)
Overseas tours: Duke of Norfolk's XI to West Indies 1969-70
Overseas teams played for: Johannesburg Municipals 1978-79
Highlights of playing career: 'Gillette Cup final, Lord's, 1969, v Derbyshire – Man
of the Match'
Cricket moments to forget: 'Can't remember'
Extras: Took part in London Marathon 1997, 1999, 2000. Retired from county cricket
in 1979 and played social cricket

Opinions on cricket: 'A little more honesty and self-analysis wouldn't go amiss. Some improvement in technique, both batting and bowling, is required if we are to compete effectively with the top international teams.'
Best batting: 140* Yorkshire v Hampshire, Portsmouth 1976
Best bowling: 1-1 Yorkshire v Middlesex, Headingley 1971

First-Class Career Performances

	M	Inn	NO	Runs	HS	Avg	100	Ct	St	Runs	Wkts	Avg	BB	5I	10M
Test															
FC	147	241	29	5373	140*	25.34	1	82	-	5	1	5.00	1-1	-	-

LLONG, N. J.

Name: <u>Nigel</u> James Llong
Born: 11 February 1969, Ashford, Kent
Height: 6ft
Nickname: Nidge
Wife and date of marriage: Melissa, 20 February 1999
Children: Andrew Stuart, 30 August 2002; Matthew James, 14 December 2004
Family links with cricket: Father and brother played local club cricket
Education: North School for Boys, Ashford
Off-season: Coaching – Duke of York School, Dover
Other sports followed: Football (Arsenal), 'generally most sports'
Relaxations: Fishing
Appointed to 1st-Class list: 2002
International panel: 2004-2006 as TV umpire; 2006 –

Tests umpired: 6 as TV umpire
ODIs umpired: 6 (plus 13 as TV umpire)
Twenty20 Ints umpired: 3
Other umpiring honours: Officiated at Twenty20 finals day at Edgbaston 2004, including standing in the final
Highlights of umpiring career: 'Twenty20 finals 2004. All international matches'
County as player: Kent
Role: Left-hand bat, right-arm off-spin bowler
County debut: 1991
County cap: 1993
One-Day 100s: 2

Overseas tours: Kent to Zimbabwe 1993

Overseas teams played for: Ashburton, Melbourne 1988-90, 1996-97; Green Point, Cape Town 1990-95

Highlights of playing career: 'B&H final 1997. Sunday League winners 1995. First Championship hundred, Lord's 1993'

Cricket moments to forget: 'Sunday League [1993], last match against Glamorgan at Canterbury – lost the match and were runners-up. Plus not making the most of my ability'

Extras: Kent Young Player of the Year 1992. Man of the Match in 2nd XI Trophy semi-final and final 1999. Retired from county cricket in September 1999 and played for Norfolk in 2000

Opinions on cricket: 'Umpires watch every ball of a game. It's amazing how little their opinions are valued!'

Best batting: 130 Kent v Hampshire, Canterbury 1996

Best bowling: 5-21 Kent v Middlesex, Canterbury 1996

First-Class Career Performances

	M	Inn	NO	Runs	HS	Avg	100	Ct	St	Runs	Wkts	Avg	BB	5I	10M
Test															
FC	68	108	11	3024	130	31.17	6	59	-	1259	35	35.97	5-21	2	-

LLOYDS, J. W.

Name: <u>Jeremy</u> William Lloyds

Born: 17 November 1954, Penang, Malaya

Height: 5ft 11in

Nickname: Jerry

Wife and date of marriage: Janine, 16 September 1997

Children: Kaeli, 16 November 1991

Family links with cricket: Father played cricket in Malaya. Brother Chris played for Somerset 2nd XI

Education: Blundell's School, Tiverton

Career outside cricket: Coaching and setting up Western Province Youth Programme 1992-95 in South Africa

Off-season: 'Getting a job'

Other sports played: Golf (6 handicap)

Other sports followed: Golf, football (Tottenham Hotspur), American football

(San Francisco 49ers), Formula One and saloon car racing, rugby (Gloucester)

Relaxations: 'Reading, music and spending time at home with my family'

Appointed to 1st-Class list: 1998
International panel: 2002-2004 as TV umpire; 2004-2006
Tests umpired: 5 (plus 10 as TV umpire)
ODIs umpired: 18 (plus 22 as TV umpire)
Twenty20 Ints umpired: 1
Other umpiring honours: Stood in the C&G final 2006
Counties as player: Somerset, Gloucestershire
Role: Left-hand bat, off-spin bowler
County debut: 1979 (Somerset), 1985 (Gloucestershire)
County cap: 1982 (Somerset), 1985 (Gloucestershire)
1000 runs in a season: 3
Overseas tours: Somerset to Antigua 1982; Gloucestershire to Barbados 1985,
to Sri Lanka 1987
Overseas teams played for: St Stithian's Old Boys, Johannesburg 1978-79; Toombull
DCC, Brisbane 1980-82; North Sydney District 1982-83; Alberton, Johannesburg
1984; Preston CC, Melbourne 1986; Orange Free State 1987; Fish Hoek CC,
Cape Town 1988-92
Highlights of playing career: 'Winning 1983 NatWest final'
Extras: Highest score in Brisbane Premier League 1980-81 (165). Britannic Player of
the Month July 1987. Gloucestershire Player of the Year 1987. Leading run-scorer in
Western Province Cricket League 1988, 1989
Opinions on cricket: 'Would take too long. I would suggest that by having central
contracts we are creating elitism. Batsmen must be allowed to bat and bowlers to bowl
whenever possible. Net bowling/batting is never quite the same.'
Best batting: 132* Somerset v Northamptonshire, Northampton 1982
Best bowling: 7-88 Somerset v Essex, Chelmsford 1982

First-Class Career Performances

	M	Inn	NO	Runs	HS	Avg	100	Ct	St	Runs	Wkts	Avg	BB	5I	10M
Test															
FC	267	408	64	10679	132*	31.04	10	229	-	12943	333	38.86	7-88	13	1

MALLENDER, N. A.

Name: <u>Neil</u> Alan Mallender
Born: 13 August 1961, Kirk Sandall,
Doncaster
Height: 6ft
Nickname: Ghostie
Marital status: Divorced
Children: Kirstie, 18; Dominic, 15; Jacob, 10
Education: Beverley Grammar School
Off-season: 'Trying to keep fit'
Other sports played: Golf (2 handicap)
Other sports followed: 'Most sports'
Relaxations: 'Watching sport; music'
Appointed to 1st-Class list: 1999
International panel: 2002-2004
Tests umpired: 3 (plus 5 as TV umpire)
ODIs umpired: 22 (plus 9 as TV umpire)
Other umpiring honours: Went with MCC
to umpire in Namibia March/April 2001.

PCA Umpire of the Year 2001, 2002, 2003, 2004, 2006. Stood in the 2002-03 World
Cup. Umpired the 2004, 2005 and 2006 C&G Trophy finals
Highlights of umpiring career: 'First ODI at Lord's, England v Pakistan – and game
went to the last ball'
Players to watch for the future: Stuart Broad, Tom Smith, Ravi Bopara
Counties as player: Northamptonshire, Somerset
Role: Right-hand bat, right-arm fast-medium bowler
County debut: 1980 (Northamptonshire), 1987 (Somerset)
County cap: 1984 (Northamptonshire), 1987 (Somerset)
Benefit: 1994 (Somerset)
Test debut: 1992
50 wickets in a season: 6
One-Day 5 w. in innings: 3
Overseas tours: England YC to West Indies 1979-80
Overseas teams played for: Kaikorai, Dunedin, New Zealand; University,
Wellington, New Zealand; Otago, New Zealand 1983-84 – 1992-93
Highlights of playing career: 'Test debut at Headingley'
Extras: Represented England YC 1980-81. Took 5-50 on Test debut v Pakistan at
Headingley in 1992. Retired from county cricket in 1996
Opinions on cricket: 'In 25 years involved in the game I have never known such
interest and enthusiasm for cricket as [in] the summer of 2005. It shows what a great
game it is and we are so lucky to be involved!'
Best batting: 100* Otago v Central Districts, Palmerston North 1991-92
Best bowling: 7-27 Otago v Auckland, Auckland 1984-85

First-Class Career Performances

	M	Inn	NO	Runs	HS	Avg	100	Ct	St	Runs	Wkts	Avg	BB	5I	10M
Test	2	3	0	8	4	2.66	-	-	-	215	10	21.50	5-50	1	-
FC	345	396	122	4709	100*	17.18	1	111	-	24654	937	26.31	7-27	36	5

PALMER, R.

Name: Roy Palmer
Born: 12 July 1942, Hampshire
Height: 6ft 3in
Nickname: Arp
Wife and date of marriage: Alyne,
5 November 1983
Children: Nick, 7 October 1968
Family links with cricket: Brother of Ken
Palmer, former Test umpire and Somerset
player; nephew Gary also played for
Somerset
Education: Southbroom Secondary Modern,
Devizes
Off-season: Golf, DIY
Relaxations: Golf
Appointed to 1st-Class list: 1980
First appointed to Test panel: 1992
Tests umpired: 2 (plus 1 as TV umpire)
ODIs umpired: 8 (plus 2 as TV umpire)
Other umpiring honours: Stood in 1983 World Cup
County as player: Somerset
Role: Right-hand bat, right-arm fast-medium bowler
County debut: 1965
50 wickets in a season: 1
One-Day 5 w. in innings: 1
Extras: Won two Man of the Match Awards in the Gillette Cup
Best batting: 84 Somerset v Leicestershire, Taunton 1967
Best bowling: 6-45 Somerset v Middlesex, Lord's 1967

First-Class Career Performances

	M	Inn	NO	Runs	HS	Avg	100	Ct	St	Runs	Wkts	Avg	BB	5I	10M
Test															
FC	74	110	32	1037	84	13.29	-	25	-	5439	172	31.62	6-45	4	-

ROBINSON, R. T.

Name: Robert Timothy (<u>Tim</u>) Robinson
Born: 21 November 1958, Sutton-in-Ashfield, Nottinghamshire
Height: 6ft
Nickname: Robbo
Marital status: Divorced
Children: Philip; Alex
Family links with cricket: 'Father, uncles all played local cricket'
Education: Dunstable GS; High Pavement GS; Sheffield University
Career outside cricket: 'Accountancy. Sports promotions'
Off-season: 'Self-employed, doing above'
Other sports played: Golf, squash
Other sports followed: Golf, rugby, football
Appointed to 1st-Class list: 2007
County as player: Nottinghamshire
Role: Right-hand opening bat
County debut: 1978
County cap: 1983
Benefit: 1992
Test debut: 1984-85
ODI debut (matches): 1984-85 (26)
1000 runs in a season: 14
1st-Class 200s: 3
One-Day 100s: 9

Overseas tours: England to India and Sri Lanka 1984-85, to West Indies 1985-86, to India and Pakistan (World Cup) 1987-88, to Pakistan 1987-88, to New Zealand and Australia 1987-88, plus two one-day tournaments in Sharjah; unofficial England XI to South Africa 1989-90
Highlights of playing career: '175 v Aussie, home Test debut 1985' (*In the first Test at Headingley*)
Cricket moments to forget: 'Retiring from first-class cricket'
Extras: One of *Wisden*'s Five Cricketers of the Year 1986. Second in the list of Nottinghamshire first-class run-scorers behind George Gunn. Captain of Nottinghamshire 1988-95. Retired from county cricket at the end of the 1999 season
Opinions on cricket: 'Should become more spectator-orientated.'
Best batting: 220* Nottinghamshire v Yorkshire, Trent Bridge 1990
Best bowling: 1-22 Nottinghamshire v Northamptonshire, Northampton 1982

	M	Inn	NO	Runs	HS	Avg	100	Ct	St	Runs	Wkts	Avg	BB	5I	10M
Test	29	49	5	1601	175	36.38	4	8	-	0	0		-	-	-
FC	425	739	85	27571	220*	42.15	63	257	-	289	4	72.25	1-22	-	-

SHARP, G.

Name: George Sharp
Born: 12 March 1950, West Hartlepool,
County Durham
Height: 5ft 11in
Nickname: Sharpy
Wife and date of marriage: Audrey,
14 September 1974
Children: Gareth James, 27 June 1984
Education: Elwick Road Secondary Modern,
Hartlepool
Career outside cricket: Watching all sports
Off-season: Working as joint director of GSB
Loams Ltd for soils and top dressing
Other sports played: Golf (8 handicap)
Other sports followed: Football (Newcastle
Utd and Middlesbrough), rugby
(Northampton Saints)
Relaxations: Golf; 'spend a lot of time in the
gym during the off-season'
Appointed to 1st-Class list: 1992
International panel: 1996-2002
Tests umpired: 15 (plus 1 as TV umpire)
ODIs umpired: 31 (plus 13 as TV umpire)
Other umpiring honours: Has umpired three B&H finals and one NatWest final and
stood in the inaugural C&G final 2001 and the 2002 final; also officiated at the
inaugural Twenty20 finals day at Trent Bridge 2003, at finals day 2005 at The Oval
and at finals day 2006 at Trent Bridge. Has stood in four overseas tournaments,
including the Singer Cup (India, Sri Lanka, Pakistan) in Singapore 1995-96 and the
Singer Champions Trophy (Pakistan, Sri Lanka, New Zealand) in Sharjah 1996-97
County as player: Northamptonshire
Role: Right-hand bat, wicket-keeper
County debut: 1967
County cap: 1973
Benefit: 1982
Overseas tours: England Counties XI to Barbados and Trinidad 1975

Best batting: 98 Northamptonshire v Yorkshire, Northampton 1983
Best bowling: 1-47 Northamptonshire v Yorkshire, Northampton 1980

First-Class Career Performances

	M	Inn	NO	Runs	HS	Avg	100	Ct	St	Runs	Wkts	Avg	BB	5I	10M
Test															
FC	306	396	81	6254	98	19.85	-	565	90	70	1	70.00	1-47	-	-

STEELE, J. F.

Name: <u>John</u> Frederick Steele
Born: 23 July 1946, Stafford
Height: 5ft 10in
Nickname: Steely
Wife and date of marriage: Susan,
17 April 1977
Children: Sarah Jane, 2 April 1982;
Robert Alfred, 10 April 1985
Family links with cricket: Uncle Stan
played for Staffordshire. Brother David
played for Northamptonshire, Derbyshire and
England. Cousin Brian Crump played for
Northamptonshire and Staffordshire
Education: Endon School, Stoke-on-Trent;
Stafford College
Other sports followed: Football (Stoke City,
Port Vale), golf
Relaxations: Music and walking
Appointed to 1st-Class list: 1997
Counties as player: Leicestershire, Glamorgan
Role: Right-hand bat, slow left-arm bowler
County debut: 1970 (Leicestershire), 1984 (Glamorgan)
County cap: 1971 (Leicestershire), 1984 (Glamorgan)
Benefit: 1983 (Leicestershire)
1000 runs in a season: 6
One-Day 100s: 1
One-Day 5 w. in innings: 4
Overseas teams played for: Springs HSOB, Northern Transvaal 1971-73;
Pine Town CC, Natal 1973-74, 1982-83; Natal 1975-76, 1978-79
Extras: Played for England U25. Was voted Natal's Best Bowler in 1975-76. First-
wicket record partnership for Leicestershire of 390 with Barry Dudleston v Derbyshire
at Leicester 1979. Won two Man of the Match Awards in the Gillette Cup and four in
the Benson and Hedges Cup. Won the award for the most catches in a season in 1984

Best batting: 195 Leicestershire v Derbyshire, Leicester 1971
Best bowling: 7-29 Natal B v Griqualand West, Umzinto 1973-74
7-29 Leicestershire v Gloucestershire, Leicester 1980

First-class career performances

	M	Inn	NO	Runs	HS	Avg	100	Ct	St	Runs	Wkts	Avg	BB	5I	10M
Test															
FC	379	605	85	15053	195	28.94	21	414	-	15793	584	27.04	7-29	16	-

WILLEY, P.

Name: Peter Willey
Born: 6 December 1949, Sedgefield,
County Durham
Height: 6ft 1in
Nickname: Will, 'many unprintable'
Wife and date of marriage: Charmaine,
23 September 1971
Children: Heather Jane, 11 September 1985;
David, 28 February 1990
Family links with cricket: Father played
local club cricket in County Durham
Education: Seaham Secondary School,
County Durham
Other sports followed: All sports
Relaxations: 'Dog-walking, keeping fit (??),
fishing'
Appointed to 1st-Class list: 1993
International panel: 1996-2003
Tests umpired: 25 (plus 7 as TV umpire)
ODIs umpired: 34 (plus 16 as TV umpire)
Other umpiring honours: Stood in the 1999 and 2002-03 World Cups, in the 1999
Benson and Hedges Super Cup final and in the 2004 C&G Trophy final. Officiated at
Twenty20 finals day at The Oval 2005, including the final. Chairman of the First-Class
Umpires' Association
Counties as player: Northamptonshire, Leicestershire
Role: Right-hand bat, off-break bowler
County debut: 1966 (Northamptonshire), 1984 (Leicestershire)
County cap: 1971 (Northamptonshire), 1984 (Leicestershire)
Benefit: 1981 (Northamptonshire)
Test debut: 1976
ODI debut (matches): 1977 (26)
1000 runs in a season: 10

50 wickets in a season: 2
1st-Class 200s: 1
One-Day 100s: 9
Overseas tours: England to Australia and India 1979-80, to West Indies 1980-81, 1985-86; unofficial England XI to South Africa 1981-82
Overseas teams played for: Eastern Province, South Africa 1982-85
Cricket moments to forget: 'First ball in first-class cricket (v Cambridge University), bowled – thought it can only get better'
Extras: Became youngest player ever to play for Northamptonshire, at 16 years 180 days, v Cambridge University in 1966. Leicestershire captain 1987. Played for Northumberland in 1992. Offered membership of the ICC Elite Panel of umpires in 2002 but declined because of the amount of time the appointment would require away from his family
Opinions on cricket: 'Too much "robot" coaching from nine-year-olds to county standard. Players don't seem to be allowed individual batting styles or bowling actions. Bowling actions changed in case of injury. Too much time spent looking at video analysis and training instead of more time spent in nets. Seems bowling length and line (Pollock, McGrath) is a thing of the past.'
Best batting: 227 Northamptonshire v Somerset, Northampton 1976
Best bowling: 7-37 Northamptonshire v Oxford University, The Parks 1975

First-Class Career Performances

	M	Inn	NO	Runs	HS	Avg	100	Ct	St	Runs	Wkts	Avg	BB	5I	10M
Test	26	50	6	1184	102*	26.90	2	3	-	456	7	65.14	2-73	-	-
FC	559	918	121	24361	227	30.56	44	235	-	23400	756	30.95	7-37	26	3

WHEN THE BALL HITS THE DECK AT 85 MPH
IT DOESN'T CARE WHAT LANGUAGE YOU SPEAK.
WHEN IT REVERSE SWINGS INTO YOUR LEG STUMP
IT DOESN'T CARE WHERE YOU GREW UP.
WHEN IT RIPS BACK THROUGH YOUR GATE
IT DOESN'T CARE WHAT YOUR RELIGIOUS BELIEFS ARE.
AND WHEN IT TRAPS YOU IN FRONT
IT CERTAINLY DOESN'T CARE WHAT COLOUR YOU ARE.

NEITHER SHOULD YOU.

APPENDICES

Roll of Honour 2006
First-class Averages 2006
Index of Players by County

ROLL OF HONOUR 2006

LIVERPOOL VICTORIA COUNTY CHAMPIONSHIP

Division One

		P	W	L	D	T	Bt	Bl	Pts
1	Sussex (I/3)	16	9	2	5	0	49	47	242
2	Lancashire (II/1)	16	6	1	9	0	58	46	224
3	Hampshire (I/2)	16	6	3	7	0	48	48	207
4	Warwickshire (I/4)	16	6	5	5	0	42	43	189
5	Kent (I/5)	16	4	4	8	0	43	44	175
6	Yorkshire (II/3)	16	3	6	7	0	43	41	154
7	Durham (II/2)	16	4	8	4	0	39	43	153.5
8	Nottinghamshire (I/1)	16	4	7	5	0	40	37	153
9	Middlesex (I/6)	16	1	7	8	0	47	42	133.5

The bottom two counties were relegated to Division Two for the 2007 season

Division Two

		P	W	L	D	T	Bt	Bl	Pts
1	Surrey (I/7)	16	10	2	4	0	62	44	262
2	Worcestershire (II/6)	16	8	4	4	0	58	43	229
3	Essex (II/5)	16	7	4	5	0	62	40	220
4	Leicestershire (II/7)	16	5	4	7	0	47	41	185.5
5	Derbyshire (II/9)	16	4	4	8	0	51	41	178.5
6	Northamptonshire (II/4)	16	3	5	8	0	52	37	163
7	Gloucestershire (I/8)	16	3	6	7	0	51	36	155.5
8	Glamorgan (I/9)	16	2	7	7	0	51	41	146.5
9	Somerset (II/8)	16	3	9	4	0	43	40	140

The top two counties were promoted to Division One for the 2007 season

The following sides incurred points deductions for slow over rates in 2006:
Hampshire 1, Durham 0.5, Middlesex 1.5; Leicestershire 0.5, Derbyshire 1.5,
Gloucestershire 1.5, Glamorgan 1.5, Somerset 1.

NATWEST PRO40 LEAGUE

Division One

		P	W	L	T	NR	Pts
1	Essex (I/1)	8	5	2	0	1	11
2	Northamptonshire (I/3)	8	5	2	0	1	11
3	Sussex (II/1)	8	5	3	0	0	10
4	Nottinghamshire (I/5)	8	4	3	0	1	9
5	Warwickshire (II/3)	8	3	4	0	1	7
6	Lancashire (I/6)	8	2	3	0	3	7
7	Glamorgan (I/4)	8	2	3	1	2	7
8	Durham (II/2)	8	2	4	1	1	6
9	Middlesex (I/2)	8	2	6	0	0	4

Essex were champions and the bottom three counties were relegated to Division Two for the 2007 season, Glamorgan (I/7) after a play-off with Hampshire (II/3)

Division Two

		P	W	L	T	NR	Pts
1	Gloucestershire (I/7)	8	6	2	0	0	12
2	Worcestershire (I/8)	8	6	2	0	0	12
3	Hampshire (I/9)	8	5	2	0	1	11
4	Surrey (II/7)	8	5	2	0	1	11
5	Kent (II/8)	8	5	3	0	0	10
6	Leicestershire (II/4)	8	3	5	0	0	6
7	Somerset (II/6)	8	2	6	0	0	4
8	Derbyshire (II/5)	8	1	6	0	1	3
9	Yorkshire (II/9)	8	1	6	0	1	3

The top three counties (see note above) were promoted to Division One for 2007

CHELTENHAM & GLOUCESTER TROPHY

Winners: Sussex   **Runners-up:** Lancashire

TWENTY20 CUP

Winners: Leicestershire   **Runners-up:** Nottinghamshire
Semi-finalists: Essex, Surrey

2006 AVERAGES (all first-class matches)

BATTING AVERAGES
Qualifying requirements: 6 completed innings and an average of over 10.00

Name	Matches	Inns	NO	Runs	HS	Avge	SR	100s	50s
MR Ramprakash	15	24	2	2278	301*	103.54	60.79	8	9
PA Jaques	8	15	2	1148	244	88.30	79.11	3	7
Mohammad Yousuf	5	9	1	666	202	83.25	61.26	3	0
DS Lehmann	15	23	1	1706	339	77.54	80.39	6	3
HD Ackerman	15	28	4	1808	309*	75.33	61.10	4	14
A Flower	17	27	6	1536	271*	73.14	61.66	7	3
JP Crawley	16	27	1	1737	189	66.80	53.76	6	7
L Klusener	16	26	7	1251	147*	65.84	72.94	6	3
Younus Khan	5	9	2	459	173	65.57	59.84	1	3
N Pothas	15	22	7	973	122*	64.86	50.86	4	5
AN Cook	13	23	5	1159	132	64.38	54.97	4	6
MW Goodwin	16	27	1	1649	235	63.42	63.42	6	7
CJL Rogers	14	24	2	1360	319	61.81	61.23	4	5
MJ Walker	16	26	3	1419	197	61.69	44.84	5	8
A McGrath	15	24	3	1293	140*	61.57	54.95	4	9
JM Kemp	6	9	3	369	124*	61.50	75.30	2	1
SR Patel	8	12	2	612	173	61.20	67.77	2	2
HJH Marshall	11	21	1	1218	168	60.90	63.93	5	7
RC Irani	16	23	5	1075	145	59.72	47.82	3	6
PA Nixon	16	23	8	895	144*	59.66	57.66	2	6
CL White	12	22	2	1190	260*	59.50	81.45	5	3
IR Bell	9	16	4	713	119	59.41	55.40	3	4
KP Pietersen	7	12	0	707	158	58.91	78.29	3	1
MB Loye	16	24	2	1296	148*	58.90	61.77	6	6
MA Butcher	17	29	4	1465	151	58.60	56.30	5	8
NJ Dexter	8	12	4	463	131*	57.87	58.68	2	1
R Clarke	13	21	3	1027	214	57.05	78.45	3	3
IJ Harvey	9	15	5	561	114	56.10	69.51	2	2
SG Law	16	23	3	1103	130	55.15	63.10	4	6
AD Brown	16	27	4	1264	215	54.95	76.97	5	4
MJ DiVenuto	14	23	1	1198	161*	54.45	64.47	3	7
T Frost	8	13	5	431	96	53.87	45.75	0	4
D Mongia	11	18	3	800	165	53.33	56.81	3	2
AJ Strauss	8	14	0	741	141	52.92	58.62	3	2
EC Joyce	14	24	1	1215	211	52.82	58.78	3	6
DM Benkenstein	17	31	2	1500	151	51.72	61.22	3	7
LD Sutton	13	16	3	666	151*	51.23	48.26	2	2

Name	Matches	Inns	NO	Runs	HS	Avge	SR	100s	50s
MJ Powell (Gm)	16	29	3	1327	299	51.03	52.57	4	2
MH Yardy	12	20	2	914	159*	50.77	46.60	3	4
CJ Adams	16	25	1	1218	155	50.75	66.37	3	7
U Afzaal	18	32	6	1315	151	50.57	53.30	4	6
MJ Cosgrove	10	19	2	856	233	50.35	81.44	2	6
SA Newman	17	29	1	1404	144*	50.14	69.16	2	10
APR Gidman	16	31	6	1244	120	49.76	57.45	4	7
SP Fleming	13	22	2	992	192	49.60	61.04	2	8
JL Sadler	15	26	5	1024	128*	48.76	51.69	1	8
GA Hick	14	23	2	1023	182	48.71	61.11	4	3
M van Jaarsveld	16	27	2	1217	116	48.68	50.47	3	10
JS Foster	17	21	4	822	103	48.35	54.36	2	6
TR Birt	14	24	2	1059	181	48.13	67.15	3	6
DJ Hussey	17	28	4	1143	164	47.62	61.25	5	1
DKH Mitchell	4	8	2	282	134*	47.00	41.04	1	2
NRD Compton	17	31	3	1315	190	46.96	47.91	6	4
L Vincent	6	11	1	469	141	46.90	71.16	2	1
DJG Sales	17	27	1	1219	225	46.88	66.39	2	5
ML Pettini	17	29	3	1218	208*	46.84	53.70	3	3
MJ Prior	14	22	2	934	124	46.70	68.62	3	4
GJ Batty	15	24	8	744	112*	46.50	57.09	1	3
VS Solanki	16	29	2	1252	222	46.37	68.04	4	4
DC Nash	8	14	4	460	68*	46.00	45.49	0	4
JHK Adams	17	31	5	1173	262*	45.11	45.09	2	4
CK Kapugedera	6	11	2	400	134*	44.44	52.77	1	1
JGE Benning	8	13	2	488	122*	44.36	90.03	2	2
CM Spearman	16	31	0	1370	192	44.19	73.41	6	2
Yasir Arafat	8	12	3	390	86	43.33	69.51	0	2
CMW Read	14	21	4	727	150*	42.76	61.14	3	3
IJ Westwood	13	23	3	850	178	42.50	45.26	2	4
SB Styris	10	17	1	677	133	42.31	70.87	1	5
MJ Lumb	16	25	2	963	144	41.86	44.37	2	7
PD Collingwood	7	12	1	460	186	41.81	43.39	1	1
IJL Trott	17	29	2	1128	177*	41.77	56.99	3	4
ET Smith	17	31	1	1209	166	40.30	64.61	5	2
RN ten Doeschate	9	12	2	403	105*	40.30	72.74	2	1
SD Peters	16	30	2	1122	178	40.07	52.60	3	5
Kadeer Ali	11	22	1	834	145	39.71	41.38	1	5
WPC Weston	13	24	1	911	130	39.60	43.31	2	6
KA Parsons	10	15	2	511	153	39.30	54.01	1	2
C White	15	23	1	859	147	39.04	42.44	3	3
DI Stevens	17	27	4	897	126*	39.00	65.71	2	6
DP Fulton	15	26	1	969	155	38.76	41.64	2	6
WJ Durston	13	23	3	765	89	38.25	52.18	0	7

Name	Matches	Inns	NO	Runs	HS	Avge	SR	100s	50s
V Chopra	9	16	1	569	106	37.93	48.09	1	4
AJ Bichel	8	8	1	265	75*	37.85	65.59	0	2
Imran Farhat	6	11	0	416	91	37.81	66.45	0	3
SM Davies	17	29	1	1052	192	37.57	60.59	3	3
BW Harmison	9	17	2	563	110	37.53	60.73	2	3
Azhar Mahmood	13	20	4	600	101	37.50	78.94	1	2
NV Knight	17	30	1	1070	126	36.89	50.61	2	6
IJ Sutcliffe	17	27	4	847	159	36.82	43.81	2	3
RWT Key	16	29	3	956	136*	36.76	47.94	2	3
BF Smith	16	27	2	915	203	36.60	56.55	2	3
KW Hogg	8	8	1	254	70	36.28	71.14	0	2
MA Carberry	15	28	2	938	104	36.07	50.18	2	5
Faisal Iqbal	7	11	3	288	82	36.00	47.13	0	2
Inzamam-ul-Haq	5	9	2	252	69	36.00	49.50	0	2
OA Shah	17	30	0	1079	126	35.96	53.92	2	7
DL Hemp	16	29	1	1003	155	35.82	56.12	3	2
NJ Astle	8	12	0	429	86	35.75	58.13	0	3
JN Batty	17	29	0	1025	133	35.34	46.44	2	7
RS Bopara	18	28	3	882	159	35.28	48.48	2	3
JP Maher	16	30	2	978	106	34.92	47.08	2	4
CR Taylor	15	26	0	908	121	34.92	48.97	3	4
JC Hildreth	14	24	1	798	227*	34.69	61.57	1	3
WU Tharanga	7	13	0	449	140	34.53	54.49	2	1
DJ Thornely	15	25	3	759	76	34.50	58.07	0	6
TJ New	6	12	0	414	85	34.50	45.44	0	5
JWM Dalrymple	12	19	0	654	96	34.42	63.31	0	5
SC Moore	16	30	2	960	97	34.28	60.60	0	9
JK Maunders	16	29	1	959	180	34.25	47.49	1	6
MA Hardinges	11	15	2	444	107*	34.15	66.26	2	1
TR Ambrose	9	14	1	443	133	34.07	47.37	1	3
SD Stubbings	18	32	1	1056	124	34.06	39.87	2	6
CC Benham	9	15	0	504	95	33.60	70.98	0	4
TT Samaraweera	5	9	1	267	114	33.37	46.67	2	0
OD Gibson	13	22	4	596	155	33.11	59.71	1	2
GW Flower	7	11	0	364	101	33.09	40.99	1	3
Hassan Adnan	18	29	2	893	117	33.07	43.96	1	5
RSC Martin-Jenkins	14	21	3	592	91	32.88	53.91	0	3
AR Adams	8	9	2	230	75	32.85	81.27	0	1
JPT Knappett	4	8	1	230	100*	32.85	47.71	1	1
JJ Sayers	13	21	3	590	122*	32.77	40.08	1	3
MJ Brown	5	8	1	229	133	32.71	52.76	1	0
P Mustard	16	27	2	816	130	32.64	71.76	2	3
RR Montgomerie	17	28	0	905	100	32.32	49.29	1	7
Salman Butt	5	10	0	323	84	32.30	54.46	0	4

Name	Matches	Inns	NO	Runs	HS	Avge	SR	100s	50s
G Chapple	14	19	1	580	82	32.22	66.36	0	3
DJ Pipe	14	20	4	515	89	32.18	56.34	0	3
MJ Chilton	16	25	1	766	131	31.91	40.46	1	4
MA Ealham	17	26	3	732	112*	31.82	56.39	2	4
BM Shafayat	17	30	2	887	118	31.67	45.93	2	5
RDB Croft	16	24	5	601	72	31.63	49.50	0	3
PN Weekes	8	15	4	348	128*	31.63	48.94	1	0
KC Sangakkara	6	12	1	347	66	31.54	45.35	0	2
DD Cherry	9	17	0	532	121	31.29	35.87	1	3
SK Warne	13	17	5	371	61*	30.91	91.15	0	2
NJ Edwards	7	10	0	309	77	30.90	44.46	0	2
JD Middlebrook	15	17	1	494	113	30.87	51.19	1	2
DDJ Robinson	13	25	1	738	106	30.75	54.06	1	3
BL Hutton	11	20	1	583	105	30.68	40.85	2	1
CD Nash	4	6	0	184	67	30.66	40.70	0	1
GM Scott	9	18	0	551	133	30.61	47.82	1	3
AGB Wharf	10	15	2	397	86	30.53	69.28	0	3
MA Wallace	16	27	4	698	72	30.34	52.40	0	5
CW Henderson	17	24	6	545	62*	30.27	50.69	0	1
AJ Tudor	11	13	1	362	144	30.16	74.18	1	1
DL Maddy	11	19	1	538	97	29.88	58.54	0	4
SJ Adshead	16	28	5	687	79*	29.86	48.10	0	4
PD Trego	12	20	0	596	135	29.80	67.19	3	2
MP Vaughan	3	6	0	178	99	29.66	47.34	0	2
AV Suppiah	12	19	0	563	99	29.63	40.82	0	4
MA Wagh	13	24	2	648	128	29.45	50.74	2	1
DJ Bicknell	18	29	0	851	95	29.34	46.50	0	4
DPMD Jayawardene	6	11	0	317	119	28.81	53.72	1	1
LC Parker	8	15	0	431	140	28.73	53.20	1	2
D Alleyne	12	20	1	543	109*	28.57	45.02	1	4
HH Streak	15	24	6	513	68*	28.50	44.18	0	2
MJ Nicholson	15	20	4	454	106*	28.37	60.69	1	1
GM Smith	5	9	1	227	86	28.37	47.99	0	1
ME Trescothick	10	18	0	510	154	28.33	50.79	2	1
JER Gallian	14	24	0	679	171	28.29	49.81	2	3
ID Fisher	5	8	2	168	45	28.00	40.28	0	0
GJ Muchall	15	28	0	778	219	27.78	57.71	2	3
SJ Walters	3	6	0	166	67	27.66	51.23	0	1
TM Dilshan	6	12	0	331	69	27.58	51.79	0	2
WR Smith	14	21	0	575	141	27.38	50.13	1	2
GP Swann	15	21	1	546	85	27.30	67.65	0	3
RJ Sillence	13	19	1	487	64	27.05	72.57	0	3
MA Sheikh	9	13	3	270	51*	27.00	31.28	0	1
GD Cross	4	6	0	162	72	27.00	86.17	0	2

Name	Matches	Inns	NO	Runs	HS	Avge	SR	100s	50s
AGR Loudon	17	26	0	681	123	26.19	46.77	1	5
CG Taylor	14	27	0	705	121	26.11	60.67	1	4
DJ Bravo	5	8	0	208	76	26.00	55.02	0	1
CD Hopkinson	17	28	0	723	74	25.82	37.46	0	6
MJ Powell (Wa)	6	11	1	256	56	25.60	42.45	0	1
Kamran Akmal	7	9	1	202	62*	25.25	61.21	0	2
SM Guy	6	8	2	150	52*	25.00	74.62	0	1
AG Botha	12	21	2	470	100	24.73	45.94	1	4
JEC Franklin	9	15	1	346	94	24.71	50.43	0	2
JN Gillespie	14	21	6	370	45	24.66	35.23	0	0
SM Ervine	15	22	3	464	50*	24.42	63.56	0	1
GG Wagg	9	14	1	317	94	24.38	52.92	0	1
AW Gale	5	9	0	219	149	24.33	53.80	1	0
IDK Salisbury	16	19	4	363	74	24.20	59.60	0	2
TT Bresnan	12	17	1	387	94	24.18	50.45	0	2
RE Watkins	14	25	2	554	87	24.08	45.15	0	2
MG Vandort	6	12	1	264	105	24.00	38.65	1	1
N Peng	8	15	0	357	59	23.80	36.69	0	2
DG Cork	14	17	2	354	154	23.60	70.94	1	1
MH Wessels	10	17	2	353	62	23.53	65.24	0	2
MJ Wood (So)	16	27	0	622	73	23.03	47.84	0	5
JO Troughton	10	18	1	390	103	22.94	36.04	1	2
TD Groenewald	6	9	2	157	76	22.42	79.29	0	1
TJ Phillips	14	17	2	336	49	22.40	44.32	0	0
GO Jones	12	17	2	336	60	22.40	51.29	0	3
BJ Phillips	17	25	2	515	75	22.39	51.09	0	4
SJP Moreton	3	6	0	134	63	22.33	46.04	0	1
JJB Lewis	9	16	0	355	99	22.18	35.57	0	2
RA White	9	14	1	288	141	22.15	68.40	1	0
PJ Franks	14	20	3	376	64	22.11	48.51	0	3
JN Snape	8	11	1	219	90	21.90	38.35	0	1
DS Harrison	13	16	3	281	64	21.61	78.49	0	1
JC Morris	4	7	0	151	81	21.57	40.59	0	1
GR Breese	17	29	0	623	110	21.48	50.40	1	1
SCJ Broad	14	17	4	279	65*	21.46	42.85	0	2
NC Saker	7	10	1	192	58*	21.33	40.00	0	1
LJ Wright	11	17	2	313	59	20.86	51.39	0	3
MF Maharoof	5	9	0	185	59	20.55	39.02	0	1
DR Brown	11	19	1	368	69	20.44	37.43	0	2
NJ O'Brien	10	13	1	241	62	20.08	42.73	0	1
DA Mascarenhas	16	24	0	474	131	19.75	60.00	1	0
MM Ali	6	9	0	177	68	19.66	49.30	0	2
G Welch	15	23	5	353	94	19.61	39.39	0	2
GJ Pratt	6	10	0	193	52	19.30	34.90	0	1

Name	Matches	Inns	NO	Runs	HS	Avge	SR	100s	50s
RL Johnson	8	12	1	211	51	19.18	75.89	0	1
A Rashid	5	6	0	115	63	19.16	48.72	0	1
BJM Scott	9	15	2	248	49	19.07	47.50	0	0
JMM Averis	4	7	0	128	53	18.28	60.66	0	1
T Henderson	6	9	1	146	59	18.25	106.56	0	1
TCP Smith	15	18	5	234	49	18.00	46.70	0	0
AKD Gray	8	11	2	162	29	18.00	39.41	0	0
J Lewis	13	17	2	269	57	17.93	75.56	0	1
RN Grant	7	11	0	196	44	17.81	41.35	0	0
MJ Wood (Y)	6	10	0	177	92	17.70	37.34	0	1
SJ Harmison	6	8	2	105	36	17.50	60.69	0	0
RJ Warren	5	8	0	140	93	17.50	54.68	0	1
NJ Lamb	4	7	1	105	62	17.50	28.07	0	1
SP Crook	8	10	2	138	44	17.25	85.18	0	0
LE Plunkett	6	7	1	103	28	17.16	41.86	0	0
CD Thorp	12	21	2	326	75	17.15	63.05	0	2
AR Caddick	16	25	5	341	68	17.05	58.89	0	1
DA Cosker	13	16	6	168	39	16.80	47.19	0	0
Naved-ul-Hasan	6	8	0	134	64	16.75	85.35	0	1
MGN Windows	5	9	1	127	48	15.87	34.32	0	0
Mushtaq Ahmed	15	19	5	222	42*	15.85	78.72	0	0
CT Peploe	10	14	1	204	46	15.69	43.31	0	0
GL Brophy	10	16	0	251	97	15.68	46.48	0	1
NM Carter	13	20	4	250	36	15.62	83.33	0	0
MAK Lawson	7	10	2	124	44	15.50	59.61	0	0
MCJ Ball	10	15	1	215	58	15.35	52.69	0	1
MA Richards	4	8	2	92	39*	15.33	42.39	0	0
CM Gazzard	13	22	2	305	35	15.25	48.95	0	0
RW Price	8	10	3	106	56	15.14	53.00	0	1
PS Jones	17	21	6	227	34*	15.13	46.32	0	0
CEW Silverwood	16	24	6	271	50	15.05	82.87	0	1
SD Udal	10	9	1	118	28	14.75	58.70	0	0
DD Masters	14	16	1	219	52	14.60	36.99	0	1
ID Hunter	14	13	6	102	48	14.57	54.83	0	0
JD Francis	5	9	0	131	41	14.55	38.87	0	0
J Louw	17	27	5	314	42	14.27	43.61	0	0
MS Mason	10	11	5	85	29*	14.16	41.26	0	0
SA Patterson	5	7	1	85	46	14.16	31.36	0	0
ML Lewis	11	18	9	127	38	14.11	79.87	0	0
SJ Cook	11	14	0	196	71	14.00	51.04	0	1
PL Harris	8	11	1	140	32	14.00	50.54	0	0
JC Tredwell	7	10	1	126	47	14.00	42.56	0	0
RJ Sidebottom	15	22	6	222	33	13.87	38.87	0	0
EJG Morgan	6	11	0	144	38	13.09	38.50	0	0

Name	Matches	Inns	NO	Runs	HS	Avge	SR	100s	50s
JA Lowe	5	10	0	130	30	13.00	34.39	0	0
MM Patel	13	16	2	179	61	12.78	50.00	0	1
CB Keegan	7	10	1	111	34*	12.33	68.09	0	0
Kabir Ali	11	16	2	168	38*	12.00	46.28	0	0
SL Malinga	5	6	0	71	26	11.83	55.46	0	0
G Onions	16	26	6	232	40	11.60	52.96	0	0
MN Malik	6	9	3	68	35	11.33	39.53	0	0
JD Lewry	16	19	11	89	27*	11.12	36.77	0	0
SI Mahmood	9	10	1	99	34	11.00	58.92	0	0
Z Khan	16	21	6	161	30*	10.73	57.70	0	0
GJ Kruis	13	17	9	85	28*	10.62	37.11	0	0
RKJ Dawson	8	13	1	127	56	10.58	51.62	0	1
MS Panesar	17	21	8	136	34	10.46	47.38	0	0

BOWLING AVERAGES
Qualifying requirements: 10 wickets taken

Name	Matches	Balls	Runs	Wkts	Avge	RPO	BB	5I
DJG Sammy	3	372	163	10	16.30	2.62	5-85	1
Naved-ul-Hasan	6	992	585	35	16.71	3.53	7-62	3
M Muralitharan	4	1136	507	28	18.10	2.67	8-70	2
Mushtaq Ahmed	15	3743	2031	102	19.91	3.25	9-48	11
MA Ealham	17	2158	956	46	20.78	2.65	5-59	2
J Lewis	13	2366	1302	60	21.70	3.30	7-38	4
A Kumble	3	840	418	19	22.00	2.98	8-100	2
MS Mason	10	1777	910	41	22.19	3.07	8-45	3
JD Lewry	16	2966	1321	57	23.17	2.67	6-68	2
AJ Hall	4	771	334	14	23.85	2.59	3-27	0
CT Tremlett	9	1586	835	34	24.55	3.15	6-89	1
CE Shreck	12	2556	1512	61	24.78	3.54	8-31	5
CD Thorp	12	1965	968	39	24.82	2.95	6-55	2
Yasir Arafat	8	1627	1019	41	24.85	3.75	5-84	2
DA Mascarenhas	16	2574	1074	43	24.97	2.50	6-65	2
A Rashid	5	1082	629	25	25.16	3.48	6-67	1
CEW Silverwood	16	3026	1591	63	25.25	3.15	6-51	4
LM Daggett	5	694	405	16	25.31	3.50	6-30	1
DG Cork	14	2335	1071	42	25.50	2.75	6-53	1
CM Willoughby	15	2991	1687	66	25.56	3.38	7-44	3
SI Mahmood	9	1612	925	36	25.69	3.44	5-52	1
RJ Sidebottom	15	2915	1307	50	26.14	2.69	5-22	1
DJ Thornely	15	1194	578	22	26.27	2.90	3-38	0
SJ Harmison	6	1101	637	24	26.54	3.47	6-19	2
SK Warne	13	3142	1571	58	27.08	3.00	7-99	4
LE Plunkett	6	974	516	19	27.15	3.17	3-17	0

Name	Matches	Balls	Runs	Wkts	Avge	RPO	BB	5I
G Keedy	15	3398	1660	61	27.21	2.93	6-40	2
G Chapple	14	2552	1124	41	27.41	2.64	6-35	1
OJ Newby	7	831	523	19	27.52	3.77	4-58	0
IDK Salisbury	16	3465	1732	62	27.93	2.99	5-46	1
ND Doshi	14	2813	1434	51	28.11	3.05	6-91	1
DR Brown	11	1947	940	33	28.48	2.89	4-45	0
MS Panesar	17	4554	2029	71	28.57	2.67	5-32	6
N Tahir	3	588	375	13	28.84	3.82	7-107	1
D Gough	7	1393	724	25	28.96	3.11	5-82	1
Kabir Ali	11	2023	1161	40	29.02	3.44	7-43	3
IJ Harvey	9	854	378	13	29.07	2.65	3-25	0
Z Khan	16	3712	2268	78	29.07	3.66	9-138	5
JTA Bruce	13	1962	1109	38	29.18	3.39	5-43	1
PL Harris	8	2084	905	31	29.19	2.60	6-80	4
A Flintoff	4	911	410	14	29.28	2.70	3-52	0
WPUJC Vaas	5	852	352	12	29.33	2.47	4-34	0
ML Lewis	11	1755	1031	35	29.45	3.52	4-69	0
OD Gibson	13	2368	1458	49	29.75	3.69	6-110	1
JM Kemp	6	666	333	11	30.27	3.00	3-72	0
AJ Harris	13	2075	1151	38	30.28	3.32	5-53	1
BV Taylor	6	699	364	12	30.33	3.12	6-32	1
A Khan	9	1873	1034	34	30.41	3.31	5-100	1
JEC Franklin	9	1510	950	31	30.64	3.77	5-68	1
TCP Smith	15	2298	1073	35	30.65	2.80	4-57	0
Mohammad Akram	14	2190	1294	42	30.80	3.54	6-34	2
AJ Bichel	8	1685	991	32	30.96	3.52	6-38	1
SCJ Broad	14	2417	1491	48	31.06	3.70	5-83	4
MN Malik	6	822	536	17	31.52	3.91	3-49	0
G Onions	16	2642	1704	54	31.55	3.86	5-45	1
HT Waters	5	669	380	12	31.66	3.40	5-86	1
PS Jones	17	3145	1871	59	31.71	3.56	6-25	1
BJ Phillips	17	2246	1081	34	31.79	2.88	6-29	1
MJ Nicholson	15	2849	1471	46	31.97	3.09	7-62	2
RDB Croft	16	4215	2112	66	32.00	3.00	7-67	3
TT Bresnan	12	1905	1058	33	32.06	3.33	5-58	1
RL Johnson	8	1174	717	22	32.59	3.66	5-37	1
JE Anyon	11	2054	1011	31	32.61	2.95	5-83	1
KA Parsons	10	586	360	11	32.72	3.54	3-33	0
MK Munday	7	1073	658	20	32.90	3.67	6-77	2
SJ Cook	11	1763	925	28	33.03	3.14	6-74	2
Mohammad Asif	9	1795	996	30	33.20	3.32	5-56	2
G Welch	15	2349	1198	36	33.27	3.06	4-33	0
GJ Batty	15	2977	1439	43	33.46	2.90	6-119	1
HH Streak	15	2680	1374	41	33.51	3.07	6-73	2

Name	Matches	Balls	Runs	Wkts	Avge	RPO	BB	5I
SL Malinga	5	747	436	13	33.53	3.50	5-79	1
JN Gillespie	14	2607	1210	36	33.61	2.78	6-37	1
Umar Gul	6	1292	816	24	34.00	3.78	5-123	1
AGR Loudon	17	2145	1097	32	34.28	3.06	5-49	2
RJ Sillence	13	1324	792	23	34.43	3.58	7-96	1
MCJ Ball	10	1847	930	27	34.44	3.02	6-134	1
TE Savill	3	585	345	10	34.50	3.53	4-62	0
MAK Lawson	7	1242	897	26	34.50	4.33	6-88	2
MJ Hoggard	11	2220	1146	33	34.72	3.09	4-27	0
RSC Martin-Jenkins	14	1297	489	14	34.92	2.26	4-78	0
KW Hogg	8	1164	528	15	35.20	2.72	2-33	0
N Killeen	9	1404	671	19	35.31	2.86	5-29	1
GJ Kruis	13	2286	1342	38	35.31	3.52	5-67	2
NGE Walker	5	913	498	14	35.57	3.27	5-59	1
JC Tredwell	7	1619	927	26	35.65	3.43	6-81	1
AR Caddick	16	3659	2259	63	35.85	3.72	5-40	4
DI Stevens	17	1415	688	19	36.21	2.91	4-36	0
MM Patel	13	2337	1171	32	36.59	3.00	4-83	0
L Klusener	16	1239	699	19	36.78	3.38	6-69	1
ID Hunter	14	2214	1328	36	36.88	3.59	4-22	0
SB Styris	10	1191	670	18	37.22	3.37	6-71	1
RH Joseph	9	1469	897	24	37.37	3.66	5-57	1
JWM Dalrymple	12	2134	1084	29	37.37	3.04	4-61	0
Azhar Mahmood	13	2020	1161	31	37.45	3.44	5-69	1
GG Wagg	9	1280	904	24	37.66	4.23	6-38	1
DD Masters	14	2795	1232	32	38.50	2.64	4-89	0
CB Keegan	7	1204	736	19	38.73	3.66	5-90	1
AG Botha	12	1995	1124	29	38.75	3.38	6-117	1
LJ Wright	11	1068	582	15	38.80	3.26	3-39	0
GJ Smith	6	812	467	12	38.91	3.45	4-75	0
DM Benkenstein	17	877	552	14	39.42	3.77	3-16	0
AR Adams	8	1669	830	21	39.52	2.98	4-72	0
DS Harrison	13	2521	1387	35	39.62	3.30	5-76	1
SP Kirby	15	3106	1944	49	39.67	3.75	5-99	1
RN ten Doeschate	9	1495	1115	28	39.82	4.47	5-143	1
Danish Kaneria	6	1842	924	23	40.17	3.00	4-32	0
SM Ervine	15	1777	1060	26	40.76	3.57	3-57	0
A McGrath	15	1296	734	18	40.77	3.39	4-62	0
NM Carter	13	2354	1392	34	40.94	3.54	6-63	1
R Clarke	13	1408	911	22	41.40	3.88	4-45	0
RJ Kirtley	8	1420	748	18	41.55	3.16	3-82	0
WJ Durston	13	675	416	10	41.60	3.69	2-31	0
JD Middlebrook	15	3381	1706	41	41.60	3.02	5-70	1
CW Henderson	17	3724	2054	49	41.91	3.30	5-69	2

Name	Matches	Balls	Runs	Wkts	Avge	RPO	BB	5I
AP Palladino	6	994	547	13	42.07	3.30	6-68	1
AJ Tudor	11	1762	1195	28	42.67	4.06	5-67	1
SD Udal	10	1254	646	15	43.06	3.09	2-12	0
MA Richards	4	636	433	10	43.30	4.08	3-62	0
MA Sheikh	9	1313	650	15	43.33	2.97	5-65	1
CJ Liddle	6	760	478	11	43.45	3.77	3-42	0
TJ Phillips	14	2578	1615	37	43.64	3.75	5-41	1
J Louw	17	3214	1890	43	43.95	3.52	5-117	1
MA Hardinges	11	1624	1011	23	43.95	3.73	4-127	0
DH Wigley	8	1110	796	18	44.22	4.30	5-77	1
GP Swann	15	2639	1247	28	44.53	2.83	4-54	0
RAG Cummins	7	858	579	13	44.53	4.08	4-46	0
APR Gidman	16	1392	762	17	44.82	3.28	3-38	0
Mohammad Sami	5	981	673	15	44.86	4.11	3-53	0
RS Bopara	18	1551	1035	23	45.00	4.00	5-75	1
DA Cosker	13	3017	1486	33	45.03	2.95	4-78	0
Mohammad Ali	5	692	453	10	45.30	3.92	2-15	0
AKD Gray	8	1150	635	14	45.35	3.31	3-106	0
SP Crook	8	1051	782	17	46.00	4.46	3-46	0
NC Saker	7	880	657	14	46.92	4.47	4-79	0
JMM Averis	4	646	473	10	47.30	4.39	4-75	0
GR Breese	17	2229	1297	27	48.03	3.49	4-75	0
CL White	12	1121	723	15	48.20	3.86	5-148	1
RE Watkins	14	1385	922	19	48.52	3.99	4-40	0
JF Brown	15	3564	1765	35	50.42	2.97	5-82	1
PD Trego	12	1457	965	19	50.78	3.97	3-87	0
DL Maddy	11	1047	564	11	51.27	3.23	3-70	0
AGB Wharf	10	1577	983	19	51.73	3.74	4-67	0
RW Price	8	1678	813	15	54.20	2.90	4-38	0
AR Griffith	5	1096	621	11	56.45	3.39	3-34	0
V Banerjee	7	1377	801	14	57.21	3.49	4-150	0
PJ Franks	14	1675	1071	18	59.50	3.83	2-24	0
ID Fisher	5	1208	755	10	75.50	3.75	3-110	0
CT Peploe	10	1694	944	12	78.66	3.34	4-31	0

THE PRIMARY CLUB

PO Box 12121, Saffron Walden
Essex CB10 2ZF
Telephone: 01799 586507
e-mail: secretary@primaryclub.or
website: www.primaryclub.org

Derek Underwood, the patron of the Primary Club, qualified f
membership in some style in 1965. Playing for Kent against th
South Africans he was out first ball twice in the same match.

However, members do not have to be playing Test or coun
cricket when the ultimate disaster strikes in order to qualify fo
the club. As long as you are out first ball at ANY level of cricke
you are eligible to join The Primary Club.

Why join? The Primary Club is a charity (Registered Charity
No. 285285) and all profits from subscriptions, donations and
the range of items for sale (ties, sweaters, shirts, mugs,
umbrellas, etc.) go to pay for sporting and recreational
facilities for the blind and partially sighted. All the club's
workers are volunteers.

For many of us sport is an important part of our every day
lives; for the blind and partially sighted, sport can mean so
much more. The confidence and sense of achievement they
get from mastering a physical skill helps them a great deal in
tackling the problems of their lives.

MEMBERSHIP APPLICATION

Name

Address

Joining subscription:	
To include City tie – £20	
To include Club tie – £20	
To include City & Club tie – £30	
To include 100% silk tie (City) – £30	
To include 100% silk tie (Country) – £30	
To include Bow tie – £20	
Lady, to include brooch – £15	
DONATION	
REMITTANCE TO 'THE PRIMARY CLUB'	£

Registered Charity No. 285285

The value of your remittance to The Prim
Club can be increased by 28p for every £
you give under Gift Aid tax reclaim
arrangements, *at no extra cost to you.*
To enable the Club to benefit from this
scheme, please sign and date the
declaration below, provided that you pay
income tax, or capital gains tax, of an
amount equal to the tax to be reclaimed.

**I wish The Primary Club to reclaim tax on
all donations I make on or after the date
this declaration.**

Signed   **Date**

It would be of great benefit to the Club if yc
pay future donations by banker's standing
order. Please tick the box and
a form will be sent to you.

INDEX OF PLAYERS BY COUNTY

*denotes not registered for the 2007 season. Where a player is known to have moved in the off-season he is listed under his new county.

DERBYSHIRE

BALLANCE, G.S.
BIRCH, D.J.
BIRT, T.R.
BORRINGTON, P.M.
BOTHA, A.G.
CUSDEN, S.M.J.
DEAN, K.J.
GODDARD, L.J.*
GRAY, A.K.D.*
HARVEY, I.J.
HASSAN ADNAN
HUGHES, L.D.
HUNTER, I.D.
KATICH, S.M.
LUNGLEY, T.
NEEDHAM, J.
PAGET, C.D.
PIPE, D.J.
RANKIN, W.B.
REDFERN, D.J.
SHEIKH, M.A.*
SMITH, G.M.
STUBBINGS, S.D.
TAYLOR, C.R.
WAGG, G.G.
WELCH, G.
WESTON, W.P.C.
WHITE, W.A.

DURHAM

BARRICK, D.J.*
BENKENSTEIN, D.M.
BREESE, G.R.
BRIDGE, G.D.*

CLAYDON, M.E.
COETZER, K.J.
COLLINGWOOD, P.D.
DAVIES, M.A.
DIVENUTO, M.J.
EVANS, L.
GIBSON, O.D.
GIDMAN, W.R.S.
HARMISON, B.W.
HARMISON, S.J.
IQBAL, M.M.
KILLEEN, N.
LEWIS, J.J.B.*
LEWIS, M.L.*
LOWE, J.A.*
MAHER, J.P.*
MAHOMED, U.
MUCHALL, G.J.
MUSTARD, P.
ONIONS, G.
PARK, G.T.
PLUNKETT, L.E.
PRATT, G.J.*
SCOTT, G.M.
SMITH, W.R.
STONEMAN, M.D.
THORP, C.D.
WISEMAN, P.J.

ESSEX

ADAMS, A.R.*
AHMED, J.S.
BICHEL, A.J.
BOPARA, R.S.
CHAMBERS, M.A.
CHOPRA, V.

COOK, A.N.
DANISH KANERIA
FLOWER, A.
FLOWER, G.W.
FOSTER, J.S.
GOUGH, D.
IRANI, R.C.
MIDDLEBROOK, J.D.
NAPIER, G.R.
NEL, A.
PALLADINO, A.P.
PETTINI, M.L.
PHILLIPS, T.J.
TEN DOESCHATE, R.N.
THOMAS, S.D.
TUDOR, A.J.
WESTFIELD, M.S.
WESTLEY, T.

GLAMORGAN

BRAGG, W.D.
CHERRY, D.D.
COSGROVE, M.J.*
COSKER, D.A.
CROFT, R.D.B.
DAVIES, A.P.
FRANKLIN, J.E.C.*
GRANT, R.N.
HARRIS, J.A.R.
HARRISON, A.J.
HARRISON, D.S.
HEMP, D.L.
JONES, S.P.
MCCULLUM, B.B.*
O'SHEA, M.P.
PENG, N.

INDEX OF PLAYERS BY COUNTY

POWELL, M.J.
REES, G.P.
SHINGLER, A.C.
TUDGE, K.D.
WALLACE, M.A.
WATERS, H.T.
WATKINS, R.E.
WHARF, A.G.B.
WRIGHT, B.J.

GLOUCESTERSHIRE

ADSHEAD, S.J.
ALI, KADEER
AVERIS, J.M.M.*
BALL, M.C.J.*
BANERJEE, V.
BROWN, D.O.
BURTON, D.A.
FISHER, I.D.
GIDMAN, A.P.R.
GREENIDGE, C.G.
HARDINGES, M.A.
HODNETT, G.P.
KIRBY, S.P.
LEWIS, J.
MARSHALL, H.J.H.
NOFFKE, A.A.
NORTH, M.J.
RUDGE, W.D.
SNELL, S.D.
SPEARMAN, C.M.
TAYLOR, C.G.
UMAR GUL
WINDOWS, M.G.N.*

HAMPSHIRE

ADAMS, J.H.K.
BALCOMBE, D.J.
BENHAM, C.C.
BROWN, M.J.
BRUCE, J.T.A.
BURROWS, T.G.
CARBERRY, M.A.
CRAWLEY, J.P.
DAWSON, L.A.
ERVINE, S.M.
GRIFFITHS, D.A.
LAMB, G.A.
LATOUF, K.J.
LUMB, M.J.
MASCARENHAS, D.A.
MCLEAN, J.J.*
MORRIS, R.K.
PIETERSEN, K.P.
POTHAS, N.
STOKES, M.S.T.
TAYLOR, B.V.
THORNELY, D.J.*
TOMLINSON, J.A.
TREMLETT, C.T.
UDAL, S.D.
WARNE, S.K.

KENT

BRAVO, D.J.*
CHAMBERS, D.J.*
COOK, S.J.
DENLY, J.L.
DENNINGTON, M.J.*
DEXTER, N.J.
DIXEY, P.G.

FULTON, D.P.*
HALL, A.J.
HENDERSON, T.*
ILES, J.A.
JONES, G.O.
JOSEPH, R.H.
KEMP, J.M.*
KEY, R.W.T.
KHAN, A.
MCLAREN, R.
NORTHEAST, S.A.
PATEL, M.M.
SAGGERS, M.J.
STEVENS, D.I.
TREDWELL, J.C.
VAN JAARSVELD, M.
WALKER, M.J.
YASIR ARAFAT

LANCASHIRE

ASTLE, N.J.*
ANDERSON, J.M.
BROWN, K.R.
CHAPPLE, G.
CHILTON, M.J.
CORK, D.G.
CROFT, S.J.
CROSS, G.D.
FLINTOFF, A.
HODGE, B.J.
HOGG, K.W.
HORTON, P.J.
KEEDY, G.
LAW, S.G.
LOYE, M.B.
MAHMOOD, S.I.
MARSHALL, S.J.
MULLANEY, S.J.

INDEX OF PLAYERS BY COUNTY

INDEX OF PLAYERS BY COUNTY

QUIZ ANSWERS

1. Andrew Strauss (E)
2. Alastair Cook (E)
3. Lawrence Rowe
4. Jacques Rudolph
5. Graham Gooch
6. Mohammad Ashraful
7. Richard Illingworth (E)
8. Bob Massie (A)
9. Damien Fleming
10. Dominic Cork (E)
11. Wilfred Rhodes (E)
12. Brian Close
13. Allan Border (A)
14. Andy Flower
15. Eric Hollies (E)
16. Alec Stewart (E)
17. Arjuna Ranatunga
18. Lance Klusener's
19. Tony Lewis
20. New Zealand
21. Tony Pigott (E)
22. Mohammad Azharuddin
23. Mark Ramprakash (Middlesex)
24. Durham's first first-class match – v Oxford University
25. The custom of beginning Test matches in England on a Thursday – the match started on a Friday
26. Darren Lehmann (Yorkshire)
27. Mark Butcher (Surrey) – his father Alan was captaining Glamorgan
28. Shivnarine Chanderpaul
29. Greg Chappell (A) – 123/109*
30. Derek Underwood
31. Bobby Simpson's (A)
32. Intikhab Alam
33. John Lever – 7-46/3-24
34. 2003; second Test v Zimbabwe
35. The Rose Bowl – 2005
36. Chris Bassano (Derbyshire) – 186*/106
37. Neil Mallender (E)
38. Nasser Hussain
39. Peter Pollock (SA) – 3-61/6-38
40. Colin Cowdrey (E)
41. Tom Graveney
42. Old Trafford
43. St Helen's, Swansea
44. Ed Joyce (E) – his brother Dominick was playing for Ireland
45. David Hemp (Glamorgan) – v Kenya in Nairobi in the ICC Inter-Continental Cup
46. Darren Gough
47. Simon Jones (E)
48. Jon (J.J.B.) Lewis
49. John Hampshire
50. Alamgir Sheriyar

51. Nick Knight
52. David Sales (Northamptonshire)
53. Michael Powell
54. Martin Saggers (E)
55. Mal Loye (E), who was playing state cricket in New Zealand
56. Steve Waugh (A)
57. Clarrie Grimmett (A)
58. Richard Hadlee (NZ)
59. Marcus Trescothick
60. Allan Border (A) – 150*/153
61. Jack Hobbs (E)
62. Desmond Haynes (WI)
63. Dimitri Mascarenhas (Hampshire)
64. Paul Collingwood – 181/105* in 2005
65. Ricky Ponting (A) – 120/143* in 2005-06
66. Sunil Gavaskar (I)
67. Sachin Tendulkar (I)
68. Muttiah Muralitharan
69. Geoffrey Boycott – 100.12 in 1971
70. Rod Marsh (A)
71. Alvin Kallicharran (Warwickshire) – 206
72. Adam Gilchrist (A/World XI)
73. Ian Harvey (Gloucestershire) – 100* from 50 balls
74. Grant Flower – 104/151
75. It was the first match in which Yorkshire fielded an overseas player – Sachin Tendulkar (I)
76. Benson and Hedges Cup
77. ICC Trophy
78. Clive Lloyd
79. Nick Knight (E)
80. Jeremy Coney – in 1986
81. Ajit Wadekar – in 1971
82. Lance Gibbs (WI)
83. Anil Kumble (I) – 10-74 at Delhi
84. Pakistan
85. Ian Botham (E)
86. Andre Nel (SA)
87. Chris Cowdrey
88. Geoff Pullar
89. Paul Allott – 52* at his home ground of Old Trafford, batting at No. 10
90. Marvan Atapattu
91. Dermot Reeve
92. Ajmal Shahzad
93. Justin Langer (A) – 54 in the second innings at Adelaide
94. Graham Thorpe – 114* in the second innings
95. Waqar Younis (P)
96. Alec Stewart – 118/143 in 1993-94
97. Steve Bucknor (WI)
98. Darren Gough (E)
99. Lee Germon
100. Chris Cairns (NZ)